COMMENTARY

ON

THE SONG OF SONGS

AND

ECCLESIASTES.

BY

FRANZ DELITZSCH, D.D.,

PROFESSOR OF THEOLOGY, LEIPSIC.

Translated from the German

BY

M. G. EASTON, A.M., D.D.

WIPF & STOCK · Eugene, Oregon

Wipf and Stock Publishers
199 W 8th Ave, Suite 3
Eugene, OR 97401

Commentary on The Song of Songs and Ecclesiastes
By Delitzsch, Franz
ISBN 13: 978-1-60608-191-4
Publication date 2/27/2009
Previously published by T & T Clark, 1885

THE TRANSLATOR'S PREFACE.

THE volume now offered to students of the Bible completes the Keil and Delitzsch series of Commentaries on the Old Testament. Like the earlier volumes, it addresses itself exclusively to theological students and the more scholarly class of readers, and will be certain to find a cordial welcome among them, whether they may be able to agree or not with the conclusions of the learned author.

In an Appendix to the German edition there are added three brief Dissertations by Wetzstein. But as the commentary is in itself complete without these, they have been omitted with Dr. Delitzsch's concurrence. I content myself by merely indicating here their import. In the first, Wetzstein aims at showing that the words פֶּלַח הָרִמּוֹן, Song iv. 3, vi. 7, signify the slice (*Spalt*, *Ritz*) of a pomegranate = the inner surface of a sliced pomegranate. In the second, he argues that the *Dudaïm* plant, Song vii. 13, is not the *mandragora vernalis* of botanists, but the *mandr. autumnalis*, which begins to bud and blossom, as is the case with most of the Palestinian flora, about the time of the first winter rains in the month of November. The passage, הד' . . . ריח־, he accordingly translates: "Already the mandragora apples give forth their fragrance," *i.e.* are already ripe; because it is only the ripe apples that are fragrant. In the third, on Eccles. xii. 5, he seeks to establish the translation of וינאץ . . . האב' by "And the almond tree flourisheth, and the locusts creep forth, and the wretched life is brought to dissolution." The first two of these clauses, he holds, denote the season of the year [the beginning of the meteorological spring. The seven days from 25th February to 3d March are called the *eijam el-'agaiz*, *i.e.* the (seven death-) days for old people] in which that which is said in the third (the death of the old man) takes place.

The Translator cannot send forth this volume without expressing his deep obligation to Dr. Delitzsch for his kindness in forwarding various important corrections and additions which have been incorporated in the translation, as well as for other valuable suggestions with reference to it. This English edition may consequently be almost regarded as a second edition of the work. It is not unlikely that in a work containing such a multiplicity of details, and involving so many minute points of criticism, several *errata* may be found; but it is believed that the scholarly reader will have no difficulty in inserting the necessary corrections. The Translator has done his best to verify the references, and to present a faithful rendering of the original, and in such a form as to allow the author to express himself in his own way, so far as the idiom of our language would permit.

DARVEL, *May* 1877.

ABBREVIATIONS.

The abbreviations and technical forms common to such critical works as this have been retained. These require no explanation. The colon (:) has been used, as in the original, to introduce a translation or a quotation. In the text-criticisms, the following abbreviations have been used:—

F. = *Cod. Francofurtensis* of 1294, described by Delitzsch in his Preface to Baer's edition of the *Psalter* of 1861 and 1874.

H. = *Cod. Heidenheimii*, a MS.

J. = *Cod. Jamanensis*, which was brought from South Arabia by Jacob Sappir, and passed into Baer's possession. *Vid.* Delitzsch's Preface to Baer's edition of *Isaiah*, 1872.

P. = *Cod. Petropolitanus* of the year 1010, now in St. Petersburg. *Vid.* Pinner's *Prospectus*, pp. 81–88.

D. = A parchment MS. of the Song placed at Delitzsch's disposal by Baer.

E^1, E^2, E^3, E^4 = The four Erfurt Manuscripts.

TABLE OF CONTENTS.

I. THE SONG OF SONGS.

	PAGE
1. INTRODUCTION TO THE SONG OF SONGS,	1
Typical but not Allegorical,	2
Its Ethical Character,	5
A Dramatic Pastoral,	8
Divisions of,	9
The Date and Authorship of,	11
An Antilegomenon,	13
2. EXPOSITION OF THE SONG,	17
Title of the Book, i. 1,	17–161
First Act—The Mutual Affection of the Lovers, i. 2–ii. 7,	19–47
(1) First Scene of the Act, i. 2–8,	19
(2) Second Scene of the Act, i. 9–ii. 7,	32
Second Act—The Mutual Seeking and Finding of the Lovers, ii. 8–iii. 5,	47–57
(1) First Scene of the Act, ii. 8–17,	47
(2) Second Scene of the Act, iii. 1–5,	57
Third Act—The Home-bringing of the Bride, and the Marriage, iii. 6–v. 1,	60–90
(1) First Scene of the Act, iii. 6–11,	60
(2) Second Scene of the Act, iv. 1–v. 1,	70
Fourth Act—Love disdained, but won again, v. 2–vi. 9,	90–113
(1) First Scene of the Act, v. 2–vi. 3,	90
(2) Second Scene of the Act, vi. 4–9,	109
Fifth Act—Shulamith the attractively fair but humble Princess, vi. 10–viii. 4,	113–140
(1) First Scene of the Act, vi. 10–vii. 6,	113
(2) Second Scene of the Act, vii. 7–viii. 4,	129

Sixth Act—*The Ratification of the Covenant of Love in Shulamith's Native Home,* viii. 5–14, ... 140–161
    (1) First Scene of the Act, viii. 5–7, ... 140
    (2) Second Scene of the Act, viii. 8–14, . . . 149

3. APPENDIX.—*Remarks on the Song by Dr. J. G. Wetzstein,* . . 162
    The Syrian Thrashing-table, ... 162
    Notes on i. 7, i. 17, ... 164
    Notes on ii. 11, iii. 11, iv. 14, ... 165–167
    Notes on v. 1, vii. 1; the Dance of Mahanaim, . . 170
    A Wedding Song (*Waṣf*) by Ḳâsim, ... 174
    Note on vii. 3, ... 176

II. THE BOOK OF ECCLESIASTES.

1. INTRODUCTION TO ECCLESIASTES, ... 179–217
    A Production of the Israelitish Chokma, . . . 180
    The Standpoint and Individuality of the Author, . . 181
    Self-Contradictions in the Book, ... 183
    Survey of the Contents of the Book, ... 185
    A Post-exilian Book, ... 189
    List of Hapaxlegomena and Words and Forms belonging to the more recent Period of the Language, ... 190
    The Style and Artistic Form of the Book, . . . 199
    The Title of the Book, ... 201
    The Epilogue proves the late Composition of the Book, . 206
    The Anonymous Author speaks as if he were Solomon—represents Solomon, ... 207
    The Date of the Book, ... 210
    The Author a Palestinian, ... 216
    Literature of the Book, ... 216

2. EXPOSITION OF THE BOOK OF ECCLESIASTES, . . 218–442
    The Title, i. 1, ... 218
    The Prologue: The Everlasting Sameness, i. 2–11, . . 218
    Koheleth's Experiences and their Results, i. 12–iv. 16—
        The Unsatisfactoriness of striving after Wisdom, i. 12–18, . 226
        The Unsatisfying Nature of Worldly Joy, ii. 1–11, . . 232

CONTENTS.

	PAGE
The End of the Wise Man the same as that of the Fool, ii. 12–17,	243
The Vanity of Wealth gathered with Care and Privation, ii. 18–23,	248
The Condition of Pure Enjoyment, ii. 24–26,	251
The Short-sightedness and Impotence of Man over against God, the All-conditioning, iii. 1–15,	254
The Godless Conduct of Men left to themselves, and their End like that of the Beasts, iii. 16–22,	265
The Wrongs suffered by Man from Man, embittering the Life of the Observer, iv. 1–3,	273
Miserable Rivalry and Restless Pursuit, iv. 4–6,	275
The Aimless Labour and Penuriousness of him who stands alone, iv. 7–12,	276
The People's Enthusiasm for the new King, and its Extinction, iv. 13–16,	278

FIRST CONCLUDING SECTION—
| Proverbs respecting the Worship of God, iv. 17 [v. 1]–v. 6 [7], | 283 |

CONTINUATION OF THE CATALOGUE OF VANITIES—
The Gradations of Oppression in Despotic States, v. 7, 8 [8, 9],	291
The Uncertainty of Riches, and the Cheerful Enjoyment of Life, v. 9 [10]–vi. 6,	295
Obtaining better than desiring, vi. 7–9,	308
The Weakness and Short-sightedness of Man over against his Destiny, vi. 10–12,	310

SECOND CONCLUDING SECTION—
Proverbs of Better Things, Things supposed to be better, Good Things, Good and Bad Days, vii. 1–14,	313
Continuation of Experiences and their Results, vii. 15–ix. 12—	
The Injuriousness of Excesses, vii. 15–18,	323
What protects him who, with all his Righteousness, is not free from Sin, and what becomes him, vii. 19–22,	326
Not-found and found—the Bitterest—a Woman, vii. 23–29,	329
Wise Conduct towards the King and under Despotic Oppression, viii. 1–9,	336
It is with the Righteous as with the Wicked—it is best to enjoy Life so long as God grants it, viii. 10–15,	345
The Fruitlessness of all Philosophizing, viii. 16, 17,	352

	PAGE
The Power of Fate, and the best possible thing for Man is his Want of Freedom, ix. 1–12, ...	354
The Incalculableness of the Issue and of the Duration of Life, ix. 11, 12, ...	365

The further setting forth of Experiences, with Proverbs intermixed, ix. 13–x. 15—

Experiences and Proverbs touching Wisdom and the Contrasts to it, ix. 13–x. 3, ...	367
The Caprice of Rulers and the Perverted World, x. 4–7, . .	374
That which is difficult exposes to Danger; that which is improper brings Trouble; that which comes too late is of no use, x. 8–11,	377
The Worthless Prating and the Aimless Labour of the Fool, x. 12–15,	382

THIRD CONCLUDING SECTION, WITH THE FINALE AND EPILOGUE—

(*A.*) Warnings against Idle Revelry and Improvidence, and a Call to a Fresh Effort after a Happy Improvement of Life, x. 16–xi. 8,	385–399
The Prosperity of a Country, its Misfortune, and Thoughtful Foresight, x. 16–20, ...	385
Act cautiously, but not too cautiously—the Future is God's; enjoy life—the Future is dark, xi. 1–8, ...	391
(*B.*) Finale, with an Epiphonema, xi. 9–xii. 7, 8, . . .	399
(*C.*) The Epilogue, xii. 9–14, ...	428

THE SONG AND ECCLESIASTES.

INTRODUCTION TO THE SONG OF SONGS.

THE *Song* is the most obscure book of the Old Testament. Whatever principle of interpretation one may adopt, there always remains a number of inexplicable passages, and just such as, if we understood them, would help to solve the mystery. And yet the interpretation of a book presupposes from the beginning that the interpreter has mastered the idea of the whole. It has thus become an ungrateful task; for however successful the interpreter may be in the separate parts, yet he will be thanked for his work only when the conception as a whole which he has decided upon is approved of.

It is a love-poem. But why such a *minne*-song in the canon? This question gave rise in the first century, in the Jewish schools, to doubts as to the canonicity of the book. Yet they firmly maintained it; for they presupposed that it was a spiritual and not a secular love-poem. They interpreted it allegorically. The Targum paraphrases it as a picture of the history of Israel from the Exodus to the coming of the Messiah. The bride is the congregation of Israel; and her breasts, to quote one example, are interpreted of the Messiah in His lowliness and the Messiah in His glory. But "Solomon" is an anthropomorphic representation of Jahve Himself. And all the instances of the occurrence of the name, with one exception, are therefore regarded as an indirect allegorical designation of the God of peace (*vid.* Norzi under i. 1). And because of its apparently erotic, but in truth mysterious contents, it was a Jewish saying, as Origen and Jerome mention, that the Song should not be studied by any one till he was thirty years of age (*nisi quis ætatem sacerdotalis ministerii, id est, tricesimum annum impleverit*). Because, according to the traditional Targ. interpretation, it begins with the departure out of Egypt, it forms a part of the liturgy for the eighth day of the Passover. The five Megilloths are arranged in the calendar according to their liturgical use.[1]

In the church this synagogal allegorizing received a new turn. They saw represented in the Song the mutual love of Christ and His church, and it thus became a mine of sacred mysticism in which men have dug to the present day. Thus Origen explains it in twelve volumes. Bernhard of Clairvaux died (1153) after he had delivered eighty-six sermons on it, and had only reached the end of the second chapter;[2] and his disciple Gilbert Porretanus carried forward the interpretation in forty-eight sermons only to v. 10, when he died. Perluigi de Palestrina gained by his twenty-nine motettoes on the Song (1584) the honoured name of *Principe della Musica*. In modern times this allegorico-mystical interpretation is represented in the department of exegesis (Hengst.), sermon (F. W. Krummacher), and poetry (Gustav Jahn), as well as of music (Neukomm's duet: *Er und sie*), and even of painting (Ludw. von Maydell).

If the Song is to be understood allegorically, then Shulamith is the personification of the congregation of Israel, and mediately of the church. All other interpretations fall below this. Hug (1813) understands by the "beloved" the kingdom of the ten tribes longing after a reunion with the house of David; and Heinr. Aug. Hahn (1852), the Japhetic heathendom. Ludw. Noack (1869) has even changed and modified the readings of the Heb. text, that he might find therein the ballads of a Tirhâka romance, *i.e.* a series of pictures of the events occurring between Samaria and her Aethiopian lover Tirhâka, of the years (B.C.) 702, 691, and 690. These are the aberrations of individuals. Only one other interpretation recommends itself. Solomon's *charisma* and aim was the Chokma. The Peshito places over the Song the superscription חכמת דחכמתא. Is Shulamith, then, the personification of wisdom, like Dante's Beatrice? Rosenmüller (1830) is the most recent representative of this view; we ought then to have in Dante's *Convito* the key to the allegorical interpretation. He there sings sweet songs of love of his mistress Philosophy. But there is nothing in the description here to show that Shulamith is Wisdom. The one expression, "Thou shalt teach me" (viii. 2), warns us against attempting to put Wisdom in the place of the church, as a reversal of the facts of the case.

---

[1] The *Song* was read on the 8th day of the Passover; *Ruth*, on the second Shabuoth [Pentecost]; *Lamentations*, on the 9th Ab; *Ecclesiastes*, on the 3d Succoth [Tabernacles]; *Esther*, between the 11th and 16th Adar [feast of Purim].

[2] *Vid.* Fernbacher's *Die Reden des. h. Bernhard über das Hohelied*, prefaced by Delitzsch. Leipzig 1862.

But if one understands the church to be meant, there yet remains much that is inexplicable. Who are the sixty queens and the eighty concubines (vi. 8) ? And why are the heroes just sixty (iii. 7) ? The synagogal and church interpretation, in spite of two thousand years' labour, has yet brought to light no sure results, but only numberless absurdities, especially where the Song describes the lovers according to their members from head to foot and from foot to head. But notwithstanding all this, it is certain that the "great mystery" (Eph. v. 32) mirrors itself in the Song. In this respect it resembles the love of Joseph and Zuleikha, often sung by the Arabian poets, which is regarded by the mystics[1] as a figure of the love of God toward the soul longing for union with Him. Shulamith is a historic personage; not the daughter of Pharaoh, as has been often maintained since the days of Theodore of Mopsuestia (died 429) and Abulfaraj (died 1286), but a country maiden of humble rank, who, by her beauty and by the purity of her soul, filled Solomon with a love for her which drew him away from the wantonness of polygamy, and made for him the primitive idea of marriage, as it is described in Gen. iii. 23 ff., a self-experienced reality. This experience he here sings, idealizing it after the manner of a poet; *i.e.*, removing the husk of that which is accidental, he goes back to its kernel and its essential nature. We have before us six dramatic figures, each in two divisions, which represent from within the growth of this delightful relation to its conclusion. This sunny glimpse of paradisaical love which Solomon experienced, again became darkened by the insatiableness of passion; but the Song of Songs has perpetuated it, and whilst all other songs of Solomon have disappeared, the providence of God has preserved this one, the crown of them all. It is a protest against polygamy, although only in the measure one might expect from the Mosaic standpoint. For the *Tôra* recognises, indeed, in its primitive history monogamy as the original form (Matt. xix. 4–6); but in its legislation, giving up the attempt to abolish polygamy, it is satisfied with its limitation (Deut. xvii. 17).

The Song celebrates paradisaical, but yet only natural love (*minne*). It stands, however, in the canon of the church, because Solomon is a type of Him of whom it can be said, " a greater than Solomon is here" (Matt. xii. 12). Referred to Him the antitype, the earthly contents receive a heavenly import and glorification. We see therein the mystery of the love of Christ and His church shadowed forth, not, however, allegorically, but typically. The allegory has to coincide throughout with that which is represented; but

[1] *Vid.* Hammer-Purgstall's *Das hohe Lied der Liebe der Araber*, 1854.

the type is always only a type *subtractis subtrahendis*, and is exceedingly surpassed by the antitype. In this sense Jul. Sturm (1854) has paraphrased the Song under the title of "*Zwei Rosen*" (two roses) (the typical and the antitypical). When my monograph on the Song appeared (1851), a notice of it in Colani's *Revue de Theologie* (1852) began with the frivolous remark: "*Ce n'est pas la première rêverie de ce genre sur le livre en question; plût à Dieu que ce fût la dernière;*" and Hitzig (1855) judged that "such a work might properly have remained unprinted; it represents nothing but a perverse inconsiderate literature which has no conception of scientific judgment and industry." But this work (long since out of print and now rare) was the fruit of many years of study. The commentary here given is based on it, but does not put it out of date. It broke with the allegorizing interpretation, the untenableness of which appears against his will in Hengstenberg's commentary (1853); it broke also with the theory which regards the poem as a history of Solomon's unsuccessful seductive efforts to gain the Shulamite's affections, a theory which Hitzig (1855) tries to exempt from the necessity of doing violence to the text by arbitrarily increasing the number of speakers and actors in the plot. I certainly succeeded in finding the right key to the interpretation of this work. Zöckler has recognised my book[1] as presenting "the only correct interpretation of its design and contents." Kingsbury, author of the notes on the Song in *The Speaker's Commentary*, has expressed the same judgment. Poets such as Stadelmann (*Das Hohelied, ein dramatisches Gedicht* = The Song of Songs: a dramatic poem, 1870) and J. Koch, late pastor of St. Mary's in Parchim (died 1873), have recognised in their beautiful German paraphrases my interpretation as natural and in conformity with the text; and for twenty years I have constantly more and more seen that the solution suggested by me is the right and only satisfactory one.

Shulamith is not Pharaoh's daughter. The range of her thoughts is not that of a king's daughter, but of a rustic maiden; she is a stranger among the daughters of Jerusalem, not because she comes from a foreign land, but because she is from the country; she is dark-complexioned, not from the sun of her more southern home, but from the open sunshine to which she has been exposed as the keeper of a vineyard; in body and soul she is born to be a princess, but in reality she is but the daughter of a humble family in a remote part of Galilee; hence the child-like simplicity and the rural character of her thoughts, her joy in the open fields, and her longing after the

[1 *Das Hohelied untersucht u. ausg.* Leipzig 1851.]

quiet life of her village home. Solomon appears here in loving fellowship with a woman such as he had not found among a thousand (Eccles. vii. 28); and although in social rank far beneath him, he raises her to an equality with himself. That which attached her to him is not her personal beauty alone, but her beauty animated and heightened by nobility of soul. She is a pattern of simple devotedness, naive simplicity, unaffected modesty, moral purity, and frank prudence,—a lily of the field, more beautifully adorned than he could claim to be in all his glory. We cannot understand the Song of Songs unless we perceive that it presents before us not only Shulamith's external attractions, but also all the virtues which make her the ideal of all that is gentlest and noblest in woman. Her words and her silence, her doing and suffering, her enjoyment and self-denial, her conduct as betrothed, as a bride, and as a wife, her behaviour towards her mother, her younger sister, and her brothers,—all this gives the impression of a beautiful soul in a body formed as it were from the dust of flowers. Solomon raises this child to the rank of queen, and becomes beside this queen as a child. The simple one teaches the wise man simplicity; the humble draws the king down to her level; the pure accustoms the impetuous to self-restraint. Following her, he willingly exchanges the bustle and the outward splendour of court life for rural simplicity, wanders gladly over mountain and meadow if he has only her; with her he is content to live in a lowly cottage. The erotic external side of the poem has thus an ethical background. We have here no "song of loves" (Ezek. xxxiii. 32) having reference to sensual gratification. The rabbinical proverb is right when it utters its threat against him who would treat this Song, or even a single verse of it, as a piece of secular literature.[1] The Song transfigures natural but holy love. Whatever in the sphere of the divinely-ordered marriage relation makes love the happiest, firmest bond uniting two souls together, is presented to us here in living pictures. "The Song," says Herder, "is written as if in Paradise. Adam's song: Thou art my second self! Thou art mine own! echoes in it in speech and interchanging song from end to end." The place of the book in the canon does not need any further justification; that its reception was favoured also by the supposition that it represented the intercourse between Jahve and the congregation of Israel, may be conjectured indeed, but is not established. The supposition, however, would have been false; for the book is not an allegory, and Solomon is by no means an *Alle-*

[1] Cf. *Tosefta Sanhedrin* xii., *Sanhedrin* iii.a, and the commencement of the tract *Kalla*.

gorumenon of God. But the congregation is truly a bride (Jer. ii. 2; Isa. lxii. 5), and Solomon a type of the Prince of peace (Isa. ix. 5; Luke xi. 31), and marriage a mystery, viz. as a pattern of the loving relation of God and His Christ to the church (Eph. v. 32). The Song has consequently not only a historico-ethical, but also a typico-mystical meaning. But one must be on his guard against introducing again the allegorical interpretation as Soltz (1850) has done, under the misleading title of the typical interpretation. The typical interpretation proceeds on the idea that the type and the antitype do not exactly coincide; the mystical, that the heavenly stamps itself in the earthly, but is yet at the same time immeasurably different from it. Besides, the historico-ethical interpretation is to be regarded as the proper business of the interpreter. But because Solomon is a type (*vaticinium reale*) of the spiritual David in his glory, and earthly love a shadow of the heavenly, and the Song a part of sacred history and of canonical Scripture, we will not omit here and there to indicate that the love subsisting between Christ and His church shadows itself forth in it.

But the prevailing view which Jacobi (1771) established, and which has predominated since Umbreit (1820) and Ewald (1826), is different from ours. According to them, the Song celebrates the victory of the chaste passion of conjugal love. The beloved of Shulamith is a shepherd, and Solomon acts toward her a part like that of Don Juan with Anna, or of Faust with Gretchen. Therefore, of course, his authorship is excluded, although Anton (1773), the second oldest representative of this so-called shepherd hypothesis, supposes that Solomon at a later period of his life recognised his folly, and now here magnanimously praises the fidelity of Shulamith, who had spurned his enticements away from her; and a Jewish interpreter, B. Holländer (1871), following Hezel (1780), supposes that Solomon represents himself as an enticer, only to exhibit the ideal of female virtue as triumphing over the greatest seduction. Similarly also Godet (1867),[1] who, resting on Ewald, sees here a very complicated mystery presented by Solomon himself, and pointing far beyond him: Solomon, the earthly Messiah; Shulamith, the true Israel; the shepherd, Jahve, and as Jahve who is about to come, the heavenly Solomon; the little sisters, heathenism—it is the old allegory, able for everything, only with changed names and a different division of the parts which here comes in again by the back-door of the seduction-history.[2]

[1] *Vid.* Jahrg. i. No. 22–24 of the Berne *Kirchenfreund*.
[2] And in this Godet stands not alone. The Jewish interpreter Malbim (1850) accepts also this seduction-history: Solomon = the sensual impulse; Shulamith =

Thus this seduction-history has not put an end to the over-ingenious allegorizing. In one point, however, at least, it has aided in the understanding of the Song. Herder saw in the Song a collection of Solomonic songs of love, which he translated (1778), as the oldest and the most beautiful, from the Orient. But Goethe, who in the *Westöst. Divan* (1819) praises the Song as the most divine of all love-songs, recognised, after the appearance of Umbreit's Comm., the unity also of the "inexplicably mysterious."

We are not conscious of any prejudice which makes it impossible for us to do justice to the interpretation to which Umbreit and Ewald gave currency. It abundantly accounts for the reception of the book into the canon, for so interpreted it has a moral motive and aim. And the personality of Solomon has certainly not merely a bright side, which is typical, but also a dark side, which is pregnant with dark issues for his kingdom; it may perhaps be possible that in the Song the latter, and not the former, is brought to view. Then, indeed, the inscription would rest on an error; for that in this case also the Solomonic authorship could be maintained, is an idea which, in the traditional-apologetical interest, mounts up to a faith in the impossible. But the truth goes beyond the tradition; the inscription would then indicate a traditional interpretation which, as is evident from the book itself, does not correspond with its original meaning and aim. "It is clear to every unprejudiced mind," says Gustav Baur,[1] "that in ii. 10–15, iv. 8–15, a different person speaks from the royal wooer; for (1) Solomon only says, 'my friend' [i. 15, etc.]; while, on the other hand, the shepherd heaps up flattering words of warmest love; (2) Solomon praises only the personal beauty of the woman; the shepherd, the sweet voice, the enchanting look, the warm love, the incorruptible chastity of his beloved;—in short, the former reveals the eye and the sensuousness of the king; the latter, the heart of a man who is animated by the divine flame of true love." We only ask, meanwhile, whether words such as iv. 13 are less sensuous than iv. 5, and whether the image of the twin gazelles is not more suitable in the mouth of the shepherd than the comparison of the attractions of Shulamith with the exotic plants of Solomon's garden? "In three passages," says Godet, "lies open the slender thread which Ewald's penetrating eye discovered under the flowers and leaves which adorn the poem: 'The king has brought me into his palace' (i. 4); 'I knew not how my heart has

the spirit-soul; the little sister = the natural soul; and Shulamith's beloved = the heavenly Friend, the Shepherd of the universe.

[1] *Literaturb. der Darmst. Kirchenzeitung*, 1851, pp. 114–146, and 1854, No. 11.

brought me to the chariots of a princely people' (vi. 12); 'I was a wall, and have found peace before his eyes' (viii. 10)." The same critic also finds in several passages an apparent contrariety between Solomon and the shepherd. "Observe," says he, "*e.g.* i. 12, 13, where the shepherd—whom Shulamith calls her spikenard, and compares to a bunch of flowers on her breast—is placed over against the king, who sits on his divan; or vii. 9 f., where, suddenly interrupting the king, she diverts the words which he speaks concerning herself to her beloved; or viii. 7, where, leaning on the arm of her beloved, she expresses her disregard for riches, with which Solomon had sought to purchase her love." But spikenard is not the figure of the shepherd, not at all the figure of a man; and she who is praised as a "prince's daughter" (vii. 2) cannot say (vi. 12) that, enticed by curiosity to see the royal train, she was taken prisoner, and now finds herself, against her will, among the daughters of Jerusalem; and he whom she addresses (viii. 12) can be no other than he with whom she now finds herself in her parents' home. The course of the exposition will show that the shepherd who is distinguished from Solomon is nothing else than a shadow cast by the person of Solomon.

The Song is a dramatic pastoral. The ancients saw in it a *carmen bucolicum mimicum*. Laurentius Peträus, in his Heb.-Danish Paraphrase (1640), calls it *carmen bucolicum, ἀμοιβαῖον* (δραματικόν); George Wachter (1722), an "opera divided into scenic parts." It acquires the character of a pastoral poem from this, that Shulamith is a shepherdess, that she thinks of Solomon as a shepherd, and that Solomon condescends to occupy the sphere of life and of thought of the shepherdess. It is not properly an idyll, nor yet properly a drama. Not an idyll, because the life-image which such a miniature drawn from life—such, *e.g.*, as the Adon. of Theocritus presents to us—unfolds itself within a brief time without interruption; in the Song, on the other hand, not merely are the places and persons interchanged, but also the times. The whole, however, does not fall into little detached pictures; but there runs through this wreath of figures a love-relation, which embodies itself externally and internally before our eyes, and attains the end of its desire, and shows itself on the summit of this end as one that is not merely sensuous, but moral. The Song is certainly not a theatrical piece:[1] the separate pieces would necessarily have been longer if the

---

[1] "Shulamith," says E. F. Friedrich (1855 and 1866), "is the oldest theatrical piece in existence." Ewald and Böttcher, who find not fewer than twelve persons mentioned in it, think that it was represented on an actual stage. Then, indeed, it

poet had had in view the changes of theatrical scenery. But at all events the theatre is not a Semitic institution, but is of Indo-Persian Greek origin. Jewish poetry attempted the drama only after it began in Alexandrinism[1] to emulate Greece. Grätz' (1871) polemic against the dramatists is so far justified. But yet we see, as in the Book of Job, so in the Song, the drama in process of formation from the lyric and narrative form of poetry, as it has developed among the Greeks from the lyric, and among the Indians from the epic. In the Book of Job the colloquies are all narrative. In the Song this is never the case;[2] for the one expression, "answered my beloved, and said to me" (ii. 10), is not to be compared with, "and Job answered and said:" the former expression indicates a monologue. And in the "Daughters of Jerusalem" (i. 5, etc.) we have already something like the chorus of the Greek drama. The ancient Greek MSS. bear involuntary testimony to this dramatic character of the Song. There are several of them which prefix to the separate addresses the names of the persons speaking, as ἡ νύμφη, ὁ νυμφίος.[3] And the Aethiopic translation makes five separate pieces, probably, as the *Cod. Sinait.* shows, after the example of the LXX., which appear as divisions into Acts.

The whole falls into the following six Acts:—

(1.) The mutual affection of the lovers, i. 2–ii. 7, with the conclusion, "I adjure you, ye daughters of Jerusalem."
(2.) The mutual seeking and finding of the lovers, ii. 8–iii. 5, with the conclusion, "I adjure you, ye daughters of Jerusalem."
(3.) The fetching of the bride, and the marriage, iii. 6–v. 1, beginning with, "Who is this . . . ?" and ending with, "Drink and be drunken, beloved."
(4.) Love scorned, but won again, v. 2–vi. 9.
(5.) Shulamith the attractively fair but humble princess, vi. 10–viii. 4, beginning with, "Who is this . . . ?" and ending with, "I adjure you, ye daughters of Jerusalem."

would be the oldest drama—older than Thespis and Kalîdasa. For the Sakuntâla and the drama *Der Kaufmann und die Bajadere* belong to the first century of our era.

[1] *Vid.* my *Prolegomena* to Luzzatto's מגדל עז (Heb Paraphrase of the *Pastors fido* of Guarini), 1837, pp. 24–32.

[2] Similar is the relation between Homer, where the speakers are introduced with narrative, and our national epics, the *Nibelungen* and *Gudrun*, which become dramatic when the action and the feeling rise to a higher elevation: the words of the different persons follow each other without introduction, so that here the manner of the singer had to become dramatic.

[3] *Vid. Repert. für bibl. u. morgenl. Lit.* viii. (1781), p. 180. The Archimandrite Porphyrios describes such a MS. in his (Russian) *Reisewerk* (1856).

(6.) The ratification of the covenant of love in Shulamith's home, viii. 5–14, beginning with, "Who is this . . . ?"

Zöckler reckons only five acts, for he comprehends v. 2–viii. 4 in one; but he himself confesses its disproportionate length; and the reasons which determine him are invalid; for the analogy of the Book of Job, which, besides, including the prologue and the epilogue, falls into seven formal parts, can prove nothing; and the question, "Who is this?" vi. 10, which he interprets as a continuation of the encomium in vi. 9, is rather to be regarded, like iii. 8, viii. 5, as a question with reference to her who is approaching, and as introducing a new act; for the supposition that vi. 9 requires to be further explained by a statement of what was included in the "blessing" and the "praising" is unwarranted, since these are ideas requiring no supplement to explain them (Gen. xxx. 13; Ps. xli. 3, cvii. 32), and the poet, if he had wished to explain the praise as to its contents, would have done this otherwise (cf. Prov. xxxi. 28 f.) than in a way so fitted to mislead. Rightly, Thrupp (1862) regards vi. 10 as the chorus of the daughters of Jerusalem. He divides as follows: (1) the Anticipation, i. 2–ii. 7; (2) the Awaiting, ii. 8–iii. 5; (3) the Espousal and its Results, iii. 6–v. 1; (4) the Absence, v. 2–8; (5) the Presence, v. 9–viii. 4; (6) Love's Triumph, viii. 5–12, with the Conclusion, viii. 13, 14. But how can v. 9 begin a new formal part? It is certainly the reply to Shulamith's adjuration of the daughters of Jerusalem, and not at all the commencement of a new scene, much less of a new act.

In our division into six parts, the separate acts, for the most part necessarily, and in every case without any violence, divide themselves into two scenes each, thus:—

Act I. i. 2–ii. 7.	Scene 1. i. 2–8.	Scene 2. i. 9–ii. 7.
„ II. ii. 8–iii. 5.	„ ii. 8 ff.	„ iii. 1–5.
„ III. iii. 6–v. 1.	„ iii. 6 ff.	„ iv. 1–v. 1.
„ IV. v. 2–vi. 9.	„ v. 2–vi. 3.	„ vi. 4–9.
„ V. vi. 10–viii. 4.	„ vi. 10–vii. 6.	„ vii. 7–viii. 4.
„ VI. viii. 5–14.	„ viii. 5–7.	„ viii. 8–14.

The first scene of the first act I formerly (1851) extended to i. 17, but it reaches only to i. 8; for up to this point Solomon is absent, but with i. 9 he begins to converse with Shulamith, and the chorus is silent—the scene has thus changed. Kingsbury in his translation (1871) rightly places over i. 9 the superscription, "The Entrance of the King."

The change of scenery is not regulated in accordance with stage decoration, for the Song is not a theatrical piece.[1] The first act is played both in the dining-room and in the wine-room appertaining to the women of the royal palace. In the second act, Shulamith is again at home. In the third act, which represents the marriage, the bride makes her entrance into Jerusalem from the wilderness, and what we further then hear occurs during the marriage festival. The locality of the fourth act is Jerusalem, without being more particularly defined. That of the fifth act is the park of Etam, and then Solomon's country house there. And in the sixth act we see the newly-married pair first in the way to Shulem, and then in Shulamith's parental home. In the first half of the dramatic pictures, Shulamith rises to an equality with Solomon; in the second half, Solomon descends to an equality with Shulamith. At the close of the first, Shulamith is at home in the king's palace; at the close of the second, Solomon is at home with her in her Galilean home.

. . . .

In our monograph on the Song (1851), we believe we have proved that it distinctly bears evidences of its Solomonic origin. The familiarity with nature, the fulness and extent of its geographical and artistic references, the mention made of so many exotic plants and foreign things, particularly of such objects of luxury as the Egyptian horses, point to such an authorship; in common with Ps. lxxii., it has the multiplicity of images taken from plants; with the Book of Job, the dramatic form; with the Proverbs, manifold allusions to Genesis. If not the production of Solomon, it must at least have been written near his time, since the author of Prov. i.–ix., the introduction to the older Book of Proverbs, for the origin of which there is no better defined period than that of Jehoshaphat (909–883 B.C.), and the author or authors of the supplement (Prov. xxii. 17–xxiv. 22), reveal an acquaintance with the Song. Ewald also, and Hitzig, although denying that Solomon is the author because it is directed against him, yet see in it a product of the most flourishing state of the language and of the people; they ascribe it to a poet of the northern kingdom about 950 B.C. Modern Jewish criticism surpasses, however, on the field of O. T. history, the anachronisms of the Tübingen school. As Zunz has recently (*Deut. Morgenl. Zeitsch.*

---

[1] Ephr. Epstein, surgeon in Cincinnati, in a review of Von Grätz' *Comm.* in *The Israelite* (1872), calls the Song quite in our sense, "a dramatic poem, though not a complete scenic drama." But the bridal procession in the third act is not of this character—he sees in it a return from a hunting expedition.

xxvii.) sought to show that the Book of Leviticus was written about a thousand years after Moses, that there never was a prophet Ezekiel, that the dates of this book are fictitious, etc.; so Grätz attempts to prove that the Song in its Graecising language and Greek customs and symbols bears evidences of the Syro-Macedonian age;[1] that the poet was acquainted with the idylls of Theocritus and the Greek erotic poets, and, so far as his Israelitish standpoint admitted, imitates them; and that he placed an ideal picture of pure Jewish love over against the immorality of the Alexandrine court and its Hellenistic partisans, particularly of Joseph b. Tobia, the collector of taxes in the time of Ptolemy Euergetes (247–221 B.C.),—a picture in which "the Shepherd,"[2] now grown into a fixed idea, renders welcome service, in contrast to Solomon, in whom the poet glances at the court of Alexandria. One is thus reminded of Kirschbaum (1833), who hears in Ezek. xxxiii. 5 an echo of Cicero's *dixi et salvavi animam*, and in the Song ii. 17, a reference to the Bethar of Barcochba. We do not deny the penetration which this chief of Jewish historians has expended on the establishment of his hypothesis; but the same penetration may prove that the Babylon.-Assyr. "*syllabaries*" of the time of Asurbanipal (667–626) belong to the Greek era, because there occurs therein the word *azamillav* (knife), and this is the Greek $\sigma\mu\iota\lambda\eta$; or that the author of Prov. i.-ix. alludes in vii. 23 to Eros and his quivers, and in ix. 1 betrays a knowledge of the seven *artes liberales*. Parallels to the Song are found wherever sensuous love is sung, also in the *Pastoralia* of Longus, without the least dependence of one author upon another. And if such a relation is found between Theocritus and the Song, then it might rather be concluded that he became acquainted with it in Alexandria from Jewish literates,[3] than that the author of the Song has imitated Greek models, as Immanuel Romi, the Arabians and Dante; besides, it is not at all the Song lying before us which Grätz expounds, but the Song modified by violent corrections of all kinds, and fitted to the supposed tendency. Thus he changes (i. 3) שְׁמָנֶיךָ (thine unguent) into בְּשָׂמָיו, and שֶׁמֶן תּוּרַק (ointment poured forth) into שֶׁמֶן תַּמְרוּק. — Shulamith says this of her beautiful shepherd, and what follows (i. 4) the damsels say to him; he changes

---

[1] So also, on linguistic grounds, Ant. Theod. Hartmann in Winer's *Zeitschr.* 1829.
[2] Epstein, in true American style, calls him "the bogus shepherd."
[3] *Vid.* my *Gesch. der jud. Poesie*, p. 205 ff. Not as Joh. Gott. Lessing (*Eclogae regis Salomonis*, 1777), the brother of Gotthold Ephraim Lessing, supposes: through the LXX. translation; for the Song was among the books latest in being translated.

מָשְׁכֵנִי into מָשְׁכֵנוּ, הֲבִיאַנִי into הֱבִיאֻנוּ, and then remarks: "Shulamith mentions it as to the praise of her beloved, that the damsels, attracted by his beauty, love him, and say to him, 'Draw us, we will run after thee; though the king brought us into his chambers, we would rejoice only with thee, and prefer thee to the king.'" His too confident conjectural criticism presents us with imaginary words, such as (iii. 10) אֲהָבִים (ebony); with unfortunate specimens of style, such as (vi. 10), "Thou hast made me weak, O daughter of Aminadab;" and with unheard-of renderings, such as (viii. 5), "There where thy mother has wounded thee;" for he supposes that Shulamith is chastised by her mother because of her love. *This* Song is certainly not written by Solomon, nor yet does it date from the Syro-Macedonian time, but was invented in Breslau in the 19th century of our era!

Grätz (1871) has placed yet farther down than the Song the Book of Ecclesiastes, in which he has also found Graecisms; the tyrannical king therein censured is, as he maintains, Herod the Great, and the last three verses (xii. 12-14) are not so much the epilogue of the book as that of the Hagiographa which closes with it. Certainly, if this was first formed by the decision of the conference in Jerusalem about 65, and of the synod in Jabne about 90, and the reception of the Books of Ecclesiastes and the Song was carried not without controversy, then it lies near to regard these two books as the most recent, originating not long before. But the fact is this: We learn from *Jud-ajim* iii. 5, iv. 6, cf. *Edujoth* v. 3, that in the decade before the destruction of Jerusalem the saying was current among the disciples of Hillel and Shammai, that "all Holy Scriptures (*Kethubîm*) pollute the hands;"[1] but that the question whether Ecclesiastes is included was answered in the negative by the school of Shammai, and in the affirmative by the school of Hillel—of the Song nothing is here said. But we learn further, that several decades later the Song also was comprehended in this controversy along with Ecclesiastes; and in an assembly of seventy-two doctors of the law in Jabne, that decree, "all Holy Scriptures (*Kethubîm*) pollute the hands," was extended to Ecclesiastes and the Song. R. Akiba

---

[1] *Vid.* for the explanation of this, my essay, "Das Hohelied verunreinigt die Hände," in the *Luth. Zeitsch.* 1854. [The *Tôra* and the *Theruma*-food, as being both reckoned holy, were usually placed together in the temple. It was discovered that the sacred books were thereby exposed to damage by mice: and hence, to prevent their being brought any longer into contact with the *Theruma*, the Rabbins decided that they were henceforth to be regarded as unclean, and they gave forth the decree, "All Holy Scriptures pollute the hand." This decree was applicable only to *holy* or *inspired* books. *Vid.* Ginsburg on the Song, p. 3, *note.*]

(or some one else) asserted, in opposition to those who doubted the canonicity of the Song, "No day in the whole history of the world is so much worth as that in which the Song of Songs was given; for all the *Kethubîm* are holy, but the Song of Songs is most holy." From this Grätz draws the conclusion that the Hagiographa was received as canonical for the first time about 65, and that its canon was finally fixed so as to include Ecclesiastes and the Song, not till about 90; but this conclusion rests on the false supposition that "Holy Scriptures" (*Kethubîm*) is to be understood exclusive of the Hagiographa, which is just as erroneous as that *Sephârim* designates the prophets, with the exclusion of the Hagiographa. Holy *Kethubîm* is a general designation, without distinction, of all the canonical books, *e.g. Bathra* i. 6, and *Sepharim* in like manner, with the exception only of the Tôra, *Megilla* i. 8, iii. 1, *Shabbath* 115b. And it rests on a misapprehension of the question discussed: the question was not whether Ecclesiastes and the Song should be admitted, but whether they had been justly admitted, and whether the same sacred character should be ascribed to them as to the other holy writings; for in *Bathra* 14b–15a (without a parallel in the Palest. Talmud) the enriching of the canon by the addition of the Books of Isaiah, Proverbs, the Song, and Ecclesiastes, is ascribed to the Hezekiah-*Collegium* (Prov. xxi. 5), and thus is dated back in the period before the rise of the great synagogue. That Philo does not cite the Song proves nothing; he cites none of the five Megilloth. But Josephus (*C. Ap.* 1, § 8; cf. Euseb. *H. E.* iii. 10), since he enumerates five books of the Mosaic law, thirteen books of prophetic history and prediction, and four books of a hymno-ethical character, certainly means by these four the Psalms, Proverbs, Ecclesiastes, and the Song, which in the Alexandrine canon stand thus connected. His work, *Cont. Apion*, was not indeed written till about 100 A.D.; but Josephus there speaks of a fact which had existed for centuries. The Song and Ecclesiastes formed part of the sacred books among the Hellenists as well as among the Palestinian Jews of the first Christian century; but, as those Talmud notices show, not without opposition. The Old Testament canon, as well as that of the New Testament, had then also its *Antilegomena*. These books were opposed not because of their late origin, but because their contents apparently militated against the truth of revelation and the spiritual nature of revealed religion. Similar doubts, though not so strong and lasting, were also uttered with reference to Proverbs, Esther, and Ezekiel.

The history of the exposition of this book is given in detail by

Christian D. Ginsburg in *The Song of Songs,* London 1857 ; and by Zöckler in "The Song," forming part of Lange's *Bibelwerk,* 1868, and supplemented by an account of the English interpretations and translations in the Anglo-American translation of this work by Green. Zunz, in the preface to Rebenstein's (Bernstein's) *Lied der Lieder,* 1834, has given an historical account of the Jewish expositors. Steinschneider's המזכיר (*Heb. Bibliograph.* 1869, p. 110 ff.) presents a yet fuller account of the Jewish commentaries. The Münich royal library contains a considerable number of these,—*e.g.* by Moses b. Tibbon, Shemariah, Immanuel Romi, Moses Calais (who embraced Christianity). Our commentary presents various new contributions to the history of the interpretation of this book. No other book of Scripture has been so much abused, by an unscientific spiritualizing, and an over-scientific unspiritual treatment, as this has. Luther says, at the close of his exposition: *Quodsi erro, veniam meretur primus labor, nam aliorum cogitationes longe plus absurditatis habent.* To inventory the *maculatur* of these absurdities is a repulsive undertaking, and, in the main, a useless labour, from which we absolve ourselves.

EXPOSITION OF THE SONG OF SONGS.

THE title of the book at once denotes that it is a connected whole, and is the work of one author.—Ch. i. 1. *The Song of Songs, composed by Solomon.* The genitival connection, "Song of Songs," cannot here signify the Song consisting of a number of songs, any more than calling the Bible "The Book of books" leads us to think of the 24 + 27 canonical books of which it consists. Nor can it mean "one of Solomon's songs;" the title, as it here stands, would then be the paraphrase of שִׁיר שִׁירֵי, chosen for the purpose of avoiding the redoubled genitives; but "one of the songs" must rather have been expressed by שִׁיר מִשִּׁירֵי. It has already been rightly explained in the *Midrash*:[1] "the most praiseworthy, most excellent, most highly-treasured among the songs." The connection is superl. according to the sense (cf. ἄῤῥητα ἀῤῥήτων of Sophocles), and signifies that song which, as such, surpasses the songs one and all of them; as "servant of servants," Gen. ix. 25, denotes a servant who is such more than all servants together. The plur. of the second word is for this superl. sense indispensable (*vid.* Dietrich's *Abhand. zur hebr. Gramm* p. 12), but the article is not necessary: it is regularly wanting where the complex idea takes the place of the predicate, Gen. ix. 25, Ex xxix. 37, or of the inner member of a genitival connection of words Jer. iii. 19; but it is also wanting in other places, as Ezek. xvi. 7 and Eccles. i. 2, xii. 8, where the indeterminate plur. denotes not totality, but an unlimited number; here it was necessary, because a definite Song—that, namely, lying before us—must be designated as the paragon of songs. The relative clause, "*asher lishlōmō*," does not refer to the single word "Songs" (Gr. Venet. τῶν τοῦ), as it would if the expression were שִׁיר מֵהַשּׁ, but to the whole idea of "the Song of Songs." A relative clause of similar formation and reference occurs at 1 Kings iv. 2: "These are the princes, *asher lo*, which belonged

[1] *Vid.* Fürst's *Der Kanon des A. T.* (1868), p. 86.

to him (Solomon)." They who deny the Solomonic authorship usually explain: The Song of Songs which concerns or refers to Solomon, and point in favour of this interpretation to LXX. B. ὅ ἐστι Σαλ., which, however, is only a latent genit., for which LXX. A. τῷ Σαλ. *Lamed* may indeed introduce the reference of a writing, as at Jer. xxiii. 9; but if the writing is more closely designated as a "Song," "Psalm," and the like, then *Lamed* with the name of a person foll. is always the *Lamed auctoris*; in this case the idea of reference to, as *e.g.* at Isa. i. 1, cf. 1 Kings v. 13, is unequivocally expressed by עַל. We shall find that the dramatized history which we have here, or as we might also say, the fable of the melodrama and its dress, altogether correspond with the traits of character, the favourite turns, the sphere of vision, and the otherwise well-known style of authorship peculiar to Solomon. We may even suppose that the superscription was written by the author, and thus by Solomon himself. For in the superscription of the Proverbs he is surnamed "son of David, king of Israel," and similarly in Ecclesiastes. But he who entitles him merely "Solomon" is most probably himself. On the other hand, that the title is by the author himself, is not favoured by the fact that instead of the שׁ, everywhere else used in the book, the fuller form *asher* is employed. There is the same reason for this as for the fact that Jeremiah in his prophecies always uses *asher*, but in the Lamentations interchanges שׁ with *asher*. This original demonstrative שׁ is old-Canaanitish, as the Phoenician אש, arrested half-way toward the form *asher*, shows.[1] In the Book of Kings it appears as a North Palest. provincialism, to the prose of the pre-exilian literature it is otherwise foreign;[2] but the pre-exilian *shir* and *kinah* (cf. also Job xix. 29) make use of it as an ornament. In the post-exilian literature it occurs in poetry (Ps. cxxii. 3, etc.) and in prose (1 Chron. v. 20, xxvii. 27); in Ecclesiastes it is already a component part of the rabbinism in full growth. In a pre-exilian book-title שׁ in place of *asher* is thus not to be expected. On the other hand, in the Song itself it is no sign of a post-exilian composition, as Grätz supposes. The history of the language and literature refutes this.

[1] From this it is supposed that *asher* is a pronom. root-cluster equivalent to אֲשֶׁל. Fleischer, on the contrary, sees in *asher* an original substantive *athar* = (Arab.) *ithr*, Assyr. *asar*, track, place, as when the vulgar expression is used, "The man where (*wo* instead of *welcher*) has said."

[2] We do not take into view here Gen. vi. 3. If בְּשַׁגָּם is then to be read, then there is in it the pronominal שׁ, as in the old proper name *Mishael* (who is what God is?).

FIRST ACT.

THE MUTUAL AFFECTION OF THE LOVERS.—CHAP. I. 2–II. 7.

FIRST SCENE OF THE ACT, I. 2–8.

The first act of the melodrama, which presents the loving relationship in the glow of the first love, now opens. i. 5, 6, are evidently the words of Shulamith. Here one person speaks of herself throughout in the singular. But in vers. 2–4 one and several together speak. Ewald also attributes vers. 2–4 to Shulamith, as words spoken by her concerning her shepherd and to him. She says, "Draw me after thee, so will we run," for she wishes to be brought by him out of Solomon's court. But how can the praise, "an ointment poured forth is thy name,"—an expression which reminds us of what is said of Solomon, 1 Kings v. 11 [1 Kings iv. 31], "and his fame was in all nations round about,"—be applicable to the shepherd? How could Shulamith say to the shepherd, "virgins love thee," and including herself with others, say to him also, "we will exult and rejoice in thee"? on which Ewald remarks: it is as if something kept her back from speaking of herself alone. How this contradicts the psychology of love aiming at marriage! This love is jealous, and does not draw in rivals by head and ears. No; in vers. 2–4 it is the daughters of Jerusalem, whom Shulamith addresses in ver. 5, who speak. The one who is praised is Solomon. The ladies of the palace are at table (*vid.* under ver. 12), and Solomon, after whom she who is placed amid this splendour which is strange to her asks longingly (ver. 7), is not now present. The two pentastichal strophes, vers. 2–4, are a scholion, the table song of the ladies; the solo in both cases passes over into a chorus.

Ver. 2. From these words with which as a solo the first strophe begins:

Let him kiss me with kisses of his mouth,

we at once perceive that she who here speaks is only one of many among whom Solomon's kisses are distributed; for *min* is partitive, as *e.g.* Ex. xvi. 27 (cf. Jer. xlviii. 32 and Isa. xvi. 9), with the underlying phrase נָשַׁק נְשִׁיקָה, *osculum osculari = figere, jungere, dare. Nashak* properly means to join to each other and to join together, particularly mouth to mouth. פִּיהוּ is the parallel form of פִּי, and is found in prose as well as in poetry; it is here preferred for the sake of the rhythm. Böttcher prefers, with Hitzig, יַשְׁקֵנִי ("let him give me to drink"); but "to give to drink with kisses" is an expression unsupported.

In line 2 the expression changes into an address:

For better is thy love than wine.

Instead of " thy love," the LXX. render " thy breasts," for they had before them the word written defectively as in the traditional text, and read דַּדֶּיךָ. Even granting that the dual דַּדַיִם or דַּדִּים could be used in the sense of the Greek μαστοί (Rev. i. 13),[1] of the breasts of a man (for which Isa. xxxii. 12, Targ., furnishes no sufficient authority); yet in the mouth of a woman it were unseemly, and also is itself absurd as the language of praise. But, on the other hand, that דָּדֶיךָ is not the true reading (" for more lovely—thus he says to me—are," etc.), R. Ismael rightly says, in reply to R. Akiba, *Aboda zara* 29b, and refers to שְׁמָנֶיךָ following (ver. 3), which requires the mas. for דֹּדֶיךָ. Rightly the Gr. Venet. οἱ σοὶ ἔρωτες, for דֹּדִים is related to אַהֲבָה, almost as ἔρως to ἀγάπη, *Minne* to *Liebe*. It is a plur. like חַיִּים, which, although a *pluraletantum*, is yet connected with the plur. of the pred. The verbal stem דּוּד is an abbreviated reduplicative stem (Ewald, § 118. 1); the root דּוּ appears to signify " to move by thrusts or pushes " (*vid.* under Ps. xlii. 5); of a fluid, " to cause to boil up," to which the word דּוּד, a kitchen-pot, is referred.[2] It is the very same verbal stem from which דָּוִד (David), the beloved, and the name of the foundress of Carthage, דִּילָה (=דִּידוֹ) *Minna*, is derived. The adj. *tov* appears here and at 3a twice in its nearest primary meaning, denoting that which is pleasant to the taste and (thus particularly in Arab.) to the smell.

This comparison *suaves prae vino*, as well as that which in line 3 of the pentastich, ver. 3,

To the smell thy ointments are sweet,

shows that when this song is sung wine is presented and perfumes are sprinkled; but the love of the host is, for those who sing, more excellent than all. It is maintained that רֵיחַ signifies fragrance emitted, and not smell. Hence Hengst., Hahn, Hölem., and Zöck. explain: in odour thy ointments are sweet. Now the words can certainly, after Josh. xxii. 10, Job xxxii. 4, 1 Kings x. 23, mean " sweet in (of) smell;" but in such cases the word with *Lamed* of reference naturally stands after that to which it gives the nearer reference, not as here before it. Therefore Hengst.: *ad odorem unguentorem tuorum quod attinet bonus est*, but such giving prominence to the subject and

---

[1] *Vid.* my *Handsch. Funde*, Heft 2 (1862).

[2] Yet it is a question whether דד, to love, and דד, the breast (Arab. *thady*, with a verb *thadiyi*, to be thoroughly wet), are not after their nearest origin such words of feeling, caressing, prattling, as the Arab. *dad*, sport (also *dadad*, the only Arab. word which consists of the same three letters); cf. Fr. *dada*, hobby-horse.

attraction (cf. 1 Sam. ii. 4a; Job xv. 20) exclude one another; the accentuation correctly places לריח out of the gen. connection. Certainly this word, like the Arab. *ryḥ*, elsewhere signifies *odor*, and the *Hiph.* הֵרִיחַ (*araḥ*) *odorari;* but why should not ריח be also used in the sense of *odoratus*, since in the post-bibl. Heb. חוּשׁ הריח means the sense of smell, and also in Germ. "*riechen*" means to emit fragrance as well as to perceive fragrance? We explain after Gen. ii. 9, where *Lamed* introduces the sense of sight, as here the sense of smell. Zöckl. and others reply that in such a case the word would have been לָרִיחַ; but the art. is wanting also at Gen. ii. 9 (cf. iii. 6), and was not necessary, especially in poetry, which has the same relation to the art. as to *asher*, which, wherever practicable, is omitted.

Thus in line 4:
An ointment poured forth is thy name.

By "thy ointments," line 3, spices are meant, by which the palace was perfumed; but the fragrance of which, as line 4 says, is surpassed by the fragrance of his name. שֵׁם (name) and שֶׁמֶן (fragrance) form a paranomasia by which the comparison is brought nearer Eccles. vii. 1. Both words are elsewhere mas.; but sooner than שׁם, so frequently and universally mas. (although its plur. is שֵׁמוֹת, but cf. אָבוֹת), שמן may be used as fem., although a parallel example is wanting (cf. *dᵉvāsh*, *mōr*, *nōphĕth*, *kĕmāh*, and the like, which are constantly mas.). Ewald therefore translates שמן תורק as a proper name: "O sweet *Salbenduft*" [Fragrance of Ointment]; and Böttcher sees in *turăk* a subst. in the sense of "sprinkling" [*Spreng-Oel*]; but a name like "*Rosenoel*" [oil of roses] would be more appropriately formed, and a subst. form תורק is, in Heb. at least, unexampled (for neither תּוּגָה nor תּוּבָל, in the name Tubal-Cain, is parallel). Fürst imagines "a province in Palestine where excellent oil was got," called *Turak*; "Turkish" *Rosenöl* recommends itself, on the contrary, by the fact of its actual existence. Certainly less is hazarded when we regard *shĕmĕn*, as here treated exceptionally, as fem.; thus, not: *ut unguentum nomen tuum effunditur*, which, besides, is unsuitable, since one does not empty out or pour out a name; but: *unguentum quod effunditur* (Hengst., Hahn, and others), an ointment which is taken out of its depository and is sprinkled far and wide is thy name. The harsh expression שמן מוּרָק is intentionally avoided; the old Heb. language is not φιλομέτοχος (fond of participles); and, besides, מורק sounds badly with מרק, to rub off, to wash away. Perhaps, also, שמן יוּרק is intentionally avoided, because of the collision of the weak sounds *n* and *j*. The name *Shēm* is derived from the verb *shāmā*, to be high, prominent, remarkable: whence also the name for the heavens (*vid.* under Ps. viii. 2). That attractive charm (lines 2, 3), and this glory (line 4), make him, the praised, an object of general love, line 5, ver. 3*b*:

Therefore virgins love thee.

This "therefore" reminds us of Ps. xlv. עֲלָמוֹת (sing. Isa. vii. 14), from עָלַם (Arab.), *ghalima, pubescere*, are maidens growing to maturity. The intrans. form אֲהֵבוּךָ, with transitive signification, indicates a pathos. The perf. is not to be translated *dilexerunt*, but is to be judged of according to Gesen. § 126. 3: they have acquired love to thee (= love thee), as the ἠγάπησάν σε of the Greek translators is to be understood. The singers themselves are the evidence of the existence of this love.

With these words the first pentastich of the table-song terminates. The mystical interpretation regards it as a song of praise and of loving affection which is sung to Christ the King, the fairest of the children of men, by the church which is His own. The Targum, in line first, thinks of the "mouth to mouth" [Num. xii. 8] in the intercourse of Moses with God. Evidence of divine love is also elsewhere thought of as a kiss: the post-bibl. Heb. calls the gentlest death the death בנשיקה, *i.e.* by which God takes away the soul with a kiss.

The second pentastich also begins with a solo:

Ver. 4 Draw me, so will we run after thee.

All recent interpreters (except Böttcher) translate, like Luther, "Draw me after thee, so we run." Thus also the Targ., but doubtfully: *Trahe nos post te et curremus post viam bonitatis tuae*. But the accentuation which gives *Tiphcha* to מָשְׁ׳ requires the punctuation to be that adopted by the Peshito and the Vulg., and according to which the passage is construed by the Greeks (except, perhaps, by the Quinta): Draw me, so will we, following thee, run (*vid.* Dachselt, *Biblia Accentuata*, p. 983 *s.*). In reality, this word needs no complement: of itself it already means, one drawing towards, or to himself; the corresponding (Arab.) *masak* signifies, *prehendere prehensumque tenere*; the root is מש, *palpare, contrectare*. It occurs also elsewhere, in a spiritual connection, as the expression of the gentle drawing of love towards itself (Hos. xi. 4; Jer. xxxi. 3); cf. ἑλκύειν, John vi. 44, xii. 32. If one connects "after thee" with "draw me," then the expression seems to denote that a certain violence is needed to bring the one who is drawn from her place; but if it is connected with "we will run," then it defines the desire to run expressed by the cohortative, more nearly than a willing obedience or following. The whole chorus, continuing the solo, confesses that there needs only an indication of his wish, a direction given, to make those who here speak eager followers of him whom they celebrate.

In what follows, this interchange of the *solo* and the *unisono* is repeated:

> Ver. 4*b* If the king has brought me into his chambers,
> So will we exult and rejoice in thee.
> We will praise thy love more than wine!
> Uprightly have they loved thee.

The cohortative נָרוּצָה (we will run) was the *apodosis imperativi;* the cohortatives here are the *apodosis perfecti hypothetici.* "Suppose that this has happened," is oftener expressed by the perf. (Ps. lvii. 7; Prov. xxii. 29, xxv. 16); "suppose that this happens," by the fut. (Job xx. 24; Ewald, § 357*b*). חֲדָרִים are the *interiora domus;* the root word *hhādăr,* as the Arab. *khadar* shows, signifies to draw oneself back, to hide; the *hhĕdĕr* of the tent is the back part, shut off by a curtain from the front space. Those who are singing are not at present in this innermost chamber. But if the king brings one of them in (הֵבִיא, from בּוֹא, *introire,* with *acc. loci*), then—they all say—we will rejoice and be glad in thee. The cohortatives are better translated by the fut. than by the conjunctive (*exultemus*); they express as frequently not what they then desire to do, but what they then are about to do, from inward impulse, with heart delight. The sequence of ideas, "exult" and "rejoice," is not a *climax descendens,* but, as Ps. cxviii. 24, etc., an advance from the external to the internal,—from jubilation which can be feigned, to joy of heart which gives it truth; for שָׂמַח —according to its root signification: to be smoothed, unwrinkled, to be glad[1]—means to be of a joyful, bright, complaisant disposition; and גִּיל, cogn. חִיל, to turn (wind) oneself, to revolve, means conduct betokening delight. The prep. בְּ in verbs of rejoicing, denotes the object on account of which, and in which, one has joy. Then, if admitted into the closest neighbourhood of the king, they will praise his love more than wine. זָכַר denotes to fix, viz. in the memory; *Hiph.*: to bring to remembrance, frequently in the way of praise, and thus directly equivalent to *celebrare, e.g.* Ps. xlv. 18. The wine represents the gifts of the king, in contradistinction to his person. That in inward love he gives himself to them, excels in their esteem all else he gives. For, as the closing line expresses, "uprightly they love thee,"—viz. they love thee, *i.e.* from a right heart, which seeks nothing besides, and nothing with thee; and a right mind, which is pleased with thee, and with nothing but thee. Heiligstedt, Zöckler, and others translate: with right they love thee. But the *pluralet.*

---

[1] *Vid.* Friedr. Delitzsch's *Indo-german.-sem. Studien* (1873), p. 99 f.

מֵישָׁרִים (from מֵישָׁר, for which the sing. מִישׁוֹר occurs) is an ethical conception (Prov. i. 3), and signifies, not: the right of the motive, but: the rightness of the word, thought, and act (Prov. xxiii. 16; Ps. xvii. 2, lviii. 2); thus, not: *jure;* but: *recte, sincere, candide.* Hengst., Thrupp, and others, falsely render this word like the LXX., Aquil., Symm., Theod., Targ., Jerome, Venet., and Luther, as subject: rectitudes [abstr. for concr.] = those who have rectitude, the upright. Hengstenberg's assertion, that the word never occurs as an adv., is set aside by a glance at Ps. lviii. 2, lxxv. 3; and, on the other hand, there is no passage in which it is used as *abstr. pro concr.* It is here, as elsewhere, an adv. acc. for which the word בְּמֵישָׁרִים might also be used.

The second pentastich closes similarly with the first, which ended with "love thee." What is there said of this king, that the virgins love him, is here more generalized; for *diligunt te* is equivalent to *diligeris* (cf. viii. 1, 7). With these words the table-song ends. It is erotic, and yet so chaste and delicate,—it is sensuous, and yet so ethical, that here, on the threshold, we are at once surrounded as by a mystical cloudy brightness. But how is it to be explained that Solomon, who says (Prov. xxvii. 2), "Let another praise thee, and not thine own mouth," begins this his Song of Songs with a song in praise of himself? It is explained from this, that here he celebrates an incident belonging to the happy beginning of his reign; and for him so far fallen into the past, although not to be forgotten, that what he was and what he now is are almost as two separate persons.

After this choral song, Shulamith, who has listened to the singers not without being examined by their inquisitive glances as a strange guest not of equal rank with them, now speaks:

Ver. 5 Black am I, yet comely, ye daughters of Jerusalem,
As the tents of Kedar, as the hangings of Solomon.

From this, that she addresses the ladies of the palace as "daughters of Jerusalem" (*Kerî* יְרוּשָׁלַיִם, a *du. fractus;* like עֶפְרַיִן for עֶפְרוֹן, 2 Chron. xiii. 19), it is to be concluded that she, although now in Jerusalem, came from a different place. She is, as will afterwards appear, from Lower Galilee;—and it may be remarked, in the interest of the mystical interpretation, that the church, and particularly her first congregations, according to the prophecy (Isa. viii. 23), was also Galilean, for Nazareth and Capernaum are their original seats;—and if Shulamith is a poetico-mystical Mashal or emblem, then she represents the synagogue one day to enter into the fellowship of Solomon —*i.e.* of the son of David, and the daughters of Jerusalem, *i.e.* the congregation already believing on the Messiah. Yet we confine ourselves to the nearest sense, in which Solomon relates a self-experience. Shulamith, the lightly esteemed, cannot boast that she is so ruddy and fair of countenance as they who have just sung how pleasant it is to be beloved by this king; but yet she is not so devoid of beauty as not to venture to love and hope to be loved: "Black am I, yet comely." These words express humility without abjectness. She calls herself "black," although she is not so dark and unchangeably black as an "Ethiopian" (Jer. xiii. 23). The verb שָׁחַר has the general primary idea of growing dark, and signifies not necessarily soot-blackness (modern Arab. *shuhwar*, soot), but blackness more or less deep, as שַׁחַר, the name of the morning twilight, or rather the morning grey, shows; for (Arab.) *saḥar*[1] denotes the latter, as distinguished from (Arab.) *fajr*, the morning twilight (*vid.* under Isa. xiv. 12, xlvii. 11). She speaks of herself as a Beduin who appears to herself as (Arab.) *sawda*, black, and calls[2] the inhabitants of the town (Arab.) *ḥawaryyat* (*cute candidas*). The *Vav* we have translated "yet" ("yet comely"); it connects the opposite, which exists along with the blackness. נָאוָה is the fem. of the adj. נָאוֶה = נָאוִי = נָאוִי, which is also formed by means of the doubling of the third stem-letter of נָאָה = נָאוּ, נָאִי (to bend forward, to aim; to be corresponding to the aim, conformable, becoming, beautiful), *e.g.* like רַעֲנָן, to be full of sap, green. Both comparisons run parallel to *nigra et bella*; she compares on the one hand the tents of Kedar, and on the other the tapestry of Solomon. אֹהֶל signifies originally, in general, the dwelling-place, as בַּיִת the place where one spends the night; these two words interchange: *ohel* is the house of the nomad, and *bäith* is the tent of him who is settled. קֵדָר (with the *Tsere*, probably from (Arab.) *kadar*, to have ability, be powerful, thought of after the Heb. manner, as Theodoret explains and Symm. also translates: σκοτασμός, from (Heb.) *Kadar, atrum esse*) is the name of a tribe of North. Arab. Ishmaelites (Gen. xxv. 13) whom Pliny speaks of (*Cedraei* in his *Hist. Nat.* v. 11), but which disappeared at the era of the rise of Islam; the Karaite Jefeth uses for it the word (Arab.) *Karysh*, for he substitutes the powerful Arab tribe from which Muhammed sprung, and rightly remarks: "She compares the colour of her skin to the blackness of the hair tents of the Koreishites,"—

---

[1] After an improbable etymology of the Arab., from *saḥar*, to turn, to depart, "the departure of the night" (Lane). Magic appears also to be called *siḥar*, as *nigromantia* (Mediaev. from *nekromantia*), the black art.

[2] The houri (damsel of paradise) is thus called *ḥawaryyt*, adj. relat. from *ḥawra*, from the black pupil of the eye in the centre of the white eyeball.

even to the present day the Beduin calls his tent his "hair-house" (*bêt wabar*, or, according to a more modern expression, *bêt sa'r*, בֵּית שֵׂעָר); for the tents are covered with cloth made of the hair of goats, which are there mostly black-coloured or grey. On the one hand, dark-coloured as the tents of the Kedarenes, she may yet, on the other hand, compare herself to the beautiful appearance of the יְרִיעוֹת of Solomon. By this word we will have to think of a pleasure-tent or pavilion for the king; *pavillon* (softened from Lat. *papilio*) is a pleasure-tent spread out like the flying butterfly. This Heb. word could certainly also mean curtains for separating a chamber; but in the tabernacle and the temple the curtains separating the Most Holy from the Holy Place were not so designated, but are called פָּרֹכֶת and מָסָךְ; and as with the tabernacle, so always elsewhere, יְרִיעוֹת (from יָרַע, to tremble, to move hither and thither) is the name of the cloths or tapestry which formed the sides of the tent (Isa. liv. 2); of the tent coverings, which were named in parall. with the tents themselves as the clothing of their framework (Hab. iii. 7; Jer. iv. 20, x. 20, xlix. 29). Such tent hangings will thus also be here meant; precious, as those described Ex. xxvi. and xxxvi., and as those which formed the tabernacle on Zion (2 Sam. vii.; cf. 1 Chron. xvii. 1) before the erection of the temple. Those made in Egypt[1] were particularly prized in ancient times.

Shulamith now explains, to those who were looking upon her with inquisitive wonder, how it is that she is swarthy:

Ver. 6a Look not on me because I am black,
Because the sun has scorched me.

If the words were אַל־תִּרְאוּ (תִּרְאֶינָה) בִּי, then the meaning would be: look not at me, stare not at me. But אַל־תִּרְאֻנִי, with שׁ (elsewhere כִּי) following, means: Regard me not that I am blackish (*subnigra*); the second שׁ is to be interpreted as co-ordin. with the first (that ... that), or assigning a reason, and that objectively (for). We prefer, with Böttch., the former, because in the latter case we would have had שֶׁהַשֶּׁמֶשׁ. The *quinqueliterum* שְׁחַרְחֹרֶת signifies, in contradistinction to שָׁחוֹר, that which is black here and there, and thus not altogether black. This form, as descriptive of colour, is diminutive; but since it also means *id quod passim est*, if the accent lies on *passim*, as distinguished from *raro*, it can be also taken as increasing instead of diminishing, as in הֲפַכְפַּךְ, יְפֵיפֶה. The LXX. trans. παρέβλεψέ (Symm. παρανέβλεψέ) με ὁ ἥλιος: the sun has looked askance on me. But why only askance? The Venet. better: κατεῖδέ με; but that is too little. The look is thought of as scorching; wherefore

[1] *Vid.* Wetzstein's *Isaiah* (1869), p. 698.

Aquila: συνέκαυσέ με, it has burnt me; and Theodotion: περιέφρυξέ με, it has scorched me over and over. שָׁזַף signifies here not *adspicere* (Job iii. 9, xli. 10) so much as *adurere*. In this word itself (cogn. שָׂדַף; Arab. *sadaf*, whence *asdaf*, black; cf. דָּעַף and זָעַף, Job xvii. 1), the looking is thought of as a scorching; for the rays of the eye, when they fix upon anything, gather themselves, as it were, into a focus. Besides, as the Scriptures ascribe twinkling to the morning dawn, so it ascribes eyes to the sun (2 Sam. xii. 11), which is itself as the eye of the heavens.[1] The poet delicately represents Shulamith as regarding the sun as fem. Its name in Arab. and old Germ. is fem., in Heb. and Aram. for the most part mas. My lady the sun, she, as it were, says, has produced on her this swarthiness.

She now says how it has happened that she is thus sunburnt:

6b My mother's sons were angry with me,
Appointed me as keeper of the vineyards—
Mine own vineyard have I not kept.

If " mother's sons " is the parallel for " brothers " (אֲחִי), then the expressions are of the same import, *e.g.* Gen. xxvii. 29; but if the two expressions stand in apposition, as Deut. xiii. 7 [6], then the idea of the natural brother is sharpened; but when "mother's sons" stands thus by itself alone, then, after Lev. xviii. 9, it means the relationship by one of the parents alone, as " father's wife " in the language of the O. T. and also 1 Cor. v. 5 is the designation of a step-mother. Nowhere is mention made of Shulamith's father, but always, as here, only of her mother, iii. 4, viii. 2, vi. 9; and she is only named without being introduced as speaking. One is led to suppose that Shulamith's own father was dead, and that her mother had been married again; the sons by the second marriage were they who ruled in the house of their mother. These brothers of Shulamith appear towards the end of the melodrama as rigorous guardians of their youthful sister; one will thus have to suppose that their zeal for the spotless honour of their sister and the family proceeded from an endeavour to accustom the fickle or dreaming child to useful activity, but not without step-brotherly harshness. The form נִחֲרוּ, Ewald, § 193c, and Olsh. p. 593, derive from חָרַר, the *Niph.* of which is either נָחַר or נִחַר (= נִחְרַר), Gesen. § 68, An. 5; but the plur. of this נִחַר should, according to rule, have been נִחֲרוּ (cf. how-

---

[1] According to the Indian idea, it is the eye of Varuna; the eye (also after Plato: ἡλιοειδέστατον τῶν περὶ τὰς αἰσθήσεις ὀργάνων) is regarded as taken from the sun, and when men die returning to the sun (Muir in the *Asiatic Journal*, 1865, p. 294, S. 309).

ever, נֵחֱלוּ, *profanantur*, Ezek. vii. 24); and what is more decisive, this נִחַר from חָרָה everywhere else expresses a different passion from that of anger; Böttch. § 1060 (2, 379). חָרָה is used of the burning of anger; and that נִחֲרוּ (from נִחֲרָה = נִחֲרוּ) can be another form for נֶחֱרוּ, is shown, *e.g.*, by the interchange of אֲחֵרוּ and אֶחֱרוּ; the form נִחֲרוּ, like נֵחֱלוּ, Amos vi. 6, resisted the bringing together of the ח and the half guttural ר. *Nĕhĕrā* (here as Isa. xli. 11, xlv. 24) means, according to the original, mid. signif. of the *Niph.*, to burn inwardly, ἀναφλέγεσθαι = ὀργίζεσθαι. Shulamith's address consists intentionally of clauses with perfects placed together: she speaks with childlike artlessness, and not "like a book;" in the language of a book, וַיִּשְׁמוּנִי would have been used instead of שָׂמֻנִי. But that she uses נֹטֵרָה (from נטר, R. טר = τηρεῖν; cf. Targ. Gen. xxxvii. 11 with Luke ii. 51), and not נֹצְרָה, as they were wont to say in Judea, after Prov. xxvii. 18, and after the designation of the tower for the protection of the flocks by the name of "the tower of the *nōtsrīm*" [the watchmen], 2 Kings xvii. 9, shows that the maid is a Galilean, whose manner of speech is Aramaizing, and if we may so say, platt-Heb. (= Low Heb.), like the Lower Saxon *plattdeutsch*. Of the three forms of the particip. נֹטְרָה, נוֹטֵרָה, נֹטֶרֶת, we here read the middle one, used subst. (Ewald, § 188*b*), but retaining the long ē (ground-form, *nâṭir*). The plur. אֶת־הַכְּ does not necessarily imply that she had several vineyards to keep, it is the categ. plur. with the art. designating the genus; *custodiens vineas* is a keeper of a vineyard. But what kind of vineyard, or better, vine-garden, is that which she calls כַּרְמִי שֶׁלִּי, *i.e. meam ipsius vineam?* The personal possession is doubly expressed; *shĕllī* is related to *cărmī* as a nearer defining apposition: my vineyard, that which belongs to me (*vid.* Fr. Philippi's *Status constr.* pp. 112–116). Without doubt the figure refers to herself given in charge to be cared for by herself: vine-gardens she had kept, but her own vine-garden, *i.e.* her own person, she had not kept. Does she indicate thereby that, in connection with Solomon, she has lost herself, with all that she is and has? Thus in 1851 I thought; but she certainly seeks to explain why she is so sunburnt. She intends in this figurative way to say, that as the keeper of a vineyard she neither could keep nor sought to keep her own person. In this connection *cărmī*, which by no means = the colourless *memet ipsam*, is to be taken as the figure of the person in its external appearance, and that of its fresh-blooming attractive appearance which directly accords with כֶּרֶם, since from the stem-word כָּרַם (Arab.), *karuma*, the idea of that which is noble and distinguished is connected with this designation of the planting of vines (for כֶּרֶם, (Arab.) *karm*, cf. *karmat*, of a single vine-stock, denotes not so much the soil in which the vines are planted, as rather the vines themselves): her *kĕrĕm* is her (Arab.) *karamat*, *i.e.* her stately attractive appearance. If we must interpret this mystically then, supposing that Shulamith is the congregation of Israel moved at some future time with love to Christ, then by the step-brothers we think of the teachers, who after the death of the fathers threw around the congregation the fetters of their human ordinances, and converted fidelity to the law into a system of hireling service, in which all its beauty disappeared. Among the allegorists, Hengstenberg here presents the extreme of an interpretation opposed to what is true and fine.

These words (vers. 5–6) are addressed to the ladies of the palace, who look upon her with wonder. That which now follows is addressed to her beloved:

Ver. 7 O tell me, thou whom my soul loveth : where feedest thou?
Where causest thou it (thy flock) to lie down at noon?
For why should I appear as one veiled
Among the flocks of thy companions!

The country damsel has no idea of the occupation of a king. Her simplicity goes not beyond the calling of a shepherd as of the fairest and the highest. She thinks of the shepherd of the people as the shepherd of sheep. Moreover, Scripture also describes governing as a tending of sheep; and the Messiah, of whom Solomon is a type, is specially represented as the future Good Shepherd. If now we had to conceive of Solomon as present from the beginning of the scene, then here in ver. 7 would Shulamith say that she would gladly be alone with him, far away from so many who are looking on her with open eyes; and, indeed, in some country place where alone she feels at home. The entreaty " O tell me" appears certainly to require (cf. Gen. xxxvii. 19) the presence of one to whom she addresses herself. But, on the other hand, the entreaty only asks that he should let her know where he is; she longs to know where his occupation detains him, that she may go out and seek him. Her request is thus directed toward the absent one, as is proved by ver. 8. The vocat., " O thou whom my soul loveth," is connected with אַתָּה, which lies hid in הַגִּידָה (" inform thou"). It is a circumlocution for " beloved" (cf. Neh. xiii. 26), or " the dearly beloved of my soul" (cf. Jer. xii. 7). The entreating request, *indica quaeso mihi ubi pascis*, reminds one of Gen. xxxvii. 16, where, however, *ubi* is expressed by אֵיפֹה, while here by אֵיכָה, which in this sense is ἅπ. λεγ. For *ubi* = אֵיפֹה, is otherwise denoted only by אֵיכֹה (אֵיכוֹ), 2 Kings vi. 13, and usually אַיֵּה, North Palest., by Hosea אֱהִי. This אֵיכָה elsewhere means *quo-*

modo, and is the key-word of the *Kîna*, as אֵיךְ is of the *Mashal* (the satire); the Song uses for it, in common with the Book of Esther, אֵיכָבָה. In themselves בֹּה and כָּה, which with אֵי preceding, are stamped as interrog. in a sense analogous to *hic, ecce*, κεῖνος, and the like; the local, temporal, polite sense rests only on a conventional *usus loq.*, Böttch. § 530. She wishes to know where he feeds, viz. his flock, where he causes it (viz. his flock) to lie down at mid-day. The verb רָבַץ (R. רב, with the root signif. of condensation) is the proper word for the lying down of a four-footed animal: *complicatis pedibus procumbere (cubare)*; *Hiph.* of the shepherd, who causes the flock to lie down; the Arab. *rab'a* is the name for the encampment of shepherds. The time for encamping is the mid-day, which as the time of the double-light, *i.e.* the most intense light in its ascending and descending, is called צָהֳרַיִם. שַׁלָּמָה, occurring only here, signifies *nam cur*, but is according to the sense = *ut ne*, like אֲשֶׁר לָמָּה, Dan. i. 10 (cf. Ezra vii. 23); לָמָּה, without *Dag. forte euphon.*, is, with the single exception of Job vii. 20, always *milra*, while with the *Dag.* it is *milel*, and as a rule, only when the following word begins with א"הע carries forward the tone to the *ult.* Shulamith wishes to know the place where her beloved feeds and rests his flock, that she might not wander about among the flocks of his companions seeking and asking for him. But what does כְּעֹטְיָה mean? It is at all events the *part. act. fem.* of עָטִי which is here treated after the manner of the strong verb, the kindred form to the equally possible עֹטָה (from *'âtaja*) and עֲטִיָה. As for the meaning, *instar errabundae* (Syr., Symm., Jerome, Venet., Luther) recommends itself; but עטה must then, unless we wish directly to adopt the reading כְּטֹעֲיָה (Böttch.), have been transposed from טעה (תעה), which must have been assumed if עטה, in the usual sense of *velare* (cf. עָטוּף), did not afford an appropriate signification. Indeed, *velans*, viz. *sese*, cannot denote one whom consciousness veils, one who is weak or fainting (Gesen. *Lex.*), for the *part. act.* expresses action, not passivity. But it can denote one who covers herself (the LXX., perhaps, in this sense ὡς περιβαλλομένη), because she mourns (Rashi); or after Gen. xxxviii. 14 (cf. Martial, ix. 32) one who muffles herself up, because by such affected apparent modesty she wishes to make herself known as a Hierodoule or harlot. The former of these significations is not appropriate; for to appear as mourning does not offend the sense of honour in a virtuous maiden, but to create the appearance of an immodest woman is to her intolerable; and if she bears in herself the image of an only beloved, she shrinks in horror from such a base appearance, not only as a debasing of herself, but also as a desecration of this sanctuary in her heart.

Shulamith calls entreatingly upon him whom her soul loveth to tell her how she might be able directly to reach him, without feeling herself wounded in the consciousness of her maidenhood and of the exclusiveness of her love. It is thereby supposed that the companions of her only beloved among the shepherds might not treat that which to her is holy with a holy reserve,—a thought to which Hattendorff has given delicate expression in his exposition of the Song, 1867. If Solomon were present, it would be difficult to understand this entreating call. But he is not present, as is manifest from this, that she is not answered by him, but by the daughters of Jerusalem.

> Ver. 8 If thou knowest not, thou fairest of women,
> Go after the footprints of the flock,
> And feed thy kids beside the shepherds' tents.

הַיָּפָה, standing in the address or call, is in the voc.; the art. was indispensable, because " the beautiful one among women" = the one distinguished for beauty among them, and thus is, according to the meaning, superlative; cf. Judg. vi. 15, Amos ii. 16, with Judg. v. 24; Luke i. 28; Ewald, § 313c. The verb יָפָה refers to the fundamental idea: *integrum, completum esse*, for beauty consists in well-proportioned fulness and harmony of the members. That the ladies of the court are excited to speak thus may arise from this, that one often judges altogether otherwise of a man, whom one has found not beautiful, as soon as he begins to speak, and his countenance becomes intellectually animated. And did not, in Shulamith's countenance, the strange external swarthiness borrow a brightness from the inner light which irradiated her features, as she gave so deep and pure an expression to her longing? But the instruction which her childlike, almost childish, *naïvete* deserved, the daughters of Jerusalem do not feel disposed to give her. לֹא יֵדַע signifies, often without the obj. supplied, *non sapere, e.g.* Ps. lxxxii. 5; Job viii. 9. The לָךְ subjoined guards against this inclusive sense, in which the phrase here would be offensive. This *dat. ethicus* (*vid.* ii. 10, 11, 13, 17, iv. 6, viii. 14), used twice here in ver. 8 and generally in the Song, reflects that which is said on the will of the subject, and thereby gives to it an agreeable cordial turn, here one bearing the colour of a gentle reproof: if thou knowest not to thee,—*i.e.* if thou, in thy simplicity and retirement, knowest it not, viz. that he whom thou thinkest thou must seek for at a distance is near to thee, and that Solomon has to tend not sheep but people,—now, then, so go forth, viz. from the royal city, and remain, although chosen to royal honours, as a shepherdess beside thine own sheep and kids. One misapprehends the answer if he supposes that they in reality point out the way to Shulamith by which she might reach her object; on the contrary, they answer her ironically, and, entering into her confusion of mind, tell her that if she cannot apprehend the position of Solomon, she may just remain what she is. עָקֵב (Arab. *'akib*), from עָקַב, to be convex, arched, is the heel; to go in the heels (the reading fluctuates between the form, with and without *Dag. dirimens* in ק) of one = to press hard after him, to follow him immediately. That they assign to her not goats or kids of goats, but kids, גְּדִיֹּת, is an involuntary fine delicate thought with which the appearance of the elegant, beautiful shepherdess inspires them. But that they name kids, not sheep, may arise from this, that the kid is a near-lying erotic emblem; cf. Gen. xxxviii. 17, where it has been fittingly remarked that the young he-goat was the proper courtesan-offering in the worship of Aphrodite (Movers' *Phönizier*, I. 680). It is as if they said: If thou canst not distinguish between a king and shepherds, then indulge thy love-thoughts beside the shepherds' tents,—remain a country maiden if thou understandest not how to value the fortune which has placed thee in Jerusalem in the royal palace.

SECOND SCENE OF THE FIRST ACT, I. 9—II. 7.

Solomon, while he was absent during the first scene, is now present. It is generally acknowledged that the words which follow were spoken by him:

> Ver. 9 To a horse in the chariot of Pharaoh
> Do I compare thee, my love.
> 10 Beautiful are thy cheeks in the chains,
> Thy neck in the necklaces.
> 11 Golden chains will we make for thee,
> With points of silver.

Till now, Shulamith was alone with the ladies of the palace in the banqueting-chamber. Solomon now comes from the banquet-hall of the men (ver. 12); and to ii. 7, to which this scene extends, we have to think of the women of the palace as still present, although not hearing what Solomon says to Shulamith. He addresses her, "my love:" she is not yet his bride. רַעְיָה (female friend), from רָעִי (רָעָה), to guard, care for, tend, ethically: to delight in something particularly, to take pleasure in intercourse with one, is formed in the same way as נַעֲרָה; the mas. is רֵעֶה (= *ra'j*), abbreviated רֵעַ, whence the fem. *ra'yāh* (Judg. xi. 37; *Chethîb*), as well as *rē'āh*, also with reference to the ground-form. At once, in the first words used by Solomon, one recognises a Philip, *i.e.* a man fond of horses,—an important feature in the character of the sage (*vid.* Sur. 38 of the Koran),—and that, one fond of Egyptian horses: Solomon carried on an extensive importation of horses from Egypt and other countries (2 Chron. ix. 28); he possessed 1400 war-chariots and 12,000 horsemen (1 Kings x. 26); the number of stalls of horses for his chariots was still greater (1 Kings v. 6) [iv. 26]. Horace (Ode iii. 11) compares a young sprightly maiden to a nimble and timid *equa trima;* Anacreon (60) addresses such an one: "thou Thracian filly;" and Theocritus says (Idyl xviii. 30, 31):

"As towers the cypress mid the garden's bloom,
As in the chariot proud Thessalian steed,
Thus graceful rose-complexioned Helen moves."

But how it could occur to the author of the Song to begin the praise of the beauty of a shepherdess by saying that she is like a horse in Pharaoh's chariot, is explained only by the supposition that the poet is Solomon, who, as a keen hippologue, had an open eye for the beauty of the horse. Egyptian horses were then esteemed as afterwards the Arabian were. Moreover, the horse was not native to Egypt, but was probably first imported thither by the Hyksos: the Egyptian name of the horse, and particularly of the mare, *ses-t, ses-mut,* and of the chariot, *markabuta,* are Semitic.[1] סוּסָה is here not *equitatus* (Jerome), as Hengst. maintains: "*Susah* does not denote a horse, but is used collectively;" while he adds, "Shulamith is compared to the whole Egyptian cavalry, and is therefore an ideal person." The former statement is untrue, and the latter is absurd. *Sūs* means *equus,* and *susā* may, indeed, collectively denote the stud (cf. Josh. xix. 5 with 1 Chron. iv. 31), but obviously it first denotes the *equa.* But is it to be rendered, with the LXX. and the Venet., "to my horse"? Certainly not; for the chariots of Pharaoh are just the chariots of Egypt, not of the king of Israel. The *Chirek* in which this word terminates is the *Ch. compag.,* which also frequently occurs where, as here and Gen. xlix. 11, the second member of the word-chain is furnished with a prep. (*vid.* under Ps. cxiii.). This *i* is an old genitival ending, which, as such, has disappeared from the language; it is almost always accented as the suff. Thus also here, where the *Metheg* shows that the accent rests on the *ult.* The plur. רִכְבֵי, occurring only here, is the amplificative poetic, and denotes state equipage. דִּמָּה is the trans. of דָּמָה, which combines the meanings *aequum* and *aequalem esse.* Although not allegorizing, yet, that

[1] Eber's *Aegypten u. die B. Mose's,* Bd. I. pp. 221 f. 226; cf. *Aeg. Zeitschr* 1864, p. 26 f.

we may not overlook the judiciousness of the comparison, we must remark that Shulamith is certainly a "daughter of Israel;" a daughter of the people who increased in Egypt, and, set free from the bondage of Pharaoh, became the bride of Jahve, and were brought by the law as a covenant into a marriage relation to Him.

The transition to ver. 10 is mediated by the effect of the comparison; for the head-frame of the horse's bridle, and the poitral, were then certainly, just as now, adorned with silken tassels, fringes, and other ornaments of silver (vid. Lane's *Modern Egypt*, I. 149). Jerome, absurdly, after the LXX.: *pulchrae sunt genae tuae sicut turturis*. The name of the turtle, תֹּר, redupl. *turtur*, is a pure onomatopoeia, which has nothing to do with תּוּר, whence דּוּר, to go round about, or to move in a circle; and turtle-dove's cheeks — what absurdity! Birds have no cheeks; and on the sides of its neck the turtle-dove has black and white variegated feathers, which also furnishes no comparison for the colour of the cheeks. תּוֹרִים are the round ornaments which hang down in front on both sides of the head-band, or are also inwoven in the braids of hair in the forehead; תּוּר, *circumire*, signifies also to form a circle or a row; in Aram. it thus denotes, *e.g.*, the hem of a garment and the border round the eye. In נָאווּ (vid. at 5*a*) the *Aleph* is silent, as in אָכַל לֵאמֹר. חֲרוּזִים are strings of pearls as a necklace; for the necklace (Arab. *kharaz*) consists of one or more, for the most part, of three rows of pearls. The verb חָרַז signifies, to bore through and to string together; *e.g.* in the Talm., fish which one strings on a rod or line, in order to bring them to the market. In Heb. and Aram. the secondary sense of stringing predominates, so that to string pearls is expressed by חרז, and to bore through pearls, by קדח; in Arab., the primary meaning of piercing through, *e.g. michraz*, a shoemaker's awl.

After ver. 11, one has to represent to himself Shulamith's adorning as very simple and modest; for Solomon seeks to make her glad with the thought of a continued residence at the royal court by the promise of costly and elegant ornaments. Gold and silver were so closely connected in ancient modes of representation, that in the old Aegypt. silver was called *nub het*, or white gold. Gold derived its name of זָהָב from its splendour, after the witty Arab. word *zahab*, to go away, as an unstable possession; silver is called כֶּסֶף, from כָּסַף, *scindere, abscindere*, a piece of metal as broken off from the motherstone, like the Arab. *dhukrat*, as set free from the lump by means of the pickaxe (cf. at Ps. xix. 11, lxxxiv. 3). The name of silver has here, not without the influence of the rhythm (cf. viii. 9), the article designating the species; the Song frequently uses this, and is generally in using the art. not so sparing as poetry commonly is.¹ עִם makes prominent the points of silver as something particular, but not separate. In נַעֲשֶׂה, Solomon includes himself among the other inhabitants, especially the women of the palace; for the *plur. majest.* in the words of God of Himself (frequently in the Koran), or persons of rank of themselves (general in the vulgar Arab.), is unknown in the O. T. They would make for her golden globules or knobs with (*i.e.* provided with . . .; cf. Ps. lxxxix. 14) points of silver sprinkled over them,—which was a powerful enticement for a plain country damsel.

Now for the first time Shulamith addresses Solomon, who is before her. It might be expected that the first word will either express the joy that she now sees him face to face, or the longing which she had hitherto cherished to see him again. The verse following accords with this expectation:

> Ver. 12 While the king is at his table,
> My nard has yielded its fragrance.

עַד שׁ or עַד אֲשֶׁר, with fut. foll., usually means: *usque eo*, until this and that shall happen, ii. 7, 17; with the perf. foll., until something happened, iii. 4. The idea connected with "until" may, however, be so interpreted that there comes into view not the end of the period as such, but the whole length of the period. So here in the subst. clause following, which in itself is already an expression of continuance, *donec = dum* (*erat*); so also עַד alone, without *asher*, with the part. foll. (Job i. 18), and the infin. (Judg. iii. 26; Ex. xxxiii. 22; Jonah iv. 2; cf. 2 Kings ix. 22); seldomer with the

---

¹ The art. denoting the idea of species in the second member of the *st. const.* standing in the sing. without a determining reference to the first, occurs in i. 13, "a bundle of (*von*) myrrh;" i. 14, "a cluster of (*von*) the cyprus-flower;" iv. 3, "a thread of (*von*) scarlet," "a piece of pomegranate;" v. 13, "a bed of balm" (but otherwise, vi. 2); vii. 9, "clusters of the vine;" vii. 3, "a bowl of roundness" (which has this property); vii. 10, "wine (of the quality) of goodness;" cf. viii. 2, "wine the (= of the) spicing." It also, in cases where the defined species to which the first undefined member of the *st. const.* belongs, stands in the pl.: ii. 9, 17, viii. 14, "like a young one of the hinds;" iv. 1, vi. 5, "a herd of goats;" iv. 2, "a flock of shorn sheep;" vi. 6, "a flock of lambs," *i.e.* consisting of individuals of this kind. Also, when the second member states the place where a thing originates or is found, the first often remains indeterminate, as one of that which is there found, or a part of that which comes from thence: ii. 1, "a meadow-saffron of Sharon," "a lily of the valleys;" iii. 9, "the wood of Lebanon." The following are doubtful: iv. 4, "a thousand bucklers;" and vii. 5, "a tower of ivory;" less so vii. 1, "the dance of Mahanaim." The following are examples of a different kind: Gen. xvi. 7, "a well of water;" Deut. xxii. 19, "a damsel of Israel;" Ps. cxiii. 9, "a mother of children;" cf. Gen. xxi. 28.

fin. foll., once with the perf. foll. (1 Sam. xiv. 19), once (for Job viii. 21 is easily explained otherwise) with the fut. foll. (Ps. cxli. 10, according to which Gen. xlix. 10 also is explained by Baur and others, but without עַד כִּי in this sense of limited duration: "so long as," being anywhere proved). מְסִבּוֹ is the inflected מֵסַב, which, like the post-bibl. מְסִבָּה, signifies the circuit of the table; for סָבַב signifies also, after 1 Sam. xvi. 11 (the LXX. rightly, after the sense οὐ μὴ κατακλιθῶμεν), to seat themselves around the table, from which it is to be remarked that not till the Greek-Roman period was the Persian custom of reclining at table introduced, but in earlier times they sat (1 Sam. xx. 5; 1 Kings xiii. 20; cf. Ps. cxxviii. 3). Reclining and eating are to be viewed as separate from each other, Amos vi. 4; הֵסֵב, "three and three they recline at table," is in matter as in language *mishnic* (*Berachoth* 42*b*; cf. *Sanhedrin* ii. 4, of the king: if he reclines at table, the Tôra must be opposite him). Thus: While (*usque eo*, so long as), says Shulamith, the king was at his table, my nard gave forth its fragrance.

נֵרְדְּ is an Indian word: *naladâ*, *i.e.* yielding fragrance, Pers. *nard* (*nârd*), Old Arab. *nardîn* (*nârdîn*), is the aromatic oil of an Indian plant *valeriana*, called *Nardostachys 'Gatâmânsi* (hair-tress nard). Interpreters are wont to represent Shulamith as having a stalk of nard in her hand. Hitzig thinks of the nard with which she who is speaking has besprinkled herself, and he can do this because he regards the speaker as one of the court ladies. But that Shulamith has besprinkled herself with nard, is as little to be thought of as that she has in her hand a sprig of nard (*spica nardi*), or, as the ancients said, an ear of nard; she comes from a region where no nard grows, and nard-oil is for a country maiden unattainable.[1] Horace promises Virgil a *cadus* (= 9 gallons) of the best wine for a small onyx-box full of nard; and Judas estimated at 300 denarii (about £8, 10s.) the genuine nard (how frequently nard was adulterated we learn from Pliny) which Mary of Bethany poured from an alabaster box on the head of Jesus, so that the whole house was filled with the odour of the ointment (Mark xiv. 5; John xii. 2). There, in Bethany, the love which is willing to sacrifice all expressed itself in the nard; here, the nard is a figure of the happiness of love, and its fragrance a figure of the longing of love. It is only in the language of flowers that Shulamith makes precious perfume a figure of the love which she bears in the recess of her heart, and which, so

---

[1] The nard plant grows in Northern and Eastern India; the hairy part of the stem immediately above the root yields the perfume. *Vid.* Lassen's *Indische Alterthumskunde*, I. 338 f., III. 41 f.

long as Solomon was absent, breathed itself out and, as it were, cast forth its fragrance[1] (cf. ii. 13, vii. 14) in words of longing. She has longed for the king, and has sought to draw him towards her, as she gives him to understand. He is continually in her mind.

> Ver. 13 A bundle of myrrh is my beloved to me,
> Which lieth between my breasts.
> 14 A bunch of cypress-flowers is my beloved to me,
> From the vine-gardens of Engedi.

Most interpreters, ignoring the lessons of botany, explain 13a of a little bunch of myrrh; but whence could Shulamith obtain this? Myrrh, מֹר (מָרַר, to move oneself in a horizontal direction hither and thither, or gradually to advance; of a fluid, to flow over the plain[2]), belongs, like the frankincense, to the amyrids, which are also exotics[3] in Palestine; and that which is aromatic in the *Balsamodendron myrrha* are the leaves and flowers, but the resin (*Gummi myrrhae*, or merely *myrrha*) cannot be tied in a bunch. Thus the myrrh here can be understood in no other way than as at v. 5; in general צְרוֹר, according to Hitzig's correct remark, properly denotes not what one binds up together, but what one ties up—thus *sacculus*, a little bag. It is not supposed that she carried such a little bag with her (cf. Isa. iii. 20), or a box of frankincense (Luth. musk-apple); but she compares her beloved to a myrrh-repository, which day and night departs not from her bosom, and penetrates her inwardly with its heart-strengthening aroma. So constantly does she think of him, and so delightful is it for her to dare to think of him as her beloved.

The 14th verse presents the same thought. כֹּפֶר is the cypress-cluster or the cypress-flowers, κύπρος (according to Fürst, from כפר = עפר, to be whitish, from the colour of the yellow-white flowers), which botanists call *Lawsonia*, and in the East *Alhennā*; its leaves yield the orange colour with which the Moslem women stain[4] their hands and feet. אֶשְׁכֹּל (from שָׁכַל, to interweave) denotes that which is woven, tresses, or a cluster or garland of their flowers. Here also we

---

[1] In Arab. نتن = נתן, to give an odour, has the specific signification, to give an ill odour (*mintin, foetidus*), which led an Arab. interpreter to understand the expression, "my nard has yielded, etc.," of the stupifying savour which compels Solomon to go away (*Mittheilung*, Goldziher's)

[2] *Vid.* Schlotmann in the *Stud. u. Krit.* (1867), p. 217.

[3] They came from Arabia and India; the better Arabian was adulterated with Indian myrrh.

[4] *Vid.* the literature of this subject in Defrémery's notice of Dozy-Engelmann's work in the *Revue Critique*, III. 2 (1868), p. 408.

have not to suppose that Shulamith carried a bunch of flowers; in her imagination she places herself in the vine-gardens which Solomon had planted on the hill-terraces of Engedi lying on the west of the Dead Sea (Eccles. ii. 4), and chooses a cluster of flowers of the cypress growing in that tropical climate, and says that her beloved is to her internally what such a cluster of cypress-flowers would be to her externally. To be able to call him her beloved is her ornament; and to think of him refreshes her like the most fragrant flowers.

In this ardour of loving devotion, she must appear to the king so much the more beautiful.

Ver. 15 Lo, thou art fair, my love.
Lo, thou art fair; thine eyes are doves.

This is a so-called *comparatio decurtata*, as we say: feet like the gazelle, *i.e.* to which the swiftness of the gazelle's feet belongs (Hab. iii. 19); but instead of "like doves," for the comparison mounts up to equalization, the expression is directly, "doves." If the pupil of the eye were compared with the feathers of the dove (Hitz.), or the sprightliness of the eye with the lively motion hither and thither of the dove (Heiligst.), then the eulogium would stand out of connection with what Shulamith has just said. But it stands in reference to it if her eyes are called doves; and so the likeness to doves' eyes is attributed to them, because purity and gentleness, longing and simplicity, express themselves therein. The dove is, like the myrtle, rose, and apple, an attribute of the goddess of love, and a figure of that which is truly womanly; wherefore יְמִימָה (the Arab. name of a dove), *Columbina*, and the like names of women, *columba* and *columbari*, are words of fondness and caressing. Shulamith gives back to Solomon his eulogium, and rejoices in the prospect of spending her life in fellowship with him.

Ver. 16 Behold, thou art comely, my beloved; yea, charming;
Yea, our couch is luxuriously green.
17 The beams of our house are cedars,
Our wainscot of cypresses.

If ver. 16 were not the echo of her heart to Solomon, but if she therewith meant some other one, then the poet should at least not have used הִנְּךָ, but הִנֵּה. Hitzig remarks, that up to "my beloved" the words appear as those of mutual politeness—that therefore נָעִים (charming) is added at once to distinguish her beloved from the king, who is to her insufferable. But if a man and a woman are together, and he says הִנָּךְ and she says הִנְּךָ, that is as certainly an interchange of address as that one and one are two and not three.

He praises her beauty; but in her eyes it is rather he who is beautiful, yea charming: she rejoices beforehand in that which is assigned to her. Where else could her conjugal happiness find its home but among her own rural scenes? The city with its noisy display does not please her; and she knows, indeed, that her beloved is a king, but she thinks of him as a shepherd. Therefore she praises the fresh green of their future homestead; cedar tops will form the roof of the house in which they dwell, and cypresses its wainscot. The bed, and particularly the bridal-bower (*D. M. Z.* xxii. 153),—but not merely the bed in which one sleeps, but also the cushion for rest, the divan (Amos vi. 4),—has the name עֶרֶשׂ, from עָרַשׂ, to cover over; cf. the "network of goats' hair" (1 Sam. xix. 13) and the κωνωπεῖον of Holofernes (Judith x. 21, xiii. 9), (whence our *kanapee* = canopy), a bed covered over for protection against the κώνωπες, the gnats. רַעֲנָן, whence here the fem. adj. accented on the *ult.*, is not a word of colour, but signifies to be extensible, and to extend far and wide, as *lentus* in *lenti salices;* we have no word such as this which combines in itself the ideas of softness and juicy freshness, of bending and elasticity, of looseness, and thus of overhanging ramification (as in the case of the weeping willow). The beams are called קֹרוֹת, from קָרָה, to meet, to lay crosswise, to hold together (cf. *contingere* and *contignare*). רַחִיטֵנוּ (after another reading, רַחִ׳, from רָחִיט, with *Kametz* immutable, or a virtual *Dag.*) is North Palest. = רִהִיט (*Keri*), for in place of רְהָטִים, troughs (Ex. ii. 16), the Samarit. has רחטים (cf. *sahar* and *sahhar, circumire, zahar* and *zahhar,* whence the Syr. name of scarlet); here the word, if it is not defect. plur. (Heiligst.), is used as collect. sing. of the hollows or panels of a wainscoted ceiling, like φάτναι, whence the LXX. φατνώματα (Symm. φατνώσεις), and like *lacunae,* whence *lacunaria,* for which Jerome has here *laquearia,* which equally denotes the wainscot ceiling Abulwalid glosses the word rightly by מרזבים, gutters (from רָהַט, to run); only this and οἱ διάδρομοι of the Gr. Venet. is not an architectural expression, like רהיטים, which is still found in the Talm. (*vid.* Buxtorf's *Lex.*). To suppose a transposition from חריטנו, from חָרַט, to turn, to carve (Ew. Heiligst. Hitz.), is accordingly not necessary. As the ח in בְּרוֹתִים belongs to the North Palest. (Galilean) form of speech,[1] so also ח for ה in this word: an exchange of the gutturals was characteristic of the Galilean idiom (*vid.* Talm. citations by Frankel, *Einl. in d. jerus. Talm.*

---

[1] Pliny, *H. N.* xxiv. 102, ed. Jan., notes *brathy* as the name of the savin-tree *Juniperus sabina.* Wetstein is inclined to derive the name of Beirut from בְּרוֹת, as the name of the sweet pine, the tree peculiar to the Syrian landscape, and which,

1870, 7b). Well knowing that a mere hut was not suitable for the king, Shulamith's fancy converts one of the magnificent nature-temples of the North Palest. forest-solitudes into a house where, once together, they will live each for the other. Because it is a large house, although not large by art, she styles it by the poet. plur. *bāttenu*. The mystical interpretation here finds in Isa. lx. 13 a favourable support.

What Shulamith now further says confirms what had just been said. City and palace with their splendour please her not; forest and field she delights in; she is a tender flower that has grown up in the quietness of rural life.

Ch. ii. 1 I am a meadow-flower of Sharon,
A lily of the valleys.

We do not render: "the wild-flower," "the lily,"... for she seeks to represent herself not as the one, but only as one of this class; the definiteness by means of the article sometimes belongs exclusively to the second number of the genit. word-chain. מלאך ה׳ may equally (*vid.* at i. 11, Hitz. on Ps. cxiii. 9, and my *Comm.* on Gen. ix. 20) mean "an angel" or "the angel of Jahve;" and בת יש׳ "a virgin," or "the virgin of Israel" (the personification of the people). For *hhăvatstsĕlĕth* (perhaps from *hhivtsĕl*, a denom. quadril. from *bĕtsĕl*, to form bulbs or bulbous knolls) the Syr. Pesh. (Isa. xxxv. 1) uses *chamṣaljotho*, the meadow-saffron, *colchicum autumnale;* it is the flesh-coloured flower with leafless stem, which, when the grass is mown, decks in thousands the fields of warmer regions. They call it *filius ante patrem*, because the blossoms appear before the leaves and the seed-capsules, which develope themselves at the close of winter under the ground. Shulamith compares herself to such a simple and common flower, and that to one in Sharon, *i.e.* in the region known by that name. *Sharon* is *per aphaer.* derived from יְשָׁרוֹן. The most celebrated plain of this name is that situated on the Mediterranean coast between Joppa and Caesarea; but there is also a trans-Jordanic Sharon, 1 Chron. v. 16; and according to Eusebius and Jerome, there is also another district of this name between Tabor and the Lake of Tiberias,[1] which is the one here intended, because Shulamith is a Galilean: she calls herself a flower from the neighbourhood of Nazareth. Aquila translates: "A rosebud of Sharon;" but שׁוֹשַׁנָּה (designedly here the fem. form of the name, which is also

---

growing on the sandy hills, prevents the town from being filled with flying sand. The cypress is now called (Arab.) *sanawbar;* regarding its old names, and their signification in the figurative language of love, *vid.* under Isa. xli. 19.

[1] *Vid.* Lagarde, *Onomastica*, p. 296; cf. Neubauer, *Géographie du Talm.* p. 47.

the name of a woman) does not mean the Rose which was brought at a later period from Armenia and Persia, as it appears,[1] and cultivated in the East (India) and West (Palestine, Egypt, Europe). It is nowhere mentioned in the canonical Scriptures, but is first found in Sir. xxiv. 14, xxxix. 13, l. 8; Wisd. ii. 8; and Esth. i. 6, LXX. Since all the *rosaceae* are five-leaved, and all the *liliaceae* are six-leaved, one might suppose, with Aben Ezra, that the name *sosan* (*susan*) is connected with the numeral שֵׁשׁ, and points to the number of leaves, especially since one is wont to represent to himself the Eastern lilies as red. But they are not only red, or rather violet, but also white: the Moorish-Spanish *azucena* denotes the white lily.[2] The root-word will thus, however, be the same as that of שֵׁשׁ, *byssus*, and שַׁיִשׁ, white marble. The comparison reminds us of Hos. xiv. 6 [5], "I shall be as the dew unto Israel: he shall grow as the lily." הָעֲמָקִים are deep valleys lying between mountains. She thinks humbly of herself; for before the greatness of the king she appears diminutive, and before the comeliness of the king her own beauty disappears—but he takes up her comparison of herself, and gives it a notable turn.

> Ver. 2 As a lily among thorns,
> So is my love among the daughters.

By הַחוֹחִים are not meant the thorns of the plant itself, for the lily has no thorns, and the thorns of the rose are, moreover, called *kotsim*, and not *hhohhim*;[3] besides, *ben* (among) contradicts that idea, since the thorns are on the plant itself, and it is not among them—thus the *hhohhim* are not the thorns of the flower-stem, but the thorn-plants that are around. חוֹחַ designates the thorn-bush, *e.g.* in the allegorical answer of King Josiah to Amaziah, 2 Kings xiv. 9. Simplicity, innocence, gentleness, are the characteristics in which Shulamith surpasses all בָּנוֹת, *i.e.* all women (*vid.* vi. 9), as the lily of the valley surpasses the thorn-bushes around it. "Although thorns surround her, yet can he see her; he sees her quiet life, he finds her beautiful." But continuing this reciprocal rivalry in the praise of mutual love, she says:

---

[1] *Vid.* Ewald, *Jahrbuch*, IV. p. 71; cf. Wüstemann, *Die Rose*, etc., 1854.

[2] *Vid.* Fleischer, *Sitzungs-Berichten d. Sächs. Gesell. d. Wissensch.* 1868, p. 305. Among the rich flora on the descent of the Hauran range, Wetstein saw (*Reisebericht*, p. 148) a dark-violet magnificent lily (*susan*) as large as his fist. We note here Rückert's "Bright lily! The flowers worship God in the garden: thou art the priest of the house."

[3] An Aramaic proverb: "from thorns sprouts the rose" (*i.e.* bad fathers have often pious children), in Heb. is קוֹץ מוֹצִיא שׁוֹשָׁן; *vid. Jalkut Samuel*, § 134.

Ver. 3a As an apple-tree among the trees of the wood,
So is my beloved among the sons.

The apple-tree, the name of which, תַּפּוּחַ, is formed from נָפַח, and denominates it from its fragrant flower and fruit, is as the king among fruit trees, in Shulamith's view. יַעַר (from יָעַר, to be rough, rugged, uneven) is the wilderness and the forest, where are also found trees bearing fruit, which, however, is for the most part sour and unpalatable. But the apple-tree unites delicious fruit along with a grateful shade; and just such a noble tree is the object of her love.

3b Under his shadow it delighted me to sit down;
And his fruit is sweet to my taste.

In *concupivi et consedi* the principal verb completes itself by the co-ordinating of a verb instead of an adv. or inf. as Isa. xlii. 21; Esth. viii. 7; Ewald, § 285. However, *concupivi et consedi* is yet more than *concupivi considere,* for thereby she not only says that she found delight in sitting down, but at the same time also in sitting down in the shadow of this tree. The *Piel* חִמֵּד, occurring only here, expresses the intensity of the wish and longing. The shadow is a figure of protection afforded, and the fruit a figure of enjoyment obtained. The taste is denoted by חֵךְ = חִנֵּךְ, from חָנַךְ, to chew, or also *imbuere;* and that which is sweet is called מָתוֹק, from the smacking connected with an agreeable relish. The *usus loq.* has neglected this image, true to nature, of physical circumstances in words, especially where, as here, they are transferred to the experience of the soul-life. The taste becomes then a figure of the soul's power of perception ($\alpha i\sigma\theta\eta\tau\iota\kappa\acute{o}\nu$); a man's fruit are his words and works, in which his inward nature expresses itself; and this fruit is sweet to those on whom that in which the peculiar nature of the man reveals itself makes a happy, pleasing impression. But not only does the person of the king afford to Shulamith so great delight, he entertains her also with what can and must give her enjoyment.

Ver. 4 He has brought me into the wine-house,
And his banner over me is love.

After we have seen the ladies of the palace at the feast, in which wine is presented, and after Solomon, till now absent, has entered the banqueting-chamber (Arab. *meǵlis*), by בֵּית הַיָּיִן we are not to understand the vineyard, which would be called *bêth hággephānim* or *bêth hā'ănāvim,* as in Acts i. 12, Pesh. the Mount of Olives, *bêth zaite.*[1] He has introduced her to the place where he royally entertains his friends. Well knowing that she, the poor and sunburnt

[1] In Heb. יין does not denote the vine as a plant, as the Aethiop. *wain,* whence *asada wain,* wine-court = vineyard, which Ewald compares; Dillmann, however,

maiden, does not properly belong to such a place, and would rather escape away from it, he relieves her from her fear and bashfulness, for he covers her with his fear-inspiring, awful, and thus surely protecting, banner; and this banner, which he waves over her, and under which she is well concealed, is "love." דֶּגֶל (from דָּגַל, to cover) is the name of the covering of the shaft or standard, *i.e. pannus*, the piece of cloth fastened to a shaft. Like a pennon, the love of the king hovers over her; and so powerful, so surpassing, is the delight of this love which pervades and transports her, that she cries out:

> Ver. 5 Support me with grape-cakes,
> Refresh me with apples:
> For I am sick with love.

She makes use of the intensive form as one in a high degree in need of the reanimating of her almost sinking life: סַמֵּךְ is the intens. of סָמַךְ, to prop up, support, or, as here, to under-prop, uphold; and רַפֵּד, the intens. of רָפַד (R. רף), to raise up from beneath (*vid.* at Prov. vii. 16), to furnish firm ground and support. The apple is the Greek attribute of Aphrodite, and is the symbol of love; but here it is only a means of refreshing; and if thoughts of love are connected with the apple-tree (ii. 3, viii. 5), that is explained from Shulamith's rural home. Böttcher understands quinces; Epstein, citrons; but these must needs have been more closely denoted, as at Prov. xxv. 11, by some addition to the expression. אֲשִׁישׁוֹת (from אָשַׁשׁ, to establish, make firm) are (cf. Isa. xvi. 7; Hos. iii. 1) grapes pressed together like cakes; different from צִמּוּקִים, dried grapes (cf. דְּבֵלָה), fig-cakes (Arab. *dabbûle*, a mass pressed together), and πλακοῦς, *placenta*, from the pressed-out form. A cake is among the gifts (2 Sam. vi. 19) which David distributed to the people on the occasion of the bringing up of the ark; date-cakes, *e.g.* at the monastery at Sinai, are to the present day gifts for the refreshment of travellers. If Shulamith's cry was to be understood literally, one might, with Noack, doubt the correctness of the text; for "love-sickness, even in the age of passion and sentimentality, was not to be cured with roses and apples." But (1) sentimentality, *i.e.* susceptibility, does not belong merely to the Romantic, but also to Antiquity, especially in the Orient, as *e.g.* is shown by the symptoms of sympathy with which the prophets were affected when uttering their threatenings of judgment; let one read such outbreaks of sorrow as Isa. xxi. 3, which, if one is disposed to scorn, may be derided as hysterical fits. Moreover, the Indian, Persian, and Arabic erotic

ineptly cites "vine-arbour," and South-Germ. "*kamerte*" = *vinea camerata*; in Heb. בֵּית הַיַּיִן is the house in which wine is drunk.

(*vid. e.g.* the Romance *Siret 'Antar*) is as sentimental as the German has at any time been. (2) The subject of the passage here is not the curing of love-sickness, but bodily refreshment: the cry of Shulamith, that she may be made capable of bearing the deep agitation of her physical life, which is the consequence, not of her love-sickness, but of her love-happiness. (3) The cry is not addressed (although this is grammatically possible, since סַמְּכוּנִי is, according to rule, = סַמְּכְנָה אֹתִי) to the daughters of Jerusalem, who would in that case have been named, but to some other person; and this points to its being taken not in a literal sense. (4) It presupposes that one came to the help of Shulamith, sick and reduced to weakness, with grapes and apple-scent to revive her fainting spirit. The call of Shulamith thus means: hasten to me with that which will revive and refresh me, for I am sick with love. This love-sickness has also been experienced in the spiritual sphere. St. Ephrem was once so overcome by such a joy that he cried out: "Lord, withdraw Thine hand a little, for my heart is too weak to receive so great joy." And J. R. Hedinger († 1704) was on his deathbed overpowered with such a stream of heavenly delight that he cried: "Oh, how good is the Lord! Oh, how sweet is Thy love, my Jesus! Oh, what a sweetness! I am not worthy of it, my Lord! Let me alone; let me alone!" As the spiritual joy of love, so may also the spiritual longing of love consume the body (cf. Job xix. 27; Ps. lxiii. 2, lxxxiv. 3); there have been men who have actually sunk under a longing desire after the Lord and eternity. It is the state of love-ecstasy in which Shulamith calls for refreshment, because she is afraid of sinking. The contrast between her, the poor and unworthy, and the king, who appears to her as an ideal of beauty and majesty, who raises her up to himself, was such as to threaten her life. Unlooked for, extraordinary fortune, has already killed many. Fear, producing lameness and even death, is a phenomenon common in the Orient.[1] If Pharaoh's daughter, if the Queen of Sheba, finds herself in the presence of Solomon, the feeling of social equality prevents all alarm. But Shulamith is dazzled by the splendour, and disconcerted;

---

[1] "*Ro'b* (לֹעַב, thus in Damascus), or *ra'b* (thus in the Hauran and among the Beduins), is a state of the soul which with us is found only in a lower degree, but which among the Arabians is psychologically noteworthy. The *wahm*, *i.e.* the idea of the greatness and irresistibility of a danger or a misfortune, overpowers the Arabian; all power of body and of soul suddenly so departs from him, that he falls down helpless and defenceless. Thus, on the 8th July 1860, in a few hours, about 6000 Christian men were put to death in Damascus, without one lifting his hand in defence, or uttering one word of supplication. That the *ro'b*

and it happens to her in type as it happened to the seer of Patmos, who, in presence of the ascended Lord, fell at His feet as one dead, Rev. i. 17. If beauty is combined with dignity, it has always, for gentle and not perverted natures, something that awakens veneration and tremor; but if the power of love be superadded, then it has, as a consequence, that combination of awe and inward delight, the psychological appearance of which Sappho, in the four strophes which begin with "Φαίνεταί μοι κῆνος ἴσος θεοῖσιν ἔμμεν ὠνήρ," has described in a manner so true to nature. We may thus, without carrying back modern sentimentality into antiquity, suppose that Shulamith sank down in a paroxysm caused by the rivalry between the words of love and of praise, and thus thanking him,—for Solomon supports and bears her up,—she exclaims:

> Ver. 6 His left hand is under my head,
> And his right hand doth embrace me.

With his left hand he supports her head that had fallen backwards, and with his right he embraces her [*herzet*], as Luther rightly renders it (as he also renders the name *Habakkuk* by "*der Herzer*" = the embracer); for חִבֵּק signifies properly to enfold, to embrace; but then generally, to embrace lovingly, to fondle, of that gentle stroking with the hand elsewhere denoted by חִלָּה, *mulcere*. The situation here is like that at Gen. xxix. 13, xlviii. 10; where, connected with the dat., it is meant of loving arms stretched out to embrace. If this sympathetic, gentle embracing exercises a soothing influence on her, overcome by the power of her emotions; so love mutually kindled now celebrates the first hour of delighted enjoyment, and the happy Shulamith calls to those who are witnesses of her joy:

> Ver. 7 I adjure you, ye daughters of Jerusalem,
> By the gazelles or the hinds of the field,
> That ye arouse not and disturb not love
> Till she pleases.

It is permitted to the Israelites to swear, נִשְׁבַּע, only by God (Gen. xxi. 23); but to adjure, הִשְׁבִּיעַ, by that which is not God, is also admissible, although this example before us is perhaps the only

---

kills in Arabia, European and native physicians have assured me; and I myself can confirm the fact. Since it frequently produces a stiffening of the limbs, with chronic lameness, every kind of paralysis is called *ro'b*, and every paralytic *mar'ûb*. It is treated medically by applying the 'terror-cup' (*tâset er-ro'b*), covered over with sentences engraved on it, and hung round with twenty bells; and since, among the Arabians, the influence of the psychical on the physical is stronger and more immediate than with us, the sympathetic cure may have there sometimes positive results."—*Wetstein.*

direct one in Scripture. צְבִי (= צְבִי, dialect. טַבְי), fem. צְבִיָּה (Aram. טָבִיתָא, Acts ix. 36), plur. *tsebaim* or *tsebajīm*, fem. *tsabaōth* (according with the pl. of צָבָא), softened from *tsebajōth*, is the name for the gazelle, from the elegance of its form and movements. אֵילוֹת is the connecting form of אַיָּלוֹת, whose consonantal *Yod* in the Assyr. and Syr. is softened to the diphthong *ailuv, ailā;* the gen. "of the field," as not distinguishing but describing, belongs to both of the animals, therefore also the first is without the article. אוֹ (after the etymon corresponding to the Lat. *vel*) proceeds, leaving out of view the repetition of this so-called Slumber-Song (iii. 5; cf. viii. 4, as also ii. 9), from the endeavour to give to the adjuration the greatest impression; the expression is varied, for the representations flit from image to image, and the one, wherever possible, is surpassed by the other (*vid.* at Prov. xxx. 31). Under this verse Hengst. remarks: "The bride would not adjure by the hinds, much more would she adjure by the stags." He supposes that Solomon is here the speaker; but a more worthless proof for this could not be thought of. On the contrary, the adjuration by the gazelles, etc., shows that the speaker here is one whose home is the field and wood; thus also not the poet (Hitz.) nor the queen-mother (Böttch.), neither of whom is ever introduced as speaking. The adjuration is that love should not be disturbed, and therefore it is by the animals that are most lovely and free, which roam through the fields. Zöckler, with whom in this one point Grätz agrees, finds here, after the example of Böttch. and Hitz., the earnest warning against wantonly exciting love in themselves (cf. Lat. *irritamenta veneris, irritata voluptas*) till God Himself awakens it, and heart finds itself in sympathy with heart. But the circumstances in which Shulamith is placed ill accord with such a general moralizing. The adjuration is repeated, iii. 5, viii. 4, and wherever Shulamith finds herself near her beloved, as she is here in his arms. What lies nearer, then, than that she should guard against a disturbance of this love-ecstasy, which is like a slumber penetrated by delightful dreams? Instead of תָּעִירוּ אֶתְכֶם, and תְּעוֹרְרוּ, should be more exactly the words תָּעֵרְנָה אֶתְכֶן, and תְּעוֹרֵרְנָה; but the gram. distinction of the *genera* is in Heb. not perfectly developed. We meet also with the very same *synallage generis*, without this adjuration formula, at v. 8, vii. 1, iv. 2, vi. 8, etc.; it is also elsewhere frequent; but in the Song it perhaps belongs to the foil of the vulgar given to the highly poetic. Thus also in the vulgar Arab. the fem. forms *jaktulna, taktulna*, corresponding to תִּקְטֹלְנָה, are fallen out of use. With הֵעִיר, *expergefacere*, there is connected the idea of an interruption of sleep; with עוֹרֵר,

excitare, the idea, which goes further, of arousing out of sleep, placing in the full activity of awakened life.¹ The one adjuration is, that love should not be awakened out of its sweet dream; the other, that it should not be disturbed from its being absorbed in itself. The *Pasek* between חעירו and the word following has, as at Lev. x. 6, the design of keeping the two *Vavs* distinct, that in reading they might not run together; it is the *Pasek* which, as Ben Asher says, serves "to secure to a letter its independence against the similar one standing next it." הָאַהֲבָה is not *abstr. pro concreto*, but love itself in its giving and receiving. Thus closes the second scene of the first act: Shulamith lies like one helpless in the arms of Solomon; but in him to expire is her life; to have lost herself in him, and in him to find herself again, is her happiness.

SECOND ACT.

THE MUTUAL SEEKING AND FINDING OF THE LOVERS.—
Chap. II. 8–III. 5.

FIRST SCENE OF THE SECOND ACT, II. 8–17.

With ii. 8 the second act begins. The so-called slumber-song (iii. 5) closes it, as it did the first act; and also the refrain-like summons to hasten to the mountains leaves no doubt regarding the close of the first scene. The locality is no longer the royal city. Shulamith, with her love-sickness, is once more at home in the house which she inhabits along with her own friends, of whom she has already (i. 6) named her brothers. This house stands alone among the rocks, and deep in the mountain range; around are the vineyards which the family have planted, and the hill-pastures on which they feed their flocks. She longingly looks out here for her distant lover.

> Ver. 8 Hark, my beloved! lo, there he comes!
> Springs over the mountains,
> Bounds over the hills.

---

¹ The distinction between these words is well explained by Lewisohn in his *Investigationes Linguae* (Wilna, 1840), p. 21 : "The מֵעִיר אֶת־הַיָּשֵׁן is satisfied that the sleeper wakes, and it is left to him fully to overcome the influence of sleep; the מְעוֹרֵר, however, arouses him at once from sleepiness, and awakes him to such a degree that he is secured against falling asleep again."

9 My beloved is like a gazelle,
Or a young one of the harts.
Lo, there he stands behind our wall!
He looks through the windows,
Glances through the lattices.

The word קוֹל, in the expression קוֹל דּוֹדִי, is to be understood of the call of the approaching lover (Böttch.), or only of the sound of his footsteps (Hitz.); it is an interjectional clause (sound of my beloved!), in which *kōl* becomes an interjection almost the same as our "*horch*" ["hear!"]. *Vid.* under Gen. iv. 10. זֶה after הִנֵּה sharpens it, as the demonst. *ce* in *ecce = en ce*. בָּא is thought of as partic., as is evident from the accenting of the fem. בָּאָה, *e.g.* Jer. x. 22. דִּלֵּג is the usual word for springing; the parallel קָפֵץ (קִפֵּץ), Aram. קְפַץ, קָפַץ, signifies properly *contrahere* (cogn. קָמַץ, whence *Kametz*, the drawing together of the mouth, more accurately, of the muscles of the lips), particularly to draw the body together, to prepare it for a spring. In the same manner, at the present day, both in the city and in the Beduin Arab. *kamaz*, for which also *famaz*, is used of the springing of a gazelle, which consists in a tossing up of the legs stretched out perpendicularly. 'Antar says similarly, as Shulamith here of the swift-footed *schêbûb* (*D. M. Zeitung*, xxii. 362): *wahu jeǵmiz ǵamazât el-ǵazâl*, it leaps away with the springing of a gazelle.

The figure used in ver. 8 is continued in ver. 9. צְבִי is the gazelle, which is thus designated after its Arab. name *ghazâl*, which has reached us probably through the Moorish-Spanish *gazela* (distinct from "ghasele," after the Pers. *ghazal*, love-poem). עֹפֶר is the young hart, like the Arab. *ghufar* (*ghafar*), the young chamois, probably from the covering of young hair; whence also the young lion may be called כְּפִיר. Regarding the effect of אוֹ passing from one figure to another, *vid.* under ii. 7*a*. The meaning would be plainer were ver. 9*a* joined to ver. 8, for the figures illustrate quick-footed speed (2 Sam. ii. 18; 1 Chron. xii. 8; cf. Ps. xviii. 34 with Hab. iii. 19 and Isa. xxxv. 6). In ver. 9*b* he comes with the speed of the gazelle, and his eyes seek for the unforgotten one. כֹּתֶל (from כָּתַל, *compingere, condensare*; whence, *e.g.*, Arab. *mukattal*, pressed together, rounded, *ramassé*; *vid.* regarding R. כת at Ps. lxxxvii. 6), Aram. כּוּתְלָא (Josh. ii. 15; Targ. word for קִיר), is meant of the wall of the house itself, not of the wall surrounding it. Shulamith is within, in the house: her beloved, standing behind the wall, stands without, before the house (Tympe: *ad latus aversum parietis*, viz. out from it), and looks through the windows,—at one time through this one, at another through that one,—that he might see her and feast his eyes on her. We have here two verbs from the fulness of Heb. synon. for one idea of seeing. הִשְׁגִּיחַ, from שָׁגַח, occurring only three times in the O. T., refers, in respect of the roots שג, שך, שק, to the idea of piercing or splitting (whence also שָׁגַע, to be furious, properly pierced, *percitum esse*; cf. *oestrus*, sting of a gadfly = madness, Arab. transferred to hardiness = madness), and means fixing by reflection and meditation; wherefore הַשְׁגָּחָה in post-bibl. Heb. is the name for Divine Providence. הֵצִיץ, elsewhere to twinkle and to bloom, appears only here in the sense of seeing, and that of the quick darting forward of the glance of the eye, as *blick* [glance] and *blitz* [lightning] (*blic*) are one word; "he saw," says Goethe in *Werther*, "the glance of the powder" (Weigand).[1] The plurs. *fenestrae* and *transennae* are to be understood also as *synechdoche totius pro parte*, which is the same as the plur. of categ.; but with equal correctness we conceive of him as changing his standing place. חַלּוֹן is the window, as an opening in the wall, from חָלַל, *perforare*. חֲרַכִּים we combine most certainly (*vid.* Prov. xii. 27) with (Arab.) *khark, fissura*, so that the idea presents itself of the window broken through the wall, or as itself broken through; for the window in the country there consists for the most part of a pierced wooden frame of a transparent nature,—not (as one would erroneously conclude, from the most significant name of a window שְׂבָכָה, now *schubbáke*, from שָׂבַךְ, to twist, to lattice, to close after the manner of our Venetian blinds) of rods or boards laid crosswise. הֵצִיץ accords with the looking out through the pierced places of such a window, for the glances of his eye are like the penetrating rays of light.

When now Shulamith continues:

Ver. 10a My beloved answered and said to me,
Arise, my love, my fair one, and go forth!

the words show that this first scene is not immediately dramatic, but only mediately; for Shulamith speaks in monologue, though in a dramatic manner narrating an event which occurred between the commencement of their love-relation and her home-bringing.[2] She does not relate it as a dream, and thus it is not one. Solomon

[1] In this sense: to look sharply toward, is הֵצִיץ (Talm.)—for Grätz alone a proof that the Song is of very recent date; but this word belongs, like סמדר, to the old Heb. still preserved in the Talm.

[2] Grätz misinterprets this in order by the supplement of similar ones to make the whole poem a chain of narrative which Shulamith declaims to the daughters of Jerusalem. Thereby it certainly ceases to be dramatic, but so much more tedious does it become by these interposed expressions, " I said," " he said," " the sons of my mother said."

again once more passes, perhaps on a hunting expedition into the northern mountains after the winter with its rains, which made them inaccessible, is over; and after long waiting, Shulamith at length again sees him, and he invites her to enjoy with him the spring season. עָנָה signifies, like ἀποκρίνεσθαι, not always to answer to the words of another, but also to speak on the occasion of a person appearing before one; it is different from ענה, the same in sound, which signifies to sing, properly to sing through the nose, and has the root-meaning of replying (of the same root as עָנָן, clouds, as that which meets us when we look up toward the heavens); but taking speech in hand in consequence of an impression received is equivalent to an answer. With קוּמִי he calls upon her to raise herself from her stupor, and with וּלְכִי־לָךְ, French va-t-en, to follow him.

> Ver. 11 For, lo! the winter is past,
> The rain is over, is gone.
> 12 The flowers appear in the land;
> The time of song has come,
> And the voice of the turtle makes itself heard in our land.
> 13 The fig-tree spices her green figs,
> And the vines stand in bloom, they diffuse fragrance;—
> Rise up, my love, my fair one, and go forth!

The winter is called סְתָו, perhaps from a verb סָתָה (of the same root as סָתַם, סָתַר, without any example, since סוּת, Gen. xlix. 11, is certainly not derived from a verb סוּת), to conceal, to veil, as the time of being overcast with clouds, for in the East winter is the rainy season; (Arab.) shataā is also used in the sense of rain itself (vid. D. M. Zeitsch. xx. 618); and in the present day in Jerusalem, in the language of the people, no other name is used for rain but shataā (not metar). The word סְתָיו, which the Kerí substitutes, only means that one must not read סְתוֹ, but סְתָו with long a; in the same way עָנָיו, humble, from עָנָה, to be bowed down, and שְׂלָיו, a quail, from שָׁלָה, to be fat, are formed and written. Rain is here, however, especially mentioned: it is called gĕshĕm, from gāshăm, to be thick, massy (cf. revivim, of density). With עָבַר, to pass by, there is interchanged חָלַף, which, like (Arab.) khalaf, means properly to press on, and then generally to move to another place, and thus to remove from the place hitherto occupied. In הָלַךְ לוֹ, with the dat. ethicus, which throws back the action on the subject, the winter rain is thought of as a person who has passed by. נִצָּן, with the noun-ending ân, is the same as נִיסָן, and signifies the flower, as the latter the flower-month, floréal; in the use of the word, נִצָּן is related to צִיץ and נִצָּה, probably as little flower is to flower. In hăzzāmīr the idea of the song of birds (Arab. gharad) appears, and this is not to be given up. The

LXX., Aquila, Symm., Targ., Jerome, and the Venet. translate *tempus putationis*: the time of the pruning of vines, which indeed corresponds to the *usus loq.* (cf. זָמַר, to prune the vine, and מִזְמְרָה, a pruning-knife), and to similar names, such as אָסִיף [ingathering of fruit], but supplies no reason for her being invited out into the open fields, and is on this account improbable, because the poet further on speaks for the first time of vines. זָמִיר (זָמַר) is an onomatopoeia, which for the most part denotes song and music; why should זָמִיר thus not be able to denote singing, like זִמְרָה,—but not, at least not in this passage, the singing of men (Hengst.), for they are not silent in winter; but the singing of birds, which is truly a sign of the spring, and as a characteristic feature, is added[1] to this lovely picture of spring? Thus there is also suitably added the mention of the turtle-dove, which is a bird of passage (*vid.* Jer. viii. 7), and therefore a messenger of spring. נִשְׁמַע is 3d pret.: it makes itself heard.

The description of spring is finished by a reference to the fig-tree and the vine, the standing attributes of a prosperous and peaceful homestead, 1 Kings v. 5; 2 Kings xviii. 31. פַּג (from פָּנַג, and thus named, not from their hardness, but their delicacy) are the little fruits of the fig-tree which now, when the harvest-rains are over, and the spring commences with the equinox of Nisan, already begin to assume a red colour; the verb חָנַט does not mean "to grow into a bulb," as Böttch. imagines; it has only the two meanings, *condire* (*condiri*, post-bibl. syn. of בָּשַׁל) and *rubescere*. From its colour, wheat has the name חִטָּה = חִנְטָה; and here also the idea of colour has the preference, for becoming fragrant does not occur in spring,—in the history of the cursing of the fig-tree at the time of the Passover, Mark (xi. 13) says, "for the time of figs was not yet." In fig-trees, by this time the green of the fruit-formation changes its colour, and the vines are סְמָדַר, blossom, *i.e.* are in a state of bloom (LXX. κυπρίζουσαι; cf. vii. 13, κυπρισμός)—it is a clause such as Ex. ix. 31, and to which "they diffuse fragrance" (ver. 13) is parallel. This word סמדר is usually regarded as a compound word, consisting of סַם, scent, and הָדָר, brightness = blossom (*vid.* Gesen. *Thes.*); it is undeniable that there are such compound formations, *e.g.* שְׁלַאֲנָן, from שָׁלָה and שָׁאַן; חַלָּמִישׁ, from (Arab.) *ḥams*, to be hard, and *hals*, to be dark-brown.[2] But the

---

[1] It is true that besides in this passage *zāmār*, of the singing of birds, is not demonstrable, the Arab. *zamar* is only used of the shrill cry of the ostrich, and particularly the female ostrich.

[2] In like manner as (Arab.) *karbsh*, *corrugare*, is formed of *karb*, to string, and *karsh*, to wrinkle, combined; and another extension of *karsh* is *kurnash*, wrinkles, and *mukarnash*, wrinkled. "One day," said Wetstein to me, "I asked an

traditional reading סְמָדַר (not סְמָדָר) is unfavourable to this view; the middle *ā* accordingly, as in צֶלְצַל, presents itself as an *ante*-tone vowel (Ewald, § 154*a*), and the stem-word appears as a quadril. which may be the expansion of סדר, to range, put in order in the sense of placing asunder, unfolding. Symm. renders the word by οἰνάνθη, and the Talm. idiom shows that not only the green five-leaved blossoms of the vine were so named, but also the fruit-buds and the first shoots of the grapes. Here, as the words "they diffuse fragrance" (as at vii. 14 of the mandrakes) show, the vine-blossom is meant which fills the vineyard with an incomparably delicate fragrance. At the close of the invitation to enjoy the spring, the call "Rise up," etc., with which it began, is repeated. The *Chethîb* לכי, if not an error in writing, justly set aside by the *Kerî*, is to be read לְכִי (cf. Syr. *bechi*, in thee, *l'votechi*, to thee, but with occult *i*)—a North Palestinism for לָךְ, like 2 Kings iv. 2, where the *Kerî* has substituted the usual form (*vid.* under Ps. ciii. introd.) for this very dialectic form, which is there undoubtedly original.

Ver. 14. Solomon further relates how he drew her to himself out of her retirement:

> My dove in the clefts of the rock,
> In the hiding-place of the cliff;
> Let me see thy countenance,
> Let me hear thy voice!
> For thy voice is sweet and thy countenance comely.

"Dove" (for which Castellio, *columbula*, like *vulticulum, voculam*) is a name of endearment which Shulamith shares with the church of God, Ps. lxxiv. 19; cf. lvi. 1; Hos. vii. 11. The wood-pigeon builds its nest in the clefts of the rocks and other steep rocky places, Jer. xlviii. 28.[1] That Shulamith is thus here named, shows that, far removed from intercourse with the world, her home was among the mountains. חַגְוֵי, from חֶגֶו, or also חָגוּ, requires a verb חָגָה = (Arab.)

Arab the origin of the word *karnasâ*, to wrinkle, and he replied that it was derived from a sheep's stomach that had lain over night, *i.e.* the stomach of a slaughtered sheep that had lain over night, by which its smooth surface shrinks together and becomes wrinkled. In fact, we say of a wrinkled countenance that it is *mathal alkarash albayt*." With right Wetstein gathers from this curious fact how difficult it is to ascertain by purely etymological considerations the view which guided the Semites in this or that designation. *Samdor* is also a strange word; on the one side it is connected with *sadr*, of the veiling of the eyes, as the effect of terror; and on the other with *samd*, of stretching oneself straight out. E. Meier takes סמדר as the name of the vine-blossom, as changed from סמסר, bristling. Just as unlikely as that סָמַד is cogn. to חָמַד, *Jesurun*, p. 221.

[1] Wetstein's *Reisebericht*, p. 182: "If the Syrian wood-pigeon does not find a

khajja, findere. סֶלַע, as a Himyar. lexicographer defines it, is a cleft into the mountains after the nature of a defile; with צוּר, only the ideas of inaccessibility and remoteness are connected; with סלע, those of a secure hiding-place, and, indeed, a convenient, pleasant residence. מַדְרֵגָה is the stairs; here the rocky stairs, as the two chalk-cliffs on the Rügen, which sink perpendicularly to the sea, are called "*Stubbenkammer*," a corruption of the Slavonic *Stupnykamen*, i.e. the Stair-Rock. "Let me see," said he, as he called upon her with enticing words, "thy countenance;" and adds this as a reason, "for thy countenance is lovely." The word מַרְאֵיךְ, thus pointed, is sing.; the *Jod otians* is the third root letter of רָאִי, retained only for the sake of the eye. It is incorrect to conclude from *ashrēch*, in Eccles. x. 17, that the *ech* may be also the plur. suff., which it can as little be as *ēhu* in Prov. xxix. 18; in both cases the sing. *ĕshĕr* has substituted itself for *ashrē*. But, inversely, *mărāīch* cannot be sing.; for the sing. is simply *marēch*. Also *mărāv*, Job xli. 1, is not sing.: the sing. is *marēhu*, Job iv. 16; Song v. 15. On the other hand, the determination of such forms as מַרְאֵיהֶם, מַרְאֵינוּ, is difficult: these forms may be sing. as well as plur. In the passage before us, מַרְאִים is just such a non-numer. plur. as פָּנִים. But while *panīm* is an extensive plur., as Böttcher calls it: the countenance, in its extension and the totality of its parts,—*marīm*, like *marōth*, vision, a stately term, Ex. xl. 2 (*vid.* Dietrich's *Abhand.* p. 19), is an amplificative plur.: the countenance, on the side of its fulness of beauty and its overpowering impression.

There now follows a *cantiuncula*. Shulamith comes forward, and, singing, salutes her beloved. Their love shall celebrate a new spring. Thus she wishes everything removed, or rendered harmless, that would disturb the peace of this love:

> Ver. 15 Catch us the foxes, the little foxes,
>   The spoilers of the vineyards;
>   For our vineyards are in bloom!
> 16 My beloved is mine, and I am his;
>   Who feeds [his flock] among the lilies.

If the king is now, on this visit of the beloved, engaged in hunting, the call: "Catch us," etc., if it is directed at all to any definite persons, is addressed to those who follow him. But this is a vine-dresser's ditty, in accord with Shulamith's experience as the keeper

---

pigeon-tower, περιστερεῶνα, it builds its nest in the hollows of rocky precipices, or in the walls of deep and wide fountains." See also his *Nord-arabien*, p. 58: "A number of scarcely accessible mountains in Arabia are called *alkunnat*, a rock-nest."

of a vineyard, which, in a figure, aims at her love-relation. The vineyards, beautiful with fragrant blossom, point to her covenant of love; and the foxes, the little foxes, which might destroy these united vineyards, point to all the great and little enemies and adverse circumstances which threaten to gnaw and destroy love in the blossom, ere it has reached the ripeness of full enjoyment. שֻׁעָלִים comprehends both foxes and jackals, which "destroy or injure the vineyards; because, by their holes and passages which they form in the ground, loosening the soil, so that the growth and prosperity of the vine suffers injury" (Hitzig). This word is from שָׁעַל (R. של), to go down, or into the depth. The little foxes are perhaps the jackals, which are called *tănnīm*, from their extended form, and in height are seldom more than fifteen inches. The word "jackal" has nothing to do with שׁוּעָל, but is the Persian-Turkish *shaghal*, which comes from the Sanscr. *crgála*, the howler (R. *krag*, like *kap-ála*, the skull; R. *kap*, to be arched). Moreover, the mention of the foxes naturally follows 14a, for they are at home among rocky ravines. Hitzig supposes Shulamith to address the foxes: hold for us = wait, ye rascals! But אֱחָז, Aram. אֲחַד, does not signify to wait, but to seize or lay hold of (synon. לָכַד, Judg. xv. 4), as the lion its prey, Isa. v. 29. And the plur. of address is explained from its being made to the king's retinue, or to all who could and would give help. Fox-hunting is still, and has been from old times, a sport of rich landowners; and that the smaller landowners also sought to free themselves from them by means of snares or otherwise, is a matter of course,—they are proverbially as destroyers, Neh. iii. 35 [iv. 3], and therefore a figure of the false prophets, Ezek. xiii. 4. מְחַבְּ' כְּרָמ' are here instead of מְחַבְּלֵי הַכְּרָמ'. The articles are generally omitted, because poetry is not fond of the article, where, as here (cf. on the other hand, i. 6), the thoughts and language permit it; and the fivefold *im* is an intentional mere *verborum sonus*. The clause וּכְרָ' סְמָדַר is an explanatory one, as appears from the *Vav* and the subj. preceding, as well as from the want of a *finitum*. סְמָדַר maintains here also, *in pausa*, the sharpening of the final syllable, as חָצ', Deut. xxviii. 42.

The 16th verse is connected with the 15th. Shulamith, in the pentast. song, celebrates her love-relation; for the praise of it extends into ver. 15, is continued in ver. 16, and not till ver. 17 does she address her beloved. Luther translates:

> My beloved is mine, and I am his;
> He feeds [his flock] among the roses.

He has here also changed the "lilies" of the Vulgate into "roses;" for of the two queens among the flowers, he gave the preference to the popular and common rose; besides, he rightly does not translate הָרֹעֶה, in the mid. after the *pascitur inter lilia* of the Vulgate: who feeds himself, *i.e.* pleases himself; for רעה has this meaning only when the object expressly follows, and it is evident that 'בַּשׁ cannot possibly be this object, after Gen. xxxvii. 2,—the object is thus to be supplied. And which? Without doubt, *gregem*; and if Heiligst., with the advocates of the shepherd-hypothesis, understands this feeding (of the flock) among the lilies, of feeding on a flowery meadow, nothing can be said against it. But at vi. 2 f., where this saying of Shulamith is repeated, she says that her beloved בַּנַּנִּים feeds and gathers lilies. On this the literal interpretation of the *qui pascit* (*gregem*) *inter lilia* is wrecked; for a shepherd, such as the shepherd-hypothesis supposes, were he to feed his flock in a garden, would be nothing better than a thief; such shepherds, also, do not concern themselves with the plucking of flowers, but spend their time in knitting stockings. It is Solomon, the king, of whom Shulamith speaks. She represents him to herself as a shepherd; but in such a manner that, at the same time, she describes his actions in language which rises above ordinary shepherd-life, and, so to speak, idealizes. She, who was herself a shepherdess, knows from her own circle of thought nothing more lovely or more honourable to conceive and to say of him, than that he is a shepherd who feeds among lilies. The locality and the surroundings of his daily work correspond to his nature, which is altogether beauty and love. Lilies, the emblem of unapproachable highness, awe-inspiring purity, lofty elevation above what is common, bloom where the lily-like (king) wanders, whom the Lily names her own. The mystic interpretation and mode of speaking takes "lilies" as the figurative name of holy souls, and a lily-stalk as the symbol of the life of regeneration. Mary, who is celebrated in song as the *rosa mystica*, is rightly represented in ancient pictures with a lily in her hand on the occasion of the Annunciation; for if the people of God are called by Jewish poets "a people of lilies," she is, within this lily-community, this *communio sanctorum*, the lily without a parallel.

Shulamith now further relates, in a dramatic, lively manner, what she said to her beloved after she had saluted him in a song:

> Ver. 17 Till the day cools and the shadows flee away,
> Turn; make haste, my beloved,
> Like a gazelle or a young one of the hinds
> On the craggy mountains.

With the perf., שֶׁ עַד (cf. עַד אִם, Gen. xxiv. 33) signifies, till something is done; with the fut., till something will be done. Thus: till the evening comes—and, therefore, before it comes—may he do what she requires of him. Most interpreters explain סֹב, *verte te*, with the supplement *ad me;* according to which Jerome, Castell., and others translate by *revertere*. But Ps. lxxi. 21 does not warrant this rendering; and if Shulamith has her beloved before her, then by סֹב she can only point him away from herself; the parall. viii. 14 has בְּרַח instead of סֹב, which consequently means, "turn thyself from here away." Rather we may suppose, as I explained in 1851, that she holds him in her embrace, as she says, and, inseparable from him, will wander with him upon the mountains. But neither that *ad me* nor this *mecum* should have been here (cf. on the contrary viii. 14) unexpressed. We hold by what is written. Solomon surprises Shulamith, and invites her to enjoy with him the spring-time; not alone, because he is on a hunting expedition, and—as denoted by "catch us" (ver. 15)—with a retinue of followers. She knows that the king has not now time to wander at leisure with her; and therefore she asks him to set forward his work for the day, and to make haste on the mountains till "the day cools and the shadows flee." Then she will expect him back; then in the evening she will spend the time with him as he promised her. The verb פּוּחַ, with the guttural letter *Hheth* and the labial *Pe,* signifies *spirare*, here of being able to be breathed, *i.e.* cool, like the expression רוּחַ הַ׳, Gen. iii. 8 (where the guttural *Hheth* is connected with *Resh*). The shadows flee away, when they become longer and longer, as if on a flight, when they stretch out (Ps. cix. 23, cii. 12) and gradually disappear. Till that takes place—or, as we say, will be done—he shall hasten with the swiftness of a gazelle on the mountains, and that on the mountains of separation, *i.e.* the riven mountains, which thus present hindrances, but which he, the "swift as the gazelle" (*vid.* ii. 9), easily overcomes. Rightly, Bochart: *montes scissionis, ita dicti propter,* ῥωχμούς *et* χάσματα. Also, Luther's "*Scheideberge*" are "mountains with peaks, from one of which to the other one must spring." We must not here think of *Bithron* (2 Sam. ii. 29), for that is a mountain ravine on the east of Jordan; nor of Bar-Cochba's בֵּיתֵר (Kirschbaum, Landau), because this mountain (whether it be sought for to the south of Jerusalem or to the north of Antipatris) ought properly to be named בֵּיתְתֵר (*vid.* Aruch). It is worthy of observation, that in an Assyrian list of the names of animals, along with *ṣabi* (gazelle) and *apparu* (the young of the gazelle or of the hind), the name *bitru* occurs, perhaps the name of the *rupicapra*. At the close of the song, the expression "mountain of spices" occurs instead of "mountain of separation," as here. There no more hindrances to be overcome lie in view, the rock-cliffs have become fragrant flowers. The request here made by Shulamith breathes self-denying humility, patient modesty, inward joy in the joy of her beloved. She will not claim him for herself till he has accomplished his work. But when he associates with her in the evening, as with the Emmaus disciples, she will rejoice if he becomes her guide through the new-born world of spring. The whole scene permits, yea, moves us to think of this, that the Lord already even now visits the church which loves Him, and reveals Himself to her; but that not till the evening of the world is His *parousia* to be expected.

SECOND SCENE OF THE SECOND ACT, III. 1–5.

In the first scene, Shulamith relates what externally happened to her one day when the evening approached. In this second scene, she now relates what she inwardly experienced when the night came. She does not indeed say that she dreamed it; but that it is a dream is seen from this, that that which is related cannot be represented as an external reality. But it at once appears as an occurrence that took place during sleep.

> Chap. iii. 1 On my bed in the nights
> I sought him whom my soul loveth:
> I sought him, and found him not.

She does not mean to say that she sought him beside herself on her couch; for how could that be of the modest one, whose home-bringing is first described in the next act—she could and might miss him there neither waking nor sleeping. The commencement is like Job xxxiii. 15. She was at night on her couch, when a painful longing seized her: the beloved of her soul appeared to have forsaken her, to have withdrawn from her; she had lost the feeling of his nearness, and was not able to recover it. לֵילוֹת is neither here nor at iii. 8 necessarily the categ. plur. The meaning may also be, that this pain, arising from a sense of being forgotten, always returned upon her for several nights through: she became distrustful of his fidelity; but the more she apprehended that she was no longer loved, the more ardent became her longing, and she arose to seek for him who had disappeared.

> Ver. 2 So I will arise, then, and go about the city,
> The markets, and the streets;
> I will seek him whom my soul loveth!—
> I sought him, and found him not.

How could this night-search, with all the strength of love, be consistent with the modesty of a maiden? It is thus a dream which she relates. And if the beloved of her soul were a shepherd, would she seek him in the city, and not rather without, in the field or in some village? No; the beloved of her soul is Solomon; and in the dream, Jerusalem, his city, is transported close to the mountains of her native home. The resolution expressed by "I will arise, then," is not introduced by "then I said," or any similar phrase: the scene consists of a monologue which dramatically represents that which is experienced. Regarding the second *Chatef-Pathach* of וָאֲם, vid. Baer's *Genesis*, p. 7. שְׁוָקִים is the plur. of שׁוּק (= *shavk*), as שְׁוָרִים of שׁוּר (= *shavr*); the root-word שׁוּק (Arab. *shak*) signifies to press on, to follow after continuously; (Arab.) *suwak* designates perhaps, originally, the place to which one drives cattle for sale, as in the desert; (Arab.) *sawak* designates the place to which one drives cattle for drink (Wetzst.). The form אֲבַקְשָׁה is without the *Daghesh*, as are all the forms of this verb except the imper.; the semi-guttural nature of the *Koph* has something opposing the simple *Sheva*.

Shulamith now relates what she further experienced when, impelled by love-sorrow, she wandered through the city:

Ver. 3 The watchmen who go about in the city found me:
"Have ye seen him whom my soul loveth?"

Here also (as in ver. 2) there is wanting before the question such a phrase as, "and I asked them, saying:" the monologue relates dramatically. If she described an outward experience, then the question would be a foolish one; for how could she suppose that the watchmen, who make their rounds in the city (Epstein, against Grätz, points for the antiquity of the order to Ps. cxxvii. 1; Isa. lxii. 6; cf. xxi. 11), could have any knowledge of her beloved! But if she relates a dream, it is to be remembered that feeling and imagination rise higher than reflection. It is in the very nature of a dream, also, that things thus quickly follow one another without fixed lineaments. This also, that having gone out by night, she found in the streets him whom she sought, is a happy combination of circumstances formed in the dreaming soul; an occurrence without probable external reality, although not without deep inner truth:

Ver. 4 Scarcely had I passed from them,
When I found him whom my soul loveth.
I seized him, and did not let him go
Until I brought him into the house of my mother,
And into the chamber of her that gave me birth.

כִּמְעַט = *paululum*, here standing for a sentence: it was as a little that I passed, etc. Without שׁ, it would be *paululum transii*; with it, *paululum fuit quod transii*, without any other distinction than that in the latter case the *paululum* is more emphatic. Since Shulamith relates something experienced earlier, אֲחַזְתִּי is not fitly rendered by *teneo*, but by *tenui*; and וְלֹא אַרְפֶּנּוּ, not by *et non dimittam eum*, but, as the neg. of וְאַרְפֶנוּ, *et dimisi eum*,—not merely *et non dimittebam eum*, but *et non dimisi eum*. In Gen. xxxii. 27 [26], we read the cogn. שַׁלַּח, which signifies, to let go ("let me go"), as הַרְפֵּה, to let loose, to let free. It is all the same whether we translate, with the subjective colouring, *donec introduxerim*, or, with the objective, *donec introduxi*; in either case the meaning is that she held him fast till she brought him, by gentle violence, into her mother's house. With בית there is the more definite parallel חֶדֶר, which properly signifies (*vid.* under i. 4), *recessus, penetrale;* with אִמִּי, the seldom occurring (only, besides, at Hos. ii. 7) הוֹרָה, *part. f. Kal* of הָרָה, to conceive, be pregnant, which poetically, with the accus., may mean *parturire* or *parere*. In Jacob's blessing, Gen. xlix. 26, as the text lies before us, his parents are called הוֹרַי; just as in Arab. *ummâni*, properly "my two mothers," may be used for "my parents;" in the Lat. also, *parentes* means father and mother zeugmatically taken together.

The closing words of the monologue are addressed to the daughters of Jerusalem.

> Ver. 5 I adjure you, O ye daughters of Jerusalem,
> By the gazelles or the hinds of the field,
> That ye awake not and disturb not love
> Till she pleases.

We are thus obliged apparently to think of the daughters of Jerusalem as being present during the relation of the dream. But since Shulamith in the following Act is for the first time represented as brought from her home to Jerusalem, it is more probable that she represented her experience to herself in secret, without any auditors, and feasting on the visions of the dream, which brought her beloved so near, that she had him by herself alone and exclusively, that she fell into such a love-ecstasy as ii. 7; and pointing to the distant Jerusalem, deprecates all disturbance of this ecstasy, which in itself is like a slumber pervaded by pleasant dreams. In two monologues dramatically constructed, the poet has presented to us a view of the thoughts and feelings by which the inner life of the maiden was moved in the near prospect of becoming a bride and being married. Whoever reads the Song in the sense in which it is incorporated with the canon, and that, too, in the historical sense fulfilled in the N. T., will not be able to read the two scenes from Shulamith's experience without finding therein a mirror of the intercourse of the soul with God in Christ, and cherishing thoughts such, *e.g.*, as are expressed in the ancient hymn:

Quando tandem venies, meus amor?
Propera de Libano, dulcis amor!
Clamat, amat sponsula: Veni, Jesu,
Dulcis veni Jesu!

THIRD ACT.

THE BRINGING OF THE BRIDE AND THE MARRIAGE.
Chap. III. 6–V. I.

FIRST SCENE OF THE THIRD ACT, III. 6–11.

In this third Act the longing of the loving one after her beloved is finally appeased. The first scene[1] represents her home-bringing into the royal city. A gorgeous procession which marches towards Jerusalem attracts the attention of the inhabitants of the city.

> Ver. 6 Who is this coming up from the wilderness
> Like pillars of smoke,
> Perfumed with myrrh and frankincense,
> With all aromatics of the merchants?

It is possible that זֹאת and עֹלָה may be connected; but זֶה עָנִי, Ps. xxxiv. 7 (this poor man, properly, this, a poor man), is not analogous, it ought to be זֹאת הָעֹלָה. Thus *zoth* will either be closely connected with מִי, and make the question sharper and more animated, as is that in Gen. xii. 18, or it will be the subject which then, as in Isa. lxiii. 1, Job xxxviii. 2, cf. below vii. 5*b*, Jonah iv. 17, Amos ix. 12, is more closely written with indeterminate participles, according to which it is rightly accented. But we do not translate with Heiligst. *quid est hoc quod adscendit*, for *mî* asks after a person, *mâ* after a thing, and only *per attract.* does *mî* stand for *mâ* in Gen. xxxiii. 8; Judg. xiii. 17; Mic. i. 5; also not *quis est hoc* (Vaih.), for *zoth* after *mi* has a personal sense, thus: *quis (quaenam) haec est.* That it is

---

[1] *Vid.* Schlottmann in the *Stud. u. Kritiken*, 1867, pp. 209–243. Rejecting the dramatic arrangement of this section, he interprets it throughout as a song of the chorus of the daughters of Jerusalem, which is already contradicted by 10*b*.

a woman that is being brought forward those who ask know, even if she is yet too far off to be seen by them, because they recognise in the festal gorgeous procession a marriage party. That the company comes up from the wilderness, it may be through the wilderness which separates Jerusalem from Jericho, is in accordance with the fact that a maiden from Galilee is being brought up, and that the procession has taken the way through the Jordan valley (Ghôr); but the scene has also a typical colouring; for the wilderness is, since the time of the Mosaic deliverance out of Egypt, an emblem of the transition from a state of bondage to freedom, from humiliation to glory (*vid.* under Isa. xl. 3; Hos. i. 16; Ps. lxviii. 5). The pomp is like that of a procession before which the censer of frankincense is swung. Columns of smoke from the burning incense mark the line of the procession before and after. תִּימְרוֹת (תִּימֲ) here and at Job iii. (*vid.* Norzi) is formed, as it appears, from יָמַר, to strive upwards, a kindred form to אָמַר; cf. Isa. lxi. 6 with xvii. 6, Ps. xciv. 4; the verb תָּמַר, whence the date-palm receives the name תָּמָר, is a secondary formation, like תָּאַב to אָבָה. Certainly this form תִּימָרָה (cf. on the contrary, תּוֹלֵדָה) is not elsewhere to be supported; Schlottm. sees in it תִּמְרוֹת, from תִּמְרָה; but such an expansion of the word for *Dag. dirimens* is scarcely to be supposed. This naming of the pillars of smoke is poet., as Jonah iii. 3; cf. "a pillar of smoke," Judg. xx. 40. She who approaches comes from the wilderness, brought up to Jerusalem, placed on an elevation, "like pillars of smoke," *i.e.* not herself likened thereto, as Schlottm. supposes it must be interpreted (with the *tertium comp.* of the slender, precious, and lovely), but encompassed and perfumed by such. For her whom the procession brings this lavishing of spices is meant; it is she who is incensed or perfumed with myrrh and frankincense. Schlottm. maintains that מְקֻטֶּרֶת cannot mean anything else than "perfumed," and therefore he reads מְקֻטֹּרֶת (as Aq. ἀπὸ θυμιάματος, and Jerome). But the word *mekuttĕrĕth* does not certainly stand alone, but with the genit. foll.; and thus as "rent in their clothes," 2 Sam. xiii. 31, signifies not such as are themselves rent, but those whose clothes are rent (Ewald, § 288*b*, compare also de Sacy, II. § 321), so מקט׳ וגו׳ can also mean those for whom (for whose honour) this incense is expended, and who are thus fumigated with it. מֹר, myrrh, (Arab.) *murr* (*vid.* above under i. 13), stands also in Ex. xxx. 23 and Ps. xlv. 9 at the head of the perfumes; it came from Arabia, as did also frankincense *levōnā*, Arab. *lubân* (later referred to benzoin); both of the names are Semitic, and the circumstance that the *Tôra* required myrrh as a component part of the holy oil, Ex. xxx. 23, and frankincense as a component part of the holy incense, Ex. xxx. 34, points to Arabia as the source whence they were obtained. To these two principal spices there is added מִכֹּל (cf. Gen. vi. 20, ix. 2) as an *et cetera*. רוֹכֵל denotes the travelling spice merchants (traders in aromatics), and traders generally. אֲבָקָה, which is related to אָבָק as powder to dust (cf. *abacus*, a reckoning-table, so named from the sand by means of which arithmetical numbers were reckoned), is the name designating single drugs (*i.e.* dry wares; cf. the Arab. *elixir* = ξηρόν).

The description of the palanquin now following, one easily attributes to another voice from the midst of the inhabitants of Jerusalem.

> Ver. 7 Lo! Solomon's palanquin,
> Threescore heroes are around it,
> Of the heroes of Israel,
> 8 All of them armed with the sword, expert in war.
> Each with his sword on his thigh,
> Against fear in the nights.

Since אַפִּרְיוֹן, 9*a*, is not by itself a word clearly intelligible, so as to lead us fully to determine what is here meant by מִטָּה as distinguished from it, we must let the connection determine. We have before us a figure of that which is called in the post-bibl. Heb. הַכְנָסַת כַּלָה (the bringing-home of the bride). The bridegroom either betook himself to her parents' house and fetched his bride thence, which appears to be the idea lying at the foundation of Ps. xlv., if, as we believe, the ivory-palaces are those of the king of Israel's house; or she was brought to him in festal procession, and he went forth to meet her, 1 Macc. ix. 39—the prevailing custom, on which the parable of the ten virgins (Matt. xxv.) is founded.[1] Here the bride comes from a great distance; and the difference in rank between the Galilean maid and the king brings this result, that he does not himself go and fetch her, but that she is brought to him. She comes, not as in old times Rebecca did, riding on a camel, but is carried in a *mittā*, which is surrounded by an escort for protection and as a mark of honour. Her way certainly led through the wilderness, where it was necessary, by a safe convoy, to provide against the possibility (*min* in *mippahad*, cf. Isa. iv. 6, xxv. 4) of being attacked by robbers; whereas it would be more difficult to understand why the marriage-bed in the palace of the king of peace (1 Chron. xxii. 9) should be surrounded by such

---

[1] Weigand explains the German word *Braut* (bride) after the Sanscr. *praudha*, "she who is brought in a carriage;" but this particip. signifies nothing more than (*aetate*) *provecta*.

an armed band for protection. That Solomon took care to have his chosen one brought to him with royal honours, is seen in the lavish expenditure of spices, the smoke and fragrance of which signalized from afar the approach of the procession,—the *mittā*, which is now described, can be no other than that in which, sitting or reclining, or half sitting, half reclining, she is placed, who is brought to him in such a cloud of incense. Thus *mittā* (from *nāthā*, to stretch oneself out), which elsewhere is also used of a bier, 2 Sam. iii. 21 (like the Talm. עֶרֶשׂ = עֶרֶס), will here signify a portable bed, a sitting cushion hung round with curtains after the manner of the Indian palanquin, and such as is found on the Turkish caiques or the Venetian gondolas. The appositional nearer definition שֶׁלִּשְׁ׳, " which belonged to Solomon " (*vid.* under i. 6b), shows that it was a royal palanquin, not one belonging to one of the nobles of the people. The bearers are unnamed persons, regarding whom nothing is said; the sixty heroes form only the guard for safety and for honour (*sauvegarde*), or the *escorte* or *convoie*. The sixty are the tenth part (the *élite*) of the royal body-guard, 1 Sam. xxvii. 2, xxx. 9, etc. (Schlottm.). If it be asked, Why just 60 ? we may perhaps not unsuitably reply: The number 60 is here, as at vi. 8, the number of Israel multiplied by 5, the fraction of 10; so that thus 60 distinguished warriors form the half of the escort of a king of Israel. אֲחֻזֵי חֶרֶב properly means, held fast by the sword so that it does not let them free, which, according to the sense = holding fast [= practised in the use of the sword]; the Syr. translation of the Apoc. renders παντοκράτωρ by " he who is held by all," *i.e.* holding it (cf. Ewald, § 149*d*).[1]

Another voice now describes the splendour of the bed of state which Solomon prepared in honour of Shulamith:

> Ver. 9 A bed of state hath King Solomon made for himself
> Of the wood of Lebanon.
> 10 Its pillars hath he made of silver,
> Its support of gold, its cushion of purple;
> Its interior is adorned from love
> By the daughters of Jerusalem.

The sound of the word, the connection and the description, led the Greek translators (the LXX., Venet., and perhaps also others) to render אַפִּרְיוֹן by φορεῖον, litter, palanquin (Vulg. *ferculum*). The *appiryon* here described has a silver pedestal and a purple cushion —as we read in Athenaeus v. 13 (II. p. 317, ed. Schweigh.) that the

---

[1] This deponent use of the *part. pass.* is common in the Mishna; *vid.* Geiger's *Lehrbuch zur Sprache der Mishna*, § 16. 5.

philosopher and tyrant Athenion showed himself "on a silver-legged φορεῖον, with purple coverlet;" and the same author, v. 5 (II. p. 253), also says, that on the occasion of a festal procession by Antiochus Epiphanes, behind 200 women who sprinkled ointments from golden urns came 80 women, sitting in pomp on golden-legged, and 500 on silver-legged, φορεῖα—this is the proper name for the costly women's-litter (Suidas: φορεῖον γυναικεῖον), which, according to the number of bearers (Mart. VI. 77: six Cappadocians and, ix. 2, eight Syrians), was called ἑξάφορον (*hexaphorum*, Mart. II. 81) or ὀκτώφορον (*octophorum*, Cicero's *Verr.* v. 10). The Mishna, *Sota* ix. 14, uses *appiryon* in the sense of *phoreion*: "in the last war (that of Hadrian) it was decreed that a bride should not pass through the town in an *appiryon* [on account of the danger], but our Rabbis sanctioned it later [for modesty's sake];" as here, "to be carried in an *appiryon*," so in Greek, προιέναι (καταστείχειν) ἐν φορείῳ. In the Midrash also, *Bamidbar rabba* c. 12, and elsewhere, *appiryon* of this passage before us is taken in all sorts of allegorical significations, in most of which the identity of the word with φορεῖον is supposed, which is also there written פּוּרְיוֹן (after Aruch), cf. Isa. xlix. 22, Targ., and is once interchanged with פַּאפִלְיוֹן, *papilio* (*pavillon*), pleasure-tent. But a Greek word in the Song is in itself so improbable, that Ewald describes this derivation of the word as a frivolous jest; so much the more improbable, as φορεῖον as the name of a litter (*lectica*) occurs first in such authors (of the κοινή) as Plutarch, Polybius, Herodian, and the like, and therefore, with greater right, it may be supposed that it is originally a Semitic word, which the Greek language adopted at the time when the Oriental and Graeco-Roman customs began to be amalgamated. Hence, if *mittā*, 7 a, means a portable bed,—as is evident from this, that it appears as the means of transport with an escort,—then *appiryon* cannot also mean a litter; the description, moreover, does not accord with a litter. We do not read of rings and carrying-poles, but, on the contrary, of pillars (as those of a tent-bed) instead, and, as might be expected, of feet. Schlottm., however, takes *mittā* and *appiryon* as different names for a portable bed; but the words, "an *appiryon* has King Solomon made," etc., certainly indicate that he who thus speaks has not the *appiryon* before him, and also that this was something different from the *mittā*. While Schlottm. is inclined to take *appiryon*, in the sense of a litter, as a word borrowed from the Greek (but in the time of the first king?), Gesen. in his *Thes.* seeks to derive it, thus understood, from פָּרָה, *cito ferri*, *currere*; but this signification of the verb is imaginary. We expect here, in accordance with the progress of the scene, the name of the bridal couch; and on the supposition that *appiryon*, Sota 12a, as in the Mishna, means the litter (Aruch) of the bride, Arab. *maziffat*, and not *torus nuptialis* (Buxt.), then there is a possibility that *appiryon* is a more dignified word for *'ĕrĕs*, i. 17, yet sufficient thereby to show that פּוּרְיָא is the usual Talm. name of the marriage-bed (*e.g. Mezia* 23b, where it stands, *per meton.*, for *concubitus*), which is wittily explained by שפרין ורבין עליה (*Kethuboth* 10b, and elsewhere). The Targ. has for it the form פּוּרְיָן (*vid.* Levy). It thus designates a bed with a canopy (a tent-bed), Deut. xxxii. 50, *Jerus;* so that the ideas of the bed of state and the palanquin (cf. כילה, canopy, and כילת חתנים, bridal-bed, *Succa* 11a) touch one another. In general, פּוּרְיָא (פּוּרִין), as is also the case with *appiryon*, must have been originally a common designation of certain household furniture with a common characteristic; for the Syr. *parautha*, plur. *parjevatha* (Wiseman's *Horae*, p. 255), or also *parha* (Castell.), signifies a cradle. It is then to be inquired, whether this word is referable to a root-word which gives a common characteristic with manifold applications. But the Heb. פָּרָה, from the R. פר, signifies to split,[1] to tear asunder, to break forth, to bring fruit, to be fruitful, and nothing further. *Pārā* has nowhere the signification to run, as already remarked; only in the Palest.-Aram. פְּרָא is found in this meaning (*vid.* Buxt.). The Arab. *farr* does not signify to run, but to flee; properly (like our "*ausreissen*" = to tear out, to break out), to break open by flight the rank in which one stands (as otherwise turned by horse-dealers: to open wide the horse's mouth). But, moreover, we do not thus reach the common characteristic which we are in search of; for if we may say of the litter that it runs, yet we cannot say that of a bed or a cradle, etc. The Arab. *farfâr*, *species vehiculi muliebris*, also does not help us; for the verb *farfar*, to vacillate, to shake, is its appropriate root-word.[2] With better results shall we compare the Arab. *fary*, which, in *Kal* and *Hiph.*, signifies to break open, to cut out (*couper, tailler une étoffe*), and also, figuratively, to bring forth something strange, something not yet existing (*yafry alfaryya*, according to the Arab. *Lex.* = *yaty bal'ajab fy 'amalh*, he accomplishes something wonderful); the primary

---

[1] *Vid.* Friedr. Delitzsch's *Indogerman.-semit. Studien*, p. 72.

[2] The Turkish *Kâmûs* says of *farfâr*: "it is the name of a vehicle (*merkeb*), like the camel-litter (*haudej*), destined merely for women." This also derives its name from rocking to and fro. So *farfâr*, for *farfara* is to the present day the usual word for *agiter, sécouer les ailes*; *farfarah*, for *légèreté*; *furfûr*, for butterfly (cf. Ital. *farfalla*); generally, the ideas of that which is light and of no value—*e.g.* a babbler—connect themselves with the root *far* in several derivatives.

SONG. E

meaning in Conj. viii. is evidently: *yftarra kidban*, to cut out lies, to meditate and to express that which is calumnious (a similar metaphor to *khar'a, findere*, viii. *fingere*, to cut out something in the imagination; French, *inventer, imaginer*). With this *fary*, however, we do not immediately reach אַפִּרְיוֹן, פּוּרְיָא; for *fary*, as well as *fara* (*farw*), are used only of cutting to pieces, cutting out, sewing together of leather and other materials (cf. Arab. *farwat*, fur; *farrā*, furrier), but not of cutting and preparing wood. But why should not the Semitic language have used פָּרָא, פָּרָה, also, in the sense of the verb בָּרָא, which signifies[1] to cut and hew, in the sense of forming (cf. *Pih.* בֵּרֵא, *sculpere*, Ezek. xxi. 24), as in the Arab. *bara* and *bary*, according to Lane, mean, "be formed or fashioned by cutting (a writing-reed, stick, bow), shaped out, or pared,"—in other words: Why should פרה, used in the Arab. of the cutting of leather, not be used, in the Heb. and Aram., of the preparing of wood, and thus of the fashioning of a bed or carriage? As חִשָּׁבוֹן signifies a machine, and that the work of an engineer, so פִּרְיוֹן signifies timber-work, carpenter-work, and, lengthened especially by *Aleph prosthet.*, a product of the carpenter's art, a bed of state. The *Aleph prosth.* would indeed favour the supposition that *appiryon* is a foreign word; for the Semitic language frequently forms words after this manner,— *e.g.* אֲמְגוּשָׁא, a magician; אִסְתֵּרָא, a stater.[2] But apart from such words as אַנְרְטֵל, oddly sounding in accord with κάρταλλος as *appiryon* with φορεῖον, אֲבַטִּיחַ and אֲבַעְבָּעָה are examples of genuine Heb. words with such a prosthesis, *i.e.* an *Aleph* added at the beginning of the word; not a formative *Aleph*, as in אַכְזָב and the like. אַפֶּדֶן, palace, Dan. xi. 45, is, for its closer amalgamation by means of *Dag.*, at least an analogous example; for thus it stands related to the Syr. *opadna*, as, *e.g.* (Syr.), *oparsons*, net, Ewald, § 163*c*, to the Jewish-Aram. אַפַּרְסְנָא or אַפַּרְסָנָא; cf. also אַפְּתֹם, "finally," in relation to the Pehlv. אַפְדוּם (Spiegel's *Literatur der Parsen*, p. 356).[3] We think we have thus proved that אַפִּרְיוֹן is a Heb. word, which, coming from the verb פָּרָה, to cut right, to make, frame, signifies[4] a bed, and that, as Ewald also renders, a bed of state.

[1] *Vid.* Friedr. Delitzsch's *Indogerm.-sem. Stud.* p. 50. We are now taught by the Assyr. that as בן goes back to בנה, so בר (Assyr. *nibru*) to ברה = ברא, to bring forth.

[2] *Vid.* Merx's *Gramm. Syr.* p. 115.

[3] אַפּוּרְיָא, quoted by Gesen. in his *Thes.*, Sanhedrin 109*b*, is not applicable here; it is contracted from אַד־פּוּרְיָא (on the bed).

[4] This derivation explains how it comes that *appiryon* can mean, in the Karaite Heb., a bird-cage or aviary, *vid.* Gottlober's בקרת ס', p. 208. We have left out of view the phrase אפריון נמטיי ליה, which, in common use, means: we present

רְפִידָה (from רָפַד, R. רפ, to lift from beneath, *sublevare*, then *sternere*) is the head of the bed; LXX. ἀνάκλιτον; Jerome, *reclinatorium*, which, according to Isidore, is the Lat. vulgar name for the *fulchra*, the reclining (of the head and foot) of the bedstead. Schlottmann here involuntarily bears testimony that *appiryon* may at least be understood of a bed of state as well as of a litter of state; for he remarks: "The four sides of the bed were generally adorned with carved work, ivory, metal, or also, as in the case of most of the Oriental divans, with drapery." "*Nec mihi tunc*," says Propertius, ii. 10, 11, "*fulcro lectus sternatur eburno*." Here the *fulcrum* is not of ivory, but of gold.

מֶרְכָּב (from רָכַב, to lie upon anything; Arab. II. *componere*; Aethiop. *adipisci*) is that which one takes possession of, sitting or lying upon it, the cushion, *e.g.* of a saddle (Lev. xv. 9); here, the divan (*vid.* Lane, *Mod. Egypt*, I. 10) arranged on an elevated frame, serving both as a seat and as a couch. Red purple is called אַרְגָּמָן, probably from רָגַם = רָקַם, as material of variegated colour. By the interior תּוֹךְ of the bed, is probably meant a covering which lay above this cushion. רָצַף, to arrange together, to combine (whence רִצְפָה, pavement; Arab. *ruṣafat*, a paved way), is here meant like στορέννυμι, στόρνυμι, στρώννυμι, whence στρῶμα. And רָצוּף אַהֲ' is not equivalent to רָצוּף אַהֲ' (after the construction 1 Kings xxii. 10; Ezek. ix. 2), inlaid with love, but is the adv. accus. of the manner; "love" (cf. *hhesed*, Ps. cxli. 5) denotes the motive: laid out or made up as a bed from love on the part of the daughters of Jerusalem, *i.e.* the ladies of the palace—these from love to the king have procured a costly tapestry or tapestries, which they have spread over the purple cushion. Thus rightly Vaihinger in his *Comm.*, and Merx, *Archiv.* Bd. II. 111–114. Schlottmann finds this interpretation of מִן "stiff and hard;" but although מִן in the pass. is not used like the Greek ὑπό, yet it can be used like ἀπό (Ewald, sec. 295*b*); and if there be no actual example of this, yet we point to Ps. xlv. in illustration of the custom of presenting gifts to a newly-married pair. He himself understands אהבה personally, as do also Ewald, Heiligst., Böttcher; "the voice of the people," says Ewald, "knows that the finest ornament with which the in-

---

to him homage (of approbation or thanks). It occurs first, as uttered by the Sassanidean king, Shabur I., *Mezia* 119*a*, *extr.*; and already Rapoport, in his *Erech Millin*, 1852, p. 183, has recognised this word *appiryon* as Pers. It is the Old Pers. *âfrîna* or *âfrivana* (from *frî*, to love), which signifies blessing or benediction (*vid.* Justi's *Handb. d. Zendsprache*, p. 51). Rashi is right in glossing it by חֵן שֶׁלָּנוּ (the testimony of our favour).

visible interior of the couch is adorned, is a love from among the daughters of Jerusalem,—*i.e.* some one of the court ladies who was raised, from the king's peculiar love to her, to the rank of a queen-consort. The speaker thus ingeniously names this newest favourite 'a love,' and at the same time designates her as the only thing with which this elegant structure, all adorned on the outside is adorned within." Relatively better Böttcher: with a love (beloved one), *prae filiis Hierus.* But even though אהבה, like *amor* and *amores*, might be used of the beloved one herself, yet רצוף does not harmonize with this, seeing we cannot speak of being paved or tapestried with persons. Schlottm. in vain refers for the personal signification of אהבה to ii. 7, where it means love and nothing else, and seeks to bring it into accord with רצוף; for he remarks, "as the stone in mosaic work fills the place destined for it, so the bride the interior of the litter, which is intended for just one person filling it." But is this not more comical, without intending to be so, than Juvenal's (i. 1. 32 s.):

> *Causidici nova cum veniat lectica Mathonis*
> *Plena ipso . . . .*

But Schlottm. agrees with us in this, that the marriage which is here being prepared for was the consummation of the happiness of Solomon and Shulamith, not of another woman, and not the consummation of Solomon's assault on the fidelity of Shulamith, who hates him to whom she now must belong, loving only one, the shepherd for whom she is said to sigh (i. 4*a*), that he would come and take her away. "This triumphal procession," says Rocke,[1] "was for her a mourning procession, the royal litter a bier; her heart died within her with longing for her beloved shepherd." Touching, if it were only true! Nowhere do we see her up to this point resisting; much rather she is happy in her love. The shepherd-hypothesis cannot comprehend this marriage procession without introducing incongruous and imaginary things; it is a poem of the time of Gellert. Solomon the seducer, and Shulamith the heroine of virtue, are figures as from Gellert's Swedish Countess; they are moral commonplaces personified, but not real human beings. In the litter sits Shulamith, and the *appiryon* waits for her. Solomon rejoices that now the reciprocal love-bond is to find its conclusion; and what Shulamith, who is brought from a lowly to so lofty a station, experiences, we shall hear her describe in the sequel.

[1] *Das Hohelied, Erstlingsdrama, u.s.w.* [The Song, a Primitive Drama from the East; or, Family Sins and Love's Devotion. A Moral Mirror for the Betrothed and Married], 1851.

At the close of the scene, the call now goes forth to the daughters of Zion, *i.e.* the women of Jerusalem collectively, to behold the king, who now shows himself to the object of his love and to the jubilant crowd, as the festal procession approaches.

> Ver. 11 Come out, ye daughters of Zion, and see
> King Solomon with the crown
> With which his mother crowned him
> On the day of his espousal,
> And on the day of the gladness of his heart.

The women of the court, as distinguished from the Galilean maiden, are called "daughters of Jerusalem;" here, generally, the women of Zion or Jerusalem (Lam. v. 11) are called "daughters of Zion." Instead of צֶאנָה (since the verb *Lamed Aleph* is treated after the manner of verbs *Lamed He*, cf. Jer. 1. 20; Ezek. xxiii. 49), צֶאֶינָה, and that defect. צֶאֶנָה,[1] is used for the sake of assonance with וּרְאֶינָה;[2] elsewhere also, as we have shown at Isa. xxii. 13, an unusual form is used for the sake of the sound. It is seen from the *Sota* (ix. 14) that the old custom for the bridegroom to wear a "crown" was abolished in consequence of the awful war with Vespasian. Rightly Epstein, against Grätz, shows from Job xxxi. 36, Isa. xxviii. 1, Ps. ciii. 4, that men also crowned themselves. בַּעֲטָרָה (with the crown) is, according to the best authorities, without the art., and does not require it, since it is determined by the relat. clause following. חֲתֻנָּה is the marriage (the word also used in the post.-bibl. Heb., and interchanging with חֻפָּה, properly νυμφών, Matt. ix. 15), from the verb חָתַן, which, proceeding from the root-idea of cutting into (Arab. *khatn*, to circumcise; R. חת, whence חָתַם, חָתַף, חָתַר), denotes the pressing into, or going into, another family; חָתָן is he who enters into such a relation of affinity, and חֹתֵן the father of her who is taken away, who also on his part is related to the husband.[3] Here also the seduction fable is shattered. The marriage with Shulamith takes place with the joyful consent of the queen-mother. In order to set aside this fatal circumstance, the "crown"

---

[1] Without the *Jod* after *Aleph* in the older ed. Thus also in J and H with the note לית וחסר [= *nonnisi h. l. et defective*] agreeing with the MS. Masora Parna. Thus also Kimchi, *Michlol* 108b.

[2] The *Resh* has in H *Chatef-Pathach*, with *Metheg* preceding. This, according to Ben-Asher's rule, is correct (cf. Ps. xxviii. 9, וּרְ). In the punctuation of the *Aleph* with Tsere or Segol the Codd. vary, according to the different views of the punctuation. J has Segol; D H, Tsere, which latter also Kimchi, *Michlol* 109a.

[3] L. Geiger (*Ursprung der Sprache*, 1869, p. 88) erroneously finds in R. חת (חתם, etc.) the meaning of binding. The (Arab.) noun *Khatan* means first a

is referred back to the time when Solomon was married to Pharaoh's daughter. *Cogitandus est Salomo*, says Heiligst., *qui cum Sulamitha pompa sollemni Hierosolyma redit, eadem corona nuptiali ornatus, qua quum filiam regis Aegyptiorum uxorem duxeret ornatus erat.* But was he then so poor or niggardly as to require to bring forth this old crown? and so basely regardless of his legitimate wife, of equal rank with himself, as to wound her by placing this crown on his head in honour of a rival? No; at the time when this youthful love-history occurred, Pharaoh's daughter was not yet married. The mention of his mother points us to the commencement of his reign. His head is not adorned with a crown which had already been worn, but with a fresh garland which his mother wreathed around the head of her youthful son. The men have already welcomed the procession from afar; but the king in his wedding attire has special attractions for the women—they are here called upon to observe the moment when the happy pair welcome one another.

SECOND SCENE OF THE THIRD ACT, IV. 1–V. 1.

This scene contains a conversation between Solomon and his beloved, whom he at first calls friend, and then, drawing always nearer to her, bride. The place of the conversation is, as v. 1 shows, the marriage hall. That the guests there assembled hear what Solomon says to Shulamith, one need not suppose; but the poet has overheard it from the loving pair. Fairer than ever does Shulamith appear to the king. He praises her beauty, beginning with her eyes.

Chap. iv. 1a Lo, thou art fair, my friend! yes, thou art fair!
Thine eyes are doves behind thy veil.

The Gr. Venet. translates, after Kimchi, "looking out from behind, thy hair flowing down from thy head like a mane." Thus also Schultens, *capillus plexus*; and Hengst., who compares πλέγμα, 1 Tim. ii. 9, and ἐμπλοκὴ τριχῶν, 1 Pet. iii. 3, passages which do not accord with the case of Shulamith; but neither עֲמָם, ﺻﻢ, nor ﻟﺐ signifies to plait; the latter is used of the hair when it is too abundant, and ready for the shears. To understand the hair as

married man, and then any relation on the side of the wife (Lane); the fundamental idea must be the same as that of *Khatn, circumcidere* (cf. Ex. iv. 25), viz that of penetrating, which חתת, *percellere*, and נחת, *descendere* (cf. *e.g. ferrum descendit haud alte in corpus*, in Livy, and Prov. xvii. 1), also exhibit.

denoted here, is, moreover, inadmissible, inasmuch as מבעד cannot be used of the eyes in relation to the braids of hair hanging before them. Symm. rightly translates צמה by κάλυμμα [veil] (in the Song the LXX. erroneously renders by σιωπήσεως [behind thy silence]), Isa. xlvii. 2. The verb צָמַם, (Arab.) ṣamm, to make firm, solid, massive, impenetrable; whence *e.g.* (Arab.) ṣimam, a stopper, and (Arab.) alṣamma, a plaid in which one veils himself, when he wraps it around him.[1] The veil is so called, as that which closely hides the face. In the Aram. צְמַם, *Palp.* צַמְצֵם, means directly to veil, as *e.g. Bereshith rabba* c. 45, *extr.*, of a matron whom the king lets pass before him it is said, צימצמה פניה. Shulamith is thus veiled. As the Roman bride wore the *velum flammeum*, so also the Jewish bride was deeply veiled; cf. Gen. xxiv. 65, where Rebecca veiled herself (Lat. *nubit*) before her betrothed. בַּעַד, constr. בְּעַד, a segolate noun, which denotes separation, is a prep. in the sense of *pone*, as in Arab. in that of *post*. Ewald, sec. 217*m*, supposes, contrary to the Arab., the fundamental idea of covering (cogn. בגד); but that which surrounds is thought of as separating, and at the same time as covering, the thing which it encompasses. From behind her veil, which covered her face (*vid.* Bachmann, under Judg. iii. 23), her eyes gleam out, which, without needing to be supplemented by עֵינֵי, are compared, as to their colour, motion, and lustre, to a pair of doves.

From the eyes the praise passes to the hair.

Ver. 1*b* Thy hair is like a flock of goats
Which repose downwards on Mount Gilead.

The hair of the bride's head was uncovered. We know from later times that she wore in it a wreath of myrtles and roses, or also a 'golden city' (עיר של זהב), *i.e.* an ornament which emblematically represented Jerusalem. To see that this comparison is not incongruous, we must know that sheep in Syria and Palestine are for the most part white; but goats, for the most part, black, or at least dark coloured, as *e.g.* the brown *gedi Mamri*.[2] The verb גָּלְשׁוּ is the Arab. جلس, which signifies, to rest upon; and is distinguished from

---

[1] Regarding this verbal stem and its derivatives, see Ethé's *Schlafgemach der Phantasie*, pp. 102–105.

[2] Burns, the Scottish poet, thinking that goats are white, transfers the comparison from the hair to the teeth:

"Her teeth are like a flock of sheep,
With fleeces newly washen clean,
That slowly mount the rising steep,
And she's twa glancin', sparklin' een."

the synon. تَعَدَ in this, that the former is used of him who has previously lain down; the latter, of one who first stands and then sits down.¹ The *nejd* bears also the name *jals*, as the high land raising itself, and like a dome sitting above the rest of the land. One has to think of the goats as having lain down, and thus with the upper parts of their bodies as raised up. מִן in מֵהַר is used almost as in מַר מִדְּלִי, Isa. xl. 15. A flock of goats encamped on a mountain (rising up, to one looking from a distance, as in a steep slope, and almost perpendicularly), and as if hanging down lengthwise on its sides, presents a lovely view adorning the landscape. Solomon likens to this the appearance of the locks of his beloved, which hang down over her shoulders. She was till now a shepherdess, therefore a second rural image follows:

> Ver. 2 Thy teeth are like a flock of shorn sheep
> Which come up from the washing
> All bearing twins,
> And a bereaved one is not among them.

The verb קָצַב is, as the Arab. shows, in the sense of *tondere oves*, the synon. of גָּזַז. With shorn (not to be shorn) sheep, the teeth in regard to their smoothness, and with washed sheep in regard to their whiteness, are compared—as a rule the sheep of Palestine are white; in respect of their full number, in which in pairs they correspond to one another, the one above to the one below, like twin births in which there is no break. The parallel passage, vi. 6, omits the point of comparison of the smoothness. That some days after the shearing the sheep were bathed, is evident from Columella vii. 4. Regarding the incorrect exchange of mas. with fem. forms, *vid.* under ii. 7. The part. *Hiph.* מַתְאִימוֹת (cf. διδυματόκος, Theocr. i. 25) refers to the mothers, none of which has lost a twin of the pair she had borne. In "which come up from the washing," there is perhaps thought of, at the same time with the whiteness, the *saliva dentium*. The moisture of the saliva, which heightens the glance of the teeth, is frequently mentioned in the love-songs of Mutenebbi, Hariri, and Deschami. And that the saliva of a clean and sound man is not offensive, is seen from this, that the Lord healed a blind man by means of His spittle.

The mouth is next praised:

> Ver. 3a Like a thread of crimson thy lips,
> And thy mouth is lovely.

---

¹ *K'ad* cannot be used of one who sits on the bed *farash*; in *jalas* lies the direction from beneath to above; in *k'ad* (properly, to heap together, to cower down), from above to beneath.

As distinguished from red-purple, אַרְגָּמָן, שָׁנִי (properly, shining, glistening; for this form has an active signification, like נָקִי, as well as a passive, like עָנִי)—fully, שְׁנִי תוֹלַעַת—signifies the *kermes* or worm-colour; the *karmese*, the red juice of the cochineal. מִדְבָּרֵךְ (מִדְבָּרֵיךְ) is translated by the LXX. "thy speech;" Jerome, *eloquium;* and the Venet. "thy dialogue;" but that would be expressed, though by a ἀπ. λεγ., by דִּבּוּרֵךְ. מִדְבָּר is here the name of the mouth, the naming of which one expects; the preform. is the *mem instrumenti:* the mouth, as the instrument of speech, as the organ by which the soul expresses itself in word and in manner of speech. The poet needed for פִּיךְ a fuller, more select word; just as in Syria the nose is not called *anf*, but *minchâr* (from *nachara*, to blow, to breathe hard).

Praise of her temples.

> Ver. 3b Like a piece of pomegranate thy temples
> Behind thy veil.

רַקָּה is the thin piece of the skull on both sides of the eyes; Lat., mostly in the plur., *tempora;* German, *schläfe*, from *schlaff*, loose, slack, *i.e.* weak = רַק. The figure points to that soft mixing of colours which makes the colouring of the so-called carnation one of the most difficult accomplishments in the art of painting. The half of a cut pomegranate (Jer. *fragmen mali punici*) is not meant after its outer side, as Zöckler supposes, for he gives to the noun *răkkā*, contrary to Judg. iv. 21, v. 26, the meaning of cheek, a meaning which it has not, but after its inner side, which presents[1] a red mixed and tempered with the ruby colour,—a figure so much the more appropriate, since the ground-colour of Shulamith's countenance is a subdued white.[2] Up to this point the figures are borrowed from the circle of vision of a shepherdess. Now the king derives them from the sphere of his own experience as the ruler of a kingdom. She who has eyes like doves is in form like a born queen.

> Ver. 4 Like the tower of David thy neck,
> Built in terraces;
> Thereon a thousand shields hang,
> All the armour of heroes.

---

[1] The interior of a pomegranate is divided by tough, leather-like white or yellow skins, and the divisions are filled with little berries, in form and size like those of the grape, in the juicy inside of which little, properly, seed-corns, are found. The berries are dark red, or also pale red. The above comparison points to the mixing of these two colours.

[2] The Moslem erotic poets compare the division of the lips to the dividing cleft into a pomegranate.

The tower of David is, as it appears, "the tower of the flock," Mic. iv. 4, from which David surveyed the flock of his people. In Neh. iii. 25 f. it is called the "tower which lieth out from the king's high house," *i.e.* not the palace, but a government house built on Zion, which served as a court of justice. But what is the meaning of the ἅπ. λεγ. תַּלְפִּיוֹת ? Grätz translates: for a prospect; but the Greek τηλωπός, of which he regards תל' as the Heb. abstr., is a word so rare that its introduction into the Semitic language is on that account improbable. Hengst. translates: built for hanging swords; and he sees in the word a compound of תַּל (from תָּלָה, with which forms such as יָד = *jadj*, שַׁד = *shadj*, שַׁל, 2 Sam. vi. 7, are compared) and פִּיוֹת; but this latter word signifies, not swords, but edges of the (double-edged) sword; wherefore Kimchi (interpreting תַל as the constr. of תֵּל, as אֵל, in בְּצַלְאֵל, is of צֵל) explains: an erection of sharp-cornered stones; and, moreover, the Heb. language knows no such *nmm. comp. appellativa*: the names of the frog, צְפַרְדֵּעַ, and the bat, עֲטַלֵּף (cf. the *Beth* in (Arab.) *sa'lab*, fox, with the added *Pe*), are not such; and also *tsalmāveth*, the shadow of death, is at a later period, for th first time, restamped [1] as such from the original *tsalmuth* (cf. Arab. *zalumat* = *tenebrae*). Gesen. obtains the same meanings; for he explains לתל' by *exitialibus* (sc. *armis*), from an adj. תַּלְפִּי, from תָּלַף = Arab. *talifa*, to perish, the inf. of which, *talaf*, is at the present day a word synon. with *halak* (to perish); (Arab.) *matlaf* (place of going down) is, like יְשִׁימוֹן, a poetic name of the wilderness. The explanation is acceptable but hazardous, since neither the Heb. nor the Aram. shows a trace of this verb; and it is thus to be given up, if תלפ' can be referred to a verbal stem to be found in the Heb. and Aram. This is done in Ewald's explanation, to which also Böttcher and Rödig. give the preference: built for close (crowded) troops (so, viz., that many hundreds or thousands find room therein); the (Arab.) verb *aff*, to wrap together (opp. *nashar*, to unfold), is used of the packing together of multitudes of troops (*liff*, plur. *lufuf*), and also of warlike hand-to-hand conflicts; תלפ' would be traced to a verb לָפָה synon. therewith, after the form תַּאֲנִיָּה. But if תלפ' were meant of troops, then they would be denoted as the garrison found therein, and it would not be merely said that the tower was built for such; for the point of comparison would then be, the imposing look of the neck, overpowering by the force of the impression proceeding from within. But now, in the Aram., and relatively in the Talm. Heb., not only לָפַף and לוּף occur, but also לְפִי (Af. אַלְפִּי), and that in

---

[1] Cf. regarding such double words belonging to the more modern Semitic language, *Jesurun*, pp. 232–236.

the sense of enclosure, *i.e.* of joining together, the one working into the other,—*e.g.* in the Targ. : of the curtain of the tabernacle (בֵּית לוֹפֵי, place of the joining together = חֹבֶרֶת or מַחְבֶּרֶת of the Heb. text); and in the Talm. : of the roofs of two houses (*Bathra* 6*a*, לוּפְתָּא, the joining[1]). Accordingly 'לְתַלְפ, if we interpret the *Lamed* not of the definition, but of the norm, may signify, " in ranks together." The *Lamed* has already been thus rendered by Döderl. : " in turns " (cf. לָפַת, to turn, to wind); and by Meier, Mr. : " in gradation ; " and Aq. and Jerome also suppose that 'תלפ refers to component parts of the building itself, for they understand [2] pinnacles or parapets (ἐπάλξεις, *propugnacula*) ; as also the Venet. : εἰς ἐπάλξεις χιλίας. But the name for pinnacles is פִּנָּה, and their points, שְׁמָשׁוֹת; while, on the contrary, 'תלפ is the more appropriate name for terraces which, connected together, rise the one above the other. Thus to build towers like terraces, and to place the one, as it were, above the other, was a Babylonian custom.[3] The comparison lies in this, that Shulamith's neck was surrounded with ornaments so that it did not appear as a uniform whole, but as composed of terraces. That the neck is represented as hung round with ornaments, the remaining portion of the description shows.

מָגֵן signifies a shield, as that which protects, like *clupeus* (*clypeus*), perhaps connected with καλύπτειν and שֶׁלֶט, from שָׁלַט = (Arab.) *shalita*, as a hard impenetrable armour. The latter is here the more common word, which comprehends, with מָגֵן, the round shield ; also צִנָּה, the oval shield, which covers the whole body ; and other forms of shields. אֶלֶף הַמָּגֵן, " the thousand shields," has the indicative, if not (*vid.* under i. 11) the generic article. The appositional כֹּל שִׁלְטֵי הַגִּ׳ is not intended to mean : all shields of (*von*) heroes, which it would if the article were prefixed to *col* and omitted before *gibborim*, or if כֻּלָּם, iii. 8, were used ; but it means : all the shields of heroes, as the accentuation also indicates. The article is also here significant. Solomon made, according to 1 Kings x. 16 f., 200 golden targets and 300 golden shields, which he put in the house of the forest of Lebanon. These golden shields Pharaoh Shishak took away with him, and Rehoboam replaced them by " shields of brass," which the guards bore when they accompanied the king on his going into the temple (1 Kings xiv. 26–28 ; cf. 2 Chron. xii. 9–11) ; these

---

[1] The Arab. *lafa*, vi., proceeding from the same root-idea, signifies to bring in something again, to bring in again, to seek to make good again.

[2] *Vid.* also Lagarde's *Onomastica*, p. 202 : Θαλπιωθ ἐπάλξη (read εἰς) ἡ ὑψηλά.

[3] *Vid.* Oppert's *Grundzüge der Assyr. Kunst* (1872), p. 11.

"shields of David," *i.e.* shields belonging to the king's house, were given to the captains of the guard on the occasion of the raising of Joash to the throne, 2 Kings xi. 10; cf. 2 Chron. xxiii. 9. Of these brazen shields, as well as of those of gold, it is expressly said how and where they were kept, nowhere that they were hung up outside on a tower, the tower of David. Such a display of the golden shields is also very improbable. We will perhaps have to suppose that 4*b* describes the tower of David, not as it actually was, but as one has to represent it to himself, that it might be a figure of Shulamith's neck. This is compared to the terraced tower of David, if one thinks of it as hung round by a thousand shields which the heroes bore, those heroes, namely, who formed the king's body-guard. Thus it is not strange that to the 200 + 300 golden shields are here added yet 500 more; the body-guard, reckoned in companies of 100 each, 2 Kings xi. 4, is estimated as consisting of 1000 men. The description, moreover, corresponds with ancient custom. The words are תְּלוּי עָלָיו, not תְּלוּי בּוֹ; the outer wall of the tower is thought of as decorated with shields hung upon it. That shields were thus hung round on tower-walls, Ezekiel shows in his prophecy regarding Tyre, xxvii. 11; cf. 1 Macc. iv. 57, and *supra foris Capitolinae aedis*, Pliny, *Hist. Nat.* xxxv. 3; and although we express the presumption that Solomon's imagination represented David's tower as more gorgeous than it actually was, yet we must confess that we are not sufficiently acquainted with Solomon's buildings to be able to pass judgment on this. These manifold inexplicable references of the Song to the unfolded splendour of Solomon's reign, are favourable to the Solomonic authorship of the book. This grandiose picture of the distinguished beauty of the neck, and the heightening of this beauty by the ornament of chains, is now followed by a beautiful figure, which again goes back to the use of the language of shepherds, and terminates the description:

> Ver. 5 Thy two breasts are like two fawns,
>   Twins of a gazelle,
>   Which feed among lilies.

The dual, originating in the inner differ. of the plur., which denotes in Heb. not two things of any sort, but two paired by nature or by art, exists only in the principal form; שָׁדַיִם, as soon as inflected, is unrecognisable, therefore here, where the pair as such is praised, the word שְׁנֵי is used. The breasts are compared to a twin pair of young gazelles in respect of their equality and youthful freshness, and the bosom on which they raise themselves is compared to a meadow covered with lilies, on which the twin-pair of young gazelles feed.

With this tender lovely image the praise of the attractions of the chosen one is interrupted. If one counts the lips and the mouth as a part of the body, which they surely are, there are seven things here praised, as Hengst. rightly counts (the eyes, the hair, teeth, mouth, temples, neck, breasts); and Hahn speaks with right of the sevenfold beauty of the bride.

Shulamith replies to these words of praise:

> Ver. 6 Until the day cools and the shadows flee,
> I will go forth to the mountain of myrrh
> And to the hill of frankincense.

All those interpreters who suppose these to be a continuation of Solomon's words, lose themselves in absurdities. Most of them understand the mountain of myrrh and the hill of frankincense of Shulamith's attractions, praised in ver. 5, or of her beauty as a whole; but the figures would be grotesque (cf. on the other hand v. 13), and אֵלֶךְ לִי אֶל prosaic, wherefore it comes that the idea of betaking oneself away connects itself with הלך לו (Gen. xii. 1; Ex. xviii. 27), or that it yet preponderates therein (Gen. xxii. 2; Jer. v. 5), and that, for אלך לי in the passage before us in reference to ii. 10, 11, the supposition holds that it will correspond with the French *jè m'en irai*. With right Louis de Leon sees in the mountain of myrrh and the hill of frankincense names of shady and fragrant places; but he supposes that Solomon says he wishes to go thither to enjoy a siesta, and that he invites Shulamith thither. But we read nothing of this invitation; and that a bridegroom should sleep a part of his marriage-day is yet more unnatural than that, *e.g.*, Wilh. Budäus, the French philologist, spent a part of the same at work in his study. That not Solomon but Shulamith speaks here is manifest in the beginning, "until the day," etc., which at ii. 17 are also Shulamith's words. Anton (1773) rightly remarks, "Shulamith says this to set herself free." But why does she seek to make herself free? It is answered, that she longs to be forth from Solomon's too ardent eulogies; she says that, as soon as it is dark, she will escape to the blooming aromatic fields of her native home, where she hopes to meet with her beloved shepherd. Thus, *e.g.*, Ginsburg (1868). But do myrrh and frankincense grow in North Palestine? Ginsburg rests on Florus' *Epitome Rerum Rom.* iii. 6, where Pompey the Great is said to have passed over Lebanon and by Damascus "*per nemora illa odorata, per thuris et balsami sylvas.*" But by these *thuris et balsami sylvae* could be meant only the gardens of Damascus; for neither myrrh nor frankincense is indigenous to North Palestine, or generally to any part of Palestine.

Friedrich (1866) therefore places Shulamith's home at Engedi, and supposes that she here once more looks from the window and dotes on the mountain of myrrh and the hill of frankincense, "where, at the approach of twilight, she was wont to look out for her betrothed shepherd." But Shulamith, as her name already denotes, is not from the south, but is a Galilean, and her betrothed shepherd is from Utopia! That myrrh and frankincense were planted in the gardens of Engedi is possible, although (i. 14) mention is made only of the *Al-henna* there. But here places in the neighbourhood of the royal palace must be meant; for the myrrh tree, the gum of which, prized as an aroma, is the Arab. *Balsamodendron Myrrha*, and the frankincense tree, the resin of which is used for incense, is, like the myrrh tree, an Arab. amyrid. The *Boswellia serrata*,[1] indigenous to the East Indies, furnishes the best frankincense; the Israelites bought it from Sheba (Isa. lx. 6; Jer. vi. 20). The myrrh tree as well as the frankincense tree were thus exotics in Palestine, as they are in our own country; but Solomon, who had intercourse with Arabia and India by his own mercantile fleet, procured them for his own garden (Eccles. ii. 5). The modest Shulamith shuns the loving words of praise; for she requests that she may be permitted to betake herself to the lonely places planted with myrrh and frankincense near the king's palace, where she thinks to tarry in a frame of mind befitting this day till the approaching darkness calls her back to the king. It is the importance of the day which suggests to her this אֵלֶךְ לִי, a day in which she enters into the covenant of her God with Solomon (Prov. ii. 17). Without wishing to allegorize, we may yet not omit to observe, that the mountain of myrrh and the hill of frankincense put us in mind of the temple, where incense, composed of myrrh, frankincense, and other spices, ascended up before God every morning and evening (Ex. xxx. 34 ff.). הַר הַמּוֹר is perhaps a not unintentional accord to הַר הַמּוֹרִיָּה (2 Chron. iii. 1), the mountain where God appeared; at all events, "mountain of myrrh" and "hill of frankincense" are appropriate names for places of devout meditation, where one holds fellowship with God.

This childlike modest disposition makes her yet more lovely in the eyes of the king. He breaks out in these words:

Ver. 7 Thou art altogether fair, my love,
And no blemish in thee.

Certainly he means, no blemish either of soul or body. In vers. 1–5 he has praised her external beauty; but in ver. 6 her soul has disclosed itself: the fame of her spotless beauty is there extended to

[1] Lassen's *Ind. Alterthumskunde*, I. 334.

her soul no less than to her external appearance. And as to her longing after freedom from the tumult and bustle of court life, he thus promises to her:

> Ver. 8 With me from Lebanon, my bride,
> With me from Lebanon shalt thou come
> Shalt look from the top of Amana,
> From the top of Shenir and Hermon,
> From dens of lions,
> From mountains of leopards.

Zöckl. interprets אִתִּי in the sense of אֵלַי, and תָּשׁוּרִי in the sense of journeying to this definite place: "he announces to her in overflowing fulness of expression, that from this time forth, instead of the lonely mountainous regions, and the dangerous caves and dens, she shall inhabit with him the royal palace." Thus also Kingsbury. But the interpretation, however plausible, cannot be supported. For (1) such an idea ought to be expressed either by אֵלַי תב' or by תב' וְאִתִּי תֵשֵׁבִי, instead of אִתִּי תָב' ; (2) Shulamith is not from Lebanon, nor from the Anti-Libanus, which looks toward Damascus; (3) this would be no answer to Shulamith's longing for lonely quietness. We therefore hold by our explanation given in 1851. He seeks her to go with him up the steep heights of Lebanon, and to descend with him from thence; for while ascending the mountain one has no view before him, but when descending he has the whole panorama of the surrounding region lying at his feet. Thus חש' is not to be understood as at Isa. lvii. 9, where it has the meaning of *migrabas*, but, as at Num. xxiii. 9, it means *spectabis*. With מֵר' the idea of prospect lies nearer than that of descending; besides, the meaning *spectare* is secondary, for שׁוּר signifies first "to go, proceed, journey," and then "going to view, to go in order to view." *Sêr* in Arab. means "the scene," and *sêr etmek* in Turkish, "to contemplate" (cf. Arab. *tamashy*, to walk, then, to contemplate). *Lebanon* is the name of the Alpine range which lies in the N.-W. of the Holy Land, and stretches above 20 (German) miles from the Leontes (*Nahr el-Kasmîe*) northwards to the Eleutheros (*Nahr el-Kebîr*). The other three names here found refer to the Anti-Libanus separated from the Lebanon by the Coelo-Syrian valley, and stretching from the Banias northwards to the plain of Hamâth.

Amana denotes that range of the Anti-Libanus from which the springs of the river Amana issue, one of the two rivers which the Syrian captain (2 Kings v. 12) named as better than all the waters of Israel. These are the *Amana* and *Pharpar*, *i.e.* the *Baradâ* and *A'wadsh*; to the union of the Baradâ (called by the Greeks *Chry-*

sorrhoas, *i.e.* "golden stream") with the *Feidshe*, the environs of Damascus owe their *ghuwḍat*, their paradisaical beauty.

Hermon (from חָרַם, to cut off; cf. Arab. *kharom* and *makhrim*, the steep projection of a mountain) is the most southern peak of the Anti-Libanus chain, the lofty mountains (about 10,000 feet above the level of the sea) which form the north-eastern border of Palestine, and from which the springs of the Jordan take their rise.

Another section of the Anti-Libanus range is called *Senir*, not *Shenir*. The name, in all the three places where it occurs (Deut. iii. 9; 1 Chron. v. 23), is, in accordance with tradition, to be written with *Sin*. The Onkelos Targum writes סריון; the Jerusalem paraphrases, טורא דמסרי פירוי (the mountain whose fruits become putrid, viz. on account of their superabundance); the Midrash explains otherwise: שהוא שונא הניר (the mountain which resists being broken up by the plough),—everywhere the writing of the word with the letter *Sin* is supposed. According to Deut. iii. 9, this was the Amorite name of Hermon. The expression then denotes that the Amorites called Hermon—*i.e.* the Anti-Libanus range, for they gave the name of a part to the whole range—by the name *Senir*; Abulfeda uses سنير as the name of the part to the north of Damascus, with which the statement of Schwarz (*Das h. Land*, p. 33) agrees, that the Hermon (Anti-Libanus) to the north-west of Damascus is called *Senir*.

נְמֵרִים, panthers, to the present day inhabit the clefts and defiles of the Lebanon, and of the Anti-Libanus running parallel to it; whereas lions have now altogether disappeared from the countries of the Mediterranean. In Solomon's time they were to be met with in the lurking-places of the Jordan valley, and yet more frequently in the remote districts of the northern Alpine chains. From the heights of these Alps Solomon says Shulamith shall alone with him look down from where the lions and panthers dwell. Near these beasts of prey, and yet inaccessible by them, shall she enjoy the prospect of the extensive pleasant land which was subject to the sceptre of him who held her safe on these cliffs, and accompanied her over these giddy heights. If "mountain of myrrh," so also "the top of Amana" is not without subordinate reference. *Amana*, proceeding from the primary idea of firmness and verification, signifies fidelity and the faithful covenant as it is established between God and the congregation, for He betrothes it to Himself באמונה ("in faithfulness"), Hos. ii. 22 [20]; the congregation of which the apostle (Eph. v. 27) says the same as is here said by

Solomon of Shulamith. Here for the first time he calls her כַּלָּה, not כַּלָּתִי; for that, according to the *usus loq.*, would mean "my daughter-in-law." Accordingly, it appears that the idea of "daughter-in-law" is the primary, and that of "bride" the secondary one. כַּלָּה, which is = כְּלוּלָה, as חַלָּה, a cake, is = חֲלוּלָה, that which is pierced through (cf. כְּלוּלוֹת, being espoused; Jer. ii. 2), appears to mean[1] (cf. what was said regarding חָתָן under iii. 11*b*) her who is comprehended with the family into which, leaving her parents' house, she enters; not her who is embraced = crowned with a garland (cf. Arab. تكلّل, to be garlanded; *tĕklîl*, garlanding; *iklîl*, Syr. *kᵉlilo*, a wreath), or her who is brought to completion (cf. the verb, Ezek. xxvii. 4, 11), *i.e.* has reached the goal of her womanly calling. Besides, כַּלָּה, like "*Braut*" in the older German (*e.g.* Gudrun), means not only her who is betrothed, but also her who has been lately married.

All that the king calls his, she now can call hers; for she has won his heart, and with his heart himself and all that is his.

> Ver. 9 Thou hast taken my heart, my sister-bride;
> Thou hast taken my heart with one of thy glances,
> With a little chain of thy necklace.

The *Piel* לִבֵּב may mean to make courageous, and it actually has this meaning in the Aram., wherefore the Syr. retains the word; Symm. renders it by ἐθάρσυνάς με. But is it becoming in a man who is no coward, especially in a king, to say that the love he cherishes gives him heart, *i.e.* courage? It might be becoming, perhaps, in a warrior who is inspired by the thought of his beloved, whose respect and admiration he seeks to gain, to dare the uttermost. But Solomon is no Antar, no wandering knight.[2] Besides, the first effect of love is different: it influences those whom it governs, not as encouraging, in the first instance, but as disarming them; love responded to encourages, but love in its beginning, which is the subject here, overpowers. We would thus more naturally render: "thou hast unhearted me;" but "to unheart," according to the Semitic and generally the ancient conception of the heart (*Psychol.* p. 254), does not so much mean to

---

[1] L. Geiger's *Ursprung d. Sprach.* p. 227; cf. 88.

[2] A specimen of Böttcher's interpretation: "What is more natural than to suppose that the keeper of a vineyard showed herself with half of her head and neck exposed at the half-opened window to her shepherd on his first attempt to set her free, when he cried, 'my dove in the clefts of the rocks,' etc., and animated him thereby to this present bold deliverance of her from the midst of robbers?" We pity the Shulamitess, that she put her trust in this moonshiny coward.

captivate the heart, as rather to deprive of understanding or of judgment (cf. Hos. iv. 11). Such denomin. *Pi.* of names of corporeal members signify not merely taking away, but also wounding, and generally any violent affection of it, as זִנֵּב, גֵּרֵם, Ewald, § 120*c;* accordingly the LXX., Venet., and Jerome: ἐκαρδίωσάς με, *vulnerasti cor meum.* The meaning is the same for "thou hast wounded my heart" = "thou hast subdued my heart" (cf. Ps. xlv. 6*b*). With one of her glances, with a little chain of her necklace, she has overcome him as with a powerful charm: *veni, visa sum, vici.* The *Kerî* changes באחד into בְּאַחַת; certainly עַיִן is mostly fem. (*e.g.* Judg. xvi. 28), but not only the non-bibl. *usus loq.*, which *e.g.* prefers רָעָה or עַיִן רָע, of a malignant bewitching look, but also the bibl. (*vid.* Zech. iii. 9, iv. 10) treats the word as of double gender. עֲנָק and צַוְּרוֹנִים are related to each other as a part is to the whole. With the subst. ending *ôn,* the designation of an ornament designed for the neck is formed from צַוָּאר, the neck; cf. שַׂהֲרוֹן, the "round tires like the moon" of the women's toilet, Isa. iii. 18 ff. עֲנָק (connected with עֻנַּק עָנָק, *cervix*) is a separate chain (Aram. עוּנְקְתָא) of this necklace. In the words אַחַד עֲנָק, אַחַד is used instead of אֶחָד, occurring also out of genit. connection (Gen. xlviii. 22; 2 Sam. xvii. 22), and the arrangement (*vid.* under Ps. lxxxix. 51) follows the analogy of the pure numerals as שָׁלֹשׁ נָשִׁים; it appears to be transferred from the vulgar language to that used in books, where, besides the passage before us, it occurs only in Dan. viii. 13. That a glance of the eye may pierce the heart, experience shows; but how can a little chain of a necklace do this? That also is intelligible. As beauty becomes unlike itself when the attire shows want of taste, so by means of tasteful clothing, which does not need to be splendid, but may even be of the simplest kind, it becomes mighty. Hence the charming attractive power of the impression one makes communicates itself to all that he wears, as, *e.g.*, the woman with the issue of blood touched with joyful hope the hem of Jesus' garment; for he who loves feels the soul of that which is loved in all that stands connected therewith, all that is, as it were, consecrated and charmed by the beloved object, and operates so much the more powerfully if it adorns it, because as an ornament of that which is beautiful, it appears so much the more beautiful. In the preceding verse, Solomon has for the first time addressed Shulamith by the title "bride." Here with heightened cordiality he calls her "sister-bride." In this change in the address the progress of the story is mirrored. Why he does not say כַּלָּתִי (my bride), has already been explained, under 8*a*, from the derivation of the word. Solomon's mother might call Shulamith *callathi*, but he gives to the relation of affinity into which Shulamith has entered a reference to himself individually, for he says *ăhhothi callā* (my sister-bride): she who as *callā* of his mother is to her a kind of daughter, is as *callā* in relation to himself, as it were, his sister.

He proceeds still further to praise her attractions.

Ver. 10 How fair is thy love, my sister-bride!
How much better thy love than wine!
And the fragrance of thy unguents than all spices!
11 Thy lips drop honey, my bride;
Honey and milk are under thy tongue;
And the fragrance of thy garments is like the fragrance of Lebanon.

Regarding the connection of the *pluralet.* דּוֹדִים with the plur. of the pred., *vid.* at i. 2*b*. The pred. יָפוּ praises her love in its manifestations according to its impression on the sight; טֹבוּ, according to its experience on nearer intercourse. As in ver. 9 the same power of impression is attributed to the eyes and to the necklace, so here is intermingled praise of the beauty of her person with praise of the fragrance, the odour of the clothing of the bride; for her soul speaks out not only by her lips, she breathes forth odours also for him in her spices, which he deems more fragrant than all other odours, because he inhales, as it were, her soul along with them. נֹפֶת, from נָפַת, *ebullire* (*vid.* under Prov. v. 3, also Schultens), is virgin honey, ἄκοιτον (*acetum*, Pliny, xi. 15), *i.e.* that which of itself flows from the combs (צוּפִים). Honey drops from the lips which he kisses; milk and honey are under the tongue which whispers to him words of pure and inward joy; cf. the contrary, Ps. cxl. 4. The last line is an echo of Gen. xxvii. 27. שַׂלְמָה is שִׂמְלָה (from שָׂמַל, *complicare, complecti*) transposed (cf. עָלָה from עוֹלָה, כַּשְׂבָּה from כִּבְשָׂה). As Jacob's raiment had for his old father the fragrance of a field which God had blessed, so for Solomon the garments of the faultless and pure one, fresh from the woods and mountains of the north, gave forth a heart-strengthening savour like the fragrance of Lebanon (Hos. iv. 7), viz. of its fragrant herbs and trees, chiefly of the balsamic odour of the apples of the cedar.

The praise is sensuous, but it has a moral consecration.

Ver. 12 A garden locked is my sister-bride;
A spring locked, a fountain sealed.

גַּן (according to rule masc. Böttch. § 658) denotes the garden from its enclosure; גַּל (elsewhere גֻּלָּה), the fountain (synon. מַבּוּעַ), the waves bubbling forth (cf. Amos v. 24); and מַעְיָן, the place, as it were an eye of the earth, from which a fountain gushes forth. Luther distinguishes rightly between *gan* and *gal*; on the contrary, all the old translators (even the Venet.) render as if the word in both cases were *gan*. The *Pasek* between *gan* and *nā'ul*, and between *gal* and *nā'ul*, is designed to separate the two *Nuns*, as *e.g.* at 2 Chron. ii. 9, Neh. ii. 2, the two *Mems;* it is the orthophonic *Pasek*, already described under ii. 7, which secures the independence of two similar or organically related sounds. Whether the sealed fountain (*fons signatus*) alludes to a definite fountain which Solomon had built for the upper city and the temple place,[1] we do not now inquire. To a locked garden and spring no one has access but the rightful owner, and a sealed fountain is shut against all impurity. Thus she is closed against the world, and inaccessible to all that would disturb her pure heart, or desecrate her pure person.[2] All the more beautiful and the greater is the fulness of the flowers and fruits which bloom and ripen in the garden of this life, closed against the world and its lust.

> Ver. 13 What sprouts forth for thee is a park of pomegranates,
>   With most excellent fruits;
>   Cypress flowers with nards;
> 14 Nard and crocus; calamus and cinnamon,
>   With all kinds of incense trees;
>   Myrrh and aloes,
>   With all the chief aromatics.

The common subject to all down to ver. 15 inclusive is שְׁלָחַיִךְ ("what sprouts for thee" = "thy plants"), as a figurative designation, borrowed from plants, of all the "phenomena and life utterances" (Böttch.) of her personality. "If I only knew here," says Rocke, "how to disclose the meaning, certainly all these flowers and fruits, in the figurative language of the Orient, in the flower-language of love, had their beautiful interpretation." In the old German poetry, also, the phrase *bluomen brechen* [to break flowers] was equivalent to: to enjoy love; the flowers and fruits named are figures of all that the *amata* offers to the *amator*. Most of the plants here named are exotics; פַּרְדֵּס (heaping around, circumvallation, enclosing) is a garden or park, especially with foreign ornamental and fragrant plants—an old Persian word, the explanation of which, after Spiegel, first given in our exposition of the Song, 1851 (from *pairi* = περί, and *dêz*, R. *diz*, a heap), has now become common property (Justi's *Handb. der Zendsprache*, p. 180). פְּרִי מְגָדִים (from מֶגֶד, which corresponds to

---

[1] *Vid.* Zschocke in the *Tübinger Quartalschrift*, 1867, 3.
[2] Seal, חֹתָם, pers. *muhr*, is used directly in the sense of maiden-like behaviour; *vid.* Perles' *etymol. Studien* (1871), p. 67.

the Arab. *mejd*, praise, honour, excellence; *vid.* Volck under Deut. xxxiii. 13) are *fructus laudum*, or *lautitiarum*, excellent precious fruits, which in the more modern language are simply called מְגָדִים (*Shabbath* 127*b*, מִינֵי מְגָדִים, all kinds of fine fruits); cf. Syr. *magdo*, dried fruit. Regarding כֹּפֶר, *vid.* under i. 14; regarding מֹר, under i. 13; also regarding נֵרְדְּ, under i. 12. The long vowel of נֵרְדְּ corresponds to the Pers. form *nârd*, but near to which is also *nard*, Indian *nalada* (fragrance-giving); the *ê* is thus only the long accent, and can therefore disappear in the plur. For נְרָדִים, Grätz reads יְרָדִים, roses, because the poet would not have named nard twice. The conjecture is beautiful, but for us, who believe the poem to be Solomonic, is inconsistent with the history of roses (*vid.* under ii. 1), and also unnecessary. The description moves forward by steps rhythmically.

כַּרְכֹּם is the *crocus stativus*, the genuine Indian *safran*, the dried flower-eyes of which yield the safran used as a colour, as an aromatic, and also as medicine; *safran* is an Arab. word, and means yellow root and yellow colouring matter. The name כַּרְכֹּם, Pers. *karkam*, Arab. *karkum*, is radically Indian, Sanscr. *kuṅkuma*. קָנֶה, a reed (from קָנָה, R. קנ, to rise up, viewed intrans.),[1] viz. sweet reed, *acorus calamus*, which with us now grows wild in marshes, but is indigenous to the Orient.

קִנָּמוֹן is the *laurus cinnamomum*, a tree indigenous to the east coast of Africa and Ceylon, and found later also on the Antilles. It is of the family of the *laurineae*, the inner bark of which, peeled off and rolled together, is the cinnamon-bark (*cannella*, French *cannelle*); Aram. קוּנְמָא, as also the Greek κιννάμωμον and κίνναμον, Lat. (*e.g.* in the 12th book of Pliny) *cinnamomum* and *cinnamum*, are interchanged, from קְנַם, probably a secondary formation from קָנֶה (like בָּם, whence בָּמָה, from בָּא), to which also ܩܘܢܡܐ, ὑπόστασις, and the Talm.-Targ. קִנּוּם קוֹנָם, an oath (cf. קָיָם), go back, so that thus the name which was brought to the west by the Phoenicians denoted not the tree, but the reed-like form of the rolled dried bark. As "nards" refer to varieties of the nard, perhaps to the Indian and the Jamanic spoken of by Strabo and others, so "all kinds of incense trees" refers definitely to Indo-Arab. varieties of the incense tree and its fragrant resin; it has its name from the white and transparent seeds of this its resin (cf. Arab. *lubân*, incense and benzoin, the resin of

---

[1] In this general sense of "reed" (Syn. *arundo*) the word is also found in the Gr. and Lat.: κάνναι (κάναι), reed-mats, κάνεον, κάναστρον, a wicker basket, *canna*, *canistrum*, without any reference to an Indo-Germ. verbal stem, and without acquiring the specific signification of an aromatic plant.

the storax tree, לִבְנֶה); the Greek λίβανος, λιβανωτός (Lat. *thus*, frankincense, from θύω), is a word derived from the Phoenicians.

אֲהָלוֹת or אֲהָלִים (which already in a remarkable way was used by Balaam, Num. xxiv. 6, elsewhere only since the time of Solomon) is the Semitized old Indian name of the aloe, *agaru* or *aguru;* that which is aromatic is the wood of the aloe-tree (*aloëxylon agallochum*), particularly its dried root (*agallochum* or *lignum aloës*, ξυλαλόη, according to which the Targ. here: אכסיל אלואין, after the phrase in Aruch) mouldered in the earth, which chiefly came from farther India.[1] עִם, as everywhere, connects things contained together or in any way united (v. 1; cf. i. 11, as Ps. lxxxvii. 4; cf. 1 Sam. xvi. 12). The concluding phrase עִם כָּל־רָ' וגו׳, *cum praestantissimis quibusque aromatibus*, is a poet. *et cetera.* רֹאשׁ, with the gen. of the object whose value is estimated, denotes what is of *meilleure qualité*; or, as the Talm. says, what is אלפא, ἄλφα, *i.e.* number one. Ezekiel, xxvii. 22, in a similar sense, says, "with chief (רֹאשׁ) of all spices."

The panegyric returns now once more to the figure of a fountain.

Ver. 15 A garden-fountain, a well of living water,
And torrents from Lebanon.

The *tertium compar.* in ver. 12 was the collecting and sealing up; here, it is the inner life and its outward activity. A fountain in gardens (גַּנִּים, categ. pl.) is put to service for the benefit of the beds of plants round about, and it has in these gardens, as it were, its proper sphere of influence. A well of living water is one in which that which it distributes springs up from within, so that it is indeed given to it, but not without at the same time being its own true property. נָזַל is related, according to the Semitic *usus loq.*, to אָזַל, as "*niedergehen*" (to go down) to "*weggehen*" (to go away) (*vid.* Prov. v. 15); similarly related are (Arab.) *sar*, to go, and *sal* (in which

---

[1] *Vid.* Lassen's *Ind. Alterthumsk.* I. 334 f. Furrer, in Schenkel's *Bib. Lex.*, understands אהלות of the *liliaceae*, indigenous to Palestine as to Arabia, which is also called *aloë*. But the drastic purgative which the succulent leaves of this plant yield is not aromatic, and the verb אחל "to glisten," whence he seeks to derive the name of this aloe, is not proved. Cf. besides, the Petersburg *Lex.* under *aguru* ("not difficult"), according to which is this name of the *amyris agallocha*, and the *aquilaria agallocha*, but of no *liliaceae*. The name *Adlerholz* ("eagle-wood") rests on a misunderstanding of the name of the Agila tree. It is called "*Paradiesholz*," because it must have been one of the paradise trees (*vid.* Bereshith rabba under Gen. ii. 8). Dioskorides says of this wood: θυμιᾶται ἀντὶ λιβανωτοῦ; the Song therefore places it along with myrrh and frankincense. That which is common to the lily-aloe and the wood-aloe, is the bitter taste of the juice of the former and of the resinous wood of the latter. The Arab. name of the aloe, *ṣabir*, is also given to the lily-aloe. The proverbs: *amarru min eṣ-ṣabir*, bitterer than the aloe, and *es-sabr sabir*, patience is the aloe, refer to the aloe-juice.

the letter *ra* is exchanged for *lam*, to express the softness of the liquid), to flow, whence *syl* (*sêl*), impetuous stream, rushing water, kindred in meaning to נֹזְלִים. Streams which come from Lebanon have a rapid descent, and (so far as they do not arise in the snow region) the water is not only fresh, but clear as crystal. All these figures understood sensuously would be insipid; but understood ethically, they are exceedingly appropriate, and are easily interpreted, so that the conjecture is natural, that on the supposition of the spiritual interpretation of the Song, Jesus has this saying in His mind when He says that streams of living water shall flow "out of the belly" of the believer, John vii. 38.

The king's praise is for Shulamith proof of his love, which seeks a response. But as she is, she thinks herself yet unworthy of him; her modesty says to her that she needs preparation for him, preparation by that blowing which is the breath of God in the natural and in the spiritual world.

> Ver. 16 Awake, thou North (wind), and come, thou South!
> Blow through my garden, cause its spices to flow—
> Let my beloved come into his garden,
> And eat the fruits which are precious to him.

The names of the north and south, denoting not only the regions of the heavens, but also the winds blowing from these regions, are of the fem. gender, Isa. xliii. 6. The east wind, קָדִים, is purposely not mentioned; the idea of that which is destructive and adverse is connected with it (*vid.* under Job xxvii. 21). The north wind brings cold till ice is formed, Sir. xliii. 20; and if the south wind blow, it is hot, Luke xii. 55. If cold and heat, coolness and sultriness, interchange at the proper time, then growth is promoted. And if the wind blow through a garden at one time from this direction and at another from that,—not so violently as when it shakes the trees of the forest, but softly and yet as powerfully as a garden can bear it,—then all the fragrance of the garden rises in waves, and it becomes like a sea of incense. The garden itself then blows, *i.e.* emits odours; for (פַּח = the Arab. *fakh, fah*, cf. *fawh*, pl. *afwâh*, sweet odours, fragrant plants) as in רוּחַ הַיּוֹם, Gen. iii. 8, the idea underlies the expression, that when it is evening the day itself blows, *i.e.* becomes cool, the causative הָפִיחִי, connected with the object-accus. of the garden, means to make the garden breezy and fragrant. נָזַל is here used of the odours which, set free as it were from the plants, flow out, being carried forth by the waves of air. Shulamith wishes that in her all that is worthy of love should be fully realized. What had to be done for Esther (Esth. ii. 12) before she could be brought in to the king, Shulamith calls on the winds to accomplish for her, which are, as it were, the breath of the life of all nature, and as such, of the life-spirit, which is the sustaining background of all created things. If she is thus prepared for him who loves her, and whom she loves, he shall come into his garden and enjoy the precious fruit belonging to him. With words of such gentle tenderness, childlike purity, she gives herself to her beloved.

She gives herself to him, and he has accepted her, and now celebrates the delight of possession and enjoyment.

> Chap. v. 1 I am come into my garden, my sister-bride;
> Have plucked my myrrh with my balsam;
> Have eaten my honeycomb with my honey;
> Have drunk my wine with my milk—
> Eat, drink, and be drunken, ye friends!

If the exclamation of Solomon, 1*a*, is immediately connected with the words of Shulamith, iv. 16, then we must suppose that, influenced by these words, in which the ardour of love and humility express themselves, he thus in triumph exclaims, after he has embraced her in his arms as his own inalienable possession. But the exclamation denotes more than this. It supposes a union of love, such as is the conclusion of marriage following the betrothal, the God-ordained aim of sexual love within the limits fixed by morality. The poetic expression בָּאתִי לְנַנִּי points to the בּוֹא אֶל, used of the entrance of a man into the woman's chamber, to which the expression (Arab.) *dakhal bihā* (he went in with her), used of the introduction into the bride's chamber, is compared. The road by which Solomon reached this full and entire possession was not short, and especially for his longing it was a lengthened one. He now triumphs in the final enjoyment which his ardent desire had found. A pleasant enjoyment which is reached in the way and within the limits of the divine order, and which therefore leaves no bitter fruits of self-reproach, is pleasant even in the retrospect. His words, beginning with "I am come into my garden," breathe this pleasure in the retrospect. Ginsburg and others render incorrectly, "I am coming," which would require the words to have been (הִנֵּה) אֲנִי בָא. The series of perfects beginning with בָּאתִי cannot be meant otherwise than retrospectively. The "garden" is Shulamith herself, iv. 12, in the fulness of her personal and spiritual attractions, iv. 16; cf. כְּרָמִי, i. 6. He may call her "my sister-bride;" the garden is then his by virtue of divine and human right, he has obtained possession of this garden, he has broken its costly rare flowers.

אָרָה (in the Mishna dialect the word used of plucking figs) signifies to pluck; the Aethiop. trans. *ararku karbê*, I have plucked myrrh ; for the Aethiop. has *arara* instead of simply ארה. בְּשָׂמִי is here בְּשָׂם deflected. While בֶּשֶׂם, with its plur. *besámim*, denotes fragrance in general, and only balsam specially, *bāsām* = (Arab.) *bashâm* is the proper name of the balsam-tree (the Mecca balsam), *amyris opobalsamum*, which, according to Forskal, is indigenous in the central mountain region of Jemen (S. Arabia); it is also called (Arab.) *balsaman;* the word found its way in this enlarged form into the West, and then returned in the forms אַפְּרְסְמָא, אֲפוֹפַלְסָמוֹן, בַּלְסְמוֹן (Syr. *afrusomo*), into the East. Balsam and other spices were brought in abundance to King Solomon as a present by the Queen of Sheba, 1 Kings x. 10; the celebrated balsam plantations of Jericho (*vid.* Winer's *Real-W.*), which continued to be productive till the Roman period, might owe their origin to the friendly relations which Solomon sustained to the south Arab. princess. Instead of the Indian aloe, iv. 14, the Jamanic balsam is here connected with myrrh as a figure of Shulamith's excellences. The plucking, eating, and drinking are only interchangeable figurative descriptions of the enjoyment of love.

"Honey and milk," says Solomon, iv. 11, "is under thy tongue." יַעַר is like יַעֲרָה, 1 Sam. xiv. 27, the comb (*favus*) or cells containing the honey,—a designation which has perhaps been borrowed from porous lava.[1] With honey and milk "under the tongue" wine is connected, to which, and that of the noblest kind, vii. 10, Shulamith's palate is compared. Wine and milk together are οἰνόγαλα, which Chloe presents to Daphnis (Longus, i. 23). Solomon and his Song here hover on the pinnacle of full enjoyment; but if one understands his figurative language as it interprets itself, it here also expresses that delight of satisfaction which the author of Ps. xix. 6*a* transfers to the countenance of the rising sun, in words of a chaste purity which sexual love never abandons, in so far as it is connected with esteem for a beloved wife, and with the preservation of mutual personal dignity. For this very reason the words of Solomon, 1*a*, cannot be thought of as spoken to the guests. Between iv. 16 and v. 1*a* the bridal night intervenes. The words used in 1*a* are Solomon's morning salutation to her who has now wholly become his own. The call addressed to the guests at the feast is given forth on the second day of the marriage, which, according to ancient custom, Gen. xxix. 28, Judg. xiv. 12, was wont to be celebrated for seven days, Tob. xi. 18. The dramatical character of the Song leads to this result, that the pauses are passed over, the scenes are quickly changed, and the times appear to be continuous.

[1] *Vid.* Wetstein in the *Zeitsch. für allgem. Erdkunde*, 1859, p. 123.

The plur. דּוֹדִים Hengst. thinks always designates "love" (*Liebe*); thus, after Prov. vii. 28, also here: Eat, friends, drink and intoxicate yourselves in love. But the summons, *inebriamini amoribus*, has a meaning if regarded as directed by the guests to the married pair, but not as directed to the guests. And while we may say רוה דדים, yet not שׁכר דו׳, for *shakar* has always only the accus. of a spirituous liquor after it. Therefore none of the old translators (except only the Venet.: μεθύσθητε ἔρωσιν) understood *dodim*, notwithstanding that elsewhere in the Song it means love, in another than a personal sense; רֵעִים and דו׳ are here the plur. of the elsewhere parallels רֵעַ and דּוֹד, *e.g.* v. 16*b*, according to which also (cf. on the contrary, iv. 16*b*) they are accentuated. Those who are assembled are, as sympathizing friends, to participate in the pleasures of the feast. The Song of Songs has here reached its climax. A Paul would not hesitate, after Eph. v. 31 f., to extend the mystical interpretation even to this. Of the antitype of the marriage pair it is said: "For the marriage of the Lamb is come, and His wife hath made herself ready" (Rev. xix. 7); and of the antitype of the marriage guests: "Blessed are they which are called unto the marriage supper of the Lamb" (Rev. xix. 9).

FOURTH ACT.

LOVE DISDAINED BUT WON AGAIN.—Chap. V. 2–VI. 9.

FIRST SCENE OF THE FOURTH ACT, V. 2–VI. 3.

In this fourth Act we are not now carried back to the time when Solomon's relation to Shulamith was first being formed. We are not placed here amid the scenes of their first love, but of those of their married life, and of their original ardour of affection maintaining itself not without trial. This is evident from the circumstance that in the first two Acts the beloved is addressed by the title רעיתי (my friend, beloved), and that the third Act rises[1] to the title כלה (bride) and אחתי כלה (my sister-bride); in the fourth Act, on the other hand, along with the title *ra'yaihi*, we hear no longer *calla*, nor *ahhothi*

---

[1] Among the Slovacs a bride is called *malducha*, "virgin-bride," before she has a cap placed on her head; and after that, *nevesta*, "bride-spouse." In England, *bride* does not designate the betrothed as such, but the betrothed when near her marriage.

calla, but simply *ahhothi*,[1]—a title of address which contributes to heighten the relation, to idealize it, and give it a mystical background. We have here presented to us pictures from the life of the lovers after their marriage has been solemnized. Shulamith, having reached the goal of her longing, has a dream like that which she had (iii. 1–4) before she reached that goal. But the dreams, however they resemble each other, are yet also different, as their issues show; in the former, she seeks him, and having found him holds him fast; here, she seeks him and finds him not. That that which is related belongs to the dream-life in ch. iii., was seen from the fact that it was inconceivable as happening in real life; here that which is related is expressly declared in the introductory words as having occurred in a dream.

> Ver. 2 I sleep, but my heart keeps waking—
> Hearken! my beloved is knocking:
> Open to me, my sister, my love,
> My dove, my perfect one;
> For my head is filled with dew,
> My locks (are) full of the drops of the night.

The partic. subst. clauses, 2*a*, indicate the circumstances under which that which is related in 2*b* occurred. In the principal sentence in hist. prose וַיִּדְפֹּק would be used; here, in the dramatic vivacity of the description, is found in its stead the interject. *vocem* = *ausculta* with the gen. foll., and a word designating[2] state or condition added, thought of as accus. according to the Semitic syntax (like Gen. iv. 10; Jer. x. 22; cf. 1 Kings xiv. 6). To sleep while the heart wakes signifies to dream, for sleep and distinct consciousness cannot be co-existent; the movements of thought either remain in obscurity or are projected as dreams. עֵר = '*awir* is formed from עוּר, to be awake

---

[1] There is scarcely any other example of the husband calling his spouse "sister" than that found in Esth. v. 9 (Apocr.), where Ahasuerus says to Esther: "What is it, Esther? I am thy brother." Still more analogous are the words of Tob. vii. 12: "From this time forth thou art her brother, and she is thy sister;" but here the relation of affinity blends itself with the marriage relationship. In Lat. *soror* frequently denotes a lover, in contrast to *uxor*. But here in the Song *ahhothi calla* comes in the place of *callathi*, which is ambiguous ("my daughter-in-law").

[2] דוֹפֵק [is knocking] is not an attribute to the determinate דּוֹדִי [my beloved] which it follows, but a designation of state or condition, and thus acc., as the Beirut translation renders it: "hear my beloved in the condition of one knocking." On the other hand, דוֹד דּוֹפֵק signifies "a beloved one knocking." But "hear a beloved one knocking" would also be expressed acc. In classical language, the designation of state, if the subst. to which it belongs is indeterminate, is placed before it, *e.g.* "at the gate stood a beloved one knocking."

(in its root cogn. to the Aryan *gar*, of like import in γρηγορεῖν, ἐγείρειν), in the same way as מֵת = *mawith* from מוּת. The שׁ has here the conj. sense of "*dieweil*" (because), like *asher* in Eccles. vi. 12, viii. 15. The ר *dag.*, which occurs several times elsewhere (*vid.* under Prov. iii. 8, xiv. 10), is one of the inconsistencies of the system of punctuation, which in other instances does not double the ר; perhaps a relic of the Babylonian idiom, which was herein more accordant with the lingual nature of the ר than the Tiberian, which treated it as a semi-guttural. קְוֻצָּה, a lock of hair, from קָץ = קָיִץ, *abscîdit*, follows in the formation of the idea, the analogy of קָצִיר, in the sense of branch, from קָצַר, *desecuit*; one so names a part which is removed without injury to the whole, and which presents itself conveniently for removal; cf. the oath sworn by Egyptian women, *lahajât muksûsi*, " by the life of my separated," *i.e.* "of my locks" (Lane, *Egypt*, etc., I. 38). The word still survives in the Talmud dialect. Of a beautiful young man who proposed to become a Nazarite, *Nedarim* 9*a* says the same as the *Jer. Horajoth* iii. 4 of a man who was a prostitute in Rome: his locks were arranged in separate masses, like heap upon heap; in *Bereshith rabba* c. lxv., under Gen. xxvii. 11, קְוֻץ, curly-haired, is placed over against קֵרֵחַ, bald-headed, and the Syr. also has *kausoto* as the designation of locks of hair,—a word used by the Peshito as the rendering of the Heb. קְוֻצּוֹת, as the Syro-Hexap. Job xvi. 12, the Greek κόμη. טַל, from טָלַל (طلّ, to moisten, viz. the ground; to squirt, viz. blood), is in Arabic drizzling rain, in Heb. dew; the drops of the night (רְסִיסֵי, from רָסַס, to sprinkle, to drizzle)[1] are just drops of dew, for the precipitation of the damp air assumes this form in nights which are not so cold as to become frosty. Shulamith thus dreams that her beloved seeks admission to her. He comes a long way and at night. In the most tender words he entreats for that which he expects without delay. He addresses her, "my sister," as one of equal rank with himself, and familiar as a sister with a brother; "my love" (רַעְיָ), as one freely chosen by him to intimate fellowship; "my dove," as beloved and prized by him on account of her purity, simplicity, and loveliness. The meaning of

---

[1] According to the primary idea: to break that which is solid or fluid into little pieces, wherefore רְסִיסִים means also broken pieces. To this root appertains also the Arab. *rashh*, to trickle through, to sweat through, II. to moisten (*e.g.* the mouth of a suckling with milk), and the Aethiop. *raseḥa*, to be stained. Drops scattered with a sprinkling brush the Arabs call *rashaḥât*; in the mystical writings, *rashaḥât el-uns* (dew-drops of intimacy) is the designation of sporadic gracious glances of the deity.

the fourth designation used by him, תַּמָּתִי, is shown by the Arab. *tam* to be "wholly devoted," whence *teim*, "one devoted" = a servant, and *mutajjam*, desperately in love with one. In addressing her תמתי, he thus designates this love as wholly undivided, devoting itself without evasion and without reserve. But on this occasion this love did not approve itself, at least not at once.

> Ver. 3 I have put off my dress,
> How shall I put it on again?
> I have washed my feet,
> How shall I defile them again?

She now lies unclothed in bed. כֻּתֹּנֶת is the χιτών worn next the body, from כתן, linen (diff. from the Arab. *kutun*, cotton, whence French *coton*, calico = cotton-stuff). She had already washed her feet, from which it is supposed that she had throughout the day walked barefooted,—how (אֵיכָכָה, how? both times with the tone on the *penult.*;[1] cf. אֵיכָה, where? i. 7) should she again put on her dress, which she had already put off and laid aside (פָּשַׁט)? why should she soil (אֲטַנְּפֵם, relating to the fem. רַגְלַי, for אטנפן) again her feet, that had been washed clean? Shulamith is here brought back to the customs as well as to the home of her earlier rural life; but although she should thus have been enabled to reach a deeper and more lively consciousness of the grace of the king, who stoops to an equality with her, yet she does not meet his love with an equal requital. She is unwilling for his sake to put herself to trouble, or to do that which is disagreeable to her. It cannot be thought that such an interview actually took place; and yet what she here dreamed had not only inward reality, but also full reality. For in a dream, that which is natural to us or that which belongs to our very constitution becomes manifest, and much that is kept down during our waking hours by the power of the will, by a sense of propriety, and by the activities of life, comes to light during sleep; for fancy then stirs up the ground of our nature and brings it forth in dreams, and thus exposes us to ourselves in such a way as oftentimes, when we waken, to make us ashamed and alarmed. Thus it was with Shulamith. In the dream it was inwardly manifest that she had

---

[1] That it has the tone on the *penult.*, like בָּכָה, e.g., v. 9, is in conformity with the paragog. nature of ה. The tone, however, when the following word in close connection begins with א, goes to the *ult.*, Esth. vii. 6. That this does not occur in איכ' אל, is explained from the circumstance that the word has the disjunctive *Tifcha*. But why not in איכ' אט'? I think it is for the sake of the rhythm. Pinsker, *Einl.* p. 184, seeks to change the accentuation in order that the *penult.* accent might be on the second אֵיךְ, but that is not necessary. Cf. Ps. cxxxvii. 7.

lost her first love. She relates it with sorrow; for scarcely had she rejected him with these unworthy deceitful pretences when she comes to herself again.

> Ver. 4 My beloved stretched his hand through the opening,
> And my heart was moved for him.

חוֹר,[1] from the verb חוּר, in the sense of to break through (R. חר, whence also חָרָה, i. 10, and חָרָם, Arab. *kharam*, part. broken through, *e.g.* of a lattice-window), signifies *foramen*, a hole, also *caverna* (whence the name of the Troglodytes, חֹרִי, and the Haurân, חַוְרָן), here the loophole in the door above (like *khawkht*, the little door for the admission of individuals in the street or house-door). It does not properly mean a window, but a part of the door pierced through at the upper part of the lock of the door (the door-bolt). מִן־הַחוֹר is understood from the standpoint of one who is within; "by the opening from without to within," thus "through the opening;" stretching his hand through the door-opening as if to open the door, if possible, by the pressing back of the lock from within, he shows how greatly he longed after Shulamith. And she was again very deeply moved when she perceived this longing, which she had so coldly responded to: the interior of her body, with the organs which, after the bibl. idea, are the seat of the tenderest emotions, or rather, in which they reflect themselves, both such as are agreeable and such as are sorrowful, groaned within her,—an expression of deep sympathy so common, that "the sounding of the bowels," Isa. lxiii. 15, an expression used, and that anthropopathically of God Himself, is a direct designation of sympathy or inner participation. The phrase here wavers between עָלָיו and עָלָי (thus, *e.g.* Nissel, 1662). Both forms are admissible. It is true we say elsewhere only *naphshi 'ālāi*, *ruhi 'ālāi*, *libbi 'ālāi*, for the *Ego* distinguishes itself from its substance (cf. *System d. bibl. Psychologie*, p. 151 f.); *meäi 'alāi*, instead of *bi* (בְּקִרְבִּ), would, however, be also explained from this, that the bowels are meant, not anatomically, but as *psychical* organs. But the old translators (LXX., Targ., Syr., Jerome, Venet.) rendered עָלָיו, which rests on later MS. authority (*vid.* Norzi and de Rossi), and is also more appropriate: her bowels are stirred, viz. over him, *i.e.* on account of him (Alkabez: בַּעֲבוּרוֹ). As she will now open to him, she is inwardly more ashamed, as he has come so full of love and longing to make her glad.

---

[1] Cf. the Arab. *ghawr* (*ghôr*), as a sinking of the earth, and *khawr* (*khôr*), as a breaking through, and, as it were, a piercing. The mouth of a river is also called *khôr*, because there the sea breaks into the river.

> Ver. 5 I arose to open to my beloved,
> And my hands dropped with myrrh,
> And my fingers with liquid myrrh,
> On the handle of the bolt.

The personal pron. אֲנִי stands without emphasis before the verb which already contains it; the common language of the people delights in such particularity. The Book of Hosea, the Ephraimite prophet's work, is marked by such a style. מוֹר עֹבֵר, with which the parallel clause goes beyond the simple *mōr*, is myrrh flowing over, dropping out of itself, *i.e.* that which breaks through the bark of the *balsamodendron myrrha*, or which flows out if an incision is made in it; *myrrha stacte*, of which Pliny (xii. 35) says: *cui nulla praefertur*, otherwise מֹר דְּרוֹר, from דָּרַר, to gush out, to pour itself forth in rich jets. He has come perfumed as if for a festival, and the costly ointment which he brought with him has dropped on the handles of the bolts (מַנְעוּל, keeping locked, after the form מַלְבּוּשׁ, drawing on), viz. the inner bolt, which he wished to withdraw. A classical parallel is found in Lucretius, iv. 1171:

> "At lacrimans exclusus amator limina saepe
> Floribus et sertis operit postesque superbos
> Unguit amaracino" . . .

Böttch. here puts to Hitzig the question, "Did the shepherd, the peasant of Engedi, bring with him oil of myrrh?" Rejecting this reasonable explanation, he supposes that the Shulamitess, still in Solomon's care, on rising up quickly dipped her hand in the oil of myrrh, that she might refresh her beloved. She thus had it near her before her bed, as a sick person her decoction. The right answer was, that the visitant by night is not that imaginary personage, but it is Solomon. She had dreamed that he stood before her door and knocked. But finding no response, he again in a moment withdrew, when it was proved that Shulamith did not requite his love and come forth to meet it in its fulness as she ought.

> Ver. 6 I opened to my beloved;
> And my beloved had withdrawn, was gone:
> My soul departed when he spake—
> I sought him, and found him not;
> I called him, and he answered me not.

As the disciples at Emmaus, when the Lord had vanished from the midst of them, said to one another: Did not our heart burn within us when He spake with us? so Shulamith says that when he spake, *i.e.* sought admission to her, she was filled with alarm, and almost terrified to death. Love-ecstasy (ἐκστῆναι, as contrast to γενέσθαι ἐν ἑαυτῷ) is not to be here understood, for in such a state she would have flown to meet him; but a sinking of the soul, such as is described by Terence (*And.* I. 5. 16):

"*Oratio haec me miseram exanimavit metu.*"

The voice of her beloved struck her heart; but in the consciousness that she had estranged herself from him, she could not openly meet him and offer empty excuses. But now she recognises it with sorrow that she had not replied to the deep impression of his loving words; and seeing him disappear without finding him, she calls after him whom she had slighted, but he answers her not. The words: "My soul departed when he spake," are the reason why she now sought him and called upon him, and they are not a supplementary remark (Zöckl.); nor is there need for the correction of the text בְּדָבְרוֹ, which should mean: (my soul departed) when he turned his back (Ewald), or, behind him (Hitz., Böttch.), from דָבַר = (Arab.) *dabara, tergum vertere, praeterire,*—the Heb. has the word דְבִיר, the hinder part, and as it appears, דִּבֶּר, to act from behind (treacherously) and destroy, 2 Chron. xxii. 10; cf. under Gen. xxxiv. 13, but not the *Kal* דָּבַר, in that Arab. signification. The meaning of חָמַק has been hit upon by Aquila (ἔκλινεν), Symmachus (ἀπονεύσας), and Jerome (*declinaverat*); it signifies to turn aside, to take a different direction, as the *Hithpa.* Jer. xxxi. 22: to turn oneself away; cf. חַמּוּקִים, turnings, bendings, vii. 2. חָבַק and אָבַק (cf. Gen. xxxii. 25), Aethiop. *ḥakafa*, Amhar. *akafa* (reminding us of נָקַף, *Hiph.* יָקִיף, are usually compared; all of these, however, signify to "encompass;" but חָמַק does not denote a moving in a circle after something, but a half circular motion away from something; so that in the Arab. the prevailing reference to fools, *aḥamḳ*, does not appear to proceed from the idea of closeness, but of the oblique direction, pushed sideways. Turning himself away, he proceeded farther. In vain she sought him; she called without receiving any answer. עָנָנִי is the correct pausal form of עֲנָנִי, *vid.* under Ps. cxviii. 5. But something worse than even this seeking and calling in vain happened to her.

> Ver. 7 The watchmen who go about in the city found me,
> They beat me, wounded me;
> My upper garment took away from me,
> The watchmen of the walls.

She sought her beloved, not "in the *midbar*" (open field), nor "in the *kepharim*" (villages), but בָּעִיר, "in the city,"—a circumstance which is fatal to the shepherd-hypothesis here, as in the other dream. There in the city she is found by the watchmen who patrol the city, and have their proper posts on the walls to watch those who approach the city and depart from it (cf. Isa. lxii. 6). These rough, regardless men,—her story returns at the close like a palindrome to those previously named,—who judge only according to that which is external, and have neither an eye nor a heart for the sorrow of a loving soul, struck (הִכָּה, from נָכָה, to pierce, hit, strike) and wounded (פָּצַע, R. פץ, to divide, to inflict wounds in the flesh) the royal spouse as a common woman, and so treated her, that, in order to escape being made a prisoner, she was constrained to leave her upper robe in their hands (Gen. xxxix. 12). This upper robe, not the veil which at iv. 1, 3 we found was called *tsammā*, is called רְדִיד. Aben Ezra compares with it the Arab. *ridâ*, a plaid-like over-garment, which was thrown over the shoulders and veiled the upper parts of the body. But the words have not the same derivation. The *ridâ* has its name from its reaching downward,—probably from the circumstance that, originally, it hung down to the feet, so that one could tread on it; but the (Heb.) *rᵉdid* (in Syr. the *dalmatica* of the deacons), from רָדַד, *Hiph.*, 1 Kings vi. 32, Targ., Talm., Syr., רְדַד, to make broad and thin, as *expansum, i.e.* a thin and light upper robe, viz. over the *cuttonĕth*, 3a. The LXX. suitably translates it here and at Gen. xxiv. 65 (*hatstsâiph*, from *tsa'aph*, to lay together, to fold, to make double or many-fold) by θέριστρον, a summer over-dress. A modern painter, who represents Shulamith as stripped naked by the watchmen, follows his own sensual taste, without being able to distinguish between *tunica* and *pallium*; for neither Luther, who renders by *schleier* (veil), nor Jerome, who has *pallium* (cf. the saying of Plautus: *tunica propior pallio est*), gives any countenance to such a freak of imagination. The city watchmen tore from off her the upper garment, without knowing and without caring to know what might be the motive and the aim of this her nocturnal walk.

All this Shulamith dreamed; but the painful feeling of repentance, of separation and misapprehension, which the dream left behind, entered as deeply into her soul as if it had been an actual external experience. Therefore she besought the daughters of Jerusalem:

> Ver. 8 I adjure you, ye daughters of Jerusalem,
>   If ye find my beloved,—
>   What shall ye then say to him?
>   "That I am sick of love."

That אִם is here not to be interpreted as the negative particle of adjuration (Böttch.), as at ii. 7, iii. 5, at once appears from the absurdity arising from such an interpretation. The *or. directa*, following " I adjure you," can also begin (Num. v. 19 f.) with the usual אִם, which is followed by its conclusion. Instead of " that ye say to him I am sick of love," she asks the question: What shall ye say to him? and adds the answer: *quod aegra sum amore*, or, as Jerome rightly renders, in conformity with the root-idea of חלה : *quia amore langueo*; while, on the other hand, the LXX.: ὅτι τετρωμένη (*saucia*) ἀγάπης ἐγώ εἰμι, as if the word were חֲלָלָה, from חָלָל. The question proposed, with its answer, inculcates in a naive manner that which is to be said, as one examines beforehand a child who has to order something. She turns to the daughters of Jerusalem, because she can presuppose in them, in contrast with those cruel watchmen, a sympathy with her love-sorrow, on the ground of their having had similar experiences. They were also witnesses of the origin of this covenant of love, and graced the marriage festival by their sympathetic love. When, therefore, they put to her the question:

> Ver. 9 What is thy beloved before another (beloved),
> Thou fairest of women?
> What is thy beloved before another (beloved),
> That thou dost adjure us thus?

the question thus asked cannot proceed from ignorance; it can only have the object of giving them the opportunity of hearing from Shulamith's own mouth and heart her laudatory description of him, whom they also loved, although they were not deemed worthy to stand so near to him as she did who was thus questioned. Böttch. and Ewald, secs. 325*a*, 326*a*, interpret the מִן in מִדּוֹד partitively: *quid amati* (as in Cicero: *quod hominis*) *amatus tuus*; but then the words would have been מַה־מִדּוֹד דּוֹדֵךְ, if such a phrase were admissible; for מַה־דּוֹד certainly of itself alone means *quid amati*, what kind of a beloved. Thus the מִן is the comparative (*prae amato*), and דּוֹד the sing., representing the idea of species or kind; מְדוֹדִים, here easily misunderstood, is purposely avoided. The use of the form הִשְׁבַּעְתָּנוּ for הִשְׁבַּעְתִּינוּ is one of the many instances of the disregard of the generic distinction occurring in this Song, which purposely, after the manner of the vulgar language, ignores pedantic regularity.

Hereupon Shulamith describes to them who ask what her beloved is. He is the fairest of men. Everything that is glorious in the kingdom of nature, and, so far as her look extends, everything in the sphere of art, she appropriates, so as to present a picture of his external appearance. Whatever is precious, lovely, and grand, is all combined in the living beauty of his person.[1] She first praises the mingling of colours in the countenance of her beloved.

Ver. 10 My beloved is dazzlingly white and ruddy,
Distinguished above ten thousand.

The verbal root צח has the primary idea of purity, *i.e.* freedom from disturbance and muddiness, which, in the stems springing from it, and in their manifold uses, is transferred to undisturbed health (Arab. *ṣahh*, cf. *baria*, of smoothness of the skin), a temperate stomach and clear head, but particularly to the clearness and sunny brightness of the heavens, to dazzling whiteness (צָחַח, Lam. iv. 7; cf. צָחֹר), and then to parched dryness, resulting from the intense and continued rays of the sun; צַח is here adj. from צָחַח, Lam. iv. 7, bearing almost the same relation to לָבָן as λαμπρός to λευκός, cogn. with *lucere*. אָדֹם, R. דם, to condense, is properly dark-red, called by the Turks *kuju kirmesi* (from *kuju*, thick, close, dark), by the French *rouge foncé*, of the same root as דָּם, the name for blood, or a thick and dark fluid. White, and indeed a dazzling white, is the colour of his flesh, and redness, deep redness, the colour of his blood tinging his flesh. Whiteness among all the race-colours is the one which best accords with the dignity of man; pure delicate whiteness is among the Caucasian races a mark of high rank, of superior training, of hereditary nobility; wherefore, Lam. iv. 7, the appearance of the nobles of Jerusalem is likened in whiteness to snow and milk, in redness to corals; and Homer, *Il.* iv. 141, says of Menelaus that he appeared stained with gore, " as when some woman tinges ivory with purple colour." In this mingling of white and red, this fulness of life and beauty, he is דָּגוּל, distinguished above myriads. The old translators render *dagul* by "chosen" (Aquila, Symm., Syr., Jerome, Luther), the LXX. by ἐκλελοχισμένος, *e cohorte selectus*; but it means "bannered" (*degel*, ii. 4), as the Venet.: σεσημαιωμένος, *i.e.* thus distinguished, as that which is furnished with a *degel*, a banner, a pennon. Grätz takes *dagul* as the Greek σημειωτός (noted). With רְבָבָה, as a designation of an inconceivable number, Rashi rightly compares Ezek. xvi. 7. Since the "ten thousand" are here thought of, not in the same manner as רְגוּלִים, the particle *min* is not the compar. *magis quam*, but, as at Gen. iii. 14, Judg. v. 24, Isa. lii. 14, *prae*, making conspicuous (cf. Virgil, *Aen.* v. 435, *prae omnibus*

---

[1] Hengstenberg finds in this eulogium, on the supposition that Solomon is the author, and is the person who is here described, incomprehensible self-praise. But he does not certainly say all this immediately of himself, but puts it into the mouth of Shulamith, whose love he gained. But love idealizes; she sees him whom she loves, not as others see him,—she sees him in her own transforming light.

unum). After this praise of the bright blooming countenance, which in general distinguished the personal appearance of her beloved, so far as it was directly visible, there now follows a detailed description, beginning with his head.

>Ver. 11 His head is precious fine gold,
>His locks hill upon hill,
>Black as the raven.

The word-connection כֶּתֶם פָּז, occurring only here, serves as a designation of the very finest pure gold; for כֶּתֶם (hiding, then that which is hidden), from כתם, R. כת (*vid*. concerning the words appertaining to this root, under Ps. lxxxvii. 6), is the name of fine gold, which was guarded as a jewel (cf. Prov. xxv. 12), and פָּז (with long *ā*) is pure gold freed from inferior metals, from פָּזַז, to set free, and generally violently to free (cf. *zahav muphaz*, 1 Kings x. 18, with *zahav tahor*, 2 Chron. ix. 17). The Targ. to the Hagiog. translate פז by אוֹבְרִיזָא (*e.g.* Ps. cxix. 127), or אוֹבְרִיזִין (*e.g.* Ps. xix. 11), ὄβρυζον, *i.e.* gold which has stood the fire-proof (*obrussa*) of the cupel or the crucible. Grammatically regarded, the word-connection *kethem paz* is not genit., like *kethem ophir*, but appositional, like *naarah bᵉthulah*, Deut. xxii. 28, *zᵉvahim shᵉlamim*, Ex. xxiv. 5, etc. The point of comparison is the imposing nobility of the fine form and noble carriage of his head. In the description of the locks of his hair the LXX. render תלתלים by ἐλάται, Jerome by *sicut elatae palmarum*, like the young twigs, the young shoots of the palm. Ewald regards it as a harder parall. form of זלזלים, Isa. xviii. 15, vine-branches; and Hitzig compares the *Thousand and One Nights*, iii. 180, where the loose hair of a maiden is likened to twisted clusters of grapes. The possibility of this meaning is indisputable, although (Arab.) *taltalat*, a drinking-vessel made of the inner bark of palm-branches, is named, not from *taltalah*, as the name of the palm-branch, but from *taltala*, to shake down, viz. in the throat. The palm-branch, or the vine-branch, would be named from תִּלְתֵּל, *pendulum esse*, to hang loosely and with a wavering motion, the freq. of תָּלָה, *pendere*. The Syr. also think on תלה, for it translates "spread out," *i.e.* waving downward; and the Venet., which translates by ἀπαιωρήματα. The point of comparison would be the freshness and flexibility of the abundant long hair of the head, in contrast to motionless close-lying smoothness. One may think of Jupiter, who, when he shakes his head, moves heaven and earth. But, as against this, we have the fact: (1) That the language has other names for palm-branches and vine-branches; the former are called in the Song vii. 9, *sansinnim*. (2) That תלתלים, immediately referred to the hair, but not in the sense of "hanging locks" (Böttch.),

CHAP. V. 12.

is still in use in the post-bibl. Heb. (vid. under v. 2b); the Targ. also, in translating דְּגוּרִין דְּגוּרִין, *cumuli cumuli*, thinks תלתלים = תלין תלין. *Menachoth* 29b. A hill is called תֵּל, (Arab.) *tall*, from תָּלַל, *prosternere*, to throw along, as of earth thrown out, sand, or rubbish; and תַּלְתַּל, after the form גַּלְגַּל, in use probably only in the plur., is a hilly country which rises like steps, or presents an undulating appearance. Seen from his neck upwards, his hair forms in undulating lines, hill upon hill. In colour, these locks of hair are black as a raven, which bears the Semitic name עוֹרֵב from its blackness (עָרַב), but in India is called *kârava* from its croaking. The raven-blackness of the hair contrasts with the whiteness and redness of the countenance, which shines forth as from a dark ground, from a black border. The eyes are next described.

Ver. 12 His eyes like doves by the water-brooks,
Bathing in milk, stones beautifully set

The eyes in their glancing moistness (cf. ὑγρότης τῶν ὀμμάτων, in Plutarch, of a languishing look), and in the movement of their pupils, are like doves which sip at the water-brooks, and move to and fro beside them. אֲפִיק, from אָפַק, *continere*, is a watercourse, and then also the water itself flowing in it (vid. under Ps. xviii. 16), as (Arab.) *wadin*, a valley, and then the river flowing in the valley, *bahr*, the sea-basin (properly the cleft), and then also the sea itself. The pred. "bathing" refers to the eyes (cf. iv. 9), not to the doves, if this figure is continued. The pupils of the eyes, thus compared with doves, seem as if bathing in milk, in that they swim, as it were, in the white in the eye. But it is a question whether the figure of the doves is continued also in יֹשְׁבוֹת עַל־מִלֵּאת. It would be the case if *milleth* meant "fulness of water," as it is understood, after the example of the LXX., also by Aquila (ἐκχύσεις), Jerome (*fluenta plenissima*), and the Arab. (*piscinas aqua refertas*); among the moderns, by Döpke, Gesen., Hengst., and others. But this pred. would then bring nothing new to 12a; and although in the Syr. derivatives from ܡܠܐ signify flood and high waters, yet the form *milleth* does not seem, especially without מַיִם, to be capable of bearing this signification. Luther's translation also, although in substance correct: *vnd stehen in der fülle* (and stand in fulness) (*milleth*, like שַׁלְמוּתָא of the Syr., πληρώσεως of the Gr. Venet., still defended by Hitz.), yet does not bring out the full force of *milleth*, which, after the analogy of כִּסֵּא, רִצְפָה, appears to have a concrete signification which is seen from a comparison of Ex. xxv. 7, xxvii. 17, 20, xxxix. 13. There מִלֻּאָה and מִלֻּאִים signify not the border with precious stones, but, as rightly maintained by Keil, against Knobel, their filling in, *i.e.* their bordering, setting. Accordingly, *milleth* will be a synon. technical expression: the description, passing from the figure of the dove, says further of the eyes, that they are firm on (in) their setting; עַל is suitable, for the precious stone is laid within the casket in which it is contained. Hitzig has, on the contrary, objected that מְלֵאָה and מִלֻּאִים denote filling up, and thus that *milleth* cannot be a filling up, and still less the place thereof. But as in the Talm. מוּלְיָתָא signifies not only fulness, but also stuffed fowls or pies, and as πλήρωμα in its manifold aspects is used not only of that with which anything is filled, but also of that which is filled (*e.g.* of a ship that is manned, and Eph. i. 23 of the church in which Christ, as in His body, is immanent),—thus also *milleth*, like the German "*Fassung*," may be used of a ring-casket (*funda* or *pala*) in which the precious stone is put. That the eyes are like a precious stone in its casket, does not merely signify that they fill the sockets,—for the *bulbus* of the eye in every one fills the *orbita*,—but that they are not sunk like the eyes of one who is sick, which fall back on their supporting edges in the *orbita*, and that they appear full and large as they press forward from wide and open eyelids. The cheeks are next described.

Ver. 13*a* His cheeks like a bed of sweet herbs,
Towers of spicy plants.

A flower-bed is called עֲרוּגָה, from עָרַג, to be oblique, inclined. His cheeks are like such a soft raised bed, and the impression their appearance makes is like the fragrance which flows from such a bed planted with sweet-scented flowers. *Migᵉdaloth* are the tower-like or pyramidal mounds, and *merkahhim* are the plants used in spicery. The point of comparison here is thus the soft elevation; perhaps with reference to the mingling of colours, but the word chosen (*merkahhim*) rather refers to the lovely, attractive, heart-refreshing character of the impression. The Venet., keeping close to the existing text: αἱ σιαγόνες αὐτοῦ ὡς πρασιὰ τοῦ ἀρώματος, πύργοι ἀρωματισμῶν (thus not ἀρωματιστῶν) according to Gebhardt's just conjecture). But is the punctuation here correct? The sing. בַּעֲרוּגַת is explained from this, that the bed is presented as sloping from its height downward on two parallel sides; but the height would then be the nose dividing the face, and the plur. would thus be more suitable; and the LXX., Symm., and other ancient translators have, in fact, read בַּעֲרוּגוֹת. But still less is the phrase *migdᵉloth merkahhim* to be comprehended; for a tower, however diminutive it may be, is not a proper figure for a soft elevation, nor even a graduated flowery walk, or a terraced flowery hill,—a tower always presents, however round one may conceive it, too much the idea of a natural chubbiness, or of a diseased tumour. Therefore the expression used by the LXX., φύουσαι μυρεψικά, i.e. מִגְדְּלוֹת מרק, commends itself. Thus also Jerome: *sicut areolae aromatum consitae a pigmentariis*, and the Targ. (which refers לְחָיִם allegorically to the לוּחֵי of the law, and *merkahhim* to the refinements of the Halacha): "like the rows of a garden of aromatic plants which produce (*gignentes*) deep, penetrating sciences, even as a (magnificent) garden, aromatic plants." Since we read כַעֲרוּגוֹת מִגְדְּלוֹת, we do not refer *migadloth*, as Hitzig, who retains כַעֲרוּגַת, to the cheeks, although their name, like that of the other members (*e.g.* the ear, hand, foot), may be fem. (Böttch. § 649), but to the beds of spices; but in this carrying forward of the figure we find, as he does, a reference to the beard and down on the cheeks. גִּדֵּל is used of suffering the hair to grow, Num. vi. 5, as well as of cultivating plants; and it is a similar figure when Pindar, *Nem.* v. 11, compares the milk-hair of a young man to the fine woolly down of the expanding vine-leaves (*vid.* Passow). In *merkahhim* there scarcely lies anything further than that this *flos juventae* on the blooming cheeks gives the impression of the young shoots of aromatic plants; at all events, the *merkahhim*, even although we refer this feature in the figure to the fragrance of the unguents on the beard, are not the perfumes themselves, to which *mᵉgadloth* is not appropriate, but fragrant plants, so that in the first instance the growth of the beard is in view with the impression of its natural beauty.

Ver. 13*b* His lips lilies,
Dropping with liquid myrrh.

Lilies, viz. red lilies (*vid.* under ii. 1), unless the point of comparison is merely loveliness associated with dignity. She thinks of the lips as speaking. All that comes forth from them, the breath in itself, and the breath formed into words, is מוֹר עֹבֵר, most precious myrrh, viz. such as of itself wells forth from the bark of the *balsamodendron*. עֹבֵר, the running over of the eyes (cf. *myrrha in lacrimis*, the most highly esteemed sort, as distinguished from *myrrha in granis*), with which Dillmann combines the Aethiop. name for myrrh, *karbê* (*vid.* under v. 5).

Ver. 14*a* His hands golden cylinders,
Filled in with stones of Tarshish.

The figure, according to Gesen., *Heb. Wörterbuch*, and literally also Heilgst., is derived from the closed hand, and the stained nails are compared to precious stones. Both statements are incorrect; for (1) although it is true that then Israelitish women, as at the present day Egyptian and Arabian women, stained their eyes with *stibium* (*vid.*

under Isa. liv. 11), yet it is nowhere shown that they, and particularly men, stained the nails of their feet and their toes with the orange-yellow of the Alhenna (Lane's *Egypt*, I. 33–35); and (2) the word used is not כַּפָּיו, but יָדָיו; it is thus the outstretched hands that are meant; and only these, not the closed fist, could be compared to "lilies," for גְּלִיל signifies not a ring (Cocc., Döpke, Böttch., etc.), but that which is rolled up, a roller, cylinder (Esth. i. 6), from גָּלַל, which properly means not κυκλοῦν (Venet., after Gebhardt: κεκυκλωμέναι), but κυλίνδειν. The hands thus are meant in respect of the fingers, which on account of their noble and fine form, their full, round, fleshy mould, are compared to bars of gold formed like rollers, garnished (מְמֻלָּאִים, like מִלֵּא, Ex. xxviii. 17) with stones of Tarshish, to which the nails are likened. The transparent horn-plates of the nails, with the *lunula*, the white segment of a circle at their roots, are certainly, when they are beautiful, an ornament to the hand, and, without our needing to think of their being stained, are worthily compared to the gold-yellow topaz. *Tarshish* is not the onyx, which derives its Heb. name שֹׁהַם from its likeness to the finger-nail, but the χρυσόλιθος, by which the word in this passage before us is translated by the Quinta and the Sexta, and elsewhere also by the LXX. and Aquila. But the chrysolite is the precious stone which is now called the topaz. It receives the name *Tarshish* from Spain, the place where it was found. Pliny, xxxviii. 42, describes it as *aureo fulgore tralucens*. Bredow erroneously interprets *Tarshish* of amber. There is a kind of chrysolite, indeed, which is called *chryselectron*, because *in colorem electri declinans*. The comparison of the nails to such a precious stone (Luther, influenced by the consonance, and apparently warranted by the *plena hyacinthis* of the Vulg., has substituted golden rings, *vol Türkissen*, whose blue-green colour is not suitable here), in spite of Hengst., who finds it insipid, is as true to nature as it is tender and pleasing. The description now proceeds from the uncovered to the covered parts of his body, the whiteness of which is compared to ivory and marble.

   Ver. 14*b* His body an ivory work of art,
    Covered with sapphires.

The plur. מֵעִים or מֵעַיִם, from מֵעָה or מְעִי (*vid.* under Ps. xl. 9), signifies properly the tender parts, and that the inward parts of the body, but is here, like the Chald. מְעִין, Dan. ii. 32, and the בֶּטֶן, vii. 3, which also properly signifies the inner part of the body, κοιλία, transferred to the body in its outward appearance. To the question how Shulamith should in such a manner praise that which is for the most part covered with clothing, it is not only to be answered that it is the poet who speaks by her mouth, but also that it is not the bride or the beloved, but the wife, whom he represents as thus speaking. עָשֵׁת (from the peculiar Hebraeo-Chald. and Targ. עֲשֵׁי, which, after Jer. v. 28, like *khalak, creare*, appears to proceed from the fundamental idea of smoothing) designates an artistic figure. Such a figure was Solomon's throne, made of שֵׁן, the teeth of elephants, ivory,[1] 1 Kings x. 18. Here Solomon's own person, without reference to a definite admired work of art, is praised as being like an artistic figure made of ivory,—like it in regard to its glancing smoothness and its fine symmetrical form. When, now, this work of art is described as covered with sapphires (מְעֻלֶּפֶת, referred to עֶשֶׁת, as apparently gramm., or as ideal, fem.), a sapphire-coloured robe is not meant (Hitzig, Ginsburg); for עלף, which only means to disguise, would not at all be used of such a robe (Gen. xxxviii. 14 ; cf. xxiv. 65), nor would the one uniform colour of the robe be designated by sapphires in the plur. The choice of the verb עלף (elsewhere used of veiling) indicates a covering shading the pure white, and in connection with סַפִּירִים, thought of as accus., a moderating of the bright glance by a soft blue. For ספיר (a genuine Semit. word, like the Chald. שַׁפִּיר; cf. regarding סְפַר = שָׁפַר, under Ps. xvi. 6) is the sky-blue sapphire (Ex. xxiv. 10), including the *Lasurstein* (*lapis lazuli*), sprinkled with golden, or rather with gold-like glistening points of pyrites, from which, with the *l* omitted, sky-blue is called *azur* (azure) (*vid.* under Job xxviii. 6). The work of art formed of ivory is quite covered over with sapphires fixed in it. That which is here compared is nothing else than the branching blue veins under the white skin.

Ver. 15a His legs white marble columns,
Set on bases of fine gold.

If the beauty of the living must be represented, not by colours, but in figurative language, this cannot otherwise be done than by the selection of minerals, plants, and things in general for the comparison, and the comparison must more or less come short, because dead soulless matter does not reach to a just and full representation of the living. Thus here, also, the description of the lower extremity, which reaches from the thighs and the legs down to the feet, of which last, in the words of an anatomist,[2] it may be said that "they form the pedestal for the bony pillars of the legs." The comparison is thus in accordance with fact; the שׁוֹקִים (from שׁוּק = (Arab.) *saḵ*, to

[1] Ivory is fully designated by the name שֶׁנְהַבִּים, Lat. *ebur*, from the Aegypt. *ebu*, the Aegypto-Indian *ibha*, elephant.

[2] Hyrtl's *Lehrbuch der Anat. des Menschen*, sec. 155.

drive: the movers forward), in the structure of the human frame, take in reality the place of "pillars," and the feet the place of "pedestals," as in the tabernacle the wooden pillars rested on small supports in which they were fastened, Ex. xxvi. 18 f. But in point of fidelity to nature, the symbol is inferior to a rigid Egyptian figure. Not only is it without life; it is not even capable of expressing the curvilinear shape which belongs to the living. On the other hand, it loses itself in symbol; for although it is in conformity with nature that the legs are compared to pillars of white (according to Aquila and Theod., Parian) marble,—שֵׁשׁ = שַׁיִשׁ, 1 Chron. xxix. 2 (material for the building of the temple), Talm. מַרְמְרָא, of the same verbal root as שׁוּשָׁן, the name of the white lily,—the comparison of the feet to bases of fine gold is yet purely symbolical. Gold is a figure of that which is sublime and noble, and with white marble represents greatness combined with purity. He who is here praised is not a shepherd, but a king. The comparisons are thus so grand because the beauty of the beloved is in itself heightened by his kingly dignity.[1]

Ver. 15. His aspect like Lebanon,
Distinguished as the cedars.

By בָּחוּר the Chald. thinks of "a young man" (from בָּחַר = בֵּנֵר, to be matured, as at Ps. lxxxix. 20); but in that case we should have expected the word כָּאֶרֶז instead of כָּאֲרָזִים. Luther, with all other translators, rightly renders "chosen as the cedars." His look, *i.e.* his appearance as a whole, is awe-inspiring, majestic, like Lebanon, the king of mountains; he (the praised one) is chosen, *i.e.* presents a rare aspect, rising high above the common man, like the cedars, those kings among trees, which as special witnesses of creative omnipotence are called "cedars of God," Ps. lxxx. 11 [10]. בָּחוּר, *electus*, everywhere else an attribute of persons, does not here refer to the look, but to him whose the look is; and what it means in union with the cedars is seen from Jer. xxii. 7; cf. Isa. xxxvii. 24. Here also it is seen (what besides is manifest), that the fairest of the children of men is a king. In conclusion, the description returns from elevation of rank to loveliness.

[1] Dillmann proposes the question, the answer to which he desiderates in Ewald, how the maiden could be so fluent in speaking of the new glories of the Solomonic era (plants and productions of art). Böttcher answers, that she had learned to know these whilst detained at court, and that the whole description has this ground-thought, that she possessed in her beloved all the splendour which the women of the harem value and enjoy. But already the first words of the description, "white and ruddy," exclude the sunburnt shepherd. To refer the gold, in the figurative description of the uncovered parts of the body, to this bronze colour is insipid.

Ver. 16a His palate is sweets [sweetnesses],
And he is altogether precious [lovelinesses].

The palate, חֵךְ, is frequently named as the organ of speech, Job vi. 30, xxxi. 30, Prov. v. 3, viii. 7; and it is also here used in this sense. The meaning, "the mouth for kissing," which Böttch. gives to the word, is fanciful; חֵךְ (=*hink*, Arab. *hanak*) is the inner palate and the region of the throat, with the *uvula* underneath the chin. Partly with reference to his words, his lips have been already praised, 13b; but there the fragrance of his breath came into consideration, his breath both in itself and as serving for the formation of articulate words. But the naming of the palate can point to nothing else than his words. With this the description comes to a conclusion; for, from the speech, the most distinct and immediate expression of the personality, advance is made finally to the praise of the person. The *pluraliatant.* מַמְתַקִּים and מַחֲמַדִּים designate what they mention in richest fulness. His palate, *i.e.* that which he speaks and the manner in which he speaks it, is true sweetness (cf. Prov. xvi. 21; Ps. lv. 15), and his whole being true loveliness. With justifiable pride Shulamith next says:

Ver. 16b This is my beloved and this my friend,
Ye daughters of Jerusalem!

The emphatically repeated "this" is here pred. (Luth.: "such an one is" . . .); on the other hand, it is subj. at Ex. iii. 15 (Luth.: "that is" . . .).

The daughters of Jerusalem now offer to seek along with Shulamith for her beloved, who had turned away and was gone.

Chap. vi. 1. Whither has thy beloved gone,
Thou fairest of women?
Whither has thy beloved turned,
That we may seek him with thee?

The longing remains with her even after she has wakened, as the after effect of her dream. In the morning she goes forth and meets with the daughters of Jerusalem. They cause Shulamith to describe her friend, and they ask whither he has gone. They wish to know the direction in which he disappeared from her, the way which he had probably taken (פָּנָה, R. פ, to drive, to urge forward, to turn from one to another), that with her they might go to seek him (*Vav* of the consequence or the object, as at Ps. lxxxii. 17). The answer she gives proceeds on a conclusion which she draws from the inclination of her beloved.

Ver. 2 My beloved has gone down into the garden,
To the beds of sweet herbs,
To feed in the gardens
And gather lilies.

He is certainly, she means to say, there to be found where he delights most to tarry. He will have gone down—viz. from the palace (vi. 11; cf. 1 Kings xx. 43 and Esth. vii. 7)—into his garden, to the fragrant beds, there to feed in his garden and gather lilies (cf. Old Germ. "to collect *rôsen*"); he is fond of gardens and flowers Shulamith expresses this in her shepherd-dialect, as when Jesus says of His Father (John xv. 1), "He is the husbandman." Flower-beds are the feeding place (*vid.* regarding לִרְעוֹת under ii. 16) of her beloved. Solomon certainly took great delight in gardens and parks, Eccles. ii. 5. But this historical fact is here idealized; the natural flora which Solomon delighted in with intelligent interest presents itself as a figure of a higher Loveliness which was therein as it were typically manifest (cf. Rev. vii. 17, where the "Lamb," "feeding," and "fountains of water," are applied as anagogics, *i.e.* heavenward-pointing types). Otherwise it is not to be comprehended why it is lilies that are named. Even if it were supposed to be implied that lilies were Solomon's favourite flowers, we must assume that his taste was determined by something more than by form and colour. The words of Shulamith give us to understand that the inclination and the favourite resort of her friend corresponded to his nature, which is altogether thoughtfulness and depth of feeling (cf. under Ps. xcii. 5, the reference to Dante :. the beautiful women who gather flowers representing the paradisaical life); lilies, the emblems of unapproachable grandeur, purity inspiring reverence, high elevation above that which is common, bloom there wherever the lily-like one wanders, whom the lily of the valley calls her own. With the words:

Ver. 3 I am my beloved's, and my beloved is mine,
Who feeds among the lilies,

Shulamith farther proceeds, followed by the daughters of Jerusalem, to seek her friend lost through her own fault. She always says, not אִישִׁי, but דּוֹדִי and רֵעִי; for love, although a passion common to mind and body, is in this Song of Songs viewed as much as possible apart from its basis in the animal nature. Also, that the description hovers between that of the clothed and the unclothed, gives to it an ideality favourable to the mystical interpretation. Nakedness is עֶרְוָה. But at the cross nakedness appears transported from the sphere of sense to that of the supersensuous.

SECOND SCENE OF THE FOURTH ACT, VI. 4—9.

With ver. 4 Solomon's address is resumed, and a new scene opens. Shulamith had found him again, and she who is beautiful in herself appears now so much the more beautiful, when the joy of seeing him again irradiates her whole being.

> Ver. 4 Beautiful art thou, my friend, as Tirzah,
> Comely as Jerusalem,
> Terrible as a battle-array.

In the praise of her beauty we hear the voice of the king. The cities which are the highest ornament of his kingdom serve him as the measure of her beauty, which is designated according to the root conceptions by יָפֶה, after the quality of completeness; by נָאוָה, after the quality of that which is well-becoming, pleasing. It is concluded, from the prominence given to Tirzah, that the Song was not composed till after the division of the kingdom, and that its author was an inhabitant of the northern kingdom; for Tirzah was the first royal city of this kingdom till the time of Omri, the founder of Samaria. But since, at all events, it is Solomon who here speaks, so great an historical judgment ought surely to be ascribed to a later poet who has imagined himself in the exact position of Solomon, that he would not represent the king of the undivided Israel as speaking like a king of the separate kingdom of Israel. The prominence given to Tirzah has another reason. Tirzah was discovered by Robinson on his second journey, 1852, in which Van de Velde accompanied him, on a height in the mountain range to the north of Nablûs, under the name *Tullûzah*. Brocardus and Breydenbach had already pointed out a village called *Thersa* to the east of Samaria. This form of the name corresponds to the Heb. better than that Arab. *Tullûzah*; but the place is suitable, and if Tullûzah lies high and beautiful in a region of olive trees, then it still justifies its ancient name, which means pleasantness or sweetness. But it cannot be sweetness on account of which Tirzah is named before Jerusalem, for in the eye of the Israelites Jerusalem was " the perfection of beauty " (Ps. l. 2; Lam. ii. 15). That there is gradation from Tirzah to Jerusalem (Hengst.) cannot be said; for נָאוָה (*decora*) and יפה (*pulchra*) would be reversed if a climax were intended. The reason of it is rather this, that Shulamith is from the higher region, and is not a daughter of Jerusalem, and that therefore a beautiful city situated in the north toward Sunem must serve as a comparison of her beauty. That Shulamith is both beautiful and terrible (אֲיֻמָּה from אֹים) is no contradition: she is terrible in the irresistible power of the impression of her personality, terrible as *nidgaloth*, i.e. as troops going forth with their banners unfurled (cf. the *Kal* of this *v. denom.*, Ps. xx. 6). We do not need to supply מַחֲנוֹת, which is sometimes fem., Ps. xxv. 3, Gen. xxxii. 9, although the attribute would here be appropriate, Num. ii. 3, cf. x. 5; still less צְבָאוֹת, which occurs in the sense of military service, Isa. xl. 2, and a war-expedition, Dan. viii. 12, but not in the sense of war-host, as fem. Much rather *nidgaloth*, thus neut., is meant of bannered hosts, as אֹרְחוֹת (not אָרְ'), Isa. xxi. 13, of those that are marching. War-hosts with their banners, their standards, go forth confident of victory. Such is Shulamith's whole appearance, although she is unconscious of it—a *veni, vidi, vici*. Solomon is completely vanquished by her. But seeking to maintain himself in freedom over against her, he cries out to her:

> Ver. 5a Turn away thine eyes from me,
> For overpoweringly they assail me.

Döpke translates, *ferocire me faciunt*; Hengst.: they make me proud; but although הִרְהִיב, after Ps. cxxxviii. 3, may be thus used, yet that would be an effect produced by the eyes, which certainly would suggest the very opposite of the request to turn them away. The verb רָהַב means to be impetuous, and to press impetuously against any one; the *Hiph.* is the intens. of this trans. signification of the *Kal*: to press overpoweringly against one, to infuse terror, *terrorem incutere*. The LXX. translates it by ἀναπτεροῦν, which is also used of the effect of terror ("to make to start up"), and the Syr. by *afred*, to put to flight, because *arheb* signifies to put in fear, as also *arhab* = *khawwaf*, *terrefacere*; but here the meaning of the verb corresponds more with the sense of رعب, to be placed in the state of *ro'b*, i.e. of paralyzing terror. If she directed her large, clear, penetrating eyes to him, he must sink his own: their glance is unbearable by him. This peculiar form the praise of her eyes here assumes; but then the description proceeds as at iv. 1b, ii. 3b. The words used there in praise of her hair, her teeth, and her cheeks, are here repeated.

> Ver. 5b Thy hair is like a flock of goats
>   Which repose downwards on Gilead.
> 6 Thy teeth like a flock of lambs
>   Which come up from the washing,
>   All of them bearing twins,
>   And a bereaved one is not among them.
> 7 Like a piece of pomegranate thy temples
>   Behind thy veil.

The repetition is literal, but yet not without change in the expression,—there, מֵהַר גִּלְ׳, here, מִן־הַגִּלְ׳; there, הַקְּצֻ׳, *tonsarum*, here, הָרְחֵ׳, *agnarum* (Symm., Venet. τῶν ἀμνάδων); for רָחֵל, in its proper signification, is like the Arab. *rachil, richl, richleh*, the female lamb, and particularly the ewe. Hitzig imagines that Solomon here repeats to Shulamith what he had said to another *donna* chosen for marriage, and that the flattery becomes insipid by repetition to Shulamith, as well as also to the reader. But the romance which he finds in the Song is not this itself, but his own palimpsest, in the style of Lucian's transformed ass. The repetition has a morally better reason, and not one so subtle. Shulamith appears to Solomon yet more beautiful than on the day when she was brought to him as his bride. His love is still the same, unchanged; and this both she and the reader or hearer must conclude from these words of praise, repeated now as they were then. There is no one among the ladies of the court whom he prefers to her,—these must themselves acknowledge her superiority.

> Ver. 8 There are sixty queens,
> And eighty concubines,
> And virgins without number.
> 9 One is my dove, my perfect one,—
> The only one of her mother,
> The choice one of her that bare her.
> The daughters saw her and called her blessed,—
> Queens and concubines, and they extolled her.

Even here, where, if anywhere, notice of the difference of gender was to be expected, הֵמָּה stands instead of the more accurate הֵנָּה (*e.g.* Gen. vi. 2). The number of the women of Solomon's court, 1 Kings xi. 3, is far greater (700 wives and 300 concubines); and those who deny the Solomonic authorship of the Song regard the poet, in this particular, as more historical than the historian. On our part, holding as we do the Solomonic authorship of the book, we conclude from these low numbers that the Song celebrates a love-relation of Solomon's at the commencement of his reign: his luxury had not then reached the enormous height to which he, the same Solomon, looks back, and which he designates, Eccles. ii. 8, as *vanitas vanitatum*. At any rate, the number of 60 מְלָכוֹת, *i.e.* legitimate wives of equal rank with himself, is yet high enough; for, according to 2 Chron. xi. 21, Rehoboam had 18 wives and 60 concubines. The 60 occurred before, at iii. 7. If it be a round number, as sometimes, although rarely, *sexaginta* is thus used (Hitzig), it may be reduced only to 51, but not further, especially here, where 80 stands along with it. פִּילֶגֶשׁ (פִּלֶּגֶשׁ), Gr. πάλλαξ, παλλακή (Lat. *pellex*), which in the form פִּלַּקְתָּא

(פִּלְקְתָא) came back from the Greek to the Aramaic, is a word as yet unexplained. According to the formation, it may be compared to חֶרְמֵשׁ, from חָרַם, to cut off; whence also the harem bears the (Arab.) name *haram*, or the separated *gynaeconitis*, to which access is denied. An ending in *is* (שׁ) is known to the Assyr., but only as an adverbial ending, which, as '*istinis* = לְבַדּוֹ, alone, *solus*, shows is connected with the pron. *su*. These two nouns appear as thus requiring to be referred to *quadrilitera*, with the annexed שׁ; perhaps פלנשׁ, in the sense of to break into splinters, from פָּלַג, to divide (whence a brook, as dividing itself in its channels, has the name of פֶּלֶג), points to the polygamous relation as a breaking up of the marriage of one; so that a concubine has the name *pillĕgĕsh*, as a representative of polygamy in contrast to monogamy.

In the first line of ver. 9 אחת is subj. (one, who is my dove, my perfect one); in the second line, on the contrary, it is pred. (one, *unica*, is she of her mother). That Shulamith was her mother's only child does not, however, follow from this; אַחַת, *unica*, is equivalent to *unice dilecta*, as יָחִיד, Prov. iv. 3, is equivalent to *unice dilectus* (cf. Keil's *Zech.* xiv. 7). The parall. בָּרָה has its nearest signification *electa* (LXX., Syr., Jerome), not *pura* (Venet.); the fundamental idea of cutting and separating divides itself into the ideas of choosing and purifying. The Aorists, 9*b*, are the only ones in this book; they denote that Shulamith's look had, on the part of the women, this immediate result, that they willingly assigned to her the good fortune of being preferred to them all,—that to her the prize was due. The words, as also at Prov. xxxi. 28, are an echo of Gen. xxx. 13,—the books of the *Chokma* delight in references to Genesis, the book of pre-Israelitish origin. Here, in vers. 8, 9, the distinction between our typical and the allegorical interpretation is correctly seen. The latter is bound to explain what the 60 and the 80 mean, and how the wives, concubines, and "virgins" of the harem are to be distinguished from each other; but what till now has been attempted in this matter has, by reason of its very absurdity or folly, become an easy subject of wanton mockery. But the typical interpretation regards the 60 and the 80, and the unreckoned number, as what their names denote,—viz. favourites, concubines, and serving-maids. But to see an allegory of heavenly things in such a herd of women—a kind of thing which the Book of Genesis dates from the degradation of marriage in the line of Cain—is a profanation of that which is holy. The fact is, that by a violation of the law of God (Deut. xvii. 17), Solomon brings a cloud over the typical representation, which is not at all to be thought of in connection with the Antitype. Solomon, as Jul. Sturm rightly remarks, is not to be considered by himself, but only in his relation to Shulamith. In Christ, on the contrary, is no imperfection; sin remains in the congregation. In the Song, the bride is purer than the bridegroom; but in the fulfilling of the Song this relation is reversed: the bridegroom is purer than the bride.

FIFTH ACT.

SHULAMITH, THE ATTRACTIVELY FAIR BUT HUMBLE PRINCESS.—
CHAP. VI. 10–VIII. 4.

FIRST SCENE OF THE FIFTH ACT, VI. 10–VII. 6.

The fourth Act, notwithstanding little disturbances, gives a clear view of the unchanging love of the newly-married pair. This fifth shows how Shulamith, although raised to a royal throne, yet remains, in her childlike disposition and fondness for nature, a lily of the valley. The first scene places us in the midst of the royal gardens. Shulamith comes to view from its recesses, and goes to the daughters of Jerusalem, who, overpowered by the beauty of her heavenly appearance, cry out:

> Ver. 10 Who is this that looketh forth like the morning-red,
> Beautiful as the moon, pure as the sun,
> Terrible as a battle-host?

The question, "Who is this?" is the same as at iii. 6. There, it refers to her who was brought to the king; here, it refers to her who moves in that which is his as her own. There, the "this" is followed by עֹלָה appositionally; here, by הַנִּשְׁקָפָה [looking forth] determ., and thus more closely connected with it; but then indeterm., and thus apposit. predicates follow. The verb שָׁקַף signifies to bend forward, to overhang; whence the *Hiph.* הִשְׁקִיף and *Niph.* נִשְׁקַף, to look out, since in doing so one bends forward (*vid.* under Ps. xiv. 2). The LXX. here translates it by ἐκκύπτουσα, the Venet. by παρακύπτουσα, both of which signify to look toward something with the head inclined forward. The point of comparison is, the rising up from the background: Shulamith breaks through the shades of the garden-grove like the morning-red, the morning dawn; or, also: she comes nearer and nearer, as the morning-red rises behind the mountains, and then fills always the more widely the whole horizon. The Venet. translates ὡς ἑωσφόρος; but the morning star is not שַׁחַר, but בֶּן־שַׁחַר, Isa. xiv. 12; *shahhar*, properly, the morning-dawn, means, in Heb., not only this, like the Arab. *shahar*, but rather, like the Arab. *fajr*, the morning-red,—*i.e.* the red tinge of the morning mist. From the morning-red the description proceeds to the moon, yet visible in the morning sky, before the sun has risen. It is usually called יָרֵחַ, as being yellow; but here it is called לְבָנָה, as being white; as also the sun, which here is spoken of as having risen (Judg. v. 31), is designated not by the word שֶׁמֶשׁ, as the unwearied (Ps. xix. 6*b*, 6*a*), but, on account of the intensity of its warming light (Ps. xix. 7*b*), is called חַמָּה. These, in the language of poetry, are favourite names of the moon and the sun, because already the primitive meaning of the two other names had disappeared from common use; but with these, definite attributive ideas are immediately connected. Shulamith appears like the morning-red, which breaks through the darkness; beautiful, like the silver moon, which in soft still majesty shines in the heavens (Job xxxi. 26); pure (*vid.* regarding בַּר, בָּרוּר in this signification: smooth, bright, pure, under Isa. xlix. 2) as the sun, whose light (cf. טָהוֹר with the Aram. טִיהֲרָא, mid-day brightness) is the purest of the pure, imposing as war-hosts with their standards (*vid.* vi. 4*b*). The answer of her who was drawing near, to this exclamation, sounds homely and childlike:

> Ver. 11 To the nut garden I went down
> To look at the shrubs of the valley,
> To see whether the vine sprouted,
> The pomegranates budded.
> Ver. 12 I knew it not that my soul lifted me up
> To the royal chariots of my people, a noble (one).

In her loneliness she is happy; she finds her delight in quietly moving about in the vegetable world; the vine and the pomegranate, brought from her home, are her favourites. Her soul—viz. love for Solomon, which fills her soul—raised her to the royal chariots of her people, the royal chariots of a noble (one), where she sits beside the king, who drives the chariot; she knew this, but she also knew it not for what she had become without any cause of her own, that she is without self-elation and without disavowal of her origin. These are Shulamith's thoughts and feelings, which we think we derive from these two verses without reading between the lines and without refining. I went down, she says, viz. from the royal palace, cf. vi. 2. Then, further, she speaks of a valley; and the whole sounds rural, so that we are led to think of Etam as the scene. This Etam, romantically (vid. Judg. xv. 8 f.) situated, was, as Josephus (*Antt.* viii. 7. 3) credibly informs us, Solomon's Belvedere. "In the royal stables," he says, "so great was the regard for beauty and swiftness, that nowhere else could horses of greater beauty or greater fleetness be found. All had to acknowledge that the appearance of the king's horses was wonderfully pleasing, and that their swiftness was incomparable. Their riders also served as an ornament to them. They were young men in the flower of their age, and were distinguished by their lofty stature and their flowing hair, and by their clothing, which was of Tyrian purple. They every day sprinkled their hair with dust of gold, so that their whole head sparkled when the sun shone upon it. In such array, armed and bearing bows, they formed a body-guard around the king, who was wont, clothed in a white garment, to go out of the city in the morning, and even to drive his chariot. These morning excursions were usually to a certain place which was about sixty stadia from Jerusalem, and which was called Etam; gardens and brooks made it as pleasant as it was fruitful." This Etam, from whence (the עיטם עֵין [1]) a watercourse, the ruins of which are still visible, supplied the temple with water, has been identified by Robinson with a village called *Artas* (by Lumley called *Urtas*), about a mile and a half to the south of Bethlehem. At the upper end of the winding valley, at a considerable height above the bottom, are three old Solomonic pools,—large, oblong basins of considerable compass placed one behind the other in terraces. Almost at an equal height with the highest pool, at a distance of several hundred steps there is a strong fountain, which is carefully built over, and to which there is a descent by means of stairs inside the building. By it principally were the pools, which are just large reservoirs, fed, and the water was conducted by a subterranean conduit into the upper pool. Riding along the way close to the aqueduct, which stills exists, one sees even at the present day the valley below clothed in rich vegetation; and it is easy to understand that here there may have been rich gardens and pleasure-grounds (Moritz Lüttke's *Mittheilung*). A more suitable place for this first scene of the fifth Act cannot be thought of; and what Josephus relates serves remarkably to illustrate not only the description of ver. 11, but also that of ver. 12.

אֱגוֹז is the walnut, *i.e.* the Italian nut tree (*Juglans regia L.*), originally brought from Persia; the Persian name is *keuz*, Aethiop. *gûz*, Arab. Syr. *gauz* (*gôz*), in Heb. with א prosth., like the Armen. *engus*. גִּנַּת אֱגוֹז is a garden, the peculiar ornament of which is the

[1] According to *Sebachim* 54b, one of the highest points of the Holy Land.

fragrant and shady walnut tree; גִּנַּת אֱגוֹז would not be a nut garden, but a garden of nuts, for the plur. signifies, Mishn. *nuces* (viz. *juglandes = Jovis glandes*, Pliny, xvii. 136, ed. Jan.), as תְּאֵנִים, figs, in contradistinction to תְּאֵנָה, a fig tree, only the Midrash uses אֱגוֹזָה here, elsewhere not occurring, of a tree. The object of her going down was one, viz. to observe the state of the vegetation; but it was manifold, as expressed in the manifold statements which follow יָרַדְתִּי. The first object was the nut garden. Then her intention was to observe the young shoots in the valley, which one has to think of as traversed by a river or brook; for נַחַל, like *Wady*, signifies both a valley and a valley-brook. The nut garden might lie in the valley, for the walnut tree is fond of a moderately cool, damp soil (Joseph. *Bell.* iii. 10. 8). But the אִבֵּי are the young shoots with which the banks of a brook and the damp valley are usually adorned in the spring-time. אֵב, shoot, in the Heb. of budding and growth, in Aram. of the fruit-formation, comes from R. אב, the weaker power of נב, which signifies to expand and spread from within outward, and particularly to sprout up and to well forth. ראה ב signifies here, as at Gen. xxxiv. 1, attentively to observe something, looking to be fixed upon it, to sink down into it. A further object was to observe whether the vine had broken out, or had budded (this is the meaning of פָּרַח, breaking out, to send forth, R. פר, to break),[1]—whether the pomegranate trees had gained flowers or flower-buds הֵנֵצוּ, not as Gesen. in his *Thes.* and *Heb. Lex.* states, the *Hiph.* of נוץ, which would be הֵנִיצוּ, but from נָצַץ instead of הֵנַצּוּ, with the same omission of *Dagesh*, after the forms הֵפֵרוּ, הֵרֵעוּ, cf. Prov. vii. 13, R. נס נץ, to glance, bloom (whence *Nisan* as the name of the flower-month, as *Ab* the name of the fruit-month).[2] Why the pomegranate tree (*Punica granatum L.*), which derives this its Latin name from its fruit being full of grains, bears the Semitic name of רִמּוֹן, (Arab.) *rummân*, is yet unexplained; the Arabians are so little acquainted with it, that they are uncertain whether *ramm* or *raman* (which, however, is not proved to exist) is to be regarded as the root-word. The question goes along with that regarding the origin and signification of *Rimmon*, the name of the Syrian god, which appears to denote[3] "sublimity;" and it is possible that the pomegranate tree has its name from this god as being consecrated to him.[4]

---

[1] *Vid.* Fried. Delitzsch, *Indo-Germ. Sem. Studien*, p. 72.

[2] Cf. my *Jesurun*, p. 149.

[3] An old Chald. king is called *Rim-Sin*; *rammu* is common in proper names, as *Ab-rammu*.

[4] The name scarcely harmonizes with רִמָּה, worm, although the pomegranate

In ver. 12, Shulamith adds that, amid this her quiet delight in contemplating vegetable life, she had almost forgotten the position to which she had been elevated. לֹא יָדַעְתִּי may, according to the connection in which it is used, mean, "I know not," Gen. iv. 9, xxi. 26, as well as "I knew not," Gen. xxviii. 16, Prov. xxiii. 35; here the latter (LXX., Aquila, Jerome, Venet., Luther), for the expression runs parallel to ירדתי, and is related to it as verifying or circumstantiating it. The connection לֹא יד' נפשי, whether we take the word נפשי as permut. of the subject (Luther: My soul knew it not) or as the accus. of the object: I knew not myself (after Job ix. 21), is objectionable, because it robs the following שָׂמַתְנִי of its subject, and makes the course of thought inappropriate. The accusative, without doubt, hits on what is right, since it gives the Rebia, corresponding to our colon, to יָד'; for that which follows with נַפְשִׁי שָׂמ' is just what she acknowledges not to have known or considered. For the meaning cannot be that her soul had placed or brought her in an unconscious way, *i.e.* involuntarily or unexpectedly, etc., for "I knew not," as such a declaration never forms the principal sentence, but, according to the nature of the case, always a subordinate sentence, and that either as a conditional clause with *Vav*, Job ix. 5, or as a relative clause, Isa. xlvii. 11; cf. Ps. xlix. 21. Thus "I knew not" will be followed by what she was unconscious of; it follows in *oratio directa* instead of *obliqua*, as also elsewhere after כִּי, ידע, elsewhere introducing the object of knowledge, is omitted, Ps. ix. 21; Amos v. 12. But if it remains unknown to her, if it has escaped her consciousness that her soul placed her, etc., then *naphshi* is here her own self, and that on the side of desire (Job xxiii. 13; Deut. xii. 15); thus, in contrast to external constraint, her own most inward impulse, the leading of her heart. Following this, she has been placed on the height on which she now finds herself, without being always mindful of it. It would certainly now be most natural to regard מַרְכְּבוֹת, after the usual constr. of the verb שׂוּם with the double accus., *e.g.* Gen. xxviii. 22, Isa. l. 2, Ps. xxxix. 9, as pred. accus. (Venet. ἔθετό με ὀχήματα), as *e.g.* Hengst.: I knew not, thus my soul brought me (*i.e.* brought me at unawares) to the chariots of my people, who are noble. But what does this mean? He adds the remark: "Shulamith stands in the place of the war-chariots of her people as their powerful protector, or by the heroic spirit residing in her." But apart from the syntactically false rendering of לא ידעתי, and the unwarrantable allegorizing, this interpretation suffers from worm-holes; the worm which pierces it bears the strange name הה (דרימוני), *Shabbath* 90a.

wrecks itself on this, that "chariots" in themselves are not for protection, and thus without something further, especially in this designation by the word מרכבות, and not by רכב (2 Kings vi. 17; cf. 2 Kings ii. 12, xiii. 14), are not war-chariots. מר׳ will thus be the accus. of the object of motion. It is thus understood, e.g., by Ewald (sec. 281d): My soul brought me to the chariots, etc. The shepherd-hypothesis finds here the seduction of Shulamith. Holländer translates: "I perceived it not; suddenly, it can scarcely be said unconsciously, I was placed in the state-chariots of Amminadab." But the Masora expressly remarks that עמי נדיב are not to be read as if forming one, but as two words, תרין מלין.[1] Hitzig proportionally better, thus: without any apprehension of such a coincidence, she saw herself carried to the chariots of her noble people, i.e. as Gesen. in his *Thes.: inter currus comitatus principis.* Any other explanation, says Hitzig, is not possible, since the accus. מרכ׳ in itself signifies only in the direction whither, or in the neighbourhood whence. And certainly it is generally used of the aim or object toward which one directs himself or strives, e.g. Isa. xxxvii. 23. *Kodĕsh*, "toward the sanctuary," Ps. cxxxiv. 2; cf. *hashshā'rā*, "toward the gate," Isa. xxii. 7. But the accus. *mārom* can also mean "on high," Isa. xxii. 16, the accus. *hashshāmaīm* "in the heavens," 1 Kings viii. 32; and as *hishlic hăiōrah* is used, Ex. i. 22, of being cast into the Nile, and *shalahh hāărĕts* of being sent into the land, Num. xiii. 27; thus may also *sīm mĕrkāvāh* be used for *sīm bᵉmĕrkāvāh*, 1 Sam. viii. 11, according to which the Syr. (*bᵉmercabto*) and the Quinta (εἰς ἅρματα) translate; on the contrary, Symm. and Jerome destroy the meaning by adopting the reading שַׂמְתְנִי (my soul placed me in confusion). The plur. *markᵉvoth* is thus meant amplifi., like *richvē*, i. 9, and *battēnu*, i. 17. As regards the subject, 2 Sam. xv. 1 is to be compared; it is the king's chariot that is meant, yoked, according to i. 9, with Egypt. horses. It is a question whether *nadiv* is related adject. to *ammi*: my people, a noble (people),—a connection which gives prominence to the attribute appositionally, Gen. xxxvii. 2; Ps. cxliii. 10; Ezek. xxxiv. 12,—or permutat., so that the first gen. is exchanged for one defining more closely: to the royal chariot of my people, a prince. The latter has the preference, not merely because (leaving out of view the proper name *Amminadab*) wherever עם and נדיב are used together

[1] עַמִּי־נָדִיב, thus in D F: עַמִּי, without the accent and connected with נָדִיב by *Makkeph*. On the contrary, P has עַמִּינָדִיב as one word, as also the Masora *parva* has here noted חדה מלה. Our Masora, however, notes לית ותרתין כתיבין, and thus Rashi and Aben Ezra testify.

they are meant of those who stand prominent above the people, Num. xxi. 18, Ps. xlvii. 10, cxiii. 8, but because this נדיב and בַּת־נָדִיב evidently stand in interchangeable relation. Yet, even though we take נדיב and עמי together, the thought remains the same. Shulamith is not one who is abducted, but, as we read at iii. 6 ff., one who is honourably brought home; and she here expressly says that no kind of external force but her own loving soul raised her to the royal chariots of her people and their king. That she gives to the fact of her elevation just this expression, arises from the circumstance that she places her joy in the loneliness of nature, in contrast to her driving along in a splendid chariot. Designating the chariot that of her noble people, or that of her people, and, indeed, of a prince, she sees in both cases in Solomon the concentration and climax of the people's glory.

Encouraged by Shulamith's unassuming answer, the daughters of Jerusalem now give utterance to an entreaty which their astonishment at her beauty suggests to them.

Chap. vii. 1 Come back, come back, O Shulamith!
Come back, come back, that we may look upon thee!

She is now (vi. 10 ff.) on the way from the garden to the palace. The fourfold "come back" entreats her earnestly, yea, with tears, to return thither with them once more, and for this purpose, that they might find delight in looking upon her; for חָזָה בְ signifies to sink oneself into a thing, looking at it, to delight (feast) one's eyes in looking on a thing. Here for the first time Shulamith is addressed by name. But הַשּׁוּ׳ cannot be a pure proper name, for the art. is vocat., as *e.g.* הַבַּת ירו׳, "O daughter of Jerusalem!" Pure proper names like שלמה are so determ. in themselves that they exclude the article; only such as are at the same time also nouns, like יַרְדֵּן and לְבָנוֹן, are susceptible of the article, particularly also of the vocat., Ps. cxiv. 5; but cf. Zech. xi. 1 with Isa. x. 34. Thus הַשּׁוּ׳ will be not so much a proper name as a name of descent, as generally nouns in î (with a few exceptions, viz. of ordinal number, הָרָרִי, יְמִנִי, etc.), are all *gentilicia*. The LXX. render השׁו׳ by ἡ Σουναμῖτις, and this is indeed but another form for הַשּׁוּנַמִּית, *i.e.* she who is from Sunem. Thus also was designated the exceedingly beautiful Abishag, 1 Kings i. 3, Elisha's excellent and pious hostess, 2 Kings iv. 8 ff. *Sunem* was in the tribe of Issachar (Josh. xix. 18), near to Little Hermon, from which it was separated by a valley, to the south-east of Carmel. This lower Galilean Sunem, which lies south from Nain, south-east from Nazareth, south-west from Tabor, is also called *Shulem*. Eusebius in his *Onomasticon* says regarding it: Σουβήμ (l. Σουλήμ) κλήρου

Ἰσσάχαρ. καὶ νῦν ἐστὶ κώμη Σουλὴμ κ.τ.λ., i.e. as Jerome translates it: *Sunem in tribu Issachar. et usque hodie vicus ostenditur nomine Sulem in quinto miliario montis Thabor contra australem plagam.* This place is found at the present day under the name of *Suwlam* (*Sôlam*), at the west end of *Jebel ed-Duhi* (Little Hermon), not far from the great plain (*Jisre'el*, now *Zer'în*), which forms a convenient way of communication between Jordan and the sea-coast, but is yet so hidden in the mountain range that the Talmud is silent concerning this Sulem, as it is concerning Nazareth. Here was the home of the Shulamitess of the Song. The ancients interpret the name by εἰρηνεύουσα, or by ἐσκυλευμένη (vid. Lagarde's *Onomastica*), the former after Aquila and the Quinta, the latter after Symm. The Targum has the interpretation: הַשְּׁלֵמָה בֶּאֱמוּנָתָהּ עִם ה׳ (vid. Rashi). But the form of the name (the Syr. writes שִׁילוּמִיתָא) is opposed to these allegorical interpretations. Rather it is to be assumed that the poet purposely used, not הַשּׁוּנ׳, but הַשּׁוּל׳, to assimilate her name to that of Solomon; and that it has the parallel meaning of one devoted to Solomon, and thus, as it were, of a passively-applied שְׁלוּמִית = Σαλώμη, is the more probable, as the daughters of Jerusalem would scarcely venture thus to address her who was raised to the rank of a princess unless this name accorded with that of Solomon.

Not conscious of the greatness of her beauty, Shulamith asks,—

1b α What do you see in Shulamith?

She is not aware that anything particular is to be seen in her; but the daughters of Jerusalem are of a different opinion, and answer this childlike, modest, but so much the more touching question,—

1b β As the dance of Mahanāïm !

They would thus see in her something like the dance of Mahanāïm. If this be here the name of the Levitical town (now *Maḥneh*) in the tribe of Gad, north of Jabbok, where Ishbosheth resided for two years, and where David was hospitably entertained on his flight from Absalom (Luthr.: "the dance to Mahanāïm"), then we must suppose in this trans-Jordanic town such a popular festival as was kept in Shiloh, Judg. xxi. 19, and we may compare *Abel-Meholah* [= meadow of dancing], the name of Elisha's birth-place (cf. also Herod. i. 16: "To dance the dance of the Arcadian town of Tegea "). But the Song delights in retrospective references to Genesis (cf. iv. 11b, vii. 11). At xxxii. 3, however, by *Mahanāïm*[1] is meant the double encampment of angels who protected Jacob's two companies

---

[1] Böttcher explains *Mahanāïm* as a plur.; but the plur. of מַחֲנֶה is מַחֲנוֹת and מַחֲנַיִם; the plur. termination *ajim* is limited to מַיִם and שָׁמַיִם.

(xxxii. 8). The town of Mahanāïm derives its name from this vision of Jacob's. The word, as the name of a town, is always without the article; and here, where it has the article, it is to be understood appellatively. The old translators, in rendering by "the dances of the camps" (Syr., Jerome, *choros castrorum*, Venet. θίασον στρατοπέδων), by which it remains uncertain whether a war-dance or a parade is meant, overlook the dual, and by exchanging מחנים with מְחֹנוֹת, they obtain a figure which in this connection is incongruous and obscure. But, in truth, the figure is an angelic one. The daughters of Jerusalem wish to see Shulamith dance, and they designate that as an angelic sight. *Mahanāïm* became in the post-bibl. dialect a name directly for angels. The dance of angels is only a step beyond the responsive song of the seraphim, Isa. vi. *Engelkoere* [angel-choir] and "heavenly host" are associated in the old German poetry.[1] The following description is undeniably that (let one only read how Hitzig in vain seeks to resist this interpretation) of one dancing. In this, according to biblical representation and ancient custom, there is nothing repulsive. The women of the ransomed people, with Miriam at their head, danced, as did also the women who celebrated David's victory over Goliath (Ex. xv. 20; 1 Sam. xviii. 66). David himself danced (2 Sam. vi.) before the ark of the covenant. Joy and dancing are, according to Old Testament conception, inseparable (Eccles. iii. 4); and joy not only as the happy feeling of youthful life, but also spiritual holy joy (Ps. lxxxvii. 7). The dance which the ladies of the court here desire to see, falls under the point of view of a play of rival individual *artistes* reciprocally acting for the sake of amusement. The play also is capable of moral nobility, if it is enacted within the limits of propriety, at the right time, in the right manner, and if the natural joyfulness, penetrated by intelligence, is consecrated by a spiritual aim. Thus Shulamith, when she dances, does not then become a Gaditanian (Martial, xiv. 203) or an *Alma* (the name given in Anterior Asia to those women who go about making it their business to dance mimic and partly lascivious dances); nor does she become a *Bajadere* (Isa. xxiii. 15 f.),[2] as also Miriam, Ex. xv. 20, Jephthah's daughter, Judg. xi. 34, the "daughters of Shiloh," Judg.

---

[1] Vid. *Walther von der Vogelweide*, 173. 28. The Indian mythology goes farther, and transfers not only the original of the dance, but also of the drama, to heaven; vid. *Götting. Anzeigen*, 1874, p. 106.

[2] *Alma* is the Arab. 'ualmah (one skilled, viz. in dancing and *jonglerie*), and *Bajadere* is the Portug. softening of *baladera*, a dancer, from *balare* (*ballare*), mediaev. Lat., and then Romanic: to move in a circle, to dance.

xxi. 21, and the women of Jerusalem, 1 Sam. xviii. 6, did not dishonour themselves by dancing; the dancing of virgins is even a feature of the times after the restoration, Jer. xxxi. 13. But that Shulamith actually danced in compliance with the earnest entreaty of the daughters of Jerusalem, is seen from the following description of her attractions, which begins with her feet and the vibration of her thighs.

After throwing aside her upper garments, so that she had only the light clothing of a shepherdess or vinedresser, Shulamith danced to and fro before the daughters of Jerusalem, and displayed all her attractions before them. Her feet, previously (v. 3) naked, or as yet only shod with sandals, she sets forth with the deportment of a prince's daughter.

Ver. 2a *How beautiful are thy steps in the shoes, O prince's daughter!*

The noun נָדִיב, which signifies noble in disposition, and then noble by birth and rank (cf. the reverse relation of the meanings in *generosus*), is in the latter sense synon. and parallel to מֶלֶךְ and שַׂר; Shulamith is here called a prince's daughter because she was raised to the rank of which Hannah, 1 Sam. ii. 8, cf. Ps. cxiii. 8, speaks, and to which she herself, vi. 12, points. Her beauty, from the first associated with unaffected dignity, now appears in native princely grace and majesty. פַּעַם (from פָּעַם, *pulsare*, as in *nunc pede libero pulsanda tellus*) signifies step and foot,—in the latter sense the poet. Heb. and the vulgar Phoen. word for רֶגֶל; here the meanings *pes* and *passus* (Fr. *pas*, dance-step) flow into each other. The praise of the spectators now turns from the feet of the dancer to her thighs:

Ver. 2b *The vibration of thy thighs like ornamental chains,*
The work of an artist's hands.

The double-sided thighs, viewed from the spine and the lower part of the back, are called מָתְנַיִם; from the upper part of the legs upwards, and the breast downwards (the lumbar region), thus seen on the front and sidewise, חֲלָצִים or יְרֵכַיִם. Here the manifold twistings and windings of the upper part of the body by means of the thigh-joint are meant; such movements of a circular kind are called חַמּוּקִים, from חָמַק, v. 6. חֲלָאִים is the plur. of חֲלִי = (Arab.) *haly*, as צְבָאִים (gazelles) of צְבִי = *zaby*. The sing. חֲלִי (or חֶלְיָה = (Arab.) *hulyah*) signifies a female ornament, consisting of gold, silver, or precious stones, and that (according to the connection, Prov. xxv. 2; Hos. ii. 15) for the neck or the breast as a whole; the plur. 'חל, occurring only here, is therefore chosen because the bendings of the loins, full of life and beauty, are compared to the free swingings to and fro of such an ornament, and thus to a connected ornament of chains; for 'חמ

are not the beauty-curves of the thighs at rest,—the connection here requires movement. In accordance with the united idea of חֵל, the appos. is not מֶעֱשֵׂי, but (according to the Palestin.) מַעֲשֵׂה (LXX., Targ., Syr., Venet.). The artist is called אָמָּן (*ommân*) (the forms אָמָּן and אָמָן are also found), Syr. *avmon*, Jewish-Aram. אוּמָּן; he has, as the master of stability, a name like יָמִין, the right hand: the hand, and especially the right hand, is the *artifex* among the members.[1] The eulogists pass from the loins to the middle part of the body. In dancing, especially in the Oriental style of dancing, which is the mimic representation of animated feeling, the breast and the body are raised, and the forms of the body appear through the clothing.

> Ver. 3 Thy navel is a well-rounded basin—
> Let not mixed wine be wanting to it
> Thy body is a heap of wheat,
> Set round with lilies.

In interpreting these words, Hitzig proceeds as if a "voluptuary" were here speaking. He therefore changes שָׁרְרֵךְ into שְׁרֵךְ, "thy pudenda." But (1) it is no voluptuary who speaks here, and particularly not a man, but women who speak; certainly, above all, it is the poet, who would not, however, be so inconsiderate as to put into the mouths of women immodest words which he could use if he wished to represent the king as speaking. Moreover (2) שׁר = (Arab.) *surr*, secret (that which is secret; in Arab. especially referred to the *pudenda*, both of man and woman), is a word that is[2] foreign to the Heb. language, which has for "*Geheimnis*" [secret] the corresponding word סוֹד (*vid.* under Ps. ii. 2, xxv. 14), after the root-signification of its verbal stem (viz. to be firm, pressed together); and (3) the reference—preferred by Döpke, Magnus, Hahn, and others, also without any change of punctuation—of שׁר to the *interfeminium mulieris*, is here excluded by the circumstance that the attractions of a woman dancing, as they unfold themselves, are here described. Like the Arab. *surr*, שֹׁר (= *shurr*), from שָׁרַר, to bind fast, denotes properly the umbilical cord, Ezek. xvi. 4, and then the umbilical scar. Thus, Prov. iii. 8, where most recent critics prefer, for לְשָׁרֶּךָ, to read, but without any proper reason, לִשְׁאֵרֶךָ = לִשְׁרֶךָ, "to thy flesh," the navel comes there into view as the centre of the body,—which it always is with new-born infants, and is almost so with grown-up persons in respect of the length of the body,—and as, indeed, the centre, whence the pleasurable feeling of health diffuses its rays of heat. This middle and prominent point of the

---

[1] *Vid.* Ryssel's *Die Syn. d. Wahren u. Guten in d. Sem. Spr.* (1873), p. 12.
[2] *Vid.* Tebrîzi, in my work entitled *Jud.-Arab. Poesien, u.s.w.* (1874), p. 24.

abdomen shows itself in one lightly clad and dancing when she breathes deeply, even through the clothing; and because the navel commonly forms a little funnel-like hollow (Böttch.: in the form almost of a whirling hollow in the water, as one may see in nude antique statues), therefore the daughters of Jerusalem compare Shulamith's navel to a "basin of roundness," *i.e.* which has this general property, and thus belongs to the class of things that are round. אַגָּן does not mean a *Becher* (a cup), but a *Bechen* (basin), *pelvis*; properly a washing basin, *ijjanah* (from אָגַן = *ajan*, to full, to wash = כָּבַס); then a sprinkling basin, Ex. xxiv. 6; and generally a basin, Isa. xxii. 24; here, a mixing basin, in which wine was mingled with a proportion of water to render it palatable (κρατήρ, from κεραννύναι, *temperare*),—according to the Talm. with two-thirds of water. In this sense this passage is interpreted allegorically, *Sanhedrin* 14*b*, 37*a*, and elsewhere (*vid.* Aruch under מזג). מֶזֶג is not spiced wine, which is otherwise designated (viii. 2), but, as Hitzig rightly explains, mixed wine, *i.e.* mixed with water or snow (*vid.* under Isa. v. 22). מָזַג is not borrowed from the Greek μίσγειν (Grätz), but is a word native to all the three chief Semitic dialects,—the weaker form of מָסַךְ, which may have the meaning of "to pour in;" but not merely "to pour in," but, at the same time, "to mix" (*vid.* under Isa. v. 22; Prov. ix. 2). סַהַר, with אַגָּן, represents the circular form (from סָהַר = סָחַר), corresponding to the navel ring; Kimchi thinks that the moon must be understood (cf. שַׂהֲרוֹן, *lunula*): a moon-like round basin; according to which the Venet., also in Gr., choosing an excellent name for the moon, translates: ῥαντιστρον τῆς ἑκάτης. But "moon-basin" would be an insufficient expression for it; Ewald supposes that it is the name of a flower, without, however, establishing this opinion. The "basin of roundness" is the centre of the body a little depressed; and that which the clause, "may not mixed wine be lacking," expresses, as their wish for her, is soundness of health, for which no more appropriate and delicate figure can be given than hot wine tempered with fresh water.

The comparison in 3*b* is the same as that of R. Johanan's of beauty, *Mezia* 84*a*: "He who would gain an idea of beauty should take a silver cup, fill it with pomegranate flowers, and encircle its rim with a garland of roses."[1] To the present day, winnowed and sifted corn is piled up in great heaps of symmetrical half-spherical form,

---

[1] See my *Gesch. d. Jüd. Poesie*, p. 30 f. Hoch (the German Solomon) reminds us of the Jewish marriage custom of throwing over the newly-married pair the contents of a vessel wreathed with flowers, and filled with wheat or corn (with money underneath), accompanied with the cry, פְּרוּ וּרְבוּ [be fruitful and multiply].

which are then frequently stuck over with things that move in the wind, for the purpose of protecting them against birds. "The appearance of such heaps of wheat," says Wetstein (*Isa.* p. 710), "which one may see in long parallel rows on the thrashing-floors of a village, is very pleasing to a peasant; and the comparison of the Song, vii. 3, every Arabian will regard as beautiful." Such a corn-heap is to the present day called *ṣubbah*, while *'aramah* is a heap of thrashed corn that has not yet been winnowed; here, with עֲרֵמָה, is to be connected the idea of a *ṣubbah, i.e.* of a heap of wheat not only thrashed and winnowed, but also sifted (riddled). סוּג, enclosed, fenced about (whence the post-bibl. סְיָג, a fence), is a part. pass. such as פוּץ, scattered (*vid.* under Ps. xcii. 12). The comparison refers to the beautiful appearance of the roundness, but, at the same time, also to the flesh-colour shining through the dress; for fancy sees more than the eyes, and concludes regarding that which is veiled from that which is visible. A wheat-colour was, according to the Moslem Sunna, the tint of the first created man. Wheat-yellow and lily-white is a subdued white, and denotes at once purity and health; by πυρός [wheat] one thinks of πῦρ—heaped up wheat developes a remarkable heat, a fact for which Biesenthal refers to Plutarch's *Quaest.* In accordance with the progress of the description, the breasts are now spoken of:

> Ver. 4 Thy two breasts are like two fawns,
> Twins of a gazelle.

iv. 5 is repeated, but with the omission of the attribute, "feeding among lilies," since lilies have already been applied to another figure. Instead of תְּאוֹמֵי there, we have here תָּאֳמֵי (*taŏme*), the former after the ground-form *ti'ăm*, the latter after the ground-form *to'm* (cf. גָּאֳלִי, Neh. xiii. 29, from גֹּאַל = גָּאַל).

> Ver. 5*a* Thy neck like an ivory tower.

The article in הַשֵּׁן may be that designating species (*vid.* under i. 11); but, as at vii. 5 and iv. 4, it appears to be also here a definite tower which the comparison has in view: one covered externally with ivory tablets, a tower well known to all in and around Jerusalem, and visible far and wide, especially when the sun shone on it; had it been otherwise, as in the case of the comparison following, the locality would have been more definitely mentioned. So slender, so dazzlingly white, so imposing, and so captivating to the eye did Shulamith's neck appear. These and the following figures would be open to the objection of being without any occasion, and monstrous, if they referred to an ordinary beauty; but they refer to Solomon's spouse, they apply to a queen, and therefore are derived from that which is most splendid in the kingdom over which, along with him, she rules; and in this they have the justification of their grandeur.

Ver. 5b α Thine eyes pools in Heshbon,
At the gate of the populous (city).

Heshbon, formerly belonging to the Amorites, but at this time to the kingdom of Solomon, lay about $5\frac{1}{2}$ hours to the east of the northern point of the Dead Sea, on an extensive, undulating, fruitful, high table-land, with a far-reaching prospect. Below the town, now existing only in heaps of ruins, a brook, which here takes it rise, flows westward, and streams towards the Ghôr as the *Nahr Hesbán*. It joins the Jordan not far above its entrance into the Dead Sea. The situation of the town was richly watered. There still exists a huge reservoir of excellent masonry in the valley, about half a mile from the foot of the hill on which the town stood. The comparison here supposes two such pools, but which are not necessarily together, though both are before the gate, *i.e.* near by, outside the town. Since שַׁעַר, except at Isa. xiv. 31, is fem., בַּת־רַבִּים, in the sense of רַבָּתִי עָם, Lam. i. 1 (cf. for the non-determin. of the adj., Ezek. xxi. 25), is to be referred to the town, not to the gate (Hitz.); Blau's[1] conjectural reading, *bath-'akrabbim*, does not recommend itself, because the craggy heights of the "ascent of Akrabbim" (Num. xxxiv. 4; Josh. xv. 3), which obliquely cross[2] the Ghôr to the south of the Dead Sea, and from remote times formed the southern boundary of the kingdom of the Amorites (Judg. i. 36), were too far off, and too seldom visited, to give its name to a gate of Heshbon. But generally the crowds of men at the gate and the topography of the gate are here nothing to the purpose; the splendour of the town, however, is for the figure of the famed cisterns like a golden border. בְּרֵכָה (from בָּרַךְ, to spread out, *vid. Genesis*, p. 98; Fleischer in *Levy*, I. 420b) denotes a skilfully built round or square pool. The comparison of the eyes to a pool means, as Wetstein[3] remarks, "either thus glistening like a water-mirror, or thus lovely in appearance, for the Arabian knows no greater pleasure than to look upon clear, gently rippling water." Both are perhaps to be taken together; the mirroring glance of the moist eyes (cf. Ovid, *De Arte Am.* ii. 722:

"*Adspicies oculos tremulo fulgore micantes,*
Ut sol a liquida saepe refulget aqua"),

and the spell of the charm holding fast the gaze of the beholder.

[1] In Merx' *Archiv.* III. 355.
[2] *Vid.* Robinson's *Phys. Geogr.* p. 51.
[3] *Zeitschr. für allgem. Erdkunde*, 1859, p. 157 f.

Ver. 5b β Thy nose like the tower of Lebanon,
Which looks towards Damascus.

This comparison also places us in the midst of the architectural and artistic splendours of the Solomonic reign. A definite town is here meant; the art. determines it, and the part. following appositionally without the art., with the expression "towards Damascus" defining it more nearly (*vid.* under iii. 6), describes it. הַלְּבָנוֹן designates here "the whole Alpine range of mountains in the north of the land of Israel" (Furrer); for a tower which looks in the direction of Damascus (פְּנֵי, accus., as אֶת־פְּנֵי, 1 Sam. xxii. 4) is to be thought of as standing on one of the eastern spurs of Hermon, or on the top of Amana (iv. 8), whence the Amana (Barada) takes its rise, whether as a watch-tower (2 Sam. viii. 6), or only as a look-out from which might be enjoyed the paradisaical prospect. The nose gives to the face especially its physiognomical expression, and conditions its beauty. Its comparison to a tower on a lofty height is occasioned by the fact that Shulamith's nose, without being blunt or flat, formed a straight line from the brow downward, without bending to the right or left (Hitzig), a mark of symmetrical beauty combined with awe-inspiring dignity. After the praise of the nose it was natural to think of Carmel; Carmel is a promontory, and as such is called *anf el-jebel* (" nose of the mountain-range ").

Ver. 6a α Thy head upon thee as Carmel.

We say that the head is "on the man" (2 Kings vi. 31; Judith xiv. 18), for we think of a man ideally as the central unity of the members forming the external appearance of his body. Shulamith's head ruled her form, surpassing all in beauty and majesty, as Carmel with its noble and pleasing appearance ruled the land and sea at its feet. From the summit of Carmel, clothed with trees (Amos ix. 3; 1 Kings xviii. 42), a transition is made to the hair on the head, which the Moslem poets are fond of comparing to long leaves, as vine leaves and palm branches; as, on the other hand, the thick leafy wood is called (*vid.* under Isa. vii. 20) *comata silva* (cf. Oudendorp's Apuleii *Metam.* p. 744). Grätz, proceeding on the supposition of the existence of Persian words in the Song, regards כרמל as the name of a colour; but (1) crimson is designated in the Heb.-Pers. not כַּרְמָל, but כַּרְמִיל, instead of תּוֹלַעַת שָׁנִי (*vid.* under Isa. i. 18; Prov. xxxi. 21); (2) if the hair of the head (if רֹאשׁךְ might be directly understood of this) may indeed be compared to the glistening of purple, not, however, to the glistening of carmese or scarlet, then red and not black hair must be meant. But it is not the locks of hair, but the hair in locks that is meant. From this the eulogium finally passes to the hair of the head itself.

Ver. 6a β The flowing hair of thy head like purple—
A king fettered by locks.

Hitzig supposes that כַּרְמֶל reminded the poet of כַּרְמִיל (carmese), and that thus he hit upon אַרְגָּמָן (purple); but one would rather think that *Carmel* itself would immediately lead him to purple, for near this promontory is the principal place where purple shell-fish are found (Seetzen's *Reisen*, IV. 277 f.). דַּלָּה (from דָּלַל, to dangle, to hang loose, Job xxviii. 4, Arab. *tadladal*) is *res pendula*, and particularly *coma pendula*. Hengst. remarks that the "purple" has caused much trouble to those who understand by דלה the hair of the head. He himself, with Gussetius, understands by it the temples, *tempus capitis*; but the word רַקָּה is used (iv. 3) for "temples," and "purple-like" hair hanging down could occasion trouble only to those who know not how to distinguish purple from carmese. Red purple, אַרְגָּמָן (Assyr. *argamannu*, Aram., Arab., Pers., with departure from the primary meaning of the word, אַרְגְּוָן), which derives this name from רָקַם = רָגַם, material of variegated colour, is dark-red, and almost glistening black, as Pliny says (*Hist. Nat.* ix. 135): *Laus ei* (the Tyrian purple) *summa in colore sanguinis concreti, nigricans adspectu idemque suspectu* (seen from the side) *refulgens, unde et Homero purpureus dicitur sanguis*. The purple hair of Nisus does not play a part in myth alone, but beautiful shining dark black hair is elsewhere also called purple, *e.g.* πυρφύρεος πλόκαμος in Lucian, πορφυραῖ χαῖται in Anacreon. With the words "like purple," the description closes; and to this the last characteristic distinguishing Shulamith there is added the exclamation: "A king fettered by locks!" For רְהָטִים, from רָהַט, to run, flow, is also a name of flowing locks, not the ear-locks (Hitz.), *i.e.* long ringlets flowing down in front the same word (i. 17) signifies in its North Palest. form רַחִיט (*Chethîb*), a water-trough, *canalis*. The locks of one beloved are frequently called in erotic poetry "the fetters" by which the lover is held fast, for "love wove her net in alluring ringlets" (Deshâmi in *Joseph and Zuleika*).[1] Goethe in his *Westöst. Divan* presents as a bold yet moderate example: "There are more than fifty hooks in each lock of thy hair;" and, on the other hand, one offensively extravagant, when it is said of a Sultan: "In the bonds of thy locks lies fastened the neck of the enemy." אָסוּר signifies also in Arab. frequently one enslaved by

---

[1] Compare from the same poet: "Alas! thy braided hair, a heart is in every curl, and a dilemma in every ring" (*Deut. Morg. Zeit.* xxiv. 581).

love: *astruha* is equivalent to her lover.[1] The mention of the king now leads from the imagery of a dance to the scene which follows, where we again hear the king's voice. The scene and situation are now manifestly changed. We are transferred from the garden to the palace, where the two, without the presence of any spectators, carry on the following dialogue.

SECOND SCENE OF THE FIFTH ACT, VII. 7–VIII. 4.

It is the fundamental thought forming the motive and aim of the Song which now expresses itself in the words of Solomon.

> Ver. 7 How beautiful art thou, and how charming,
> O love, among delights!

It is a truth of all-embracing application which is here expressed. There is nothing more admirable than love, *i.e.* the uniting or mingling together of two lives, the one of which gives itself to the other, and so finds the complement of itself; nor than this self-devotion, which is at the same time self-enrichment. All this is true of earthly love, of which Walther v. d. Vogelweide says: "*minne ist zweier herzen wünne*" [love is the joy of two hearts], and it is true also of heavenly love; the former surpasses all earthly delights (also such as are purely sensuous, Eccles. ii. 8), and the latter is, as the apostle expresses himself in his spiritual "Song of Songs," 1 Cor. xiii. 13, in relation to faith and hope, "greater than these," greater than both of them, for it is their sacred, eternal aim. In יָפִית it is indicated that the ideal, and in נָעַמְתְּ that the eudaemonistic feature of the human soul attains its satisfaction in love. The LXX., obliterating this so true and beautiful a promotion of love above all other joys, translate ἐν ταῖς τρυφαῖς σου (in the enjoyment which thou impartest). The Syr., Jerome, and others also rob the Song of this its point of light and of elevation, by reading אֲהֻבָה (O beloved!) instead of אַהֲבָה. The words then declare (yet contrary to the spirit of the Hebrew language, which knows neither אֲהוּבָה nor אֲהוּבָתִי as vocat.) what we already read at iv. 10; while, according to the traditional form of the text, they are the prelude of the love-song, to love as such, which is continued in viii. 6 f.

When Solomon now looks on the wife of his youth, she stands before him like a palm tree with its splendid leaf-branches, which the Arabians call *ucht insân* (the sisters of men); and like a vine

[1] Samachshari, *Mufaṣṣal*, p. 8.

which climbs up on the wall of the house, and therefore is an emblem of the housewife, Ps. cxxviii. 3.

> Ver. 8 Thy stature is like the palm tree;
> And thy breasts clusters.
> 9 I thought: I will climb the palm,
> Grasp its branches;
> And thy breasts shall be to me
> As clusters of the vine,
> And the breath of thy nose like apples,
> 10a α And thy palate like the best wine.

Shulamith stands before him. As he surveys her from head to foot, he finds her stature like the stature of a slender, tall date-palm, and her breasts like the clusters of sweet fruit, into which, in due season, its blossoms are ripened. That קוֹמָתֵךְ (thy stature) is not thought of as height apart from the person, but as along with the person (cf. Ezek. xiii. 18), scarcely needs to be remarked. The palm derives its name, *tāmār*, from its slender stem rising upwards (*vid.* under Isa. xvii. 9, lxi. 6). This name is specially given to the *Phoenix dactylifera*, which is indigenous from Egypt to India, and which is principally cultivated (*vid.* under Gen. xiv. 7), the female flowers of which, set in panicles, develope into large clusters of juicy sweet fruit. These dark-brown or golden-yellow clusters, which crown the summit of the stem and impart a wonderful beauty to the appearance of the palm, especially when seen in the evening twilight, are here called אַשְׁכֹּלוֹת (connecting form at Deut. xxxii. 32), as by the Arabians '*ithkal*, plur. '*ithakyl* (*botri dactylorum*). The perf. דָּמְתָה signifies *aequata est = aequa est;* for דָּמָה, R. דם, means, to make or to become plain, smooth, even. The perf. אָמַרְתִּי, on the other hand, will be meant retrospectively. As an expression of that which he just now purposed to do, it would be useless; and thus to notify with emphasis anything beforehand is unnatural and contrary to good taste and custom. But looking back, he can say that in view of this august attractive beauty the one thought filled him, to secure possession of her and of the enjoyment which she promised; as one climbs (עָלָה with בְּ, as Ps. xxiv. 3) a palm tree and seizes (אָחַז, fut. יֹאחֵז, and אֹחֲזָה with בְּ, as at Job xxiii. 11) its branches (סַנְסִנִּים, so called, as it appears,[1] after the feather-like pointed leaves proceeding from the mid-rib on both sides), in order to break off the fulness of the sweet fruit under its leaves. As the cypress (*sarwat*), so also the palm is with the Moslem poets the figure of a loved one, and with the mystics, of God;[2]

---

[1] Also that סנסן is perhaps equivalent to סלסל (תלתל, זלזל), to wave hither and thither, comes here to view.

[2] *Vid.* Hâfiz, ed. Brockhaus, II. p. 46.

and accordingly the idea of possession is here particularly intended. וִיהִי־נָא denotes what he then thought and aimed at. Instead of בְּחָמָר, 9a, the punctuation בַּחָמָר is undoubtedly to be preferred. The figure of the palm tree terminates with the words, "will grasp its branches." It was adequate in relation to stature, but less so in relation to the breasts; for dates are of a long oval form, and have a stony kernel. Therefore the figure departs from the date clusters to that of grape clusters, which are more appropriate, as they swell and become round and elastic the more they ripen. The breath of the nose, which is called אַף, from breathing hard, is that of the air breathed, going in and out through it; for, as a rule, a man breathes through his nostrils with closed mouth. Apples present themselves the more naturally for comparison, that the apple has the name תַּפּוּחַ (from נָפַח, after the form תִּמְכוּף), from the fragrance which it exhales.

יֵין הַטּוֹב is wine of the good kind, i.e. the best, as אֵשֶׁת רָע, Prov. vi. 24, a woman of a bad kind, i.e. a bad woman; the neut. thought of as adject. is both times the gen. of the attribute, as at Prov. xxiv. 25 it is the gen. of the *substratum.* The punctuation כְּיֵין הַטּוֹב (Hitz.) is also possible; it gives, however, the common instead of the delicate poetical expression. By the comparison one may think of the expressions, *jungere salivas oris* (Lucret.) and *oscula per longas jungere pressa moras* (Ovid). But if we have rightly understood iv. 11, v. 16, the palate is mentioned much rather with reference to the words of love which she whispers in his ears when embracing her. Only thus is the further continuance of the comparison to be explained, and that it is Shulamith herself who continues it.

The dramatic structure of the Song becomes here more strongly manifest than elsewhere before. Shulamith interrupts the king, and continues his words as if echoing them, but again breaks off.

Ver. 10a β b Which goes down for my beloved smoothly,
Which makes the lips of sleepers move.

The LXX. had here לרודי in the text. It might notwithstanding be a spurious reading. Hitzig suggests that it is erroneously repeated, as if from ver. 11. Ewald also (*Hohesl.* p. 137) did that before,— Heiligstedt, as usual, following him. But, as Ewald afterwards objected, the line would then be "too short, and not corresponding to that which follows." But how shall לרודי now connect itself with Solomon's words? Ginsburg explains: "Her voice is not merely compared to wine, because it is sweet to everybody, but to such wine as would be sweet to a friend, and on that account is more valuable and pleasant." But that furnishes a thought digressing εἰς ἄλλο γένος; and besides, Ewald rightly remarks that Shulamith always uses the word דודי of her beloved, and that the king never uses it in a similar sense. He contends, however, against the idea that Shulamith here interrupts Solomon; for he replies to me (*Jahrb.* IV. 75): "Such interruptions we certainly very frequently find in our ill-formed and dislocated plays; in the Song, however, not a solitary example of this is found, and one ought to hesitate in imagining such a thing." He prefers the reading לְדוֹדִים [beloved ones], although possibly לדודי, with *î*, abbreviated after the popular style of speech from *îm*, may be the same word. But is this *l^edodim* not a useless addition? Is excellent wine good to the taste of friends merely; and does it linger longer in the palate of those not beloved than of those loving? And is the circumstance that Shulamith interrupts the king, and carries forward his words, not that which frequently also occurs in the Greek drama, as *e.g.* Eurip. *Phoenissae*, v. 608? The text as it stands before us requires an interchange of the speakers, and nothing prevents the supposition of such an interchange. In this idea Hengstenberg for once agrees with us. The *Lamed* in *l^edodi* is meant in the same sense as when the bride drinks to the bridegroom, using the expression *l^edodi*. The *Lamed* in לְמֵישָׁרִים is that of the defining norm, as the *Beth* in בְמִי, Prov. xxiii. 31, is that of the accompanying circumstance: that which tastes badly sticks in the palate, but that which tastes pleasantly glides down directly and smoothly. But what does the phrase דּוֹבֵב שִׂפְ' וגו' mean? The LXX. translate by ἱκανούμενος χείλεσί μου καὶ ὀδοῦσιν, "accommodating itself (Sym. προστιθέμενος) to my lips and teeth." Similarly Jerome (omitting at least the false μου), *labiisque et dentibus illius ad ruminandum*, in which דִּבָּה, *rumor*, for דּוֹבֵב, seems to have led him to *ruminare*. Equally contrary to the text with Luther's translation: "which to my friend goes smoothly down, and speaks of the previous year;" a rendering which supposes יְשָׁנִים (as also the Venet.) instead of יְשֵׁנִים (good wine which, as it were, tells of former years), and, besides, disregards שפתי. The translation: "which comes at unawares upon the lips of the sleepers," accords with the language (Heiligst., Hitz.). But that gives no meaning, as if one understood by יְשֵׁנִים, as Gesen. and Ewald do, *una in eodem toro cubantes;* but in this case the word ought to have been שֹׁכְבִים. Since, besides, such a thing is known as sleeping through drink or speaking in sleep, but not of drinking in sleep, our earlier translation approves itself: which causes the lips of sleepers to speak. This interpretation is also supported by a proverb in the Talm. *Jebamoth* 97a, *Jer. Moëd Katan*, iii. 7, etc., which, with reference to the passage under review, says that if any one in this world adduces the saying of a righteous man in his name (שפתותיו דובבות בקבר, מרחשות or רוחשות). But it is an error inherited from Buxtorf, that דובבות means there *loquuntur*, and, accordingly, that דובב of this passage before us means *loqui faciens*. It rather means (vid. Aruch), *bullire, stillare, manare* (cogn. טף, זב, Syn. רחש), since, as that proverb signifies, the deceased experiences an after-taste of his saying, and this experience expresses itself in the smack of the lips; and דּוֹבֵב, whether it be part. *Kal* or *Po.* = מְדוֹבֵב, thus: brought into the condition of the overflowing, the after-experience of drink that has been partaken of, and which returns again, as it were, *ruminando*. The meaning "to speak" is, in spite of Parchon and Kimchi (whom the Venet., with its φθεγγόμενος, follows), foreign to the verb; for דִּבָּה also means, not discourse, but sneaking, and particularly sneaking calumny, and, generally, *fama repens*. The calumniator is called in Arab. *dabûb*, as in Heb. רָכִיל. We now leave it undecided whether in דובב, of this passage before us, that special idea connected with it in the Gemara is contained; but the roots דב and זב are certainly cogn., they have the fundamental idea of a soft, noiseless movement generally, and modify this according as they are referred to that which is solid or fluid. Consequently דָּבַב, as it means in *lente incedere* (whence the bear has the name דֹּב), is also capable of being interpreted *leniter se movere*, and trans. *leniter movere*, according to which the Syr. here translates, *quod commovet labia mea et dentes meos* (this absurd bringing in of the teeth is from the LXX. and Aq.), and the Targ. allegorizes, and whatever also in general is the meaning of the Gemara as far as it exchanges דובבות for רוחשות (vid. Levy under רָחַשׁ). Besides, the translations *qui commovet* and *qui loqui facit* fall together according to the sense. For when it is said of generous wine, that it makes the lips of sleepers move, a movement is meant expressing itself in the sleeper speaking. But generous wine is a figure of the love-responses of the beloved, sipped in, as it were, with pleasing satisfaction, which hover still around the sleepers in delightful dreams, and fill them with hallucinations.

It is impossible that לדודי in ver. 10 has any other reference than it has in ver. 11, where it is without doubt Shulamith who speaks.

Ver. 11 I am my beloved's,
And to me goeth forth his desire.

After the words "I am my beloved's," we miss the "and my beloved is mine" of vi. 3, cf. ii. 16, which perhaps had dropped out. The second line here refers back to Gen. iii. 16, for here, as there, תְּשׁוּקָה, from שׁוּק, to impel, move, is the impulse of love as a natural power.

When a wife is the object of such passion, it is possible that, on the one side, she feels herself very fortunate therein; and, on the other side, if the love, in its high commendations, becomes excessive, oppressed, and when she perceives that in her love-relation she is the observed of many eyes, troubled. It is these mingled feelings which move Shulamith when she continues the praise so richly lavished on her in words which denote what she might be to the king, but immediately breaks off in order that, as the following verse now shows, she might use this superabundance of his love for the purpose of setting forth her request, and thus of leading into another path; her simple, child-like disposition longs for the quietness and plainness of rural life, away from the bustle and display of city and court life.

Ver. 12 **Up, my lover; we will go into the country,**
Lodge in the villages.

Hitzig here begins a new scene, to which he gives the superscription: "Shulamith making haste to return home with her lover." The advocate of the shepherd-hypothesis thinks that the faithful Shulamith, after hearing Solomon's panegyric, shakes her head and says: "I am my beloved's." To him she calls, "Come, my beloved;" for, as Ewald seeks to make this conceivable: the golden confidence of her near triumph lifts her in spirit forthwith above all that is present and all that is actual; only to him may she speak; and as if she were half here and half already there, in the midst of her rural home along with him, she says, "Let us go out into the fields," etc. In fact, there is nothing more incredible than this Shulamitess, whose dialogue with Solomon consists of Solomon's addresses, and of answers which are directed, not to Solomon, but in a monologue to her shepherd; and nothing more cowardly and more shadowy than this lover, who goes about in the moonlight seeking his beloved shepherdess whom he has lost, glancing here and there through the lattices of the windows and again disappearing. How much more justifiable is the drama of the Song by the French Jesuit C. F. Menestrier (born in Sion 1631, died 1705), who, in his two little works on the opera and the ballet, speaks of Solomon as the creator of the opera, and regards the Song as a shepherd-play, in which his love-relation to the daughter of the king of Egypt is set forth under the allegorical figures of the love of a shepherd and a shepherdess![1] For Shulamith is thought of as a רֹעָה [shepherdess], i. 8, and she thinks of Solomon

---

[1] *Vid.* Eugène Despris in the *Revue politique et litteraire* 1873. The idea was not new. This also was the sentiment of **Fray Luis de Leon**; *vid.* his *Biographie* by Wilkens (1866), p. 209.

as a רֹעָה [shepherd]. She remains so in her inclination even after her elevation to the rank of a queen. The solitude and glory of external nature are dearer to her than the bustle and splendour of the city and the court. Hence her pressing out of the city to the country. הַשָּׂדֶה is local, without external designation, like *rus* (to the country). כְּפָרִים (here and at 1 Chron. xxvii. 25) is plur. of the unused form כָּפָר (const. כְּפַר, Josh. xviii. 24) or כְּפָר, Arab. *kafar* (cf. the Syr. dimin. *kafrûno*, a little town), instead of which it is once pointed כֹּפֶר, 1 Sam. vi. 18, of that name of a district of level country with which a multitude of later Palest. names of places, such as כְּפַר נָחוּם, are connected. Ewald, indeed, understands *k*pharim* as at iv. 13: we will lodge among the fragrant Al-henna bushes. But yet בַּכְּפָ' cannot be equivalent to תַּחַת הַכְּפָרִים; and since לִין (probably changed from לִיל) and הַשְּׁכֵּים, 13*a*, stand together, we must suppose that they wished to find a bed in the henna bushes; which, if it were conceivable, would be too gipsy-like, even for a pair of lovers of the rank of shepherds (*vid.* Job xxx. 7). No. Shulamith's words express a wish for a journey into the country: they will there be in freedom, and at night find shelter (בכפ', as 1 Chron. xxvii. 25 and Neh. vi. 2, where also the plur. is similarly used), now in this and now in that country place. Spoken to the supposed shepherd, that would be comical, for a shepherd does not wander from village to village; and that, returning to their home, they wished to turn aside into villages and spend the night there, cannot at all be the meaning. But spoken of a shepherdess, or rather a vine-dresser, who has been raised to the rank of queen, it accords with her relation to Solomon,—they are married,—as well as with the inexpressible impulse of her heart after her earlier homely country-life. The former vine-dresser, the child of the Galilean hills, the lily of the valley, speaks in the verses following.

> Ver. 13 In the morning we will start for the vineyards,
> See whether the vine is in bloom,
> Whether the vine-blossoms have opened,
> The pomegranates budded—
> There will I give thee my love.
> 14 The mandrakes breathe a pleasant odour,
> And over our doors are all kinds of excellent fruits,
> New, also old,
> Which, my beloved, I have kept for thee.

As the rising up early follows the tarrying over night, the description of that which is longed for moves forward. As הִשְׁכִּים is denom. of שְׁכֶם, and properly signifies only to shoulder, *i.e.* to rise, make oneself ready, when early going forth needs to be designated it has generally בַּבֹּקֶר (cf. Josh. vi. 15) along with it; yet this word may also be wanting, 1 Sam. ix. 26, xvii. 16. נֹשְׁכּ׳ וְנֵלֵךְ לכר׳ = נַשְׁכּ׳ לַבְּר׳, an abbreviation of the expression which is also found in hist. prose, Gen. xix. 27; cf. 2 Kings xix. 9. They wished in the morning, when the life of nature can best be observed, and its growth and progress and striving upwards best contemplated, to see whether the vine had opened, *i.e.* unfolded (thus, vi. 11), whether the vine-blossom (*vid.* at ii. 13) had expanded (LXX. ἤνθησεν ὁ κυπρισμός), whether the pomegranate had its flowers or flower-buds (הֵנֵצוּ; as at vi. 11); פִּתַּח is here, as at Isa. xlviii. 8, lx. 11, used as internally transitive: to accomplish or to undergo the opening, as also (Arab.) *fattaḥ*[1] is used of the blooming of flowers, for (Arab.) *taftṭaḥ* (to unfold). The vineyards, inasmuch as she does not say כְּרָמֵינוּ, are not alone those of her family, but generally those of her home, but of *her* home; for these are the object of her desire, which in this pleasant journey with her beloved she at once in imagination reaches, flying, as it were, over the intermediate space. There, in undisturbed quietness, and in a lovely region consecrating love, will she give herself to him in the entire fulness of her love. By דֹּדַי she means the evidences of her love (*vid.* under iv. 10, i. 2), which she will there grant to him as thankful responses to his own. Thus she speaks in the spring-time, in the month Ijjar, corresponding to our *Wonnemond* (pleasure-month, May), and seeks to give emphasis to her promise by this, that she directs him to the fragrant "mandragoras," and to the precious fruits of all kinds which she has kept for him on the shelf in her native home.

דּוּדַי (after the form לֵילַי), love's flower, is the *mandragora officinalis*, L., with whitish green flowers and yellow apples of the size of nutmegs, belonging to the Solanaceae; its fruits and roots are used as an aphrodisiac, therefore this plant was called by the Arabs *abd al-sal'm*, the servant of love, *postillon d'amour*; the son of Leah found such mandrakes (LXX. Gen. xxx. 14, μῆλα μανδραγορῶν) at the time of the vintage, which falls in the month of Ijjar; they have a strong but pleasant odour. In Jerusalem mandrakes are rare; but so much the more abundantly are they found growing wild in Galilee, whither Shulamith is transported in spirit. Regarding the מְגָדִים (from מֶגֶד, occurring in the sing. exclusively in the blessing of Moses, Deut. xxxiii.), which in the Old Testament is peculiar to the Song, *vid.* iv. 13, 16. From "over our doors," down to "I have kept for thee," is, according to the LXX., Syr., Jerome, and others, one sentence, which in itself is not inadmissible; for the object can precede

[1] *Vid.* Fleischer, *Makkari*, 1868, p. 271.

its verb, iii. 3*b*, and can stand as the subject between the place mentioned and the verb, Isa. xxxii. 13*a*, also as the object, 2 Chron. xxxi. 6, which, as in the passage before us, may be interpunctuated with *Athnach* for the sake of emphasis; in the bibl. Chald. this inverted sequence of the words is natural, *e.g.* Dan. ii. 17*b*. But such a long-winded sentence is at least not in the style of the Song, and one does not rightly see why just "over our doors" has the first place in it. I therefore formerly translated it as did Luther, dividing it into parts: "and over our doors are all kinds of precious fruits; I have," etc. But with this departure from the traditional division of the verse nothing is gained; for the "keeping" (laying up) refers naturally to the fruits of the preceding year, and in the first instance can by no means refer to fruits of this year, especially as Shulamith, according to the structure of the poem, has not visited her parental home since her home-bringing in marriage, and now for the first time, in the early summer, between the barley harvest and the wheat harvest, is carried away thither in her longing. Therefore the expression, "my beloved, I have kept for thee," is to be taken by itself, but not as an independent sentence (Böttch.), but is to be rendered, with Ewald, as a relative clause; and this, with Hitz., is to be referred to יְשָׁנִים (old). *Col* refers to the many sorts of precious fruits which, after the time of their ingathering, are divided into "new and old" (Matt. xiii. 52). The plur. "our doors" which as amplif. poet. would not be appropriate here, supposes several entrances into her parents' home; and since "I have kept" refers to a particular preserving of choice fruits, *al* does not (Hitzig) refer to a floor, such as the floor above the family dwelling or above the barn, but to the shelf above the inner doors, a board placed over them, on which certain things are wont to be laid past for some particular object. She speaks to the king like a child; for although highly elevated, she yet remains, without self-elation, a child.

If Solomon now complies with her request, yields to her invitation, then she will again see her parental home, where, in the days of her first love, she laid up for him that which was most precious, that she might thereby give him joy. Since she thus places herself with her whole soul back again in her home and amid its associations, the wish expressed in these words that follow rises up within her in the childlike purity of her love:

>   Chap. viii. 1 O that thou wert like a brother to me,
>   Who sucked my mother's breasts!
>   If I found thee without, I would kiss thee;
>   They also could not despise me.

2 I would lead thee, bring thee into my mother's house;
Thou wouldest instruct me—
I would give thee to drink spiced wine,
The must of my pomegranates.

Solomon is not her brother, who, with her, hung upon the same mother's breast; but she wishes, carried away in her dream into the reality of that she wished for, that she had him as her brother, or rather, since she says, not אָח, but כְּאָח (with כְּ, which here has not, as at Ps. xxxv. 14, the meaning of *tanquam*, but of *instar*, as at Job xxiv. 14), that she had in him what a brother is to a sister. In that case, if she found him without, she would kiss him (hypoth. fut. in the protasis, and fut. without *Vav* in the apodosis, as at Job xx. 24; Hos. viii. 12; Ps. cxxxix. 18)—she could do this without putting any restraint on herself for the sake of propriety (cf. the kiss of the wanton harlot, Prov. vii. 13), and also (גַּם) without needing to fear that they who saw it would treat it scornfully (בּוּז לְ, as in the reminiscence, Prov. vi. 30). The close union which lies in the sisterly relationship thus appeared to her to be higher than the near connection established by the marriage relationship, and her childlike feeling deceived her not: the sisterly relationship is certainly purer, firmer, more enduring than that of marriage, so far as this does not deepen itself into an equality with the sisterly, and attain to friendship, yea, brotherhood (Prov. xvii. 17), within. That Shulamith thus feels herself happy in the thought that Solomon was to her as a brother, shows, in a characteristic manner, that "the lust of the flesh, the lust of the eye, and the pride of life," were foreign to her. If he were her brother, she would take him by the hand,[1] and bring him into her mother's house, and he would then, under the eye of their common mother, become her teacher, and she would become his scholar. The LXX. adds, after the words "into my mother's house," the phrase, καὶ εἰς ταμεῖον τῆς συλλαβούσης με, cf. iii. 4. In the same manner also the Syr., which has not read the words διδάξεις με following, which are found in some Codd. of the LXX. Regarding the word $t^e lamm^e d\bar{e}ne$ (thou wouldest instruct me) as incongruous, Hitzig asks: What should he then teach her? He refers it to her mother: "who would teach me," namely, from her own earlier experience, how I might do everything rightly for him. "Were the meaning," he adds, "*he* should do it, then also it is she who ought to be represented as led home by him

---

[1] Ben-Asher punctuates אֶנְהָֽגֲךָ. Thus also P. rightly. Ben-Naphtali, on the contrary, punctuates אֶנְהָֽגֲךָ. Cf. *Genesis* (1869), p. 85, note 3.

CHAP. VIII. 1, 2.

into his house, the bride by the bridegroom." But, correctly, Jerome, the Venet., and Luther: "Thou wouldest (shouldest) instruct me;" also the Targ.: "I would conduct thee, O King Messiah, and bring Thee into the house of my sanctuary; and Thou wouldest teach me (וּתְאַלֵּף יָתִי) to fear God and to walk in His ways." Not her mother, but Solomon, is in possession of the wisdom which she covets; and if he were her brother, as she wishes, then she would constrain him to devote himself to her as her teacher. The view, favoured by Leo Hebraeus (*Dialog. de amore*, c. III.), John Pordage (*Metaphysik*, III. 617 ff.), and Rosenmüller, and which commends itself, after the analogy of the Gîtagovinda, Boethius, and Dante, and appears also to show itself in the Syr. title of the book, "Wisdom of the Wise," that Shulamith is wisdom personified (cf. also viii. 2 with Prov. ix. 2, and viii. 3, ii. 6 with Prov. iv. 8), shatters itself against this תלמדני; the fact is rather the reverse: Solomon is wisdom in person, and Shulamith is the wisdom-loving soul,[1]—for Shulamith wishes to participate in Solomon's wisdom. What a deep view the "Thou wouldest teach me" affords into Shulamith's heart! She knew how much she yet came short of being to him all that a wife should be. But in Jerusalem the bustle of court life and the burden of his regal duties did not permit him to devote himself to her; but in her mother's house, if he were once there, he would instruct her, and she would requite him with her spiced wine and with the juice of the pomegranates. יַיִן הָרֶקַח, *vinum conditura*, is appos. = genitiv. יֵין הרקח, *vinum conditurae* (ἀρωματίτης in Dioscorides and Pliny), like יֵין תַּרְ, Ps. vi. 5, מַיִם לַחַץ, 1 Kings xxii. 27, etc., *vid.* Philippi's *Stat. Const.* p. 86. אַשְׁקְךָ carries forward אֶשָּׁקְךָ in a beautiful play upon words. עָסִיס designates the juice as pressed out: the Chald. עֲסֵי corresponds to the Heb. דָּרַךְ, used of treading the grapes. It is unnecessary to render רִמֹּנִי as apoc. plur., like מֵי, Ps. xlv. 9 (Ewald, § 177a); *rimmoni* is the name she gives to the pomegranate trees belonging to her,—for it is true that this word, *rimmon*, can be used in a collective sense (Deut. viii. 8); but the connection with the possessive suff. excludes this; or by *'asis rimmoni* she means the pomegranate must (cf. ῥοίτης = *vinum e punicis*, in Dioscorides and Pliny) belonging to her. Pomegranates are not to be thought of as an erotic symbol;[2] they are named as something beautiful and precious. "O Ali," says a proverb of

---

[1] Cf. my *Das Hohelied unter. u. ausg.* (1851), pp. 65-73.

[2] *Vid.* Porphyrius, *de Abstin.* iv. 16, and Inman in his smutty book, *Ancient Faiths*, vol. I. 1868, according to which the pomegranate is an emblem of "a full womb."

Sunna, "eat eagerly only pomegranates (Pers. *anâr*), for their grains are from Paradise."[1]

Resigning herself now dreamily to the idea that Solomon is her brother, whom she may freely and openly kiss, and her teacher besides, with whom she may sit in confidential intercourse under her mother's eye, she feels herself as if closely embraced by him, and calls from a distance to the daughters of Jerusalem not to disturb this her happy enjoyment:

> Ver. 3 His left hand is under my head,
> And his right doth embrace me:
> 4 I adjure you, ye daughters of Jerusalem,
> That ye awake not and disturb not love
> Till she please!

Instead of תַּחַת לְ, "underneath," there is here, as usual, תַּחַת (cf. 5b). Instead of אִם ... וְאִם in the adjuration, there is here the equivalent מַה ... וּמַה; the interrogative מָה, which in the Arab. *mâ* becomes negat., appears here, as at Job xxxi. 1, on the way toward this change of meaning. The *per capreas vel per cervas agri* is wanting, perhaps because the natural side of love is here broken, and the ἔρως strives up into ἀγάπη. The daughters of Jerusalem must not break in upon this holy love-festival, but leave it to its own course.

SIXTH ACT.

THE RATIFICATION OF THE COVENANT OF LOVE IN SHULAMITH'S NATIVE HOME.—Chap. VIII. 5-14.

FIRST SCENE OF THE SIXTH ACT, VIII. 5-7.

Shulamith's longing wish attains its satisfaction. Arm in arm with Solomon, she comes forth and walks with him on her native ground. Sunem (Sulem), at the west end of Little Hermon (*'Gebel ed-Duhî*), lay something more than $1\frac{1}{2}$ hour[2] to the north of Jezreel (*Zera'în*), which also lay at the foot of a mountain, viz. on a N.-W. spur of Gilboa. Between the two lay the valley of Jezreel in the "great plain," which was called, 2 Chron. xxxv. 22, Zech. xii. 11, "the valley of *Megiddo*" [Esdraelon], now *Merj ibn 'Amir*—an extensive level plain, which, seen from the south Galilean hills in the spring-

---

[1] *Vid.* Fleischer's *Catal. Codd. Lips.* p. 428.
[2] *Vid.* "Jisreel" in Schenkel's *Bib. Lex.*

time, appears "like a green sea encompassed by gently sloping banks." From this we will have to suppose that the loving pair from the town of Jezreel, the highest point of which afforded a wide, pleasant prospect, wandered on foot through the "valley of Jezreel," a beautiful, well-watered, fruitful valley, which is here called מדבר, as being uncultivated pasture land. They bend their way toward the little village lying in the valley, from which the dark sloping sides of Little Hermon rise up suddenly. Here in this valley are the countrymen (*populares*) of these wanderers, as yet unrecognised from a distance, into whose mouth the poet puts these words:

> Ver. 5a Who is this coming up out of the wilderness,
> Leaning on her beloved?

The third Act, iii. 6, began with a similar question to that with which the sixth here commences. The former closed the description of the growth of the love-relation, the latter closes that of the consummated love-relation. Instead of "out of the wilderness," the LXX. has "clothed in white" (λελευκανθισμένη); the translator has gathered מִתְחַוֶּרֶת from the illegible consonants of his MS. before him. On the contrary, he translates מתרפקת correctly by ἐπιστηριζομένη (Symm. ἐπερειδομένη, Venet. κεκμηκυῖα ἐπί, wearily supporting herself on . . .), while Jerome renders it unsuitably by *deliciis affluens*, interchanging the word with מִתְפַּנֶּקֶת. But הִתְרַפֵּק, common to the Heb. with the Arab. and Aethiop., signifies to support oneself, from רָפַק, *sublevare* (French, *soulager*), Arab. *rafaka*, *rafuka*, to be helpful, serviceable, compliant, viii. *irtafaka*, to support oneself on the elbow, or (with the elbow) on a pillow (cf. *rafîk*, fellow-traveller, *rufka*, a company of fellow-travellers, from the primary idea of mutually supporting or being helpful to each other); Aethiop. *rafaka*, to encamp for the purpose of taking food, ἀνακλίνεσθαι (cf. John xiii. 23). That Shulamith leant on her beloved, arose not merely from her weariness, with the view of supplementing her own weakness from his fulness of strength, but also from the ardour of the love which gives to the happy and proud Solomon, raised above all fears, the feeling of his having her in absolute possession. The road brings the loving couple near to the apple tree over against Shulamith's parental home, which had been the witness of the beginning of their love.

> Ver. 5b Under the apple tree I waked thy love:
> There thy mother travailed with thee;
> There travailed she that bare thee.

The words, "under the apple tree I waked thee," עוֹרַרְתִּיךָ, might be regarded as those of Shulamith to Solomon: here, under this apple tree, where Solomon met with her, she won his first love; for the words cannot mean that she wakened him from sleep under the apple tree, since עוֹרֵר has nowhere the meaning of הֵקִיץ and הֵעִיר here given to it by Hitzig, but only that of "to stir, to stir up, to arouse;" and only when sleep or a sleepy condition is the subject, does it mean "to shake out of sleep, to rouse up" (vid. under ii. 7). But it is impossible that "there" can be used by Shulamith even in the sense of the shepherd hypothesis; for the pair of lovers do not wander to the parental home of the lover, but of his beloved. We must then here altogether change the punctuation of the text, and throughout restore the fem. suffix forms as those originally used: עוֹרַרְתִּיךְ, חִבְּלָתֶךְ אִמֵּךְ,[1] and יְלָדַתֶךְ (cf. שׂוֹ, Isa. xlvii. 10), in which we follow the example of the Syr. The allegorizing interpreters also meet only with trouble in regarding the words as those of Shulamith to Solomon. If התפוח were an emblem of the Mount of Olives, which, being wonderfully divided, gives back Israel's dead (Targ.), or an emblem of Sinai (Rashi), in both cases the words are more appropriately regarded as spoken to Shulamith than by her. Aben-Ezra correctly reads them as the words of Shulamith to Solomon, for he thinks on prayers, which are like golden apples in silver bowls; Hahn, for he understands by the apple tree, Canaan, where with sorrow his people brought him forth as their king; Hengstenberg, rising up to a remote-lying comparison, says, "the mother of the heavenly Solomon is at the same time the mother of Shulamith." Hoelemann thinks on Sur. xix. 32 f., according to which 'Isa, Miriam's son, was born under a palm tree; but he is not able to answer the question, What now is the meaning here of the apple tree as Solomon's birthplace? If it were indeed to be interpreted allegorically, then by the apple tree we would rather understand the "tree of knowledge" of Paradise, of which Aquila, followed by Jerome, with his ἐκεῖ διεφθάρη, appears to think,—a view which recently Godet approves of;[2] there Shulamith, i.e. poor humanity,

---

[1] חִבְּלָתֶךְ, penult. accented, and *Lamed* with *Pathach* in P. This is certainly right. *Michlol* 33a adduces merely יְלָדַתֶךְ of the verse as having Kametz, on account of the pause, and had thus in view 'חִבְּ, with the *Pathach* under *Lamed*. But P. has also 'לְ, with *Pathach* under *Daleth*, and so also has H, with the remark ב׳ פתחין (viz. here and Jer. xxii. 26). The *Biblia Rabbinica* 1526 and 1615 have also the same pointing, *Pathach* under *Daleth*. In the printed list of words having *Pathach* in pause, this word is certainly not found. But it is found in the MS. list of the *Ochla veochla*, at Halle.

[2] Others, *e.g.* Bruno von Asti († 1123) and the Waldensian Exposition, edited

awakened the compassionate love of the heavenly Solomon, who then gave her, as a pledge of this love, the *Protevangelium*, and in the neighbourhood of this apple tree, *i.e.* on the ground and soil of humanity fallen, but yet destined to be saved, Shulamith's mother, *i.e.* the pre-Christian O. T. church, brought forth the Saviour from itself, who in love raised Shulamith from the depths to regal honour. But the Song of Songs does not anywhere set before us the task of extracting from it by an allegorizing process such far-fetched thoughts. If the masc. suff. is changed into the fem., we have a conversation perfectly corresponding to the situation. Solomon reminds Shulamith by that memorable apple tree of the time when he kindled within her the fire of first love; עוֹרֵר elsewhere signifies energy (Ps. lxxx. 3), or passion (Prov. x. 12), put into a state of violent commotion; connected with the accus. of the person, it signifies, Zech. ix. 13, excited in a warlike manner; here, placed in a state of pleasant excitement of love that has not yet attained its object. Of how many references to contrasted affections the reflex. התע׳ is capable, is seen from Job xvii. 8, xxxi. 29; why not thus also עוֹרֵר ?

With שָׁמָּה Solomon's words are continued, but not in such a way as that what follows also took place under the apple tree. For Shulamith is not the child of Beduins, who in that case might even have been born under an apple tree. Among the Beduins, a maiden accidentally born at the watering-place (*menhîl*), on the way (*rahîl*), in the dew (*tall*) or snow (*thelg*), is called from that circumstance *Munêhil, Ruhêla, Talla*, or *Thelga*.[1] The birthplace of her love is not also the birthplace of her life. As הַתַּפּוּחַ points to the apple tree to which their way led them, so שמה points to the end of their way, the parental home lying near by (Hitzig). The LXX. translates well : ἐκεῖ ὠδίνησέ σε ἡ μήτηρ σου, for while the Arab. *ḥabida* means *concipere*, and its *Pi., ḥabbada*, is the usual word for *gravidam facere*, חִבֵּל in the passage before us certainly appears to be[2] a denom.

by Herzog in the *Zeit. für hist. Theol.* 1861 : *malum = crux dominica*. Th. Harms (1870) quotes ii. 3, and remarks : The church brings forth her children under the apple tree, Christ. Into such absurdities, in violation of the meaning of the words, do the allegorizing interpreters wander.

[1] *Vid.* Wetstein's *Inschriften* (1864), p. 336.

[2] The Arab. *ḥabilat*, she has conceived, and is in consequence pregnant, accords in the latter sense with *ḥamilat*, she bears, *i.e.* is pregnant, without, however, being, as Hitzig thinks, of a cognate root with it. For *ḥamal* signifies to carry ; *ḥabal*, on the contrary, to comprehend and to receive (whence also the cord, figuratively, the tie of love, *liaison*, as enclosing, embracing, is called *ḥabl* , חֶבֶל), and like the Lat. *concipere* and *suscipere*, is used not only in a sexual, but also in an ethical sense, to

Pi. in the sense of " to bring forth with sorrow " (חֶבְלֵי הַיּוֹלֵדָה). The LXX. further translates: ἐκεῖ ὠδίνησέ σε ἡ τεκοῦσά σε, in which the σε is inserted, and is thus, as also by the Syr., Jerome, and Venet., translated, with the obliteration of the finite יְלָדַתְךָ, as if the reading were יֹלַדְתְּךָ. But not merely is the name of the mother intentionally changed, it is also carried forward from the labour, *eniti,* to the completed act of birth.

After Solomon has thus called to remembrance the commencement of their love-relation, which receives again a special consecration by the reference to Shulamith's parental home, and to her mother, Shulamith answers with a request to preserve for her this love.

> Ver. 6 Place me as a signet-ring on thy heart,
> As a signet-ring on thine arm!
> For strong as death is love;
> Inexorable as hell is jealousy:
> Its flames are flames of fire,
> A flame of Jah.
> 7 Mighty waters are unable
> To quench such love,
> And rivers cannot overflow it.
> If a man would give
> All the wealth of his house for love,—
> He would only be contemned.

The signet-ring, which is called חוֹתָם (חָתַם, to impress), was carried either by a string on the breast, Gen. xxxviii. 18, or also, as that which is called טַבַּעַת denotes (from טָבַע, to sink into), on the hand, Jer. xxii. 24, cf. Gen. xli. 42, Esth. iii. 12, but not on the arm, like a bracelet, 2 Sam. i. 10; and since it is certainly permissible to say "hand" for "finger," but not "arm" for "hand," so we may not refer "on thine arm" to the figure of the signet-ring, as if Shulamith had said, as the poet might also introduce her as saying: Make me like a signet-ring (כְּחוֹתָם) on thy breast; make me like a signet-ring "on thy hand," or "on thy right hand." The words, "set me on thy heart," and "(set me) on thine arm," must thus also, without regard to "as a signet-ring," express independent thoughts, although שִׂימֵנִי is chosen (*vid.* Hag. ii. 23) instead of קָחֵנִי, in view of the comparison.[1] Thus, with right, Hitzig finds the

---

conceive anger, to take up and cherish sorrow. The Assyr. *habal*, corresponding to the Heb. בן, is explained from this Arab. *habl, concipere.* On the supposition that the Heb. had a word, חבל, of the same meaning as the Arab. *habl,* then חֶבֶל might mean *concipiendo generare;* but the Heb. sentence lying before us leads to the interpretation *eniti.*

[1] Of the copy of the *Tôra,* which was to be the king's *vade-mecum,* it is said,

thought therein expressed: "Press me close to thy breast, enclose me in thine arms." But it is the first request, and not the second, which is in the form עַל־זְרוֹעֶךָ, and not עַל־זְרוֹעֹתֶיךָ (שִׂימֵנִי), which refers to embracing, since the subject is not the relation of person and thing, but of person and person. The signet-ring comes into view as a jewel, which one does not separate from himself; and the first request is to this effect, that he would bear her thus inalienably (the art. is that of the specific idea) on his heart (Ex. xxviii. 29); the meaning of the second, that he would take her thus inseparably as a signet-ring on his arm (cf. Hos. xi. 3: "I have taught Ephraim also to go, taking them by their arms"), so that she might lie always on his heart, and have him always at her side (cf. Ps. cx. 5): she wishes to be united and bound to him indissolubly in the affection of love and in the community of life's experience.

The reason for the double request following כִּי, abstracted from the individual case, rises to the universality of the fact realized by experience, which specializes itself herein, and celebrates the praise of love; for, assigning a reason for her "set me," she does not say, "my love," nor "thy love," but אַהֲבָה, "love" (as also in the address at vii. 7). She means love undivided, unfeigned, entire, and not transient, but enduring; thus true and genuine love, such as is real, what the word denotes, which exhausts the conception corresponding to the idea of love.

קִנְאָה, which is here parallel to "love," is the jealousy of love asserting its possession and right of property; the reaction of love against any diminution of its possession, against any reserve in its response, the "self-vindication of angry love."[1] Love is a passion, i.e. a human affection, powerful and lasting, as it comes to light in "jealousy." *Zelus*, as defined by Dav. Chyträus, *est affectus mixtus ex amore et ira, cum videlicet amans aliquid irascitur illi, a quo laeditur res amata*, wherefore here the adjectives עַזָּה (strong) and קָשָׁה (hard, inexorable, firm, severe) are respectively assigned to "love" and "jealousy," as at Gen. xlix. 7 to "anger" and "wrath." It is much more remarkable that the energy of love, which, so to say, is the life of life, is compared to the energy of death and Hades; with at least equal right מִפָּוֶת and מִשְּׁאוֹל might be used, for love scorns both, outlasts both, triumphs over both (Rom. viii. 38 f.; 1 Cor. xv. 54 f.). But the text does not speak of surpassing, but of equality; not of love and jealousy that they surpass death and Hades,

Sanhedrin 21b: עָשָׂה אוֹתָהּ כְּמִין קָמֵעַ וּתְלָאָהּ בִּזְרוֹעַ, but also there the amulet is thought of not as fastened to the finger, but as wound round the arm.

[1] Vid. my *Prolegomena* to Weber's *Vom Zorne Gottes* (1862), p. 35 ss.

but that they are equal to it. The point of comparison in both cases is to be obtained from the predicates. עַז, powerful, designates the person who, being assailed, cannot be overcome (Num. xiii. 28), and, assailing, cannot be withstood (Judg. xiv. 18). Death is obviously thought of as the assailer (Jer. ix. 20), against which nothing can hold its ground, from which nothing can escape, to whose sceptre all must finally yield (*vid.* Ps. xlix.). Love is like it in this, that it also seizes upon men with irresistible force (Böttcher: "He whom Death assails must die, whom Love assails must love"); and when she has once assailed him, she rests not till she has him wholly under her power; she kills him, as it were, in regard to everything else that is not the object of his love. קָשָׁה, hard (opposed to רַךְ, 2 Sam. iii. 39), σκληρός, designates one on whom no impression is made, who will not yield (Ps. xlviii. 4, xix. 4), or one whom stern fate has made inwardly stubborn and obtuse (1 Sam. i. 15). Here the point of comparison is inflexibility; for *Sheol*, thought of with שאל, to ask (*vid.* under Isa. v. 14), is the God-ordained messenger of wrath, who inexorably gathers in all that are on the earth, and holds them fast when once they are swallowed up by him. So the jealousy of love wholly takes possession of the beloved object not only in arrest, but also in safe keeping; she holds her possession firmly, that it cannot be taken from her (Wisd. ii. 1), and burns relentlessly and inexorably against any one who does injury to her possession (Prov. vi. 34 f.). But when Shulamith wishes, in the words, "set me," etc., to be bound to the heart and to the arm of Solomon, has she in the clause assigning a reason the love in view with which she loves, or that with which she is loved? Certainly not the one to the exclusion of the other; but as certainly, first of all, the love with which she wishes to fill, and believes that she does fill, her beloved. If this is so, then with "for strong as death is love," she gives herself up to this love on the condition that it confesses itself willing to live only for her, and to be as if dead for all others; and with "inexorable as hell is jealousy," in such a manner that she takes shelter in the jealousy of this love against the occurrence of any fit of infidelity, since she consents therein to be wholly and completely absorbed by it.

To קנאה, which proceeds from the primary idea of a red glow, there is connected the further description of this love to the sheltering and protecting power of which she gives herself up: "its flames, רְשָׁפֶיהָ, are flames of fire;" its sparkling is the sparkling of fire. The verb רשף signifies, in Syr. and Arab., to creep along, to make short steps; in Heb. and Chald., to sparkle, to flame, which in Samar. is referred to impetuosity. Symmachus translates, after the Samar. (which Hitzig approves of): αἱ ὁρμαὶ αὐτοῦ ὁρμαὶ πύρινοι; the Venet., after Kimchi, ἄνθρακες, for he exchanges רֶשֶׁף with the probably non.-cogn. רִצְפָּה; others render it all with words which denote the bright glancings of fire. רִשְׁפֵּי (so here, according to the Masora; on the contrary, at Ps. lxxvi. 4, רִשְׁפֵי) are effulgurations; the pred. says that these are not only of a bright shining, but of a fiery nature, which, as they proceed from fire, so also produce fire, for they set on fire and kindle.[1] Love, in its flashings up, is like fiery flashes of lightning; in short, it is שַׁלְהֶבֶתְיָה,[2] which is thus to be written as one word with ה raphatum, according to the Masora; but in this form of the word יה is also the name of God, and more than a meaningless superlative strengthening of the idea. As לֶהָבָה is formed from the Kal לָהַב, to flame (R. לב, to lick, like לָהַט, R. לט, to twist), so is שַׁלְהֶבֶת, from the Shafel שַׁלְהֵב, to cause to flame; this active stem is frequently found, especially in the Aram., and has in the Assyr. almost wholly supplanted the Afel (vid. Schrader in Deut. Morg. Zeit. xxvi. 275). שלהבת is thus related primarily to להבה, as inflammatio to (Ger.) Flamme; יה thus presents itself the more naturally to be interpreted as gen. subjecti. Love of a right kind is a flame not kindled and inflamed by man (Job xx. 26), but by God—the divinely-influenced free inclination of two souls to each other, and at the same time, as is now further said, 7a, 7b, a situation supporting all adversities and assaults, and a pure personal relation conditioned by nothing material. It is a fire-flame which mighty waters (רַבִּים, great and many, as at Hab. iii. 15; cf. עַזִּים, wild, Isa. xliii. 16) cannot extinguish, and streams cannot overflow it (cf. Ps. lxix. 3, cxxiv. 4) or sweep it away (cf. Job xiv. 19; Isa. xxviii. 17). Hitzig adopts the latter signification, but the figure of the fire makes the former more natural; no heaping up of adverse circumstances can extinguish true love, as many waters extinguish elemental

---

[1] The Phoen. Inscriptions, Citens. xxxvii., xxxviii., show a name for God, רשפי חץ, or merely רשף, which appears to correspond to Ζεὺς Κεραύνιος on the Inscriptions of Larnax (vid. Vogué's Mélanges Archéologiques, p. 19). רשפי are thus not the arrows themselves (Grätz), but these are, as it were, lightnings from His bow (Ps. lxxvi. 4).

[2] Thus in the Biblia Rabbinica and P. H. with the note מלהחדא ולא מפיק. Thus by Ben-Asher, who follows the Masora. Cf. Liber Psalmorum Hebr. atque Lat. p. 155, under Ps. cxviii. 5; and Kimchi, Wörterb., under אפל and שלהב. Ben-Naphtali, on the other hand, reads as two words, שַׁלְהֶבֶת יָהּ. [Except in this word, the recensions of Ben-Asher and Ben-Naphtali differ only "de punctis vocalibus et accentibus." Strack's Prolegomena, p. 28.]

fire; no earthly power can suppress it by the strength of its assault, as streams drench all they sweep over in their flow—the flame of Jah is inextinguishable.

Nor can this love be bought; any attempt to buy it would be scorned and counted madness. The expression is like Prov. vi. 30 f.; cf. Num. xxii. 18; 1 Cor. xiii. 3. Regarding הוֹן (from הון, (Arab.) *han, levem esse*), convenience, and that by which life is made comfortable, *vid.* at Prov. i. 13. According to the shepherd-hypothesis, here occurs the expression of the peculiar point of the story of the intercourse between Solomon and Shulamith; she scorns the offers of Solomon; her love is not to be bought, and it already belongs to another. But of offers we read nothing beyond i. 11, where, as in the following ver. 12, it is manifest that Shulamith is in reality excited in love. Hitzig also remarks under i. 12: "When the speaker says the fragrance of her nard is connected with the presence of the king, she means that only then does she smell the fragrance of nard, *i.e.* only his presence awakens in her heart pleasant sensations or sweet feelings." Shulamith manifestly thus speaks, also emphasizing vi. 12, the spontaneousness of her relation to Solomon; but Hitzig adds: "These words, i. 12, are certainly spoken by a court lady." But the Song knows only a chorus of the "Daughters of Jerusalem"—that court lady is only a phantom, by means of which Hitzig's ingenuity seeks to prop up the shepherd-hypothesis, the weakness of which his penetration has discerned. As we understand the Song, ver. 7 refers to the love with which Shulamith loves, as decidedly as 6b to the love with which she is loved. Nothing in all the world is able to separate her from loving the king; it is love to his person, not love called forth by a desire for riches which he disposes of, not even by the splendour of the position which awaited her, but free, responsive love with which she answered free love making its approach to her. The poet here represents Shulamith herself as expressing the idea of love embodied in her. That apple tree, where he awaked first love in her, is a witness of the renewal of their mutual covenant of love; and it is significant that only here, just directly here, where the idea of the whole is expressed more fully, and in a richer manner than at vii. 7, is God denoted by His name, and that by His name as revealed in the history of redemption. Hitzig, Ewald, Olshausen, Böttcher, expand this concluding word, for the sake of rhythmic symmetry, to שַׁלְהֶבֶת יָהּ שַׁלְהֲבֹתֶיהָ [its flames are flames of Jah]; but a similar conclusion is found at Ps. xxiv. 6, xlviii. 7, and elsewhere.

"I would almost close the book," says Herder in his *Lied der*

Lieder (Song of Songs), 1778, " with this divine seal. It is even as good as closed, for what follows appears only as an appended echo." Daniel Sanders (1845) closes it with ver. 7, places ver. 12 after i. 6, and cuts off vers. 8–11, 13, 14 as not original. Anthologists, like Döpke and Magnus, who treat the Song as the Fragmentists do the Pentateuch, find here their confused medley sanctioned. Umbreit also, 1820, although as for the rest recognising the Song as a compact whole, explains viii. 8–12, 13, 14 as a fragment, not belonging to the work itself. Hoelemann, however, in his *Krone des Hohenliedes* [Crown of the Song], 1856 (thus he names the "concluding Act," viii. 5–14), believes that there is here represented, not only in vers. 6, 7, but further also in vers. 8–12, the essence of true love—what it is, and how it is won; and then in viii. 13 f. he hears the Song come to an end in pure idyllic tones. We see in ver. 8 ff. the continuation of the love story practically idealized and set forth in dramatic figures. There is no inner necessity for this continuance. It shapes itself after that which has happened; and although in all history divine reason and moral ideas realize themselves, yet the material by means of which this is done consists of accidental circumstances and free actions passing thereby into reciprocal action. But ver. 8 ff. is the actual continuance of the story on to the completed conclusion, not a mere appendix, which might be wanting without anything being thereby missed. For after the poet has set before us the loving pair as they wander arm in arm through the green pasture-land between Jezreel and Sunem till they reach the environs of the parental home, which reminds them of the commencement of their love relations, he cannot represent them as there turning back, but must present to us still a glimpse of what transpired on the occasion of their visit there. After that first Act of the concluding scene, there is yet wanting a second, to which the first points.

SECOND SCENE OF THE FIFTH ACT, VIII. 8–14.

The locality of this scene is Shulamith's parental home. It is she herself who speaks in these words:

> Ver. 8 We have a sister, a little one,
> And she has no breasts:
> What shall we do with our sister
> In the day when she will be sued for?

Between vers. 8 and 7 is a blank. The figure of the wanderers is followed by the figure of the visitors. But who speaks here? The interchange of the scene permits that Shulamith conclude the one scene and begin the other, as in the first Act; or also that at the same time with the change of scene there is an interchange of persons, as *e.g.* in the third Act. But if Shulamith speaks, all her words are not by any means included in what is said from ver. 8 to ver. 10. Since, without doubt, she also speaks in ver. 11 f., this whole second figure consists of Shulamith's words, as does also the second of the second Act, iii. 1–5. But there Shulamith's address presents itself as the narrative of an experience, and the narrative dramatically framed in itself is thoroughly penetrated by the *I* of the speaker; but here, as *e.g.* Ewald, Heiligst., and Böttch. explain, she would begin with a dialogue with her brothers referable to herself, one that had formerly taken place—that little sister, Ewald remarks under ver. 10, stands here now grown up; she took notice of that severe word formerly spoken by her brothers, and can now joyfully before all exclaim, taking up the same flowery language, that she is a wall, etc. But that a monologue should begin with a dialogue without any introduction, is an impossibility; in this case the poet ought not to have left the expression, " of old my mother's sons said," to be supplemented by the reader or hearer. It is true, at iii. 2, v. 3, we have a former address introduced without any formal indication of the fact; but it is the address of the narrator herself. With ver. 8 there will thus begin a colloquy arising out of present circumstances. That in this conversation ver. 8 appertains to the brothers, is evident. This harsh *entweder oder* (*aut . . . aut*) is not appropriate as coming from Shulamith's mouth; it is her brothers alone, as Hoelemann rightly remarks, who utter these words, as might have been expected from them in view of i. 6. But does ver. 8 belong also to them? There may be two of them, says Hitzig, and the one may in ver. 9 reply to the question of the other in ver. 8; Shulamith, who has heard their conversation, suddenly interposes with ver. 10. But the transition from the first to the second scene is more easily explained if Shulamith proposes the question of ver. 8 for consideration. This is not set aside by Hitzig's questions: " Has she to determine in regard to her sister? and has she now for the first time come to do nothing in haste?" For (1) the dramatic figures of the Song follow each other chronologically, but not without blanks; and the poet does not at all require us to regard ver. 8 as Shulamith's first words after her entrance into her parental home; (2) but it is altogether seeming for Shulamith, who has now become independent, and who has been raised so high, to throw out this question of loving care for her sister. Besides, from the fact that with ver. 8 there commences the representation of a present occurrence, it is proved that the sister here spoken of is not Shulamith herself. If it were Shulamith herself, the words of vers. 8, 9 would look back to what had previously taken place, which, as we have shown, is impossible. Or does vi. 9 require that we should think of Shulamith as having no sister? Certainly not, for so understood, these words would be purposeless. The "only one," then, does not mean the only one numerically, but, as at Prov. iv. 3, it is emphatic (Hitzig); she is called by Solomon the "only one" of her mother in this sense, that she had not one her equal.

Thus it is Shulamith who here speaks, and she is not the "sister" referred to. The words, "we have a sister . . .," spoken in the family circle, whether regarded as uttered by Shulamith or not, have something strange in them, for one member of a family does not need thus to speak to another. We expect: With regard to our sister, who is as yet little and not of full age, the question arises, What will be done when she has grown to maturity to guard her innocence? Thus the expression would have stood, but the poet separates it into little symmetrical sentences; for poetry presents facts in a different style from prose. Hoelem. has on this remarked that the words are not to be translated: we have a little sister, which the order of the words אָחוֹת קָ׳ וּגוֹ׳ would presuppose, Gen. xl. 20; cf. 2 Sam. iv. 4, xii. 2 f.; Isa. xxvi. 1, xxxiii. 21. "Little" is not immediately connected with "sister," but follows it as an apposition; and this appositional description lays the ground for the question: We may be now without concern; but when she is grown up and will be courted, what then? "Little" refers to age, as at 2 Kings v. 2; cf. Gen. xliv. 20. The description of the child in the words, "she has no breasts," has neither in itself nor particularly for Oriental feeling anything indecent in it (cf. *mammae sororiarunt*, Ezek. xvi. 7). The ל following מַה־נַּעֲשֶׂה is here not thus purely the *dat. commodi*, as *e.g.* Isa. lxiv. 3 (to act for some one), but indiff. dat. (what shall we do for her?); but מה is, according to the connection, as at Gen. xxvii. 37, 1 Sam. x. 2, Isa. v. 4, equivalent to: What conducing to her advantage? Instead of בַּיּוֹם, the form בְּיוֹם lay syntactically nearer (cf. Ex. vi. 28); the art. in בַּיּוֹם is, as at Eccles. xii. 3, understood demonst.: that day when she will be spoken for, *i.e.* will attract the attention of a suitor. בְּ after דֻּבַּר may have manifold significations (*vid.* under Ps. lxxxvii. 3); thus the general signification of "concerning," 1 Sam. xix. 3, is modified in the sense of courting a wife, 1 Sam. xxv. 39. The brothers now take speech in hand, and answer Shulamith's question as to what will have to be done for the future safety of their little sister when the time comes that she shall be sought for:

> Ver. 9 If she be a wall,
> We will build upon her a pinnacle of silver;
> And if she be a door,
> We will block her up with a board of cedar-wood.

The brothers are the nearest guardians and counsellors of the sister, and, particularly in the matter of marriage, have the precedence even of the father and mother, Gen. xxiv. 50, 55, xxxiv. 6–8. They suppose two cases which stand in contrast to each other, and announce their purpose with reference to each case. Hoelem. here affects a synonymous instead of the antithetic parallelism; for he maintains that אִם (וְאִם)... אִם nowhere denotes a contrast, but, like *sive ... sive*, essential indifference. But examples such as Deut. xviii. 3 (*sive bovem, sive ovem*) are not applicable here; for this correl. אִם ... אִם, denoting essential equality, never begins the antecedents of two principal sentences, but always stands in the component parts of one principal sentence. Wherever אִם ... וְאִם commences two parallel conditional clauses, the parallelism is always, according to the contents of these clauses, either synonymous, Gen. xxxi. 50, Amos ix. 2–4, Eccles. xi. 3 (where the first וְאִם signifies *ac si*, and the second *sive*), or antithetic, Num. xvi. 29 f.; Job xxxvi. 11 f.; Isa. i. 19 f. The contrast between חוֹמָה (from חָמָה, Arab. *haman*, Modern Syr. *chamo*, to preserve, protect) and דֶּלֶת (from דָּלַל, to hang loose, of doors, Prov. xxvi. 14, which move hither and thither on their hinges) is obvious. A wall stands firm and withstands every assault if it serves its purpose (which is here presupposed, where it is used as a figure of firmness of character). A door, on the contrary, is moveable; and though it be for the present closed (דלת is intentionally used, and not פֶּתַח, *vid.* Gen. xix. 6), yet it is so formed that it can be opened again. A maiden inaccessible to seduction is like a wall, and one accessible to it is like a door. In the apodosis, 9a, the LXX. correctly renders טִירַת by ἐπάλξεις; Jerome, by *propugnacula*. But it is not necessary to read טִירַת. The verb טוּר, cogn. דוּר, signifies to surround, whence *tirah* (= Arab. *duâr*), a round encampment, Gen. xxv. 16, and, generally, a habitation, Ps. lxix. 25; and then also, to range together, whence טוּר, a rank, row (cf. Arab. *thur* and *daur*, which, in the manifoldness of their meanings, are parallel with the French *tour*), or also *tirah*, which, Ezek. xlvi. 23 (*vid.* Keil), denotes the row or layer of masonry,—in the passage before us, a row of battlements (Ew.), or a crown of the wall (Hitz.), *i.e.* battlements as a wreath on the summit of a wall. Is she a wall,—*i.e.* does she firmly and successfully withstand all immoral approaches?— then they will adorn this wall with silver pinnacles (cf. Isa. liv. 12), *i.e.* will bestow upon her the high honour which is due to her maidenly purity and firmness; silver is the symbol of holiness, as gold is the symbol of nobility. In the apodosis 9*b*, צוּר עַל is not otherwise meant than when used in a military sense of enclosing by means of besieging, but, like Isa. xxix. 3, with the obj.-accus., of that which is pressed against that which is to be excluded; צוּר here means, forcibly to press against, as סגר, Gen. ii. 21, to unite by closing up.

לוּחַ אֶרֶז is a board or plank (cf. Ezek. xxvii. 5, of the double planks of a ship's side) of cedar wood (cf. Zeph. ii. 14, אַרְזָה, cedar wainscot). Cedar wood comes here into view not on account of the beautiful polish which it takes on, but merely because of its hardness and durability. Is she a door, *i.e.* accessible to seduction? they will enclose this door around with a cedar plank, *i.e.* watch her in such a manner that no seducer or lover will be able to approach her. By this morally stern but faithful answer, Shulamith is carried back to the period of her own maidenhood, when her brothers, with good intention, dealt severely with her. Looking back to this time, she could joyfully confess:

>Ver. 10 I was a wall,
>And my breasts like towers;
>Then I became in his eyes
>Like one who findeth peace.

In the language of prose, the statement would be: Your conduct is good and wise, as my own example shows; of me also ye thus faithfully took care; and that I met this your solicitude with strenuous self-preservation, has become, to my joy and yours, the happiness of my life. That in this connection not חומה אני, but אני חומה has to be used, is clear: she compares herself with her sister, and the praise she takes to herself she takes to the honour of her brothers. The comparison of her breasts to towers is suggested by the comparison of her person to a wall; Kleuker rightly remarks that here the comparison is not of thing with thing, but of relation with relation: the breasts were those of her person, as the towers were of the wall, which, by virtue of the power of defence which they conceal within themselves, never permit the enemy, whose attention they attract, to approach them. The two substantival clauses, *murus et ubera mea instar turrium*, have not naturally a retrospective signification, as they would in a historical connection (*vid.* under Gen. ii. 10); but they become retrospective by the following "then I became," like Deut. xxvi. 5, by the historical tense following. where, however, it is to be remarked that the expression, having in itself no relation to time, which is incapable of being expressed in German, mentions the past not in a way that excludes the present, but as including it. She was a wall, and her breasts like the towers, *i.e.* all seductions rebounded from her, and ventured not near her awe-inspiring attractions; then (אָז, temporal, but at the same time consequent; thereupon, and for this reason, as at Ps. xl. 8, Jer. xxii. 15, etc.) she became in his (Solomon's) eyes as one who findeth peace. According to the shepherd-hypothesis, she says here: he deemed it good to forbear any further attempts, and to let me remain in peace (Ewald, Hitz., and others). But how is that possible? מצא שָׁלוֹם בְעֵינֵי is a variation of the frequently occurring מצא חֵן בְעֵינֵי, which is used especially of a woman gaining the affections of a man, Esth. ii. 17, Deut. xxiv. 1, Jer. xxxi. 2 f.; and the expression here used, "thus I was in his eyes as one who findeth peace," is only the more circumstantial expression for, "then I found (אז מָצָאתִי) in his eyes peace," which doubtless means more than: I brought it to this, that he left me further unmolested; שָׁלוֹם in this case, as syn. of חֵן, means inward agreement, confidence, friendship, as at Ps. xli. 10; there it means, as in the salutation of peace and in a hundred other cases, a positive good. And why should she use שָׁלוֹם instead of חֵן, but that she might form a play upon the name which she immediately, 11*a*, thereafter utters, שְׁלֹמֹה, which signifies, 1 Chron. xxii. 9, "The man of peace." That *Shulamith* had found *shalom* (peace) with *Sh'lomoh* (Solomon), cannot be intended to mean that uninjured she escaped from him, but that she had entered into a relation to him which seemed to her a state of blessed peace. The delicate description, "in his eyes," is designed to indicate that she appeared to him in the time of her youthful discipline as one finding peace. The כ is כ *veritatis, i.e.* the comparison of the fact with its idea, Isa. xxix. 2, or of the individual with the general and common, Isa. xiii. 6; Ezek. xxvi. 10; Zech. xiv. 3. Here the meaning is, that Shulamith appeared to him corresponding to the idea of one finding peace, and thus as worthy to find peace with him. One "finding peace" is one who gains the heart of a man, so that he enters into a relation of esteem and affection for her. This generalization of the idea also opposes the notion of a history of seduction. מוֹצְאֵת is from the ground-form *matsiat*, the parallel form to מוֹצֵאת, 2 Sam. xviii. 22. Solomon has won her, not by persuasion or violence; but because she could be no other man's, he entered with her into the marriage covenant of peace (cf. Prov. ii. 17 with Isa. liv. 10).

It now lies near, at least rather so than remote, that Shulamith, thinking of her brothers, presents her request before her royal husband:

> Ver. 11 Solomon had a vineyard in Baal-hamon;
> He committed the vineyard to the keepers,
> That each should bring for its fruit
> A thousand in silver.
> 12 I myself disposed of my own vineyard:
> The thousand is thine, Solomon,
> And two hundred for the keepers of its fruit!

The words כֶּרֶם הָיָה לִשׁ׳ are to be translated after כרם ונו׳, 1 Kings xxi. 1, and לְדִידִי ..., Isa. v. 1, "Solomon had a vineyard" (cf. 1 Sam. ix. 2; 2 Sam. vi. 23, xii. 2; 2 Kings i. 17; 1 Chron. xxiii. 17, xxvi. 10), not "Solomon has a vineyard," which would have required the words כרם לשׁ׳, with the omission of היה. I formerly explained, as also Böttcher : 'a vineyard became his, thus at present is his possession; and thus explaining, one could suppose that it fell to him, on his taking possession of his government, as a component part of his domain; but although in itself היה לו can mean, "this or that has become one's own" (e.g. Lev. xxi. 3), as well as "it became his own," yet here the historical sense is necessarily connected by היה with the נתן foll.: Solomon has had ..., he has given; and since Solomon, after possessing the vineyard, would probably also preserve it, Hitzig draws from this the conclusion, that the poet thereby betrays the fact that he lived after the time of Solomon. But these are certainly words which he puts into Shulamith's mouth, and he cannot at least have forgotten that the heroine of his drama is a contemporary of Solomon; and supposing that he had forgotten this for a moment, he must have at least once read over what he had written, and could not have been so blind as to have allowed this היה which had escaped him to stand. We must thus assume that he did not in reality retain the vineyard, which, as Hitzig supposes, if he possessed it, he also "probably" retained, whether he gave it away, or exchanged it, or sold it, we know not; but the poet might suppose that Shulamith knew it, since it refers to a piece of land lying not far from her home. For בַּעַל הָמוֹן, LXX. Βεελαμών, is certainly the same as that mentioned in Judith viii. 3, according to which Judith's husband died from sunstroke in Bethulia, and was buried beside his fathers "between *Dothaim* and *Balamōn*"[1]

---

[1] This is certainly not the *Baal-Meon* (now *Maïn*) lying half an hour to the south of Heshbon; there is also, however, a *Meon* (now *Maïn*) on this [the west] side of Jordan, Nabal's Maon, near to Carmel. *Vid.* art. "Maon," by Kleuker in Schenkel's *Bibl. Lex.*

(probably, as the sound of the word denotes, *Belmen,* or, more accurately, *Belmaïn,* as it is also called in Judith iv. 4, with which Kleuker in Schenkel's *Bibl. Lex.,* de Bruyn in his *Karte,* and others, interchange it; and חַמֹּן, Josh. xix. 28, lying in the tribe of Asher). This *Balamōn* lay not far from Dothan, and thus not far from *Esdrälon;* for Dothan lay (cf. Judith iii. 10) south of the plain of Jezreel, where it has been discovered, under the name of *Tell Dotan,* in the midst of a smaller plain which lies embosomed in the hills of the south.[1] The ancients, since Aquila, Symm., Targ., Syr., and Jerome, make the name of the place Baal-hamon subservient to their allegorizing interpretation, but only by the aid of soap-bubble-like fancies; *e.g.* Hengst. makes *Baal-hamon* designate the world; *nothrim* [keepers], the nations; the 1000 pieces in silver, the duties comprehended in the ten commandments. *Hamon* is there understood of a large, noisy crowd. The place may, indeed, have its name from the multitude of its inhabitants, or from an annual market held there, or otherwise from revelry and riot; for, according to Hitzig,[2] there is no ground for co-ordinating it with names such as *Baal-Gad* and *Baal-Zephon,* in which *Baal* is the general, and what follows the special name of God. *Amon,* the Sun-God, specially worshipped in Egyptian Thebes, has the bibl. name אָמוֹן, with which, after the sound of the word, accords the name of a place lying, according to *Jer. Demaï* ii. 1, in the region of Tyrus, but not המן. The reference to the Egypt. *Amon Ra,* which would direct rather to Baalbec, the Coele-Syrian Heliupolis, is improbable; because the poet would certainly not have introduced into his poem the name of the place where the vineyard lay, if this name did not call forth an idea corresponding to the connection. The Shulamitess, now become Solomon's, in order to support the request she makes to the king, relates an incident of no historical value in itself of the near-lying Sunem (Sulem), situated not far from Baal-hamon to the north, on the farther side of the plain of Jezreel. She belongs to a family whose inheritance consisted in vineyards, and she herself had acted in the capacity of the keeper of a vineyard, i. 6,—so much the less therefore is it to be wondered at that she takes an interest in the vineyard of Baal-hamon, which Solomon had let out to keepers on the condition that they should pay to him for its fruit-harvest the sum of 1000 shekels of silver (*shekel* is, according to Ges. § 120. 4, Anm. 2, to be supplied). יָבִא, since we have interpreted היה retro-

---

[1] *Vid.* Robinson's *Physical Geogr. of the Holy Land,* p. 113; Morrison's *Recovery of Jerusalem* (1871), p. 463, etc.

[2] Cf. also Schwarz' *Das heilige Land,* p. 37.

spectively, might also indeed be rendered imperfect. as equivalent to *afferebat*, or, according to Ewald, § 136*c*, *afferre solebat;* but since נָתַן = ἐξέδοτο, Matt. xxi. 33, denotes a gift laying the recipients under an obligation, יָבִא is used in the sense of (אֲשֶׁר) יָבִא לְמַעַן; however, לְמַעַן is not to be supplied (Symm. ἐνέγκῃ), but יָבִא in itself signifies *afferre debebat* (he ought to bring), like יֵעָ, Dan. i. 5, they should stand (wait upon), Ewald, § 136*g*. Certainly נטרים does not mean tenants, but watchers,—the post-bibl. language has חָכַר, to lease, קִבֵּל, to take on lease, חִכּוּר, rent, *e.g. Mezîa* ix. 2,—but the subject here is a *locatio conductio;* for the vine-plants of that region are entrusted to the "keepers" for a rent, which they have to pay, not in fruits but in money, as the equivalent of a share of the produce (the ב in בְּפִרְ׳ is the ב *pretii*). Isa. vii. 23 is usually compared; but there the money value of a particularly valuable portion of a vineyard, consisting of 1000 vines, is given at "1000 silverlings" (1 shekel); while, on the other hand, the 1000 shekels here are the rent for a portion of a vineyard, the extent of which is not mentioned. But that passage in Isaiah contains something explanatory of the one before us, inasmuch as we see from it that a vineyard was divided into portions of a definite number of vines in each. Such a division into *meḳomoth* is also here supposed. For if each "keeper" to whom the vineyard was entrusted had to count 1000 shekels for its produce, then the vineyard was at the same time committed to several keepers, and thus was divided into small sections (Hitzig). It is self-evident that the gain of the produce that remained over after paying the rent fell to the "keepers;" but since the produce varied, and also the price of wine, this gain was not the same every year, and only in general are we to suppose from 12*b*, that it yielded on an average about 20 per cent. For the vineyard which Shulamith means in 12*b* is altogether different from that of Baal-hamon. It is of herself she says, i. 6, that as the keeper of a vineyard, exposed to the heat of the day, she was not in a position to take care of her own vineyard. This her own vineyard is not her beloved (Hoelem.), which not only does not harmonize with i. 6 (for she there looks back to the time prior to her elevation), but her own person, as comprehending everything pleasant and lovely which constitutes her personality (iv. 12–v. 1), as *kerem* is the sum-total of the vines which together form a vineyard.

Of this figurative vineyard she says: כַּרְמִי שֶׁלִּי לְפָנָי. This must mean, according to Hitzig, Hoelem., and others, that it was under her protection; but although the idea of affectionate care may, in certain circumstances, be connected with לִפְנֵי, Gen. xvii. 18, Prov.

iv. 3, yet the phrase: this or that is לְפָנַי, wherever it has not merely a local or temporal, but an ethical signification, can mean nothing else than: it stands under my direction, Gen. xiii. 9, xx. 15, xlvii. 6; 2 Chron. xiv. 6; Gen. xxiv. 51; 1 Sam. xvi. 16. Rightly Heiligst., after Ewald: *in potestate mea est.* Shulamith also has a vineyard, which she is as free to dispose of as Solomon of his at Baal-hamon. It is the totality of her personal and mental endowments. This vineyard has been given over with free and joyful cordiality into Solomon's possession. This vineyard also has keepers (one here sees with what intention the poet has chosen in 11*a* just that word נטרים) — to whom Shulamith herself and to whom Solomon also owes it that as a chaste and virtuous maiden she became his possession. These are her brothers, the true keepers and protectors of her innocence. Must these be unrewarded? The full thousands, she says, turning to the king, which like the annual produce of the vineyard of Baal-hamon will thus also be the fruit of my own personal worth, shall belong to none else, O Solomon, than to thee, and two hundred to the keepers of its fruit! If the keepers in Baal-hamon do not unrewarded watch the vineyard, so the king owes thanks to those who so faithfully guarded his Shulamith. The poetry would be reduced to prose if there were found in Shulamith's words a hint that the king should reward her brothers with a gratification of 200 shekels. She makes the case of the vineyard in Baal-hamon a parable of her relation to Solomon on the one hand, and of her relation to her brothers on the other. From מָאתַיִם, one may conclude that there were two brothers, thus that the rendering of thanks is thought of as מַעֲשֵׂר (a tenth part); but so that the 200 are meant not as a tax on the thousand, but as a reward for the faithful rendering up of the thousand.

The king, who seems to this point to have silently looked on in inmost sympathy, now, on being addressed by Shulamith, takes speech in hand; he does not expressly refer to her request, but one perceives from his words that he heard it with pleasure. He expresses to her the wish that she would gratify the companions of her youth who were assembled around her, as well as himself, with a song, such as in former times she was wont to sing in these mountains and valleys.

> Ver. 13 O thou (who art) at home in the gardens,
> Companions are listening for thy voice;
> Let me hear!

We observe that in the rural paradise with which she is surrounded, she finds herself in her element. It is a primary feature of her character which herein comes to view: her longing after quietness and peace, her love for collectedness of mind and for contemplation; her delight in thoughts of the Creator suggested by the vegetable world, and particularly by the manifold soft beauty of flowers; she is again once more in the gardens of her home, but the address, "O thou at home in the gardens!" denotes that wherever she is, these gardens are her home as a fundamental feature of her nature. The חֲבֵרִים are not Solomon's companions, for she has come hither with Solomon alone, leaning on his arm. Also it is indicated in the expression: "are listening for thy voice," that they are such as have not for a long time heard the dear voice which was wont to cheer their hearts. The חבר׳ are the companions of the former shepherdess and keeper of a vineyard, i. 6 f., the playmates of her youth, the friends of her home. With a fine tact the poet does not represent Solomon as saying חֲבֵרָיִךְ nor חֲבֵרֵינוּ: the former would be contrary to the closeness of his relation to Shulamith, the latter contrary to the dignity of the king. By חברים there is neither expressed a one-sided reference, nor is a double-sided excluded. That "for thy voice" refers not to her voice as speaking, but as the old good friends wish, as singing, is evident from הַשְׁמִיעִנִי in connection with ii. 14, where also קוֹלֵךְ is to be supplied, and the voice of song is meant. She complies with the request, and thus begins:

> Ver. 14 Flee, my beloved,
> And be thou like a gazelle,
> Or a young one of the harts,
> Upon spicy mountains.

Hitzig supposes that with these words of refusal she bids him away from her, without, however, as "my beloved" shows, meaning them in a bad sense. They would thus, as Renan says, be bantering coquetry. If it is Solomon who makes the request, and thus also he who is addressed here, not the imaginary shepherd violently introduced into this closing scene in spite of the words "(the thousand) is thine, Solomon" (ver. 12), then Shulamith's ignoring of his request is scornful, for it would be as unseemly if she sang of her own accord to please her friends, as it would be wilful if she kept silent when requested by her royal husband. So far the Spanish author, Soto Major, is right (1599): *jussa et rogata id non debuit nec potuit recusare.* Thus with "flee" she begins a song which she sings, as at ii. 15 she commences one, in reponse to a similar request, with "catch us." Hoelem. finds in her present happiness, which fills her more than ever, the thought here expressed that her beloved, if he again went from her for a moment, would yet very speedily return to his longing, waiting bride.[1] But apart from the circumstance that Shulamith is no longer a bride, but is married, and that the wedding festival is long past, there is not a syllable of that thought in the text; the words must at least have been בְּרַח אֵלַי, if ברח signified generally to hasten hither, and not to hasten forth. Thus, at least as little as סֹב, ii. 17, without אֵלַי, signifies "turn thyself hither," can this בְּרַח mean "flee hither." The words of the song thus invite Solomon to disport himself, *i.e.* give way to frolicsome and aimless mirth on these spicy mountains. As *sov l*e*cha* is enlarged to *sov d*e*meh-l*e*cha*, ii. 17, for the sake of the added figures (*vid.* under ii. 9), so here *b*e*rahh-l*e*cha* (Gen. xxvii. 43) is enlarged to *b*e*rahh ud*e*meh* (*ud*ă*meh*) *l*e*cha*. That "mountains of spices" occurs here instead of "cleft mountains," ii. 17*b*, has its reason, as has already been there remarked, and as Hitzig, Hoelem., and others have discovered, in the aim of the poet to conclude the pleasant song of love that has reached perfection and refinement with an absolutely pleasant word.

But with what intention does he call on Shulamith to sing to her beloved this בְּרַח, which obviously has here not the meaning of escaping away (according to the fundamental meaning, *transversum currere*), but only, as where it is used of fleeting time, Job ix. 25, xiv. 2, the sense of hastening? One might suppose that she whom he has addressed as at home in gardens replies to his request with the invitation to hasten forth among the mountains,—an exercise which gives pleasure to a man. But (1) Solomon, according to ii. 16, vi. 2 f., is also fond of gardens and flowers; and (2) if he took pleasure in ascending mountains, it doubled his joy, according to iv. 8, to share this joy with Shulamith; and (3) we ask, would this closing scene, and along with it the entire series of dramatic pictures, find a satisfactory conclusion, if either Solomon remained and gave no response to Shulamith's call, or if he, as directed, disappeared alone, and left Shulamith by herself among the men who surrounded her? Neither of these two things can have been intended by the poet, who shows himself elsewhere a master in the art of composition. In ii. 17 the matter lies otherwise. There the love-relation is as yet in progress, and the abandonment of love to uninterrupted fellowship places a limit to itself. Now, however, Shulamith is married, and the summons is unlimited. It reconciles itself neither

---

[1] Similarly Godet: The earth during the present time belongs to the earthly power; only at the end shall the bridegroom fetch the bride, and appear as the heavenly Solomon to thrust out the false and fleshly, and to celebrate the heavenly marriage festival.

with the strength of her love nor with the tenderness of the relation, that she should with so cheerful a spirit give occasion to her husband to leave her alone for an indefinite time. We will thus have to suppose that, when Shulamith sings the song, "Flee, my beloved," she goes forth leaning on Solomon's arm out into the country, or that she presumes that he will not make this flight into the mountains of her native home without her. With this song breaking forth in the joy of love and of life, the poet represents the loving couple as disappearing over the flowery hills, and at the same time the sweet charm of the Song of Songs, leaping gazelle-like from one fragrant scene to another, vanishes away.

APPENDIX.

REMARKS ON THE SONG BY DR. J. G. WETZSTEIN.

THE following aphoristic elucidations of the Song are partly collected from epistolary communications, but for the most part are taken from my friend's "Treatise on the Syrian thrashing-table" (in Bastian's *Zeitsch. für Ethnographie*, 1873), but not without these extracts having been submitted to him, and here and there enlarged by him.

The thrashing-table (*lô^{a}h ed-derâs*) is an agricultural implement in common use from ancient times in the countries round the Mediterranean Sea. It consists of two boards of nut-tree wood or of oak, bound together by two cross timbers. These boards are bent upwards in front, after the manner of a sledge, so as to be able to glide without interruption over the heaps of straw; underneath they are set with stones (of porous basalt) in oblique rows, thus forming a rubbing and cutting apparatus, which serves to thrash out the grain and to chop the straw; for the thrashing-table drawn by one or two animals yoked to it, and driven by their keeper, moves round on the straw-heaps spread on the barn floor. The thrashing-table may have sometimes been used in ancient times for the purpose of destroying prisoners of war by a horrible death (2 Sam. xii. 31); at the present day it serves as the seat of honour for the bride and bridegroom, and also as a bier whereon the master of the house is laid when dead. The former of these its two functions is that which has given an opportunity to Wetzstein to sketch in that Treatise, under the title of "The Table in the King's-week," a picture of the marriage festival among the Syrian peasantry. This sketch contains not a few things that serve to throw light on the Song, which we here place in order, intermixed with other remarks by Wetzstein with reference to the Song and to our commentary on it.

i. 6. In August 1861, when on a visit to the hot springs *El-hamma*, between *Domeir* and *Roheiba* to the north of Damascus, I was the guest of the Sheik *'Id*, who was encamped with his tribe, a branch of the *Solêb*, at the sulphurous stream there (*nahar el-mukebret*).

Since the language of this people (who inhabited the Syrian desert previous to the Moslem period, were longest confessors of Christianity among the nomads, and therefore kept themselves free from intermingling with the tribes that at a later period had migrated from the peninsula) possesses its own remarkable peculiarities, I embraced the opportunity of having dictated and explained to me, for three whole days, Solebian poems. The introduction to one of these is as follows : " The poet is *Solêbî Tuwês,* nephew of (the already mentioned) *Râshid.* The latter had had a dispute with a certain *Bishr;* that Tuwês came to know, and now sent the following *kasidah* (poem) to Bishr, which begins with praise in regard to his uncle, and finally advises Bishr to let that man rest, lest he (Tuwês) should become his adversary and that of his party." The last verse is in these words :

" That say I to you, I shall become the adversary of the disturber of the peace,
Bend my right knee before him, and, as a second Zir, show myself on the field of battle (the *menâch*)."

Zir is a hero celebrated in the Dîwân of Benî Hilâl; and to bend the right knee is to enter into a conflict for life or death : the figure is derived from the sword-dance.[1]

So much regarding the poem of Ṣolêbî. From this can nothing be gained for the explanation of נֶחֱרוּ־בִי of the Song ? This is for the most part interpreted as the *Niph.* of חָרָה or חָרַר (to be inflamed, to be angry with one) ; but why not as the *Pih.* of נָחַר ? It is certainly most natural to interpret this נחר in the sense of *nakhar,* to breathe, snort ; but the LXX., Symm., Theod., in rendering by μαχέσαντο (διεμαχέσαντο), appear to have connected with *nihharu* the meaning

[1] If this dance, *e.g.*, is danced to celebrate a victory, it not seldom happens that the spectators call out to a young man particularly struck by the dancer : Kneel to her. He who is thus challenged steps into the circle, sinks down on his right knee, in which inconvenient attitude he endeavours to approach the dancer, who on her part falls down on both her knees ; sliding and fencing according to the beat of the music, she retreats, and at the same time seeks with all her might to keep her assailant back with a sword. He parries the strokes with his left arm, while he attempts to gain his object. viz. with his right hand to touch the head of the dancer. If he succeeds in this, he cries out, " Dancer, I touch ! " With that the play ends, and the victor leaves the arena amid the approving shouts of the throng, often bleeding from many wounds. Many a one has forfeited his life in his attempt to touch a celebrated beauty. Since such death was self-chosen, the maiden goes unpunished. If the assailant, as often happens, is the brother or father's brother's son of the dancer, in which case the venture is less perilous, he has the right to kiss the vanquished damsel, which is always for the spectator a great amusement.

of that (Arab.) *tanaḥar*, which comes from *taḥrn*, the front of the neck. The outstretched neck of the camel, the breast, the head, the face, the brow, the nose, are, it is well known in the Arab., mere symbols for that which stands forward according to place, time, and rank. Of this *nahrn*, not only the Old Arab. (vid. *Kâmûs* under the word) but also the Modern Arab. has denom. verbal forms. In Damascus they say, *alsyl naḥara min alystan*, " the torrent tore away a part of the garden opposing it ;" and according to the *Deutsch. morg. Zeitschr.* xxii. 142, *naḥḥar flana* is " to strive forward after one." Hence *tanaḥarua*, to step opposite to (in a hostile manner), like *takabalua*, then to contend in words, to dispute; and *nahir* is, according to a vulgar mode of expression, one who places himself *coram* another, sits down to talk, discourses with him. These *denominativa* do not in themselves and without further addition express in the modern idioms the idea of " to take an opponent by the neck," or " to fight hand to hand with him."

i. 7. For עֲטִיָה the Arab. עֲצִיָה presents itself for comparison ; with inhabitants of the town, as well as of the desert (*Haḍar* and *Bedu*), *alghadwat*, " the (maiden) languishing with love," a very favourite designation for a maiden fatally in love ; the mas. *alghady* (plur. *alghudat*) is used in the same sense of a young man. According to its proper signification, it denotes a maiden with a languishing eye, the deeply sunk glimmerings of whose eyelids veil the eye. In Damascus such eyes are called *'iwan dubbal*, " pressed down eyes ;" and in the Haurân, *'iwan mugharribat*, " broken eyes ;" and they are not often wanting in love songs there. Accordingly, she who speaks seeks to avoid the neighbourhood of the shepherds, from fear of the *hatkalsitr*, i.e. for fear lest those who mocked would thus see the secret of her love, in accordance with the verse :

> " By its symptoms love discovers itself to the world,
> As musk which one carries discovers itself by its aroma."

i. 17. The cypress never bears the name *ṣnawbar*, which always denotes only the pine, one of the pine tribe. The cypress is only called *serwa*, collect. *seru*. Since it is now very probable that ברות (ברוש) is the old Heb. name of the cypress, and since there can at no time have been cypresses on the downs of Beirût, the connection of بيروت with ברות is to be given up. Instead of the difficult Heb. word *rahhithēnu*, there is perhaps to be read *vᵉhhēthēnu* (from *hhāith* = *hhāits*), " and our walls." The word-form حَايِط may have come from the idiom of the Higâz, or from some other impure source, into the written language; the living language knows only *hayt*

(חִיט), plur. ḥîṭân (Syr. Egypt.) and ḥijûṭ (Berbery). The written language itself has only the plur. ḥîṭân, and uses חַיט as an actual sing. For the transition of the letter *tsade* into *teth* in the Song, cf. נטר.

ii. 11. "For lo, the winter is past, the rain is over—is gone."

These are the words of the enticing love of the bridegroom to his beloved, whom he seeks to raise to the rank of queen. "The fairest period in the life of a Syrian peasant," thus Wetzstein's description begins, "are the first seven days after his marriage, in which, along with his young wife, he plays the part of king (*melik*) and she of queen (*melika*), and both are treated and served as such in their own district and by the neighbouring communities." The greater part of village weddings take place for the most part in the month of March, the most beautiful month of the Syrian year, called from its loveliness (*sahhᵃr*) *âdâr* = "*prachtmonat*" (magnificent month), to which the proverb refers: "If any one would see Paradise in its flowery splendour (*fî ezhârihâ*), let him contemplate the earth in its month of splendour (*fî âdârihâ*). Since the winter rains are past, and the sun now refreshes and revives, and does not, as in the following months, oppress by its heat, weddings are celebrated in the open air on the village thrashing-floor, which at this time, with few exceptions, is a flowery meadow. March is also suitable as the season for festivals, because at such a time there is little field labour, and, moreover, everything then abounds that is needed for a festival. During the winter the flocks have brought forth their young,—there are now lambs and kids, butter, milk, and cheese, and cattle for the slaughter, which have become fat on the spring pasture; the neighbouring desert yields for it brown, yellow, and white earth-nuts in such abundance, that a few children in one day may gather several camel-loads." The description passes over the marriage day itself, with its pomp, the sword-dance of the bride, and the great marriage feast, and begins where the newly married, on the morning after the marriage night,—which the young husband, even to this day, like the young Tobiah, spends sometimes in prayer,—appear as king and queen, and in their wedding attire receive the representative of the bride's-men, now their minister (*mezêr*), who presents them with a morning meal. Then the bride's-men come, fetch the thrashing-table ("corn-drag") from the straw storehouse (*metben*), and erect a scaffolding on the thrashing-floor, with the table above it, which is spread with a variegated carpet, and with two ostrich-feather cushions studded with gold, which is the seat of honour (*merteba*) for the king and queen during the seven days. This beautiful custom has a good reason for it, and also fulfils a noble end. For the more oppressive, troublesome, and unhappy the condition of the Syro-Palestinian peasant, so much the more reasonable does it appear that he should be honoured for a few days at least, and be celebrated and made happy. And considering the facility and wantonness of divorces in the Orient, the recollection of the marriage week, begun so joyfully, serves as a counterpoise to hinder a separation.

iii. 11. עֲטָרָה. The custom of crowning the bridegroom no longer exists in Syria. The bride's crown, called in Damascus *tâg-el-'arûs*, is called in the Haurân *'orga* (עֲרָגָה). This consists of a silver circlet, which is covered with a net of strings of corals of about three fingers' breadth. Gold coins are fastened in rows to this net, the largest being on the lowest row, those in the other rows upward becoming always smaller. At the wedding feast the hair of the bride is untied, and falls freely down over her neck and breast; and that it might not lose its wavy form, it is only oiled with some fragrant substances. The crowning thus begins: the headband is first bound on her head,—which on this day is not the *Sembar* (vid. Deut. morg. Zeit. xxii. 94), but the *Kesmâja*, a long, narrow, silken band, interwoven with dark-red and gold, and adorned at both ends with fringes, between which the *Ṣumûch*, silver, half-spherical little bells, hang down. The ends of the Kesmâja fall on both sides of the head, the one on the breast and the other on the back, so that the sound of the *Ṣumûch* is distinctly perceptible only during the sword-dance of the bride. Over the Kesmâja the crown is now placed in such a way that it rests more on the front of the head, and the front gold pieces of the under row come to lie on the naked brow. In the *Saḥka*, partly referred to under vii. 2, the poet addresses the goldsmith:

"And beat (for the bride) little bells, which constantly swing and ring like the tymbals (*nakkârât*);[1]
And (beat) the crown, one of four rows, and let Gihâdîs[2] be on the brow."

---

[1] By *nakkârât* are meant those little tymbals (kettledrums) which are used to keep time with the dancing-song, when that is not done by the tambourine. The ladies of Damascus take them with them to every country party, where frequently, without any singing, they are the only accompaniment of the dance. They are thus used: a damsel seats herself on the bare ground, places the two (scarcely is there ever only one) saucers—large copper hemispheres—before her breast, and beats against them with two wooden mallets. Their strings are made of the skins of goats or gazelles, while, for the tambourine, preference is given to the throat-bag of the pelican. These tymbals, like our own, have an unequal sound; when out of tune, they are rectified by being heated over a brazier.

[2] The *Gihâdî* is a rare Turkish gold piece of money, of old and beautiful

Etymologically considered, I believe that the word *'orga* must be regarded as parallel with *'argûn* (עֲרֻנוֹ), which in the Haurân is the foot-buckle; so that, from the root *'arag*, "to be bent," it is the designation of a bow or circlet, which the word *taj* also certainly means. However, on one occasion in Korêa (to the east of Bosrâ), while we were looking at a bride's crown, one said to me: "They call it *'orga*, because the coral strings do not hang directly down, but, running oblique (*mu'arwajat*), form a net of an elongated square."

iv. 14. אֲהָלוֹת. Who recognises in the Moorish *nif*, "the nose," the Heb. אַף? And yet the two words are the same. The word אֲנִף, *enf*, "the nose," is used by the wandering Arabs, who are fond of the dimin. אֲנֵיף, *"nêf*, which is changed into נֵיף; for א in the beginning of a word, particularly before a grave and accented syllable, readily falls away. From *nêf* (*neif*), finally, comes *nif*, because the idiom of the Moorish Arabians rejects the diphthong *ei*.

Thus, also, it fared with the word אֲהָלוֹת, "the little tent," "the little house," as the three-cornered capsules of the cardamum are called,—an aromatic plant which is to the present day so ardently loved by the Hadar and the Bedu, on account of its heat, and especially its sweet aroma, that one would have been led to wonder if it were wanting in this passage of the Song. From אֹהֶל there is formed the dimin. אֲהֵיל, and this is shortened into *hêl*, which is at the present day the name of the cardamum, while the unabbreviated *°hêl* is retained as the caritative of the original meaning,—we say, *jâ °hêli*, "my dear tent- (*i.e.* tribal) companions." This linguistic process is observable in all the Semitic languages; it has given rise to a mass of new roots. That it began at an early period, is shown by the Phoenician language; for the bibl. names *Hiram* and *Huram* are abbreviated from *Ahi-ram* and *Ahu-ram*; and the Punic stones supply many analogues, *e.g.* the proper names *Himilcath* (= *Ahhi-Milcath, restrictus reginae coeli*) with *Hethmilcath* (= *Ahith-Milcath*) and the like. On one of the stones which I myself brought from Carthage is found the word דֹן instead of אֲדֹן, "sir, master." In a similar way, the watering-place which receives so many diverse names by travellers, the *Wêba* (*Weibu*), in the Araba valley, will be an abbreviation of אֲוֵיבָה, and this the dimin. of אֹבוֹת, the name of an encampment of the Israelites in the wilderness (Num. xxi. 10). It had the name *'ên ovoth*, "the fountain of the water-bottles," perhaps

coinage, thin but very large, and of the finest gold. It was carried as a charm against the evil eye. On a bride's crown it forms the lowermost row of coins.

from the multitude of water-bottles filled here by water-drawers, waiting one after another. This encampment has been sought elsewhere—certainly incorrectly. Of the harbour-town *Elath* (on the Red Sea), it has been said, in the geography of *Ibn el-Bennâ* (MSS. of the Royal Lib. in Berlin, Sect. Spr. Nr. 5), published in Jerusalem about the year 1000: "*Weila*, at the north end of the (eastern) arm of the Red Sea; prosperous and distinguished; rich in palms and fishes; the harbour of Palestine, and the granary of Ḥigâz; is called *Aila* by the common people; but *Aila* is laid waste,—it lies quite in the neighbourhood." Thus it will be correct to say, that the name *Weila* is abbreviated from אֲוֵילָה, "Little-Aila," and designated a settlement which gradually grew up in the neighbourhood of the old Aila, and to which, when the former was at last destroyed, the name was transferred, so that "Little-Aila" became Aila; therefore it is that the later Arab. geographers know nothing of *Weila*. I have already elsewhere mentioned, that at the root of the name of the well-known Port *Suês* lies the Arab. ʽ*sâs* (= אָשִׁישׁ), which, among all the Syrian tribes, has lost the initial letter *Elif*, and takes the form of *Sâs*. Hence the name *Suês* (*Suwês*), the diminutive. The place has its name from this, that it was built on the foundations of an older harbour.

Silv. de Sacy already (*vid.* Gesen. *Thes.* p. 33*b*) conjectured that אהלות means cardamums. But, as it appears, he based his proof less on the identity of the two words *hêl* and *ahalôt*, than on the circumstance that he found the word *ḳâkula*—the Jemanic, and perhaps originally Indian name of cardamums — in the *hâhula* of the Egyptians of the present day. But the Egyptian does not pronounce the *k* like *h;* he does not utter it at all, or at most like a *Hamza*, so that *ḳâkula* is sounded by him not *hâhula*, but *ʼâʼula*. And who could presuppose the antiquity of this word, or that of its present pronunciation, in a land which has so radically changed both its language and its inhabitants as Egypt? And why should the Palestinians have received their Indian spices, together with their names, from Egypt? Why not much rather from *Aila*, to which they were brought from Jemen, either by ships or by the well-organized caravans (*vid.* Strabo, xvi. 4) which traded in the maritime country *Tihâma?* Or from *Têma*, the chief place in the desert (Job vi. 19; Isa. xxi. 14), whither they were brought from ʼ*Aḳir*, the harbour of *Gerrha*, which, according to Strabo (as above), was the great Arab. spice market? But if Palestine obtained its spices from thence, it would also, with them, receive the foreign name for them unchanged,—*kakula*,—since all the Arab tribes express the *ḳ* sound very distinctly. In short, the word אהלות has nothing to do with *ḳâkula;* it is shown to be a pure Semitic word by the plur. formations *ahaloth* and *ahalim* (Prov. vii. 17). The punctuation does not contradict this. The inhabitants of Palestine received the word, with the thing itself, through the medium of the Arabs, among whom the Heb. אֹהֶל is at the present time, as in ancient times, pronounced אָהֵל; thus the Arab vocalization is simply retained to distinguish it from אֹהֶל in its proper signification, without the name of the spice becoming thereby a meaningless foreign word. That the living language had a sing. for "a cardamum capsule" is self-evident. Interesting is the manner and way in which the modern Arabs help themselves with reference to this sing. Since *hêl* does not discover the mutilated אהל, and the Arab. اهل, besides, has modified its meaning (it signifies tent- and house-companions), the *nom. unit. hêla,* "a cardamum capsule," is no longer formed from *hêl;* the word *geras*, "the little bell," is therefore adopted, thereby forming a comparison of the firmly closed seed capsules, in which the loose seeds, on being shaken, give forth an audible rustling, with the little bells which are hung round the bell-wether and the leading camel. Thus they say: take three or four little bells (*egrâs*), and not: *telât, arba' hêlât* (which at most, as a mercantile expression, would denote, "parcels or kinds" of cardamum); they speak also of *geras-el-hêl* ("*hêl* little bells") and *geras-et-ṭib* ("*spice* little bells"). This "little bell" illustrates the ancient אהל. Supposing that *ḳâkula* might have been the true name of the cardamum, then these would have been called אהלות קקלה, "*ḳakula*-capsules," by the Heb. traders in spicery, who, as a matter of course, knew the foreign name; while, on the contrary, the people, ignoring the foreign name, would use the words אֲהָלוֹת (אֳהָלֵי) בֹּשֶׂם, "spice-capsules," or only *ahaloth.* Imported spices the people named from their appearance, without troubling themselves about their native names. An Arabian called the nutmeg *gôz-et-ṭib,* "spice-nut," which would correspond to a Heb. אֱגוֹז בֹּשֶׂם. So he called the clove-blossom *mismâr-et-ṭib,* "spice-cloves," as we do, or merely *mismâr,* "clove." The spice-merchant knows only the foreign word *gurumful,* "clove." It is very probable that *hêl,* divested of its appellative signification by the word *geras,* in process of time disappeared from the living language.

That pounded cardamum is one of the usual ingredients in Arab. coffee, we see from a poem, only a single very defective copy of which could be obtained by Wallin (*vid. Deutsch. morg. Zeit.*

vi. 373). The verse alluded to, with a few grammatical and metrical changes which were required, is as follows:

"With a pot (of coffee) in which must be cardamum and nutmeg,
And twenty cloves, the right proportion for connoisseurs."

The nut is not, as Wallin supposes, the cocoa-nut (*gôz-el-Hind*), but the nutmeg; and '*ûd* = "the small piece of wood," is the clove, as Wallin also, rightly; elsewhere '*ûd* and '*ûda* is the little stalk of the raisin.

v. 1. "Eat, friends, drink and be drunken, beloved." With רֵעִים here is compared מֵרֵעִים, Judg. xiv. 11, where thirty companions are brought to Samson when he celebrated for seven days his marriage in Timnath, the so-called bride's-men, who are called in post-bibl. Heb. שׁוֹשְׁבְּנִים, and at the present day in Syria, *shebâb el-'arîs, i.e.* the bridegroom's young men; their chief is called the *Shebîn*. "The designation 'bride's-men' (Nymphagogen) is not wholly suitable. Certainly they have also to do service to the bride; and if she is a stranger, they form the essential part of the armed escort on horseback which heads the marriage procession (*el-fârida*), and with mock fighting, which is enacted before the bride and the bride's-maids (*el-ferrâdât*), leads it into the bridegroom's village; but the chief duties of the *shebâb* on the marriage day and during the 'king's week' belong properly to the bridegroom. This escort must be an ancient institution of the country. Perhaps it had its origin in a time of general insecurity in the land, when the 'young men' formed a watch-guard, during the festival, against attacks." The names רֵעַ and מֵרֵעַ Wetzstein derives from a רִיעַ, "to be closely connected," which is nearly related to רעה; for he takes רֵיעַ, Job vi. 27, as the etymologically closer description of the former, and מֵרֵעַ (= מִרְיָע) he places parallel to the Arab. word *mirjá'*, which signifies "the inseparable companion," and among all the Syrian nomad tribes is the designation of the bell-wether, because it follows closely the steps of the shepherd, carries his bread-pouch, and receives a portion at every meal-time.

vii. 1. What would ye see in Shulamith?—
"As the dance of Mahanaim."

"The sports during the days of the marriage festival are from time to time diversified with dances. The various kinds of dances are comprehended under the general names of *sahka* and *debka*. The *sahka*, pronounced by the Beduin *sahée* (= *sahtsche*), is a graceful solitary dance, danced by a single person, or in itself not involving several persons. The *debka*, "hanging dance," because the dancers link themselves together by their little fingers; if they were linked together by their hands, this would give the opportunity of pressing hands, which required to be avoided, because Arab ladies would not permit this from men who were strangers to them. For the most part, the *debka* appears as a circular dance. If it is danced by both sexes, it is called *debka muwadda'a* = 'the variegated *debka*.' The *saḥka* must be of Beduin origin, and is accordingly always danced with a *kasidah* (poem or song) in the nomad idiom; the *debka* is the peculiar national dance of the Syrian peasantry (*Hadarî*), and the songs with which it is danced are exclusively in the language of the *Hadarî*. They have the prevailing metre of the so-called Andalusian ode (— ∪ — — | — ∪ — — | — ∪ —), and it is peculiar to the *debka*, that its strophes hang together like the links of a chain, or like the fingers of the dancers, while each following strophe begins with the words with which the preceding one closes [similar to the step-like rhythm of the psalms of degrees; *vid. Psalmen*, ii. 257]. For the *saḥka* and the *debka* they have a solo singer. Whenever he has sung a verse, the chorus of dancers and spectators takes up the *kehrvers* (*meredd*), which in the *debka* always consists of the two last lines of the first strophe of the poem. Instrumental music is not preferred in dancing; only a little timbrel (*deff*), used by the solo singer, who is not himself (or herself) dancing, gently accompanies the song to give the proper beat" (cf. Ex. xv. 20 f., and Ps. lxviii. 26).

To the *saḥka*, which is danced after a *kasidah* (for the most part with the metre — — ∪ — | — — ∪ — | — — ∪ — | — — ∪ —) without the *kehrvers* in ¾ time, belongs the sword-dance, which the bride dances on her marriage day. Wetzstein thus describes it in *Deutsch. morg. Zeit.* xxii. 106, having twice witnessed it: "The figure of the dancer (*el-hâshî*, 'she who fills the ring,' or *abû ḥᵒwêsh*, 'she who is in the ring'), the waving dark hair of her locks cast loose, her serious noble bearing, her downcast eyes, her graceful movements, the quick and secure step of her small naked feet, the lightning-like flashing of the blade, the skilful movements of her left hand, in which the dancer holds a handkerchief, the exact keeping of time, although the song of the *munshid* (the leader) becomes gradually quicker and the dance more animated—this is a scene which has imprinted itself indelibly on my memory. It is completed by the ring (*ḥᵒwêsh*), the one half of which is composed of men and the other of women. They stand upright, gently move their shoulders, and accompany the beat of the time with a swaying to and fro of the upper part of their bodies, and a gentle beating of their hands stretched upwards before their breasts. The whole scene is brightened by a fire that has been kindled. The constant repetition of the words *jâ ḥalâlî jâ mâlî*, O my own, O my possession! [*vid. Psalmen*, ii. 384, Anm.], and the sword with which the husband protects his family and his property in the hand of the maiden, give to the *saḥka*, celebrated in the days of domestic happiness, the stamp of an expression of thanks and joy over the possession of that which makes life pleasant—the family and property; for with the *Hadarî* and the *Bedawî* the word *ḥalâl* includes wife and child."

"When the *saḥka* is danced by a man, it is always a sword-dance. Only the form of this dance (it is called *saḥkat el-Gawâfina*), as it is performed in Gôf, is after the manner of the *contre*-dance, danced by two rows of men standing opposite each other. The dancers do not move their hands, but only their shoulders; the women form the ring, and sing the refrain of the song led by the *munshid*, who may here be also one of the dancers."

vii. 2. "How beautiful are thy steps in the shoes, O prince's daughter!"

After the maidenhood of the newly married damsel has been established (cf. Deut. xxii. 13–21) before the tribunal (*dîvân*) of the wedding festival, there begins a great dance; the song sung to it refers only to the young couple, and the inevitable *waṣf*, *i.e.* a description of the personal perfections and beauty of the two, forms its principal contents. Such a *waṣf* was sung also yesterday during the sword-dance of the bride; that of to-day (the first of the seven wedding-festival days) is wholly in praise of the queen; and because she is now a wife, commends more those attractions which are visible than those which are veiled. In the Song, only vii. 2–6 [1] is compared to this *waṣf*. As for the rest, it is the lovers themselves who reciprocally sing. Yet this may also have been done under the

---

[1] According to Wetzstein's opinion, v. 2 ff. is also a *waṣf*, to which the narrative, vv. 5–7, aims at giving only an agreeable commencement; the songs of the Song which he does not regard as Solomonic, nor as a dramatic united whole, particularly the *Waṣf*-portions, appear to him to have been received into the Canon in order to preserve for the people some beautiful hallowed marriage songs, and to give good examples for imitation to the occasional poets whose productions may in ancient times, among the Hebrews, as in our own day among ourselves, have overstepped the limits of propriety and good taste. The allegorical or mystical interpretation appeared later, and was in this case something lying far nearer than *e.g.* with those love-songs which were sung by the singers of the mosque of the Omajads at the festival *thalilat*, at the grave of John the Baptist. "Place, time, and circumstance," says the Damascene, "give to a song its meaning."

influence of the custom of the *waṣf*. The repetition, iv. 1–5 and vi. 4–7, are wholly after the manner of the *waṣf;* in the Syrian wedding songs also, these encomiums are after one pattern.

We quote here by way of example such an encomium. It forms the conclusion of a *saḥka*, which had its origin under the following circumstances: When, some forty years ago, the sheik of *Nawâ* gave away his daughter in marriage, she declared on her wedding day that she would dance the usual sword-dance only along with a *kasidah*, composed specially for her by a noted Hauran poet. Otherwise nothing was to be done, for the Hauranian chief admired the pride of his daughter, because it was believed it would guard her from errors, and afford security for her family honour. The most distinguished poet of the district at that time was *Kasîm el-Chinn*, who had just shortly before returned from a journey to Mesopotamia to the phylarch of the *Gerbâ* tribe, who had bestowed on him royal gifts. He lived in the district of *Gâsim*,[1] famed from of old for its poets, a mile (German) to the north of *Nawâ*. A messenger on horseback was sent for him. The poet had no time to lose; he stuck some writing materials and paper into his girdle, mounted his ass, and composed his poem whilst on the way, the messenger going before him to announce his arrival. When Ḳâsim came, the fire was already kindled on the ground, the wedding guests were waiting, and the dancer in bridal attire, and with the sword in her hand, stood ready. Ḳâsim kissed her hand and took the place of leader of the song, since from want of time no one could repeat the poem; moreover, Ḳâsim had a fine voice. When the dance was over, the bride took her *kesmâja* from off her head, folded twenty *Gâzi* (about thirty thalers) in it, and threw it to the poet,—a large present considering the circumstances, for the *kesmâja* of a rich bride is costly. On the other hand, she required the poem to be delivered up to her. The plan of the poem shows great skill. *Nawâ*, lying in the midst of the extremely fruitful Batanian plain, is interested in agriculture to an extent unequalled in any other part of Syria and Palestine; its sheik is proud of the fact that formerly Job's 500 yoke ploughed there, and *Nawâ* claims to be Job's town.[2] Since the peasant, according to the well-known proverb, *de bobus arator*, has thought and concern for nothing more than for agriculture; so the poet might

[1] Abû-Temmâm, the collector of the Hamâsa, was also a native of *Gâsim*. [*Vid.* Delitzsch's *Jud.-Arab. Poesien* of the pre-Muhammed period, p. 1.]

[2] It is not improbable that *Nawâ* is an abbreviation of נְוֵה־אִיּוֹב, as *Medina* is of *Medînat-en-Nebi*. Regarding the supposed grave of Job in the neighbourhood of *Nawâ*, vid. *Comment. on Job* by Fr. Delitzsch.

with certainty reckon on an understanding and an approbation of his poem if he makes it move within the sphere of country life. He does this. He begins with this, that a *shekâra*, *i.e.* a benefice, is sown for the dancer, which is wont to be sown only to the honour of one of great merit about the place. That the benefice might be worthy of the recipient, four *sauwâmen* (a *sauwâma* consists of six yoke) are required, and the poet has opportunity to present to his audience pleasing pictures of the great *shekâra*, of harvests, thrashings, measuring, loading, selling. Of the produce of the wheat the portion of the dancer is now bought, first the clothes, then the ornaments; both are described. The *waṣf* forms the conclusion, which is here given below. In the autumn of 1860, I received the poem from a young man of Nawâ at the same time along with other poems of Kâsim's, all of which he knew by heart. The rest are much more artistic and complete in form than the *saḥka*. Who can say how many of the (particularly metrically) weak points of the latter are to be attributed to the poet, and to the rapidity with which it was composed; and how many are to be laid to the account of those by whom it was preserved?

> " Here hast thou thy ornament, O beautiful one ! put it on, let nothing be forgotten!
> Put it on, and live when the coward and the liar are long dead.
> She said: Now shalt thou celebrate me in song, describe me in verse from head to foot!
> I say: O fair one, thine attractions I am never able to relate,
> And only the few will I describe which my eyes permit me to see:
> Her head is like the crystal goblet, her hair like the black night,
> Her black hair like the seven nights, the like are not in the whole year;[1]
> In waves it moves hither and thither, like the rope of her who draws water,
> And her side locks breathe all manner of fragrance, which kills me.
> The new moon beams on her brow, and dimly illuminated are the balances,[2]

---

[1] These seven nights are the last four of February and the first three of March (of the old calendar). They are very cloudy, rainy, and dark, and are called *el-mustaḳridât*, "the borrowing nights," either because they have a share of the clouds, rain, and darkness of all the other nights of the year, as if borrowed from them, or because the seven reciprocally dispose of their shares, so that, *e.g.*, the darkness of each of these nights is sevenfold. The frequent hail which falls during these cold disagreeable days is called " old wives' teeth " (*asnân-el-'agâiz*), because many old people die during these days.

[2] While sometimes the light of the new moon is weak and that of the balances is very strong ; the contrary is the case here. The balances are two constellations: the one is called the right balance (*mîzân-el-ḥakk*), and consists of three very bright stars; the other is called the false balance (*m. el-butl*), and consists of two bright and one dimmer star.

And her eyebrows like the arch of the *Nûn* drawn by an artist's hand.[1]
The witchery of her eyes makes me groan as if they were the eyes of a Kufic lady;[2]
Her nose is like the date of Irâk,[3] the edge of the Indian sword;
Her face like the full moon, and heart-breaking are her cheeks.
Her mouth is a little crystal ring, and her teeth rows of pearls,
And her tongue scatters pearls; and, ah me, how beautiful her lips!
Her spittle pure virgin honey, and healing for the bite of a viper.
Comparable to elegant writing, the *Seijal*[4] waves downwards on her chin,
Thus black seeds of the fragrant *Kezḥa*[5] show themselves on white bread.
The *Mâni* draws the neck down to itself with the spell written in Syrian letters;
Her neck is like the neck of the roe which drinks out of the fountain of *Kanawât*.[6]
Her breast like polished marble tablets, as ships bring them to *Ṣê lâ* (Sidon),
Thereon like apples of the pomegranate two glittering piles of jewels.
Her arms are drawn swords, peeled cucumbers—oh that I had such!
And incomparably beautiful her hands in the rose-red of the *Hinnâ*-leaf;
Her smooth, fine fingers are like the writing reed not yet cut;
The glance of her nails like the Dura-seeds which have lain overnight in milk;[7]
Her body is a mass of cotton wool which a master's hand has shaken into down,[8]
And her legs marble pillars in the sacred house of the Omajads.

---

[1] The eyebrows are compared to the arch of the Arab. letter ن inverted; this comparison, in which the rural poets imitate the insipid city poets, is only admissible when one has before him a *Nûn* written by a caligraphic hand.

[2] The eyes of the Kufic or Babylonian lady (*bâbilija*) are perfectly black, which for the Arabians are particularly dangerous. Also with the Babylonian sorceress *Zuhara*, who led astray the two angels *Hârût* and *Mârût* (vid. *Ḳorân* ii. 26), her charms lay in her black eyes.

[3] The date of 'Irâḳ is white and small, not too long and very sweet.

[4] The *Seijal* is a *daḳḳa*, i.e. a tattooed arabesque in the form of final *Mim's* (م) standing over one another. The *Mânî* (ver. 20), another *daḳḳa*, is applied to the top of the windpipe. It consists for the most part of a ring, in which is engraved as a talisman a Syrian, i.e. a feigned angel's name ending in ىٮ.

[5] The *Ḳezah*, n. unit. *Ḳezḥa*, is the *nigella sativa* with which fine pastry is sprinkled.

[6] Here it is not the well of the *Wâdy Kanawât* on the Haurân range that is meant, but the *Ḳanawât* stream, an arm of the *Baradâ*, which fills the tanks of the Damascus houses, so that the thought would be that the neck of the bride is white like that of a lady of the city, not brown like that of a peasant.

[7] The *Dura* of the Haurân is the millet, which, when laid in milk, receives a white glance, and enlarges, so that it may be compared to a finger-nail.

[8] The upholsterer (*neddâf*, usually called *ḥallâg*) has a bow above one fathom long, the string of which, consisting of a very thick gut-string, he places in contact with the wool or cotton-wool which is to be shaken loose, and then

> There hast thou, fair one, thy attractions, receive this, nothing would be forgotten,
> And live and flourish when the coward and the liar are long ago dead!"

vii. 3. "Thy body a heap of wheat, set round with lilies."

In the fifth Excursus regarding the winnowing shovel and the winnowing fork in my *Comment. on Isaiah*, Wetzstein's illustration of this figure was before me. The dissertation regarding the thrashing-table contains many instructive supplements thereto. When the grain is thrashed, from that which is thrashed (*derîs*), which consists of corn, chopped straw, and chaff, there is formed a new heap of winnowings, which is called ʽ*arama*. "According to its derivation (from ʽ*aram*, to be uncovered), ʽ*arama* means heaps of rubbish destitute of vegetation; ʽ*arama*, ʽ*oreima*, ʽ*irâm*, are, in the Haurân and Golân, proper names of several *Puys* (conical hills formed by an eruption) covered with yellow or red volcanic rubbish. In the terminology of the thrashing-floor, the word always and without exception denotes the *derîs*-heaps not yet winnowed; in the Heb., on the contrary, corn-heaps already winnowed. Such a heap serves (Ruth iii. 7) Boaz as a pillow for his head when he lay down and watched his property. Luther there incorrectly renders by 'behind a *Mandel*,' *i.e.* a heap of (fifteen) sheaves; on the contrary, correctly at the passage before us (Song vii. 3), 'like a heap of wheat,' viz. a heap of winnowed wheat. The wheat colour (*el-lôn el-ḥinṭi*) is in Syria regarded as the most beautiful colour of the human body."

strikes it with a short wooden mallet. By the violent and rapid vibration of the string, the wool, however closely it may have been pressed together and entangled, is changed with surprising quickness into the finest down.

THE BOOK OF ECCLESIASTES.

THE BOOK OF ECCLESIASTES.

INTRODUCTION.

F we look at the world without God, it appears what it is,—a magnificent, graduated combination of diverse classes of beings, connected causes and effects, well-calculated means and ends. But thus contemplated, the world as a whole remains a mystery. If, with the atheist, we lay aside the idea of God, then, notwithstanding the law of causation, which is grounded in our mental nature, we abandon the question of the origin of the world. If, with the pantheist, we transfer the idea of God to the world itself, then the effect is made to be as one with the cause,—not, however, without the conception of God, which is inalienable in man, reacting against it; for one cannot but distinguish between substance and its phenomena. The mysteries of the world which meet man as a moral being remain, under this view of the world, altogether without solution. For the moral order of the world presupposes an absolutely good Being, from whom it has proceeded, and who sustains it; it demands a Lawgiver and a Judge. Apart from the reference to this Being, the distinction between good and evil loses its depth and sharpness. Either there is no God, or all that is and happens is a moment in the being and life of God Himself, who is identical with the world: thus must the world-destructive power of sin remain unrecognised. The opinion as to the state of the world will, from a pantheistic point of view, rise to optimism; just as, on the other hand, from an atheistic point of view, it will sink to pessimism. The commanding power of goodness even the atheist may recognise by virtue of the inner law peculiar to man as a moral being, but the divine consecration is wanting to this goodness; and if human life is a journey from nothing to nothing, then this will be the best

of all goodness: that man set himself free from the evil reality, and put his confidence in nothing. "Him who views the world," says Buddhism, "as a water-bubble, a phantom, the king of death does not terrify. What pleasure, what joy is in this world? Behold the changing form—it is undone by old age; the diseased body—it dissolves and corrupts! 'I have sons and treasures; here will I dwell in the season of the cold, and there in the time of the heat:' thus thinks the fool; and cares not for, and sees not, the hindrances thereto. Him who is concerned about sons and treasures,—the man who has his heart so entangled,—death tears away, as the torrent from the forest sweeps away the slumbering village."

The view taken of the world, and the judgment formed regarding it, in the Book of Ecclesiastes, are wholly different. While in the Book of Esther faith in God remains so much in the background that there is nowhere in it express mention made of God, the name of God occurs in Ecclesiastes no fewer than thirty-seven times,[1] and that in such a way that the naming of Him is at the same time the confession of Him as the True God, the Exalted above the world, the Governor and the Ruler over all. And not only that: the book characterizes itself as a genuine product of the Israelitish Chokma by this, that, true to its motto, it places the command, "Fear thou God," v. 6 [7], xii. 13, in the foremost rank as a fundamental moral duty; that it makes, viii. 12, the happiness of man to be dependent thereon; that it makes, vii. 18, xi. 9, xii. 14, his final destiny to be conditioned by his fearing God; and that it contemplates the world as one that was created by God very good, iii. 11, vii. 29, and as arranged, iii. 14, and directed so that men should fear Him. These primary principles, to which the book again and again returns, are of special importance for a correct estimate of it.

Of like decisive importance for the right estimate of the theistic, and at the same time also the pessimistic, view of the world presented by Koheleth is this, that he knows of no future life compensating for the troubles of the present life, and resolving its mystery. It is true that he says, xii. 7, that the life-spirit of the man who dies returns to God who gave it, as the body returns to the dust of which it is formed; but the question asked in iii. 21 shows that this preferring of the life-spirit of man to that of a beast was not, in his regard, raised above all doubt. And what does this return to

---

[1] הָאֱלֹהִים, ii. 24, 26, iii. 11, 14 (twice), 15, 17, 18, iv. 17, v. 1, 5, 6, 17, 18*a*, 19, vi. 2 (twice), vii. 13, 14, 26, 29, viii. 15, 17, ix. 1, 7, xi. 5, 9, xii. 7, 13, 14. אֱלֹהִים, iii. 10, 13, v. 3, 18*b*, vii. 18, viii. 2, 13.

God mean? By no means such a return unto God as amounts to the annihilation of the separate existence of the spirit of man; for, in the first place, there is the supposition of this separate existence running through the Bible; in the second place, נתח, xii. 7*b*, does not point to an emanation; and in the third place, the idea of Hades prevailing in the consciousness of the ages before Christ, and which is also that of Koheleth, proves the contrary. Man exists also beyond the grave, but without the light and the force of thought and activity characterizing his present life, ix. 5, 10. The future life is not better, but is worse than the present, a dense darkness enduring "for ever," ix. 6, xi. 8, xii. 5*b*. It is true, indeed, that from the justice of God, and the experiences of the present life as standing in contradiction thereto, viii. 14, the conclusion is drawn, xii. 14, xi. 9, that there is a last decisive judgment, bringing all to light; but this great thought, in which the interest of the book in the progress of religious knowledge comes to a climax, is as yet only an abstract postulate of faith, and not powerful enough to brighten the future; and therefore, also, not powerful enough to lift us above the miseries of the present.

That the author gives utterance to such thoughts of the future as xii. 7 and xi. 9, xii. 14,—to which Wisd. iii. 1 ("The souls of the righteous are in God's hand, and no trouble moves them") and Dan. xii. 2 ("Many that sleep in the dust of the earth shall awake, some to everlasting life, and some to shame and everlasting contempt") are related, as being their expansion,—warrants the supposition that he disputes as little as Job does in chap. xiv. the reality of a better future; but only that the knowledge of such a future was not yet given to him. In general, for the first time in the N. T. era, the hope of a better future becomes a common portion of the church's creed, resting on the basis of faith in the history of redemption warranting it; and is advanced beyond the isolated prophetic gleams of light, the mere postulates of faith that were ventured upon, and the unconfirmed opinions, of the times preceding Christ. The N. T. Scripture shows how altogether different this world of sin and of change appears to be since a world of recompense and of glory has been revealed as its background; since the Lord has pronounced as blessed those who weep, and not those who laugh; and since, with the apostle (Rom. viii. 18), we may be convinced that the sufferings of this present time are not worthy to be compared with the glory that shall be revealed to us. The goal of human life, with its labour and its sufferings, is now carried beyond the grave. That which is done under the sun appears only as a segment of the universal and everlasting operation, governed by the wisdom of God, the separate portions of which can only be understood in their connection with the whole. The estimate taken of this present world, apart from its connection with the future, must be one-sided. There are two worlds: the future is the solution of the mystery of the present.

A N. T. believer would not be able to write such a book as that of Job, or even as that of Ecclesiastes, without sinning against revealed truth; without renouncing the better knowledge meanwhile made possible; without falling back to an O. T. standpoint. The author of the Book of Ecclesiastes is related to revealed religion in its O. T. manifestation,—he is a believer before the coming of Christ; but not such an one as all, or as most were, but of peculiar character and position. There are some natures that have a tendency to joyfulness, and others to sadness. The author of this book does not belong to the latter class; for if he did, the call to rejoice, xi. 9, viii. 15, etc., would not as it does pervade his book, as the χαίρετε, though in a deeper sense, pervades the Epistle to the Philippians. Neither does he belong to those superficial natures which see almost everything in a rosy light, which quickly and easily divest themselves of their own and of others' sorrows, and on which the stern earnestness of life can make no deep and lasting impressions. Nor is he a man of feeling, whom his own weakness makes a prophet of evil; not a predominatingly passive man, who, before he could fully know the world, withdrew from it, and now citicises it from his own retired corner in a careless, inattentive mood; but a man of action, with a penetrating understanding and a faculty of keen observation; a man of the world, who, from his own experience, knows the world on all its sides; a restless spirit, who has consumed himself in striving after that which truly satisfies. That this man, who was forced to confess that all that science and art, all that table dainties, and the love of women, and riches, and honour yielded him, was at last but vanity and vexation of spirit, and who gained so deep an insight into the transitoriness and vanity of all earthly things, into the sorrows of this world of sin and death, and their perplexing mysteries, does not yet conclude by resigning himself to atheism, putting "Nothing" (*Nirvâna*), or blind Fate, in the place of God, but firmly holds that the fear of God is the highest duty and the condition of all true prosperity, as it is the highest truth and the surest knowledge—that such is the case with him may well excite our astonishment; as well as this also, that he penetrates the known illusory character of earthly things in no overstrained manner, despising the world in itself, and also the gifts of God in it, but that he places his ultimatum as to the pure enjoyment of life within the limits of the fear of God, and extends it as widely as God permits. One might therefore call the Book of Koheleth, "The Song of the Fear of God," rather than, as H. Heine does, "The Song of Scepticism;" for however great the sorrow of the world which is therein expressed, the religious conviction of the author remains in undiminished strength; and in the midst of all the disappointments in the present world, his faith in God, and in the rectitude of God, and in the victory of the good, stands firm as a rock, against which all the waves dash themselves into foam. "This book," says another recent author,[1] "which contains almost as many contradictions as verses, may be regarded as the Breviary of the most modern materialism, and of extreme licentiousness." He who can thus speak has not read the book with intelligence. The appearance of materialism arises from this, that the author sees in the death of man an end similar to that of beasts; and that is certainly so far true, but it is not the whole truth. In the knowledge of the reverse side of the matter he does not come beyond the threshold, because His hand was not yet there—viz. the hand of the Arisen One—which could help him over it. And as for the supposed licentiousness, ix. 7-9 shows, by way of example, how greatly the fear of God had guarded him from concluding his search into all earthly things with the disgust of a worn-out libertine.

But there are certainly self-contradictions in the Book of Ecclesiastes. They have a twofold ground. They are, on the one hand, the reflection of the self-contradicting facts which the author affirms. Thus, *e.g.*, iii. 11, he says that God has set eternity in the heart of man, but that man cannot find out from the beginning to the end the work which God maketh; iii. 12, 13, that the best thing in this world is for a man to enjoy life; but to be able to do this, is a gift of God; viii. 12, 14, that it goes well with them that fear God, but ill with the godless. But there is also the contrary—which is just the ground-tone of the book, that everything has its *But;* only the fear of God, after all that appertains to the world is found to be as *vanitas vanitatum*, remains as the kernel without the shell, but the commandment of the fear of God as a categorical imperative, the knowledge that the fear of God is in itself the highest happiness, and fellowship with God the highest good, remain unexpressed; the fear of God is not combined with the love of God, as *e.g.* in Ps. lxxiii. it serves only for warning and not for comfort. On the

---

[1] Hartmann's *Das Lied vom Ewigen*, St. Galle 1859, p. 12.

other hand, the book also contains contradictions, which consist in contrasts which the author is not in a condition to explain and adjust. Thus, *e.g.*, the question whether the spirit of a dying man, in contrast to that of a beast, takes its way upwards, iii. 21, is proposed as one capable of a double answer; but xii. 7 answers it directly in the affirmative; the author has good grounds for the affirmative, but yet no absolute proofs. And while he denies the light of consciousness and the energy of activity to those who have gone down to Hades, ix. 10, he maintains that there is a final decisive judgment of a holy and righteous God of all human conduct, xi. 9, xii. 14, which, since there is frequently not a righteous requital given on earth, viii. 14, and since generally the issue here does not bring to light, ix. 2, the distinction between the righteous and the wicked, will take place in eternity; but it is difficult to comprehend how he has reconciled the possibility of such a final judgment with the shadowy nature of existence after death.

The Book of Koheleth is, on the one side, a proof of the power of revealed religion which has grounded faith in God, the One God, the All-wise Creator and Governor of the world, so deeply and firmly in the religious consciousness, that even the most dissonant and confused impressions of the present world are unable to shake it; and, on the other side, it is a proof of the inadequacy of revealed religion in its O. T. form, since the discontent and the grief which the monotony, the confusion, and the misery of this earth occasion, remain thus long without a counterbalance, till the facts of the history of redemption shall have disclosed and unveiled the heavens above the earth. In none of the O. T. books does the Old Covenant appear as it does in the Book of Koheleth, as "that which decayeth and waxeth old, and is ready to vanish away" (Heb. viii. 13). If the darkness of earth must be enlightened, then a New Covenant must be established; for heavenly love, which is at the same time heavenly wisdom, enters into human nature and overcomes sin, death, and Hades, and removes the turning-point of the existence of man from this to the future life. The finger of prophecy points to this new era. And Koheleth, from amid his heaps of ruins, shows how necessary it is that the heavens should now soon open above the earth.

It is a view of the world, dark, and only broken by scattered gleams of light, not disowning its sullenness even where it recommends the happy enjoyment of life, which runs through the book in a long series of dissonances, and gives to it a peculiar character. It is thus intentionally a homogeneous whole; but is it also divided into separate parts according to a plan? That we may be able to answer this question, we subject the contents of the book to a searching analysis, step by step, yet steadily keeping the whole in view. This will at the same time also serve as a preparation for the exposition of the book.

Here below, all things under the sun are vanity. The labour of man effects nothing that is enduring, and all that is done is only a beginning and a vanishing away again, repeating itself in a never-ending circle: these are the thoughts of the book which stand as its motto, i. 2—11.

Koheleth-Solomon, who had been king, then begins to set forth the vanity of all earthly things from his own experience. The striving after secular knowledge, i. 12 ff., has proved to him unsatisfactory, as has also the striving after happiness in pleasure and in procuring the means of all imaginable gratifications, ii. 1—11; wisdom is vanity, for the wise man falls under the stroke of death as well as the fool, and is forgotten, ii. 12—17; and riches are vanity, for they become the inheritance, one knows not whether of a worthy or of an unworthy heir, ii. 18—21; and, besides, pure enjoyment, like wisdom and knowledge, depends not merely on the will of man, but both are the gift of God, ii. 22 ff. Everything has its time appointed by God, but man is unable to survey either backwards or forwards the work of God, which fills eternity, notwithstanding the impulse to search into it which is implanted within him; his dependence in all things, even in pure enjoyment, must become to him a school in which to learn the fear of God, who maintains all things unchangeably, who forms the course of that which is done, iii. 1—15. If he sees injustice prevailing in the place of justice, God's time for righteous interference has not yet come, iii. 16, 17. If God wishes to try men, they shall see that they are dependent like the beasts, and liable to death without any certain distinction from the beasts—there is nothing better than that this fleeting life should be enjoyed as well as may be, iii. 18 ff.

Koheleth now further records the evils that are under the sun: oppression, in view of which death is better than life, and not to have been at all is better than both, iv. 1—3; envy, iv. 4; the restlessness of labour, from which only the fool sets himself free, iv. 5, 6; the aimless trouble and parsimony of him who stands alone, iv. 7—12; the disappointment of the hopes placed on an upstart who has reached the throne, iv. 13—16.

Up to this point there is connection. There now follow rules, externally unconnected, for the relation of man to Him who is the Disposer of all things; regarding his frequenting the house of God, iv. 17 [v. 1]; prayer, v. 2; and praise, v. 3—6.

Then a catalogue of vanities is set forth: the insatiable covetous plundering of the lowly by those who are above them in despotic states, whereat the author praises, v. 7, 8, the patriarchal state based on agriculture; and the nothingness and uncertainty of riches, which do not make the rich happier than the labourer, v. 9–11; which sometimes are lost without any to inherit them, v. 12–14; and which their possessor, at all events, must leave behind him when he dies, v. 15, 16. Riches have only a value when by means of them a purer enjoyment is realized as the gift of God, v. 17 ff. For it happens that God gives to a man riches, but to a stranger the enjoyment thereof, vi. 1, 2. An untimely birth is better than a man who has an hundred children, a long life, and yet who has no enjoyment of life even to his death, vi. 3–6. Desire stretching on into the future is torment; only so much as a man truly enjoys has he of all his labour, vi. 7–9; what man shall be is predestinated, all contendings against it are useless: the knowledge of that which is good for him, and of the future, is in the power of no man, vi. 10 ff.

There now follow, without a premeditated plan, rules for the practical conduct of life, loosely connecting themselves with the "what is good," vi. 12, by the catchword "good:" first six (probably originally seven) proverbs of two things each, whereof the one is better than the other, vii. 1–9; then three with the same catchword, but without comparison, vii. 10, 11–12, 13–14. This series of proverbs is connected as a whole, for their ultimatum is a counsel to joy regulated by the fear of God within the narrow limits of this life, constituted by God of good and bad days, and terminating in the darkness of death. But this joy is also itself limited, for the deep seriousness of the *memento mori* is mingled with it, and sorrow is declared to be morally better than laughter.

With vii. 15, the *I*, speaking from personal experience, again comes into the foreground; but counsels and observations also here follow each other aphoristically, without any close connection with each other. Koheleth warns against an extreme tendency to the side of good as well as to that of evil: he who fears God knows how to avoid extremes, vii. 15–18. Nothing affords a stronger protection than wisdom, for (?) with all his righteousness a man makes false steps, vii. 19, 20. Thou shalt not always listen, lest thou hear something about thyself,—also thou thyself hast often spoken harshly regarding others, vii. 21, 22. He has tried everything, but in his strivings after wisdom, and in his observation of the distinction between wisdom and folly, he has found nothing more dangerous than the snares of women; among a thousand men he found one man; but one woman such as she ought to be, he found not; he found in general that God made men upright, but that they have devised many kinds of by-ways, vii. 23 ff.

As the wise man considers women and men in general, wisdom teaches him obedience to the king to whom he has sworn fealty, and, under despotic oppression, patient waiting for the time of God's righteous interference, viii. 1–9. In the time of despotic domination, it occurs that the godless are buried with honour, while the righteous are driven away and forgotten, viii. 10. God's sentence is to be waited for, the more deliberately men give themselves to evil; God is just, but, in contradiction to His justice, it is with the righteous as with the wicked, and with the wicked as with the righteous, here on earth, viii. 11–14. In view of these vanities, then, it is the most desirable thing for a man to eat and drink, and enjoy himself, for that abides with him of his labour during the day of his life God has given him, viii. 15. Restless labour here leads to nothing; all the efforts of man to comprehend the government of God are in vain, viii. 16 ff. For on closer consideration, it appears that the righteous also, with all their actions, are ruled by God, and generally that in nothing, not even in his affections, is man his own master; and, which is the worst thing of all, because it impels men to a wicked, mad abuse of life, to the righteous and the unrighteous, death at last comes alike; it is also the will of God towards man that he should spend this transient life in cheerful enjoyment and in vigorous activity before it sinks down into the night of Hades, ix. 1–10. The fruits of one's labour are not to be gained by force, even the best ability warrants it not, an incomprehensible fate finally frustrates all, ix. 11, 12.

There now follows, but in loose connection as to thought with the preceding, a section relating to wisdom and folly, and the discordances as to the estimate of both here below, along with diverse kinds of experiences and proverbs, ix. 13–x. 15. Only one proverb is out of harmony with the general theme, viz. x. 4, which commends resignation under the ebullition of the wrath of the ruler. The following proverb, x. 5, 6, returns to the theme, but connecting itself with the preceding; the relation of rulers and the ruled to each other is kept principally in view by Koheleth.

With a proverb relating to kings and princes, good and bad, a new departure is made. Riotous living leads to slothfulness; and in contrast to this (but not without the intervention of a warning not to curse the king) follow exhortations to provident, and, at the same time, bold and all-attempting activity; for the future is God's, and not to be reckoned on, x. 16–xi. 6. The light is sweet; and life, however long it may last, in view of the uncertain dark future, is worthy of being enjoyed, xi. 7, 8. Thus Koheleth, at the end of this last series of proverbs, has again reached his *Ceterum censeo;* he formulates it, in an exhortation to a young man to enjoy his life—but without forgetting God, to whom he owes it, and to whom he has to render an account—before grey-haired old age and death overtake him, into a full-toned *finale,* xi. 9–xii. 7. The last word of the book, xii. 8, is parallel with the first (i. 1): "O! vanity of vanities; All is vain!"

An epilogue, from the same hand as the book, seals its truth: it is written as from the very soul of Solomon; it issues from the same fountain of wisdom. The reader must not lose himself in reading many books, for the sum of all knowledge that is of value to man is comprehended in one sentence: "Fear God, for He shall bring every work into judgment," xii. 9 ff.

If we look back on this compendious reproduction of the contents and of the course of thought of the book, there appears everywhere the same view of the world, along with the same *ultimatum;* and as a pictorial *overture* opens the book, a pictorial *finale* closes it. But a gradual development, a progressive demonstration, is wanting, and so far the grouping together of the parts is not fully carried out; the connection of the thoughts is more frequently determined by that which is external and accidental, and not unfrequently an incongruous element is introduced into the connected course of kindred matters. The Solomonic stamp impressed on chap. i. and ii. begins afterwards to be effaced. The connection of the confessions that are made becomes aphoristic in chap. iii.; and the proverbs that are introduced do not appropriately fall into their place. The grounds, occasions, and views which determine the author to place confessions and moral proverbs in such an order after one another, for the most part withdraw themselves from observation. All attempts to show, in the whole, not only oneness of spirit, but also a genetic progress, an all-embracing plan, and an organic connection, have hitherto failed, and must fail.[1]

---

[1] "*Ajunt Hebraei, quum inter cetera scripta Salomonis, quae antiquata sunt nec in memoria duraverunt, et hic liber obliterandus videretur, et quod vanas assereret Dei creaturas et totum putaret esse pro nihilo, et potum et cibum et delicias transeuntes praeferret omnibus, ex hoc uno capitulo* (xii. 13) *meruisse auctoritatem, ut in divinorum voluminum numero poneretur.*"—JEROME.

In presenting this view of the spirit and plan of the Book of Koheleth, we have proceeded on the supposition that it is a post-exilian book, that it is one of the most recent of the books of the O. T. It is true, indeed, that tradition regards it as Solomonic. According to *Bathra* 15*a*, the Hezekiah - *Collegium* [*vid.* Del. on *Proverbs*, vol. I. p. 5] must have "written"—that is, collected into a written form—the Book of Isaiah, as also of the Proverbs, the Song, and Koheleth. The Midrash regards it as Solomon's, and as written in the evening of his days; while the Song was written in his youth, and the Proverbs when he was in middle age (*Jalkut*, under i. 1). If in *Rosch haschana* 21*b* it is said that Koheleth sought to be a second Moses, and to open the one of the fifty gates of knowledge which was unopened by Moses, but that this was denied to him, it is thereby assumed that he was the incomparable king, as Moses was the incomparable prophet. And Bloch, in his work on the origin and era of the Book of Koheleth (1872), is right in saying that all objections against the canonicity of the book leave the Solomonic authorship untouched. In the first Christian century, the Book of Koheleth was an *antilegomenon*. In the Introduction to the Song (p. 14) we have traced to their sources the two collections of legal authorities according to which the question of the canonicity of the Book of Koheleth is decided. The Synod of Jabne (Jamnia), about 90, decided the canonicity of the book against the school of Shammai. The reasons advanced by the latter against the canonicity are seen from *Shabbath* 30*b*, and *Megilla* 7*a*. From the former we learn that they regarded the words of the book, particularly ii: 2 (where they must have read מְהֻלָּל, "worthy to be praised"), cf. vii. 3, and viii. 15, cf. 22, as contradictory (cf. *Proverbs*, vol. I. p. 44); and from the latter, that they hence did not recognise its inspiration. According to the *Midrash Koheleth*, under xi. 9, they were stumbled also by the call to the enjoyment of pleasure, and to walk in the way of the desire of the heart, which appeared to stand in contradiction to the *Tôra* (cf. xi. 9 with Num. xv. 39), and to savour of heresy. But belief in the Solomonic authorship remained, notwithstanding, uninjured; and the admonitions to the fear of God, with reference to the future judgment, carried them over the tendency of these observations. Already, at the time of Herod the Great (*Bathra* 4*a*), and afterwards, in the time of R. Gamaliel (*Shabbath* 30*b*), the book was cited as Holy Scripture; and when, instead of the book, the author was named, the formula of citation mentioned the name of Solomon; or the book was treated as equally Solomonic with Proverbs and the Song (*Erubin* 21*b*).

Even the doubtfulness of its contents could give rise to no manner of doubt as to the author. Down till the new era beginning with Christianity, and, in the main, even till the Reformation-century, no attention was paid to the inner and historico-literary marks which determine the time of the origin of a book. The Reformation first called into existence, along with the criticism of dogmatic traditions, at the same time also biblical criticism, which it raised to the place of an essential part of the science of Scripture. Luther, in his *Tischreden* (*Table-Talk*), is the first who explained the Preacher as one of the most recent books of the O. T.: he supposed that the book had not reached us in its completed form; that it was written by Sirach rather than by Solomon; and that it might be, "as a Talmud, collected from many books, perhaps from the library of King Ptolemy Euergetes, in Egypt."[1] These are only passing utterances, which have no scientific value; among his contemporaries, and till the middle of the century following, they found no acceptance. Hugo Grotius (1644) is the first who, like Luther, rejects its Solomonic authorship, erroneously supposing, with him, that it is a collection of diverse sayings of the wise, περὶ τῆς εὐδαιμονίας; but on one point he excellently hits the nail on the head: *Argumentum ejus rei habeo multa vocabula, quae non alibi quam in Daniele, Esdra et Chaldaeis interpretibus reperias.* This observation is warranted. If the Book of Koheleth were of old Solomonic origin, then there is no history of the Hebrew language. But Bernstein (*Quaestiones nonnullae Kohelethanae*, 1854) is right in saying that the history of the Hebrew language and literature is certainly divided into two epochs by the Babylonish exile, and that the Book of Koheleth bears the stamp of the post-exilian form of the language.

List of the Hapaxlegomena, and of the Words and Forms in the Book of Koheleth belonging to a more recent Period of the Language.

Aviyonah, xii. 5; cf. Ma'seroth iv. 6, Berachoth 36a.
Adam, opp. ishah, only at vii. 28.
Izzen, Pi., only xii. 9; not Talm.
אִ, x. 16; אִילוּ, iv. 10, instead of the older אוּ; cf. הִי, Ezek. ii. 10; like אִ לְ, Shemoth rabba, c. 46; אִ מִ, "Alas, how bad!"

---

[1] *Tischreden*, ed. Förstemann-Bindseil, p. 400 f. The expression here almost appears as if Luther had confounded *Ecclesiastes* (Koheleth) with *Ecclesiasticus* (Sirach). At a later period he maintained that the book contained a collection of Solomonic sayings, not executed, however, by Solomon himself.

Targ. Jer. ii., Lev. xxvi. 29; אי ע׳, "Alas for the meek!" *Berachoth* 6b; cf. *Sanhedrin* 11a.

Illu, "if," vi. 6; Esth. vii. 4, of אם (אין) and לו (לא, read לֹא, Ezek. iii. 6); Targ. Deut. xxxii. 29 = Heb. לו, common in the Mishna, *e.g. Maccoth* i. 10.

Asurim, only vii. 26; cf. Judg. xv. 14; *Seder olam rabba*, c. 25; cf. at iv. 14.

Baale asupoth, only xii. 11; cf. *Sanhedrin* 12a, *Jer. Sanhedrin* x. 1.

Bihel, only v. 1, vii. 9; as *Hiph.* Esth. vi. 14; cf. the transitive use of the *Pih.* Esth. ii. 9, like Targ. *bahel* (= *ithbᵉhel*) and *bᵉhilu,* haste.

Bur, only ix. 1; cf. the Talm. *al buriv,* altogether free from error and sin.

Bᵉhuroth, only xi. 9, xii. 1; cf. *Mibᵉhurav,* Num. xi. 28.

Batel, xii. 3; elsewhere only in the Chald. of Ezra; common in the Mishna, *e.g. Aboth* i. 5.

Beth olam (cf. Ezek. xxvi. 20), xii. 5; cf. *Tosifta Berachoth* iii., Targ. Isa. xiv. 18, xlii. 11.

Bᵉchen, viii. 10; Esth. iv. 16; elsewhere only Targ., *e.g.* Isa. xvi. 5.

Baal hallashon, x. 11; cf. *baal bashar,* corpulent, *Berachoth* 13b; *baal hahhotam,* the large-nosed, carrying the nose high, *Taanith* 29a.

Gibber, only at x. 10, to exert oneself; elsewhere: to prevail.

Gummats, only x. 8, Syr., and in the Targ. of the Hag. (cf. Targ. Ps. vii. 16).

Divrath, vid. under ש.

Hoveh, ii. 22; cf. *Shabbath* vi. 6, *Erubin* i. 10, *Jebamoth* xv. 2.

Holeloth, i. 17, ii. 12, vii. 25, ix. 3; and *holeluth,* madness, only in the Book of Koheleth, x. 13.

Zichron, as primary form, i. 11, ii. 16; *vid.* at Lev. xxiii. 24, the connecting form.

Zᵉman, iii. 1; Neh. ii. 6; Esth. ix. 27, 31; elsewhere only in the bib. Chald. with שָׁעָה, ὥρα, the usual Mishnic word for καιρός and χρόνος.

Holah (*malum*), *aegrum,* v. 12, 15; for this *nahhlah* is used in Isa. xvii. 11; Nah. iii. 19; Jer. x. 19, xiv. 17.

Ben-hhorim (*liber,* in contrast to *ĕvĕd, servus*), x. 17; cf. חרות (freedom) on the coins of the Revolution of the Roman period; the usual Talm. word, even of possessions, such as *praedium liberum, aedes liberae* of the Roman law.

Hhuts min, only at ii. 25 (Chald. *bar min*); frequent in the Mishna, *e.g. Middoth* ii. 3.

Hhush, ii. 25; in the Talm. and Syr. of sorrowful experiences; here (cf. Job xx. 2), of the experiences derived from the senses, and experiences in general, as in the Rabb. the five senses are called חושים.

Hhayalim, x. 10 ; everywhere else, also in Aram., meaning war-hosts, except at Isa. xxx. 6, where it denotes *opes*, treasures.

Hhesron, i. 15, a common word in the post-bibl. language.[1]

Hēphĕts, iii. 1, 17, v. 7, viii. 6 ; cf. Isa. lviii. 3, 13. The primary unweakened meaning is found at v. 3, xii. 1, 10. The weakening of the original meaning may have already early begun ; in the Book of Koheleth it has advanced as far as in the language of the Mishna, *e.g. Mezia* iv. 6.

Hheshbon, vii. 25, 27, ix. 10. Plur. at vii. 29, *machinationes ;* only in 2 Chron. xxvi. 15 in the sense of *machinae bellicae ;* but as in Koheleth, so also in *Shabbath* 150*a*.

Hhathhhatim, only at xii. 5.

Tahhanah, xii. 4 ; cf. *tᵉhhon*, Lam. v. 3, which is foreign to the Mishna, but is used as corresponding to the older *rehhaim*, in the same way as the vulgar Arab. *mathanat* and *tahwan*, instead of the older *raha*.[2]

יאשׁ, *Pih.*, only ii. 20. Talm. *Nithpa.* נִתְיָאֵשׁ, to abandon hope, *e.g. Kelim* xxvi. 8.

Yᵉgiyah, only xii. 12 ; an abstract such as may be formed from all verbs, and particularly is more frequently formed in the more modern than in the more ancient language.

Yother, as a participial adj.: "that which remains" (cf. 1 Sam. xv. 15) = "gain," vi. 11, vii. 11 ; or "superiority," vi. 8. As an adv.: "more" (cf. Esth. vi. 6), "particularly," ii. 15, vii. 16 ; xii. 9, xii. 12. In the Talm. Heb., used in the sense of "remaining over" (*Kiddushin* 24*b*) ; and as an adv., in the sense of *plus* or *magis* (*e.g. Chullin* 57*b*).

Yaphĕh, iii. 11, v. 17, as *e.g. Jer. Pesachim* ix. 9 (*b. Pesachim* 99*a*) : "Silence is well-becoming (יפה) the wise ; how much more fools !"

Yithron, ii. 13 (twice), vii. 12 (synon. *mothar*, iii. 1) ; more frequently "real gain," i. 3, ii. 11, iii. 9, v. 15, x. 10 ; "superiority and gain," v. 8. Peculiar (= Aram. *yuthran*) to the Book of Koheleth, and in Rabb., whence it is derived.

Kᵉĕhhad, xi. 6, Isa. lxv. 25, Chron., Ezra, Nehem., the Chald. *kahhada ;* Syr. *okchado;* frequent in the Mish., *e.g. Bechoroth* vii. 4 ; *Kilajim* i. 9.

---

[1] Vid. my *Geschichte der jüd. Poesie*, p. 187 f.
[2] Vid. Eli Smith in my *Jud.-Arab. Poesien aus vormuh. Zeit.* (1874), p. 40.

INTRODUCTION. 193

Kᵉvar, adv., i. 10, ii. 12, 16, iii. 15, iv. 2, vi. 10, ix. 6, 7; common in the Mishna, *e.g. Erubin* iv. 2, *Nedarim* v. 5; in Aram., more frequently in the sense of "perhaps" than of "formerly."

Kasher, xi. 6, Esth. viii. 5; in the Mishna, the word commonly used of that which is legally admissible; *Hiph.* verbal noun, *hachshēr*, only at x. 10; in the Mishna, of arranging according to order; in the superscription of the tract, *macshirin*, of making susceptible of uncleanness. Cf. *e.g. Menachoth* 48*b*. The word is generally pointed הֶכְשֵׁר, but more correctly הַכְשֵׁר.¹

Kishron, only at ii. 21, iv. 4, v. 10; not found in the Mishna.

Lᵉvad, tantummodo, vii. 29; similar, but not quite the same, at Isa. xxvi. 13.

Lăhăg, exclusively xii. 12; not Talm.; from the verb *lāhăg* (R. לה), to long eagerly for; Syr. *lahgoz*, vapour (of breathing, exhalare); cogn. *higgāyon* (hĕgĕh), according to which it is explained in *Jer. Sanhedrin* x. 1 and elsewhere.

Lavah, viii. 15, as in the Mishna: to conduct a guest, to accompany a traveller; whence the proverb: לוואיי לוניה, he who gives a convoy to the dead, to him it will be given, *Kethuboth* 72*a*; cf. שם לוּגי, a standing surname, *Negaïm* xiv. 6.

Mᵉdinah, v. 7, and in no book besides before the Exile.

Madda', x. 20; elsewhere only in the Chron. and Dan.; Targ. מַנְדַּע.

Mᵉleah, gravida, only xi. 5, as in the Mishna, *e.g. Jebamoth* xvi. 1.

Mălāk, v. 5; cf. Mal. ii. 7, in the sense of the later *shᵉluahh shamaïm*, delegated of God.²

Miskēn, only iv. 13, ix. 15, 16; but cf. *miskenuth*, Deut. viii. 9, and *mᵉsukan*, Isa. xl. 20.

Masmᵉroth, xii. 11 = מַסְ׳, Jer. x. 4; cf. Isa. xli. 7; 1 Chron. xxii. 3; 2 Chron. iii. 9.

Mᵉattim, v. 1; a plur. only at Ps. cix. 8.

Mikrĕh, more frequently in the Book of Koheleth than in any other book; and at iii. 19, used as explained in the Comm.

Mērots, exclusively ix. 11 (elsewhere *mᵉrutsah*).

Māshăk, ii. 3; cf. *Chagiga* 14*a*, *Sifri* 135*b*, ed. Friedmann.

Mishlahhath, viii. 8 (cf. Ps. lxxviii. 49).

Nāgă', *Hiph.* with *ĕl*, viii. 14, as at Esth. ix. 26; Aram. מְטָא לְ, *e.g.* Targ. Jer. to Ex. xxxiii. 13.

---
¹ *Vid.* my *Heb. Römerbrief*, p. 79. Cf. Stein's *Talm. Termin.* (1869), under כָּשֵׁר and הֶכְשֵׁר.

² *Vid.* my "Discussion der Amtsfrage in Mishna u. Gemara," *Luth. Zeitsch.* (1854), pp. 446–449.

ECCLES.

Nāhăg, ii. 3, as in the Mishna, *e.g. Aboda Zara* iii. 4, 54*b*; cf. Targ. Koh. x. 4.

Nahhath, vi. 5, as in the common phrase *nahhath ruahh*; cf. 'נוח לו וגו, "It were better for him," etc., *Jer. Berachoth* i. 2. This נח לו, for Koheleth's נחת לו, is frequent.

Nātă', xii. 11 (for which, Isa. xxii. 23, *tākă*'; Mishna, קבע; *Jer. Sanhedrin* x. 1), as Dan. xi. 45.

סבל, *Hithpa.*, only at xii. 5.

Sof, iii. 11, vii. 2, xii. 13; Joel ii. 20; 2 Chron. xx. 16, the more modern word which later displaced the word *ahharith*, vii. 8, x. 13 (cf. *Berachoth* i. 1), but which is not exactly equivalent to it; for *sof dāvār*, xii. 13,[1] which has the meaning of *summa summarum, ahharith davar*, would be inapplicable.

Sāchāl, ii. 19, vii. 17, x. 3 (twice), 14; Jer. iv. 22, v. 21; in the Book of Koheleth, the synon. of the yet more frequently used כְּסִיל, the Targ. word.

Sěchěl, exclusively x. 6.

Sichluth, i. 17 (here with שׂ), ii. 3, 12, 13, vii. 25, x. 1, 13 (synon. *kěsiluth*, Prov. ix. 13).

סכן, *Niph.* x. 9; cf. *Berachoth* i. 3. The Targ.-Talm. *Ithpa.* אִסְתַּכַּן, "to be in danger," corresponds with the *Niph.*

'Avād, exclusively ix. 1, like the Syr. *'bad*, Jewish-Aram. עוֹבֵד.

'Adĕn (formed of עַד־הֵן), *adhuc*, with לֹא, *nondum*, iv. 3.

'Adĕnāh (of *ăd-hēnnāh*), *adhuc*, iv. 2; Mishnic עֲדַיִן, *e.g. Nedarim* xi. 10.

עות, *Hithpa.* only at xii. 3.

'Amăd, ii. 9, viii. 3, as Jer. xlviii. 11; Ps. cii. 27.

Ummăth, *vid.* under שׁ.

'Anāh, v. 19, x. 19.

Inyān, exclusively in the Book of Koheleth, i. 13, ii. 23, 26, iii. 10, iv. 8, v. 2, 13, viii. 16, one of the most extensive words of the post-bibl. Heb.; first, of the object of employment, *e.g. Kiddushin* 6*a*, "occupied with this object;" also Aram. *Bathra* 114*b*.

'Atsăltăyim, double impurity, *i.e.* where the one hand is as impure as the other, only at x. 18.

'Asāh, with *lĕhhĕm*, x. 19, as at Dan. v. 1: *ăvăd lĕhhĕm*; in the N. T. Mark vi. 21, ποιεῖν δεῖπνον. Otherwise Ezek. iv. 15, where *asah lehhem* is used of preparing food. With the obj. of the time of life, vi. 12; cf. Acts xv. 33. With *tov*, not

[1] Vid. *Heb. Römerbrief*, pp. 81, 84.

INTRODUCTION. 195

only "to do good," vii. 20, but also "to act well," "to spend a pleasant life," iii. 12.

Pardēs (Song iv. 13; Neh. ii. 8), plur. ii. 5, flower-gardens, parks, as *Mezīʿa* 103*a*, פרדיסי.

Pēshĕr, *explicatio*, viii. 1, elsewhere only in the Chald. parts of Dan. Aram. for the older פִּתְרוֹן and שֵׁבֶר, of which the Targ. word is פְּשַׁר and פּוּשָׁרָן, Talm. פְּשָׁרָה, "adjustment of a controverted matter."

Pithgam in the Chald. parts of Ezra and Daniel, but only as a Hebraised Persian word in viii. 11, Esth. i. 20; common in the Targ. and in the Syr., but not in the Talm.

Kilkăl (*Kālāl*, Ezek. i. 7; Dan. x. 6), exclusively at x. 10 (on the contrary, at Ezek. xxi. 26, it means "to agitate").

Rᵉuth, only v. 10; *Keri*, for which *Chethîb* רָאִית, which may be read רָאִיַת, רָאִיַת (cf. Ezek. xxviii. 17), or רְאִיַת; the latter two of these forms are common in the Mishna, and have there their special meanings proceeding from the fundamental idea of seeing.

רדף, *Niph. part.*, only iii. 15.

Rᵉuth, besides the Chald. parts of Ezra, occurs only seven times in the Book of Koheleth, i. 14, ii. 11, 17, 26, iv. 4, 6, vi. 9.

Ra⁽yon, i. 17, ii. 22, iv. 16; elsewhere only in the Chald. parts of Daniel and in the Targ.

שׁ, this in and of itself is in no respect modern, but, as the Babyl.-Assyr. *sa*, the Phoen. אש, shows, is the relative (originally demonstrative) belonging to the oldest period of the language, which in the Mishna has altogether supplanted the אֲשֶׁר of the older Heb. book-language. It is used in the Book of Koheleth quite in the same way as in the Mishna, but thus, that it stands first on the same line (rank) with אשר, and makes it doubtful whether this or that which occurs more frequently in the book (שׁ, according to Herzfeld, 68 times, and אשר 89 times) has the predominance (cf. *e.g.* i. 13 f., viii. 14, x. 14, where both are used *promiscue*). The use of *asher* as a relative pronoun and relative conjunction is not different from the use of this in the older literature: *'ad asher lo*, in the sense of "before," xii. 1, 2, 6, Mishnic עד שלא, is only a natural turn to the fundamental meaning "till that not" (2 Sam. xvii. 13; 1 Kings xvii. 17); and *mibᵉli asher lo* = *nisi quod non*, iii. 11 (cf. *bilti*, Dan. xi. 18), for which the Mishnic ובלבד שלא (*e.g. Erubin* i. 10), is only accidentally not further demonstrable. But how far the use of שׁ has extended, will be seen by the following survey, from which we exclude שׁ, standing alone as a relative pronoun or relative conjunction:—

Beshekvar, ii. 16. *Beshel asher, eo quod*, viii. 17 (cf. Jonah i. 7, 8, 12), corresponding to the Talm. בְּדִיל דְּ. *Kol* שׁ, ii. 7, 9, and xi. 8. *Kol-ummath* שׁ, v. 15, corresponding to the Chald. *kol-kavel* דִּי, Dan. ii. 40, etc. כְּשׁ, v. 14, xii. 7, and in the sense of *quum*, ix. 12, x. 3. *mah-*שׁ, i. 9, iii. 15, vi. 10, vii. 24, viii. 7, x. 14; *meh* שׁ, iii. 22. מִשּׁ, v. 4. *'Al-divrath shello*, vii. 14 (cf. iii. 18, viii. 2). *Shĕgam*, ii. 15, viii. 14.

Shiddah and plur. *Shiddoth*, exclusively ii. 8.

Shaharuth, exclusively xi. 10, to be understood after *Nedarim* iii. 8, "the black-headed," opposed to בעלי השיבות, "the grey-haired."

שׂכח, *Hithpa.*, only viii. 10, the usual word in the Talm., *e.g. Sanhedrin* 13*b*.

Shalat, ii. 19, viii. 9, besides only in Nehemiah and Esther (cf. *Bechoroth*, vii. 6, etc.); *Hiph.* v. 18, vi. 2, elsewhere only Ps. cxix. 133.

Shilton, viii. 4, 8, nowhere else in O. T. Heb., but in the Mishna, *e.g. Kiddushin* iii. 6.

Shallith, with בּ, only viii. 8 (cf. Ezek. xvi. 30); on the contrary, vii. 19, x. 5, as Gen. xlii. 6, in the political signification of a ruler.

שׁמם, *Hithpo.*, vii. 16.

Shiphluth, x. 18, elsewhere only Targ. Jer. xlix. 24.

Shithi, only x. 17.

Tahath hashshĕmĕsh, i. 3, agreeing with the Greek ὑφ' ἡλίῳ, or ὑπὸ τὸν ἥλιον.

Takkiph, in O. T. Heb. only vi. 10; elsewhere in the Chald., Targ., Talm.

Takan, i. 15; *Pih.* vii. 13, xii. 9, a Mishna-word used in the *Pih.* and *Hiph.*, whence *tikkun* ("putting right," *e.g.* in the texthist. *terminus technicus, tikkun sopherim*, and " arrangement," *e.g. Gittin* iv. 2, " the ordering of the world ") and *tikkānāh* (*e.g. Gittin* iv. 6, " welfare," frequently in the sense of " direction," " arrangement ").

This survey of the forms peculiar to the Book of Koheleth, and only found in the most recent books of the O. T., partly only in the Chaldee portions of these, and in general use in the Aramaic, places it beyond all doubt that in this book we have a product of the post-exilian period, and, at the earliest, of the time of Ezra-Nehemiah. All that Wagenmann (*Comm.* 1856), von Essen (*Der Predeger Salomo's*, 1856), Böhl (*De Aramaismis libri Coheleth*, 1860), Hahn (*Comm.* 1860), Reusch (*Tübinger Quartalschr.* 1860), Warminski (*Verfasser u. Abfassungszeit des B. Koheleth*, 1867), Prof. Taylor Lewis (in the American ed. of Lange's *Bibelwerk*, 1869), Schäfer (*Neue Untersuchungen ü d. B. Koheleth*, 1870), Vegni (*L'Ecclesiaste secondo il testo Ebraico*, Florenz 1871) have advanced to the contrary, rests on grounds that are altogether untenable. If we possessed the original work of Sirach, we should then see more distinctly than from fragments[1] that the form of the language found in Koheleth, although older, is yet one that does not lie much further back; it is connected, yet loosely, with the old language, but at the same time it is in full accord with that new Heb. which we meet with in the Mishna and the Barajtha-Literature, which groups itself around it. To the modern aspects of the Heb. language the following forms belong:—

1. Verbs *Lamed-Aleph*, which from the first interchange their forms with those of verbs *Lamed-He*, are regularly treated in certain forms of inflexion in the Mishna as verbs *Lamed-He*; e.g. יָצְאָה is not used, but יָצְתָה.[2] This interchange of forms found in the later language reveals itself here in יצא, x. 5, used instead of יָצָאת; and if, according to the Masora, חוֹטֵא (חֹטֵא) is to be always written like מוֹצֵא at vii. 26 (except vii. 26b), the traditional text herein discloses a full and accurate knowledge of the linguistic character of the book. The Aram. יִשְׁנָא for יִשְׁנֶה, at viii. 1, is not thus to be accounted for.

2. The richness of the old language in mood-forms is here disappearing. The optative of the first person (the cohortative) is only represented by אֶחְכָּמָה, vii. 23. The form of the subjunctive (jussive) is found in the prohibitive clauses, such as vii. 16, 17, 18, x. 4; but elsewhere the only certain examples found are שֶׁיִּקַּח, *quod auferat secum*, v. 14, and וַיַּגֵּד, x. 10. In xii. 7, וְיָשֹׁב may also be read, although וְיָשֻׁב, under the influence of "ere ever" (xii. 6), is also admissible. On the contrary, יְהוּא, xi. 3, is indic. after the Mishn. יְהֵא, and so also is וְיָנֵץ (derived from נֵץ, not נוץ), xii. 5. Yet more characteristic, however, is the circumstance that the historic tense,

---
[1] *Vid.* the collection of the Heb. fragments of the Book of Ben-Sira in my *Gesch. der jüd. Poesie*, p. 204 f.

[2] *Vid.* Geiger's *Lehrbuch der Mishna-Sprache*, p. 46.

the so-called *fut. consecutivum*, which has wholly disappeared from the Mishna-language, also here, notwithstanding the occasions for its frequent use, occurs only three times, twice in the unabbreviated form, iv. 1, 7, and once in the form lengthened by the intentional *ah*, i. 17, which before its disappearance was in frequent use. It probably belonged more to the written than to the spoken language of the people (cf. the Song vi. 9*b*).

3. The complexion of the language peculiar to the Book of Koheleth is distinguished also by this, that the designation of the person already contained in the verbal form is yet particularly expressed, and without there being a contrast occasioning this emphasis, by the personal pronoun being added to and placed after it, *e.g.* i. 16, ii. 1, 11, 12, 13, 15, 18, 20, iii. 17, 18, iv. 1, 4, 7, v. 17, vii. 25, viii. 15, ix. 15. Among the more ancient authors, Hosea has the same peculiarity (cf. the Song v. 5); but there the personal pronoun stands always before the verb, *e.g.* viii. 13, xii. 11. The same thing is found in Ps. xxxix. 11, lxxxii. 6, etc. The inverse order of the words is found only at ii. 14, after the scheme of Job i. 15, as also ii. 15 follows the scheme of Gen. xxiv. 27. Mishna-forms of expressions such as מוֹדְרַנִי, *Nedarim* i. 1, מְקַבְּלָנִי, *Jebamoth* xvi. 7, are not homogeneous with that manner of subordinating the personal pronoun (cf. vii. 26, iv. 2). Thus we have here before us a separation of the subject and the predicate, instead of which, in the language of the Mishna, the form הָיִיתִי אֹמֵר (אֲנִי) and the like (*e.g. Berachoth* i. 5) is used, which found for itself a place in the language of Koheleth, in so far as this book delights in the use of the participle to an extent scarcely met with in any other book of Scripture (*vid. e.g.* i. 6, viii. 12, x. 19).

4. The use of the demonstrative pronoun זֶה bears also a Mishnic stamp. We lay no particular stress on the fact that the author uses it, as regularly as the Mishna, always without the article; but it is characteristic that he always, where he does not make use of the masculine form in a neuter sense (as vii. 10, 18, 29, viii. 9, ix. 1, xi. 6, keeping out of view cases determined by attraction), employs no other feminine form than זֹה, Mishnic זוֹ, in this sense, ii. 2, v. 15, 18, vii. 23, ix. 13. In other respects also the use of the pronouns approaches the Mishna language. In the use of the pronoun also in i. 10 and v. 18 there is an approach to the Mishnic זֶהוּ, *hic est*, and זֹהִי, *haec est*. And the use of הוּא and הֵמָּה for the personal verb reaches in iii. 18, ix. 4 (*vid.* Comm.), the extreme.

The enumeration of linguistic peculiarities betokening a late origin is not yet exhausted; we shall meet with many such in the course of the Exposition. Not only the language, however, but also the style and the artistic form of the book, show that it is the most recent product of the Bibl. *Chokma* literature, and belongs to a degenerate period of art. From the fact that the so-called metrical accent system of the three books—Psalms, Job, and Proverbs—is not used in Ecclesiastes, it does not follow that it is not a poetical book in the fullest sense of the word; for the Song and Lamentations, these masterpieces of the שיר and קינה, the Minnesong and the Elegy, are also excluded from that more elevated, more richly expressive, and more melodious form of discourse, perhaps to preserve the spiritual character of the one, and not to weaken the elegiac character of the other, to which a certain melancholy monotone *andante* is suitable. So also, to apply that system of accentuation to the Book of Koheleth was not at all possible, for the symmetrical stichs to which it is appropriate is for the most part wanting in Koheleth, which is almost wholly written in eloquent prose: unfolding its instruction in the form of sentences without symmetrical stichs.—It is, so to speak, a philosophical treatise in which "I saw," and the like, as the expression of the result of experience; "I said," as the expression of reflection on what was observed; "I perceived," as the expression of knowledge obtained as a conclusion from a process of reasoning; and "this also," as the expression of the result,—repeat themselves nearly terminologically. The reasoning tone prevails, and where the writer passes into gnomic poetry he enters into it suddenly, *e.g.* v. 9*b*, or holds himself ready to leave it quickly again, *e.g.* v. 12, vii. 13 f. Always, indeed, where the Mashal note is struck, the discourse begins to form itself into members arranged in order; and then the author sometimes rises in language, and in the order of his words, into the true classic form of the proverb set forth in parallel members, *e.g.* vii. 7, 9, ix. 8. The symmetry of the members is faultless, v. 5, viii. 8, ix. 11; but in other places, as v. 1, vii. 26, xi. 9, it fails, and in the long run the book, altogether peculiar in its stylistic and artistic character, cannot conceal its late origin: in the elevated classical style there quickly again intermingles that which is peculiar to the author, as representing the age in which he lived, *e.g.* vii. 19, x. 2 f., 6, 8–10, 16 f., xi. 3, 6. That in the age of the Mishna they knew how to imitate classic masterpieces, is seen from the beautiful enigma, in the form of a heptastich, by Bar-Kappara, *jer. Moëd katan* iii. 1, and the elegy, in the form of a hexastich on the death of R. Abina, by Bar-Kippuk, *b. Moëd katan*

25b.[1] One would thus be in error if he regarded such occasional classical pieces in the Book of Koheleth as borrowed. The book, however fragmentary it may seem to be on a superficial examination, is yet the product of one author.[2] In its oratorical ground-form, and in the proverbs introduced into it, it is a side-piece to Prov. i.–ix. We have shown, in the introduction to the Book of Proverbs, that in these proverbial discourses which form the introduction to the older Solomonic Book of Proverbs, which was probably published in the time of Jehoshaphat, the Mashal appears already rhetorically decomposed. This decomposition is much further advanced in the Book of Ecclesiastes. To it is applicable in a higher degree what is there (*Proverbs*, vol. I. 12 f.) said of Prov. i.–ix. The distich is represented in the integral, vii. 13, synonymous, xi. 4, and synthetic, vii. 1, and also, though rarely, in the antithetic form, vii. 4; but of the emblematic form there is only one example, x. 1. The author never attempted the beautiful numerical and priamel forms; the proverbial form also, beyond the limits of the distich, loses the firmness of its outline. The tetrastich, x. 20, is, however, a beautiful exception to this. But splendour of form would not be appropriate to such a sombre work as this is. Its external form is truly in keeping with its spirit. In the checkered and yet uniform manner of the book is reflected the image of the author, who tried everything and yet was satisfied with nothing; who hastened from one thing to another because nothing was able to captivate him. His style is like the view he takes of the world, which in its course turned to him only its dark side. He holds fast to the fear of God, and hopes in a final judgment; but his sceptical world-sorrow remains unmitigated, and his forced eudaemonism remains without the right consecration: these two stars do not turn the night into day; the significance of the book, with reference to the history of redemption, consists in the actual proof that humanity, in order to its being set free from its unhappiness, needs to be illuminated by the sun of a new revelation. But although the manner of the author's representation is the reflection of his own inner relation to the things represented, yet here and there he makes his representation, not without con-

---

[1] Given and translated in *Wissenchaft, Kunst, Judenthum* (1838), p. 231 f.

[2] Renan, in his *Histoire des Langues Sémitiques*, supposes that a work of so bold a scepticism as Ecclesiastes could not have originated in the post-exilian period of the severely legal rabbinical Judaism; it may be an old Solomonic work, but as it now lies before us, revised by a more recent hand,—an untenable expedient for establishing an arbitrary supposition.

sciousness and art, the picture of his own manner of thought. Thus, *e.g.*, the drawling tautologies in viii. 14, ix. 9, certainly do not escape from him against his will. And as was rightly remarked under Gen. ii. 1–3, that the discourse there is extended, and forms itself into a picture of rest after the work of the creation, so Koheleth, in i. 4–11 and xii. 2–7, shows himself a master of eloquence; for in the former passage he imitates in his style the everlasting unity of the course of the world, and in the latter he paints the exhausted and finally shattered life of man.

Not only, however, by the character of its thought and language and manner of representation, but also by other characteristic features, the book openly acknowledges that it was not written by Solomon himself, but by a Jewish thinker of a much later age, who sought to conceive of himself as in Solomon's position, and clothed his own life-experiences in the confessions of Solomon. The very title of the book does not leave us in doubt as to this. It is in these words: *The words of Koheleth, the son of David, king in Jerusalem.* The apposition, "king in Jerusalem," appertains, like *e.g.* 2 Chron. xxxv. 3, to the name of the speaker who is introduced; for nothing is here said as to the place in life held by David, but to that held by him who is thus figuratively named. The indeterminate "king" of itself would be untenable, as at Prov. xxxi. 1. As there the words "king of Massa" are to be taken together, so here "king" is determined by "in Jerusalem" added to it, so far that it is said what kind of king Koheleth was. That by this name Solomon is meant, follows, apart from i. 12 ff., from this, that David had only one son who was king, viz. Solomon. The opinion of Krochmal, that a later David, perhaps a governor of Jerusalem during the Persian domination, is meant,[1] is one of the many superfluities of this learned author. Koheleth is Solomon, but he who calls him "king in Jerusalem" is not Solomon himself. Solomon is called "king of Israel," *e.g.* 2 Kings xxiii. 13; and as in i. 12 he names himself "king over Israel," so, Neh. xiii. 26, he is called "king of Israel," and along with this designation, "king over all Israel;" but the title, "king in Jerusalem," nowhere else occurs. We read that Solomon "reigned in Jerusalem over all Israel," 1 Kings xi. 42, cf. xiv. 21; the title, "king in Jerusalem," is quite peculiar to the title of the book before us. Eichhorn supposes that it corresponds to the time subsequent to the division of the kingdom, when there were two different royal residences;

---

[1] Vid. *Kerem chemed* v. 89, and his *More neboche ha-seman* (*Director errantium nostrae aetatis*), edited by Zunz, 1851, 4.

but against this view Bloch rightly remarks, that the contrasted "in Samaria" occurs only very rarely (as 2 Kings xiv. 23). We think that in this expression, "king in Jerusalem," there is revealed a time in which Israel had ceased to be an independent kingdom, in which Jerusalem was no more a royal city.

That the book was not composed immediately by Solomon, is indicated by the circumstance that he is not called Solomon, nor Jedidiah (2 Sam. xii. 25), but is designated by a hitherto unheard of name, which, by its form, shows that it belongs, at earliest, to the Ezra-Nehemiah age, in which it was coined. We consider the name, first, without taking into account its feminine termination. In the Arab., *kahal* (cogn. *kaḥal*) signifies to be dry, hard, from the dryness and leather-like toughness of the skin of an old man; and, accordingly, Dindorf (*Quomodo nomen Coheleth Salomoni tribuatur*, 1791) and others understand *Koheleth* of an old man whose life is worn out; Coccejus and Schultens, with those of their school, understand it of the penitent who is dead to the world. But both views are opposed by this, that the form קָהֵל (קָהֵל, cf. בְּהֵל) would be more appropriate; but above all by this, that קהל, in this meaning, *aridum, marcidum esse*, is a verbal stem altogether foreign to the northern Semitic. The verb קהל signifies, in the Heb., Aram., and Assyr., to call (cf. the Syr. *kahlonitho*, a quarrelsome woman), and particularly to call together; whence קָהָל, of the same Sanscrit-Semit. root as the words ἐκ-κλη-σία and *con-cil-ium*,[1]—an extension of the root קל, which, on another side, is extended in the Arab. *kalaḥ*, Aethiop. *kalʿha*, to cry. This derivation of the name Koheleth shows that it cannot mean συναθροιστής (Grotius, not Aquila), in the sense of *collector sententiarum*; the Arab. translation *alajam'at* (also van Dyk) is faultless, because *jam'* can signify, to collect men as well as things together; but קהל is not used in that sense of *in unum redigere*. In close correspondence with the Heb. word, the LXX. translates, ὁ ἐκκλησιαστής; and the Graec. Venet., ἡ ἐκκλησιάστρια (xii. 9 : ἡ ἐκκλησιάζουσα). But in the nearest signification, "the collector," this would not be a significant name for the king represented as speaking in this book. In Solomon's reign there occurred an epoch-making assembly in Jerusalem, 1 Kings viii. 1, 2 Chron. v. 2—viz. for the purpose of consecrating the temple. The O. T. does not afford any other historical reference for the name; for although, in Prov. v. 14, xxvi. 26, בְּקָהָל signifies *coram populo, publice*, yet it does not occur directly of the public appearance of Wisdom; the expressions for this are different, i. 20 f.,

[1] *Vid.* Friedr. Delitzsch's *Indogermanisch-Semitische Studien*, p. 90.

viii. 1–4, ix. 3, though cognate. But on that great day of the consecration of the temple, Solomon not only called the people together, but he also preached to them,—he preached indirectly, for he consecrated the temple by prayer; and directly, for he blessed the people, and exhorted them to faithfulness, 1 Kings viii. 55–61. Thus Solomon appears not only as the assembler, but also as the preacher to those who were assembled; and in this sense of a teacher of the people (cf. xii. 9), *Koheleth* is an appropriate name of the king who was famed for his wisdom and for his cultivation of the popular Mashal. It is known that in proper names the *Kal* is frequently used in the sense of the *Hiph.* Thus *Koheleth* is not immediately what it may be etymologically = קֹרֵא, caller, proclaimer; but is = מַקְהֵלָה, from הִקְהִיל, to assemble, and to speak to the assembly, *contionari;* according to which Jerome, under i. 1, rightly explains: ἐκκλησιαστής, *Graeco sermone appellatur qui coetum, id est ecclesiam congregat, quem nos nuncupare possumus contionatorem, eo quod loquatur ad populum et ejus sermo non specialiter ad unum, sed ad universos generaliter dirigatur.* The interpretation: assembly = academy or *collectivum,* which Döderlein (*Salomon's Prediger u. Hoheslied,* 1784) and Kaiser (*Koheleth, Das Collectivum der Davidischen Könige in Jerusalem,* 1823) published, lightly disregards the form of the *n. agentis;* and Spohn's (*Der Prediger Salomo,* 1785) "O vanity of vanities, said the philosopher," itself belongs to the vanities.

Knobel in his Comm. (1836) has spoken excellently regarding the feminine form of the name; but when, at the close, he says: "Thus *Koheleth* properly signifies preaching, the office and business of the public speaker, but is then = קֹהֵל, מַקְהִיל, public speaker before an assembly," he also, in an arbitrary manner, interchanges the *n. agentis* with the *n. actionis.* His remark, that "the rule that *concreta,* if they have a fem. termination, become *abstracta,* must also hold for *participia,*" is a statement that cannot be confirmed. As חֹתֶמֶת signifies that which impresses (a seal), and כֹּתֶרֶת that which twines about (chapiter), so also חֹבֶרֶת, Ex. xxvi. 10, that which joins together (the coupling); one can translate such fem. particip., when used as substantives, as *abstracta, e.g.* בַּלָּה (from בָּלָה), destruction, utter ruin; but they are *abstracta* in themselves as little as the *neutra* in τὸ ταὐτόν, which may be translated by "identity," or in *immensum altitudinis,* by immensity (in height). Also Arab. names of men with fem. forms are *concreta.* To the participial form *Koheleth* correspond, for the most part, such names as (Arab.) *rawiyaton,* narrator of tradition (fem. of *rawyn*); but essentially cogn.

also are such words as *'allamat,* greatly learned man; also *khalyfaton,* which is by no means an inf. noun, like the Heb. חֲלִיפָה, but is the fem. of the verbal adj. *khalyf,* successor, representative. The Arabic grammarians say that the fem. termination gives to the idea, if possible, a collective signification, *e.g. jarrar,* the puller, *i.e.* the drawer of a ship (*helciarius*), and *jarrarat,* the multitude drawing, the company (*taife*) drawing the boat up the stream; or it also serves " as an exhaustive designation of the properties of the genus ;" so that, *e.g., 'allamat* means one who unites in himself that which is peculiar to the very learned, and represents in his own person a plurality of very learned men. They also say that the fem. termination serves in such cases to strengthen the idea. But how can this strengthening result from a change in the gender? Without doubt the fem. in such cases discharges the function of a neut.; and since *doctissimus* is heightened to *doctissimum,* it is thereby implied that such an one is a pattern of a learned man,—the reality of the idea, or the realized ideal of such an one.

From these Arab. analogues respecting the import of the name *Koheleth,* it follows that the fem. is not to be referred to *Chokma* in such a way as that Solomon might be thereby designated as the representative, and, as it were, the incarnation of wisdom (Ewald, Hitzig, etc.),—an idea which the book by no means supports; for if the author had designed, in conformity with that signification of the name, to let Wisdom herself speak through Solomon's mouth, he would have let him speak as the author of Prov. i.-ix. speaks when he addresses the reader by the title, " my son," he would not have put expressions in his mouth such as i. 16-18, vii. 23 f. One should not appeal to vii. 27; for there, where the subject is the dangers of the love of women, *Koheleth,* in the sense of Wisdom preaching, is as little appropriate as elsewhere; just here was the masculine gender of the speaker to be accented, and *Amrah Koheleth* is thus an incorrect reading for *Amar Hakkoheleth* (xii. 8). The name Koheleth, without *Chokma* being supplied, is a man's name, of such recent formation as *Sophereth,* Neh. vii. 5, for which Ezra ii. 55, *Hassophereth;* cf. also Ezra ii. 57, פֹּ֫כֶרֶת הַצְּ׳. The Mishna goes yet further in the coining of such names for men *generis fem.* As it generally prefers to use the *part. passivi* in an active sense, *e.g.* סָבוּר, thinking; רָכוּב, riding; שָׁתוּי, having drunk; so also it forms fem. plurals with a masculine signification,—as *Hadruchoth,* press-treaders, *Terumoth* iii. 4; *Hammᵉshuhhoth,* surveyors, *Erubin* iv. 11; *Hallᵉuzoth,* speakers in a foreign tongue, *Megilla* ii. 1,—and construes these with mas. predicates.¹ In these there can be nowhere anything said of a heightening of the idea effected by the transition to fem. forms. But the persons acting, although they are men, are thought of as neut.; and they appear, separated from the determination of their gender, as the representatives of the activity spoken of. According to this, *Koheleth* is, without regard to the gender, a preaching person. The Book of Koheleth thus bears, in its second word, as on its very forehead, the stamp of the Ezra-Nehemiah era to which it belongs.

As the woman of Endor, when she raised Samuel out of Hades at the request of Saul, sees "gods ascending out of the earth" (1 Sam. xxviii. 13), so it is not the veritable Solomon who speaks in this book, but his spirit, for which this neut. name *Koheleth* is appropriate. When he says, i. 12, " I, Koheleth, have been king over Israel in Jerusalem," he recognises himself not as the reigning monarch, but as having been king. The Talmudic *Aggada* has joined to this הייתי, the fable that Solomon was compelled to descend from the throne on account of his transgression of the law, which was then occupied by an angel in his stead, but externally bearing his likeness; and that he now went about begging, saying: " I, Koheleth, have been king over Israel in Jerusalem;" but that they struck him with a stick, and set before him a plate of groats; for they said to him: "How canst thou speak thus? There the king sits in his palace on his throne." ² In this fiction there is at least grammatical intelligence. For it is a vain delusion for one to persuade himself that Solomon in his advanced age could say, with reference to the period of his life as ruler, " I have been king," *fui rex*—he was certainly always so during the forty years of his reign, and on to the last moment of his life. Or can the words הייתי מלך mean *sum rex?* The case is as follows: הייתי is never the expression of the abstract present, or of existence without regard to time; " I am a king" is expressed in this sense by the substantival clause *ani mĕlĕk*. In every case where one can translate הייתי by " I am," *e.g.* Ps. lxxxviii. 5, the present being is thought of as the result of an historical past (*sum = factus sum*). But at the most, הייתי, when it looks from the present back upon the past, out of which it arose, signifies " I have become," Gen. xxxii. 11; Ps. xxx. 8; Jer. xx. 7; or when it looks back into the past as

---

¹ *Vid.* Geiger, *Lehrbuch*, § xvi. 6, and cf. Weiss' *Studien*, p. 90, who arbitrarily explains away this linguistic usage. Duke, in his *Sprache der Mishna*, p. 75, avoids the difficulty by the supposition of inadmissible ellipses.

² *Jer. Sanhedrin* ii. 6 goes further into the story; *b. Gittin* 68*b*, where the angel is designated by the Persian name *Ashmodee*, cf. Jellinek's *Sammlung kleiner Midrashim* 2. xxvi.

such, "I have been," Josh. i. 5; Judg. xii. 2; Ps. xxxvii. 25. Whether this word, in the former sense, corresponds to the Greek perfect, and in the latter to the Greek aorist, is determined only by the situation and connection. Thus in Ex. ii. 22 it signifies, "I have become a stranger" (γέγονα = εἰμί); while, on the other hand, in Deut. xxiii. 8, "thou hast been a stranger" (ἐγένου, fuisti). That where the future is spoken of, הייתי can, by virtue of the *consecutio temporum*, also acquire the meaning of "I shall become, I shall be," *e.g.* 1 Kings i. 21, cf. 1 Chron. xix. 12, is of no importance to us here. In the more modern language the more delicate syntax, as well as that idea of "becoming," primarily inherent in the verb היה, is disappearing, and הייתי signifies either the past purely, "I have been," Neh. xiii. 6, or, though not so frequently, the past along with the present, "I was," *e.g.* Neh. i. 11. Accordingly, Solomon while still living would be able to say הייתי מלך only in the sense of "I have become (and still am) king;" but that does not accord with the following retrospective perfects.[1] This also does not harmonize with the more modern linguistic usage which is followed by Koheleth, *e.g.* i. 9, 'מה־ש, *id quod fuit*; i. 10, כבר היה, *pridem fuit*. In conformity with this, the LXX. translates הייתי by ἐγενόμην, and the Graec. Venet. by ὑπῆρξα. But "I have been king," Solomon, yet living, cannot say, only *Salomo redivivus* here introduced, as the preacher can use such an expression.

The epilogue, xii. 9 ff., also furnishes an argument in favour of the late composition of this book, on the supposition that it is an appendix, not by another hand, but by the author himself. But that it is from the author's own hand, and does not, as Grätz supposes, belong to the period in which the school of Hillel had established the canonicity of the book, follows from this, that it is composed in a style of Hebrew approaching that used in the Mishna, yet of an earlier date than the Mishna; for in the Talmuds it is, clause by clause, a subject of uncertain interpretation,— the language used is plainly, for the Talmudic authorities, one that is antiquated, the expressions of which, because not immediately and unambiguously clear, need, in order to their explanation, to be translated into the language then in use. The author of the book makes it thus manifest that here in the epilogue, as in the book itself, Solomon is intentionally called *Koheleth;* and that the manner of expression, as well as of the formation of the sentences in this

---

[1] If וְאָהֵן followed, then הייתי (as Reusch and Hengstenberg interpret) might be a circumstantial perfect; *vid.* under Gen. i. 2.

epilogue, can in all particulars be supported from the book itself. In "fear God," xii. 13a, the saying in v. 6, which is similarly formed, is repeated; and "this is the whole of man," xii. 13b, a thought written as it were more in cipher than *in extenso*, is in the same style as vi. 10a. The word יותר ("moreover"), frequently used by the author, and בעל, used in the formation of attributive names, x. 11, 20, v. 10, 12, viii. 8, we meet with also here. And as at xii. 9, 10, 11 a third idea connected ἀσυνδέτως follows two ideas connected by *vav*, so also at i. 7, vi. 5. But if this epilogue is the product of the author's own hand, then, in meaning and aim, it presents itself as its sequel. The author says that the *Koheleth* who appears in this book as "wise" is the same who composed the beautiful people's-book *Mishle;* that he sought out not only words of a pleasing form, but also all words of truth; that the words of the wise are like goads and nails which stand in collected rows and numbers—they are given from one Shepherd. The author of the book thereby denotes that the sentences therein collected, even though they are not wholly, as they lie before us, the words of Solomon, yet that, with the Proverbs of Solomon, and of the wise men generally, they go back to one giver and original author. The epilogue thus, by its historic reference to Solomon, recognises the fiction, and gives the reader to understand that the book loses nothing in its value from its not having been immediately composed by Solomon.

Of untruthfulness, of a so-called *pia fraus*, we cannot therefore speak. From early times, within the sphere of the most ancient Israelitish authorship, it was regarded as a justifiable undertaking for an author to reproduce in a rhetorical or poetical form the thoughts and feelings of memorable personages on special occasions. The Psalter contains not a few psalms bearing the superscription *le-David*, which were composed not by David himself, but by unknown poets, placing themselves, as it were, in David's position, and representing him, such *e.g.* as cxliv., which in the LXX. excellently bears the superscription πρὸς τὸν Γολιάδ. The chronicler, when he seeks to give the reader an idea of the music at the festival of the consecration of the tabernacle and then of the completed temple, allows himself so great freedom, that he puts into the mouth of David the Beracha of the fourth book of the Psalms (cvi. 48), along with the preceding verse of Ps. cvi. (1 Chron. xvi. 35 f.), and into Solomon's mouth verses of Ps. cxxxii. (2 Chron. vi. 41 f.). And the prophetical discourses communicated in the O. T. historical books are certainly partly of this sort, that they either may be regarded as original, as *e.g.* 1 Sam. ii. 27 ff., or must be so regarded, as 2 Kings xviii.–xx.;

but not merely where the utterances of the prophets are in general terms reproduced, as at Judg. vi. 8–10, 2 Kings xvii. 13, xxi. 10–15, but also elsewhere in most of the prophetic discourses which we read in the Books of Kings and Chronicles, the style of the historian makes itself perceptible. Consequently (as also Caspari in his work on the Syro-Ephraimite War, 1849, finds) the discourses in the Chronicles, apart from those which are common to them, bear an altogether different homogeneous character from those of the Book of Kings. It is the same as with the speeches, for instance, which are recorded in Thucydides, Dionysius of Halicarnassus, Livy, and other Greek and Roman historians. Classen may be right in the opinion, that the speeches in Thucydides are not mere inventions, but that, nevertheless, as they lie before us, they are the work of the historian; even the letters that passed between Pausanias and Xerxes bear his stamp, although he composed them on the ground of the verbal reports of the Spartans. It is thus also with the speeches found in Tacitus. They are more Ciceronian than his own style is, and the discourses of Germans have less elaborated periods than those of the Romans; but so greatly was the writing of history by the ancients influenced by this custom of free reproduction, that even a speech of the Emperor Claudius, which is found engraven on brass, is given by Tacitus not in this its original, but in another and freer form, assimilated to his own manner of representation. So also sacred history, which in this respect follows the general ancient custom, depends not on the identity of the words, but of the spirit: it does not feign what it represents the historical person as saying, it follows traditions; but yet it is the power of its own subjectivity which thus recalls the past in all that was essential to it in actual life. The aim is not artistically to represent the imitation which is made as if it were genuine. The arts by which it is sought to impart to that which is introduced into a more recent period the appearance of genuineness, were unknown to antiquity. No pseudonymous work of antiquity shows any such imitation of an ancient style as, *e.g.*, does Meinhold's *Bernsteinhexe*, or such a forgery as Wagenfeld's *Sanchuniathon*. The historians reproduce always in their own individual way, without impressing on the speeches of different persons any distinct individual character. They abstain from every art aimed at the concealment of the actual facts of the case. It is thus also with the author of the Book of Koheleth. As the author of the "*Wisdom of Solomon*" openly gives himself out to be an Alexandrian, who makes Solomon his organ, so the author of the

Book of Koheleth is so little concerned purposely to veil the fiction of the Solomon-discourse, in which he clothes his own peculiar life-experiences, that he rather in diverse ways discovers himself as one and the same person with the *Salomo redivivus* here presenting himself.

We do not reckon along with these such proverbs as have for their object the mutual relationship between the king and his subjects, viii. 3–5, x. 4, 16 f., 20, cf. v. 8; these do not betray in the speaker one who is an observer of rulers and not a ruler himself; for the two collections of "Proverbs of Solomon" in the Book of Proverbs contain a multitude of proverbs of the king, xvi. 10, 12–15, xix. 12, xx. 2, 8, 26, 28, xxv. 2, 3, 4 f., 6 f., which, although objectively speaking of the king, may quite well be looked on as old Solomonic,—for is there not a whole princely literature regarding princely government, as *e.g.* Friedrich II.'s *Anti-Machiavel*? But in the complaints against unrighteous judgment, iii. 16, iv. 1, v. 7, one is to be seen who suffers under it, or who is compelled to witness it without the power to change it; they are not appropriate in the mouth of the ruler, who should prevent injustice. It is the author himself who here puts his complaints into the mouth of Solomon; it is he who has to record life-experiences such as x. 5–7. The time in which he lived was one of public misgovernment and of dynastic oppression, in contrast with which the past shone out in a light so much the rosier, vii. 10, and it threw long dark shadows across his mind when he looked out into the world, and mediately also upon the confessions of his Koheleth. This Koheleth is not the historical Solomon, but an abstraction of the historical; he is not the theocratic king, but the king among the wise men; the actual Solomon could not speak, ii. 18, of the heir to his throne as of "the man that shall be after him,"—and he who was led astray by his wives into idolatry, and thus became an apostate (1 Kings xi. 4), must have sounded an altogether different note of penitential contrition from that which we read at vii. 26–28. This Solomon who tasted all, and in the midst of his enjoyment maintained the position of a wise man (ii. 9), is described by the author of this book from history and from sayings, just as he needs him, so as to make him an organ of himself; and so little does he think of making the fiction an illusion difficult to be seen through, that he represents Koheleth, i. 16, ii. 7, 9, as speaking as if he had behind him a long line of kings over the whole of Israel and Judah, while yet not he, but the author of the book, who conceals himself behind *Salomo redivivus*, could look back on such a series of kings in Jerusalem.

When did this anonymous author, who speaks instead of his Solomon, live and write? Let us first of all see what conclusion may be gathered regarding the book from the literary references it contains. In its thoughts, and in the form of its thoughts, it is an extremely original work. It even borrows nothing from the Solomonic Book of Proverbs, which in itself contains so many repetitions; proverbs such as vii. 16–18 and Prov. iii. 7 are somewhat like, but only accidentally. On the contrary, between v. 14 and Job i. 21, as well as between vii. 14 and Job ii. 10, there undoubtedly exists some kind of connection; here there lie before us thoughts which the author of the Book of Koheleth may have read in the Book of Job, and have quoted them from thence—also the mention of an untimely birth, vi. 3, cf. Job iii. 16, and the expression "one among a thousand," vii. 28, cf. Job ix. 3, xxxiii. 23, may perhaps be reminiscences from the Book of Job occurring unconsciously to the author. This is not of any consequence as to the determination of the time of the composition of the Book of Koheleth, for the Book of Job is in any case much older. Dependence on the Book of Jeremiah would be of greater importance, but references such as vii. 2, cf. Jer. xvi. 8, ix. 11, cf. Jer. ix. 22, are doubtful, and guide to no definite conclusion. And who might venture, with Hitzig, to derive the golden lamp, xii. 10, from the vision of Zechariah, iv. 2, especially since the figure in the one place has an altogether different signification from what it has in the other? But we gain a more certain *terminus a quo* by comparing v. 5 with Mal. ii. 7. Malachi there designates the priests as messengers (delegated) of Jahve of hosts, along with which also there is the designation of the prophets as God's messengers, iii. 1, Hag. i. 13. With the author of the Book of Koheleth "the messenger" is already, without any name of God being added, a priestly title not to be misunderstood; מלאך [1] (messenger) denotes the priest as *vicarius Dei*, the delegate of God, שלוח דרחמנא, according to the later title (*Kiddushin* 23b). And a *terminus ad quem*, beyond which the reckoning of the time of its composition cannot extend, is furnished by the "Wisdom of Solomon," which is not a translation, but a work written originally in Alexandrine Greek; for that this book is older than the Book of Koheleth, as Hitzig maintains, is not only in itself improbable, since the latter shows not a trace of Greek influence, but in the light of the history of doctrine is altogether impossible, since it represents, in the history of the development of the doctrine of wisdom and the

---

[1] *Vid.* my dissertation: Die Discussion der Amtsfrage im M˙shna u. Gemara, in the *Luth. Zeitschrift* 1854, pp. 446–449.

last things, the stage immediately preceding the last B.C., as Philo does the last; it is not earlier than the beginning of the persecution of the Jews by the Egyptians under Ptolemy VII., Physkon (Joseph. c. Ap. ii. 5), and at all events was written before Philo, since the combination of the *Sophia* and the *Logos* is here as yet incomplete. This Book of Wisdom must stand in some kind of historical relation to the Book of Koheleth. The fact that both authors make King Solomon the organ of their own peculiar view of the world, shows a connection that is not accidental. Accident is altogether excluded by the circumstance that the Alexandrian author stands in the same relation to the Palestinian that James stands in to the Pauline letters. As James directs himself not so much against Paul as against a Paulinism misleading to fatal consequences, so the Book of Wisdom is certainly not directly a work in opposition to the Book of Koheleth, as is assumed by J. E. Ch. Schmidt (*Salomo's Prediger*, 1794), Kelle (*Die salom. Schriften*, 1815), and others; but, as Knobel and Grimm assert, against a one-sided extreme interpretation of views and principles as set forth by Koheleth, not without an acquaintance with this book. The lovers of pleasure, who speak in Wisd. ii. 1–9, could support that saying by expressions from the Book of Koheleth, and the concluding words there sound like an appropriation of the words of Koheleth iii. 22, v. 17 (cf. LXX.); it is true they break off the point of the Book of Koheleth, for the exhortation to the fear of God, the Judge of the world, is not echoed; but to break off this point did not lie remote, since the old Chokma watchword, "fear God," hovered over the contents of the book rather than penetrated them. It is as if the author of the Book of Wisdom, i.-v., wished to show to what danger of abuse in the sense of a pure materialistic eudaemonism the wisdom presented in the Book of Koheleth is exposed. But he also opposes the pessimistic thoughts of Koheleth in the decided assertions of the contrary: (1) Koheleth says: "There is one event to the righteous and to the wicked," ix. 2; but he says: there is a difference between them wide as the heavens, Wisd. iii. 2 f., iv. 7, v. 15 f.; (2) Koheleth says: "He that increaseth knowledge increaseth sorrow," i. 18; but he says: wisdom bringeth not sorrow, but pure joy with it, Wisd. viii. 16; (3) Koheleth says that wisdom bringeth neither respect nor favour, ix. 11; but he says: it brings fame and honour, Wisd. viii. 10; (4) Koheleth says: "There is no remembrance of the wise more than of the fool for ever," ii. 16; but he says of wisdom in contrast to folly: "I shall obtain by it a deathless name, and shall leave to my descendants an everlasting remembrance," Wisd. viii. 13.

The main distinction between the two books lies in this, that the comfortless view of Hades running through the Book of Koheleth is thoroughly surmounted by a wonderful rising above the O. T. standpoint by the author of the Book of Wisdom, and that hence there is in it an incomparably more satisfying *Theodicee* (cf. Wisd. xii. 2–18 with Eccles. vii. 15, viii. 14), and a more spiritual relation to this present time (cf. Wisd. viii. 21, ix. 17, with Eccles. ii. 24, iii. 13, etc.). The " Wisdom of Solomon " has indeed the appearance of an anti-Ecclesiastes, a side-piece to the Book of Koheleth, which aims partly at confuting it, partly at going beyond it; for it represents, in opposition to Koheleth not rising above earthly enjoyment with the *But* of the fear of God, a more ideal, more spiritual Solomon. If Koheleth says that God "hath made everything beautiful in his time," iii. 11, and hath made man upright, vii. 29; so, on the other hand, Solomon says that He hath made all things $\epsilon i\varsigma\ \tau\grave{o}\ \epsilon\tilde{i}\nu\alpha\iota$, Wisd. i. 14, and hath made man $\epsilon\pi$' $\dot{\alpha}\phi\theta\alpha\rho\sigma\acute{\iota}\alpha$, ii. 23. There are many such parallels, *e.g.* v. 9, cf. Koh. viii. 13; viii. 5, cf. Koh. vii. 12; ix. 13–16, cf. Koh. iii. 10 f., but particularly Solomon's confession, vii. 1–21, with that of Koheleth, i. 12–18. Here, wisdom appears as a human acquisition; there (which agrees with 1 Kings iii. 11–13), as a gracious gift obtained in answer to prayer, which brings with it all that can make happy. If one keeps in his eye this mutual relation between the two books, there can be no doubt as to which is the older and which the younger. In the Book of Koheleth the Old Covenant digs for itself its own grave. It is also a "schoolmaster to Christ," in so far as it awakens a longing after a better Covenant than the first.[1] But the Book of Wisdom is a precursor of this better covenant. The composition of the Book of Koheleth falls between the time of Malachi, who lived in the time of Nehemiah's second arrival at Jerusalem, probably under Darius Nothus (423–405 B.C.), and the Book of Wisdom, which at the earliest was written under Ptolemy Physkon (145–117), when the O. T. was already for the most part translated into the Greek language.[2]

Hitzig does not venture to place the Book of Koheleth so far back into the period of the Ptolemies; he reaches with his chain of evidence only the year 204, that in which Ptolemy Epiphanes (204–181) gained, under the guardianship of the Romans, the throne of his father,—he must be the minor whom the author has in his eye, x. 16. But the first link of his chain of proof is a *falsum*. For it is not true that Ptolemy Lagus was the first ruler who exacted from the Jews the "oath of God," viii. 2, *i.e.* the oath of fidelity; for

---

[1] *Vid.* Oehler's *Theol. des A. T.*, II. p. 324.
[2] Cf. ii. 12*a* with Isa. iii. 10, LXX., and xv. 10*a* with Isa. xliv. 20, LXX.

Josephus (*Antt.* xii. 1. 1) says directly, that Ptolemy Lagus did this with reference to the fidelity with which the Jews had kept to Alexander the Macedonian the oath of allegiance they had sworn to Darius, which he particularly describes, *Antt.* xi. 8. 3; besides, the covenant, *e.g.* 2 Sam. v. 3, concluded in the presence of Jahve with their own native kings included in it the oath of allegiance, and the oath of vassalage which, *e.g.*, Zedekiah swore to Nebuchadnezzar, 2 Chron. xxxvi. 13, cf. Ezek. xvii. 13–19, had at the same time binding force on the citizens of the state that was in subjection. Also that "the oath of God" must mean the oath of allegiance sworn to a foreign ruler, and not that sworn to a native ruler, which would rather be called "the oath of Jahve," does not stand the test: the author of the Book of Koheleth drives the cosmopolitism of the Chokma so far, that he does not at all make use of the national name of God connected with the history of redemption, and Nehemiah also, xiii. 25, uses an oath "of God" where one would have expected an oath "of Jahve." The first link of Hitzig's chain of proof, then, shows itself on all sides to be worthless. The author says, viii. 2, substantially the same as Paul, Rom. xiii. 5, that one ought to be subject to the king, not only from fear of punishment, but for conscience' sake.

Thus, then, viii. 10 will also stand without reference to the carrying away of the Jews captive by Ptolemy Lagus, especially since the subject there is by no means that of a mass-deportation; and, besides, those who were carried into Egypt by Lagus were partly from the regions round about Jerusalem, and partly from the holy city itself (Joseph. *Antt.* 12. 1. 1). And the old better times, vii. 10, were not those of the first three Ptolemies, especially since there are always men, and even in the best and most prosperous times, who praise the old times at the expense of the new. And also women who were a misfortune to their husbands or lovers there have always been, so that in vii. 26 one does not need to think of that Agathoclea who ruled over Ptolemy Philopator, and even had in her hands the power of life and death. Passages such as vii. 10 and vii. 26 afford no help in reference to the chronology. On the other hand, the author in ix. 13–16 relates, to all appearance, what he himself experienced. But the little city is certainly not the fortified town of Dora, on the sea-coast to the west of Carmel, which was besieged by Antiochus the Great (Polybius, v. 66) in the year 218, as at a later period, in the year 138, it was by Antiochus VII., Sidetes (Joseph. *Bell.* i. 2. 2); for this Dora was not then saved by a poor wise man within it,—of whom Polybius knows nothing,—but "by the strength of the place, and the help of those with Nicholaus." A definite historical event is also certainly found in iv. 13–16. Hitzig sees in the old foolish king the spiritually contracted, but so much the more covetous, high priest Onias, under Ptolemy Euergetes; and in the poor but wise youth, Joseph (the son of Tobias), who robbed Onias of his place in the state, and raised himself to the office of general farmer of taxes. But here nothing agrees but that Onias was old and foolish, and that Joseph was then a young wise man (Joseph. *Antt.* xii. 4. 2); of the poverty of the latter nothing is heard—he was the nephew of Onias. And besides, he did not come out of the house "of prisoners" (הָסוּרִים); this word is pointed by Hitzig so as to mean, out of the house "of fugitives" (הַסּוּרִים), perhaps, as he supposes, an allusion to the district $\Phi\iota\chi\delta\lambda a$, which the author thus interprets as if it were derived from $\phi\epsilon\acute{u}\gamma\epsilon\iota\nu$. Historical investigation has here degenerated into the boldest subjectivism. The Heb. tongue has never called "fugitives" הסורים; and to whom could the Heb. word פיקולה (cf. *Berachoth* 28*b*) suggest—as $\Phi\acute{u}\gamma\epsilon\lambda a$ did to Pliny and Mela—the Greek $\phi\epsilon\acute{u}\gamma\epsilon\iota\nu$!

We have thus, in determining the time of the authorship of this book, to confine ourselves to the period subsequent to the Diadochs. It may be regarded as beyond a doubt that it was written under the Persian domination. Kleinert (*Der Prediger Salomo*, 1864) is in general right in saying that the political condition of the people which the book presupposes, is that in which they are placed under Satraps: the unrighteous judgment, iii. 16; and the despotic oppression, iv. 1, viii. 9, v. 7; the riotous court-life, x. 16–19; the raising of mean men to the highest places of honour, x. 5–7; the inexorable severity of the law of war-service, viii. 8;[1] the prudence required by the organized system of espionage[2] existing at such a time,—all these things were characteristic of this period. But if the Book of Koheleth is not at all older than Malachi, then it was written somewhere within the last century of the Persian kingdom, between Artaxerxes I., Longimanus (464–424), and Darius Codomannus (335–332): the better days for the Jewish people, of the Persian supremacy under the first five Achaemenides, were past (vii. 10). Indeed, in vi. 3 there appear to be reminiscences of Artaxerxes II., Mnemon (died about 360), who was 94 years old, and, according to Justin (x. 1), had 115 sons, and of Artaxerxes III., Ochus his successor, who was poisoned by the chief eunuch Bagoas, who, according to Aelian, *Var. Hist.* vi. 8, threw his (Ochus') body to the cats, and

---

[1] *Vid.* Herod. iv. 84, vii. 38 f.
[2] *Vid.* Duncker's *Gesch. des Alterthums*, Bd. 2 (1867), p. 894.

caused sword-handles to be made from his bones. The book altogether contains many examples to which concrete instances in the Persian history correspond, from which they might be abstracted, in which strict harmony on all sides with historical fact is not to be required, since it did not concern the author. The event recorded iv. 13-16 refers to Cyrus rising to the supremacy of world-ruler (after dispossessing the old Median King Astyages), who left[1] nothing but misery to posterity. Such a rich man as is described in vi. 2, who had to leave all his treasures to a stranger, was Croesus, to whom Solon, as vii. 8*a* (cf. Herod. i. 32. 86), said that no one ought to be praised before his end. A case analogous at least to ix. 14-16, was the deliverance of Athens by the counsel of Themistocles (Justin, ii. 12), who finally, driven from Athens, was compelled to seek the protection of the Persian king, and ended his life in despair.[2] If we were not confined, for the history of the Persian kingdom and its provinces, from Artaxerxes I. to the appearance of Alexander of Macedon, to only a few and scanty sources of information (we know no Jewish events of this period, except the desecration of the temple by Bagoses, described by Josephus, *Antt.* xi. 7), we might probably be better able to understand many of the historical references of the Book of Koheleth. We should then be able to say to whom the author refers by the expression, "Woe to thy land when thy king is a child," x. 16; for Artaxerxes I., who, although only as yet a boy at the time of the murder of his father Xerxes (Justin, iii. 1), soon thereafter appeared manly enough, cannot be thought of. We should then, perhaps, be also in possession of the historical key to viii. 10; for with the reference to the deportation of many thousands of Jewish prisoners (Josephus, *c. Ap.* i. 22)—which, according to Syncellus and Orosius, must have occurred under Artaxerxes III., Ochus—the interpretation of that passage does not accord.[3] We should then also, perhaps, know to what political arrangement the

---

[1] According to Nicolaus of Damascus (Müller's *Fragm. hist. Graec.* III. 398), Cyrus was the child of poor parents; by "prison-house" (iv. 14), reference is made to his confinement in Persia, where access to him was prevented by guards (Herod. i. 123). Justin, i. 5: "A letter could not be openly brought to him, since the guards appointed by the king kept possession of all approaches to him."

[2] *Vid.* Spiegel's *Erânische Alterthumskunde*, II. pp. 409, 413. Bernstein suggests the deliverance of Potidea (Herod. viii. 128) or Tripolis (Diodor. xvi. 41); but neither of these cities owed its deliverance to the counsel of a wise man. Burger (*Comm. in Ecclesiasten*, 1864) thinks, with greater probability, of Themistocles, who was celebrated among the Persians (Thucyd. i. 138), which Ewald also finds most suitable, provided the author had a definite fact before his eye.

[3] *Vid.* Bernstein's *Quaestiones Kohelethanae*, p. 66.

author points when he says, vii. 19, that wisdom is a stronger protection to a city than "ten mighty men;" Grätz refers this to the *decuriones* of the Roman municipal cities and colonies; but probably it refers to the dynasties[1] (cf. Assyr. *salaṭ*, governor) placed by the Persian kings over the cities of conquered countries. And generally, the oppressed spirit pervading the book would be so much clearer if we knew more of the sacrifices which the Jewish people in the later time of the Persians had to make, than merely that the Phoenicians, at the same time with "the Syrians in Palestine," had to contribute (Herod. vii. 87) to Xerxes for his Grecian expedition three hundred triremes; and also that the people who "dwelt in the Solymean mountains" had to render him assistance in his expedition against Greece (Joseph. *c. Ap.* i. 22).

The author was without doubt a Palestinian. In iv. 17 he speaks of himself as dwelling where the temple was, and also in the holy city, viii. 10; he lived, if not actually in it, at least in its near neighbourhood, x. 15; although, as Kleinert remarks, he appears, xi. 1, to make use of a similitude taken from the corn trade of a seaport town. From iv. 8 the supposition is natural that he was alone in the land, without children or brothers or sisters; but from the contents and spirit of the whole book, it appears more certain that, like his Koheleth, he was advanced in years, and had behind him a long checkered life. The symptoms of approaching death presenting themselves in old age, which he describes to the young, xii. 2 ff., he probably borrowed from his own experience. The whole book bears the marks of age, — a production of the Old Covenant which was stricken in age, and fading away.

The literature, down to 1860, of commentaries and monographs on the Book of Koheleth is very fully set forth in the English Commentary of Ginsburg, and from that time to 1867, in Zöckler's Commentary, which forms a part of Lange's *Bibelwerk*. Keil's *Einleitung*, 3d ed. 1873, contains a supplement to these, among which, however, the *Bonner Theolog. Literaturblatt*, 1874, Nr. 7, misses Pusey's and Reusch's (cf. the *Tübingen Theol. Quartalschrift*, 1860, pp. 430–469). It is not possible for any man to compass this literature. Zedner's *Catalogue of the Hebrew books in the Library of the British Museum*, 1867, contains a number of Jewish commentaries omitted by Ginsburg and Zöckler, but far from all. For example, the Commentary of Ahron B. Josef (for the first time printed at Eupatoria, 1834) now lies before me, with those of Moses Frankel (Dessau, 1809), and of Samuel David Luz-

---

[1] *Vid.* Duncker's *Gesch. des Alterthums*, II. p. 910.

zatto, in the journal, *Ozar Nechmad* 1864. Regarding the literature of English interpretation, see the American translation, by Tayler Lewis (1870), of Zöckler's Commentary. The catalogue there also is incomplete, for in 1873 a Commentary by Thomas Pelham Dale appeared; and a Monograph on chap. xii., under the title of *The Dirge of Coheleth*, by the Orientalist C. Taylor, appeared in 1874. The fourth volume of the *Speaker's Commentary* contains a Commentary on the Song by Kingsbury, and on Ecclesiastes by W. T. Bullock, who strenuously maintains its Solomonic authorship. The opinion that the book represents the conflict of two voices, the voice of true wisdom and that of pretended wisdom, has lately found advocates not only in a Hebrew Commentary by Ephraim Hirsch (Warsaw, 1871), but also in the article "Koheleth" by Schenkel in his *Bibellexikon* (vol. III., 1871). For the history and refutation of this attempt to represent the book in the form of a dialogue, we might refer to Zöckler's Introd. to his Commentary.

The old translations have been referred to at length by Ginsburg. Frederick Field, in his *Hexapla* (Poet. vol. 1867), has collected together the fragments of the Greek translations. Ge. Janichs, in his *Animadversiones criticae* (Breslau, 1871), has examined the Peshito of Koheleth and Ruth; *vid.* with reference thereto, Nöldeke's *Anzeige* in the *Liter. Centralblatt* 1871, Nr. 49, and cf. Middeldorpf's *Symbolae exegetico-criticae ad librum Ecclesiastis*, 1811. The text of the *Graecus Venetus* lies before us now in a more accurate form than that by Villoison (1784), in Gebhardt's careful edition of certain Venetian manuscripts (Leipzig, Brockhaus 1874), containing this translation of the O. T. books.

EXPOSITION OF THE BOOK OF ECCLESIASTES.

"*Ostendit omnia esse vanitati subjecta: in his quae propter homines facta sunt vanitas est mutabilitatis; in his quae ab hominibus facta sunt vanitas est curiositatis; in his quae in hominibus facta sunt vanitas mortalitatis.*"

HUGO OF ST. VICTOR († 1140).

HE title, i. 1, *The words of Koheleth, son of David, king in Jerusalem,* has been already explained in the Introduction. The verse, which does not admit of being properly halved, is rightly divided by "son of David" by the accent *Zakef;* for the apposition, "king in Jerusalem," does not belong to "David," but to "Koheleth." In several similar cases, such as Ezek. i. 3, the accentuation leaves the designation of the oppositional genitive undefined; in Gen. x. 21b it proceeds on an erroneous supposition; it is rightly defined in Amos i. 1b, for example, as in the passage before us. That "king" is without the article, is explained from this, that it is determined by "in Jerusalem," as elsewhere by "of Israel" ("Judah"). The expression (cf. 2 Kings xiv. 23) is singular.

PROLOGUE: THE EVERLASTING SAMENESS.—I. 2—11.

The book begins artistically with an opening section of the nature of a preamble. The ground-tone of the whole book at once sounds in ver. 2, which commences this section, "O vanity of vanities, saith Koheleth, O vanity of vanities! All is vain." As at Isa. xl. 1 (*vid. l.c.*) it is a question whether by "saith" is meant a future or a present utterance of God, so here and at xii. 8 whether "saith" designates the expression of Koheleth as belonging to history or as presently given forth. The language admits both interpretations, as *e.g.* "saith," with God as the subject, 2 Sam. xxiii. 3, is meant historically, and in Isa. xlix. 5 of the present time. We understand "saith" here, as *e.g.* Isa. xxxvi. 4, "Thus saith ... the king of Assyria," of something said now, not of something said previously, since it is those presently living to whom the Solomon *redivivus*, and through him the author of this book, preaches the vanity of all earthly things. The old translators take "vanity of vanities" in the nominative, as if it were the predicate; but the repetition of the expression shows that it is an exclamation = *O vanitatem vanitatum*. The abbreviated connecting form of הֶבֶל is here not punctuated הֲבֵל, after the form חֲדַר (חֶדֶר) and the like, but הַבֵל, after the manner of the Aram. ground-form עֲבַד; cf. Ewald, § 32*b*. Jerome read differently: *In Hebraeo pro vanitate vanitatum ABAL ABALIM scriptum est, quod exceptis LXX. interpretibus omnes similiter transtulerunt ἀτμὸς ἀτμίδων sive ἀτμῶν*. *Hĕvĕl* primarily signifies a breath, and still bears this meaning in post-bibl. Heb., *e.g. Schabbath* 119*b*: "The world exists merely for the sake of the breath of school-children" (who are the hope of the future). Breath, as the contrast of that which is firm and enduring, is the figure of that which has no support, no continuance. Regarding the superlative expression, "Vanity of vanities," *vid.* the Song i. 1. "Vanity of vanities" is the *non plus ultra* of vanity,—vanity in the highest degree. The double exclamation is followed by a statement which shows it to be the result of experience. "All is vain"—the whole (of the things, namely, which present themselves to us here below for our consideration and use) is vanity.

Ver. 3. With this verse commences the proof for this exclamation and statement: "What profit hath a man of all his labour which he laboureth in under the sun?!" An interrogative exclamation, which leads to the conclusion that never anything right, *i.e.* real, enduring, satisfying, comes of it. יִתְרוֹן, profit, synon. with *mothar*, iii. 19, is peculiar to this book (= Aram. יִתְרָן). A primary form, יִתְרֹה, is unknown. The punctator Simson (Cod. 102*a* of the Leipzig University Lib. f. 5*a*) rightly blames those who use וְיִתְרוֹן, in a liturgical hymn, of the Day of Atonement. The word signifies that which remains over, either, as here, clear gain, profit, or that which has the pre-eminence, *i.e.* superiority, precedence, or is the foremost. "Under the sun" is the designation of the earth peculiar to this book,—the world of men, which we are wont to call the sublunary world. שׁ has not the force of an accusative of manner, but of the obj. The author uses the expression, "Labour wherein I have laboured," ii. 19, 20, v. 17, as Euripides, similarly, μοχθεῖν μόχθον. He now proceeds to justify the negative contained in the question, "What profit?"

Ver. 4. "One generation passeth away, and another generation cometh: and the earth remaineth for ever." The meaning is not that the earth remains standing, and thus (Hitz.) approaches no limit (for what limit for it could be had in view?); it is by this very immoveable condition that it fulfils, according to the ancient notion, its destiny, Ps. cxix. 90. The author rather intends to say that in this sphere nothing remains permanent as the fixed point around which all circles; generations pass away, others appear, and the earth is only the firm territory, the standing scene, of this ceaseless change. In reality, both things may be said of the earth: that it stands for ever without losing its place in the universe, and that it does not stand for ever, for it will be changed and become something else. But the latter thought, which appertains to the history of redemption, Ps. cii. 26 f., is remote from the Preacher; the stability of the earth appears to him only as the foil of the growth and decay everlastingly repeating themselves. Elster, in this fact, that the generations of men pass away, and that, on the contrary, the insensate earth under their feet remains, rightly sees something tragic, as Jerome had already done: *Quid hac vanius vanitate, quam terram manere, quae hominum causa facta est, et hominem ipsum, terrae dominum, tam repente in pulverem dissolvi?* The sun supplies the author with another figure. This, which he thinks of in contrast with the earth, is to him a second example of ceaseless change with perpetual sameness. As the generations of men come and go, so also does the sun.

Ver. 5. "And the sun ariseth, the sun goeth down, and it hasteth (back) to its place, there to rise again." It rises and sets again, but its setting is not a coming to rest; for from its place of resting in the west it must rise again in the morning in the east, hastening to fulfil its course. Thus Hitzig rightly, for he takes "there to rise again" as a relative clause; the words may be thus translated, but strictly taken, both participles stand on the same level; שׁוֹאֵף (panting, hastening) is like בָּא in ver. 4, the expression of the present, and 'זו that of the *fut. instans: ibi (rursus) oriturus;* the accentuation also treats the two partic. as co-ordinate, for *Tiphcha* separates more than *Tebir;* but it is inappropriate that it gives to וְאֶל־מְ׳ the greater disjunctive *Zakef Quaton* (with *Kadma* going before). Ewald adopts this sequence of the accents, for he explains: the sun goes down, and that to its own place, viz. hastening back to it just by its going down, where, panting, it again ascends. But that the sun goes down to the place of its ascending, is a distorted thought. If "to its place" belongs to "goeth," then it can refer only to the place of the going down, as e.g. Benjamin el-Nahawendi (Neubauer, *Aus der Petersb. Bibl.* p. 108) explains: "and that to its place," viz. the place of the going down appointed for it by the Creator, with reference to Ps. civ. 19, "the sun knoweth his going down." But the שָׁם, which refers back to "its place," opposes this interpretation; and the phrase שֹׁאֵף cannot mean "panting, rising," since שָׁאַף in itself does not signify to pant, but to snatch at, to long eagerly after anything, thus to strive, panting after it (cf. Job vii. 2; Ps. cxix. 131), which accords with the words "to its place," but not with the act of rising. And how unnatural to think of the rising sun, which gives the impression of renewed youth, as panting! No, the panting is said of the sun that has set, which, during the night, and thus without rest by day and night, must turn itself back again to the east (Ps. xix. 7), there anew to commence its daily course. Thus also Rashi, the LXX., Syr., Targ., Jerome, Venet., and Luther. Instead of שֹׁאֵף, Grätz would read שָׁב אַף, *redit (atque) etiam;* but שֹׁאֵף is as characteristic of the Preacher's manner of viewing the world as סוֹבֵב וְגוֹ׳, 6b, and יֵשׁ, 8a. Thus much regarding the sun. Many old interpreters, recently Grätz, and among translators certainly the LXX., refer also 6a to the sun. The Targ. paraphrases the whole verse of the state of the sun by day and night, and at the spring and autumn equinox, according to which Rashi translates הָרוּחַ, *la volonté (du soleil).* But along with the sun, the wind is also referred to as a third example of restless motion always renewing itself. The division of the verses is correct; 6a used of the sun would overload the figure, and the whole of ver. 6 therefore refers to the wind.

Ver. 6. "It goeth to the south, and turneth to the north; the wind goeth ever circling, and the wind returneth again on its circuits." Thus designedly the verse is long-drawn and monotonous. It gives the impression of weariness. שָׁב may be 3d pret. with the force of an abstract present, but the relation is here different from that in 5a, where the rising, setting, and returning stand together, and the two former lie backwards indeed against the latter; here, on the contrary, the circling motion and the return to a new beginning stand together on the same line; שָׁב is thus a part., as the Syr. translates it. The participles represent continuance in motion. In ver. 4 the subjects stand foremost, because the ever anew beginning motion belongs to the subject; in vv. 5 and 6, on the contrary, the pred. stands foremost, and the subject in ver. 6 is therefore placed thus far back, because the first two pred. were not sufficient, but required a third for their completion. That the wind goes from the south (דָּרוֹם, R. דר, the region of the most intense light) to the north (צָפוֹן, R. צָפַן, the region of darkness), is not so exclusively true of it as it is of the sun that it goes from the east to the west; this expression requires the generalization "circling, circling goes the wind," *i.e.* turning in all directions here and there; for the repetition denotes that the circling movement exhausts all possibilities. The near defining part. which is subordinated to "goeth," elsewhere is annexed by "and," *e.g.* Jonah i. 11; cf. 2 Sam. xv. 30; here סוֹבֵב ׀ סֹבֵב, in the sense of סָבִיב ׀ סָבִיב, Ezek. xxxvii. 2 (both times with *Pasek* between the words), precedes. סְבִיבָה is here the *n. actionis* of סבב. And "on its circuits" is not to be taken adverbially: it turns back on its circuits, *i.e.* it turns back on the same paths (Knobel and others), but עַל and שָׁב are connected, as Prov. xxvi. 11; cf. Mal. iii. 24; Ps. xix. 7: the wind returns back to its circling movements to begin them anew (Hitzig). "The wind" is repeated (cf. ii. 10, iv. 1) according to the figure Epanaphora or Palindrome (*vid.* the Introd. to Isaiah, c. xl.–lxvi.). To all regions of the heavens, to all directions of the compass, its movement is ceaseless, ever repeating itself anew; there is nothing permanent but the fluctuation, and nothing new but that the old always repeats itself. The examples are thoughtfully chosen and arranged. From the currents of air, the author now passes to streams of water.

Ver. 7. "All rivers run into the sea, and the sea becomes not full; to the place whence the rivers came, thither they always return again." Instead of *nᵉhhárim*, *nᵉhhalim* was preferred, because it is the more general name for flowing waters, brooks, and rivers; נַחַל (from נחל, *cavare*), אָפִיק (from אפק, *continere*), and (Arab.) *wadin* (from the root-idea of stretching, extending), all three denote the channel or bed, and then the water flowing in it. The sentence, "all rivers run into the sea," is consistent with fact. Manifestly the author does not mean that they all immediately flow thither; and by "the sea" he does not mean this or that sea; nor does he think, as the Targ. explains, of the earth as a ring (גּוּשְׁפַּנְקָא, Pers. *angusht-báne*, properly "finger-guard") surrounding the ocean: but the sea in general is meant, perhaps including also the ocean that is hidden. If we include this internal ocean, then the rivers which lose themselves in hollows, deserts, or inland lakes, which have no visible outlet, form no exception. But the expression refers first of all to the visible sea-basins, which gain no apparent increase by these masses of water being emptied into them: "the sea, it becomes not full;" אֵינֶנּוּ

(Mishn. אֵינוֹ) has the reflex. pron., as at Ex. iii. 2, Lev. xiii. 34, and elsewhere. If the sea became full, then there would be a real change; but this sea, which, as Aristophanes says (*Clouds*, 1294 f.), οὐδὲν γίγνεται ἐπιρρεόντων τῶν ποταμῶν πλείων, represents also the eternal sameness. In ver. 7*b*, Symm., Jer., Luther, and also Zöckler, translate שׁ in the sense of "from whence;" others, as Ginsburg, venture to take שָׁם in the sense of מִשָּׁם; both interpretations are linguistically inadmissible. Generally the author does not mean to say that the rivers return to their sources, since the sea replenishes the fountains, but that where they once flow, they always for ever flow without changing their course, viz. into the all-devouring sea (Elst.); for the water rising out of the sea in vapour, and collecting itself in rain-clouds, fills the course anew, and the rivers flow on anew, for the old repeats itself in the same direction to the same end. מָקוֹם is followed by what is a virtual genitive (Ps. civ. 8); the accentuation rightly extends this only to הֹלְכִים; for אֲשֶׁר, according to its relation, signifies in itself *ubi*, Gen. xxxix. 20, and *quo*, Num. xiii. 27; 1 Kings xii. 2 (never *unde*). שָׁם, however, has after verbs of motion, as *e.g.* Jer. xxii. 27 after שׁוּב, and 1 Sam. ix. 6 after הלך, frequently the sense of שָׁמָּה. And שׁוּב with לְ and the infin. signifies to do something again, Hos. xi. 9, Job vii. 7; thus: to the place whither the rivers flow, thither they flow again, *eo rursus eunt*. The author here purposely uses only participles, because although there is constant change, yet that which renews itself is ever the same. He now proceeds, after this brief but comprehensive induction of particulars, to that which is general.

Ver. 8. "All things are in activity; no man can utter it; the eye is not satisfied with seeing, and the ear is not full with hearing." All translators and interpreters who understand *d^evarim* here of words (LXX., Syr., and Targ.) go astray; for if the author meant to say that no words can describe this everlasting sameness with perpetual change, then he would have expressed himself otherwise than by "all words weary" (Ew., Elst., Hengst., and others); he ought at least to have said לָרִיק יג׳. But also "all things are wearisome" (Knob., Hitz.), or "full of labour" (Zöck.), *i.e.* it is wearisome to relate them all, cannot be the meaning of the sentence; for יָגֵעַ does not denote that which causes weariness, but that which suffers weariness (Deut. xxv. 18; 2 Sam. vii. 2); and to refer the affection, instead of to the narrator, to that which is to be narrated, would be even for a poet too affected a *quid pro quo*. Rosenmüller essentially correctly: *omnes res fatigantur h. e. in perpetua versantur vicissitudine, qua fatigantur quasi*. But יְגֵעִים is not appropriately rendered by *fatigantur;* the word means, becoming wearied, or perfectly feeble, or also: wearying oneself (cf. x. 15, xii. 12), working with a strain on one's strength, fatiguing oneself (cf. יְגִיעַ, that which is gained by labour, work). This is just what these four examples are meant to show, viz. that a restless activity reaching no visible conclusion and end, always beginning again anew, pervades the whole world—all things, he says, summarizing, are in labour, *i.e.* are restless, hastening on, giving the impression of fatigue. Thus also in strict sequence of thought that which follows: this unrest in the outer world reflects itself in man, when he contemplates that which is done around him; human language cannot exhaust this coming and going, this growth and decay in constant circle, and the *quodlibet* is so great, that the eye cannot be satisfied with seeing, nor the ear with hearing; to the unrest of things without corresponds the unrest of the mind, which through this course, in these ever repeated variations, always bringing back the old again to view, is kept in ceaseless activity. The object to *dābbēr* is the totality of things. No words can comprehend this, no sensible perception exhaust it. That which is properly aimed at here is not the unsatisfiedness of the eyes (Prov. xxvii. 20), and generally of the mind, thus not the ever-new attractive power which appertains to the eye and the ear of him who observes, but the force with which the restless activity which surrounds us lays hold of and communicates itself to us, so that we also find no rest and contentment. With שָׂבַע, to be satisfied, of the eye, there is appropriately interchanged נִמְלָא, used of the funnel-shaped ear, to be filled, *i.e.* to be satisfied (as at vi. 7). The *min* connected with this latter word is explained by Zöck. after Hitz., "away from hearing," *i.e.* so that it may hear no more. This is not necessary. As *sāvă'* with its *min* may signify to be satisfied with anything, *e.g.* vi. 3, Job xix. 22, Ps. civ. 13; so also *nimlă*, with its *min*, to be full of anything, Ezek. xxxii. 6; cf. *Kal*, Isa. ii. 6, *Pih.* Jer. li. 34, Ps. cxxvii. 5: Thus *mishsh^emoa'* is understood by all the old translators (*e.g.* Targ. מִלְּמִשְׁמַע), and thus also, perhaps, the author meant it: the eye is not satisfied with seeing, and the ear is not filled (satisfied) with hearing; or yet more in accordance with the Heb. expression: there is not an eye, *i.e.* no eye is satisfied, etc., restlessly hastening, giving him who looks no rest, the world goes on in its circling course without revealing anything that is in reality new.

Ver. 9. "That which hath been is that which shall be, and that which is done is that which shall be done; and there is nothing new under the sun."—The older form of the language uses only אֲשֶׁר instead of מַה־שֶּׁ, in the sense of *id quod*, and in the sense of *quid-*

quid, כל אשר (vi. 10, vii. 24) ; but *mâh* is also used by it with the extinct force of an interrogative, in the sense of *quodcunque*, Job xiii. 13, *aliquid* (*quidquam*), Gen. xxxix. 8, Prov. ix. 13 ; and *mi* or *mi asher*, in the sense of *quisquis*, Ex. xxiv. 14, xxxii. 33. In הוא שׁ (cf. Gen. xlii. 14) are combined the meanings *id* (*est*) *quod* and *idem* (*est*) *quod* ; *hu* is often the expression of the equality of two things, Job iii. 19, or of self-sameness, Ps. cii. 28. The double clause, *quod fuit . . . quod factum est*, comprehends that which is done in the world of nature and of men,—the natural and the historical. The bold clause, *neque est quidquam novi sub sole*, challenges contradiction; the author feels this, as the next verse shows.

Ver. 10. "Is there anything whereof it may be said: See, this is new ?—it was long ago through the ages (aeons) which have been before us." The Semit. substantive verb יֵשׁ (Assyr. *isu*) has here the force of a hypothetical antecedent: supposing that there is a thing of which one might say, etc. The זֶ֫, with *Makkeph*, belongs as subject, as at vii. 27, 29 as object, to that which follows. כְּבָר (*vid.* List, p. 193) properly denotes length or greatness of time (as כִּבְרָה, length of way). The לְ of לְעֹ is that of measure: this "long ago" measured (Hitz.) after infinitely long periods of time. מִלְּ, *ante nos*, follows the usage of מִלְּפָ, Isa. xli. 26, and לִפָּ, Judg. i. 10, etc.; the past time is spoken of as that which was before, for it is thought of as the beginning of the succession of time (*vid.* Orelli, *Synon. der Zeit u. Ewigkeit*, p. 14 f.). The singular הָיָה may also be viewed as pred. of a *plur. inhumanus* in order; but in connection, ii. 7, 9 (Gesen. § 147, An. 2), it is more probable that it is taken as a neut. verb. That which newly appears has already been, but had been forgotten; for generations come and generations go, and the one forgets the other.

Ver. 11. "There is no remembrance of ancestors; and also of the later ones who shall come into existence, there will be no remembrance for them with those who shall come into existence after them." With זָכָּרוֹן (with *Kametz*) there is also זִכְרוֹן, the more common form by our author, in accordance with the usage of his age; Gesen., Elst., and others regard it here and at ii. 16 as constr., and thus לְרִא as virtually object-gen. (Jerome, *non est priorum memoria*); but such refinements of the old *syntaxis ornata* are not to be expected in our author: he changes (according to the traditional punctuation) here the initial sound, as at i. 17 the final sound, to *oth* and *uth*. אֵין לְ is the contrast of הָיָה לְ : to attribute to one, to become partaker of. The use of the expression, "for them," gives emphasis to the statement. "With those who shall come after," points from the generation that is future to a remoter future, cf. Gen. xxxiii. 2. The

Kametz of the prep. is that of the recompens. art.; cf. Num. ii. 31, where it denotes "the last" among the four hosts; for there הָא֑ is meant of the last in order, as here it is meant of the remotely future time.

KOHELETH'S EXPERIENCES AND THEIR RESULTS.—I. 12–IV. 16.

The Unsatisfactoriness of striving after Wisdom, i. 12–18.

After this prelude regarding the everlasting sameness of all that is done under the sun, Koheleth-Solomon unfolds the treasure of his life-experience as king.

Ver. 12. "I, Koheleth, have been king over Israel in Jerusalem." That of the two possible interpretations of הָיִ֫יתִי, "I have become" and "I have been," not the former (Grätz), but the latter, is to be here adopted, has been already shown (p. 205). We translate better by "I have been"—for the verb here used is a pure perfect —than by "I was" (Ew., Elst., Hengst., Zöck.), with which Bullock (*Speaker's Comm.*, vol. IV., 1873) compares the expression *Quand j'étois roi!* which was often used by Louis XIV. towards the end of his life. But here the expression is not a cry of complaint, like the "*fuimus Troes*," but a simple historical statement, by which the Preacher of the vanity of all earthly things here introduces himself,—it is Solomon, resuscitated by the author of the book, who here looks back on his life as king. "Israel" is the whole of Israel, and points to a period before the division of the kingdom; a king over Judah alone would not so describe himself. Instead of "king עַל (over) Israel," the old form of the language uses frequently simply "king of Israel," although also the former expression is sometimes found; cf. 1 Sam. xv. 26; 2 Sam. xix. 23; 1 Kings xi. 37. He has been king,— king over a great, peaceful, united people; king in Jerusalem, the celebrated, populous, highly-cultivated city,—and thus placed on an elevation having the widest survey, and having at his disposal whatever can make a man happy; endowed, in particular, with all the means of gaining knowledge, which accorded with the disposition of his heart searching after wisdom (cf. 1 Kings iii. 9–11, v. 9).

But in his search after worldly knowledge he found no satisfaction.

Ver. 13. "And I gave my heart to seek and to hold survey with wisdom over all that is done under the sun: a sore trouble it is which God has given to the children of men to be exercised therewith." The synonyms דָּרַשׁ (to seek) and תּוּר (to hold survey over) do not represent a lower and a higher degree of search (Zöck.), but two kinds of searching: one penetrating in depth, the other going out in extent; for the former of these verbs (from the root-idea of grinding, testing) signifies to investigate an object which one already has in hand, to penetrate into it, to search into it thoroughly; and the latter verb (from the root-idea of moving round about)[1] signifies to hold a survey,—look round in order to bring that which is unknown, or not comprehensively known, within the sphere of knowledge, and thus has the meaning of *bǎkkēsh*, one going the rounds. It is the usual word for the exploring of a country, *i.e.* the acquiring personal knowledge of its as yet unknown condition; the passing over to an intellectual search is peculiar to the Book of Koheleth, as it has the phrase נָתַן לֵב, *animum advertere*, or *applicare ad aliquid*, in common only with Dan. x. 12. The *beth* of *bahhochᵉmah* is that of the instrument; wisdom must be the means (*organon*) of knowledge in this searching and inquiry. With עַל is introduced the sphere into which it extends. Grotius paraphrases: *Historiam animalium et satorum diligentissime inquisivi*. But נַעֲשָׂה does not refer to the world of nature, but to the world of men; only within this can anything be said of actions, only this has a proper history. But that which offers itself for research and observation there, brings neither joy nor contentment. Hitzig refers הוּא to human activity; but it relates to the research which has this activity as its object, and is here, on that account, called "a sore trouble," because the attainment and result gained by the laborious effort are of so unsatisfactory a nature. Regarding עִנְיָן, which here goes back to עָנָה בְ, to fatigue oneself, to trouble oneself with anything, and then to be engaged with it, *vid.* p. 194. The words עִנְיַן רָע would mean trouble of an evil nature (*vid.* at Ps. lxxviii. 49; Prov. vi. 24); but better attested is the reading עִנְיָן רָע, "a sore trouble." הוּא is the subj., as at ii. 1 and elsewhere; the author uses it also in expressions where it is pred. And as frequently as he uses *asher* and שׁ, so also, when form and matter commend it, he uses the scheme of the attributive clause (elliptical relative clause), as here (cf. iii. 16), where certainly, in conformity with the old style, נְתָנוֹ was to be used.

Ver. 14. He adduces proof of the wearisomeness of this work of research: "I saw all the works that are done under the sun; and, behold, all is vanity and striving after the wind." The point of the sentence lies in וְהִנֵּה = וְהֵ׳ וָאֶרְאֶה, so that thus *raîthi* is the expression of the parallel fact (circumst. perfect). The result of his seeing,

---

[1] *Vid.* the investigation of these roots (Assyr. *utîr*, he brought back) in Ethé's *Schlafyemach der Phantasie*, pp. 86–89.

and that, as he has said ver. 13, of a by no means superficial and limited seeing, was a discovery of the fleeting, unsubstantial, fruitless nature of all human actions and endeavours. They had, as *hevel* expresses, no reality in them; and also, as denoted by *rʿuth ruahh* (the LXX. render well by προαίρεσις πνεύματος), they had no actual consequences, no real issue. Hos. xii. 2 [1] also says: "Ephraim feedeth on wind," *i.e.* follows after, as the result of effort obtains, the wind, *roëh ruahh;* but only in the Book of Koheleth is this sentence transformed into an abstract *terminus technicus* (*vid.* under *Rʿuth*, p. 195).

Ver. 15. The judgment contained in the words, "vanity and a striving after the wind," is confirmed: "That which is crooked cannot become straight; and a deficit cannot be numerable," *i.e.* cannot be taken into account (thus Theod., after the Syro-Hex.), as if as much were present as is actually wanting; for, according to the proverb, "Where there is nothing, nothing further is to be counted." Hitzig thinks, by that which is crooked and wanting, according to vii. 13, of the divine order of the world: that which is unjust in it, man cannot alter; its wants he cannot complete. But the preceding statement refers only to labour under the sun, and to philosophical research and observation directed thereto. This places before the eyes of the observer irregularities and wants, brings such irregularities and wants to his consciousness,—which are certainly partly brought about and destined by God, but for the most part are due to the transgressions of man himself,—and what avails the observer the discovery and investigation?—he has only lamentation over it, for with all his wisdom he can bring no help. Instead of לִתְקֹן (*vid.* under תקן, p. 196), לְתַקֵּן was to be expected. However, the old language also formed intransitive infinitives with transitive modification of the final vowels, *e.g.* יָבֹשׁ, etc. (cf. יִישַׁן, v. 11).

Having now gained such a result in his investigation and research by means of wisdom, he reaches the conclusion that wisdom itself is nothing.

Vv. 16–18. "I have communed with mine own heart, saying: Lo, I have gained great and always greater wisdom above all who were before me over Jerusalem; and my heart hath seen wisdom and knowledge in fulness. And I gave my heart to know what was in wisdom and knowledge, madness and folly—I have perceived that this also is a grasping after the wind." The evidence in which he bears witness to himself that striving after wisdom and knowledge brings with it no true satisfaction, reaches down to the close of ver. 17; יָדַעְתִּי is the conclusion which is aimed at. The manner of expression is certainly so far involved, as he speaks of his heart to his heart what it had experienced, and to what he had purposely directed it. The אֲנִי leads us to think that a king speaks, for whom it is appropriate to write a capital *I*, or to multiply it into *we;* vid. regarding this "I," more pleonastic than emphatic, subordinated to its verb, § 3, p. 198. It is a question whether עִם־לִבִּי, after the phrase (אֶת) דִּבֶּר עִם, is meant of speaking with any one, *colloqui*, or of the place of speaking, as in "thou shalt consider in thine heart," Deut. viii. 5, it is used of the place of consciousness; cf. Job xv. 9, היה עִמִּי (עִמָּדִי) = σύνοιδα ἐμαυτῷ, and what is said in my *Psychol.* p. 134, regarding συνείδησις, consciousness, and συμμαρτυρεῖν. בְּלִבִּי, interchanging with עִם־לִבִּי, ii. 1, 15, cf. xv. 1, commends the latter meaning: in my heart (LXX., Targ., Jerome, Luther); but the cogn. expressions, *mᵉdabbĕrĕth ăl-libbah*, 1 Sam. i. 13, and *lᵉdabbēr ăl-libbi*, Gen. xxiv. 45, suggest as more natural the former rendering, viz. as of a dialogue, which is expressed by the Gr. Venet. (more distinctly than by Aquila, Symm., and Syr.): διείλεγμαι ἐγὼ ξὺν τῇ καρδίᾳ μου. Also לֵאמֹר, occurring only here in the Book of Koheleth, brings it near that the following *oratio directa* is directed to the heart, as it also directly assumes the form of an address, ii. 1, after בלבי. The expression, הִגְ׳ הכ׳, "to make one's wisdom great," *i.e.* "to gain great wisdom," is without a parallel; for the words, הִגְ׳ תו׳, Isa. xxviii. 29, quoted by Hitzig, signify to show and attest truly useful (beneficial) knowledge in a noble way. The annexed וְהוֹ׳ refers to the continued increase made to the great treasure already possessed (cf. ii. 9 and 1 Kings x. 7). The *al* connected therewith signifies, "above" (Gen. xlix. 26) all those who were over Jerusalem before me. This is like the *sarrâni ălik mahrija*, "the kings who were my predecessors," which was frequently used by the Assyrian kings. The Targumist seeks to accommodate the words to the actual Solomon by thus distorting them: "above all the wise men who have been in Jerusalem before me," as if the word in the text were בִּירוּשָׁלַם,[1] as it is indeed found in several Codd., and according to which also the LXX., Syr., Jerome, and the Venet. translate. Rather than think of the wise (חַכִּימַיָּא), we are led to think of all those who from of old stood at the head of the Israelitish community. But there must have been well-known great men with whom Solomon measures

---

[1] In F the following note is added: "Several Codd. have, erroneously, *birushalam* instead of *al-yᵉrushalam*." Kennicott counts about 60 such Codd. It stands thus also in J; and at first it thus stood in H, but was afterwards corrected to *al-yᵉrushalam*. Cf. Elias Levita's *Masoreth hamasoreth*, II. 8, at the end.

himself, and these could not be such dissimilarly great men as the Canaanitish kings to the time of Melchizedek; and since the Jebusites, even under Saul, were in possession of Zion, and Jerusalem was for the first time completely subdued by David (2 Sam. v. 7, cf. Josh. xv. 63), it is evident that only one predecessor of Solomon in the office of ruler over Jerusalem can be spoken of, and that here an anachronism lies before us, occasioned by the circumstance that the *Salomo redivivus*, who has behind him the long list of kings whom in truth he had before him, here speaks. Regarding אֲשֶׁר הָיָה, *qu'il y eut*, for הָיוּ אֲשֶׁר, *qui furent*, vid. at i. 10*b*. The seeing here ascribed to the heart (here = νοῦς, *Psychol.* p. 249) is meant of intellectual observation and apprehension; for "all perception, whether it be mediated by the organs of sense or not (as prophetic observing and contemplating), comprehends all, from mental discernment down to suffering, which veils itself in unconsciousness, and the Scripture designates it as a seeing" (*Psychol.* 234); the Book of Koheleth also uses the word רָאָה of every kind of human experience, bodily or mental, ii. 24, v. 17, vi. 6, ix. 9. It is commonly translated: "My heart saw much wisdom and knowledge" (thus *e.g.* Ewald); but that is contrary to the gram. structure of the sentence (Ew. § 287*c*). The adject. *harbēh*[1] is always, and by Koheleth also, ii. 7, v. 6, 16, vi. 11, ix. 18, xi. 8, xii. 9, 12, placed after its subst.; thus it is here adv., as at v. 19, vii. 16 f. Rightly the Venet.: ἡ καρδία μου τεθέαται κατὰ πολὺ σοφίαν καὶ γνῶσιν. *Chokma* signifies, properly, solidity, compactness; and then, like πυκνότης, mental ability, secular wisdom; and, generally, solid knowledge of the true and the right. *Dáăth* is connected with *chokma* here and at Isa. xxxiii. 6, as at Rom. xi. 33 γνῶσις is with σοφία. Baumgarten-Crusius there remarks that σοφία refers to the general ordering of things, γνῶσις to the determination of individual things; and Harless, that σοφία is knowledge which proposes the right aim, and γνῶσις that which finds the right means thereto. In general, we may say that *chokma* is the fact of a powerful knowledge of the true and the right, and the property which arises out of this intellectual possession; but *dáăth* is knowledge penetrating into the depth of the essence of things, by which wisdom is acquired and in which wisdom establishes itself.

Ver. 17. By the consecutive *modus* וָאֶתְּנָה (aor. with *ah*, like Gen. xxxii. 6, xli. 11, and particularly in more modern writings; vid. p. 198, regarding the rare occurrence of the aorist form in the Book of Koheleth) he bears evidence to himself as to the end

---

[1] Regarding the form הַרְבֵּה, which occurs once (Jer. xlii. 2), vid. Ew. § 240*e*.

which, thus equipped with wisdom and knowledge, he gave his heart to attain unto (cf. 13*a*), *i.e.* toward which he directed the concentration of his intellectual strength. He wished to be clear regarding the real worth of wisdom and knowledge in their contrasts; he wished to become conscious of this, and to have joy in knowing what he had in wisdom and knowledge as distinguished from madness and folly. After the statement of the object *lādăăth*, stands *v^edaath*, briefly for ולדעת. Ginsburg wishes to get rid of the words *holēloth v^esikluth*, or at least would read in their stead תְּבוּנִית וְשִׂכְלוּת (rendering them "intelligence and prudence"); Grätz, after the LXX. παραβολὰς καὶ ἐπιστήμην, reads מְשָׁלוֹת וְשִׂכלוֹת. But the text can remain as it is: the object of Koheleth is, on the one hand, to become acquainted with wisdom and knowledge; and, on the other, with their contraries, and to hold these opposite to each other in their operations and consequences. The LXX., Targ., Venet., and Luther err when they render *sikluth* here by ἐπιστήμη, etc. As *sikluth*, insight, intelligence, is in the Aram. written with the letter *samek* (instead of *sin*), so here, according to the Masora סכלות, madness is for once written with ס, being everywhere else in the book written with שׂ; the word is an ἐναντιόφωνον,[1] and has, whether written in the one way or in the other, a verb, *sakal* (שׂכל, סכל), which signifies "to twist together," as its root, and is referred partly to a complication and partly to a confusion of ideas. הֹלֵלוֹת, from הָלַל, in the sense of "to cry out," "to rage," always in this book terminates in *ôth*, and only at x. 13 in *ûth* (*vid.* p. 191); the termination *ûth* is that of the abstr. sing.; but *ôth*, as we think we have shown at Prov. i. 20, is that of a fem. plur., meant intensively, like *bogdoth*, Zeph. ii. 4; *binoth, chokmoth*, cf. *bogdim*, Prov. xxiii. 28; *hhovlim*, Zech. xi. 7, 14; *toqim*, Prov. xi. 15 (Böttch. § 700*g* E). Twice *v^esikluth* presents what, speaking to his own heart, he bears testimony to before himself. By *yādă'ti*, which is connected with *dibbarti* (ver. 16) in the same rank, he shows the *facit*. זֶה refers to the striving to become conscious of the superiority of secular wisdom and science to the love of pleasure and to ignorance. He perceived that this striving also was a grasping after the wind; with רְעוּת, 14*b*, is here interchanged רַעְיוֹן (*vid.* p. 195). He proves to himself that nothing showed itself to be real, *i.e.* firm and enduring, unimpeachable and imperishable. And why not?

Ver. 18. "For in much wisdom is much grief; and he that increaseth knowledge increaseth sorrow." The German proverb: "Much wisdom causeth headache," is compared, xii. 12*b*, but not

[1] *Vid.* Th. M. Redslob's *Die Arab. Wörter, u.s.w.* (1873).

here, where כַּעַס and מַכְאוֹב express not merely bodily suffering, but also mental grief. Spinoza hits one side of the matter in his *Ethics*, IV. 17, where he remarks: "*Veram boni et mali cognitionem saepe non satis valere ad cupiditates coercendas, quo facto homo imbecillitatem suam animadvertens cogitur exclamare: Video meliora proboque, deteriora sequor.*" In every reference, not merely in that which is moral, there is connected with knowledge the shadow of a sorrowful consciousness, in spite of every effort to drive it away. The wise man gains an insight into the thousand-fold woes of the natural world, and of the world of human beings, and this reflects itself in him without his being able to change it; hence the more numerous the observed forms of evil, suffering, and discord, so much greater the sadness (כַּעַס, R. כס, cogn. הם, *perstringere*) and the heart-sorrow (מַכְאוֹב, *crève-cœur*) which the inutility of knowledge occasions. The form of 18a is like v. 6, and that of 18b like *e.g.* Prov. xviii. 22a. We change the clause *v^eyosiph daath* into an antecedent, but in reality the two clauses stand together as the two members of a comparison: if one increaseth knowledge, he increaseth (at the same time) sorrow. "יוֹסִיף, Isa. xxix. 14, xxxviii. 5, Eccles. ii. 18," says Ewald, § 169a, "stands alone as a *part. act.*, from the stem reverting from *Hiph.* to *Kal* with י— instead of ־ִ." But this is not unparalleled; in הֹנֵ יוֹסִף the verb יוֹסִף is fin., in the same manner as יְפָד, Isa. xxviii. 16; תּוֹמִיךְ, Ps. xvi. 5, is *Hiph.*, in the sense of *amplificas*, from יָמַךְ; יָפִיחַ, Prov. vi. 19 (*vid. l.c.*), is an attribut. clause, *qui efflat*, used as an adj.; and, at least, we need to suppose in the passage before us the confusion that the *ē* of *kātēl* (from *kātil*, originally *kātal*), which is only long, has somehow passed over into *î*. Böttcher's remark to the contrary, "An impersonal *fiens* thus repeated is elsewhere altogether without a parallel," is set aside by the proverb formed exactly thus: "He that breathes the love of truth says what is right," Prov. xii. 17.

The Unsatisfying Nature of Worldly Joy, ii. 1–11.

After having proved that secular wisdom has no superiority to folly in bringing true happiness to man, he seeks his happiness in a different way, and gives himself up to cheerful enjoyment.

ii. 1. "I have said in mine heart: Up then, I will prove thee with mirth, and enjoy thou the good! And, lo, this also is vain." Speaking in the heart is not here merely, as at i. 16, 17a, speaking to the heart, but the words are formed into a direct address of the heart. The Targ. and Midrash obliterate this by interpreting as if the word were אֲנַסֶּנָּה, "I will try it" (vii. 23). Jerome also, in rendering by *vadam et affluam deliciis et fruar bonis*, proceeds contrary to the usual reading of אָסֵּ֫ךְ (*Niph.* of נסך, *vid.* at Ps. ii. 6), as if this could mean, "I will pour over myself." It is an address of the heart, and ב is, as at 1 Kings x. 1, that of the means: I will try thee with mirth, to see whether thy hunger after satisfaction can be appeased with mirth. וּרְאֵה also is an address; Grätz sees here, contrary to the Gramm., an infin. continuing the בְּשִׂ׳: *ūrēh*, Job x. 15, is the connect. form of the particip. adj. *rāĕh;* and if *rᵉēh* could be the inf. after the forms *naqqēh, hinnāqqēh,* it would be the *inf. absol.*, instead of which וּרְאוֹת was to be expected. It is the imper.: See good, sinking thyself therein, *i.e.* enjoy a cheerful life. Elsewhere the author connects ראה less significantly with the accus.-obj., v. 17, vi. 6, ii. 24.

This was his intention; but this experiment also to find out the *summum bonum* proves itself a failure: he found a life of pleasure to be a hollow life; that also, viz. devotedness to mirth, was to him manifestly vanity.

Ver. 2. "To laughter I said: It is mad; and to mirth: What doth it issue in?" Laughter and mirth are personified; *mᵉholāl* is thus not neut. (Hitz., a foolish matter), but mas. The judgment which is pronounced regarding both has not the form of an address; we do not need to supply אַתָּה and אַתְּ, it is objectively like an *oratio obliqua:* that it is mad; cf. Ps. xlix. 12. In the midst of the laughter and revelling in sensual delight, the feeling came over him that this was not the way to true happiness, and he was compelled to say to laughter, It has become mad (*part. Poal*, as at Ps. cii. 9), it is like one who is raving mad, who finds his pleasure in self-destruction; and to joy (mirth), which disregards the earnestness of life and all due bounds, he is constrained to say, What does it result in? = that it produces nothing, *i.e.* that it brings forth no real fruit; that it produces only the opposite of true satisfaction; that instead of filling, it only enlarges the inner void. Others, *e.g.* Luther, "What doest thou?" *i.e.* How foolish is thy undertaking! Even if we thus explain, the point in any case lies in the inability of mirth to make man truly and lastingly happy,—in the inappropriateness of the means for the end aimed at. Therefore עֹשָׂה is thus meant just as in עֹשֵׂה פְרִי (Hitz.), and מעשׂה, effect, Isa. xxxii. 17. Thus Mendelssohn: What profit dost thou bring to me? Regarding זֹה, *vid.* p. 198; מַה־זֹּה is = *mah-zoth*, Gen. iii. 13, where it is shown that the demonstrative pronoun serves here to sharpen the interrogative: What then, what in all the world!

After this revelling in sensual enjoyment has been proved to be a fruitless experiment, he searches whether wisdom and folly cannot be bound together in a way leading to the object aimed at.

Ver. 3. "I searched in my heart, (henceforth) to nourish my body with wine, while my heart had the direction by means of wisdom; and to lay hold on folly, till I might see what it was good for the children of men that they should do, all the number of the days of their life." After he became conscious that unbridled sensual intoxication does not lead to the wished-for end, he looked around him farther, and examined into the following receipt for happiness. Inappropriately, Zöckl., with Hengst.: "I essayed in my heart to nourish . . ." תּוּר does not mean *probare*, but *explorare*, to spy out, Num. x. 33, and frequently in the Book of Koheleth (here and at i. 13, vii. 25) of mental searching and discovery (Targ. אַלֵּל). With לִמְשׁוֹךְ there then follows the new thing that is contrived. If we read מֹשֵׁךְ and נֹהֵג in connection, then the idea of drawing a carriage, Isa. v. 18, cf. Deut. xxi. 3, and of driving a carriage, 2 Sam. vi. 3, lies near; according to which Hitzig explains: "Wine is compared to a draught beast such as a horse, and he places wisdom as the driver on the box, that his horse may not throw him into a ditch or a morass." But *moshēk* is not the wine, but the person himself who makes the trial; and *nohēg* is not the wisdom, but the heart,—the former thus only the means of guidance; no man expresses himself thus: I draw the carriage by means of a horse, and I guide it by means of a driver. Rightly the Syr.: "To delight (למבסם, from בָּסֵם, *oblectare*) my flesh with wine." Thus also the Targ. and the Venet., by "drawing the flesh." The metaphor does not accord with the Germ. *ziehen* = to nourish by caring for (for which רִבָּה is used); it is more natural, with Gesen., to compare the passing of *trahere* into *tractare*, *e.g.* in the expression *se benignius tractare* (Horace, *Ep.* i. 17); but apart from the fact that *trahere* is a word of doubtful etymology,[1] *tractare* perhaps attains the meaning of attending to, using, managing, through the intermediate idea of moving hither and thither, which is foreign to the Heb. מָשַׁךְ, which means only to draw,—to draw to oneself, and hold fast (*attractum sive prehensum tenere*). As the Talm. מָשַׁךְ occurs in the sense of "to refresh," *e.g. Chagiga* 14*a*: "The Haggadists (in contradistinction to the Halachists) refresh the heart of a man as with water" (*vid.* p. 193); so here, "to draw the flesh" = to bring it into willing obedience by means of pleasant attractions.[2]

[1] *Vid.* Corssen's *Nachtr. zur lat. Formenlehre*, pp. 107–109.
[2] Grätz translates: to embrocate my body with wine, and remarks that in

The phrase which follows: *vᵉlibbi noheg bahhochmāh*, is conditioning: While my heart had the direction by means of wisdom; or, perhaps in accordance with the more modern *usus loq.* (*vid.* p. 194): While my heart guided, demeaned, behaved itself with wisdom. Then the inf. *limshok*, depending on *tarti* as its obj., is carried forward with *vᵉlěehhoz bᵉsichluth*. Plainly the subject treated of is an intermediate thing (Bardach: מְמֻצָּעַת). He wished to have enjoyment, but in measure, without losing himself in enjoyment, and thereby destroying himself. He wished to give himself over to sweet *desipere*, but yet with wise self-possession (because it is sadly true that *ubi mel ibi fel*) to lick the honey and avoid the gall. There are drinkers who know how to guide themselves so that they do not end in drunken madness; and there are habitual pleasure-seekers who yet know how so far to control themselves, that they do not at length become *roués*. Koheleth thus gave himself to a foolish life, yet tempered by wisdom, till there dawned upon him a better light upon the way to true happiness.

The expression of the *donec viderem* is old Heb. Instead of אֵי־זֶה טוֹב, *quidnam sit bonum* in indirect interrog. (as xi. 6, cf. Jer. vi. 16), the old form מַה־טּוֹב (vi. 12) would lie at least nearer. *Asher yăăsu* may be rendered: *quod faciant* or *ut faciant;* after ii. 24, iii. 22, v. 4, vii. 18, the latter is to be assumed. The accus. designation of time, "through the number of the days of their life," is like v. 17., vi. 12. We have not, indeed, to translate with Knobel: "the few days of their life," but yet there certainly lies in מִסְפַּר the idea that the days of man's life are numbered, and that thus even if they are not few but many (vi. 3), they yet do not endure for ever.

The king now, in the verse following, relates his undertakings for the purpose of gaining the joys of life in fellowship with wisdom, and first, how he made architecture and gardening serviceable to this new style of life.

Vv. 4—6. " I undertook great works, built me houses, planted me vineyards. I made me gardens and parks, and planted therein all kinds of fruit-trees. I made me water-pools to water therewith a forest bringing forth trees." The expression, "I made great my works," is like i. 16; the verb contains the adj. as its obj. The love of wisdom, a sense of the beautiful in nature and art, a striving after splendour and dignity, are fundamental traits in Solomon's character.

this lies a *raffinement*. But why does he not rather say, "to bathe in wine"? If מָשַׁח can mean "to embrocate," it may also mean "to bathe," and for יַיִן may be read יְוָנִי: in Grecian, *i.e.* Falernian, Chian, wine.

His reign was a period of undisturbed and assured peace. The nations far and near stood in manifold friendly relations with him. Solomon was "the man of rest," 1 Chron. xxii. 9; his whole appearance was as it were the embodied glory itself that had blossomed from out of the evils and wars of the reign of David. The Israelitish commonwealth hovered on a pinnacle of worldly glory till then unattained, but with the danger of falling and being lost in the world. The whole tendency of the time followed, as it were, a secular course, and it was Solomon first of all whom the danger of the love of the world, and of worldly conformity to which he was exposed, brought to ruin, and who, like so many of the O. T. worthies, began in the spirit and ended in the flesh. Regarding his buildings,—the house of the forest of Lebanon, the pillared hall (porch), the hall of judgment, the palace intended for himself and the daughter of Pharaoh,—*vid.* the description in 1 Kings vii. 1–12, gathered from the annals of the kingdom; 1 Kings ix. 15–22 = 2 Chron. viii. 3–6, gives an account of Solomon's separate buildings (to which also the city of Millo belongs), and of the cities which he built; the temple, store-cities, treasure-cities, etc., are naturally not in view in the passage before us, where it is not so much useful buildings, as rather buildings for pleasure (1 Kings ix. 19), that are referred to. Vineyards, according to 1 Chron. xxvii. 27, belonged to David's royal domain; a vineyard in Baal-hamon which Solomon possessed, but appears at a later period to have given up, is mentioned at the close of the Song. That he was fond of gardening, appears from manifold expressions in the Song; delight in the life and movements of the natural world, and particularly in plants, is a prominent feature in Solomon's character, in which he agrees with Shulamith. The Song, vi. 2, represents him in the garden at the palace. We have spoken under the Song, vi. 11 f., of the gardens and parks at Etam, on the south-west of Bethlehem. Regarding the originally Persian word *pardēs* (plur. *pardesim*, Mishnic *pardesoth*), *vid.* under Song iv. 13; regarding the primary meaning of *bᵉrēchah* (plur. const. *bᵉrēchoth*, in contradistinction to *birchoth*, blessings), the necessary information is found under Song vii. 5. These Solomonic pools are at the present day to be seen near old Etam, and the clause here denoting a purpose, "to water from them a forest which sprouted trees, *i.e.* brought forth sprouting trees," is suitable to these; for verbs of flowing and swarming, also verbs of growing, thought of transitively, may be connected with obj.-accus., Ewald, § 281*b*; cf. under Isa. v. 6. Thus, as he gave himself to the building of houses, the care of gardens, and the erection of pools, so also to the cultivation of forests, with the raising of new trees.

Another means, wisely considered as productive of happiness, was a large household and great flocks of cattle, which he procured for himself.

Ver. 7. "I procured servants and maidens, and also I obtained servants born in the house; also the possession of flocks; I obtained many horned and small cattle before all who were in Jerusalem before me." The obtaining of these possessions is, according to Gen. xvii. 12 ff., to be understood of purchase. There is a distinction between the slaves, male and female (*mancipia*), obtained by purchase, and those who were home-born (*vernae*), the בֵּית (יְלִידֵי) בְּנֵי, who were regarded as the chief support of the house (Gen. xiv. 14), on account of their attachment to it, and to this day are called (Arab.) *fada wayyt*, as those who offer themselves a sacrifice for it, if need be. Regarding היה לי, in the sense of increasing possession, *vid*. Song, p. 155; and regarding הָיָה for הָיוּ, *vid*. at i. 10, 16; at all events, the sing. of the pred. may be explained from this, that the persons and things named are thought of in the mass, as at Zech. xi. 5, Joel i. 20 (although the idea there may be also individualizing); but in the use of the pass., as at Gen. xxxv. 26, Dan. ix. 24, the Semite custom is different, inasmuch as for it the passive has the force of an active without a definite subject, and thus with the most general subject; and as to the case lying before us in ver. 7, we see from Ex. xii. 49, cf. Gen. xv. 17, that היה (יהיה) in such instances is thought of as neut. According to Gen. xxvi. 14 and the passage before us, מִקְנֵה lay nearer than מִקְנֶה, but the primary form instead of the connecting form is here the traditional reading; we have thus apposition (*Nebenordnung*) instead of subordination (*Annexion*), as in *zᵉvahim shᵉlamim*, Ex. xxiv. 5, and in *habbaqar hannᵉhhosheth*, 2 Kings xvi. 17, although *vaqar vatson* may also be interpreted as the accus. of the more accurate definition: the possession of flocks consisting in cattle and sheep. But this manner of construction is, for a book of so late an origin, too artificial. What it represents Solomon as saying is consistent with historical fact; at the consecration of the temple he sacrificed hecatombs, 1 Kings viii. 63; and the daily supply for the royal kitchen, which will at the same time serve to show the extent of the royal household, was, according to 1 Kings v. 2 f., enormous.

There now follows the enumeration of riches and jewels which were a delight to the eye; and finally, the large provision made for revelling in the pleasures of music and of sensual love.

Ver. 8. "I heaped up for myself also silver and gold, and the peculiar property of kings and of countries; I gat me men singers and women singers, and the delights of the children of men: mistress and mistresses." The verb כָּנַשׁ בָּנַס, συνάγειν, is common to all Semitic dialects (also to the Assyr.), and especially peculiar to the more recent Heb., which forms from it the name of the religious community συναγωγή, כְּנֵסֶת; it is used here of that which is brought together merely for the purpose of possession. S^egūllah (from sagal, Targ., to make oneself possess), properly possession, and that something which specially and peculiarly belongs to one as his property; the word is here meant collect., as at 1 Chron. xxix. 3: that which only kings and individual countries possess. The interchange of m^elachim, which is without the article, with the determ. hamm^edinoth, is arbitrary: something special, such as that which a king possesses, the specialities which countries possess,—one country this, and another that. The hamm^edinoth are certainly not exclusively the regions embraced within the dominion of Solomon (Zöckl.), as, according to Esth. i. 1, the Persian kingdom was divided into 127 m^edinoth. Solomon had a fleet which went to Ophir, was in a friendly relation with the royal house of Tyre, the metropolis of many colonies, and ruled over a widely-extended kingdom, bound by commerce with Central Asia and Africa.—His desires had thus ample opportunity to stretch beyond the limits of his own kingdom, and facilities enough for procuring the peculiar natural and artistic productions which other lands could boast of. M^edinah is, first of all, a country, not as a territory, but as under one government (cf. v. 7); in the later philosophical language it is the Heb. word for the Greek πολιτεία; in the passage before us, m^edinoth is, however, not different from אֲרָצוֹת.

From the singing men and singing women who come into view here, not as appertaining to the temple service (vid. the Targ.), with which no singing women were connected, but as connected with the festivities of the court (2 Sam. xix. 36; cf. Isa. v. 12), advance is made to shiddah v^eshiddoth; and since these are designated by the preceding וְתַעֲנֻגוֹת (not וְתַעֲנֻגוֹת) b^ene hāādam, especially as objects and means of earthly pleasure, and since, according to vii. 7, sexual love is the fairest and the most pleasant, in a word, the most attractive of all earthly delights (Solomon's luxus, also here contradicting the law of the king, Deut. xvii. 17, came to a height, according to 1 Kings xi. 3, after the example of Oriental rulers, in a harem of not fewer than one thousand women, princesses and concubines), of necessity, the expression shiddah v^eshiddoth must denote a multitude of women whom the king possessed for his own pleasure. Cup-bearers, male and female (Syr., LXX.), cannot at all be understood, for although it may be said that the enumeration thus connects itself with the before-named בָּנִים, yet this class of female attendants are not numbered among the highest human pleasures; besides, with such an explanation one must read שָׂרָה וְשָׂרוֹת, and, in addition, שְׁרָא (to throw, to pour to, or pour out), to which this Heb. שדה may correspond, is nowhere used of the pouring out of wine. Rather might שדה, like שרא, *hydria*, be the name of a vessel from which one pours out anything, according to which Aq. translates by κυλίκιον καὶ κυλίκια, Symmachus, after Jerome, by *mensurarum* (read *mensarum*[1]) *species et appositiones*, and Jerome, *scyphos et urceos in ministerio ad vina fundenda*; but this word for *kᵉlē mashkēh*, 1 Kings x. 21 (= 2 Chron. ix. 20), is not found. Also the Targ., which translates by *dimasaya uvē vᵉnavan*, public baths (δημόσια), and *balneae*, vindicates this translation by referring the word to the verb שְׁרָא, "with pipes which pour out (דְּשָׁרְיָן) tepid water, and pipes which pour out hot water." But this explanation is imaginary; שִׁדָּה occurs in the Mishna, *Mikwaoth* (of plunge-baths) vi. 5, but there it denotes a chest which, when it swims in the water, makes the plunge-bath unsuitable. Such an untenable conceit also is the translation suggested by Kimchi, כְּלִי זֶמֶר, according to which the Venet. σύστημα καὶ συστήματα (in a musical sense: *concentus*), and Luther: "all kinds of musical instruments;" the word has not this meaning; Orelli, *Sanchuniathon*, p. 33, combines therewith Σιδών, according to the Phoenician myth, the inventress of the artistic song. The explanation by Kimchi is headed, "Splendour of every kind;" Ewald, Elster, and Zöckler find therein a general expression, following *taanugoth*: great heap and heaps = in great abundance [*die Hülle und Fülle*]. But the synon. of כָּבוֹד, "splendour," is not שֵׁד, but עֹז; and that שדד, like עצם, is referred to a great number, is without proof. Thus *shiddah vᵉshiddoth* will denote something definite; besides, "a large number" finds its expression in the climactic union of words. In the Jerus. Talm. *Taanith* iv. 5, *shiddah* must, according to the gloss, be the name of a chariot, although the subject there is not that of motion forward, or moving quickly; it is there announced that *Sichin*, not far from Sepphoris, a place famed also for its pottery, formerly possessed 80 such *shiddoth* wholly of metal. The very same word is explained by Rashi, *Baba kamma* ix. 3, *Shabbath* 120*a*, *Erubin* 30*b*, *Gittin* 8*b*, 68*a*, *Chagiga* 25*a*, and elsewhere, of a carriage of wood, and especially of a chariot for

[1] Thus, according to Vallarsi, a *Cod. Vat.* and *Cod. Palat.* of the first hand.

women and distinguished persons. The combination of the synonyms, *shiddah uthivah umigdal*, does not in itself mean more than a chest; and Rashi himself explains, *Kethuboth* 65a, *quolphi dashidah* of the lock of a chest (*argaz*); and the author of *Aruch* knows no other meaning than that of a repository such as a chest. But in passages such as *Gittin* 8b, the *shiddah* is mentioned as a means of transport; it is to all appearance a chest going on wheels, moved forward by means of wheels, but on that very account not a state-chariot. Rashi's tradition cannot be verified. Böttcher, in the *Neue Aehrenlese*, adduces for comparison the Syr. *Shydlo*, which, according to Castelli, signifies *navis magna, corbita, arca;* but from a merchant ship and a portable chest, it is a great way to a lady's palanquin. He translates: palanquin and palanquins = one consignment to the harem after another. Gesen., according to Rödiger, *Thes.* 1365b, thinks that women are to be understood; for he compares the Arab. *z'ynat*, which signifies a women's carriage, and then the woman herself (cf. our *Frauenzimmer*, women's apartment, women, like *Odaliske*, from the Turk. *oda*, apartment). But this all stands or falls with that gloss of Rashi's: *'agalah l^emerkavoth nashim usarim*. Meanwhile, of all the explanations as yet advanced, this last [of splendid coaches, palanquins] is the best; for it may certainly be supposed that the words *shiddah v^eshiddoth* are meant of women. Aben Ezra explains on this supposition, *shiddoth = sh^evuyoth*, females captured in war; but unwarrantably, because as yet Solomon had not been engaged in war; others (*vid.* Pinsker's *Zur Gesch. des Karaismus*, p. 296), recently Bullock, connect it with *shadāim*, in the sense of (Arab.) *nahidah* (a maiden with swelling breast); Knobel explains after *shadad*, to barricade, to shut up, *occlusa*, the female held in custody (cf. *b^ethulah*, the separated one, virgin, from *bathal*, cogn. *badal*); Hitzig, "cushions," "bolsters," from *shanad*, which, like (Arab.) *firash*, λέχος, is then transferred to the *juncta toro*. Nothing of all that is satisfactory. The Babyl. Gemara, *Gittin* 68a, glosses וְתַעֲנֻגוֹת by "reservoirs and baths," and then further says that in the west (Palestine) they say שִׁידְתָא, chests (according to Rashi: chariots); but that here in this country (*i.e.* in Babylon) they translate *shiddah v^eshiddoth* by *shēdah v^eshēdathin*, which is then explained, "demons and demonesses," which Solomon had made subservient to him.[1] This haggadic-mytholog. interpreta-

---

[1] A demon, and generally a superhuman being, is called, as in Heb. שֵׁד, so in the Babyl.-Assyr. *sidu*, *vid.* Norris' *Assyrian Dictionary*, II. p. 668; cf. Schrader, in the *Jena. Lit. Zeit.* 1874, p. 218 f., according to which *sidu*, with *alap*, is the usual name of Adar formed like an ox.

tion is, linguistically at least, on the right track. A demon is not so named from fluttering or moving to and fro (Levy, Schönhak), for there is no evidence in the Semitic language of the existence of a verb שׁוּד, to flee; also not from a verb *sadad*, which must correspond to the Heb. הִשְׁתַּחֲוָה, in the sense of to adore (Oppert's *Inscription du palais de Khorsabad*, 1863, p. 96); for this meaning is more than doubtful, and, besides, שֵׁד is an active, and not a passive idea,— much rather שֵׁד, Assyr. *sîd*, Arab. *sayyid*, signifies the mighty, from שׁוּד, to force, Ps. xci. 6.[1] In the Arab. (cf. the Spanish *Cid*) it is uniformly the name of a lord, as subduing, ruling, mastering (*sabid*), and the fem. *sayyidat*, of a lady, whence the vulgar Arab. *sitti* = my lady, and *sîdi* = my lord. Since שָׁדַד means the same as שׁוּד, and in Heb. is more commonly used than it, so also the fem. form שָׁדָה is possible, so much the more as it may have originated from שִׁידָה, v. שִׁיד = שֵׁד, by a sharpening contraction, like סֻמִּים, from סִינִים (Olsh. § 83c), perhaps intentionally to make שֵׁדָה, a demoness, and the name of a lady (*donna* = *domina*) unlike. Accordingly we translate, with Gesen. and Meyer in their *Handwört.*: "lady and ladies;" for we take *shiddoth* as a name of the ladies of the harem, like *shēglath* (Assyr. *saklâti*) and *l^ehhenath* in the book of Daniel, on which Ahron b. Joseph the Karaite remarks: *shedah hinqaroth shagal*.

The connection expressing an innumerable quantity, and at the same time the greatest diversity, is different from the genitival *dor dorim*, generation of generations, *i.e.* lasting through all generations, Ps. lxxii. 5, from the permutative heightening the idea: *rahham rahhamathaim*, one damsel, two damsels, Judg. v. 30, and from that formed by placing together the two gram. genders, comprehending every species of the generic conception: *mash'ēn umash'enah*, Isa. iii. 3 (*vid.* comm. *l.c.*, and Ewald, § 172b). Also the words cited by Ewald (Syr.), *rogo urógo*, " all possible pleasures " (Cureton's *Spicil.* p. 10), do not altogether accord with this passage, for they heighten, like *m^eod m^eod*, by the repetition of the same expression. But similar is the Arab. scheme, *mal wamwal*, " possession and possessions," *i.e.* exceeding great riches, where the collective idea, in itself affording by its indetermination free scope to the imagination, is multiplied by the plur. being further added.

After Koheleth has enumerated all that he had provided for the purpose of gratifying his lusts, but without losing himself therein, he draws the conclusion, which on this occasion also shows a perceptible deficit.

[1] *Vid.* Friedrich Delitzsch's *Assyr. Thiernamen*, p. 37.

Vv. 9–11. "And I became great, and was always greater than all that were before me in Jerusalem: also my wisdom remained with me. And all that mine eyes desired I kept not from them, I refused not any kind of joy to my heart; for my heart had joy of all my labour: and this was my portion of all my labour. And I turned myself to all the works which my hands had done, and to the labour which I had laboured to accomplish: and, behold, all was vain, and windy effort, and there was no true profit under the sun." In v‘hosaphti there is here no obj. as at i. 16; the obj. is the g‘dullah, the greatness, to be concluded and thought of from v‘gadalti, "and I became great." To the impers. הָיָה for הָיוּ, 7b, cf. 7a, i. 16, 10. He became great, and always greater, viz. in the possession of all the good things, the possession of which seemed to make a man happy on this earth. And what he resolved upon, in the midst of this *dulcis insania*, viz. to deport himself as a wise man, he succeeded in doing: his wisdom forsook him not, viz. the means adapted to the end, and ruling over this colossal apparatus of sensual lust; אַף, as *e.g.* at Ps. xvi. 6, belongs to the whole clause; and עמד, with ל, does not mean here to stand by, sustain (Herzfeld, Ewald, Elster), which it might mean as well as עמד על, Dan. xii. 1, but to continue (*vid.* p. 194), as Jerome, and after him, Luther, translates: *sapientia quoque perseveravit mecum*; the Targ. connects the ideas of continuance (LXX., Syr., Venet.) and of help; but the idea intended is that of continuance, for נהג, *e.g.*, does not refer to helping, but self-maintaining.

Ver. 10. Thus become great and also continuing wise, he was not only in a condition to procure for himself every enjoyment, but he also indulged himself in everything; all that his eyes desired, *i.e.* all that they saw, and after which they made him lust (Deut. xiv. 26) (cf. 1 John ii. 16), that he did not refuse to them (אָצַל, *subtrahere*), and he kept not back his heart from any kind of joy (מָנַע, with *min* of the thing refused, as at Num. xxiv. 11, etc., oftener with *min*, of him to whom it is refused, *e.g.* Gen. xxx. 2), for (here, after the foregoing negations, coinciding with *immo*) his heart had joy of all his work; and this, viz. this enjoyment in full measure, was his part of all his work. The palindromic form is like i. 6, iv. 1; cf. *Isa.* p. 411. We say in Heb. as well as in German: to have joy in (*an*, ב) anything, joy over (*über*, על) anything, or joy of (*von*, מן) anything; Koheleth here purposely uses *min*, for he wishes to express not that the work itself was to him an object and reason of joy, but that it became to him a well of joy (cf. Prov. v. 18; 2 Chron. xx. 27). Falsely, Hahn and others: after my work (*min*, as *e.g.*

Ps. lxxiii. 20), for thereby the causative connection is obliterated: *min* is the expression of the mediate cause, as the concluding sentence says: Joy was that which he had of all his work—this itself brought care and toil to him; joy, made possible to him thereby, was the share which came to him from it.

Ver. 11. But was this חֵלֶק a יִתְרוֹן—was this gain that fell to him a true, satisfying, pure gain? With the words *uphanithi ani* (vid. p. 198) he proposes this question, and answers it. פָּנָה (to turn to) is elsewhere followed by expressions of motion to an end; here, as at Job vi. 28, by בְּ, by virtue of a *constructio praegnans*: I turned myself, fixing my attention on all my works which my hands accomplished. *La'asoth* is, as at Gen. ii. 3 (*vid. l.c.*), equivalent to *perficiendo*, carrying out, viz. such works of art and of all his labour. The exclamation "behold" introduces the *summa summarum*. Regarding יִתְרוֹן, *vid.* i. 3. Also this way of finding out that which was truly good showed itself to be false. Of all this enjoyment, there remained nothing but the feeling of emptiness. What he strove after appeared to him as the wind; the satisfaction he sought to obtain at such an expense was nothing else than a momentary delusion. And since in this search after the true happiness of life he was in a position more favourable for such a purpose than almost any other man, he is constrained to draw the conclusion that there is no יתרון, *i.e.* no real enduring and true happiness, from all labour under the sun.

The End of the Wise Man the same as that of the Fool, ii. 12–17.

After Koheleth has shown, i. 12 ff., that the striving after wisdom does not satisfy, inasmuch as, far from making men happy, its possession only increases their inward conflicts, he proposes to himself the question, whether or not there is a difference between wisdom and folly, whether the former does not far excel the latter. He proceeds to consider this question, for it is more appropriate to him, the old much-experienced king, than to others.

Ver. 12. "And I turned myself to examine wisdom, and madness, and folly: for what is the man who could come after the king, him whom they have made so long ago!" Mendelssohn's translation, 12*a*: "I abandoned my design of seeking to connect wisdom with folly and madness," is impossible, because for such a rendering we should have had at least מִלְּרְאוֹת instead of לִרְאוֹת. Hitzig, otherwise followed by Stuart: "I turned myself to examine me wisdom, and, lo, it was madness as well as folly." This rendering is impossible also, for in such a case וְהִנֵּה ought to have stood as the result, after

חכמה. The passage, Zech. xiv. 6, cited by Hitz., does not prove the possibility of such a brachyology, for there we read not $v^eqaroth$ $v^eqeppayon$, but ^eqaroth $iq^eppaūn$ (the splendid ones, i.e. the stars, will draw themselves together, i.e. will become dark bodies). The two *vavs* are not correlative, which is without example in the usage of this book, but copulative: he wishes to contemplate (Zöckler and others) wisdom on the one side, and madness and folly on the other, in their relation to each other, viz. in their relative worth. Hitzig's ingenuity goes yet further astray in 12*b*: "For what will the man do who comes after the king? (He shall do) what was long ago his (own) doing, i.e. inheriting from the king the throne, he will not also inherit his wisdom." Instead of $āsūhū$, he reads $ǎsōhū$, after Ex. xviii. 18; but the more modern author, whose work we have here before us, would, instead of this anomalous form, use the regular form עשׂיתו; but, besides, the expression $ēth$ $asher$-k^evar '$asotho$, "(he will do) what long ago was his doing,", is not Heb.; the words ought to have been $k^easotho$ k^evar $khen$ i^esah, or at least '$asāhū$. If we compare 12*b* with 18*b*, the man who comes after the king appears certainly to be his successor.[1] But by this supposition it is impossible to give just effect to the relation (assigning a reason or motive) of 12*b* to 12*a* expressed by כִּי. When I considered, Knobel regards Koheleth as saying, that a fool would be heir to me a wise man, it appeared strange to me, and I was led to compare wisdom and folly to see whether or not the wise man has a superiority to the fool, or whether his labour and his fate are vanity, like those of the fool. This is in point of style absurd, but it is much more absurd logically. And who then gave the interpreter the right to stamp as a fool the man who comes after the king? In the answer: "That which has long ago been done," must lie its justification; for this that was done long ago naturally consists, as Zöckler remarks, in foolish and perverse undertakings, certainly in the destruction of that which was done by the wise predecessor, in the lavish squandering of the treasures and goods collected by him. More briefly, but in the same sense, Burger: *Nihil quod a solita hominum agendi ratione recedit.* But in ver. 19, Koheleth places it as a question whether his successor will be a wise man or a fool, while here he would presuppose that "naturally," or as a matter of course, he will be a fool. In the matter of style, we have nothing to object to the translation on which Zöckler, with Ramb., Rosenm., Knobel, Hengst.,

---

[1] The LXX. and Symm. by $hamm\breve{e}l\bar{e}k$ think of m^elak, counsel, βουλή, instead of $m\breve{e}l\breve{e}k$, king; and as Jerome, so also Bardach understands by the king the *rex factor*, i.e. God the Creator.

and others, proceeds; the supplying of the verb יַעֲשֶׂה to *meh hāādām* [= what can the man do?] is possible (cf. Mal. ii. 15), and the neut. interpret. of the suffix of עָשׂוּהוּ is, after vii. 13, Amos i. 3, Job xxxi. 11, admissible; but the reference to a successor is not connected with the course of the thoughts, even although one attaches to the plain words a meaning which is foreign to them. The words אֵת ... עָשׂוּהוּ are accordingly not the answer to the question proposed, but a component part of the question itself. Thus Ewald, and with him Elster, Heiligst., construes: "How will the man be who will follow the king, compared with him whom they made (a king) long ago, *i.e.* with his predecessor?" But אֵת, in this pregnant sense, "compared with," is without example, at least in the Book of Koheleth, which generally does not use it as a prep.; and, besides, this rendering, by introducing the successor on the throne, offends against the logic of the relation of 12*b* to 12*a*. The motive of Koheleth's purpose, to weigh wisdom and folly against each other as to their worth, consists in this, that a king, especially such an one as Solomon was, has in the means at his disposal and in the extent of his observation so much more than every other, that no one who comes after him will reach a different experience. This motive would be satisfactorily expressed on the supposition that the answer begins with אֵת, if one should read עָשָׂהוּ for עָשׂוּהוּ: he will be able to do (accomplish) nothing but what he (the king) has long ago done, *i.e.* he will only repeat, only be able to confirm, the king's report. But if we take the text as it here stands, the meaning is the same; and, besides, we get rid of the harsh ellipsis *meh hāādām* for *meh yăăsĕh hāādām*. We translate: for what is the man who might come after the king, him whom they have made so long ago! The king whom they made so long ago is Solomon, who has a richer experience, a more comprehensive knowledge, the longer the time (viz. from the present time backwards) since he occupied the throne. Regarding the expression *eth asher* = *quem*, instead of the *asher* simply, *vid.* Köhler under Zech. xii. 10. עָשׂוּהוּ, with the most general subj., is not different from נַעֲשָׂה, which, particularly in the Book of Daniel (*e.g.* iv. 28 f.), has frequently an active construction, with the subject unnamed, instead of the passive (Gesen. § 137, margin). The author of the Book of Koheleth, alienated from the theocratic side of the kingdom of Israel, makes use of it perhaps not unintentionally; besides, Solomon's elevation to the throne was, according to 1 Kings i., brought about very much by human agency; and one may, if he will, think of the people in the word *'asuhu* also, according to 1 Kings i. 39, who at last decided the matter. *Meh* before the letters *hheth* and *ayin* commonly occurs : according to the Masora, twenty-four times ; before other initial letters than these, eight times, and three of these in the Book of Koheleth before the letter *he*, ii. 12, 22, vii. 10. The words are more an exclamation than a question ; the exclamation means : What kind of a man is that who could come after the king ! cf. " What wickedness is this ! " etc., Judg. xx. 12, Josh. xxii. 16, Ex. xviii. 14, 1 Kings ix. 13, *i.e.* as standing behind with reference to me—the same figure of *extenuatio*, as *mah adam*, Ps. cxliv. 3 ; cf. viii. 5.

There now follows an account of what, on the one side, happened to him thus placed on a lofty watch-tower, such as no other occupied.

Vv. 13, 14*a*. " And I saw that wisdom has the advantage over folly, as light has the advantage over darkness. The wise man has eyes in his head ; but the fool walketh in darkness." In the sacred Scriptures, " light " is generally the symbol of grace, Ps. xliii. 3, but also the contrast of an intellectually and morally darkened state, Isa. li. 4. To know a thing is equivalent to having light on it, and seeing it in its true light (Ps. xxxvi. 10) ; wisdom is thus compared to light ; folly is once, Job xxxviii. 19, directly called " darkness." Thus wisdom stands so much higher than folly, as light stands above darkness. יִתְרוֹן, which hitherto denoted actual result, enduring gain, signifies here preference (*vid.* p. 192) ; along with בְּיִתְרוֹן [1] there is also found the form בִּיתְרוֹן [2] (*vid.* Prov. xxx. 17). The fool walks in darkness : he is blind although he has eyes (Isa. xliii. 8), and thus has as good as none,—he wants the spiritual eye of understanding (x. 3) ; the wise man, on the other hand, his eyes are in his head, or, as we also say : he has eyes in his head,—eyes truly seeing, looking at and examining persons and things. That is the one side of the relation of wisdom to folly as put to the test.

The other side of the relation is the sameness of the result in which the elevation of wisdom above folly terminates.

Vv. 14*b*, 15. " And I myself perceived that one experience happeneth to them all. And I said in my heart, As it will happen to the fool, it will happen also to me ; and why have I then been specially wise ? Thus I spake then in my heart, that this also is vain." Zöckler gives to גַּם an adversative sense ; but this *gam* (= ὅμως, *similiter*) stands always at the beginning of the clause, Ewald, § 354*a*. *Gam-ani* corresponds to the Lat. *ego idem*, which gives two predicates to one subject ; while *et ipse* predicates the same of the one of two subjects as it does of the other (Zumpt, § 697). The second *gam*-

---
[1] Thus written, according to J and other authorities.
[2] Thus Ven. 1515, 1521 ; *vid.* Comm. under Gen. xxvii. 28, 29 ; Ps. xlv. 10.

ani serves for the giving of prominence to the object, and here precedes, after the manner of a substantival clause (cf. Isa. xlv. 12; Ezek. xxxiii. 17; 2 Chron. xxviii. 10), as at Gen. xxiv. 27; cf. Gesen. § 121. 3. *Miqrěh* (from קָרָה, to happen, to befall) is *quiquid alicui accidit* (in the later philosoph. terminol. *accidens*; Venet. συμβεβηκός); but here, as the connection shows, that which finally puts an end to life, the final event of death. By the word יָדַ׳ the author expresses what he had observed on reflection; by בְּלִ׳ ... אָמַ׳, what he said inwardly to himself regarding it; and by בְּלִבִּ׳ דִּבַּ׳, what sentence he passed thereon with himself. *Lammah* asks for the design, as *maddu'a* for the reason. אָז is either understood temporally: then when it is finally not better with me than with the fool (Hitz. from the standpoint of the dying hour), or logically: if yet one and the same event happeneth to the wise man and to the fool (Elst.); in the consciousness of the author both are taken together. The זֶה of the conclusion refers, not, as at i. 17, to the endeavouring after and the possession of wisdom, but to this final result making no difference between wise men and fools. This fate, happening to all alike, is הֶבֶל, a vanity rendering all vain, a nullity levelling down all to nothing, something full of contradictions, irrational. Paul also (Rom. viii. 20) speaks of this destruction, which at last comes upon all, as a ματαιότης.

The author now assigns the reason for this discouraging result.

Ver. 16. "For no remembrance of the wise, as of the fool, remains for ever; since in the days that are to come they are all forgotten. And how dieth the wise man? as the fool!" As in i. 11, so here זִכְרוֹן is the principal form, not different from זִכָּרוֹן. Having no remembrance for ever, is equivalent to having no eternal endurance, having simply no onward existence (ix. 6). עִם is both times the comparat. combin., as at vii. 11; Job ix. 26, xxxvii. 18; cf. יַחַד, Ps. xlix. 11. There are, indeed, individual historically great men, the memory of whom is perpetuated from generation to generation in words and in monuments; but these are exceptions, which do not always show that posterity is able to distinguish between wise men and fools. As a rule, men have a long appreciating recollection of the wise as little as they have of the fools, for long ago (*vid. bᵉshekvar*, p. 196) in the coming days (הַיָּמִים הַבָּ׳, accus. of the time, like the ellipt. 'הב, Isa. xxvii. 6) all are forgotten; הַכֹּל is, as at Ps. xiv. 3, meant personally: the one as the other; and נִשְׁכָּח is rendered by the Masora, like ix. 6, 'כְּבָר אָב, as the pausal form of the finite; but is perhaps thought of as part., denoting that which only in the coming days will become too soon a completed fact, since those who survive go from the burial of the one, as well as from that of the other, to the ordinary duties of the day. Death thus sinks the wise man, as it does the fool, in eternal oblivion; it comes to both, and brings the same to both, which extorted from the author the cry: How dieth the wise man? as the fool! Why is the fate which awaits both thus the same! This is the pointed, sarcastic אֵיךְ (how!) of the satirical Mashal, e.g. Isa. xiv. 4, Ezek. xxvi. 17; and יָמוּת is = *moriendum est*, as at 2 Sam. iii. 3, *moriendum erat*. Rambach well: אֵיךְ *est h. l. particula admirationis super rei indignitate.*

What happened to the author from this sorrowful discovery he now states.

Ver. 17. "Then life became hateful to me; for the work which man accomplishes under the sun was grievous to me: because all is vain and windy effort." He hated life; and the labour which is done under the sun, *i.e.* the efforts of men, including the fate that befalls men, appeared to him to be evil (repugnant). The LXX. translate: πονηρὸν ἐπ' ἐμέ; the Venet.: κακὸν ἐπ' ἐμοί; and thus Hitzig: as a woful burden lying on me. But רַע עָלַי is to be understood after *tov al*, Esth. iii. 9, etc., cf. Ps. xvi. 6, and as synon. with בְּעֵינַי or לִפְנֵי (cf. Dan. iii. 32), according to which Symmachus: κακὸν γάρ μοι ἐφάνη. This *al* belongs to the more modern *usus loq.*, cf. Ewald, § 217*i*. The end of the song was also again the grievous *ceterum censeo*: Vanity, and a labour which has wind as its goal, wind as its fruit.

The Vanity of Wealth gathered with Care and Privation, ii. 18–23.

In view of death, which snatches away the wise man equally with the fool, and of the night of death, which comes to the one as to the other, deep dejection came upon him from another side.

Ver. 18. "And I hated all my labour with which I laboured under the sun, that I should leave it to the man who shall be after me;" *i.e.* not: who shall come into existence after me, but: who shall occupy my place after me. The fiction discovers itself here in the expression: "The king," who would not thus express himself indefinitely and unsympathetically regarding his son and successor on the throne, is stripped of his historical individuality. The first and third שׁ are relat. pron. (*quem*, after the *schema etymologicum* עָמָל עָמַל, ver. 11, ix. 9, and *qui*), the second is relat. conj. (*eo*) *quod*. The suffix of שֶׁאַנִּי refers to the labour in the sense of that which is obtained by wearisome labour, accomplished or collected with

CHAP. II. 19—21.

labour; cf. כֹּחַ, product, fruit, Gen. iv. 12; עֲבוּדָה, effect, Isa. xxxii. 17.

How this man will be circumstanced who will have at his disposal that for which he has not laboured, is uncertain.

Ver. 19. "And who knoweth whether he shall be wise or foolish? and he will have power over all my labour with which I had wearied myself, and had acted wisely, under the sun: this also is vain." הֲ ... אוֹ, instead of הֲ ... אִם, in the double question, as at Job xvi. 3. What kind of a man he will be no one can previously know, and yet this person will have free control (cf. שַׁלָּט, p. 196) over all the labour that the testator has wisely gained by labour—a hendiadys, for חָכַם with the obj. accus. is only in such a connection possible: "my labour which I, acting wisely, gained by labour."

In view of this doubtful future of that which was with pains and wisely gained by him, his spirit sank within him.

Ver. 20. "Then I turned to give up my heart on account of [= to despair of] all the labour with which I wearied myself under the sun." As at 1 Sam. xxii. 17 f., Song ii. 17, Jer. xli. 14, סבב has here the intrans. meaning, to turn about (LXX. ἐπέστρεψα = ἐπεστρεψάμην). Hitzig remarks that פנה and שׁוב signify, "to turn round in order to see," and סבב, on the contrary, "to turn round in order to do." But פנה can also mean, "to turn round in order to do," e.g. Lev. xxvi. 9; and סבב, "to turn in order to examine more narrowly," vii. 25. The distinction lies in this, that פנה signifies a clear turning round; סבב, a turning away from one thing to another, a turning in the direction of something new that presents itself (iv. 1, 7, ix. 11). The phrase, וַיֵּאָשׁ אֶת־לִבּוֹ,[1] closely corresponds to the Lat. despondet animum, he gives up his spirits, lets them sink, i.e. he despairs. The old language knows only נוֹאַשׁ, to give oneself up, i.e. to give up hope in regard to anything; and נוֹאָשׁ, given up, having no prospect, in despair. The Talm., however, uses along with nithyāēsh (vid. p. 192) not only noāsh, but also יֵאֵשׁ, in the sense of despair, or the giving up of all hope (subst. יֵאוּשׁ), Mezîa 21b, from which it is at once evident that יֵאֵשׁ is not to be thought of as causative (like the Arab. ajjasa and aiasa), but as simply transitive, with which, after the passage before us, לבו is to be thought of as connected. He turned round to give up all heart. He had no more any heart to labour.

---

[1] With Pathach under the yod in the text in Biblia Rabb. and the note לֹ. Thus also in the MS. Parva Masora, and e.g. Cod. P.

Ver. 21. "For there is a man who labours with wisdom, and knowledge, and ability; and to a man who has not laboured for it, must he leave it as his portion: also that is vain, and a great evil." Ewald renders: whose labour aims after wisdom. But בְּחָ׳ וגו׳ do not denote obj. (for the obj. of עמל is certainly the portion which is to be inherited), but are particular designations of the way and manner of the labour. Instead of שֶׁעָמַל, there is used the more emphatic form of the noun: שֶׁעֲמָלוֹ, who had his labour, and performed it; 1 Sam. vii. 17, cf. Jer. ix. 5 [6], "Thine habitation is in the midst of deceit," and Hitz. under Job ix. 27. *Kishron* is not ἀνδρεία (LXX.), manliness, moral energy (Elster), but aptness, ability, and (as a consequence connecting itself therewith) success, good fortune, thus skilfulness conducting to the end (*vid.* p. 193). בּוֹ refers to the object, and יִתְּנֶנּוּ to the result of the work; חֶלְקוֹ is the second obj.-accus., or, as we rather say, pred.-accus.: as his portion, viz. inheritance.

That what one has gained by skill and good fortune thus falls to the lot of another who perhaps recklessly squanders it, is an evil all the greater in proportion to the labour and care bestowed on its acquisition.

Vv. 22, 23. "For what has man of all his labour, and the endeavours of his heart with which he wearies himself under the sun? All his days are certainly in sorrows, and his activity in grief; his heart resteth not even in the night: also this is vain." The question literally is: What is (comes forth, results) to a man from all his labour; for "to become, to be, to fall to, happen to," is the fundamental idea of הוה (whence here הֹוֶה, γινόμενον, as at Neh. vi. 6, γενησόμενος) or היה, the root signification of which is *deorsum ferri, cadere,* and then *accidere, fieri,* whence הַוָּה, eagerness precipitating itself upon anything (*vid.* under Prov. x. 3), or object.: fall, catastrophe, destruction. Instead of שֶׁהוּא, there is here to be written שֶׁהוּא,[1] as at iii. 18 שֶׁהֵם. The question looks forward to a negative answer. What comes out of his labour for man? Nothing comes of it, nothing but disagreeableness. This negative contained in the question is established by כִּי, 23*a*. The form of the clause, "all his days are sorrows," viz. as to their condition, follows the scheme, "the porch was 20 cubits," 2 Chron. iii. 4, viz. in measurement; or, "their feast is music and wine," Isa. v. 12, viz. in its combination (*vid.* Philippi's *Stat. Const.* p. 90 ff.). The parallel clause is וְכַעַס עִנְיָנוֹ, not וְכ׳; for the final syllable, or that having the accent on the penult., immediately preceding the *Athnach*-word, takes *Kametz,* as

---

[1] Thus according to tradition, in H, J, P, *vid. Michlol* 47*b*, 215*b*, 216*a*; *vid.* also Norzi.

e.g. Lev. xviii. 5; Prov. xxv. 3; Isa. lxv. 17 (cf. Olsh. § 224, p. 440).[1] Many interpreters falsely explain: *at aegritudo est velut quotidiana occupatio ejus.* For the sake of the parallelism, עִנְיָנוֹ (from ענה, to weary oneself with labour, or also to strive, aim; *vid. Psalmen,* ii. 390) is subj. not pred.: his endeavour is grief, *i.e.* brings only grief or vexation with it. Even in the night he has no rest; for even then, though he is not labouring, yet he is inwardly engaged about his labour and his plans. And this possession, acquired with such labour and restlessness, he must leave to others; for equally with the fool he falls under the stroke of death: he himself has no enjoyment, others have it; dying, he must leave all behind him,—a threefold הבל, vv. 17, 21, 23, and thus הבל הבלים.

The Condition of Pure Enjoyment, ii. 24–26.

Is it not then foolish thus restlessly and with so much self-torment to labour for nothing? In view of the night of darkness which awaits man, and the uncertain destiny of our possessions, it is better to make use of the present in a way as pleasant to ourselves as possible.

Ver. 24. "There is nothing better among men, than that one eat and drink, and that he should pamper his soul by his labour: this also have I seen, that it is in the hand of God." The LXX., as well as the other Greek transl., and Jerome, had before them the words באדם שיאכל. The former translates: "Man has not the good which he shall eat and drink," *i.e.* also this that he eats … is for him no true good; but the direct contrary of this is what Koheleth says. Jerome seeks to bring the thought which the text presents into the right track, by using the form of a question: *nonne melius est comedere …*; against this iii. 12, 22, viii. 15, are not to be cited where אין טוב stands in the dependent sentence; the thought is not thus to be improved; its form is not this, for טוב, beginning a sentence, is never interrog., but affirm.; thus אין טוב is not = הלא טוב, but is a negative statement. It is above all doubt, that instead of באדם שֶׁיּ׳ we must read באדם מִשֶּׁיּ׳, after iii. 12, 22, viii. 15; for, as at Job xxxiii. 17, the initial letter *mem* after the terminal *mem* has dropped out. Codd. of the LXX. have accordingly corrected ὃ into πλὴν ὃ or εἰ μὴ ὃ (thus the Compl. Ald.), and the Syr. and Targ. render שׁ here by אלא דְ and אלהן דְ [unless that he eat];

---

[1] But cf. also וְלֹא with *Zakeph Katan,* 2 Kings v. 17; וָאֹר׳ וְנוּ׳ with *Tiphcha,* Isa. xxvi. 19; and וְרִיב under Ps. lv. 10.

Jerome also has *non est bonum homini nisi quod* in his *Comm.*; only the Venet. seeks to accommodate itself to the traditional text. Besides, only מ is to be inserted, not כי אם; for the phrase כי אם לֶאֱכֹל is used, but not כי אם שֶׁ. Instead of *bāādām*, the form *lāādām* would be more agreeable, as at vi. 12, viii. 15. Hitzig remarks, without proof, that *bāādām* is in accordance with later grammatical forms, which admit ב = "for" before the object. ב, x. 17, is neither prep. of the object, nor is ἐν, Sir. iii. 7, the exponent of the dative (*vid.* Grimm). *Bāādām* signifies, as at 2 Sam. xxiii. 3, and as ἐν ἀνθ., Sir. xi. 14, *inter homines;* also iii. 12 designates by טוב בָּם what among them (men) has to be regarded as good. It is interesting to see how here the ancient and the modern forms of the language run together, without the former wholly passing over into the latter; מִשֶּׁי, *quam ut edat*, is followed by norm. perfects, in accordance with that comprehensive peculiarity of the old syntax which Ewald, by an excellent figure, calls the dissolution of that which is coloured into grey. הַרְ' ... טוֹב is equivalent to הֱי' לוֹ, Ps. xlix. 19, the causative rendering of the phrase רָאָה טוֹב, iii. 13, or ר' טוֹבָה, v. 17, vi. 6. It is well to attend to בַּעֲמָלוֹ [by his labour], which forms an essential component part of that which is approved of as good. Not a useless sluggard-life, but a life which connects together enjoyment and labour, is that which Koheleth thinks the best in the world. But this enjoyment, lightening, embellishing, seasoning labour, has also its *But : etiam hoc vidi e manu Dei esse* (*pendere*). The order of the words harmonizes with this Lat.; it follows the scheme referred to at Gen. i. 4; cf. on the contrary, iii. 6. Instead of נַּם־זֶה, neut. by attraction, there is here the immediately neut. נַּם־זֹה; the book uniformly makes use of this fem. form instead of זֹאת (*vid.* p. 198). This or that is "in the hand of God," *i.e.* it is His gift, iii. 13, v. 18, and it is thus conditioned by Him, since man cannot give it to himself; cf. *minni*, Isa. xxx. 1; *mimménni*, Hos. viii. 4; *mimménnu*, 1 Kings xx. 33.

This dependence of the enjoyment of life on God is established.

Ver. 25. "For who can eat, and who can have enjoyment, without [= except from] Him?" Also here the traditional text is untenable: we have to read חוץ ממנו, after the LXX. (which Jerome follows in his *Comm.*) and the Syr. If we adopt the text as it lies before us, then the meaning would be, as given by Gumpel,[1] and thus translated by Jerome: *Quis ita devorabit et deliciis effluet ut ego?* But (1) the question thus understood would require יוֹתֵר מִמֶּנִּי, which Gumpel and others silently substitute in place of 'חוץ מ;

---

[1] *Vid.* regarding his noteworthy *Comm.* on Koheleth, my *Jesurun*, pp. 183 and 195. The author bears the name among Christians of Professor Levisohn.

(2) this question, in which the king adjudicates to himself an unparalleled right to eat and to enjoy himself, would stand out of connection with that which precedes and follows. Even though with Ginsburg, after Rashi, Aben Ezra, and Rashbam, we find in ver. 25 the thought that the labourer has the first and nearest title to the enjoyment of the fruit of his labour (מ׳ חוץ thus exemplif. as iv. 8, 'ע . . . למי), the continuation with כִּי, ver. 26, is unsuitable; for the natural sequence of the thoughts would then be this: But the enjoyment, far from being connected with the labour as its self-consequence and fruit, is a gift of God, which He gives to one and withholds from another. If we read מִמֶּנּוּ, then the sequence of the thoughts wants nothing in syllogistic exactness. חוּשׁ here has nothing in common with חוּשׁ = حاس, to proceed with a violent, impetuous motion, but, as at Job xx. 2, is = حس, *stringere* (whence *hiss*, a sensible impression); the experience (*vid.* p. 191) here meant is one mediated by means of a pleasant external enjoyment. The LXX., Theod., and Syr. translate: (and who can) drink, which Ewald approves of, for he compares (Arab.) *hasa* (inf. *hasy*), to drink, to sip. But this Arab. verb is unheard of in Heb.; with right, Heiligst. adheres to the Arab., and at the same time the modern Heb. *hass*, חוּשׁ, *sentire*, according to which Schultens, *quis sensibus indulserit*. חוּץ ממנו is not = ולא מ׳, "except from him" (Hitz., Zöckl.), but חוּץ מן together mean "except;" cf. *e.g.* the Mishnic למ׳, חוץ לזמנה וחוץ, beyond the time and place suitable for the thank-offering, חוץ מאחד מהם, excepting one of the same, *Menachoth* vii. 3, for which the old Heb. would in the first case use בלא, and in the second זולת or לְבַד מִן (= Aram. בַּר מִן) (*vid.* p. 191). Accordingly חוּץ ממנו means *praeter eum* (*Deum*), *i.e.* unless he will it and make it possible, Old Heb. מִבַּלְ׳, Gen. xli. 44.

In enjoyment man is not free, it depends not on his own will: labour and the enjoyment of it do not stand in a necessary connection; but enjoyment is a gift which God imparts, according as He regards man as good, or as a sinner.

Ver. 26. "For to a man who appears to Him as good, He gave wisdom, and knowledge, and joy; but to the sinner He gave the work of gathering and heaping up, in order to give it to him who appears to Him as good: this also is vain, and grasping after the wind;" viz. this striving after enjoyment in and of the labour—it is "vain," for the purpose and the issue lie far apart; and "striving after the wind," because that which is striven for, when one thinks that he has it, only too often cannot be grasped, but vanishes into nothing. If we refer this sentence to a collecting and heaping up

(Hengst., Grätz, and others), then the author would here come back to what has already been said, and that too in the foregoing section; the reference also to the arbitrary distribution of the good things of life on the part of God (Knobel) is inadmissible, because "this, although it might be called הבל, could not also be called רעות רוח" (Hitz.); and perfectly inadmissible the reference to the gifts of wisdom, knowledge, and joy (Bullock), for referred to these the sentence gains a meaning only by introducing all kinds of things into the text which here lie out of the connection. Besides, what is here said has indeed a deterministic character, and לפניו, especially if it is thought of in connection with 'ולח,[1] sounds as if to the good and the bad their objective worth and distinction should be adjudicated; but this is not the meaning of the author; the unreasonable thought that good or bad is what God's arbitrary ordinance and judgment stamp it to be, is wholly foreign to him. The "good before Him" is he who appears as good before God, and thus pleases Him, because he is truly good; and the חוטא, placed in contrast, as at vii. 26, is the sinner, not merely such before God, but really such; here לפניו has a different signification than when joined with טוב: one who sins in the sight of God, *i.e.* without regarding Him (Luke xv. 18, ἐνώπιον), serves sin. Regarding עָנְיָן, *vid.* under 23*a*: it denotes a business, *negotium*; but here such as one fatigues himself with, *quod negotium facessit*. Among the three *charismata*, joy stands last, because it is the turning-point of the series of thoughts: joy connected with wise, intelligent activity, is, like wisdom and intelligence themselves, a gift of God. The obj. of לָתֵת (that He may give it) is the store gathered together by the sinner; the thought is the same as that at Prov. xiii. 22, xxviii. 8, Job xxvii. 16 f. The perfect we have so translated, for that which is constantly repeating itself is here designated by the general expression of a thing thus once for all ordained, and thus always continued.

The Short-sightedness and Impotence of Man over against God the All-conditioning, iii. 1–15.

As pure enjoyment stands not in the power of man, much rather is a gift of God which He bestows or denies to man according to His own will, so in general all happens when and how God wills, according to a world-plan, comprehending all things which man can

---

[1] Written with *segol* under ט in P, *Biblia Rabb.*, and elsewhere. Thus correctly after the Masora, according to which this form of the word has throughout the book *segol* under ט, with the single exception of vii. 26. Cf. *Michlol* 124*b*, 140*b*.

neither wholly understand, nor in any respect change,—feeling himself in all things dependent on God, he ought to learn to fear Him.

All that is done here below is ordered by God at a time appointed, and is done without any dependence on man's approbation, according to God's ordinance, arrangement, and providence.

iii. 1. "Everything has its time, and every purpose under the heavens its hour." The Germ. language is poor in synonyms of time. Zöckler translates: Everything has its *Frist* . . ., but by *Frist* we think only of a fixed term of duration, not of a period of beginning, which, though not exclusively, is yet here primarily meant; we have therefore adopted Luther's excellent translation. Certainly זְמָן (from זָמַן, cogn. סָמַן, *signare*), belonging to the more modern Heb. (*vid.* p. 191), means a *Frist* (*e.g.* Dan. ii. 16) as well as a *Zeitpunkt*, point of time; in the Semit. (also Assyr. *simmu, simanu*, with ס) it is the most common designation of the idea of time. עֵת is abbreviated either from עֶדֶת (וָעַד, to determine) or from עֶנֶת (from עָנָה, cogn. אנה, to go towards, to meet). In the first case it stands connected with מוֹעֵד on the one side, and with עִדָּן (from עָדַד, to count) on the other; in the latter case, with עוֹנָה, Ex. xxi. 10 (perhaps also עַ and עֱנָת in בְּעַן, בְּעֱנָת). It is difficult to decide this point; proportionally more, however, can be said for the original עֱנָת (Palest.-Aram. עִנְתָּא), as also the prep. of participation אֶת is derived from אָנָת[1] (meeting, coming together). The author means to say, if we have regard to the root signification of the second conception of time—(1) that everything has its fore-determined time, in which there lies both a determined point of time when it happens, and a determined period of time during which it shall continue; and (2) that every matter has a time appointed for it, or one appropriate, suitable for it. The Greeks were guided by the right feeling when they rendered זְמָן by χρόνος, and עֵת by καιρός. Olympiodorus distinguishes too sharply when he understands the former of duration of time, and the latter of a point of time; while the state of the matter is this, that by χρόνος the idea comprehends the *termini a quo* and *ad quem*, while by καιρός it is limited to the *terminus a quo*. Regarding חֵפֶץ, which proceeds from the ground-idea of being inclined to, and intention, and thus, like πρᾶγμα and χρῆμα, to the general signification of design, undertaking, *res gesta, res, vid.* p. 192.

The illustration commences with the beginning and the ending

---

[1] *Vid.* Orelli's work on the *Heb. Synon. der Zeit u. Ewigkeit*, 1871. He decides for the derivation from וָעַד; Fleischer (Levy's *Chald. W.B.* II. 572) for the derivation from עָנָה, the higher power of אָנָה, whence (Arab.) *inan*, right time. We have, under Job xxiv. 1, maintained the former derivation.

of the life of man and (in near-lying connection of thought) of plants.

Ver. 2.[1] "To be born has its time, and to die has its time; to plant has its time, and to root up that which is planted has its time." The inf. לֶדֶת signifies nothing else than to bring forth; but when that which is brought forth comes more into view than she who brings forth, it is used in the sense of being born (cf. Jer. xxv. 34, לְטֶ' = לְהִטָּבֵחַ); *ledah*, Hos. ix. 11, is the birth; and in the Assyr., *li-id-tu, li-i-tu, li-da-a-tu*, designates posterity, *progenies*. Since now *lālĕdĕth* has here *lāmuth* as contrast, and thus does not denote the birth-throes of the mother, but the child's beginning of life, the translation, "to be born has its time," is more appropriate to what is designed than "to bring forth has its time." What Zöckler, after Hitzig, objects that by *lĕdĕth* a חֵפֶץ [an undertaking], and thus a conscious, intended act must be named, is not applicable; for כֹּל standing at the beginning comprehends doing and suffering, and death also (apart from suicide) is certainly not an intended act, frequently even an unconscious suffering. Instead of לָמֵעַת (for which the form לַמֵעַת [2] is found, cf. לָמוֹט, Ps. lxvi. 9), the older language uses לִנְטֹעַ, Jer. i. 10. In still more modern Heb. the expression used would be לִיטַע, i.e. לְפַע (*Shebîith* ii. 1). עָקַר has here its nearest signification: to root up (denom. of עֶקֶר, root), like עֵקֵר, 2 Kings iii. 25, where it is the Targ. word for הַפִּיל (to fell trees).

From out-rooting, which puts an end to the life of plants, the transition is now made to putting to death.

Ver. 3. "To put to death has its time, and to heal has its time; to pull down has its time, and to build has its time." That *harog* (to kill) is placed over against "to heal," Hitzig explains by the remark that *harog* does not here include the full consequences of the act, and is fitly rendered by "to wound." But "to put to death" is nowhere = "nearly to put to death,"—one who is *harug*

---

[1] These seven verses, 2–8, are in Codd and Edd., like Josh. xii. 9 ff., and Esth. ix. 7 ff., arranged in the form of a song, so that one עֵת (time) always stands under another, after the scheme described in *Megilla* 16b, *Massecheth Sofrim* xiii. 3, but without any express reference to this passage in Koheleth. J has a different manner of arranging the words, the first four lines of which we here adduce [read from right to left]:—

'ēth	lāmoth veeth	lalĕdĕth 'ēth
'ēth	nathu'ă lă'ăqor veeth	lathă'ăth
'ēth	lirpō veeth	lăhărog
'ēth	livnoth veeth	liphrots

[2] This Abulwalîd found in a correct Damascus MS., *Michlol* 81b.

CHAP. III. 4, 5.   257

is not otherwise to be healed than by resurrection from the dead, Ezek. xxxvii. 6. The contrast has no need for such ingenuity to justify it. The striking down of a sound life stands in contrast to the salvation of an endangered life by healing, and this in many situations of life, particularly in war, in the administration of justice, and in the defence of innocence against murder or injury, may be fitting. Since the author does not present these details from a moral point of view, the time here is not that which is morally right, but that which, be it morally right or not, has been determined by God, the Governor of the world and Former of history, who makes even that which is evil subservient to His plan. With the two pairs of γένεσις καὶ φθορά there are two others associated in ver. 3; with that, having reference, 2b, to the vegetable world, there here corresponds one referring to buildings; to פְּרוֹץ (synon. הֲרוֹס, Jer. i. 10) stands opposed בְּנוֹת (which is more than גְּדוֹר), as at 2 Chron. xxxii. 5.

These contrasts between existence and non-existence are followed by contrasts within the limits of existence itself:—

Ver. 4. "To weep has its time, and to laugh has its time; to mourn has its time, and to dance has its time." It is possible that the author was led by the consonance from *livnoth* to *livkoth*, which immediately follows it; but the sequence of the thoughts is at the same time inwardly mediated, for sorrow kills and joy enlivens, Sir. xxxii. 21-24. סְפוֹד is particularly lamentation for the dead, Zech. xii. 10; and רְקוֹד, dancing (in the more modern language the usual word for *hholēl*, *kirkēr*, *hhāgāg*) at a marriage festival and on other festal occasions.

It is more difficult to say what leads the author to the two following pairs of contrasts:—

Ver. 5. "To throw stones has its time, and to gather together stones has its time; to embrace has its time, and to refrain from embracing has its time." Did the old Jewish custom exist at the time of the author, of throwing three shovelfuls of earth into the grave, and did this lead him to use the phrase הַשְׁלֵ׳ אֲבָ׳? But we do not need so incidental a connection of the thought, for the first pair accords with the specific idea of life and death; by the throwing of stones a field is destroyed, 2 Kings iii. 35, or as expressed at ver. 19, is marred; and by gathering the stones together and removing them (which is called סִקֵּל), it is brought under cultivation. Does לְחַ׳, to embrace, now follow because it is done with the arms and hands? Scarcely; but the loving action of embracing stands beside the hostile, purposely injurious throwing of stones into a

ECCLES.   R

field, not exclusively (2 Kings iv. 16), but yet chiefly (as *e.g.* at Prov. v. 20) as referring to love for women; the intensive in the second member is introduced perhaps only for the purpose of avoiding the paronomasia *lirhhoq mahhavoq.*

The following pair of contrasts is connected with the avoiding or refraining from the embrace of love:—

Ver. 6. "To seek has its time, and to lose has its time; to lay up has its time, and to throw away has its time." Vaihinger and others translate לְאַבֵּד, to give up as lost, which the *Pih.* signifies first as the expression of a conscious act. The older language knows it only in the stronger sense of bringing to ruin, making to perish, wasting (Prov. xxix. 3). But in the more modern language, אִבֵּד, like the Lat. *perdere,* in the sense of "to lose," is the trans. to the intrans. אָבַד, *e.g. Tahoroth* viii. 3, "if one loses (הַמְאַבֵּד) anything," etc.; *Sifri,* at Deut. xxiv. 19, "he who has lost (מְאַבֵּד) a shekel," etc. In this sense the Palest.-Aram. uses the *Aphel* אוֹבֵד, *e.g. Jer. Mezia* ii. 5, "the queen had lost (אובדת) her ornament." The intentional giving up, throwing away from oneself, finds its expression in לְהַשׁ׳.

The following pair of contrasts refers the abandoning and preserving to articles of clothing:—

Ver. 7*a*. "To rend has its time, and to sew has its time." When evil tidings come, when the tidings of death come, then is the time for rending the garments (2 Sam. xiii. 31), whether as a spontaneous outbreak of sorrow, or merely as a traditional custom. —The tempest of the affections, however, passes by, and that which was torn is again sewed together.

Perhaps it is the recollection of great calamities which leads to the following contrasts:—

Ver. 7*b*. "To keep silence has its time, and to speak has its time." Severe strokes of adversity turn the mind in quietness back upon itself; and the demeanour most befitting such adversity is silent resignation (cf. 2 Kings ii. 3, 5). This mediation of the thought is so much the more probable, as in all these contrasts it is not so much the spontaneity of man that comes into view, as the predetermination and providence of God.

The following contrasts proceed on the view that God has placed us in relations in which it is permitted to us to love, or in which our hatred is stirred up:—

Ver. 8. "To love has its time, and to hate has its time; war has its time, and peace has its time." In the two pairs of contrasts here, the contents of the first are, not exclusively indeed (Ps. cxx. 7), but yet chiefly referred to the mutual relations of peoples. It is the result of thoughtful intention that the *quodlibet* of 2 × 7 pairs terminates this *for* and *against* in " peace ;" and, besides, the author has made the termination emphatic by this, that here "instead of infinitives, he introduces proper nouns" (Hitz.).

Ver. 9. Since, then, everything has its time depending not on human influence, but on the determination and providence of God, the question arises: "What gain hath he that worketh in that wherewith he wearieth himself?" It is the complaint of i. 3 which is here repeated. From all the labour there comes forth nothing which carries in it the security of its continuance; but in all he does man is conditioned by the change of times and circumstances and relations over which he has no control. And the converse of this his weakness is short-sightedness.

Vers. 10, 11. " I saw the travail, which God gave to the children of men to fatigue themselves with it—: He hath well arranged everything beautiful in its appointed time; He hath also put eternity in their heart, so that man cannot indeed wholly search through from beginning to end the work which God accomplisheth." As at i. 14, רָאִיתִי is here seeing in the way of research, as elsewhere, *e.g.* at ii. 24, it is as the result of research. In ver. 10 the author says that he closely considered the labour of men, and in ver. 11 he states the result. It is impossible to render the word עִנְיָן everywhere by the same German (or English) word: i. 13, wearisome trouble; ii. 26, business; here: *Geschäftigkeit*,—the idea is in all the three places the same, viz. an occupation which causes trouble, costs effort. What presented itself to the beholder was—(1) that He (viz. God, cf. ver. 10 and ver. 11) has made everything beautiful in its time. The author uses יָפֶה as synon. of טוֹב (v. 17); also in other languages the idea of the beautiful is gradually more and more generalized. The suffix in בְּעִתּוֹ does not refer to God, but to that which is in the time; this word is = ἐν καιρῷ ἰδίῳ (Symm.), at its proper time (*vid.* Ps. i. 3, civ. 27; Jer. v. 24, etc.), since, as with יַחְדָּו (together with) and כֻּלּוֹ (every one), the suffix is no longer thought of as such. Like יפה, בעתו as pred. conception belongs to the verb: He has made everything beautiful; He has made everything (falling out) at its appointed time.—The beauty consists in this, that what is done is not done sooner or later than it ought to be, so as to connect itself as a constituent part to the whole of God's work. The pret. עָשָׂה is to be also interpreted as such: He "has made," viz. in His world-plan, all things beautiful, falling out at the appointed time; for that which acquires an actual form in the course of history has a previous ideal existence in the knowledge and will of God (*vid.* under Isa. xxii. 11, xxxvii. 26).

That which presented itself to the beholder was—(2) the fact that He (God) had put אֶת־הָעֹלָם in their hearts (*i.e.* the hearts of men). Gaab and Spohn interpret *'olam* in the sense of the Arab. *'ilam*, knowledge, understanding; and Hitz., pointing the word accordingly עֶלֶם, translates: "He has also placed understanding in their heart, without which man," etc. The translation of מִבְּלִי אֲשֶׁר is not to be objected to; מִבְּ is, however, only seldom a conjunction, and is then to be translated by *eo quod*, Ex. xiv. 11, 2 Kings i. 3, 6, 16, which is not appropriate here; it will thus be here also a prep., and with *asher* following may mean "without which," as well as "without this, that" = "besides that" (Venet. ἄνευ τοῦ ὅτι, "except that"), as frequently אֶפֶס כִּי, *e.g.* at Amos ix. 8. But that Arab. *'ilam* is quite foreign to the Heb., which has no word עָלַם in the sense of "to rise up, to be visible, knowable," which is now also referred [1] to for the Assyr. as the stem-word of עֵילָם = highland. It is true Hitzig believes that he has found the Heb. עֹלֶם = wisdom, in Sir. vi. 21, where there is a play on the word with נעלם, "concealed:" σοφία γὰρ κατὰ τὸ ὄνομα αὐτῆς ἐστι, καὶ οὐ πολλοῖς ἐστι φανερά. Drusius and Eichhorn have here already taken notice of the Arab. *'ilam;* but Fritzsche with right asks, "Shall this word as Heb. be regarded as traceable only here and falsely pointed only at Eccles. iii. 11, and shall no trace of it whatever be found in the Chald., Syr., and Rabbin.?" We have also no need of it. That Ben-Sira has etymologically investigated the word חכמה as going back to חכם, R. חכ, "to be firm, shut up, dark" (*vid.* at Ps. x. 8), is certainly very improbable, but so much the more probable (as already suggested by Drusius) that he has introduced [2] into חכמה, after the Aram. אֲכַם, *nigrescere*, the idea of making dark. Does *eth-ha'olam* in this passage before us then mean "the world" (Jerome, Luther, Ewald), or "desire after the knowledge of the world" (Rashi), or "worldly-mindedness" (Gesen., Knobel)? The answer to this has been already given in my *Psychol.* p. 406 (2d ed.): "In post-bibl. Heb. *'olam* denotes not only 'eternity' backwards and forwards as

---

[1] *Vid.* Fried. Delitzsch's *Assyr. Stud.* (1874), p. 39. Otherwise Fleischer, who connects *'alima*, "to know," with *'alam*, "to conceal," so that to know = to be concealed, sunk deep, initiated in something (with *ba* of the obj., as *sh'ar*, whence *shâ'ir*, the poet as "one who marks").

[2] Grätz translates *eth-ha'olam* by "ignorance" (*vid.* Orelli, p. 83). R. Achwa in the Midrash has added here the *scriptio defectiva* with the remark, שהועלם וגו׳, "for the mysterious name of God is concealed from them."

infinite duration, but also 'the world' as that which endures for ever (αἰών, seculum); the world in this latter sense is, however, not yet known[1] to the bibl. language, and we will thus not be able to interpret the words of Koheleth of the impulse of man to reflect on the whole world." In itself, the thought that God has placed the whole world in man's heart is not untrue: man is, indeed, a *microcosmos*, in which the *macrocosmos* mirrors itself (Elster), but the connection does not favour it; for the discussion does not proceed from this, that man is only a member in the great universe, and that God has given to each being its appointed place, but that in all his experience he is conditioned by time, and that in the course of history all that comes to him, according to God's world-plan, happens at its appointed time. But the idea by which that of time, אֵת (זְמָן), is surpassed is not the world, but eternity, to which time is related as part is to the whole (Cicero, *Inv.* i. 26. 39, *tempus est pars quaedam aeternitatis*). The Mishna language contains, along with the meaning of world, also this older meaning of *'olam*, and has formed from it an adv. עוֹלָמִית, *aeterne*. The author means to say that God has not only assigned to each individually his appointed place in history, thereby bringing to the consciousness of man the fact of his being conditioned, but that He has also established in man an impulse leading him beyond that which is temporal toward the eternal: it lies in his nature not to be contented with the temporal, but to break through the limits which it draws around him, to escape from the bondage and the disquietude within which he is held, and amid the ceaseless changes of time to console himself by directing his thoughts to eternity.

This saying regarding the *desiderium aeternitatis* being planted in the heart of man, is one of the profoundest utterances of Koheleth. In fact, the impulse of man shows that his innermost wants cannot be satisfied by that which is temporal. He is a being limited by time, but as to his innermost nature he is related to eternity. That which is transient yields him no support, it carries him on like a rushing stream, and constrains him to save himself by laying hold on eternity. But it is not so much the practical as the intellectual side of this endowment and this peculiar dignity of human nature which Koheleth brings here to view.

It is not enough for man to know that everything that happens has its divinely-ordained time. There is an instinct peculiar to his

---

[1] In the Phoen. also, *'olam*, down to a late period, denotes not the world, but eternity: *melek 'olam*, βασιλεὺς αἰῶνος (αἰώνιος), *seculo frugifero* on a coin = the fruit-bringing *'olam* (Αἰών).

nature impelling him to pass beyond this fragmentary knowledge and to comprehend eternity; but his effort is in vain, for (3) " man is unable to reach unto the work which God accomplisheth from the beginning to the end." The work of God is that which is completing itself in the history of the world, of which the life of individual men is a fragment. Of this work he says, that God has wrought it עָשָׂה; because, before it is wrought out in its separate "time," it is already completed in God's plan. Eternity and this work are related to each other as the accomplished and the being accomplished, they are interchangeably the πλήρωμα to each other. יִמְצָא is potential, and the same in conception as at viii. 17, Job xi. 7, xxxvii. 23; a knowledge is meant which reaches to the object, and lays hold of it. A laying hold of this work is an impossibility, because eternity, as its name 'olam denotes, is the concealed, *i.e.* is both forwards and backwards immeasurable. The *desiderium aeternitatis* inherent in man thus remains under the sun unappeased. He would raise himself above the limits within which he is confined, and instead of being under the necessity of limiting his attention to isolated matters, gain a view of the whole of God's work which becomes manifest in time; but this all-embracing view is for him unattainable.

If Koheleth had known of a future life—which proves that as no instinct in the natural world is an illusion, so also the impulse toward the eternal, which is natural to man, is no illusion—he would have reached a better *ultimatum* than the following:—

Ver. 12. "Thus I then perceived that among them (men) there is nothing better than to enjoy themselves, and indulge themselves in their life." The resignation would acquire a reality if לַעֲ' טוֹב meant "to do good," *i.e.* right (LXX. Targ. Syr. Jer. Venet.); and this appears of necessity to be its meaning according to vii. 20. But, with right, Ginsburg remarks that nowhere else—neither at ii. 24, nor iii. 22, v. 17, viii. 15, ix. 7—is this moral rendering given to the *ultimatum;* also וְ' טוֹב, 13*a*, presupposes for לַעֲ' טוֹב a eudemonistic sense. On the other hand, Zöckler is right in saying that for the meaning of עֲשׂוֹת טוֹב, in the sense of "to be of good cheer" (Luth.), there is no example. Zirkel compares εὖ πράττειν, and regards it as a Graecism. But it either stands ellipt. for לַעֲ' לוֹ טוֹב (= לְהֵיטִיב לוֹ), or, with Grätz, we have to read לִרְאוֹת טוֹב; in any case, an ethical signification is here excluded by the nearest connection, as well as by the parallels; it is not contrary to the view of Koheleth, but this is not the place to express it. *Bam* is to be understood after *baadam*, ii. 24. The plur., comprehending men, here, as at ver. 11, wholly passes over into the individualizing sing.

But this enjoyment of life also, Koheleth continues, this advisedly the best portion in the limited and restrained condition of man, is placed beyond his control :—

Ver. 13. "But also that he should eat and drink, and see good in all his labour, is for every man a gift of God." The inverted and yet anacoluthistic formation of the sentence is quite like that at v. 18. כָּל־הָאָ֑ signifies, properly, the totality of men = all men, e.g. Ps. cxvi. 11; but here and at v. 18, xii. 13, the author uses the two words so that the determ. second member of the *st. constr.* does not determine the first (which elsewhere sometimes occurs, as *bᵉthulath Israel*, a virgin of Israel, Deut. xxii. 19): every one of men (cf. πᾶς τις βροτῶν). The subst. clause *col-haadam* is subject: every one of men, in this that he eats ... is dependent on God. Instead of מִיַּד the word מַתַּת (abbrev. from מַתְּנַת) is here used, as at v. 18. The connection by *vᵉgam* is related to the preceding adversat.: and (= but) also (= notwithstanding that), as at vi. 7, Neh. v. 8, cf. Jer. iii. 10; where *gam* is strengthened by *bᵉcol-zoth*. As for the rest, it follows from ver. 13, in connection with ii. 24–26, that for Koheleth εὐποΐα and εὐθυμία reciprocally condition each other, without, however, a conclusion following therefrom justifying the translation "to do good," 12*b*. Men's being conditioned in the enjoyment of life, and, generally, their being conditioned by God the Absolute, has certainly an ethical end in view, as is expressed in the conclusion which Koheleth now reaches :—

Ver. 14. "Thus I discerned it then, that all that God will do exists for ever; nothing is to be added to it, and nothing taken from it: God has thus directed it, that men should fear before Him." This is a conclusion derived from the facts of experience, a truth that is valid for the present and for the time to come. We may with equal correctness render by *quidquid facit* and *quidquid faciet.* But the pred. shows that the fut. expression is also thought of as fut.; for הוּא יִהְיֶה לְעֹ׳ does not mean: that is for ever (Hitz.), which would be expressed by the subst. clause הוּא לְעוֹלָם; but: that shall be for ever (Zöck.), *i.e.* will always assert its validity. That which is affirmed here is true of God's directing and guiding events in the natural world, as well as of the announcements of His will and His controlling and directing providence in the history of human affairs. All this is removed beyond the power of the creature to alter it. The meaning is not that one ought not to add to or to take from it (Deut. xiii. 1; Prov. xxx. 6), but that such a thing cannot be done (*vid.* Sir. xviii. 5). And this unchangeableness characterizing the arrangements of God has this as its aim, that men should fear Him who is the All-conditioning and is Himself unconditioned: He has done it that they (men) should fear before Him, שֶׁ עָשָׂה, *fecit ut;* cf. Ezek. xxxvi. 27. ποιεῖν ἵνα, Rev. xiii. 15; and "fear before Him," as at viii. 12 f.; cf. 1 Chron. xvi. 30 with Ps. xcvi. 9. The unchangeableness of God's action shows itself in this, that in the course of history similar phenomena repeat themselves; for the fundamental principles, the causal connections, the norms of God's government, remain always the same.

Ver. 15. "That which is now hath been long ago; and that which will be hath already been: God seeketh after that which was crowded out." The words: "hath been long ago" (כְּבָר הוּא), are used of that which the present represents as something that hath been, as the fruit of a development; the words: "hath already been" (כְּבָר הָיָה), are used of the future (אֲשֶׁר לְ, τὸ μέλλον, *vid.* Gesen. § 132. 1), as denying to it the right of being regarded as something new. The government of God is not to be changed, and does not change; His creative as well as His moral ordering of the world produces with the same laws the same phenomena (the וְ corresponds to this line of thought here, as at 14*b*)—God seeks אֶת־נִרְ (cf. vii. 7; Ewald, § 277*d*). Hengstenberg renders: God seeks the persecuted (LXX. Symm. Targ. Syr.), *i.e.* visits them with consolation and comfort. *Nirdaph* here denotes that which is followed, hunted, pressed, by which we may think of that which is already driven into the past; that God seeks, seeks it purposely, and brings it back again into the present; for His government remains always, and brings thus always up again that which hath been. Thus Jerome: *Deus instaurat quod abiit;* the Venet.: ὁ θεὸς ζητήσει τὸ ἀπεληλαμένον; and thus Geier, among the post-Reform. interpreters: *praestat ut quae propulsa sunt ac praeterierunt iterum innoventur ac redeant;* and this is now the prevailing exposition, after Knobel, Ewald, and Hitzig. The thought is the same as if we were to translate: God seeks after the analogue. In the Arab., one word in relation to another is called *muradif,* if it is cogn. to it; and *mutaradifat* is the technical expression for a synonym. In Heb. the expression used is שֵׁמוֹת נִרְדָּפִים, they who are followed the one by another,—one of which, as it were, treads on the heels of another. But this designation is mediated through the Arab. In evidence of the contrary, ancient examples are wanting.

The godless Conduct of Men left to themselves, and their End like that of the Beasts, iii. 16–22.

Ver. 16. "And, moreover, I saw under the sun the place of judgment, that wickedness was there; and the place of righteousness, that wickedness was there." The structure of the verse is palindromic, like i. 6, ii. 10, iv. 1. We might also render מְקוֹם as the so-called *casus absol.*, so that 'שָׁמָּ ... 'מק is an emphatic בִּמְקוֹם (Hitz.), and the construction like Jer. xlvi. 5; but the accentuation does not require this (cf. Gen. i. 1); and why should it not be at once the object to רָאִיתִי, which in any case it virtually is? These two words שָׁמָּה הָרֶשַׁע might be attribut. clauses: where wickedness (prevails), for the old scheme of the attributive clause (the *sifat*) is not foreign to the style of this book (vid. i. 13, nathan = n^ethano; and v. 12, raithi = r^eithiha); but why not rather virtual pred. accus.: *vidi locum juris (quod) ibi impietas?* Cf. Neh. xiii. 23 with Ps. xxxvii. 25. The place of "judgment" is the place where justice should be ascertained and executed; and the place of "righteousness," that where righteousness should ascertain and administer justice; for *mishpat* is the rule (of right), and the objective matter of fact; *tsedek*, a subjective property and manner of acting. רֶשַׁע is in both cases the same: wickedness (see under Ps. i. 1), which bends justice, and is the contrary of *tsĕdĕk*, i.e. upright and moral sternness. רֶשַׁע elsewhere, like *mĕlĕk*, *tsĕdĕk*, preserves *in p.* its *e*, but here it takes rank along with חֶסֶד, which in like manner fluctuates (cf. Ps. cxxx. 7 with Prov. xxi. 21). שָׁמָּה is here = שָׁם, as at Ps. cxxii. 5, etc.; the locative *ah* suits the question Where? as well as in the question Whither?—He now expresses how, in such a state of things, he arrived at satisfaction of mind.

Ver. 17. "I said in mine heart: God shall judge the righteous as well as the wicked: for there is there a time for every purpose and for every work." Since "the righteous" stands first, the word יִשְׁפֹּט has here the double sense of judging [*richtens* = setting upright] = acting uprightly, justly by one, as in the *shofteni* of Ps. vii. 9, xxvi. 1, etc., and of judging = inflicting punishment. To the righteous, as well as to the wicked,[1] God will administer that which of right belongs to them. But this does not immediately happen, and has to be waited for a long time, for there is a definite time for every undertaking

---

[1] The LXX. (in Aquila's manner): σὺν τὸν δίκαιον καὶ σὺν τὸν ἀσεβῆ—according to the Talm. hermeneut. rule, that where the obj. is designated by אֵת, with that which is expressly named, something else is associated, and is to be thought of along with it.

(iii. 1), and for (עַל, in the more modern form of the language, interchanges *promiscue* with אֶל and לְ, *e.g.* Jer. xix. 15; Ezek. xxii. 3; Ewald, § 217*i*) every work there is a "time." This שָׁם, defended by all the old interpreters, cannot have a temporal sense: *tunc = in die judicii* (Jerome, Targ.), cf. Ps. xiv. 5, xxxvi. 13, for " a time of judgment there is for all one day" is not intended, since certainly the שָׁם (day of judgment) is this time itself, and not the time of this time. Ewald renders שָׁם as pointing to the past, for he thus construes: the righteous and the unrighteous God will judge (for there is a time for everything), and judge (*vav* thus explicat., " and that too," " and indeed ") every act there, *i.e.* everything done before. But this שָׁם is not only heavy, but also ambiguous and purposeless; and besides, by this parenthesizing of the words כִּי עֵת וגו' [for there is a time for everything], the principal thought, that with God everything, even His act of judgment, has its time, is robbed of its independence and of the place in the principal clause appropriate to it. But if שָׁם is understood adverbially, it certainly has a local meaning connected with it: there, viz. with God, *apud Deum*; true, for this use of the word Gen. xlix. 24 affords the only example, and it stands there in the midst of a very solemn and earnest address. Therefore it lies near to read, with Houbig., Döderl., Palm., and Hitz., שָׂם, " a definite time ... has He (God) ordained;" שׂוֹם (שִׂים) is the usual word for the ordinances of God in the natural world and in human history (Prov. viii. 29; Ex. xxi. 13; Num. xxiv. 23; Hab. i. 12, etc.), and, as in the Assyr. *simtuv*, so the Heb. שִׂימָה (שׂוּמָה), 2 Sam. xiii. 32, signifies lot or fate, decree.[1] With this reading, Elster takes exception to the position of the words; but at Judg. vi. 19 also the object goes before שָׁם, and " unto every purpose and for every work" is certainly the complement of the object-conception, so that the position of the words is in reality no other than at x. 20*a*; Dan. ii. 17*b*. Quite untenable is Herzfeld's supposition (Fürst, Vaih.), that שָׂם has here the Talm. signification: *aestimat, taxat*, for (1) this שׂוּם = Arab. *sham*, has not עַל, but the accus. after it; (2) the thought referring to the time on which ver. 18 rests is thereby interrupted. Whether we read שָׂם, or take שָׁם in the sense of עִמּוֹ (Job xxv. 2, xxiii. 14, etc.), the thought is the same, and equally congruous: God will judge the innocent and the guilty; it shall be done some time, although not so soon as one might wish it, and think necessary, for God has for every undertaking and for every work its fixed time, also its judicial decision (*vid*. at Ps. lxxv. 3); He

---

[1] *Vid.* Schrader's *Keilsch. u. A. T.* p. 105, *simtu ubilsu*, *i.e.* fate snatched him away) Heb. *simah hovilathhu*), cf. Fried. Delitzsch's *Assyr. Stud.* p. 66 f.

permits wickedness, lets it develope itself, waits long before He interposes (*vid.* under Isa. xviii. 4 f.).

Reflecting on God's delay to a time hidden from men, and known only to Himself, Koheleth explains the matter to himself in the following verse :—

Ver. 18. "Thus I said then in mine heart : (it happeneth) for the sake of the children of men that God might sift them, and that they might see that they are like the cattle, they in themselves." Regarding עַל־דִּבְ׳ [for the sake of = on account of] as at viii. 2, *vid.* under Ps. cx. 4, where it signifies after (κατά) the state of the matter, and above at p. 195. The infin. לְבָ׳ is not derived from בּוּר.—לָבוּר, ix. 1, is only the metaplastic form of לָבֹר or לִבְרֹר,—but only from בָּרַר, whose infin. may take the form בַּר, after the form רַד, to tread down, Isa. xlv. 1, שַׁח, to bow, Jer. v. 26 ; but nowhere else is this infin. form found connected with a suff.; קָחָם, Hos. xi. 3, would be in some measure to be compared, if it could be supposed that this = בְּקַחְתָּם, *sumendo eos.* The root בר proceeds, from the primary idea of cutting, on the one side to the idea of separating, winnowing, choosing out; and, on the other, to that of smoothing, polishing, purifying (*vid.* under Isa. xlix. 2). Here, by the connection, the meaning of winnowing, *i.e.* of separating the good from the bad, is intended, with which, however, as in לְבָרֵר, Dan. xi. 35, the meaning of making clear, making light, bringing forward into the light, easily connects itself (cf. *Shabbath* 138a, 74a), of which the meaning to winnow (cf. לְהָבַר, Jer. iv. 11) is only a particular form ;[1] cf. Sanhedrin 7b: "when a matter is clear, בָרוּר, to thee (free from ambiguity) as the morning, speak it out; and if not, do not speak it." In the expression הָאֱלֹ׳ לֵב, the word הָאֱלֹ׳ is, without doubt, the subject, according to Gesen. § 133. 2. 3 ; Hitz. regards הָאֱלֹ׳ as genit., which, judged according to the Arab., is correct; it is true that for *li-imtiḥânihim allahi* (with genit. of the subj.), also *allahu* (with nominat. of the subj.) may be used; but the former expression is the more regular and more common (*vid.* Ewald's *Gramm. Arab.* § 649), but not always equally decisive with reference to the Heb. *usus loq.* That God delays His righteous interference till the time appointed beforehand, is for the sake of the children of men, with the intention, viz., that God may sift them, *i.e.* that, without breaking in upon the free development of their characters before the time, He may permit the distinction between the good and the bad to become manifest. Men,

---

[1] Not "to sift," for not בָּרַר, but רִקֵּד, means "to sift" (properly, "to make to leap up," "to agitate"); cf. *Shebiith* v. 9.

who are the obj. to לב׳, are the subject to וְלִרְאוֹת to be supplied: *et ut videant*; it is unnecessary, with the LXX., Syr., and Jerome, to read וְלִרְאוֹת (= וּלְהַרְ׳): *ut ostenderet*. It is a question whether הֵמָּה[1] is the expression of the copula: *sunt (sint)*, or whether *hēmmah lahĕm* is a closer definition, co-ordinate with *shĕhem bĕhemah*. The remark of Hitzig, that *lahĕm* throws back the action on the subject, is not clear. Does he suppose that *lahem* belongs to *liroth?* That is here impossible. If we look away from *lahem*, the needlessly circumstantial expression שה׳...המ׳ can still be easily understood: *hemmah* takes up, as an echo, *bĕhemah*, and completes the comparison (compare the battology in Hos. xiii. 2). This play upon words musically accompanying the thought remains also, when, according to the accentuation שֶׁה׳ בהמ׳ הֵ׳ לָה׳, we take *hemmah* along with *lahem*, and the former as well as the latter of these two words is then better understood. The ל in להם is not that of the pure dat. (Aben Ezra: They (are like beasts) to themselves, *i.e.* in their own estimation), but that of reference, as at Gen. xvii. 20, "as for Ishmael;" cf. Ps. iii. 3; 2 Kings v. 7; cf. אֶל, 1 Sam. i. 27, etc. Men shall see that they are cattle (beasts), they in reference to themselves, *i.e.* either they in reference to themselves mutually (Luther: among themselves), or: they in reference to themselves. To interpret the reference as that of mutual relation, would, in looking back to ver. 16, commend itself, for the condemnation and oppression of the innocent under the appearance of justice is an act of human brutishness. But the reason assigned in ver. 19 does not accord with this reciprocal rendering of *lahem*. Thus *lahem* will be meant reflexively, but it is not on that account pleonastic (Knobel), nor does it ironically form a climax: *ipsissimi = höchstselbst* (Ewald, § 315*a*); but "they in reference to themselves" is = they in and of themselves, *i.e.* viewed as men (viewed naturally). If one disregards the idea of God's interfering at a future time with the discordant human history, and, in general, if one loses sight of God, the distinction between the life of man and of beast disappears.

Ver. 19. "For the children of men are a chance, and the beast a chance, and they both have once chance: as the death of the one, so the death of the other, and they have all one breath; and there is no advantage to a man over a beast, for all is vain." If in both instances the word is pointed מִקְרֶה (LXX.), the three-membered sentence would then have the form of an emblematical proverb (as

---

[1] שֶׁהֵם בְּהֵמָה הֵמָּה thus accented rightly in F. Cf. *Michlol* 216*a*.

e.g. Prov. xxv. 25): "For as the chance of men, so (*vav* of comparison) the chance of the beast; they have both one chance." מִקְרֶה with *segol* cannot possibly be the connecting form (Luzz.), for in cases such as מַעֲשֵׂ׳ ט׳, Isa. iii. 24, the relation of the words is appositional, not genitival. This form מִקְרֵ׳, thus found three times, is vindicated by the Targ. (also the Venet.) and by Mss.; Joseph Kimchi remarks that " all three have *segol*, and are thus forms of the *absolutus*." The author means that men, like beasts, are in their existence and in their death influenced accidentally, *i.e.* not of necessity, and are wholly conditioned, not by their own individual energy, but by a power from without—are dependent beings, as Solon (Herod. i. 32) says to Croesus: "Man is altogether συμφορή," *i.e.* the sport of accident. The first two sentences mean exclusively neither that men (apart from God) are, like beasts, the birth of a blind accident (Hitz.), nor that they are placed under the same law of transitoriness (Elst.); but of men, in the totality of their being, and doing, and suffering, it is first said that they are accidental beings; then, that which separates them from this, that they all, men like beasts, are finally exposed to one, *i.e.* to the same fate. As is the death of the one, so is the death of the other; and they all have one breath, *i.e.* men and beasts alike die, for this breath of life (רוּחַ חַיִּים, which constitutes a beast—as well as a man a נֶפֶשׁ חַיָּה) departs from the body (Ps. civ. 29). In זֶה ... זֶה (as at vi. 5, Ex. xiv. 20, and frequently), לָהֶם (mas. as *genus potius*) is separately referred to men and beasts. With the Mishnic כְּמוֹת = bibl. כְּמוֹ (cf. *Maaser Sheni*, v. 2), the כְּמוֹת here used has manifestly nothing to do. The noun מוֹתָר, which in the Book of Proverbs (xiv. 23, xxi. 5, not elsewhere) occurs in the sense of profit, gain, is here in the Book of Koheleth found as a synon. of יִתְרוֹן, " preference," advantage which is exclusively peculiar to it. From this, that men and beasts fall under the same law of death, the author concludes that there is no preference of a man to a beast; he doubtless means that in respect of the end man has no superiority; but he expresses himself thus generally because, as the matter presented itself to him, all-absorbing death annulled every distinction. He looks only to the present time, without encumbering himself with the historical account of the matter found in the beginning of the *Tôra;* and he adheres to the external phenomenon, without thinking, with the Psalmist in Ps. xlix., that although death is common to man with the beast, yet all men do not therefore die as the beast dies. That the beast dies because it must, but that in the midst of this necessity of nature man can maintain his freedom, is for him out of view.

הֲבֵל הַבָּל, the ματαιότης, which at last falls to man as well as to the beast, throws its long dark shadows across his mind, and wholly shrouds it.

Ver. 20. "All goes hence to one place; all has sprung out of the dust, and all returns to the dust again." The "one place" is (as at vi. 6) the earth, the great graveyard which finally receives all the living when dead. The art. of the first הֶעָפָר is that denoting species; the art. of the second is retrospective: to the dust whence he sprang (cf. Ps. civ. 29, cxlvi. 4); otherwise, Gen. iii. 19 (cf. Job xxxiv. 15), "to dust shalt thou return," shalt become dust again. From dust to dust (Sir. xl. 11, xli. 10) is true of every living corporeal thing. It is true there exists the possibility that with the spirit of the dying man it may be different from what it is with the spirit of the dying beast, but yet that is open to question.

Ver. 21. "Who knoweth with regard to the spirit of the children of men, whether it mounteth upward; and with regard to the spirit of a beast, whether it goeth downward to the earth?" The interrogative meaning of הָעֹלָה and הַיֹּרֶדֶת is recognised by all the old translators: LXX., Targ., Syr., Jerome, Venet., Luther. Among the moderns, Heyder (*vid. Psychol.* p. 410), Hengst., Hahn, Dale, and Bullock take the ה in both cases as the article: "Who knoweth the spirit of the children of men, that which goeth upward . . . ?" But (1) thus rendered the question does not accord with the connection, which requires a sceptical question; (2) following "who knoweth," after ii. 19, vi. 12, cf. Josh. ii. 14, an interrogative continuance of the sentence was to be expected; and (3) in both cases הִיא stands as designation of the subject only for the purpose of marking the interrogative clause (cf. Jer. ii. 14), and of making it observable that *ha'olah* and *hayorĕdĕth* are not appos. belonging as objects to רוּחַ and וְרוּחַ. It is questionable, indeed, whether the punctuation of these words, הָעֹלָה and הַיֹּרֶדֶת, as they lie before us, proceeds from an interrogative rendering. Saadia in *Emunoth* c. vi., and Juda Halevi in the *Kuzri* ii. 80, deny this; and so also do Aben Ezra and Kimchi. And they may be right. For instead of הָעֹלָה, the pointing ought to have been הַעֹלָה (cf. הַעֲלֶה, Job xiii. 25) when used as interrog. *an ascendens;* even before א the compens. lengthening of the interrog. *ha* is nowhere certainly found[1] instead of the virtual reduplication; and thus also the parallel הֲיֹרֵד is not to be judged after הֲיִי, Lev.

---

[1] For ה is to be read with a *Pattach* in Judg. vi. 31, xii. 5; Neh. vi. 11; cf. under Gen. xix. 9, xxvii. 21. In Num. xvi. 22 the ה of הָאִישׁ is the art., the question is not formally designated. Cf. also הַעֵי with ה interrog., Jer. xii. 9; and הֲעֵי with ה as the art., Gen. xv. 11.

x. 19, 'הַךְ, Ezek. xviii. 29,—we must allow that the punctation seeks, by the removal of the two interrog. הֲ (ה), to place that which is here said in accord with xii. 7. But there is no need for this. For מִי יוֹדֵעַ does not quite fall in with that which Lucretius says (*Lib.* I.):

> "*Ignoratur enim quae sit natura animai,*
> *Nata sit an contra nascentibus insinuetur?*
> *An simul intereat nobiscum morte diremta?*"

It may certainly be said of *mi yode'a*, as of *ignoratur*, that it does not exclude every kind of knowledge, but only a sure and certain knowledge resting on sufficient grounds; *interire* and יֵרֵד לְמַ' are also scarcely different, for neither of the two necessarily signifies annihilation, but both the discontinuance of independent individual existence. But the putting of the question by Koheleth is different, for it discloses more definitely than this by Lucretius, the possibility of a different end for the spirit of a man from that which awaits the spirit of a beast, and thus of a specific distinction between these two principles of life. In the formation even of the dilemma: Whether upwards or downwards, there lies an inquiring knowledge; and it cannot surprise us if Koheleth finally decides that the way of the spirit of a man is upwards, although it is not said that he rested this on the ground of demonstrative certainty. It is enough that, with the moral necessity of a final judgment beyond the sphere of this present life, at the same time also the continued existence of the spirit of man presented itself to him as a postulate of faith. One may conclude from the *desiderium aeternitatis* (iii. 11) implanted in man by the Creator, that, like the instincts implanted in the beasts, it will be calculated not for deception, but for satisfaction; and from the לְמַעְלָה, Prov. xv. 24,—*i.e.* the striving of a wise man rising above earthly, temporary, common things,—that death will not put an end to this striving, but will help it to reach its goal. But this is an indirect proof, which, however, is always inferior to the direct in force of argument. He presupposes that the Omnipotence and Wisdom which formed the world is also at the same time Love. Thus, though at last, it is faith which solves the dilemma, and we see from xii. 7 that this faith held sway over Koheleth. In the Book of Sirach, also, the old conception of Hades shows itself as yet dominant; but after the οὐκ ἀθάνατος υἱὸς ἀνθρώπου, xvii. 25, we read towards the end, where he speaks of Elias: καὶ γὰρ ἡμεῖς ζωῇ ζησόμεθα, xlviii. 11. In the passage before us, Koheleth remains in doubt, without getting over it by the hand of faith. In a certain reference the question he here proposes is to the present day unanswered; for the soul, or, more correctly, according to the biblical mode of conception, the spirit from which the soul-life of all corporeal beings proceeds, is a monas, and as such is indestructible. Do the future of the beast's soul and of man's soul not then stand in a solidaric mutual relation to each other? In fact, the future life presents to us mysteries the solution of which is beyond the power of human thought, and we need not wonder that Koheleth, this sober-minded, intelligent man, who was inaccessible to fantastic self-deception, arrives, by the line of thought commenced at ver. 16, also again at the *ultimatum*.

Ver. 22. "Thus I then saw that there is nothing better than that a man should rejoice in his works, for that is his portion; for who can bring him to this, that he gains an insight into that which shall be after him?" Hengstenberg, who has decided against the interrog. signification of the twice-repeated ה in ver. 21, now also explains בַּמֶּה ... אַחֲרָיו, not: What shall become of him after it (his death)? but: What further shall be done after the state in which he now finds himself? Zöckler, although rightly understanding both ה as well as אחריו (after him = when he will be separated, or separates from this life, vii. 14, ix. 3; cf. Gen. xxiv. 67), yet proceeds on that explanation of Hengstenberg's, and gives it the rendering: how things shall be on the earth after his departure. But (1) for this thought, as vi. 12 shows, the author had a more suitable form of expression; (2) this thought, after the author has, ver. 21, explained it as uncertain whether the spirit of a man in the act of death takes a different path from that of a beast, is altogether aside from the subject, and it is only an apologetic tendency not yet fully vanquished which here constrains him. The chain of thought is however this: How it will be with the spirit of a man when he dies, who knows? What will be after death is thus withdrawn from human knowledge. Thus it is best to enjoy the present, since we connect together (ii. 24) labour and enjoyment mediated thereby. This joy of a man in his work—*i.e.* as v. 18: which flows from his work as a fountain, and accompanies him in it (viii. 15)—is his portion, *i.e.* the best which he has of life in this world. Instead of בַּמֶּה־שׁ, the punctuation is בַּמֶּה, because שיהיה אחריו is a kindred idea; *vid.* regarding מֶה under ii. 22. And לראות בְּ is used, because it is not so much to be said of the living, that he cannot foresee how it shall be with him when he dies, as that he can gain no glimpse into that world because it is an object that has for him no fixity.

The Wrongs suffered by Man from Man embittering the Life of the Observer, iv. 1—3.

From unjust decisions a transition is now made to the subject of the haughty, unmerciful cruelty of the wide-extended oppressions inflicted by men.

iv. 1. "And again I saw all the oppressions that are done under the sun: and behold there the tears of the oppressed, and they have no comforter; and from the hand of their oppressors goeth forth violence; and they have no comforter." Incorrectly Hahn: And anew I saw,—the observation is different from that of iii. 16, though cognate. Thus: And again I saw,—the expression follows the syntactic scheme of Gen. xxvi. 18; regarding the *fut. consec.* brought into view here and at ver. 7, *vid.* above, p. 197, 2. The second הָעֲשֻׁ is *part. pass.*; the first, as at Job xxxv. 9, and also at Amos iii. 9, is abstract (*i.e.* bringing the many separate instances under one general idea) *pluraletantum* (cf. פְּדוּיֵי, *redemti*, Isa. xxxv. 10; and *redemtio, pretium redemtionis*, Num. iii. 46); the plur. אֲשֶׁר נַעֲ need not appear strange, since even חַיִּים is connected with the plur. of the pred., *e.g.* Ps. xxxi. 11, lxxxviii. 4. דִּמְעַת has, as at Isa. xxv. 8 (cf. Rev. xxiv. 4, πᾶν δάκρυον), a collective sense. The expression וּמִיַּד . . . כֹּחַ is singular. According to the most natural impression, it seems to signify: "and from the hand of their oppressors no power of deliverance" (carrying forward אֵין); but the parallelism of the palindromically constructed verse (as at i. 6, ii. 10, iii. 16) excludes this meaning. Thus כֹּחַ is here once—nowhere else—used, like the Greek βία, in the sense of violence; Luzzatto prefers the reading וּבְיַד, by which the expression would be in conformity with the linguistic usage; but also מִיד is explained: the force which they have in their hands is, in going forth from their hands, thought of as abused, and, as taking the form of שֹׁד or חָזְקָה. In view of this sorrow which men bring upon their fellow-men, life for Koheleth lost all its worth and attraction.

Vers. 2, 3. "And I praised the dead who were long ago dead, more than the living who are yet in life; and as happier than both, him who has not yet come into existence, who hath not seen the evil work which is done under the sun." וְשַׁבֵּחַ is hardly thought of as part., like יֻקָּשִׁים = מְיֻקָּשִׁים, ix. 12; the מ of the *part. Pih.* is not usually thrown away, only מַהֵר, Zeph. i. 14, is perhaps = מְמַהֵר, but for the same reason as בֵּית־אֵל, 2 Kings ii. 3, is = בְּבֵית־אֵל. Thus וְשַׁבֵּחַ, like וְנָתוֹן, viii. 9, is *inf. absol.*, which is used to continue, in an adverbially subord. manner, the preceding finite with the same subject,[1] Gen. xli. 43; Lev. xxv. 14; Judg. vii. 19, etc.; cf. especially Ex. viii. 11: "Pharaoh saw ... and hardened (וְהִכְבֵּד) his heart;" just in the same manner as וְשַׁבֵּחַ here connects itself with יֵשׁ אֲנִי׳ אֲ׳. Only the annexed designation of the subject is peculiar; the syntactic possibility of this connection is established by Num. xix. 35, Ps. xv. 5, Job xl. 2, and, in the second rank, by Gen. xvii. 10, Ezek. v. 14. Yet אֲנִי might well enough have been omitted had יֵשׁ אֲנִי וֹ׳ not stood too remote. Regarding עֲדֶנָה[2] and עֲדֶן, *adhuc, vid.* p. 194. The circumstantial form of the expression: *prae vivis qui vivi sunt adhuc*, is intentional: they who are as yet living must be witnesses of the manifold and comfortless human miseries.

It is a question whether ver. 3 begins a new clause (LXX., Syr., and Venet.) or not. That אֵת, like the Arab. *aiya*, sometimes serves to give prominence to the subject, cannot be denied (*vid.* Böttcher, § 516, and Mühlau's remarks thereto). The Mishnic expressions אוֹתוֹ הַיּוֹם, that day, אוֹתָהּ הָאָרֶץ, that land, and the like (Geiger, § 14. 2), presuppose a certain preparation in the older language; and we might, with Weiss (*Stud. ueber d. Spr. der Mishna*, p. 112), interpret אֵת אֲשֶׁר in the sense of אוֹתִי אֲשֶׁר, *is qui*. But the accus. rendering is more natural. Certainly the expression שַׁבֵּחַ טוֹב, "to praise," "to pronounce happy," is not used; but to טוֹב it is natural to suppose וְקָרָאתִי added. Jerome accordingly translates: *et feliciorem utroque judicavi qui necdum natus est.* הָרָע has the double *Kametz*, as is generally the case, except at Ps. liv. 7 and Mic. vii. 3.[3] Better than he who is born is the unborn, who does not become conscious of the wicked actions that are done under the sun. A similar thought, with many variations in its expression, is found in Greek writers; see regarding these shrill discordances, which run through all the joy of the beauty and splendour of Hellenic life, my *Apologetik*, p. 116. Buddhism accordingly gives to *nirvâna* the place of the highest good. That we find Koheleth on the same path (cf. vi. 3, vii. 1), has its reason in this, that so long as the central point of man's existence lies in the present life, and this is not viewed as the fore-court of eternity, there is no enduring consolation to lift us above the miseries of this present world.

---

[1] Also 1 Chron. v. 20, the subject remains virtually the same: *et ita quidem ut exaudirentur*.

[2] Thus punctuated with *Segol* under *Daleth*, and נ, *raphatum*, in F. H. J. P. Thus also Kimchi in *W.B.* under עֶד.

[3] *Vid.* Heidenheim, *Meor Enajim*, under Deut. xvii. 7.

Miserable Rivalry and Restless Pursuit, iv. 4-6.

There follow two other observations, mutually related and issuing in "windy effort:"—

Ver. 4. "And I saw all the labour and all the skill of business, that it is an envious surpassing of the one by the other: also this is vain and windy effort." The הִיא refers to this exertion of vigorous effort and skill. The Graec. Venet., by rendering here and at ii. 24 כִּשְׁרוֹן by καθαρότης, betrays himself as a Jew. With כִּי, *quod*, that which forms the pred. follows the object. The *min* in *mere'ehu* is as in *amatz min*, Ps. xviii. 18, and the like—the same as the compar.: *aemulatio qua unus prae altero eminere studet*. All this expenditure of strength and art has covetousness and envy, with which one seeks to surpass another, as its poisoned sting.

Ver. 5. There ought certainly to be activity according to our calling; indolence is self-destruction: "The fool foldeth his hands, and eateth his own flesh." He layeth his hands together (Prov. vi. 10 = xxiv. 33),—placeth them in his bosom, instead of using them in working,—and thereby he eateth himself up, *i.e.* bringeth ruin upon himself (Ps. xxvii. 2; Mic. iii. 3; Isa. xlix. 26); for instead of nourishing himself by the labour of his hands, he feeds on his own flesh, and thus wasteth away. The emphasis does not lie on the subject (the fool, and only the fool), but on the pred.

Ver. 6. The fifth verse stands in a relation of contrast to this which follows: "Better is one hand full of quietness, than both fists full of labour and windy effort." Mendelssohn and others interpret ver. 5 as the objection of the industrious, and ver. 6 as the reply of the slothful. Zöckler agrees with Hitz., and lapses into the hypothesis of a dialogue otherwise rejected by him (*vid.* above, p. 217). As everywhere, so also here it preserves the unity of the combination of thoughts. נַחַת signifies here, as little as it does anywhere else, the rest of sloth; but rest, in contrast to such activity in labour as robs a man of himself, to the hunting after gain and honour which never has enough, to the rivalry which places its goal always higher and higher, and seeks to be before others—it is rest connected with well-being (vi. 5), gentle quietness (ix. 17), resting from self-activity (Isa. xxx. 15); cf. the post-bibl. נַחַת רוּחַ, satisfaction, contentment, comfort. In a word, *nahath* has not here the sense of being idle or lazy. The sequence of the thoughts is this: The fool in idleness consumes his own life-strength; but, on the other hand, a little of true rest is better than the labour of windy effort, urged on by rivalry yielding no rest. כַּף is the open hollow hand, and חֹפֶן

(Assyr. *hupunnu*) the hand closed like a ball, the fist. "Rest" and "labour and windy effort" are the accusatives of that to which the designation of measure refers (Gesen. § 118. 3); the accus. connection lay here so much the nearer, as מְלֹא is connected with the accus. of that with which anything is full. In "and windy effort" lies the reason for the judgment pronounced. The striving of a man who laboriously seeks only himself and loses himself in restlessness, is truly a striving which has wind for its object, and has the property of wind.

The Aimless Labour and Penuriousness of him who stands alone,
iv. 7–12.

Another sorrowful spectacle is the endless labour and the insatiable covetousness of the isolated man, which does good neither to himself nor to any other:

Vers. 7, 8. "There is one without a second, also son and brother he has not; and there is no end of his labour; his eyes nevertheless are not satisfied with riches: For whom do I labour, then, and deny all good to my soul? Also this is vain, and it is a sore trouble." That וְאַיִן, as in Ps. civ. 25, cv. 34, has the meaning of בְּאַיִן, *absque*, Nolde has already observed in his *Partik.-Concordanz:* a *solitarius*, without one standing by his side, a second standing near him, *i.e.* without wife and without friend; also, as the words following show, without son and brother. Regarding וְאַיִן, for which, with the connect. accus., וְאֵין might be expected (cf. also ii. 7, וְאַיִן with *Mahpach*; and, on the other hand, ii. 23, וָכַעַס with *Pashta*), *vid.* under Ps. lv. 10. *Gam* may be interpreted in the sense of "also" as well as of "nevertheless" (Ewald, 354*a*); the latter is to be preferred, since the endless labour includes in itself a restless striving after an increase of possession. The *Kerî*, in an awkward way, changes עיניו into עֵינוֹ; the taking together the two eyes as one would here be unnatural, since the avaricious man devours gold, silver, and precious things really with both his eyes, and yet, however great be his wealth, still more does he wish to see in his possession; the sing. of the pred. is as at 1 Sam. iv. 15; Mic. iv. 11. With *ulmi ani,* Koheleth puts himself in the place of such a friendless, childless man; yet this change of the description into a self-confession may be occasioned by this, that the author in his old age was really thus isolated, and stood alone. Regarding חָסֵר with the accus. of the person, to whom, and *min* of the matter, in respect of which there is want, *vid.* under Ps. viii. 6. That the author stands in sympathy with the sorrowful condition here exposed, may also be remarked from the fact that he now proceeds to show the value of companionship and the miseries of isolation :

Ver. 9. "Better are two together than one, seeing they have a good reward in their labour." By *hashsh^enäim*, the author refers to such a pair ; *häehhad* is one such as is just described. The good reward consists in this, that each one of the two has the pleasant consciousness of doing good to the other by his labour, and especially of being helpful to him. In this latter general sense is grounded the idea of the reward of faithful fellowship :

Ver. 10. "For if they fall, the one can raise up his fellow : but woe to the one who falleth, and there is not a second there to lift him up." Only the Targ., which Grätz follows, confounds אִילוֹ [1] with אֱלִי (*vid.* above, pp. 191 and 192); it is equivalent to אוֹי לוֹ, Isa. iii. 9, or הוֹי לוֹ, Ezek. xiii. 18. *Häehhad* is appos. connecting itself to the pronominal suff., as, *e.g.*, in a far more inappropriate manner, Ps. lxxxvi. 2 ; the prep. is not in appos. usually repeated, Gen. ii. 19, ix. 4 (exceptions : Ps. xviii. 51, lxxiv. 14). Whether we translate שֶׁיִּפֹּל by *qui ceciderit* (xi. 3), or by *quum ceciderit* (Jerome), is all one. יָקִים is potential : it is possible and probable that it will be done, provided he is a חָבֵר טוֹב, *i.e.* a true friend (*Pirke aboth*, ii. 13).

Ver. 11. "Moreover, if two lie together, then there is heat to them : but how can it be warm with one who is alone?" The marriage relation is not excluded, but it remains in the background ; the author has two friends in his eye, who, lying in a cold night under one covering (Ex. xxii. 26 ; Isa. xxviii. 20), cherish one another, and impart mutual warmth. Also in *Aboth de-Rabbi Nathan*, c. 8, the sleeping of two together is spoken of as an evidence of friendship. The *vav* in *v^ehham* is that of the consequent ; it is wanting, 10*a*, according to rule, in *häehhad*, because it commonly comes into use with the verb, seldom (*e.g.* Gen. xxii. 1) with the preceding subj.

Ver. 12. "And if one shall violently assail him who is alone, two shall withstand him ; and (finally) a threefold cord is not quickly broken asunder." The form *yithq^epho* for *yithq^ephehu*, Job xv. 24, is like *yird^epho*, Hos. viii. 3 = *yird^ephehu*, Judg. ix. 40. If we take תקף in the sense of to overpower, then the meaning is : If one can overpower him who is alone, then, on the contrary, two can maintain their ground against him (Herzf.); but the two אִם, vers. 10, 11, which are equivalent to *ἐάν*, exclude such a pure logical *εἰ*. And why should תקף, if it can mean overpowering, not also

---

[1] With *Munach* and *Rebia* in one word, which, according to the Masora, occurs in only four other places. *Vid. Mas. magna* under this passage, and *Mishpete hateamin* 26*a*.

mean doing violence to by means of a sudden attack? In the Mishnic and Arab. it signifies to seize, to lay hold of; in the Aram. הֶחֱזִיק = אֲתְקֵף, and also at Job xiv. 20, xv. 24 (vid. Comm.), it may be understood of a violent assault, as well as of a completed subjugation; as נשׂא means to lift up and carry; עמד, to tread and to stand. But whether it be understood inchoat. or not, in any case הָאֶחָד is not the assailant, who is much rather the unnamed subj. in יִתְקְפוֹ, but the one (the *solitarius*) who, if he is alone, must succumb; the construction of *yithq^epho häehhad* follows the scheme of Ex. ii. 6, "she saw it, the child." To the assault expressed by תקף, there stands opposed the expression עמד נגד, which means to withstand any one with success; as עמד לפני, 2 Kings x. 4, Ps. cxlvii. 17, Dan. viii. 7, means to maintain one's ground. Of three who hold together, 12a says nothing; the advance from two to three is thus made in the manner of a numerical proverb (vid. *Proverbs*, vol. I. p. 13). If two hold together, that is seen to be good; but if there be three, this threefold bond is likened to a cord formed of three threads, which cannot easily be broken. Instead of the definite specific art. 'הַחֲ 'הַמ, we make use of the indefinite. *Funiculus triplex difficile rumpitur* is one of the winged expressions used by Koheleth.

The People's Enthusiasm for the new King, and its Extinction, iv. 13–16.

A political observation follows in an aphoristic manner the observations relating to social life, viz. how popularity vanishes away and passes even into its opposite. The author, who here plainly quotes from actual events, begins with a general statement:

Ver. 13. "Better is a youth poor and wise, than a king old and foolish, who no longer understands how to be warned,"—*i.e.* who increases his folly by this, that he is "wise in his own eyes," Prov. xxvi. 12; earlier, as עוֹד denotes, he was, in some measure, accessible to the instruction of others in respect of what was wanting to him; but now in his advanced age he is hardened in his folly, bids defiance to all warning counsel, and undermines his throne. The connection of the verb ידע with ל and the inf. (for which elsewhere only the inf. is used) is a favourite form with the author; it means to know anything well, v. 1, vi. 8, x. 15; here is meant an understanding resting on the knowledge of oneself and on the knowledge of men. נִזְהָר is here and at xii. 12, Ps. xix. 12, a *Niph. tolerativum*, such as the synon. נוֹסָר, Ps. ii. 10: to let oneself be cleared up, made wiser, enlightened, warned. After this contrast, the idea connected with חכם also defines itself. A young man (יֶלֶד, as at Dan. i. 4, but also Gen. iv. 23) is meant who (vid. above, p. 193, under *misken*) yet excels the old imbecile and childish king, in that he perceives the necessity of a fundamental change in the present state of public matters, and knows how to master the situation to such a degree that he raises himself to the place of ruler over the neglected community.

Ver. 14. "For out of the prison-house he goeth forth to reign as king, although he was born as a poor man in his kingdom." With כִּי the properties of poverty and wisdom attributed to the young man are verified,—wisdom in this, that he knew how to find the way from a prison to a throne. As *harammim*, 2 Chron. xxii. 5 = *haarammim*, 2 Kings viii. 28, so *hasurim* = *haasurim* (cf. *masoreth* = *maasoreth*, Ezek. xx. 37); *beth haasirim* (*Kerî*: *haasurim*), Judg. xvi. 21, 25, and *beth haesur*, Jer. xxxvii. 15, designate the prison; cf. *Moēd katan*, iii. 1. The modern form of the language prefers this elision of the א, e.g. אֶפְלוּ = אִלּוּ אַף, אַלְתַּר = אַל־אֲתַר, בָּתַר = בַּאֲתַר post = contra, etc. The perf. יָצָא is also thought of as such; for the comparison, ver. 13, would have no meaning if the poor and wise youth were not thought of as having reached the throne, and having pre-eminence assigned to him as such. He has come forth from the prison to become king, רָשׁ ... כִּי. Zöckler translates: "Whereas also he that was born in his kingdom was poor," and adds the remark: "כי גם, after the כי of the preceding clause, does not so much introduce a verification of it, as much rather an intensification; by which is expressed, that the prisoner has not merely transitorily fallen into such misery, but that he was born in poor and lowly circumstances, and that in his own kingdom בְּמַ׳, i.e. in the same land which he should afterwards rule as king." But כי גם is nowhere used by Koheleth in the sense of "*ja auch*" (= whereas also); and also where it is thus to be translated, as at Jer. xiv. 18, xxiii. 11, it is used in the sense of "*denn auch*" (= for also), assigning proof. The fact is, that this group of particles, according as כי is thought of as demonst. or relat., means either "*denn auch*," iv. 16, vii. 22, viii. 16, or "*wenn auch*" = ἐὰν καί, as here and at viii. 12. In the latter case, it is related to גַּם כִּי (sometimes also merely גַּם, Ps. xcv. 9; Mal. iii. 15), as ἐὰν (εἰ) καί, although, notwithstanding, is to καὶ ἐάν (εἰ), even although.[1] Thus 14*b*, connecting itself with לִמְלֹךְ, is to be translated: "although he was born (נוֹלָד, not נוֹלַד) in his kingdom as a poor man."[2] We cannot also concur with Zöckler in the view

---

[1] That the accentuation separates the two words כי גם־ is to be judged from this, that it almost everywhere prefers כי אם־ (vid. under Comm. to Ps. i. 2).

[2] נולד רש cannot mean "to become poor." Grätz appeals to the Mishnic

that the suff. of בּמ׳ refers to the young upstart: in the kingdom which should afterwards become his; for this reason, that the suff. of תח׳, ver. 16b, refers to the old king, and thus also that this designation may be mediated, בּמ׳ must refer to him. מלכות signifies kingdom, reign, realm; here, the realm, as at Neh. ix. 35, Dan. v. 11, vi. 29. Grätz thinks vers. 13–16 ought to drive expositors to despair. But hitherto we have found no room for despair in obtaining a meaning from them. What follows also does not perplex us. The author describes how all the world hails the entrance of the new youthful king on his government, and gathers together under his sceptre.

Vers. 15, 16a. "I saw all the living which walk under the sun on the side of the youth, the second who shall enter upon the place of the former: no end of all the people, all those at whose head he stands." The author, by the expression "I saw," places himself back in the time of the change of government. If we suppose that he represents this to himself in a lively manner, then the words are to be translated: of the second who shall be his successor; but if we suppose that he seeks to express from the standpoint of the past that which, lying farther back in the past, was now for the first time future, then the future represents the time to come in the past, as at 2 Kings iii. 27; Ps. lxxviii. 6; Job xv. 28 (Hitz.): of the second who should enter on his place (עָמַד, to step to, to step forth, of the new king, Dan. viii. 23, xi. 2 f.; cf קוּם, 1 Kings viii. 20). The designation of the crowd which, as the pregnant עַם expresses, gathered by the side of the young successor to the old king, by "all the living, those walking under the sun (הַמְה׳, perhaps intentionally the pathetic word for הֹלְכִים, Isa. xlii. 5)," would remain a hyperbole, even although the throne of the Asiatic world-ruler had been intended; still the expression, so absolute in its universality, would in that case be more natural (vid. the conjectural reference to Cyrus and Astyages, above, at p. 215). הַשֵּׁנִי, Ewald refers to the successor to the king, the second after the king, and translates: "to the second man who should reign in his stead;" but the second man in this sense has certainly never been the child of fortune; one must then think of Joseph, who, however, remains the second man. Hitzig rightly: "The youth is the second שֵׁנִי, not אַחֵר, in contrast to the king, who, as his predecessor, is the first." "Yet," he continues, "הילד should be the appos. and השני the principal word," i.e. instead of: with the second youth, was to be expected: with the second, the youth. It language; but no intelligent linguist will use נולד רש of a man in any other sense than that he is originally poor.

is true, we may either translate: with the second youth, or: with the second, the youth,—the form of expression has in it something incorrect, for it has the appearance as if it treated of two youths. But similar are the expressions, Matt. viii. 21, ἕτερος κ.τ.λ., "another, and that, too, one of His disciples;" and Luke xxiii. 32, ἤγοντο κ.τ.λ. All the world ranks itself by the side (thus we may also express it) of the second youthful king, so that he comes to stand at the head of an endless multitude. The LXX., Jerome, and the Venet. render incorrectly the all (the multitude) as the subject of the relative clause, which Luther, after the Syr., corrects by reading לְפָנָיו for לִפְנֵיהֶם: of the people that went for him there was no end. Rightly the Targ.: at whose head (= בְּרֵישֵׁיהוֹן) he had the direction, לִפְנֵי, as with יָצָא וּבָא, 1 Sam. xviii. 16; 2 Chron. i. 10; Ps. lxviii. 8, etc. All the world congregates about him, follows his leadership; but his history thus splendidly begun, viewed backwards, is a history of hopes falsified.

Ver. 16b. "And yet they who come after do not rejoice in him: for that also is vain, and a grasping after the wind." For all that, and in spite of that (*gam* has here this meaning, as at vi. 7; Jer. vi. 15; Ps. cxxix. 2; Ewald, § 354a), posterity (הָא, as at i. 11; cf. Isa. xli. 4) has no joy in this king,—the hopes which his contemporaries placed in the young king, who had seized the throne and conquered their hearts, afterwards proved to be delusions; and also this history, at first so beautiful, and afterwards so hateful, contributed finally to the confirmation of the truth, that all under the sun is vain. As to the historical reminiscence from the time of the Ptolemies, in conformity with which Hitzig (in his *Comm.*) thinks this figure is constructed, *vid.* above, p. 213; Grätz here, as always, rocks himself in Herodian dreams. In his *Comm.*, Hitz. guesses first of Jeroboam, along with Rehoboam the יֶלֶד שֵׁנִי, who rebelled against King Solomon, who in his old age had become foolish. In an essay, "Zur Exeg. u. Kritik des B. Koheleth," in Hilgenfeld's *Zeitschr.* XIV. 566 ff., Saul, on the contrary, appears to him to be the old and foolish king, and David the poor wise youth who rose to the throne, and took possession of the whole kingdom, but in his latter days experienced desertion and adversities; for those who came after (the younger men) had no delight in him, but rebelled against him. But in relation to Saul, who came from the plough to be king, David, who was called from being a shepherd, is not נוֹלַד רָשׁ; and to Jewish history this Saul, whose nobler self is darkened by melancholy, but again brightens forth, and who to his death maintained the dignity of a king of Israel, never at any time appears as מֶלֶךְ ... וּכְסִיל. Moreover, by both combinations of that which is related with the בֵּית הָסוּרִים (for which 'הַס is written) of the history of the old Israelitish kings, a meaning contrary to the usage of the language must be extracted. It is true that סוּר, as the so-called *particip. perfecti*, may mean " gone aside (to a distance)," Isa. xlix. 21, Jer. xvii. 13; and we may, at any rate, by סוּרִים, think on that poor rabble which at first gathered around David, 1 Sam. xxii. 2, regarded as outcasts from honourable society. But בית will not accord therewith. That David came forth from the house (home) of the estranged or separated, is and remains historically an awkward expression, linguistically obscure, and not in accordance with the style of Koheleth. In order to avoid this incongruity, Böttcher regards Antiochus the Great as the original of the ילד. He was the second son of his father, who died 225. When a hopeful youth of fifteen years of age, he was recalled to the throne from a voluntary banishment into Farther Asia, very soon gained against his old cousin and rival Achaeus, who was supported by Egypt, a large party, and remained for several years esteemed as a prince and captain; he disappointed, however, at a later time, the confidence which was reposed in him. But granting that the voluntary exile of Antiochus might be designated as בית האם', he was yet not a poor man, born poor, but was the son of King Seleucus Callinicus; and his older relative and rival Achaeus wished indeed to become king, but never attained unto it. Hence השני is not the youth as second son of his father, but as second on the throne, in relation to the dethroned king reckoned as the first. Thus, far from making it probable that the Book of Koheleth originated in the time of the Diadochs, this combination of Böttcher's also stands on a feeble foundation, and falls in ruins when assailed.

The section i. 12–iv. 16, to which we have prefixed the superscription, "Koheleth's Experiences and their Results," has now reached its termination, and here for the first time we meet with a characteristic peculiarity in the composition of the book: the narrative sections, in which Koheleth, on the ground of his own experiences and observations, registers the vanities of earthly life, terminate in series of proverbs in which the *I* of the preacher retires behind the objectivity of the exhortations, rules, and principles obtained from experience, here recorded. The first of these series of proverbs which here follows is the briefest, but also the most complete in internal connection.

FIRST CONCLUDING SECTION.

PROVERBS REGARDING THE WORSHIP OF GOD.—IV. 17 [V. 1]–V. 6 [7]

As an appendix and interlude, these proverbs directly follow the personal section preceding. The first rule here laid down refers to the going to the house of God.

iv. 17 [v. 1]. "Keep thy foot when thou goest to the house of God, and to go to hear is better than that fools give a sacrifice; for the want of knowledge leads them to do evil." The "house of God" is like the "house of Jahve," 2 Sam. xii. 20, Isa. xxxvii. 1, the temple; אֵל, altogether like אֶל־מִ־אֵל, Ps. lxxiii. 17. The *Chethîb* רַגְלֶיךָ is admissible, for elsewhere also this plur. ("thy feet") occurs in a moral connection and with a spiritual reference, *e.g.* Ps. cxix. 59; but more frequently, however, the comprehensive sing. occurs, Ps. cxix. 105, Prov. i. 15, iv. 26 f., and the *Kerî* thus follows the right note. The correct understanding of what follows depends on כִּי־רָע... Interpreters have here adopted all manner of impossible views. Hitzig's translation: "for they know not how to be sorrowful," has even found in Stuart at least one imitator; but עֲשׂוֹת רָע would, as the contrast of *'asoth tov*, iii. 12, mean nothing else than, "to do that which is unpleasant, disagreeable, bad," like *'asah ra'ah*, 2 Sam. xii. 18. Gesen., Ewald (§ 336*b*), Elster, Heiligst., Burger, Zöckl., Dale, and Bullock translate: "they know not that they do evil;" but for such a rendering the words ought to have been עֲשׂוֹתָם רָע (cf. Jer. xv. 15); the only example for the translation of לַעֲשׂוֹת after the manner of the *acc. c. inf.* = *se facere malum*—viz. at 1 Kings xix. 4— is incongruous, for לָמוּת does not here mean *se mori*, but *ut moreretur*. Yet more incorrect is the translation of Jerome, which is followed by Luther: *nesciunt quid faciant mali*. It lies near, as at ii. 24 so also here, to suppose an injury done to the text. Aben Ezra introduced רַק before לַעְשׂ׳, but Koheleth never uses this limiting particle; we would have to write כִּי אִם־לַעֲשׂוֹת, after iii. 12, viii. 15. Anything thus attained, however, is not worth the violent means thus used; for the ratifying clause is not ratifying, and also in itself, affirmed of the כְּסִילִים, who, however, are not the same as the *r^esha'im* and the *hattāim*, is inappropriate. Rather it might be said: they know not to do good (thus the Syr.); or: they know not whether it be good or bad to do, *i.e.* they have no moral feeling, and act not from moral motives (so the Targ.). Not less violent than this remodelling of the text is the expedient of Herzberg, Philippson, and Ginsburg, who from לִשְׁמֹעַ derive the subject-conception of the obedient (הַשֹּׁמְעִים): "For those understand not at all to do evil;" the subj. ought to have been expressed if it must be something different from the immediately preceding כְּסִילִים. We may thus render *enam yod'im*, after Ps. lxxxii. 5, Isa. lvi. 10, as complete in itself: they (the fools) are devoid of knowledge to do evil = so that they do evil; *i.e.*, want of knowledge brings them to this, that they do evil. Similarly also Knobel: they concern themselves not,—are unconcerned (viz. about the right mode of worshipping God),—so that they do evil, with the correct remark that the consequence of their perverse conduct is here represented as their intention. But לֹא יֵדַע, absol., does not mean to be unconcerned (wanton), but to be without knowledge. Rashbam, in substance correctly: they are predisposed by their ignorance to do evil; and thus also Hahn; Mendelssohn translates directly: "they sin because they are ignorant." If this interpretation is correct, then for לִשְׁמֹעַ it follows that it does not mean "to obey" (thus *e.g.* Zöckler), which in general it never means without some words being added to it (cf. on the contrary, 1 Sam. xv. 22), but "to hear,"—viz. the word of God, which is to be heard in the house of God,—whereby, it is true, a hearing is meant which leads to obedience. In the word הוֹרוֹת, priests are not perhaps thought of, although the comparison of ver. 5 (הַמַּלְאָךְ) with Mal. ii. 7 makes it certainly natural; priestly instruction limited itself to information regarding the performance of the law already given in Scripture, Lev. x. 11, Deut. xxxiii. 9 f., and to deciding on questions arising in the region of legal praxis, Deut. xxiv. 8; Hag. ii. 11. The priesthood did not belong to the teaching class in the sense of preaching. Preaching was never a part of the temple cultus, but, for the first time, after the exile became a part of the synagogue worship. The preachers under the O. T. were the prophets,—preachers by a supernatural divine call, and by the immediate impulse of the Spirit; we know from the Book of Jeremiah that they sometimes went into the temple, or there caused their books of prophecy to be read; yet the author, by the word לִשְׁמֹעַ of the foregoing proverb, scarcely thinks of them. But apart from the teaching of the priests, which referred to the realization of the letter of the law, and the teaching of the prophets to the realization of the spirit of the law, the word formed an essential part of the sacred worship of the temple: the *Tefilla*, the *Beracha*, the singing of psalms, and certainly, at the time of Koheleth, the reading of certain sections of the Bible. When thou goest to the house of God, says Koheleth, take heed to thy step, well reflecting whither thou goest and how thou hast there to appear;

and (with this וְ he connects with this first *nota bene* a second) drawing near to hear exceeds the sacrifice-offering of fools, for they are ignorant (just because they hear not), which leads to this result, that they do evil. מִן, *prae*, expresses also, without an adj., precedence in number, Isa. x. 10, or activity, ix. 17, or worth, Ezek. xv. 2. קָרוֹב is *inf. absol.* Böttcher seeks to subordinate it as such to שְׁמֹר: take heed to thy foot ... and to the coming near to hear more than to ... But these obj. to שמר would be incongruous, and מתת ונו׳ clumsy and even distorted in expression; it ought rather to be מִתִּתְּךָ כִּכְסִילִים זֶבַח. As the *inf. absol.* can take the place of the obj., Isa. vii. 15, xlii. 24, Lam. iii. 45, so also the place of the subj. (Ewald, § 240*a*), although Prov. xxv. 27 is a doubtful example of this. That the use of the *inf. absol.* has a wide application with the author of this book, we have already seen under iv. 2. Regarding the sequence of ideas in זֶבַח ... מִתֵּת (first the subj., then the obj.), *vid.* Gesen. § 133. 3, and cf. above at iii. 18. זֶבַח (וְזָבְחִים), along with its general signification comprehending all animal sacrifices, according to which the altar bears the name מִזְבֵּחַ, early acquired also a more special signification: it denotes, in contradistinction to עוֹלָה, such sacrifices as are only partly laid on the altar, and for the most part are devoted to a sacrificial festival, Ex. xviii. 12 (cf. Ex. xii. 27), the so-called *sh^elamim*, or also *zivhhe sh^elamim*, Prov. vii. 14. The expression נתן זבח makes it probable that here, particularly, is intended the festival (1 Kings i. 41) connected with this kind of sacrifice, and easily degenerating to worldly merriment (*vid.* under Prov. vii. 14); for the more common word for תֵּת would have been הִקְרִיב or שָׁחוֹט; in תֵּת it seems to be indicated that it means not only to present something to God, but also to give at the same time something to man. The most recent canonical Chokma-book agrees with Prov. xxi. 3 in this depreciation of sacrifice. But the Chokma does not in this stand alone. The great word of Samuel, 1 Sam. xv. 22 f., that self-denying obedience to God is better than all sacrifices, echoes through the whole of the Psalms. And the prophets go to the utmost in depreciating the sacrificial cultus.

The second rule relates to prayer.

v. 1, 2 [2, 3]. "Be not hasty with thy mouth, and let not thy heart hasten to speak a word before God: for God is in heaven, and thou art upon earth; therefore let thy words be few. For by much business cometh dreaming, and by much talk the noise of fools." As we say in German: *auf Flügeln fliegen* [to flee on wings], *auf Einem Auge nicht sehen* [not to see with one eye], *auf der Flöte blasen* [to blow on the flute], so in Heb. we say that one slandereth with (*auf*) his tongue (Ps. xv. 3), or, as here, that he hasteth with his mouth, *i.e.* is forward with his mouth, inasmuch as the word goes before the thought. It is the same usage as when the post-bibl. Heb., in contradistinction to שֶׁבִּכְתָב הַתּוֹרָה, the law given in the Scripture, calls the oral law תּוֹ' שֶׁבְּעַל־פֶּה, *i.e.* the law mediated עַל־פֶּה, *oraliter* = *oralis traditio* (*Shabbath* 31a; cf. *Gittin* 60b). The instrument and means is here regarded as the *substratum* of the action — as that which this lays as a foundation. The phrase: "to take on the lips," Ps. xvi. 4, which needs no explanation, is different. Regarding בְּהֵל, *festinare*, which is, like מָהַר, the intens. of *Kal*, vid. above, p. 191; once it occurs quite like our "*sich beeilen*" [to hasten], with reflex. accus. suff., 2 Chron. xxxv. 21. Man, when he prays, should not give the reins to his tongue, and multiply words as one begins and repeats over a form which he has learnt, knowing certainly that it is God of whom and to whom he speaks, but without being conscious that God is an infinitely exalted Being, to whom one may not carelessly approach without collecting his thoughts, and irreverently, without lifting up his soul. As the heavens, God's throne, are exalted above the earth, the dwelling-place of man, so exalted is the heavenly God above earthly man, standing far beneath him; therefore ought the words of a man before God to be few, — few, well-chosen reverential words, in which one expresses his whole soul. The older language forms no plur. from the subst. מְעַט (fewness) used as an adv.; but the more recent treats it as an adj., and forms from it the plur. מְעַטִּים (here and in Ps. cix. 8, which bears the superscription *le-david*, but has the marks of Jeremiah's style); the post-bibl. places in the room of the apparent adj. the particip. adj. מוֹעֵט with the plur. מוֹעֲטִים (מוֹעֲטִין), *e.g. Berachoth* 61a: "always let the words of a man before the Holy One (blessed be His name!) be few" (מוּעָט). Few ought the words to be; for where they are many, it is not without folly. This is what is to be understood, ver. 2, by the comparison; the two parts of the verse stand here in closer mutual relation than vii. 1, — the proverb is not merely synthetical, but, like Job v. 7, parabolical. The בְּ is both times that of the cause. The dream happens, or, as we say, dreams happen בְּרֹב עִנְיָן; not: by much labour; for labour in itself, as the expenditure of strength making one weary, has as its consequence, v. 11, sweet sleep undisturbed by dreams; but: by much self-vexation in a man's striving after high and remote ends beyond what is possible (Targ., in manifold project-making); the care of such a man transplants itself from the waking to the sleeping life, if it does not wholly deprive him of sleep, v. 11b, viii. 16, — all kinds of images of the labours of the day, and fleeting phantoms and terrifying pictures hover before his mind. And as dreams of such a nature appear when a man wearies himself inwardly as well as outwardly by the labours of the day, so, with the same inward necessity, where many words are spoken folly makes its appearance. Hitzig renders כסיל, in the connection קוֹל כְּ׳, as adj.; but, like אֱוִיל (which forms an adj. *evîlî*), כסיל is always a subst., or, more correctly, it is a name occurring always only of a living being, never of a thing. There is sound without any solid content, mere blustering bawling without sense and intelligence. The talking of a fool is in itself of this kind (x. 14); but if one who is not just a fool falls into much talk, it is scarcely possible but that in this flow of words empty bombast should appear.

Another rule regarding the worship of God refers to vowing.

Vers. 3 [4]–6 [7]. "When thou hast made a vow to God, delay not to fulfil it; for there is no pleasure in fools: that which thou hast vowed fulfil. Better that thou vowest not, than that thou vowest and fulfillest not. Let not thy mouth bring thy body into punishment; and say not before the messenger of God that it was precipitation: why shall God be angry at thy talk, and destroy the work of thy hands? For in many dreams and words there are also many vanities: much rather fear God!" If they abstained, after *Shabbath* 30*b*, from treating the Book of Koheleth as apocryphal, because it begins with דברי תורה (cf. at i. 3) and closes in the same way, and hence warrants the conclusion that that which lies between will also be דברי תורה, this is in a special manner true of the passage before us regarding the vow which, in thought and expression, is the echo of Deut. xxiii. 22–24. Instead of *kaashĕr tiddor*, we find there the words *ki tiddor*; instead of *lelohim* (= *lĕĕlohim*, always only of the one true God), there we have *lahovah ĕlohĕcha*; and instead of *al-t^eahher*, there *lo t^eahher*. There the reason is: "for the Lord thy God will surely require it of thee; and it would be sin in thee;" here: for there is no pleasure in fools, *i.e.* it is not possible that any one, not to speak of God, could have a particular inclination toward fools, who speak in vain, and make promises in which their heart is not, and which they do not keep. Whatever thou vowest, continues Koheleth, fulfil it; it is better (Ewald, § 336*a*) that thou vowest not, than to vow and not to pay; for which the *Tôra* says: "If thou shalt forbear to vow, it shall be no sin in thee" (Deut. xxiii. 22). נֶדֶר, which, according to the stem-word, denotes first the vow of conse- cration or setting apart (cogn. Arab. *nadar*, to separate, נזר, whence נָזִיר), the so-called אֱסָר [*vid.* Num. xxx. 3], is here a vow in its widest sense; the author, however, may have had, as there, the law (cf. ver. 24), especially *shalme nĕdĕr*, in view, *i.e.* such peace-offerings as the law does not enjoin, but which the offerer promises (cogn. with the *shalme nᵉdavah, i.e.* such as rest on free-will, but not on any obligation arising from a previous promise) from his own inclination, for the event that God may do this or that for him. The verb שִׁלֵּם is not, however, related to this name for sacrifices, as חָטָא is to חַטָּאת, but denotes the fulfilling or discharge as a performance fully accordant with duty. To the expression חָטָא ... היה (twice occurring in the passage of Deut. referred to above) there is added the warning: let not thy mouth bring thy body into sin. The verb *nathan*, with *Lamed* and the inf. following, signifies to allow, to permit, Gen. xx. 6; Judg. i. 34; Job xxxi. 30. The inf. is with equal right translated: not to bring into punishment; for חָטָא—the syncop. *Hiph.* of which, according to an old, and, in the Pentateuch, favourite form, is לַחֲטִיא—signifies to sin, and also (*e.g.* Gen. xxxix. 9; cf. the play on the word, Hos. viii. 11) to expiate sin; sin-burdened and guilty, or liable to punishment, mean the same thing. Incorrectly, Ginsburg, Zöck., and others: "Do not suffer thy mouth to cause thy flesh to sin;" for (1) the formula: "the flesh sins," is not in accordance with the formation of O. T. ideas; the N. T., it is true, uses the expression σὰρξ ἁμαρτίας, Rom. viii. 3, but not ἁμαρτάνουσα, that which sins is not the flesh, but the will determined by the flesh, or by fleshly lust; (2) the mouth here is not merely that which leads to sin, but the person who sins through thoughtless haste,—who, by his haste, brings sin upon his flesh, for this suffers, for the breach of vow, by penalties inflicted by God; the mouth is, like the eye and the hand, a member of the ὅλον τὸ σῶμα (Matt. v. 24 f.), which is here called בשׂר; the whole man in its sensitive nature (*opp.* לֵב, ii. 3, xi. 10; Prov. xiv. 30) has to suffer chastisement on account of that which the mouth hath spoken. Gesen. compares this passage, correctly, with Deut. xxiv. 4, for the meaning *peccati reum facere;* Isa. xxix. 21 is also similar.

The further warning refers to the lessening of the sin of a rash vow unfulfilled as an unintentional, easily expiable offence: "and say not before the messenger of God that it was a שְׁגָגָה, a sin of weakness." Without doubt *hammălâch* is an official byname of a priest (*vid.* above, p. 193), and that such as was in common use at the time of the author (*vid.* p. 210). But as for the rest, it is not easy to make the matter of the warning clear. That it is not easy, may be concluded from this, that with Jewish interpreters it lies remote to think of a priest in the word *hammălāch*. By this word the Targ. understands the angel to whom the execution of the sentence of punishment shall be committed on the day of judgment; Aben Ezra: the angel who writes down all the words of a man; similarly Jerome, after his Jewish teacher. Under this passage Ginsburg has an entire excursus regarding the angels. The LXX. and Syr. translate "before God," as if the words of the text were נֶגֶד אֵל, Ps. cxxxviii. 1, or as if *hammalach* could of itself mean God, as presenting Himself in history. Supposing that *hammalach* is the official name of a man, and that of a priest, we appear to be under the necessity of imagining that he who is charged with the obligation of a vow turns to the priest with the desire that he would release him from it, and thus dissolve (bibl. הֵפִיר, Mishnic הִתִּיר) the vow. But there is no evidence that the priests had the power of releasing from vows. Individual cases in which a husband can dissolve the vow of his wife, and a father the vow of his daughter, are enumerated in Num. xxx.; besides, in the traditional law, we find the sentence: "A vow, which one who makes it repents of, can be dissolved by a learned man (חכם), or, where none is present, by three laymen," *Bechoroth* 36*b*; the matter cannot be settled by any middle person (שליח), but he who has taken the vow (הנודר) must appear personally, *Jore deah* c. 228, § 16. Of the priest as such nothing is said here. Therefore the passage cannot at all be traditionally understood of an official dissolution of an oath. Where the Talm. applies it juristically, *Shabbath* 32*b*, etc., Rashi explains *hammalach* by *gizbar shĕl-haqdesh*, *i.e.* treasurer of the revenues of the sanctuary; and in the *Comm.* to Koheleth he supposes that some one has publicly resolved on an act of charity (צדקה), *i.e.* has determined it with himself, and that now the representative of the congregation (שליח) comes to demand it. But that is altogether fanciful. If we proceed on the idea that *liphne hammalach* is of the same meaning as *liphne hakkohen*, Lev. xxvii. 8, 11, Num. ix. 6, xxvii. 2, etc., we have then to derive the figure from such passages relating to the law of sacrifice as Num. xv. 22—26, from which the words *ki shĕgagah hi* (Num. xv. 25*b*) originate. We have to suppose that he who has made a vow, and has not kept it, comes to terms with God with an easier and less costly offering, since in the confession (וִהִי) which he makes before the priest he explains that the vow was a *shĕgagah*, a declaration that inconsiderately escaped him. The author, in giving it to be understood that under these circumstances the offering of the sacrifice is just the direct contrary of a good work, calls to the conscience of the inconsiderate נודר: why should God be angry on account of thy voice with which thou dost excuse thy sins of omission, and destroy (*vid.* regarding חִבֵּל under Isa. x. 27) the work of thy hands (*vid.* under Ps. xc. 17), for He destroys what thou hast done, and causes to fail what thou purposest? The question with *lammah* resembles those in Ezra iv. 22, vii. 23, and is of the same kind as at vii. 16 f.; it leads us to consider what a mad self-destruction that would be (Jer. xliv. 7, cf. under Isa. i. 5).

The reason [for the foregoing admonition] now following places the inconsiderate vow under the general rubric of inconsiderate words. We cannot succeed in interpreting ver. 6 [7] (in so far as we do not supply, after the LXX. and Syr. with the Targ.: *ne credas;* or better, with Ginsburg, היא = it is) without taking one of the *vavs* in the sense of "also." That the Heb. *vav,* like the Greek καί, the Lat. *et,* may have this comparative or intensifying sense rising above that which is purely copulative, is seen from *e.g.* Num. ix. 14, cf. also Josh. xiv. 11. In many cases, it is true, we are not under the necessity of translating *vav* by "also;" but since the "and" here does not merely externally connect, but expresses correlation of things homogeneous, an "also" or a similar particle involuntarily substitutes itself for the "and," *e.g.* Gen. xvii. 20 (Jerome): *super Ismael quoque;* Ex. xxix. 8: *filios quoque;* Deut. i. 32: *et nec sic quidem credidistis;* ix. 8: *nam et in Horeb;* cf. Josh. xv. 19; 1 Sam. xxv. 43; 2 Sam. xix. 25; 1 Kings ii. 22, xi. 26; Isa. xlix. 6, "I have also given to thee." But there are also passages in which it cannot be otherwise translated than by "also." We do not reckon among these Ps. xxxi. 12, where we do not translate "also my neighbours," and Amos iv. 10, where the words are to be translated, "and that in your nostrils." On the contrary, Isa. xxxii. 7 is scarcely otherwise to be translated than "also when the poor maketh good his right," like 2 Sam. i. 23, "also in their death they are not divided." In 2 Chron. xxvii. 5, in like manner, the two *vavs* are scarcely correlative, but we have, with Keil, to translate, "also in the second and third year." And in Hos. viii. 6, וְהוּא, at least according to the punctuation, signifies "also it," as Jerome translates: *ex Israele et ipse est.* According to the interpunction of the passage before us, וְדִ׳ הַ׳ is the pred., and thus, with the Venet., is to be translated: "For in many dreams and vanities there are also many words." We could at all events render the *vav,* as also at x. 11, Ex. xvi. 6, as *vav apod.;* but בְּרֹב וגו׳ has not the character of a virtual antecedent,—the meaning of the expression remains as for the rest the same; but Hitzig's objection is of force against it (as also against Ewald's disposition of the words, like that of Symmachus, Jerome, and Luther: "for where there are many dreams, there are also vanities, and many words"), that it does not accord with the connection, which certainly in the first place requires a reason referable to inconsiderate talk, and that the second half is, in fact, erroneous, for between dreams and many words there exists no necessary inward mutual relation. Hitzig, as Knobel before him, seeks to help this, for he explains: "for in many dreams are also vanities, *i.e.* things from which nothing comes, and (the like) in many words." But not only is this assumed carrying forward of the ב doubtful, but the principal thing would be made a secondary matter, and would drag heavily. The relation in ver. 2 is different where *vav* is that of comparison, and that which is compared follows the comparison. Apparently the text (although the LXX. had it before them, as it is before us) has undergone dislocation, and is thus to be arranged: כי ברב חלמות ודברים הרבה והבלים : for in many dreams and many words there are also vanities, *i.e.* illusions by which one deceives himself and others. Thus also Bullock renders, but without assigning a reason for it. That dreams are named first, arises from a reference back to ver. 2, according to which they are the images of what a man is externally and mentally busied and engaged with. But the principal stress lies on ודברים הרבה, to which also the too rash, inconsiderate vows belong. The pred. והבלים, however, connects itself with " vanity of vanities," which is Koheleth's final judgment regarding all that is earthly. The כי following connects itself with the thought lying in 6*a*, that much talk, like being much given to dreams, ought to be avoided: it ought not to be; much rather (*imo*, Symm. ἀλλά) fear God, Him before whom one should say nothing, but that which contains in it the whole heart.

CONTINUATION OF THE CATALOGUE OF VANITIES.

THE GRADATIONS OF OPPRESSION IN DESPOTIC STATES.—V. 7, 8 [8, 9].

"Fear God," says the proverb (Prov. xxiv. 21), "and the king." The whole Book of Koheleth shows how full its author is of this fundamental thought. Thus the transition to the theme now following was at least inwardly mediated. The state-government, however, although one should be subject to it for conscience' sake, corresponds very little to his idea: the ascending scale of the powers is an ascending scale of violence and oppression.

Ver. 7 [8]. "If thou seest the oppression of the poor and the robbery of right and of justice in the state, marvel not at the matter: for one higher watches over him who is high; and others are high above both." Like *rash, mishpat vatsĕdĕq* are also the gen. of the obj.; "robbery of the right and of justice" is an expression not found elsewhere, but not on that account, as Grätz supposes, impossible: *mishpat* is right, rectitude, and conformity to law; and *tsĕdĕq*, judicial administration, or also social deportment according to these norms; גֵּזֶל, a wicked, shameless depriving of a just claim, and withholding of the showing of right which is due. If one gets a sight of such things as these in a *mᵉdinah, i.e.* in a territorial district under a common government, he ought not to wonder at the matter. תָּמַהּ means to be startled, astonished, and, in the sense of "to wonder," is the word commonly used in modern Heb. But חֵפֶץ has here the colourless general signification of *res*, according to which the Syr. translates it (*vid.* under iii. 1); every attempt in passages such as this to retain the unweakened primary meaning of the word runs out into groundless and fruitless subtlety. Cf. *Berachoth* 5a, אדם... חפץ לח, "a man who buys a thing from another." On the other hand, there is doubt about the meaning of the clause assigning the reason. It seems to be intended, that over him who is high, who oppresses those under him, there stands one who is higher, who in turn oppresses him, and thereby becomes the executor of punishment upon him; and that these, the high and the higher, have over them a Most High, viz. God, who will bring them to an account (Knobel, Ew., Elst., Vaih., Hengst., Zöckl.). None of the old translators and expositors rises, it is true, to the knowledge that גְּבֹהִים may be *pl. majestatis*,[1] but the first גָּבֹהַּ the Targ. renders by אֵל אַדִּיר. This was natural to the Jewish *usus loq.*, for גבוה in the post-bibl. Heb. is a favourite name for God, *e.g. Beza* 20b, *Jebamoth* 87a, *Kamma* 13a: "from the table of God" (משלחן נבוה), *i.e.* the altar (cf. Heb. xiii. 10; 1 Cor. x. 21).[2] The interpretation of גב, however, as the *pl. majest.*, has in the Book of Koheleth itself a support in בוֹרְאֶיךָ, xii. 1; and the thought in which 7b climactically terminates accords essentially with iii. 17. This explanation, however, of 7b does not stand the test. For if an unrighteous

---

[1] That is surprising, since the Talm. interpretation, *Menachoth* 110a, even brings it about that 'לב, v. 10, is to be understood of God.

[2] חלק נבוה is also a common Rabbin. name for the tithes and offerings (cf. *e.g.* Nachmani under Gen. xiv. 20). Along with הגבוה חלק, the sacrifices are also called (in Hurwitz' work on the Heb. rites, known by the abbreviated title ש"לה) המורם לגבוה; *vid.* 85b of the ed. 1764, and 23b of the Amsterdam ed. 1707 of the abridgment.

administration of justice, if violence is in vogue instead of right, that is an actual proof that over him who is high no human higher one watches who may put a check upon him, and to whom he feels that he is responsible. And that above them both one who is Most High stands, who will punish injustice and avenge it, is a consolatory argument against vexation, but is no explanatory reason of the phenomenon, such as we expect after the *noli mirari;* for אל־תתמה does not signify "be not offended" (John xvi. 1), or, "think it not strange" (1 Pet. iv. 12), which would be otherwise expressed (cf. under Ps. xxxvii. 1), but μὴ θαυμάσῃς (LXX.). Also the contrast, ver. 8, warrants the conclusion that in ver. 7 the author seeks to explain the want of legal order from the constitution of a despotic state as distinguished from patriarchal government. For this reason שֹׁמֵר will not be meant of over-watching, which has its aim in the execution of legal justice and official duty, but of egoistic watching,—not, however, as Hitzig understands it: "they mutually protect each other's advantage; one crow does not peck out the eyes of another,"—but, on the contrary, in the sense of hostile watching, as at 1 Sam. xix. 11, 2 Sam. xi. 16, as B. Bardach understands it: " he watches for the time when he may gain the advantage over him who is high, who is yet lower than himself, and may strengthen and enrich himself with his flesh or his goods." Over the one who is high, who oppresses the poor and is a robber in respect of right and justice, there stands a higher, who on his part watches how he can plunder him to his own aggrandisement; and over both there are again other high ones, who in their own interest oppress these, as these do such as are under them. This was the state of matters in the Persian Empire in the time of the author. The satrap stood at the head of state officers. In many cases he fleeced the province to fatten himself. But over the satrap stood inspectors, who often enough built up their own fortunes by fatal denunciations; and over all stood the king, or rather the court, with its rivalry of intrigues among courtiers and royal women. The cruel death-punishments to which disagreeable officials were subjected were fearful. There was a gradation of bad government and arbitrary domination from high to low and from low to high, and no word is more fitting for this state of things in Persia than שֹׁמֵר; for watching, artfully lurking as spies for an opportunity to accomplish the downfall of each other, was prevalent in the Persian Empire, especially when falling into decay.

Ver. 8 [9]. The author, on the other hand, now praises the patriarchal form of government based on agriculture, whose king takes pride, not in bloody conquests and tyrannical caprice, but in the peaceful promotion of the welfare of his people: "But the advantage of a country consists always in a king given to the arable land." What impossibilities have been found here, even by the most recent expositors! Ewald, Heiligst., Elster, Zöckl. translate: *rex agro factus = terrae praefectus;* but, in the language of this book, not עבד but עשׂה מלך is the expression used for "to make a king." Gesen., Win., de Wette, Knobel, Vaih. translate: *rex qui colitur a terra (civibus).* But could a country, in the sense of its population in subjection to the king, be more inappropriately designated than by שָׂדֶה? Besides, עבד certainly gains the meaning of *colere* where God is the object; but with a human ruler as the object it means *servire* and nothing more, and נֶעֱבָד[1] can mean nothing else than "*dienstbar gemacht*" [made subject to], not "honoured." Along with this signification, related denom. to עָבַד, נעבד, referred from its primary signification to שָׂדֶה, the open fields (from שָׂדָה, to go out in length and breadth), may also, after the phrase עבד האדמה, signify cultivated, wrought, tilled; and while the phrase "made subject to" must be certainly held as possible (Rashi, Aben Ezra, and others assume it without hesitation), but is without example, the *Niph.* occurs, *e.g.* at Ezek. xxxvi. 9, in the latter signification, of the mountains of Israel: "ye shall be tilled." Under 8*a*, Hitzig, and with him Stuart and Zöckler, makes the misleading remark that the *Chethîb* is בְּכָל־הִיא, and that it is = בְּכָל־זֹאת, according to which the explanation is then given: the protection and security which an earthly ruler secures is, notwithstanding this, not to be disparaged. But היא is *Chethîb*, for which the *Kerî* substitutes הוא; בַּכֹּל is *Chethîb* without *Kerî*; and that בְּכֹל is thus a modification of the text, and that, too, an objectionable one, since בכל־היא, in the sense of "in all this," is unheard of. The *Kerî* seeks, without any necessity, to make the pred. and subj. like one another in gender; without necessity, for היא may also be neut.: the advantage of a land is this, viz. what follows. And how בַּכֹּל is to be understood is seen from Ezra x. 17, where it is to be explained: And they prepared [2] the sum of the men, *i.e.* the list of the men, of such as had married strange wives; cf. 1 Chron. vii. 5. Accordingly בכל here means, as the author generally uses הכל mostly in the impersonal sense of *omnia: in omnibus*, in all things = by all means; or: *in universum,*

---

[1] Thus pointed rightly in J., with *Sheva* quiesc. and *Dagesh* in *Beth*; vid. Kimchi in *Michlol* 63*a*, and under עבד.

[2] That כלה בְּ may mean "to be ready with anything," Keil erroneously points to Gen. xliv. 12; and Philippi, *St. Const.* p. 49, thinks that *văkol ănāshim* can be taken together in the sense of *vakol haanashim*.

in general. Were the words accentuated מֶלֶךְ לְשָׂדֶה נֶעֱבָד, the adject. connection of לְשׂ׳ נע׳ would thereby be shown; according to which the LXX. and Theod. translate τοῦ ἀγροῦ εἰργασμένου; Symm., with the Syr., τῇ χώρᾳ εἰργασμένῃ: "a king for the cultivated land," *i.e.* one who regards this as a chief object. Luzz. thus indeed accentuates; but the best established accentuation is מֶלֶךְ לְשָׂדֶה נֶעֱבָד. This separation of נֶעֱבָד from לְשׂ׳ can only be intended to denote that נֶעֱבָד is to be referred not to it, but to מֶלֶךְ, according to which the Targ. paraphrases. The meaning remains the same: a king subject (who has become a *servus*) to the cultivated land, *rex agro addictus*, as Dathe, Rosenm., and others translate, is a still more distinct expression of that which "a king for the well-cultivated field" would denote: an agriculture-king,—one who is addicted, not to wars, lawsuits, and sovereign stubbornness in his opinions, but who delights in the peaceful advancement of the prosperity of his country, and especially takes a lively interest in husbandry and the cultivation of the land. The order of the words in 8*b* is like that at ix. 2; cf. Isa. viii. 22, xxii. 2. The author thus praises, in contrast to a despotic state, a patriarchal kingdom based on agriculture.

THE UNCERTAINTY OF RICHES, AND THE CHEERFUL ENJOYMENT OF LIFE WHICH ALONE IS PRAISEWORTHY.—V. 9 [10]–VI. 6.

If we fix our attention on the word תְּבוּאָה, 9*a*, which properly denotes that which comes into the barn from without (*e.g.* Prov. xiv. 4), ver. 9 seems to continue the praise of husbandry, as Rashi, Aben Ezra, Luzzatto, Bardach, and others have already concluded. But the thought that one cannot eat money is certainly not that which is intended in 9*a*; and in 9*b* the thought would be awkwardly and insufficiently expressed, that it is vain to love riches, and not, on the contrary, the fruit of agriculture. Therefore we are decidedly of opinion that here (cf. above, p. 182), with ver. 9, the foregoing series of proverbs does not come to a close, but makes a new departure.

Ver. 9 [10]. "He who loveth silver is not satisfied with silver; and he whose love cleaveth to abundance, hath nothing of it: also this is vain." The transition in this series of proverbs is not unmediated; for the injustice which, according to ver. 7, prevails in the state as it now is becomes subservient to covetousness, in the very nature of which there lies insatiableness: *semper avarus eget, hunc nulla pecunia replet*. That the author speaks of the "*sacra fames argenti*" (not *auri*) arises from this, that not זָהָב, but כֶּסֶף, is the specific word for coin.[1] Mendelssohn-Friedländer also explains: "He who loveth silver is not satisfied with silver," *i.e.* it does not make him full; that might perhaps be linguistically possible (cf. *e.g.* Prov. xii. 11), although the author would in that case probably have written the words מִן־הַכֶּסֶף, after vi. 3; but "to be not full of money" is, after i. 8, and especially iv. 8, Hab. ii. 5, cf. Prov. xxvii. 20 = never to have enough of money, but always to desire more.

That which follows, 9 *a β*, is, according to Hitz., a question: And who hath joy in abundance, which bringeth nothing in? But such questions, with the answer to be supplied, are not in Koheleth's style; and what would then be understood by capital without interest? Others, as Zöckler, supply יִשְׂבַּע: and he that loveth abundance of possessions (is) not (full) of income; but that which is gained by these hard ellipses is only a tautology. With right, the Targ., Syr., Jerome, the Venet., and Luther take *lo t^evuah* as the answer or conclusion: and who clings to abundance of possessions with his love?—he has no fruit thereof; or, with a weakening of the interrog. pronoun into the relative (as at i. 9; cf. under Ps. xxxiv. 13): he who ... clings has nothing of it. *Hamon* signifies a tumult, a noisy multitude, particularly of earthly goods, as at Ps. xxxvii. 16; 1 Chron. xxix. 16; Isa. lx. 5. The connection of אהב with בְּ, occurring only here, follows the analogy of חָפֵץ בְּ and the like. The conclusion is synon. with *l^evilti ho'il*; *e.g.* Isa. xliv. 10; Jer. vii. 8. All the Codd. read לֹא; לוֹ in this sense would be meaningless.[2] The designation of advantage by *t^evuah* may be occasioned by the foregoing agricultural proverb. In the *t^evuah*, the farmer enjoys the fruit of his labour; but he who hangs his heart on the continual tumult, noise, pomp of more numerous and greater possessions if possible, to him all real profit—*i.e.* all pleasant, peaceful enjoyment—is lost. With the increase of the possessions there is an increase also of unrest, and the possessor has in reality nothing but the sight of them.

Ver. 10 [11]. "When property and goods increase, they become many who consume them; and what advantage hath the owner thereof but the sight of [them with] his eyes?" The verb רָבָה signifies to increase, and רָבַב, to be many; but also (which Böttch. denies) inchoatively: to become many, Gen. vi. 1; rightly, the LXX., ἐπληθύν-

---

[1] A Jewish fancy supposes that כסף is chosen because it consists of letters rising in value (20, 60, 80); while, on the contrary, זהב consists of letters decreasing in value (7, 5, 2).

[2] In *Maccoth* 10a, לו is read three times in succession; the Midrash *Wajikra*, c. 22, reads לֹא, and thus it is always found without *Kerî* and without variation.

θησαν. The author has not a miser in view, who shuts up his money in chests, and only feeds himself in looking at it with closed doors; but a covetous man, of the sort spoken of in Ps. xlix. 12, Isa. v. 8. If the *hattovah*, the possession of such an one, increases, in like manner the number of people whom he must maintain increases also, and thus the number of those who eat of it along with him, and at the same time also his disquiet and care, increase; and what advantage, what useful result (*vid.* regarding *Kishron*, above, p. 193, and under ii. 21) has the owner of these good things from them but the beholding of them (r^e*ith*; Kerî, r^e*uth*; cf. the reverse case, Ps. cxxvi. 4)?—the possession does not in itself bring happiness, for it is never great enough to satisfy him, but is yet great enough to fill him with great care as to whether he may be able to support the demands of so great a household: the fortune which it brings to him consists finally only in this, that he can look on all he has accumulated with proud self-complacency.

Ver. 11 [12]. He can also eat that which is good, and can eat much; but he does not on that account sleep more quietly than the labourer who lives from hand to mouth: "Sweet is the sleep of the labourer, whether he eats little or much; but, on the contrary, the abundance of the rich does not permit him to sleep." The LXX., instead of "labourer," uses the word "slave" (δούλου), as if the original were הָעֶבֶד. But, as a rule, sound sleep is the reward of earnest labour; and since there are idle servants as well as active masters, there is no privilege to servants. The Venet. renders rightly by "of the husbandman" (ἐργάτου), the עֹבֵד הָאֲדָמָה; the "labourer" in general is called עָמֵל, iv. 8 and Judg. v. 26, post-bibl. פֹּעֵל. The labourer enjoys sweet, *i.e.* refreshing, sound sleep, whether his fare be abundant or scanty—the labour rewards him by sweet sleep, notwithstanding his poverty; while, on the contrary, the sleep of the rich is hindered and disturbed by his abundance, not: by his satiety, viz. repletion, as Jerome remarks: *incocto cibo in stomachi angustiis aestuante;* for the labourer also, if he eats much, eats his fill; and why should sufficiency have a different result in the one from what it has in the other? As שָׂבֵעַ means satiety, not over-satiety; so, on the other hand, it means, objectively, sufficient and plentifully existing fulness to meet the wants of man, Prov. iii. 10, and the word is meant thus objectively here: the fulness of possession which the rich has at his disposal does not permit him to sleep, for all kinds of projects, cares, anxieties regarding it rise within him, which follow him into the night, and do not suffer his mind to be at rest, which is a condition of sleep. The expression הַשָּׂ' לֶעָ' is the *circum-*

locutio of the genit. relation, like לְב׳ ... חֵל׳, Ruth ii. 3 ; נַ֫ע׳ ... אִמ׳ (LXX. Ἀμνὼν τῆς Ἀχινόαμ), 2 Sam. iii. 2. Heiligstedt remarks that it stands for שֶׁבַע הֶעָשִׁיר ; but the nouns צָמָא, רָעֵב, שָׂבֵע form no *const.*, for which reason the *circumloc.* was necessary ; שָׂבֵע is the *constr.* of שָׂבֵעַ. Falsely, Ginsburg: "*aber der Ueberfluss den Reichen—er lässt ihn nicht schlafen*" [but superabundance the rich—it doth not suffer him to sleep]; but this construction is neither in accordance with the genius of the German nor of the Heb. language. Only the subject is resumed in אֵינֶנּוּ (as in i. 7); the construction of הִפִּ֫יחַ is as at 1 Chron. xvi. 21 ; cf. Ps. cv. 14. Of the two *Hiphil* forms, the properly Heb. הֵנִיחַ and the Aramaizing הִנִּיחַ, the latter is used in the weakened meaning of ἐᾶν, *sinere*.

After showing that riches bring to their possessor no real gain, but, instead of that, dispeace, care, and unrest, the author records as a great evil the loss, sometimes suddenly, of wealth carefully amassed.

Vers. 12, 13 [13, 14]. "There is a sore evil which I have seen under the sun, riches kept by their possessor to his hurt: the same riches perish by an evil event; and he hath begotten a son, thus this one hath nothing in his hand." There is a gradation of evils. רָעָה חוֹלָה (cf. חֳלִי רָע, vi. 2) is not an ordinary, but a morbid evil, *i.e.* a deep hurtful evil; as a wound, not a common one, but one particularly severe and scarcely curable, is called נַחְלָה, *e.g.* Nah. iii. 19. רָא֫ ... הֹשׁ׳ is, as at x. 5, an ellipt. relat. clause ; cf. on the other hand, vi. 1; the author elsewhere uses the scheme of the relat. clause without relat. pron. (*vid.* under i. 13, iii. 16); the old language would use רְאִיתִיהָ, instead of ראיתי, with the reflex. pron. The great evil consists in this, that riches are not seldom kept by their owner to his own hurt. Certainly שָׁמוּר לְ can also mean that which is kept for another, 1 Sam. ix. 24; but how involved and constrained is Ginsburg's explanation : " hoarded up (by the rich man) for their (future) owner," viz. the heir to whom he intends to leave them ! That לְ can be used with the passive as a designation of the subj., *vid.* Ewald, § 295*c* ; certainly it corresponds as little as מִן with the Greek ὑπό, but in Greek we say also πλοῦτος φυλαχθεὶς τῷ κεκτημένῳ, *vid.* Rost's *Syntax*, § 112. 4. The suff. of *l^era'atho* refers to *b^ealav*, the plur. form of which can so far remain out of view, that we even say *adonim qosheh*, Isa. xix. 4, etc. "To his hurt," *i.e.* at the last suddenly to lose that which has been carefully guarded. The narrative explanation of this, " to his hurt," begins with *vav explic.* Regarding *'inyan ra'*, *vid.* above, p. 194. It is a *casus adversus* that is meant, such a stroke upon stroke as destroyed Job's possessions. The perf. וְהוֹ׳ supposes the case that the man thus suddenly made poor is the father of a son; the clause is logically related to that which follows as hypothet. antecedent, after the scheme, Gen. xxxiii. 13b. The loss of riches would of itself make one who is alone unhappy, for the misfortune to be poor is less than the misfortunes to be rich and then to become poor; but still more unfortunate is the father who thought that by well-guarded wealth he had secured the future of his son, and who now leaves him with an empty hand.

What now follows is true of this rich man, but is generalized into a reference to every rich man, and then is recorded as a second great evil. As a man comes naked into the world, so also he departs from it again without being able to take with him any of the earthly wealth he has acquired.

Ver. 14 [15]. "As he came forth from his mother's womb, naked shall he again depart as he came, and not the least will he carry away for his labour, which he could take with him in his hand." In 13a the author has the case of Job in his mind; this verse before us is a reminiscence from Job i. 21, with the setting aside of the difficult word שָׁמָּה found there, which Sirach xl. 1 exhibits. With "naked" begins emphatically the main subject; כַּאֲשֶׁר בָּא = כְּשֶׁבָּא is the intensifying resumption of the comparison; the contrast of לָכֶת, going away, *excedere vitâ*, is בִּיא of the entrance on life, coming into the world. מְאוּמָה (according to the root meaning and use, corresponding to the French *point*, Olsh. § 205a) emphatically precedes the negation, as at Judg. xiv. 6 (cf. the emphasis reached in a different way, Ps. xlix. 18). נשׂא signifies here, as at ver. 18, Ps. xxiv. 5, to take hence, to take forth, to carry away. The בּ of בַּעֲמָלוֹ is not partitive (Aben Ezra compares Lev. viii. 32), according to which Jerome and Luther translate *de labore suo*, but is the *Beth pretii*, as *e.g.* at 1 Kings xvi. 34, as the Chald. understands it; Nolde cites for this *Beth pretii* passages such as ii. 24, but incorrectly. Regarding the subjunctive שֶׁיֹּלֵךְ, *quod auferat*, vid. above, No. 2, p. 197. We might also with the LXX. and Symm. punctuate שֶׁיֵּלֵךְ : which might accompany him in his hand, but which could by no means denote, as Hitzig thinks: (for his trouble), which goes through his hand. Such an expression is not used; and Hitzig's supposition, that here the rich man who has lost his wealth is the subject, does not approve itself.

Ver. 15 [16]. A transition is now made to rich men as such, and the registering formula which should go before ver. 14 here follows: "And this also is a sore evil: altogether exactly as he came, thus shall he depart: and what gain hath he that laboureth in the wind?"

Regarding חִי, *vid.* above, No. 4, p. 198; and regarding בְּלִ־עֵ֫י,[1] *vid.* p. 196. The writing of these first two as one word [*vid.* note below] accords with Ibn-Giat's view, accidentally quoted by Kimchi, that the word is compounded of כְּ of comparison, and the frequently occurring לְעֻמַּת always retaining its לְ, and ought properly to be pointed בְּלָעֵ֫ (cf. מִלְּ, 1 Kings vii. 20). עֻמָּה signifies combination, society, one thing along with or parallel to another; and thus לְעֻמַּת bears no כְּ, since it is itself a word of comparison, כָּל־עֻמָּת "altogether parallel," "altogether the same." The question: what kind of advantage (*vid.* i. 3) is to him (has he) of this that ..., carries its answer in itself. Labouring for the wind or in the wind, his labour is (רַעְיוֹן) רְעוּת רוּחַ, and thus fruitless. And, moreover, how miserable an existence is this life of labour leading to nothing!

Ver. 16 [17]. "Also all his life long he eateth in darkness and grieveth himself much, and oh for his sorrow and hatred!" We might place ver. 16 under the regimen of the שׁ of שֶׁעִיֵּו of ver. 15*b*; but the Heb. style prefers the self-dependent form of sentences to that which is governed. The expression 16*a* has something strange. This strangeness disappears if, with Ewald and Heiligst., after the LXX. and Jerome, for יֹאכֵל we read וְאֵבֶל: καὶ ἐν πένθει; Böttch. prefers וָאֹפֶל, "and in darkness." Or also, if we read יֵלֵךְ for יֹאכֵל; thus the Midrash here, and several codd. by Kennicott; but the Targ., Syr., and Masora read יֹאכֵל. Hitzig gets rid of that which is strange in this passage by taking כָּל־יָמָיו as accus. of the obj., not of the time: all his days, his whole life he consumes in darkness; but in Heb. as in Lat. we say: *consumere dies vitae*, Job xxi. 13, xxxvi. 11, but not *comedere*; and why should the expression, "to eat in darkness," not be a figurative expression for a faithless, gloomy life, as elsewhere "to sit in darkness" (Mic. vii. 8), and "to walk in darkness"? It is meant that all his life long he ate לֶחֶם אוֹנִים, the bread of sorrow, or לֶחֶם לַחַץ, prison fare; he did not allow himself pleasant table comforts in a room comfortably or splendidly lighted, for it is unnecessary to understand חֹשֶׁךְ subjectively and figuratively (Hitz., Zöck.).

In 16*b* the traditional punctuation is וְכָעַס.[2] The *perf.* ruled by the preceding *fut.* is syntactically correct, and the verb כָּעַס is common with

---

[1] In H. written as one word: בְּלָעֻמַּת. Parchon (*Lex.* under עמת) had this form before him. In his *Lex.* Kimchi bears evidence in favour of the correct writing as two words.

[2] Thus in correct texts, in H. with the note: ב׳ מלרע, viz. here and at Ps. cxii. 10, only there ע has, according to tradition, the *Kametz*. Cf. *Mas. fin.* 52*b*, and Baer's Ed. of Psalter, under Ps. cxii. 10.

the author, vii. 9. Hitzig regards the text as corrupt, and reads בְּחָלְיוֹ and כָּעַס, and explains: and (he consumes or swallows) much grief in his, etc.; the phrase, "to eat sorrow," may be allowed (cf. Prov. xxvi. 6, cf. Job xv. 16); but יאכל, as the representative of two so bold and essentially different metaphors, would be in point of style in bad taste. If the text is corrupt, it may be more easily rectified by reading וְכַעַס הַרְבֵּה וָחֳלִי לוֹ וק׳: and grief in abundance, and sorrow has he, and wrath. We merely suggest this. Ewald, Burger, and Böttch. read only וכעס הרבה וחלי; but לו is not to be dispensed with, and can easily be reduced to a mere vav. Elster retains וכעס, and reads, like Hitzig, בחליו: he grieves himself much in his sorrow and wrath; but in that case the word וקצפו was to be expected; also in this way the ideas do not psychologically accord with each other. However the text is taken, we must interpret וחליו וקצף as an exclamation, like 'חָף, Isa. xxix. 16; 'תֹּף, Jer. xlix. 16; Ewald, § 328a, as we have done above. That 'וְחָ of itself is a subst. clause = וחלי לו is untenable; the rendering of the noun as forming a clause, spoken of under ii. 21, is of a different character.[1] He who by his labour and care aims at becoming rich, will not only lay upon himself unnecessary privations, but also have many sorrows; for many of his plans fail, and the greater success of others awakens his envy, and neither he himself nor others satisfy him; he is morbidly disposed, and as he is diseased in mind, so also in body, and his constantly increasing dissatisfaction becomes at last קצף, he grumbles at himself, at God, and all the world. From observing such persons, Paul says of them (1 Tim. vi. 6 f.): "They have pierced themselves through (transfoderunt) with many sorrows."

In view of these great evils, with which the possession of riches also is connected: of their deceitful instability, and their merely belonging to this present life, Koheleth returns to his *ceterum censeo*.

Ver. 17 [18]. "Behold then what I have seen as good, what as beautiful (is this): that one eat and drink and see good in all his labour with which he wearieth himself, under the sun, throughout the number of the days of his life which God hath given him; for that is his portion." Toward this seeing, *i.e.* knowing from his own experience, his effort went forth, according to ii. 3; and what he here, vers. 17, 18, expresses as his *resultat*, he has already acknowledged at ii. 24 and iii. 12 f. With "behold" he here returns to it; for he says, that from the observations just spoken of, as from others, no

---

[1] Rashi regards וחליו as a form like חִיָּתוֹ. This o everywhere appears only in a gen. connection.

other *resultat* befell him. Instead of ר' טוֹבָה (here and at vi. 6), he as often uses the words ראה טוב, iii. 13, ii. 24, or בְּטוֹב, ii. 1. In 'רָא, the seeing is meant of that of mental apperception; in 'לרא, of immediate perception, experience. Our translation above does not correspond with the accentuation of the verse, which belongs to the class of disproportionably long verses without *Athnach;* cf. Gen. xxi. 9; Num. ix. 1; Isa. xxxvi. 1; Jer. xiii. 13, li. 37; Ezek. xlii. 10; Amos v. 1; 1 Chron. xxvi. 26, xxviii. 1; 2 Chron. xxiii. 1. The sentence הנה ... אָנִי (with pausal *āni* with *Rebia*) constitutes the beginning of the verse, in the form, as it were, of a superscription; and then its second part, the main proposition, is divided by the disjunctives following each other: *Telisha Gedhola, Geresh, Legarmeh, Rebia, Tebir, Tifcha, Silluk* (cf. Jer. viii. 1, where *Pazer* instead of *Telisha Gedhola;* but as for the rest, the sequence of the accents is the same). Among the moderns, Hengst. holds to the accents, for he translates in strict accordance therewith, as Tremellius does: "Behold what I have seen: that it is fine and good (Trem. *bonum pulchrum*) to eat ..." The *asher* in the phrase, *tov asher-yapheh*, then connects it together: good which is at the same time beautiful; Grätz sees here the Greek καλὸν κἀγαθόν. But the only passage to which, since Kimchi, reference is made for this use of *asher,* viz. Hos. xii. 8, does not prove it; for we are not, with Drusius, to translate there by: *iniquitas quae sit peccatum*, but by *quae poenam mereat.* The accentuation here is not correct. The second *asher* is without doubt the resumption of the first; and the translation—as already Dachselt in his *Biblia Accentuata* indicated: *ecce itaque quod vidi bonum, quod pulchrum (hoc est ut quis edat)*—presents the true relation of the component parts of the sentence. The suffix of עֲמָלוֹ refers to the general subj. contained in the inf.; cf. viii. 15. The period of time denoted by מִסְפַּר is as at ii. 3, vi. 12. Also we read חֶל־ ... כִּי־, iii. 22, in the same connection.

Ver. 18 [19]. This verse, expressing the same, is constructed anakolouthistically, altogether like iii. 13: "Also for every man to whom God hath given riches and treasures, and hath given him power to eat thereof, and to take his portion, and to rejoice in his labour; just this is a gift of God." The anakolouthon can be rendered [into English] here as little as it can at iii. 13; for if we allow the phrase, "also every man," the "also" remains fixed to the nearest conception, while in the Heb. it governs the whole long sentence, and, at the nearest, belongs to זֹה. Cheerful enjoyment is in this life that which is most advisable; but also it is not made possible in itself by the possession of earthly treasures,—it is yet a special gift of God added thereto. *Nᵉchasim*, besides here, occurs also in Josh. xxii. 8 ; 2 Chron. i. 11 f. ; and in the Chald. of the Book of Ezra, vi. 8, vii. 26. Also *hishlit*, to empower, to make possible, is Aram., Dan. ii. 38, 48, as well as Heb., Ps. cxix. 133 ; the prevalence of the verbal stem שלט is characteristic of the Book of Koheleth. *Helqo*, " his portion," is just the cheerful enjoyment as that which man has here below of life, if he has any of it at all.

Ver. 19 [20]. Over this enjoyment he forgets the frailty and the darkened side of this life. It proves itself to be a gift of God, a gift from above : " For he doth not (then) think much of the days of his life ; because God answereth the joy of his heart." Such an one, permitted by God to enjoy this happiness of life, is thereby prevented from tormenting himself by reflections regarding its transitoriness. Incorrectly, Hengst.: Remembrance and enjoyment of this life do not indeed last long, according to Ewald, who now, however, rightly explains : He will not, by constant reflection on the brevity of his life, too much embitter this enjoyment ; because God, indeed, grants to him true heart-joy as the fairest gift. The meaning of 19*b* is also, in general, hit upon. The LXX. translates : " because God occupies him with the joy of his heart ; " but for that we ought to have had the word מַעֲנֵהוּ ; Jerome helps it, for he reads בשמחה instead of בשמחת : *eo quod Deus occupet deliciis cor ejus*. But also, in this form, this explanation of מענה is untenable ; for עָנָה בְּ, the causat. of which would be מענה, signifies, in the style of Koheleth, not in general to busy oneself with something, but to weary oneself with something ; hence ענה בש׳ cannot mean : to be occupied with joy, and thereby to be drawn away from some other thing. And since the explanation : " he makes him sing," needs no argument to dispose of it, מענה thus remains only as the *Hiph.* of ענה, to meet, to respond to, grant a request. Accordingly, Hitz., like Aben Ezra and Kimchi, comparing Hos. ii. 23 f. : God makes to answer, *i.e.* so works that all things which have in or of themselves that which can make him glad, must respond to his wish. But the omission of the obj.—of which Hitz. remarks, that because indefinite it is left indefinite—is insufferably hard, and the explanation thus ambiguous. Most interpreters translate : for God answers (Gesen. *Heb. Wört. B.*, incorrectly: answered) him with joy of his heart, *i.e.* grants this to him in the way of answer. Ewald compares Ps. lxv. 6 ; but that affords no voucher for the expression : to answer one with something = to grant it to him ; for ענה is there connected with a double accus., and בְּצֶדֶק is the adv. statement of the way and manner. But above all, against this interpretation is the fact of the want of the personal obj.

The author behoved to have written מַעֲנֵהוּ or מַעֲנֵה אֹתוֹ. We take the *Hiph.* as in the sense of the *Kal*, but give it its nearest signification: to answer, and explain, as in a similar manner Seb. Schmid, Rambam, and others have already done: God answers to the joy of his heart, *i.e.* He assents to it, or (using an expression which is an exact equivalent), He corresponds to it. This makes the joy a heart-joy, *i.e.* a joy which a man feels not merely externally, but in the deepest recess of his heart, for the joy penetrates his heart and satisfies it (Song iii. 11; Isa. xxx. 29; Jer. xv. 16). A similar expression, elsewhere not found, we had at ver. 9 in אהב בְּ. Why should not עָנָה בְּ (הַעֲנָה) be possible with עָנָהוּ, just as ἀμείβεσθαι πρός τι is with ἀμείβεσθαί τινα? For the rest, 'בש 'לב is not needed as obj.; we can take it also as an expression of the state or condition: God gives answer in the heart-joy of such an one. In ענה, to answer, to hear the answer, is thought of as granting a request; here, as giving assent to. Job xxxv. 9 affords a twofold suitable example, that the *Hiph.* can have an enlarged *Kal* signification.

After the author has taken the opportunity of once more expressing his *ultimatum*, he continues to register the sad evils that cling to wealth.

vi. 1, 2. "There is an evil which I have seen under the sun, and in great weight it lies upon man: a man to whom God giveth riches, and treasures, and honour, and he wanteth nothing for his soul of all that he may wish, but God giveth him not power to have enjoyment of it, for a strange man hath the enjoyment: that is vanity and an evil disease." The author presents the result of personal observation; but inasmuch as he relates it in the second tense, he generalizes the matter, and places it scenically before the eyes of the reader. A similar introduction with יֵשׁ, but without the unnecessary *asher*, is found at v. 12, x. 5. Regarding רַבָּה, *vid.* under viii. 6; עַל does not denote the subj., as at ii. 17: it appears great to a man, but it has its nearest lying local meaning; it is a great (ii. 21) evil, pressing in its greatness heavily upon man. The evil is not the man himself, but the condition in which he is placed, as when, *e.g.*, the kingdom of heaven is compared to a merchant (Matt. xiii. 45 f.),—not the merchant in himself, but his conduct and life is a figure of the kingdom of heaven.

Ver. 2. To עֹשֶׁר וּנְכָסִים, as at 2 Chron i. 11, וְכָ׳ [and honour] is added as a third thing. What follows we do not translate: "and there is nothing wanting . . .;" for that אֵינֶנּוּ with the pleonastic suff. may mean: "there is not," is not to be proved from Gen. xxxix. 9, thus: and he spares not for his soul (LXX. καὶ οὐκ κ.τ.λ.) what he always desires. חָסֵר is adj. in the sense of wanting, lacking, as at 1 Sam. xxi. 16; 1 Kings xi. 22; Prov. xii. 9. לְנַפְשׁוֹ, "for his soul," *i.e.* his person, is = the synon. לְעַצְמוֹ found in the later usage of the language; מִן (different from the *min*, iv. 8) is, as at Gen. vi. 2, partitive. The נָכְרִי, to whom this considerable estate, satisfying every wish, finally comes, is certainly not the legal heir (for that he enters into possession, in spite of the uncertainty of his moral character, ii. 19, would be in itself nothing less than a misfortune, yet perfectly in order, v. 13 [14]), but some stranger without any just claim, not directly a foreigner (Heiligst.), but, as Burger explains: *talis qui proprie nullum habet jus in bona ejus cui* נכרי *dicitur* (cf. נָכְרִיָּה of the unmarried wife in the Book of Proverbs).

That wealth without enjoyment is nothing but vanity and an evil disease, the author now shows by introducing another historical figure, and thereby showing that life without enjoyment is worse than never to have come into existence at all:

Ver. 3. "If a man begat an hundred, and lived many years, and the amount of the days of his years was great, and his soul satisfied not itself in good, and also he had no grave, then I say: Better than he is the untimely birth." The accentuation of 3*a* is like that of 2*a*. The disjunctives follow the *Athnach*, as at 2 Kings xxiii. 13, only that there *Telisha Gedhola* stands for *Pazer*. Hitzig finds difficulty with the clause וְגַם־ . . . לֹ, and regards it as a marginal gloss to 5*a*, taken up into the text at a wrong place. But just the unexpected form and the accidental nature, more than the inward necessity of this feature in the figure, leads us to conclude that the author here connects together historical facts, as conjecturally noted above at pp. 214, 215, into one fanciful picture. מֵאָה is obviously to be supplemented by (וּבָנוֹת) בָּנִים; the Targ. and Midrash make this man to be Cain, Ahab, Haman, and show at least in this that they extend down into the time of the Persian kingdom a spark of historical intelligence. שְׁנֵי רַב' interchanges with שְׁנֵי הַר', xi. 8, as at Neh. xi. 30. In order to designate the long life emphatically, the author expresses the years particularly in days: "and if it is much which (Heiligst.: *multum est quod*) the days of his years amount to;" cf. וַיִּהְיוּ יְמֵי in Gen. v. With *v*ᵉ*naphsho* there follows the reverse side of this long life with many children: (1) his soul satisfies not itself, *i.e.* has no self-satisfying enjoyment of the good (*min*, as at Ps. civ. 13, etc.), *i.e.* of all the good things which he possesses,—in a word, he is not happy in his life; and (2) an honourable burial is not granted to him, but קְב' חֲמ', Jer. xxii. 19, which is the contrary of a burial such as becomes a man (the body of Artaxerxes Ochus

ECCLES. U

was thrown to the cats); whereupon Elster rightly remarks that in an honourable burial and an honourable remembrance, good fortune, albeit shaded with sadness, might be seen. But when now, to one so rich in children and so long-lived, neither enjoyment of his good fortune nor even this shaded glory of an honourable burial is allowed, the author cannot otherwise judge than that the untimely birth is better than he. In this section regarding the uncertainty of riches, we have already, v. 14, fallen on a reminiscence from the Book of Job; it is so much the more probable that here also Job iii. 16 has an influence on the formation of the thought. נֵפֶל is the foetus which comes lifeless from the mother's womb.

Vers. 4, 5. The comparison of an untimely birth with such a man is in favour of the former: "For it cometh in nothingness and departeth in darkness; and with darkness its name is covered. Moreover, it hath not seen the sun, and hath not known: it is better with it than with that other." It has entered into existence, בַּהֶבֶל, because it was a lifeless existence into which it entered when its independent life should have begun; and בַּחֹשֶׁךְ, it departeth, for it is carried away in all quietness, without noise or ceremony, and "with darkness" its name is covered, for it receives no name and remains a nameless existence, and is forgotten as if it had never been. Not having entered into a living existence, it is also (*gam*) thus happy to have neither seen the sun nor known and named it, and thus it is spared the sight and the knowledge of all the vanities and evils, the deceptions and sorrows, that are under the sun. When we compare its fate with the long joyless life of that man, the conclusion is apparent: מִ׳ ... נַחַת, *plus quietis est huic quam illi*, which, with the generalization of the idea of rest (Job iii. 13) in a wider sense (*vid.* above, p. 194), is = *melius est huic quam illi* (זֶה ... זֶה, as at iii. 19). The generalization of the idea proceeds yet further in the Mishn. נוח ל׳, *e.g.*: "It is better (נוח לו לאדם) for a man that he throw himself into a lime-kiln than that (ואל), etc." From this usage Symm. renders מִ׳ ... נַחַת as obj. to לֹא ידע, and translates: οὐδὲ ἐπειράθη διαφορᾶς ἑτέρου πράγματος πρὸς ἕτερον; and Jerome: *neque cognovit distantiam boni et mali*,—a rendering which is to be rejected, because thus the point of the comparison in which it terminates is broken, for 5*b* draws the *facit*. It is true that this contains a thought to which it is not easy to reconcile oneself. For supposing that life were not in itself, as over against non-existence, a good, there is yet scarcely any life that is absolutely joyless; and a man who has become the father of an hundred children, has, as it appears, sought the enjoyment of life principally in sexual love, and then also has found it richly. But also, if we consider his life less as relating to sense : his children, though not all, yet partly, will have been a joy to him ; and has a family life, so lengthened and rich in blessings, only thorns, and no roses at all ? And, moreover, how can anything be said of the rest of an untimely birth, which has been without motion and without life, as of a rest excelling the termination of the life of him who has lived long, since rest without a subjective reflection, a rest not felt, certainly does not fall under the point of view of more or less, good or evil ? The saying of the author on no side bears the probe of exact thinking. In the main he designs to say : Better, certainly, is no life than a joyless life, and, moreover, one ending dishonourably. And this is only a speciality of the general clause, iv. 2 f., that death is better than life, and not being born is better than both. The author misunderstands the fact that the earthly life has its chief end beyond itself; and his false eudaemonism, failing to penetrate to the inward fountain of true happiness, which is independent of the outward lot, makes exaggerated and ungrateful demands on the earthly life.

Ver. 6. A life extending to more than even a thousand years without enjoyment appears to him worthless: "And if he has lived twice a thousand years long, and not seen good—Do not all go hence to one place ?" This long period of life, as well as the shortest, sinks into the night of Sheol, and has advantage over the shortest if it wants the 'ראות ט, i.e. the enjoyment of that which can make man happy. That would be correct if "good" were understood inwardly, ethically, spiritually; but although, according to Koheleth's view, the fear of God presides over the enjoyment of life, regulating and hallowing it, yet it remains unknown to him that life deepened into fellowship with God is in itself a most real and blessed, and thus the highest good. Regarding אִלּוּ (here, as at Esth. vii. 4, with perf. foll.: *etsi vixisset, tamen interrogarem: nonne*, etc.), vid. above, p. 191 ; it occurs also in the oldest liturgical *Tefilla*, as well as in the prayer *Nishmath* (vid. Baer's Siddur, *Abodath Jisrael*, p. 207). 'פ ... אֶלֶף, a thousand years twice, and thus an Adam's life once and yet again. Otherwise Aben Ezra : 1000 years multiplied by itself, thus a million, like עֶשְׂרִים פְּעָמִים, $20 \times 20 = 400$; cf. Targ. Isa. xxx. 26, which translates שִׁבְעָתַיִם by $343 = 7 \times 7 \times 7$. Perhaps that is right ; for why was not the expression אַלְפַּיִם שָׁנָה directly used ? The "one place" is, as at iii. 20, the grave and Hades, into which all the living fall. A life extending even to a million of years is worthless, for it terminates at last in nothing. Life has only as much value as it yields of enjoyment.

OBTAINING BETTER THAN DESIRING.—VI. 7-9.

All labour aims at enjoyment, and present actual enjoyment is always better than that which is sought for in the future.

Ver. 7. "All the labour of man is for his mouth, and yet his soul has never enough;" or, properly, it is not filled, so that it desires nothing further and nothing more; נִמְלָא used as appropriately of the soul as of the ear, i. 8; for that the mouth and the soul are here placed opposite to one another as "organs of the purely sensual and therefore transitory enjoyment, and of the deeper and more spiritual and therefore more lasting kind of joys" (Zöck.), is an assertion which brings out of the text what it wishes to be in it,—נֶפֶשׁ and פֶּה stand here so little in contrast, that, as at Prov. xvi. 26, Isa. v. 14, xxix. 8, instead of the soul the stomach could also be named; for it is the soul longing, and that after the means from without of self-preservation, that is here meant; נפש יפה, "beautiful soul," *Chullin* iv. 7, is an appetite which is not fastidious, but is contented. וְגַם, καὶ ὅμως, ὅμως δέ, as at iii. 13; Ps. cxxix. 2. All labour, the author means to say, is in the service of the impulse after self-preservation; and yet, although it concentrates all its efforts after this end, it does not bring full satisfaction to the longing soul. This is grounded in the fact that, however in other respects most unlike, men are the same in their unsatisfied longing.

Ver. 8. "For what hath the wise more than the fool; what the poor who knoweth to walk before the living?" The old translators present nothing for the interpretation, but defend the traditional text; for Jerome, like the Syr., which translates freely, follows the Midrash (fixed in the Targ.), which understands החיים, contrary to the spirit of the book, of the blessed future. The question would be easier if we could, with Bernst. and Ginsburg, introduce a comparat. *min* before יוֹדֵעַ; we would then require to understand by him who knows to walk before the living, some one who acts a part in public life; but how strange a designation of distinguished persons would that be! Thus, as the text stands, יודע is attrib. to לֶעָנִי, what preference hath the poor, such an one, viz., as understands (*vid.* regarding יודע instead of היודע, under Ps. cxliii. 10); not: who is intelligent (Aben Ezra); יודע is not, as at ix. 11, an idea contained in itself, but by the foll. 'לְהַ ... חַי (cf. iv. 13, 17; and the inf. form, Ex. iii. 19; Num. xxii. 13; Job xxxiv. 23) obtains the supplement and colouring required: the sequence of the accents (*Zakeph, Tifcha, Silluk,* as *e.g.* at Gen. vii. 4) is not against this. How the LXX. understood its πορευθῆναι κατέναντι τῆς ζωῆς, and the Venet. its ἀπιέναι ἀντικρὺ τῆς ζωῆς, is not clear; scarcely as Grätz, with Mendelss.: who, to go against (נגד, as at iv. 12) life, to fight against it, has to exercise himself in self-denial and patience; for "to fight with life" is an expression of modern coinage. הַֽחַיִּ֫ signifies here, without doubt, not life, but the living. But we explain now, not as Ewald, who separates יודע from the foll. inf. להלך: What profit has then the wise man, the intelligent, patient man, above the fool, that he walks before the living?—by which is meant (but how does this interrog. form agree thereto?), that the wise, patient man has thereby an advantage which makes life endurable by him, in this, that he does not suffer destroying eagerness of desire so to rule over him, but is satisfied to live in quietness. Also this meaning of a quiet life does not lie in the words 'הלך ... הח'. "To know to walk before the living" is, as is now generally acknowledged = to understand the right rule of life (Elst.), to possess the *savoir vivre* (Heiligst.), to be experienced in the right art of living. The question accordingly is: What advantage has the wise above the fool; and what the poor, who, although poor, yet knows how to maintain his social position? The matter treated of is the insatiable nature of sensual desire. The wise seeks to control his desire; and he who is more closely designated poor, knows how to conceal it; for he lays upon himself restraints, that he may be able to appear and make something of himself. But desire is present in both; and they have in this nothing above the fool, who follows the bent of his desire and lives for the day. He is a fool because he acts as one not free, and without consideration; but, in itself, it is and remains true, that enjoyment and satisfaction stand higher than striving and longing for a thing.

Ver. 9. "Better is the sight of the eyes than the wandering of the soul: also this is vain and windy effort." We see from the inf. הֲלָךְ־נָ֫ interchanging with מֵרְ֫ that the latter is not meant of the object (xi. 9), but of the action, viz. the "rejoicing in that which one has" (Targ.); but this does not signify *grassatio*,—i.e. *impetus animae appetentis*, ὁρμὴ τῆς ψυχῆς (cf. Marcus Aurelius, iii. 16), which Knobel, Heiligst., and Ginsburg compare (for הלך means *grassari* only with certain subjects, as fire, contagion, and the like; and in certain forms, as יְהַלֵּךְ for יֵלֵךְ, to which הֲלָךְ = לֶ֫כֶת does not belong),—but *erratio*, a going out in extent, roving to a distance (cf. הֵלֶךְ, wanderer), ῥεμβασμὸς ἐπιθυμίας, Wisd. iv. 12.—Going is the contrast of rest; the soul which does not become full or satisfied goes out, and seeks and reaches not its aim. This insatiableness, characteristic of the soul, this endless unrest, belongs also to the miseries of this present life; for to have and to enjoy is better than this constant

Hungern und Lungern [hungering and longing]. More must not be put into 9*a* than already lies in it, as Elster does: "the only enduring enjoyment of life consists in the quiet contemplation of that which, as pleasant and beautiful, it affords, without this mental joy mingling with the desire for the possession of sensual enjoyment." The conception of "the sight of the eyes" is certainly very beautifully idealized, but in opposition to the text. If 9*a* must be a moral proverb, then Luther's rendering is the best: "It is better to enjoy the present good, than to think about other good."

THE WEAKNESS AND SHORT-SIGHTEDNESS OF MAN OVER AGAINST HIS DESTINY.—VI. 10–12.

The future, toward which the soul stretches itself out to find what may satisfy it, is not man's: a power against which man is helpless fashions it.

Ver. 10. "That which hath been, its name hath long ago been named; and it is determined what a man shall be: and he cannot dispute with Him who is stronger than he." According to the usage of the tense, it would be more correct to translate: That which (at any time) has made its appearance, the name of which was long ago named, *i.e.* of which the *What?* and the *How?* were long ago determined, and, so to speak, formulated. This שֶׁ ... כְּבָר does not stand parallel to כבר היה, i. 10; for the expression here does not refer to the sphere of that which is done, but of the predetermination. Accordingly, וְנוֹ׳ ... אָדָם is also to be understood. Against the accents, inconsistently periodizing and losing sight of the comprehensiveness of אדם ... אשׁר, Hitzig renders: "and it is known that, if one is a man, he cannot contend," etc., which is impossible for this reason, that הוא אדם cannot be a conditional clause enclosed within the sentence יוּכל ... אשׁר. Obviously וְנוֹדָע, which in the sense of *constat* would be a useless waste of words, stands parallel to נקרא שׁמו, and signifies known, viz. previously known, as passive of ידע, in the sense of Zech. xiv. 7; cf. Ps. cxxxix. 1 f. Bullock rightly compares Acts xv. 18. After ידע, *asher*, like *ki*, which is more common, may signify "that," viii. 12, Ezek. xx. 26; but neither "that he is a man" (Knobel, Vaih., Luzz., Hengst., Ginsb.), nor "that he is the man" (Ewald, Elst., Zöckler), affords a consistent meaning. As *mah* after *yada'* means *quid*, so *asher* after it may mean *quod* = that which (cf. Dan. viii. 19, although it does not at all stand in need of proof); and *id quod homo est* (we cannot render הוא without the expression of a definite conception of time) is intended to mean that the whole being of a man, whether of this one or that one, at all times and on all sides, is previously known; cf. to this pregnant substantival sentence, xii. 13. Against this formation of his nature and of his fate by a higher hand, man cannot utter a word.

The thought in 10b is the same as that at Isa. xlv. 9; Rom. ix. 20 f. The *Chethîb* שֶׁהִתַּקִּיף [1] is not inadmissible, for the stronger than man is מִמֶּנּוּ ... מָרִי. Also הִתְקִיף might in any case be read: with one who overcomes him, has and manifests the ascendency over him. There is indeed no *Hiph*. 'הִתְ found in the language of the Bible (Herzf. and Fürst compare הִגְ, Ps. xii. 5); but in the Targ., אִתְקֵף is common; and in the school-language of the Talm., 'הִתְ is used of the raising of weighty objections, *e.g. Kamma* 71a. The verb, however, especially in the perf., is in the passage before us less appropriate. In לֹא־יוּכַל lie together the ideas of physical (cf. Gen. xliii. 32; Deut. xii. 17, xvi. 5, etc.) and moral inability.

Ver. 11. "For there are many words which increase vanity: What cometh forth therefrom for man?" The dispute (objection), רִיב, takes place in words; דְּבָרִים here will thus not mean "things" (Hengst., Ginsb., Zöckl., Bullock, etc.), but "words." As that wrestling or contending against God's decision and providence is vain and worthless, nothing else remains for man but to be submissive, and to acknowledge his limitation by the fear of God; thus there are also many words which only increase yet more the multitude of vanities already existing in this world, for, because they are resultless, they bring no advantage for man. Rightly, Elster finds herein a hint pointing to the influence of the learning of the Jewish schools already existing in Koheleth's time. We know from Josephus that the problem of human freedom and of God's absoluteness was a point of controversy between opposing parties: the Sadducees so emphasized human freedom, that they not only excluded (*Antt.* xiii. 5. 9; *Bell.* ii. 8. 14) all divine predetermination, but also co-operation; the Pharisees, on the contrary, supposed an interconnection between divine predetermination (εἱμαρμένη) and human freedom (*Antt.* xiii. 5. 9, xviii. 1. 3; *Bell.* ii. 8. 14). The Talm. affords us a glance at this controversy; but the statement in the Talm. (in *Berachôth* 33a, and elsewhere), which conditions all by the power of God manifesting itself in history, but defends the freedom of the religious-moral self-determination of man, may be regarded as a Pharisaic maxim. In Rom. ix., Paul places himself on

---

[1] With *He* unpointed, because it is omitted in the *Kerî*, as in like manner in 'כְּשֶׁה, x. 3, 'שֶׁה, Lam. v. 18. In the bibl. Rabb., the ה is noted as superfluous.

this side; and the author of the Book of Koheleth would subscribe this passage as his testimony, for the "fear God" is the "*kern und stern*" [kernel and star] of his pessimistic book.

Ver. 12. Man ought to fear God, and also, without dispute and murmuring, submit to His sway: "For who knoweth what is good for man in life during the number of the days of his vain life, and which he spendeth like a shadow? No one can certainly show a man what shall be after him under the sun." We translate אֲשֶׁר only by "*ja*" ("certainly"), because in Germ. no interrogative can follow "*dieweil*" ("because"). The clause with *asher* (as at iv. 9, viii. 11, x. 15; cf. Song, under v. 2), according to its meaning not different from *ki*, is related in the way of proof to that beginning with *ki*. Man is placed in our presence. To be able to say to him what is good for him,—*i.e.* what position he must take in life, what direction he must give to his activity, what decision he must adopt in difficult and important cases,—we ought not only to be able to penetrate his future, but, generally, the future; but, as *Tropfen* [drops] in the stream of history, we are poor *Tröpfe* [simpletons], who are hedged up within the present. Regarding the accus. of duration, מִסְפַּר וְגו׳, pointing to the brevity of human life, *vid.* at ii. 3. With הֶבְלוֹ, the attribute of breath-like transitiveness is assigned to life (as at vii. 15, ix. 9) (as already in the name given to Abel, the second son of Adam), which is continued by וְיַעֲשֵׂ בְּ with the force of a relative clause, which is frequently the case after preceding part. attrib., *e.g.* Isa. v. 23. We translate: which he spendeth like the (a) shadow [in the nom.] (after viii. 13; Job xiv. 2); not: like a shadow [in the accus.]; for although the days of life are also likened to a shadow, Ps. cxliv. 4, etc., yet this use of עָשָׂה does not accord therewith, which, without being a Graecism (Zirkel, Grätz), harmonises with the Greek phrase, ποιεῖν χρόνον, Acts xv. 33; cf. Prov. xiii. 23, LXX. (also with the Lat. *facere dies* of Cicero, etc.). Thus also in the Syr. and Palest.-Aram. *lacad* is used of time, in the sense of *transigere*. *Aharav* does not mean: after his present condition (Zöckl.); but, as at iii. 22, vii. 14: after he has passed away from this scene. Luzz. explains it correctly: Whether his children will remain in life? Whether the wealth he has wearied himself in acquiring will remain and be useful to them? But these are only illustrations. The author means to say, that a man can say, neither to himself nor to another, what in definite cases is the real advantage; because, in order to say this, he must be able to look far into the future beyond the limits of the individual life of man, which is only a small member of a great whole.

SECOND CONCLUDING SECTION.

PROVERBS OF BETTER THINGS, THINGS SUPPOSED TO BE BETTER, GOOD THINGS, GOOD AND BAD DAYS.—VII. 1–14.

We find ourselves here in the middle of the book. Of its 220 verses, vi. 10 is that which stands in the middle, and with vii. 1 begins the third of the four *Sedarim*[1] into which the Masora divides the book. The series of proverbs here first following, vii. 1–10, has, as we remarked above, p. 189, the word *tov* as their common catchword, and *mah-tov*, vi. 12, as the hook on which they hang. But at least the first three proverbs do not stand merely in this external connection with the preceding; they continue the lowly and dark estimate of the earthly life contained in vi. 3 ff.

The first proverb is a synthetic distich. The thought aimed at is that of the second half of the distich.

vii. 1. " Better is a name than precious ointment; and better is the day of death than the day when one is born." Like רָאָה and יָרֵא, so שֵׁם and שֶׁמֶן stand to each other in the relation of a paronomasia (*vid.* Song under i. 3). Luther translates: " *Ein gut Gerücht ist besser denn gute Salbe* " [" a good odour (= reputation) is better than good ointment]. If we substitute the expression *denn Wolgeruch* [than sweet scent], that would be the best possible rendering of the paronomasia. In the arrangement שֵׁם טוֹב ... טוֹב, *tov* would be adj. to *shem* (a good reputation goes beyond sweet scent); but *tov* standing first in the sentence is pred., and *shem* thus in itself alone, as in the cogn. prov., Prov. xxii. 1, signifies a good, well-sounding, honourable, if not venerable name; cf. *anshē hashshem*, Gen. vi. 4; *v^eli-shem*, nameless, Job xxx. 8. The author gives the dark reverse to this bright side of the distich: the day of death better than the day in which one (a man), or he (the man), is born; cf. for this reference of the pronoun, iv. 12, v. 17. It is the same lamentation as at iv. 2 f., which sounds less strange from the mouth of a Greek than from that of an Israelite; a Thracian tribe, the Trausi, actually celebrated their birthdays as days of sadness, and the day of death as a day of rejoicing (*vid.* Bähr's Germ. translat. of *Herodotus*, v. 4).—Among the people of the Old Covenant this was not possible; also a saying such as 1*b* is not in the spirit of the O. T. revelation of religion;

---

[1] Of three books the Masora gives only the number of verses: Ruth, 85 verses; Shir (the Song), 117 verses; and Kinoth (Lamentations), 154; but no sections (*Sedarim*).

yet it is significant that it was possible [1] within it, without apostasy from it; within the N. T. revelation of religion, except in such references as Matt. xxvi. 24, it is absolutely impossible without apostasy from it, or without rejection of its fundamental meaning.

Ver. 2. Still more in the spirit of the N. T. (cf. *e.g.* Luke vi. 25) are these words of this singular book which stands on the border of both Testaments: " It is better to go into a house of mourning than to go into a house of carousal (drinking) : for that is the end of every man ; and the living layeth it to heart." A house is meant in which there is sorrow on account of a death; the lamentation continued for seven days (Sirach xxii. 10), and extended sometimes, as in the case of the death of Aaron and Moses, to thirty days; the later practice distinguished the lamentations (אֲנִינוּת) for the dead till the time of burial, and the mournings for the dead (אֲבֵלוּת), which were divided into seven and twenty-three days of greater and lesser mourning; on the return from carrying away the corpse, there was a *Trostmahl* (a comforting repast), to which, according as it appears to an ancient custom, those who were to be partakers of it contributed (Jer. xvi. 7 ; Hos. ix. 4 ; Job iv. 17, *funde vinum tuum et panem tuum super sepulchra justorum*).[2] This feast of sorrow the above proverb leaves out of view, although also in reference to it the contrast between the " house of carousal " and " house of mourning " remains, that in the latter the drinking must be in moderation, and not to drunkenness.[3] The going into the house of mourning is certainly thought of as a visit for the purpose of showing sympathy and of imparting consolation during the first seven days of mourning (John xi. 31).[4] Thus to go into the house of sorrow, and to show one's sympathy with the mourners there, is better than to go into a house of drinking, where all is festivity and merriment; viz. because the former (that he is mourned over as dead) is the end of every man, and the survivor takes it to heart, viz. this, that he too must die. הוּא follows attractionally the gender of סוֹף (cf. Job xxxi. 11, *Keri*). What is said at iii. 13 regarding כָּל־הָ is appropriate to the passage before us. יִתֵּן is rightly vocalised ; regarding the

---

[1] " The reflections of the Preacher," says Hitzig (*Süd. deut. ev. protest. Woch. Blatt*, 1864, No. 2), " present the picture of a time in which men, participating in the recollection of a mighty religious past, and become sceptical by reason of the sadness of the present time, grasping here and there in uncertainty, were in danger of abandoning that stedfastness of faith which was the first mark of the religion of the prophets."

[2] Cf. Hamb. *Real Encyc. für Bibel u. Talmud* (1870), article " Trauer."

[3] Maimuni's *Hilchoth Ebel*, iv. 7, xiii. 8.

[4] *Ibid*. xiii. 2.

form הָתַי, vid. Baer in the critical remarks of our ed. of *Isaiah* under iii. 22. The phrase נָתַן אֶל־לֵב here and at ix. 1 is synon. with שִׂים עַל־לֵב, שִׂים אֶל־לֵב (e.g. Isa. lvii. 1) and שִׂים בְּלֵב. How this saying agrees with Koheleth's *ultimatum*: There is nothing better than to eat and drink, etc. (ii. 24, etc.), the Talmudists have been utterly perplexed to discover; Manasse ben-Israel in his *Conciliador* (1632) loses himself in much useless discussion.[1] The solution of the difficulty is easy. The *ultimatum* does not relate to an unconditional enjoyment of life, but to an enjoyment conditioned by the fear of God. When man looks death in the face, the two things occur to him, that he should make use of his brief life, but make use of it in view of the end, thus in a manner for which he is responsible before God.

Vers. 3, 4. The joy of life must thus be not riot and tumult, but a joy tempered with seriousness: "Better is sorrow than laughter: for with a sad countenance it is well with the heart. The heart of the wise is in the house of mourning, and the heart of fools in the house of mirth." Grief and sorrow, כַּעַס, whether for ourselves or occasioned by others, is better, viz. morally better, than extravagant merriment; the heart is with רֹעַ פָּ' (inf. as רֵעַ, Jer. vii. 6; cf. פְּנֵ' רָ', Gen. xl. 7; Neh. ii. 2), a sorrowful countenance, better than with laughter, which only masks the feeling of disquiet peculiar to man, Prov. xiv. 13. Elsewhere יִיטַב לֵב = "the heart is (may be) of good cheer," *e.g.* Ruth iii. 7, Judg. xix. 6; here also joyful experience is meant, but well becoming man as a religious moral being. With a sad countenance it may be far better as regards the heart than with a merry countenance in boisterous company. Luther, in the main correct, after Jerome, who on his part follows Symmachus: "The heart is made better by sorrow." The well-being is here meant as the reflex of a moral: *bene se habere*.

Sorrow penetrates the heart, draws the thought upwards, purifies, transforms. Therefore is the heart of the wise in the house of sorrow; and, on the other hand, the heart of fools is in the house of joy, *i.e.* the impulse of their heart goes thither, there they feel themselves at home; a house of joy is one where there are continual feasts, or where there is at the time a revelling in joy. That ver. 4 is divided not by *Athnach*, but by *Zakef*, has its reason in this, that of the words following אֵבֶל, none consists of three syllables; cf. on the contrary, vii. 7, חָכָם. From this point forward the internal relation of the contents is broken up, according to which this series of

---

[1] *Vid.* the English translation by Lindo (London 1842), vol. ii. pp. 306–309.

sayings as a concluding section hangs together with that containing the observations going before in ch. vi.

Vers. 5, 6. A fourth proverb of that which is better (טוֹב מִן) presents, like the third, the fools and the wise over against each other: "Better to hear the reproof of a wise man, than that one should hear the song of fools. For like the crackling of *Nesseln* (nettles) under the *Kessel* (kettle), so the laughter of the fool: also this is vain." As at Prov. xiii. 1, xvii. 10, גְּעָרָה is the earnest and severe words of the wise, which impressively reprove, emphatically warn, and salutarily alarm. שִׁיר in itself means only song, to the exclusion, however, of the plaintive song; the song of fools is, if not immoral, yet morally and spiritually hollow, senseless, and unbridled madness. Instead of מִשְׁמֹעַ, the words מֵאִ׳ שׁ׳ are used, for the twofold act of hearing is divided between different subjects. A fire of thorn-twigs flickers up quickly and crackles merrily, but also exhausts itself quickly (Ps. cxviii. 12), without sufficiently boiling the flesh in the pot; whilst a log of wood, without making any noise, accomplishes this quietly and surely. We agree with Knobel and Vaihinger in copying the paronomasia [*Nessel—Kessel*]. When, on the other hand, Zöckler remarks that a fire of nettles could scarcely crackle, we advise our friend to try it for once in the end of summer with a bundle of stalks of tall dry nettles. They yield a clear blaze, a quickly expiring fire, to which here, as he well remarks, the empty laughter of foolish men is compared, who are devoid of all earnestness, and of all deep moral principles of life. This laughter is vain, like that crackling. There is a hiatus between vers. 6 and 7. For how ver. 7 can be related to ver. 6 as furnishing evidence, no interpreter has as yet been able to say. Hitzig regards 6*a* as assigning a reason for ver. 5, but 6*b* as a reply (as ver. 7 containing its motive shows) to the assertion of ver. 5,—a piece of ingenious thinking which no one imitates. Elster translates: "Yet injustice befools a wise man," being prudently silent about this "yet." Zöckler finds, as Knobel and Ewald do, the mediating thought in this, that the vanity of fools infects and also easily befools the wise. But the subject spoken of is not the folly of fools in general, but of their singing and laughter, to which ver. 7 has not the most remote reference. Otherwise Hengst.: "In ver. 7, the reason is given why the happiness of fools is so brief; first, the *mens sana* is lost, and then destruction follows." But in that case the words ought to have been יְהוֹלֵל כְּסִיל; the remark, that חכם here denotes one who ought to be and might be such, is a pure *volte*. Ginsburg thinks that the two verses are co-ordinated by כִּי; that ver. 6 gives the reason for

5*b*, and ver. 7 that for 5*a*, since here, by way of example, one accessible to bribery is introduced, who would act prudently in letting himself therefore be directed by a wise man. But if he had wished to be thus understood, the author would have used another word instead of חכם, 7*a*, and not designated both him who reproves and him who merits reproof by the one word—the former directly, the latter at least indirectly. We do not further continue the account of the many vain attempts that have been made to bring ver. 7 into connection with vers. 6 and 5. Our opinion is, that ver. 7 is the second half of a tetrastich, the first half of which is lost, which began, as is to be supposed, with *tov*. The first half was almost the same as Ps. xxxvii. 16, or better still, as Prov. xvi. 8, and the whole proverb stood thus:

טוֹב מְעַט בִּצְדָקָה
מֵרֹב תְּבוּאוֹת בְּלֹא מִשְׁפָּט:

[and then follows ver. 7 as it lies before us in the text, formed into a distich, the first line of which terminates with חָכָם]. We go still further, and suppose that after the first half of the tetrastich was lost, that expression, "also this is vain," added to ver. 6 by the punctuation, was inserted for the purpose of forming a connection for כי עשק: Also this is vain, that, etc. (כי, like *asher*, viii. 14).

Ver. 7. Without further trying to explain the mystery of the כי, we translate this verse: "... For oppression maketh wise men mad, and corruption destroyeth the understanding." From the lost first half of the verse, it appears that the subject here treated of is the duties of a judge, including those of a ruler into whose hands his subjects, with their property and life, are given. The second half is like an echo of Ex. xxiii. 8, Deut. xvi. 19. That which שֹׁחַד there means is here, as at Prov. xv. 27, denoted by מַתָּנָה; and עֹשֶׁק is accordingly oppression as it is exercised by one who constrains others who need legal aid and help generally to purchase it by means of presents. Such oppression for the sake of gain, even if it does not proceed to the perversion of justice, but only aims at courting and paying for favour, makes a wise man mad (יְהוֹלֵל, as at Job xii. 17; Isa. xliv. 25), *i.e.* it hurries him forth, since the greed of gold increases more and more, to the most blinding immorality and regardlessness; and such presents for the purpose of swaying the judgment, and of bribery, destroys the heart, *i.e.* the understanding (cf. Hos. iv. 11, *Bereschith rabba*, ch. lvi.), for they obscure the judgment, blunt the conscience, and make a man the slave of his passion. The conjecture הָעֹשֶׁר (riches) instead of the word

הָעֹשֶׁק (Burger, as earlier Ewald) is accordingly unnecessary; it has the parallelism against it, and thus generally used gives an untrue thought. The word הוֹלֵל does not mean "gives lustre" (Desvoeux), or "makes shine forth = makes manifest" (Tyler); thus also nothing is gained for a better connection of ver. 7 with ver. 6. The Venet. excellently: ἐκστήσει. Aben Ezra supposes that מתנה is here = דְּבַר מֵת; Mendelssohn repeats it, although otherwise the consciousness of the syntactical rule, Gesen. § 147a, does not fail him.

Vers. 8, 9. There now follows a fourth, or, taking into account the mutilated one, a fifth proverb of that which is better: "Better the end of a thing than its beginning; better one who forbears than one who is haughty. Hasten thyself not in thy spirit to become angry: for anger lieth down in the bosom of fools." The clause 8a is first thus to be objectively understood as it stands. It is not without limitation true; for of a matter in itself evil, the very contrary is true, Prov. v. 4, xxiii. 32. But if a thing is not in itself evil, the end of its progress, the reaching to its goal, the completion of its destination, is always better than its beginning, which leaves it uncertain whether it will lead to a prosperous issue. An example of this is Solon's saying to Croesus, that only he is to be pronounced happy whose good fortune it is to end his life well in the possession of his wealth (*Herod.* i. 32).

The proverb 8b will stand in some kind of connection with 8a, since what it says is further continued in ver. 9. In itself, the frequently long and tedious development between the beginning and the end of a thing requires expectant patience. But if it is in the interest of a man to see the matter brought to an issue, an אֶרֶךְ אַף will, notwithstanding, wait with self-control in all quietness for the end; while it lies in the nature of the גְּבַהּ רוּחַ, the haughty, to fret at the delay, and to seek to reach the end by violent means; for the haughty man thinks that everything must at once be subservient to his wish, and he measures what others should do by his own measureless self-complacency. We may with Hitzig translate: "Better is patience (אָרֵךְ = אֶרֶךְ) than haughtiness" (גְּבַהּ, inf., as שְׁפַל, xii. 4; Prov. xvi. 19). But there exists no reason for this; גְּבַהּ is not to be held, as at Prov. xvi. 5, and elsewhere generally, as the connecting form of גָּבֹהַּ, and so אֶרֶךְ for that of אָרֵךְ; it amounts to the same thing whether the two properties (characters) or the persons possessing them are compared.

Ver. 9. In this verse the author warns against this pride which, when everything does not go according to its mind, falls into passionate excitement, and thoughtlessly judges, or with a violent rude hand anticipates the end. אַל־תְּבַ֫' : do not overturn, hasten not, rush not, as at v. 1. Why the word בְּרוּחֲךָ, and not בנפשך or בלבך, is used, vid. Psychol. pp. 197-199: passionate excitements overcome a man according to the biblical representation of his spirit, Prov. xxv. 28, and in the proving of the spirit that which is in the heart comes forth in the mood and disposition, Prov. xv. 13. כְּעוֹס is an infin., like יְשׁוֹן, v. 11. The warning has its reason in this, that anger or (כעס, taken more potentially than actually) fretfulness rests in the bosom of fools, *i.e.* is cherished and nourished, and thus is at home, and, as it were (thought of personally, as if it were a wicked demon), feels itself at home (יָנוּחַ, as at Prov. xiv. 33). The haughty impetuous person, and one speaking out rashly, thus acts like a fool. In fact, it is folly to let oneself be impelled by contradictions to anger, which disturbs the brightness of the soul, takes away the considerateness of judgment, and undermines the health, instead of maintaining oneself with equanimity, *i.e.* without stormy excitement, and losing the equilibrium of the soul under every opposition to our wish.

From this point the proverb loses the form "better than," but *tov* still remains the catchword of the following proverbs. The proverb here first following is so far cogn., as it is directed against a particular kind of *ka'as* (anger), viz. discontentment with the present.

Ver. 10. "Say not: How comes it that the former times were better than these now? for thou dost not, from wisdom, ask after this." Cf. these lines from Horace (*Poet.* 173, 4):

"*Difficilis, querulus, laudator temporis acti
Se puero, censor castigatorque minorum.*"

Such an one finds the earlier days—not only the old days described in history (Deut. iv. 32), but also those he lived in before the present time (cf. *e.g.* 2 Chron. ix. 29)—thus by contrast so much better than the present ones, that in astonishment he asks: "What is it = how comes it that?" etc. The author designates this question as one not proceeding from wisdom: מֶה, like the Mishnic מִתּוֹךְ חכמה, and שָׁאַל עַל, as at Neh. i. 2; *'al-zeh* refers to that question, after the ground of the contrast, which is at the same time an exclamation of wonder. The כי, assigning a reason for the dissuasion, does not mean that the cause of the difference between the present and the good old times is easily seen; but it denotes that the supposition of this difference is foolish, because in truth every age has its bright and its dark sides; and this division of light and shadow between the past and the present betrays a want of understanding of the signs of the times and of the ways of God. This proverb does not furnish any point of support for the determination of the date of the authorship of the Book of Koheleth (*vid.* above, p. 213). But if it was composed in the last century of the Persian domination, this dissatisfaction with the present times is explained, over against which Koheleth leads us to consider that it is self-deception and one-sidedness to regard the present as all dark and the past as all bright and rosy.

Vers. 11, 12. Externally connecting itself with "from wisdom," there now follows another proverb, which declares that wisdom along with an inheritance is good, but that wisdom is nevertheless of itself better than money and possessions: "Wisdom is good with family possessions, and an advantage for those who see the sun. For wisdom affordeth a shadow, money affordeth a shadow; yet the advantage of knowledge is this, that wisdom preserveth life to its possessor." Most of the English interpreters, from Desvoeux to Tyler, translate: "Wisdom is as good as an inheritance;" and Bullock, who translates: "with an inheritance," says of this and the other translations: "The difference is not material." But the thought is different, and thus the distinction is not merely a formal one. Zöckl. explains it as undoubted that עִם here, as at ii. 16 (*vid, l.c.*), means *aeque ac;* but (1) that *aeque ac* has occurred to no ancient translator, till the Venet. and Luther, nor to the Syr., which translates: "better is wisdom than weapons (מאנא זינא)," in a singular way making 11a a *duplette* of ix. 18a; (2) instead of "wisdom is as good as wealth," would much rather be said: "wisdom is better than wealth," as *e.g.* Prov. viii. 11; (3) the proverb is formed like *Aboth* ii. 2, "good is study connected with a citizen-like occupation," and similar proverbs; (4) one may indeed say: "the wise man dieth with (together with) the fool" = just as well as the fool; but "good is wisdom with wealth" can neither be equivalent to "as well as wealth," nor: "in comparison with wealth" (Ewald, Elster), but only: "in connection with wealth (possessions);" *aeque ac* may be translated for *una cum* where the subject is common action and suffering, but not in a substantival clause consisting of a subst. as subject and an adj. as pred., having the form of a categorical judgment. נַחֲלָה denotes a possession inherited and hereditary (cf. Prov. xx. 21); and this is evidence in favour of the view that עִם is meant not of comparison, but of connection; the expression would otherwise be עִם־עֹשֶׁר. וְיֹתֵר is now also explained. It is not to be rendered: "and better still" (than wealth), as Herzf., Hitz., and Hengst. render it; but in spite of Hengst., who decides in his own way, "יותר never means advantage, gain," it denotes a prevailing good, *avantage* (*vid.* above, p. 192); and it is explained also why men are here named "those who see the sun"—certainly not merely thus describing them poetically, as in Homer ζώειν is described and coloured by ὁρᾶν φάος ἠελίοιο. To see the sun, is = to have entered upon this earthly life, in which, along with wisdom, also no inheritance is to be despised. For wisdom affords protection as well as money, but the former still more than the latter. So far, the general meaning of ver. 12 is undisputed. But how is 12*a* to be construed? Knobel, Hitz., and others regard ב as the so-called *beth essentiae:* a shadow (protection) is wisdom, a shadow is money,—very expressive, yet out of harmony, if not with the language of that period, yet with the style of Koheleth; and how useless and misleading would this doubled ב be here! Hengstenberg translates: in the shadow of wisdom, in the shadow of silver; and Zöckler introduces between the two clauses "it is as." But (1) here the shadow of wisdom, at least according to our understanding of ver. 11, is not likened to the shadow of silver; but in conformity with that עם, it must be said that wisdom, and also that money, affords a shadow; (2) but that interpretation goes quite beyond the limits of gnomic brachyology. We explain: for in the shadow (בְּצֵל, like בְּצֵל, Jonah iv. 5) is wisdom, in the shadow, money; by which, without any particularly bold poetic licence, is meant that he who possesses wisdom, he who possesses money, finds himself in a shadow, *i.e.* of pleasant security; to be in the shadow, spoken of wisdom and money, is = to sit in the shadow of the persons who possess both.

Ver. 12*b*. The exposition of this clause is agreed upon. It is to be construed according to the accentuation: and the advantage of knowledge is this, that "wisdom preserveth life to its possessors." The Targ. regards דעת החכמה as connected genit.; that might be possible (cf. i. 17, viii. 16), but yet is improbable. Wherever the author uses דעת as subst., it is an independent conception placed beside 'חב, i. 16, ii. 26, etc. We now translate, not: wisdom gives life (LXX., Jerome, Venet., Luther) to its possessors; for חיה always means only either to revive (thus Hengst., after Ps. cxix. 25; cf. lxxi. 20) or to keep in life; and this latter meaning is more appropriate to this book than the former,—thus (cf. Prov. iii. 18): wisdom preserves in life,—since, after Hitzig, it accomplishes this, not by rash utterances of denunciation,—a thought lying far behind ver. 10, and altogether too mean,—but since it secures it against self-destruction by vice and passions and emotions, *e.g.* anger (ver. 9), which consume life. The shadow in which wisdom (the wise man) sits keeps it fresh and sound,—a result which the shadow in which money (the capitalist) sits does not afford: it has frequently the directly contrary effect.

Vers. 13, 14. There now follows a proverb of devout submission to the providence of God, connecting itself with the contents of ver. 10: "Consider the work of God: for who can make that straight which He hath made crooked! In the good day be of good cheer, and in the day of misfortune observe: God hath also made this equal to that, to the end that man need not experience anything (further) after his death." While רְאֵה, i. 10, vii. 27, 29, is not different from הַגֵּה, and in ix. 9 has the meaning of "enjoy," here the meaning of contemplative observation, mental seeing, connects itself both times with it. כִּי before מִי can as little mean *quod*, as *asher*, vi. 12, before *mi* can mean *quoniam*. "Consider God's work" means: recognise in all that is done the government of God, which has its motive in this, that, as the question leads us to suppose, no creature is able (cf. vi. 10 and i. 15) to put right God's work in cases where it seems to contradict that which is right (Job viii. 3, xxxiv. 12), or to make straight that which He has made crooked (Ps. cxlvi. 9).

Ver. 14*a a*. The call here expressed is parallel to Sir. xiv. 14 (Fritz.): "Withdraw not thyself from a good day, and let not thyself lose participation in a right enjoyment." The ב of בְּטוֹב is, as little as that of בְּצֵל, the *beth essentiae*—it is not a designation of quality, but of condition: in good, *i.e.* cheerful mood. He who is, Jer. xliv. 17, personally *tov*, cheerful (= *tov lev*), is *b*ᵉ*tov* (cf. Ps. xxv. 13, also Job xxi. 13). The reverse side of the call, 14*aβ*, is of course not to be translated: and suffer or bear the bad day (Ewald, Heiligst.), for in this sense we use the expression רָאָה רָעָה, Jer. xliv. 17, but not רָאָה בְרָעָה, which much rather, Obad. 13, means a malicious contemplation of the misfortune of a stranger, although once, Gen. xxi. 16, ראה ב also occurs in the sense of a compassionate, sympathizing look, and, moreover, the parall. shows that ביום רעה is not the obj., but the adv. designation of time. Also not: look to = be attentive to (Salomon), or bear it patiently (Burger), for רְאֵה cannot of itself have that meaning.[1] But: in the day of misfortune observe, *i.e.* perceive and reflect: God has also made (cf. Job ii. 10) the latter לְעֻמַּת corresponding, parallel, like to (cf. under v. 15) the former.

So much the more difficult is the statement of the object of this mingling by God of good and evil in the life of man. It is translated: that man may find nothing behind him; this is literal, but it is meaningless. The meaning, according to most interpreters, is

---

[1] Similarly also Sohar (Par. מצורע): הוי וגו', *i.e. cave et circumspice*, viz. that thou mayest not incur the judgment which is pronounced.

this: that man may investigate nothing that lies behind his present time,—thus, that belongs to the future; in other words: that man may never know what is before him. But *aharav* is never (not at vi. 12) = in the future, lying out from the present of a man; but always = after his present life. Accordingly, Ewald explains, and Heiligst. with him: that he may find nothing which, dying, he could take with him. But this rendering (cf. v. 14) is here unsuitable. Better, Hitzig: because God wills it that man shall be rid of all things after his death, He puts evil into the period of his life, and lets it alternate with good, instead of visiting him therewith after his death. This explanation proceeds from a right interpretation of the words: *idcirco ut* (cf. iii. 18) *non inveniat homo post se quidquam, scil. quod non expertus sit,* but gives a meaning to the expression which the author would reject as unworthy of his conception of God. What is meant is much more this, that God causes man to experience good and evil that he may pass through the whole school of life, and when he departs hence that nothing may be outstanding (in arrears) which he has not experienced.

CONTINUATION OF EXPERIENCES AND THEIR RESULTS.—VII. 15–IX. 12.

The Injuriousness of Excesses, vii. 15–18.

The concluding section, vii. 1–14, is now followed by *I*-sections, *i.e.* advices in the form of actually experienced facts, in which again the *I* of the author comes into the foreground.

Vers. 15–18. The first of these counsels warns against extremes, on the side of good as well as on that of evil: "All have I seen in the days of my vanity: there are righteous men who perish by their righteousness, and there are wicked men who continue long by their wickedness. Be not righteous over-much, and show not thyself wise beyond measure: why wilt thou ruin thyself? Be not wicked over-much, and be no fool: why wilt thou die before thy time is? It is good that thou holdest thyself to the one, and also from the other withdrawest not thine hand: for he that feareth God accomplisheth it all." One of the most original English interpreters of the Book of Koheleth, T. Tyler (1874), finds in the thoughts of the book—composed, according to his view, about 200 B.C.—and in their expression, references to the post-Aristotelian philosophy, particularly to the Stoic, variously interwoven with orientalism. But here, in vers. 15–18, we perceive, not so much the principle of the Stoical ethics—τῇ φύσει ὁμολογουμένως ζῆν—as that of the Aristotelian, according to which virtue consists in the art μέσως ἔχειν, the art of holding the middle between extremes.[1] Also, we do not find here a reference to the contrasts between Pharisaism and Sadduceeism (Zöckl.), viz. those already in growth in the time of the author; for if it should be also true, as Tyler conjectures, that the Sadducees had such a predilection for Epicurism,—as, according to Josephus (*Vit.* c. 2), "the doctrine of the Pharisees is of kin to that of the Stoics," —yet צדקה and רִשְׁעָה are not apportioned between these two parties, especially since the overstraining of conformity to the law by the Pharisees related not to the moral, but to the ceremonial law. We derive nothing for the right understanding of the passsge from referring the wisdom of life here recommended to the tendencies of the time. The author proceeds from observation, over against which the O. T. saints knew not how to place any satisfying theodicee. יְמֵי הֶבְלִי (*vid.* vi. 12) he so designates the long, but for the most part uselessly spent life lying behind him. אֶת־הַכֹּל is not "everything possible" (Zöckl.), but "all, of all kinds" (Luth.), which is defined by 15*b* as of two kinds; for 15*a* is the introduction of the following experience relative to the righteous and the unrighteous, and thus to the two classes into which all men are divided. We do not translate: there are the righteous, who by their righteousness, etc. (Umbr., Hitzig, and others); for if the author should thus commence, it would appear as if he wished to give unrighteousness the preference to righteousness, which, however, was far from him. To perish in or by his righteousness, to live long in or by his wickedness (מַאֲרִיךְ, *scil.* יָמִים, viii. 13, as at Prov. xxviii. 2), is = to die in spite of righteousness, to live in spite of wickedness, as *e.g.* Deut. i. 32: "in this thing" = in spite of, etc. Righteousness has the promise of long life as its reward; but if this is the rule, it has yet its exceptions, and the author thence deduces the doctrine that one should not exaggerate righteousness; for if it occurs that a righteous man, in spite of his righteousness, perishes, this happens, at earliest, in the case in which, in the practice of righteousness, he goes beyond the right measure and limit. The relative conceptions הַרְבֵּה and יוֹתֵר have here, since they are referred to the idea of the right measure, the meaning of *nimis*. חִתְחַכֵּם could mean, "to play the wise man;" but that, whether more or less done, is objectionable. It means, as at Ex. i. 10, to act wisely (cf. Ps. cv. 25, הִתְ, to act cunningly). And יִשֹּׁ, which is elsewhere used of being inwardly torpid, *i.e.* being astonished, *obstupescere*, has here the meaning of placing oneself in a

---

[1] Cf. Luthardt's *Lectures on the Moral Truths of Christianity*, 2d ed. Edin., T. and T. Clark.

benumbed, disordered state, or also, passively, of becoming disconcerted; not of becoming desolate or being deserted (Hitz., Ginsburg, and others), which it could only mean in highly poetic discourse (Isa. liv. 1). The form תִּשּׁוֹמֵם is syncop., like תֻּפ׳, Num. xxi. 27; and the question, with לָמָּה, here and at 17b, is of the same kind as v. 5; Luther, weakening it: "that thou mayest not destroy thyself."

Ver. 17. Up to this point all is clear: righteousness and wisdom are good and wholesome, and worth striving for; but even in these a transgressing of the right measure is possible (Luther remembers the *summum jus summa injuria*), which has as a consequence, that they become destructive to man, because he thereby becomes a caricature, and either perishes rushing from one extreme into another, or is removed out of the way by others whose hatred he provokes. But it is strange that the author now warns against an excess in wickedness, so that he seems to find wickedness, up to a certain degree, praiseworthy and advisable. So much the stranger, since "be no fool" stands as contrast to "show not thyself wise," etc.; so that "but also be no wicked person" was much rather to be expected as contrast to "be not righteous over-much." Zöckler seeks to get over this difficulty with the remark: "Koheleth does not recommend a certain moderation in wickedness as if he considered it allowable, but only because he recognises the fact as established, that every man is by nature somewhat wicked." The meaning would then be: man's life is not free from wickedness, but be only not too wicked! The offensiveness of the advice is not thus removed; and besides, 18a demands, in a certain sense, an intentional wickedness,—indeed, as 18b shows, a wickedness in union with the fear of God. The correct meaning of "be not wicked over-much" may be found if for תִּרְשַׁע we substitute תֶּחֱטָא; in this form the good counsel at once appears as impossible, for it would be immoral, since "sinning," in all circumstances, is an act which carries in itself its own sentence of condemnation. Thus רֶשַׁע must here be a setting oneself free from the severity of the law, which, although sin in the eyes of the over-righteous, is yet no sin in itself; and the author here thinks, in accordance with the spirit of his book, principally of that fresh, free, joyous life to which he called the young, that joy of life in its fulness which appeared to him as the best and fairest reality in this present time; but along with that, perhaps also of transgressions of the letter of the law, of shaking off the scruples of conscience which conformity to God-ordained circumstances brings along with it. He means to say: be not a narrow rigorist,—enjoy life, accommodate thyself to life; but let not the reins be too loose; and be no fool who wantonly places himself above law and discipline: Why wilt thou destroy thy life before the time by suffering vice to kill thee (Ps. xxxiv. 22), and by want of understanding ruin thyself (Prov. x. 21)?[1]

Ver. 18. "It is good that thou holdest fast to the one,"—viz. righteousness and wisdom,—and withdrawest not thy hand from the other,—viz. a wickedness which renounces over-righteousness and over-wisdom, or an unrestrained life;—for he who fears God accomplishes all, *i.e.* both, the one as well as the other. Luther, against the Vulg.: "for he who fears God escapes all." But what "all"? Tyler, Bullock, and others reply: "All the perplexities of life;" but no such thing is found in the text here, however many perplexities may be in the book. Better, Zöckler: the evil results of the extreme of false righteousness as of bold wickedness. But that he does not destroy himself and does not die before his time, is yet only essentially one thing which he escapes; also, from ver. 15, only one thing, אָבַד, is taken. Thus either: the extremes (Umbr.), or: the extremes together with their consequences. The thought presents a connected, worthy conclusion. But if *ēth-kullam*, with its retrospective suffix, can be referred to that which immediately precedes, this ought to have the preference. Ginsburg, with Hitzig: "Whoso feareth God will make his way with both;" but what an improbable phrase! Jerome, with his vague *nihil negligit*, is right as to the meaning. In the Bible, the phrase יָצָא הָ..., *egressus est urbem*, Gen. xliv. 4, cf. Jer. x. 20, is used; and in the Mishna, יָצָא אֶת־יְדֵי חוֹבָתוֹ, *i.e.* he has discharged his duty, he is quit of it by fulfilling it. For the most part, יָצָא merely is used: he has satisfied his duty; and לֹא יָצָא, he has not satisfied it, *e.g.* Berachoth ii. 1. Accordingly יָצָא—since *ēth-kullam* relates to, "these ought ye to have done, and not to leave the other undone," Matt. xxiii. 23—here means: he who fears God will set himself free from all, will acquit himself of the one as well as of the other, will perform both, and thus preserve the golden *via media*.

What protects him who with all his Righteousness is not free from Sin, and what becomes him, vii. 19–22.

The thought with which the following sentence is introduced is not incongruous to that going before. But each one of these moral proverbs and aphorisms is in itself a little whole, and the deeper connections, in the discovery of which interpreters vie with each other,

---

[1] An old proverb, *Sota* 3a, says: "A man commits no transgression unless there rules in him previously the spirit of folly."

are destitute of exegetical value. One must not seek to be over-wise; but the possession of wisdom deserves to be highly valued.

Ver. 19. "Wisdom affords strong protection to the wise man more than ten mighty men who are in the city." We have to distinguish, as is shown under Ps. xxxi. 3, the verbs עָזַז, to be strong, and עוּז, to flee for refuge; תָּעֹז is the fut. of the former, whence מָעוֹז, stronghold, safe retreat, protection, and with לְ, since עָזַז means not only to be strong, but also to show oneself strong, as at ix. 20, to feel and act as one strong; it has also the trans. meaning, to strengthen, as shown in Ps. lxviii. 29, but here the intrans. suffices: wisdom proves itself strong for the wise man. The ten *shallithim* are not, with Gins-burg, to be multiplied indefinitely into "many mighty men." And it is not necessary, with Desvoeux, Hitz., Zöckl., and others, to think of ten chiefs (commanders of forces), including the portions of the city garrison which they commanded. The author probably in this refers to some definite political arrangement (*vid.* above, p. 216), perhaps to the ten archons, like those Assyrian *salaṭ*, vice-regents, after whom as eponyms the year was named by the Greeks. שַׁלִּיטִים, in the Asiatic kingdom, was not properly a military title. And did a town then need protection only in the time of war, and not also at other times, against injury threatening its trade, against encroachments on its order, against the spread of infectious diseases, against the force of the elements? As the Deutero-Isaiah (lx. 17) says of Jerusalem: "I will make thy officers peace, and thine exactors righteousness," so Koheleth says here that wisdom affords a wise man as strong a protection as a powerful decemvirate a city; cf. Prov. xxiv. 5*a*: "A wise man is *baʿoz*," *i.e.* mighty.

Ver. 20. "For among men there is not a righteous man on the earth, who doeth good, and sinneth not." The original passage, found in Solomon's prayer at the consecration of the temple, is briefer, 1 Kings viii. 46: "There is no man who sinneth not." Here the words might be אֵין אָדָם צַדִּיק וגו׳, there is no righteous man ... *Adam* stands here as representing the species, as when we say in Germ.: *Menschen gibt es keine gerechten auf Erden* [men, there are none righteous on earth]; cf. Ex. v. 16: "Straw, none was given." The verification of ver. 19 by reference to the fact of the common sinfulness from which even the most righteous cannot free himself, does not contradict all expectation to the same degree as the *ki* in vii. 7; but yet it surprises us, so that Mercer and Grätz, with Aben Ezra, take ver. 20 as the verification of ver. 16, here first adduced, and Knobel and Heiligst. and others connect it with vers. 21, 22, translating: "Because there is not a just man ..., therefore it is also the part of wisdom to take no heed unto all words," etc. But these are all forced interpretations; instead of the latter, we would rather suppose that ver. 20 originally stood after ver. 22, and is separated from its correct place. But yet the sequence of thought lying before us may be conceived, and that not merely as of necessity, but as that which was intended by the author. On the whole, Hitzig is correct: "For every one, even the wise man, sins; in which case virtue, which has forsaken him, does not protect him, but wisdom proves itself as his means of defence." Zöckler adds: "against the judicial justice of God;" but one escapes from this by a penitent appeal to grace, for which there is no need for the personal property of wisdom; there is thus reason rather for thinking on the dangerous consequences which often a single false step has for a man in other respects moral; in the threatening complications in which he is thereby involved, it is wisdom which then protects him and delivers him. Otherwise Tyler, who by the עֹז, which the wise has in wisdom, understands power over evil, which is always moving itself even in the righteous. But the sinning spoken of in ver. 20 is that which is unavoidable, which even wisdom cannot prevent or make inefficacious. On the contrary, it knows how to prevent the destruction which threatens man from his transgressions, and to remove the difficulties and derangements which thence arise. The good counsel following is connected by *gam* with the foregoing. The exhortation to strive after wisdom, contained in ver. 19, which affords protection against the evil effects of the failures which run through the life of the righteous, is followed by the exhortation, that one conscious that he himself is not free from transgression, should take heed to avoid that tale-bearing which finds pleasure in exposing to view the shortcomings of others.

Vers. 21, 22. "Also give not thy heart to all the words which one speaketh, lest thou shouldest hear thy servant curse thee. For thy heart knoweth in many cases that thou also hast cursed others." The talk of the people, who are the indef. subj. of יְדַבֵּרוּ (LXX., Targ., Syr. supply ἀσεβεῖς), is not about "thee who givest heed to the counsels just given" (Hitz., Zöckl.), for the restrictive עָלֶיךָ is wanting; and why should a servant be zealous to utter imprecations on the conduct of his master, which rests on the best maxims? It is the babbling of the people in general that is meant. To this one ought not to turn his heart (לְ ... נָתַן, as at i. 13, 17, viii. 9, 16), *i.e.* give wilful attention, *ne* (אֲשֶׁר לֹא = פֶּן, which does not occur in the Book of Koheleth) *audias servum tuum tibi maledicere;* the particip. expression of the pred. obj. follows the analogy of Gen. xxi. 9, Ewald, § 284*b*, and is not a Graecism; for since in this place hearing is meant, not immediately, but mediated through others, the expression would not in good Greek be with the LXX. ... τοῦ δούλου σου καταρωμένου σε, but τὸν δοῦλόν σου καταρᾶσθαι σε. The warning has its motive in this, that by such roundabout hearing one generally hears most unpleasant things; and on hearsay no reliance can be placed. Such gossiping one should ignore, should not listen to it at all; and if, nevertheless, something so bad is reported as that our own servant has spoken words of imprecation against us, yet we ought to pass that by unheeded, well knowing that we ourselves have often spoken harsh words against others. The expression יָדַע וגו׳, " thou art conscious to thyself that," is like פֶּעָ׳ רַ׳, 1 Kings ii. 44, not the obj. accus. dependent on יָדַע (Hitz.), "many cases where also thou ...," but the adv. accus. of time to קִלְלְךָ; the words are inverted (Ewald, § 336b), the style of Koheleth being fond of thus giving prominence to the chief conception (ver. 20, v. 18, iii. 13). The first *gam*, although it belongs to "thine, thy," as at 22b it is also connected with "thou,"[1] stands at the beginning of the sentence, after such syntactical examples as Hos. vi. 11; Zech. ix. 11; and even with a two-membered sentence, Job ii. 10.

The not-found, and the found the bitterest—a Woman, vii. 23–29.

The author makes here a pause, looks back at the teaching regarding prudence, already given particularly from ver. 15, and acknowledges wisdom as the goal of his effort, especially, however, that for him this goal does not lie behind him, but before him in the remote distance.

Ver. 23. "All this have I proved by wisdom: I thought, Wise I will become; but it remained far from me." The בְּ in בַּחָכְמָה is, as at i. 13, that designating the *organon*, the means of knowledge. Thus he possessed wisdom up to a certain degree, and in part; but his purpose, comprehended in the one word אֶחְכָּמָה (*vid.* above, p. 197, § 2), was to possess it fully and completely; *i.e.* not merely to be able to record observations and communicate advices, but to adjust the contradictions of life, to expound the mysteries of time and eternity, and generally to solve the most weighty and important questions which perplex men. But this wisdom was for him still in the remote distance. It is the wisdom after which Job, chap. xxviii., made

---

[1] גַּם־אָתְּ, on account of the half pause, accented on the penult. according to the Masora.

inquiry in all regions of the world and at all creatures, at last to discover that God has appointed to man only a limited share of wisdom. Koheleth briefly condenses Job xxviii. 12–22 in the words following:

Ver. 24. "For that which is, is far off, and deep,—yes, deep; who can reach it?" Knobel, Hitz., Vaih., and Bullock translate: for what is remote and deep, deep, who can find it? *i.e.* investigate it; but *mah-shehayah* is everywhere an idea by itself, and means either *id quod fuit*, or *id quod exstitit*, i. 9, iii. 15, vi. 10; in the former sense it is the contrast of *mah-shĕ‘ihyĕh*, viii. 7, x. 14, cf. iii. 22; in the latter, it is the contrast of that which does not exist, because it has not come into existence. In this way it is also not to be translated: For it is far off what it (wisdom) is (Zöckl.) [= what wisdom is lies far off from human knowledge], or: what it is (the essence of wisdom), is far off (Elst.)—which would be expressed by the words מַה־שֶּׁהִיא. And if מה־שהיה is an idea complete in itself, it is evidently not that which is past that is meant (thus *e.g.* Rosenm., *quod ante aderat*), for that is a limitation of the obj. of knowledge, which is unsuitable here, but that which has come into existence. Rightly, Hengst.: that which has being, for wisdom is τῶν ὄντων γνῶσις ἀψευδής, Wisd. vii. 17. He compares Judg. iii. 11, "the work which God does," and viii. 17, "the work which is done under the sun." What Koheleth there says of the totality of the historical, he here says of the world of things: this (in its essence and its grounds) remains far off from man; it is for him, and also in itself and for all creatures, far too deep (עָמֹק עָמֹק, the ancient expression for the superlative): Who can intelligibly reach (יִמְצָ, from מָצָא, *assequi*, in an intellectual sense, as at iii. 11, viii. 17; cf. Job xi. 7) it (this all of being)? The author appears in the book as a teacher of wisdom, and emphatically here makes confession of the limitation of his wisdom; for the consciousness of this limitation comes over him in the midst of his teaching.

Ver. 25. But, on the other side, he can bear testimony to himself that he has honestly exercised himself in seeking to go to the foundation of things: "I turned myself, and my heart was there to discern, and to explore, and to seek wisdom, and the account, and to perceive wickedness as folly, and folly as madness." Regarding *sabbothi*, *vid.* under ii. 20: a turning is meant to the theme as given in what follows, which, as we have to suppose, was connected with a turning away from superficiality and frivolity. Almost all interpreters—as also the accentuation does—connect the two words אֲנִי וְלִבִּי; but "I and my heart" is so unpsychological an expression, without example, that many Codd. (28 of Kennicott, 44 of de Rossi) read בְּלִבִּי [with my heart]. The erasure of the *vav* (as *e.g.* Luther: "I applied my heart") would at the same time require the change of סבותי into הֲסִבּוֹתִי. The Targ., Jerome, and the Venet. render the word בלבי; the LXX. and Syr., on the contrary, ולבי; and this also is allowable, if we place the disjunctive on אני and take ולבי as consequent: my heart, *i.e.* my striving and effort, was to discern (Aben Ezra, Herzf., Stuart),—a substantival clause instead of the verbal וְנָתַתִּי אֶת־לִבִּי, i. 13, i. 17. Regarding *tur* in an intellectual sense, *vid.* i. 13. *Hhĕshbon* (*vid.* above, p. 192), with *hhochmah*, we have translated by "*Rechenschaft*" [account, *ratio*]; for we understand by it a knowledge well grounded and exact, and able to be established,—the *facit* of a calculation of all the facts and circumstances relating thereto; נתן חשבין is Mishnic, and = the N. T. λόγον ἀποδιδόναι. Of the two accus. 25*b* following לָדַעַת, the first, as may be supposed, and as the determination in the second member shows, is that of the obj., the second that of the pred. (Ewald, § 284*b*): that רֶשַׁע, *i.e.* conduct separating from God and from the law of that which is good, is *kĕsĕl*, *Thorheit*, folly (since, as Socrates also taught, all sinning rests on a false calculation, to the sinner's own injury); and that *hassichluth*, *Narrheit*, foolishness, *stultitia* (*vid.* *sachal*, p. 194, and i. 17), is to be thus translated (in contradistinction to כֶּסֶל), *i.e.* an intellectual and moral obtuseness, living for the day, rising up into foolery, not different from *holeloth*, fury, madness, and thus like a physical malady, under which men are out of themselves, rage, and are mad. Koheleth's striving after wisdom thus, at least in the second instance (ולדעת), with a renunciation of the transcendental, went towards a practical end. And now he expresses by וּמוֹצֵא one of the experiences he had reached in this way of research. How much value he attaches to this experience is evident from the long preface, by means of which it is as it were distilled. We see him there on the way to wisdom, to metaphysical wisdom, if we may so speak—it remains as far off from him as he seeks to come near to it. We then see him, yet not renouncing the effort after wisdom, on the way toward practical wisdom, which exercises itself in searching into the good and the bad; and that which has presented itself to him as the bitterest of the bitter is— a woman.

Ver. 26. "And I found woman more bitter than death; she is like hunting-nets, and like snares is her heart, her hands are bands: he who pleaseth God will escape from her; but the sinner is caught by them." As יֵשׁ אֲ׳, iv. 2, so here וּמ׳ אֲ׳ (*vid.* above, p. 197, 1, and

198, 3) gains by the preceding וְסַבּוֹתִי אֲנִי a past sense;[1] the particip. clause stands frequently thus, not only as a circumstantial clause, Gen. xiv. 12 f., but also as principal clause, Gen. ii. 10, in an historical connection. The preceding pred. מַר, in the mas. ground-form, follows the rule, Gesen. § 147. Regarding the construction of the relative clause, Hitzig judges quite correctly: "הִיא is copula between subj. and pred., and precedes for the sake of the contrast, giving emphasis to the pred. It cannot be a nomin., which would be taken up by the suff. in לִבָּהּ, since if this latter were subject also to מצ׳, הִיא would not certainly be found. Also *asher* here is not a conj." This הוּא (הִיא), which in relative substantival clauses represents the copula, for the most part stands separated from *asher*, *e.g.* Gen. vii. 2, xvii. 12, Num. xvii. 5, Deut. xvii. 15; less frequently immediately with it, Num. xxxv. 31; 1 Sam. x. 19; 2 Kings xxv. 19; Lev. xi. 26; Deut. xx. 20. But this *asher hu* (*hi*) never represents the subj., placed foremost and again resumed by the reflex. pronoun, so as to be construed as the accentuation requires: *quae quidem retia et laquei cor ejus* = *cujus quidem cor sunt retia et laquei* (Heiligst.). מָצוֹד is the means of searching, *i.e.* either of hunting: hunting-net (*mitsodah*, ix. 12), or of blockading: siege-work, bulwarks, ix. 14; here it is the plur. of the word in the former meaning. חֲרָם, Hab. i. 14, plur. Ezek. xxvi. 5, etc. (perhaps from חרם, to pierce, bore through), is one of the many synon. for fishing-net. אֲסוּרִים, fetters, the hands (arms) of voluptuous embrace (cf. above, p. 191). The primary form, after Jer. xxxvii. 15, is אָסוּר, אֵסוּר; cf. אֵבוּס, אֵב׳, Job xxxix. 9. Of the three clauses following *asher*, *vav* is found in the second and is wanting to the third, as at Deut. xxix. 22, Job xlii. 9, Ps. xlv. 9, Isa. i. 13; cf. on the other hand, Isa. xxxiii. 6. Similar in their import are these Leonine verses:

"*Femina praeclara facie quási pestis amara,*
Et quasi fermentum corrumpit cor sapientum."

That the author is in full earnest in this harsh judgment regarding woman, is shown by 26b: he who appears to God as good (cf. ii. 26) escapes from her (the fut. of the consequence of this his relation to God); but the sinner (וְחוֹטֵא, cf. above, p. 254, note) is caught by her, or, properly, in her, viz. the net-like woman, or the net to which she is compared (Ps. ix. 16; Isa. xxiv. 18). The harsh judgment is, however, not applicable to woman as such, but

---

[1] With reference to this passage and Prov. xviii. 22, it was common in Palestine when one was married to ask מצא או מוצא = happy or unhappy? *Jebamoth* 63b.

to woman as she is, with only rare exceptions; among a thousand women he has not found one corresponding to the idea of a woman.

Vers. 27, 28. "Behold what I have found, saith Koheleth, adding one thing to another, to find out the account: What my soul hath still sought, and I have not found, (is this): one man among a thousand have I found; and a woman among all these have I not found." It is the ascertained result, "one man, etc.," which is solemnly introduced by the words preceding. Instead of אָמְ׳ קֹהֶ׳, the words אָמַר הַקֹּהֶ are to be read, after xii. 8, as is now generally acknowledged; errors of transcription of a similar kind are found at 2 Sam. v. 2; Job xxxviii. 12. Ginsburg in vain disputes this, maintaining that the name *Koheleth*, as denoting wisdom personified, may be regarded as fem. as well as mas.; here, where the female sex is so much depreciated, was the fem. self-designation of the stern judge specially unsuitable (cf. above, p. 204). Hengst. supposes that *Koheleth* is purposely fem. in this one passage, since true wisdom, represented by Solomon, stands opposite to false philosophy. But this reason for the fem. rests on the false opinion that woman here is heresy personified; he further remarks that it is significant for this fem. personification, that there is "no writing of female authorship in the whole canon of the O. and N. T." But what of Deborah's triumphal song, the song of Hannah, the *magnificat* of Mary? We hand this absurdity over to the Clementines! The woman here was flesh and blood, but *pulchra quamvis pellis est mens tamen plena procellis*; and *Koheleth* is not incarnate wisdom, but the official name of a preacher, as in Assyr., for חַנָּנִים, curators, overseers, *hazanâti*[1] is used. זֶה, 27*a*, points, as at i. 10, to what follows. אַחַת לְ׳, one thing to another (cf. Isa. xxvii. 12), must have been, like *summa summarum* and the like, a common arithmetical and dialectical formula, which is here subordinate to מְצֹא, since an adv. inf. such as לָקוֹחַ is to be supplemented: taking one thing to another to find out the חֶשְׁבּוֹן, *i.e.* the balance of the account, and thus to reach a *facit*, a *resultat*.[2]

That which presented itself to him in this way now follows. It was, in relation to woman, a negative experience: "What my soul sought on and on, and I found not, (is this)." The words are like the superscription of the following result, in which finally the זֶה of 27*a* terminates. Ginsburg, incorrectly: "what my soul is still seeking," which would have required מְבַקְשָׁה. The pret. בִּקְשָׁה (with

---

[1] *Vid.* Fried. Delitzsch's *Assyr. Stud.* (1874), p. 132.
[2] Cf. *Aboth* iv. 29, לִיתֵּן וגו׳, "to give account;" הכל וגו׳, "all according to the result."

ק without *Dagesh*,[1] as at ver. 29) is retrospective; and עוֹד, from עוּד, means *redire*, again and again, continually, as at Gen. xlvi. 29. He always anew sought, and that, as *biqshah naphshi* for בִּקְשָׁתִי denotes, with urgent striving, violent longing, and never found, viz. a woman such as she ought to be: a man, one of a thousand, I have found, etc. With right, the accentuation gives *Garshayim* to *adam*; it stands forth, as at ver. 20, as a general denominator—the sequence of accents, *Geresh*, *Pashta*, *Zakef*, is as at Gen. i. 9. "One among a thousand" reminds us of Job xxxiii. 23, cf. ix. 3; the old interpreters (*vid.* Dachselt's *Bibl. Accentuata*), with reference to these parallels, connect with the one man among a thousand all kinds of incongruous christological thoughts. Only, here *adam*, like the Romanic *l'homme* and the like, means man in sexual contrast to woman. It is thus ideally meant, like *ish*, 1 Sam. iv. 9, xlvi. 15, and accordingly also the parall. אִשָּׁה. For it is not to be supposed that the author denies thereby perfect human nature to woman. But also Burger's explanation: "a human being, whether man or woman," is a useless evasion. Man has the name *adam* κατ' ἐξ. by primitive hist. right: "for the man is not of the woman, but the woman of the man," 1 Cor. xi. 8. The meaning, besides, is not that among a thousand human beings he found one upright man, but not a good woman (Hitz.),—for then the thousand ought to have had its proper denominator, בני אדם,—but that among a thousand persons of the male sex he found only one man such as he ought to be, and among a thousand of the female sex not one woman such as she ought to be; "among all these" is thus = among an equal number. Since he thus actually found the ideal of man only seldom, and that of woman still seldomer (for more than this is not denoted by the round numbers), the more surely does he resign himself to the following *resultat*, which he introduces by the word לְבַד (only, alone), as the clear gain of his searching:

Ver. 29. "Lo, this only have I found, that God created man upright; but they seek many arts." Also here the order of the words is inverted, since זֶה, belonging as obj. to מָצָ֣א (have I found), which is restricted by לְבַד (*vid.* above, p. 193), is amalgamated with רְאֵה (Lo! see!). The author means to say: Only this (*solummodo hocce*) have I found, that . . . ; the רְאֵה is an interjected *nota bene*. The expression: God has made man יָשָׁר, is dogmatically significant. Man, as he came from the Creator's hand, was not placed in the state of moral decision,

---

[1] As generally the *Piel* forms of the root בקשׁ, Masor. all have *Raphe* on the ק, except the imper. בַּקְּשׁוּ; *vid.* Luzzatto's *Gramm.* § 417.

nor yet in the state of absolute indifference between good and evil; he was not neither good nor bad, but he was טוב, or, which is the same thing, ישׁר; *i.e.* in every respect normal, so that he could normally develope himself from this positively good foundation. But by the expression עשׂה ישׁר, Koheleth has certainly not exclusively his origin in view, but at the same time his relative continuation in the propagation of himself, not without the concurrence of the Creator; also of man after the fall the words are true, עשׂה ישׁר, in so far as man still possesses the moral ability not to indulge sinful affections within him, nor suffer them to become sinful actions. But the sinful affections in the inborn nature of weak sinful man have derived so strong a support from his freedom, that the power of the will over against this power of nature is for the most part as weakness; the dominance of sin, where it is not counteracted by the grace of God, has always shown itself so powerful, that Koheleth has to complain of men of all times and in all circles of life: they seek many arts (as Luther well renders it), or properly, calculations, inventions, devices (*hhishsh^{e}vonoth*,[1] as at 2 Chron. xxvi. 15, from *hhishsh^{e}von*, which is as little distinguished from the formation *hh$\check{e}$shbon*, as *hhizzayon* from *hh$\check{e}$zyon*), viz. of means and ways, by which they go astray from the normal natural development into abnormities. In other words: inventive refined degeneracy has come into the place of moral simplicity, ἁπλότης (2 Chron. xi. 3). As to the opinion that caricatures of true human nature, contrasts between the actual and that which ought to be (the ideal), are common, particularly among the female sex, the author has testimonies in support of it from all nations. It is confirmed by the primitive history itself, in which the woman appears as the first that was led astray, and as the seducer (cf. *Psychol.* pp. 103-106). With reference to this an old proverb says: "Women carry in themselves a frivolous mind," *Kiddushin* 80b.[2] And because a woman, when she has fallen into evil, surpasses a man in fiendish superiority therein, the Midrash reckons under this passage before us fifteen things of which the one is worse than the other; the thirteenth is death, and the fourteenth a bad woman.[3] Hitzig supposes that the author has before him as his model Agathoclea, the mistress of the fourth Ptolemy Philopator. But also the history of the Persian Court affords dreadful examples of the truth of the proverb: "Woe to the age whose leader is a woman;"[4] and generally the harem is a den of female wickedness.

---

[1] If we derive this word from *hh$\check{e}$shbon*, the *Dagesh* in the שׁ is the so-called *Dag. diriniens.*   [2] Cf. Tendlau's *Sprichw.* (1860), No. 733.
[3] Duke's *Rabb. Blumenl.* (1844), No. 32.   [4] *Ibid.* No. 118.

Wise Conduct towards the King and under Despotic Oppression,
viii. 1–9.

If now the sentence first following sings the praise of wisdom, it does not stand out of connection with the striving after wisdom, which the author, vii. 23 f., has confessed, and with the experiences announced in vii. 25 ff., which have presented themselves to him in the way of the search after wisdom, so far as wisdom was attainable. It is the incomparable superiority of the wise man which the first verse here announces and verifies.

viii. 1. "Who is like the wise? and who understandeth the interpretation of things? The wisdom of a man maketh his face bright, and the rudeness of his face is changed." Unlike this saying: "Who is like the wise?" are the formulas מִי חָכָם, Hos. xiv. 10, Jer. xi. 11, Ps. cvii. 43, which are compared by Hitzig and others. "Who is like the wise?" means: Who is equal to him? and this question, after the scheme מִי־כָמֹכָה, Ex. xv. 11, presents him as one who has not his like among men. Instead of כְּהֶ֫ the word כֶּחָכָם might be used, after לֶחָכָם, ii. 16, etc. The syncope is, as at Ezek. xl. 25, omitted, which frequently occurs, particularly in the more modern books, Ezek. xlvii. 22; 2 Chron. x. 7, xxv. 10, xxix. 27; Neh. ix. 19, xii. 38. The regular giving of *Dagesh* to כְּ after מִי, with *Jethib*, not *Mahpach*, is as at ver. 7 after כִּי; *Jethib* is a disjunctive. The second question is not וּמִי כְּיוֹדֵעַ, but וּמִי יוֹדֵעַ, and thus does not mean: who is like the man of understanding, but: who understands, viz. as the wise man does; thus it characterizes the incomparably excellent as such. Many interpreters (Oetinger, Ewald, Hitz., Heiligst., Burg., Elst., Zöck.) persuade themselves that פֵּשֶׁר דָּבָר is meant of the understanding of the proverb, 8*b*. The absence of the art., says Hitzig, does not mislead us: of a proverb, viz. the following; but in this manner determinate ideas may be made from all indeterminate ones. Rightly, Gesenius: *explicationem ullius rei;* better, as at vii. 8: *cujusvis rei*. Ginsburg compares נְבוֹן דָּבָר, 1 Sam. xvi. 18, which, however, does not mean him who has the knowledge of things, but who is well acquainted with words. It is true that here also the chief idea פֵּשֶׁר first leads to the meaning *verbum* (according to which the LXX., Jer., the Targ., and Syr. translate; the Venet.: ἑρμηνείαν λόγου); but since the unfolding or explaining (*pēshĕr*) refers to the actual contents of the thing spoken, *verbi* and *rei* coincide. The wise man knows how to explain difficult things, to unfold mysterious things; in short, he understands how to go to the foundation of things.

What now follows, 1*b*, might be introduced by the confirming

כִּי, but after the manner of synonymous parallelism it places itself in the same rank with 1a, since, that the wise man stands so high, and no one like him looks through the centre of things, is repeated in another form: "Wisdom maketh his face bright" is thus to be understood after Ps. cxix. 130 and xix. 9, wisdom draws the veil from his countenance, and makes it clear; for wisdom is related to folly as light is to darkness, ii. 13. The contrast, יְשֻׁ ... וְעֹז ("and the rudeness of his face is changed"), shows, however, that not merely the brightening of the countenance, but in general that intellectual and ethical transfiguration of the countenance is meant, in which at once, even though it should not in itself be beautiful, we discover the educated man rising above the common rank. To translate, with Ewald: and the brightness of his countenance is doubled, is untenable; even supposing that יְשֻׁנֶּא can mean, like the Arab. *yuthattay, duplicatur*, still עֹז, in the meaning of brightness, is in itself, and especially with פָּנָיו, impossible, along with which it is, without doubt, to be understood after *az panim*, Deut. xxviii. 50, Dan. viii. 23, and *hē'ēz panim*, Prov. vii. 13, or *b'phanim*, Prov. xxi. 29, so that thus עֹז פנים has the same meaning as the post-bibl. עַזּוּת פנים, stiffness, hardness, rudeness of countenance = boldness, want of bashfulness, regardlessness, *e.g. Shabbath* 30b, where we find a prayer in these words: O keep me this day from עַזֵּי פנים and from פ' עַזּוּת (that I may not incur the former or the latter). The Talm. *Taanith* 7b, thus explaining, says: "Every man to whom פ' עַזּוּת belongs, him one may hate, as the scripture says, וְעֹז ... יִשָּׂנֵא (do not read יְשֻׁנֶּא)." The LXX. translates μισηθήσεται [will be hated], and thus also the Syr.; both have thus read as the Talm. has done, which, however, bears witness in favour of יְשֻׁנֶּא as the traditional reading. It is not at all necessary, with Hitzig, after Zirkel, to read יְשֻׁנֶּא: but boldness disfigureth his countenance; עֹז in itself alone, in the meaning of boldness, would, it is true, along with פניו as the obj. of the verb, be tenable; but the change is unnecessary, the passive affords a perfectly intelligible meaning: the boldness, or rudeness, of his visage is changed, viz. by wisdom (Böttch., Ginsb., Zöckl.). The verb שָׁנָה (שְׁנָא, Lam. iv. 1) means, Mal. iii. 6, merely "to change, to become different;" the *Pih.* שִׁנָּה, Jer. lii. 33, שִׁנָּא, 2 Kings xxv. 29, denotes in these two passages a change *in melius*, and the proverb of the Greek, Sir. xiii. 24,—

Καρδία ἀνθρώπου ἀλλοιοῖ τὸ πρόσωπον αὐτοῦ,
ἐάν τε εἰς ἀγαθὰ ἐάν τε εἰς κακά,

is preserved to us in its original form thus:

לֵב אָדָם יְשַׁנֶּא פָּנָיו
בֵּין לְטוֹב וּבֵין לְרָע:

so that thus שַׁנֵּא, in the sense of being changed as to the sternness of the expression of the countenance, is as good as established. What Ovid says of science: *emollit mores nec sinit esse feros*, thus tolerably falls in with what is here said of wisdom: Wisdom gives bright eyes to a man, a gentle countenance, a noble expression; it refines and dignifies his external appearance and his demeanour; the hitherto rude external, and the regardless, selfish, and bold deportment, are changed into their contraries. If, now, ver. 1 is not to be regarded as an independent proverb, it will bear somewhat the relation of a prologue to what follows. Luther and others regard 1a as of the nature of an epilogue to what goes before; parallels, such as Hos. xiv. 10, make that appear probable; but it cannot be yielded, because the words are not מי חכם, but מי כהח׳. But that which follows easily subordinates itself to ver. 1, in as far as fidelity to duty and thoughtfulness amid critical social relations are proofs of that wisdom which sets a man free from impetuous rudeness, and fits him intelligently and with a clear mind to accommodate himself to the time.

Ver. 2. The faithfulness of subjects, Koheleth says, is a religious duty: "I say: Observe well the king's command, and that because of the oath of God." The author cannot have written 2a as it here stands; אֲנִי hovers in the air. Hitzig reads, with Jerome, שְׁמֹר, and hears in vers. 2–4 a servile person speaking who veils himself in the cloak of religion; in vers. 5–8 follows the *censura* of this corrupt theory. But we have already (*vid.* above, p. 213) remarked that ver. 2 accords with Rom. xiii. 5, and is thus not a corrupt theory; besides, this distribution of the expressions of the Book of Koheleth between different speakers is throughout an expedient resting on a delusion. Luther translates: I keep the word of the king, and thus reads אֶשְׁמֹר; as also does the *Jer. Sanhedrin* 21b, and *Koheleth rabba*, under this passage: I observe the command of the king, of the queen. In any case, it is not God who is meant here by "the king;" the words: "and that because of the oath of God," render this impossible, although Hengst. regards it as possible; for (1) "the oath of God" he understands, against all usage, of the oath which is taken to God; and (2) he maintains that in the O. T. scarcely any passage is to be found where obedience to a heathen master is set forth as a religious duty. But the prophets show themselves as morally great men, without a stain, just in this, that they decidedly condemn and unhesitatingly chastise any breach of faith committed against the Assyrian or Chaldean oppressor, *e.g.* Isa. xxviii. 15, xxx. 1; Ezek. xvii. 15; cf. Jer. xxvii. 12. However, although we understand *mĕlĕk* not of the heavenly, but of an earthly king, yet אֲשְׁמֹר does not recommend itself, for Koheleth records his experience, and derives therefrom warnings and admonitions; but he never in this manner presents himself as an example of virtue. The paraenetic imper. שְׁמֹר is thus not to be touched. Can we then use *ani* elliptically, as equivalent to "I say as follows"? Passages such as Jer. xx. 10 (Elst.), where לאמר is omitted, are not at all the same. Also Ezek. xxxiv. 11, where הנני is strengthened by *ani*, and the expression is not elliptical, is not in point here. And Isa. v. 9 also does not apply to the case of the supposed ellipsis here. In an ingenious bold manner the Midrash helps itself in Lev. xviii. and Num. xiv., for with reference to the self-introduction of royal words like אני פרעה it explains: "Observe the *I* from the mouth of the king." This explanation is worthy of mention, but it has little need of refutation; it is also contrary to the accentuation, which gives *Pashta* to *ani*, as to רָאֹה, vii. 27, and לְבַד, vii. 29, and thus places it by itself. Now,

since this elliptical *I*, after which we would place a colon, is insufferably harsh, and since also it does not recommend itself to omit it, as is done by the LXX., the Targ., and Syr.,—for the words must then have a different order, שְׁמֹר פי המלך,—it is most advisable to supply אָמַרְתִּי, and to write אני אָמ׳ or אָמ׳, after ii. 1, iii. 17, 18. We find ourselves here, besides, within an *I* section, consisting of sentences interwoven in a Mashal form. The admonition is solemnly introduced, since Koheleth, himself a king, and a wise man in addition, gives it the support of the authority of his person, in which it is to be observed that the religious motive introduced by ו *explic.* (vid. Ewald, § 340b) is not merely an appendix, but the very point of the admonition. Kleinert, incorrectly: "Direct thyself according to the mouth of the king, and that, too, as according to an oath of God." Were this the meaning, then we might certainly wish that it were a servile Alexandrian court-Jew who said it. But why should that be the meaning? The meaning "*wegen*" [because of], which is usually attributed to the word-connection על־דברת here and at iii. 18, vii. 14, Kleinert maintains to be an arbitrary invention. But it alone fits these three passages, and why an arbitrary invention? If עַל־דְּבַר, Ps. xlv. 5, lxxix. 9, etc., means "*von wegen*" [on account of], then also על־דברת will signify "*propter rationem, naturam*," as well as (Ps. cx. 4) *ad rationem*. שֶׁבַּ אֶל is, as elsewhere שב׳ יח׳, *e.g.* Ex. xxii. 10, a promise given under an appeal to God, a declaration or promise strengthened by an oath. Here it is the oath of obedience which is meant, which the covenant between a king and his people includes, though it is not expressly entered into by individuals. The king is designated neither as belonging to the nation, nor as a foreigner; that which is said is valid also in the case of the latter. Daniel, Nehemiah, Mordecai, etc., acted in conformity with the words of Koheleth, and the oath of vassalage which the kings of Israel and Judah swore to the kings of Assyria and of Babylon is regarded by the prophets of both kingdoms as binding on king and people (*vid.* above, p. 213).

Ver. 3. The warning, corresponding to the exhortation, now follows: One must not thoughtlessly avoid the duty of service and homage due to the king: "Hasten not to go away from him: join not in an evil matter; for he executeth all that he desireth." Regarding the connection, of two verbs with one idea, lying before us in תֵּלֵךְ ... אַל, as *e.g.* at Zech. viii. 15, Hos. i. 6, *vid.* Gesen. § 142. 3*b*. Instead of this sentence, we might use אַל־תבהל לָלֶכֶת מִפָּנָיו, as *e.g. Aboth* v. 8: "The wise man does not interrupt another, and hastens not to answer," *i.e.* is not too hasty in answering. As with עִם, to be with the king, iv. 15 = to hold with him, so here הלך מפניו means to take oneself away from him, or, as it is expressed in x. 4, to leave one's station; cf. Hos. xi. 2: "They (the prophets of Jahve) called to them, forthwith they betook themselves away from them." It is possible that in the choice of the expression, the phrase נבהל מפני, "to be put into a state of alarm before any one," Job xxiii. 15, was not without influence. The indef. דָּבָר רָע, Deut. xvii. 1, xxiii. 10, cf. xiii. 12, xix. 20, 2 Kings iv. 41, etc., is to be referred (with Rosenm., Knobel, Bullock, and others) to undertakings which aim at resisting the will of the king, and reach their climax in conspiracy against the king's throne and life (Prov. xxiv. 21*b*). אַל־תַּעֲמֹד בְּ might mean: persist not in it; but the warning does not presuppose that the entrance thereon had already taken place, but seeks to prevent it, thus: enter not, go not, engage not, like *'amad b*ederek*, Ps. i. 1; *'amad babrith*, 2 Kings xxiii. 3; cf. Ps. cvi. 23; Jer. xxiii. 18. Also the Arab. *'amada li = intendit, proposuit sibi rem*, is compared; it is used in the general sense of "to make toward something, to stretch to something." Otherwise Ewald, Elst., Ginsb., and Zöckl.: stand not at an evil word (of the king), provoking him to anger thereby still more,—against ver. 5, where דבר רע, as generally (cf. Ps. cxli. 4), means an evil thing, and against the close connection of עמד בְּ, which is to be presupposed. Hitzig even: stand not at an evil command, *i.e.* hesitate not to do even that which is evil, which the king commands, with the remark that here a *servilismus* is introduced as speaking, who, in saying of the king, "All that pleaseth him he doeth," uses words which are used only of God the Almighty, John i. 14, Ps. xxxiii. 9, etc. Hengst., Hahn, Dale, and others therefore dream of the heavenly King in the text. But proverbs of the earthly king, such as Prov. xx. 2, say the very same thing; and if the Mishna *Sanhedrin* ii. 2, to which Tyler refers, says of the king, "The king cannot himself be a judge, nor can any one judge him; he does not give evidence, and no evidence can be given against him," a sovereignty is thus attributed to the king, which is formulated in 3*b* and established in the verse following.

Ver. 4. "Inasmuch as the word of a king is powerful; and who can say to him: What doest thou?" The same thing is said of God, Job ix. 12, Isa. xlv. 9, Dan. iv. 32, Wisd. xii. 12, but also of the king, especially of the unlimited monarch of a despotic state. *Baasher* verifies as בְּשֶׁ at ii. 16; cf. Gen. xxxix. 9, 23; Greek, ἐν ᾧ and ἐφ' ᾧ. Burger arbitrarily: *quae dixit* (דִּבֶּר for דָּבָר), *rex, in ea potestatem habet*. The adjectival impers. use of the noun *shilton = potestatem habens*, is peculiar; in the Talm. and Midrash, *shilton*, like the Assyr. *siltannu*,[1] means the ruler (*vid.* under v. 8). That which now follows is not, as Hitzig supposes, an opposing voice which makes itself heard, but as ver. 2 is compared with Rom. xiii. 5, so is ver. 5 with Rom. xiii. 3.

Ver. 5. "Whoso remaineth true to the commandment will experience nothing evil; and the heart of the wise man will know a time and judicial decision." That by מִצְוָה is here to be understood not the commandment of God, at least not immediately, as at Prov. xix. 16 (Ewald), but that of the king, and generally an injunction and appointment of the superior authority, is seen from the context, which treats not of God, but of the ruler over a state. Knobel and others explain: He who observeth the commandment engageth not with an evil thing, and the wise mind knoweth time and right. But ידע is never thus used (the author uses for this, עָמַד בְּ), and the same meaning is to be supposed for the repeated יֵדַע: it means to arrive at the knowledge of; in the first instance: to suffer, Ezek. xxv. 14; cf. Isa. ix. 8; Hos. ix. 7; in the second, to experience, Josh. xxiv. 31; Ps. xvi. 11. It may also, indeed, be translated after ix. 12: a wise heart knoweth time and judgment, viz. that they will not fail; but why should we not render יֵדַע both times fut., since nothing stands in the way? We do not translate: a wise heart,

---

[1] *Vid.* Fried. Delitzsch's *Assyr. Stud.* p. 129 f.

a wise mind (Knobel), although this is possible, 1 Kings iii. 12 (cf. Ps. xc. 12), but: the heart of a wise man, which is made more natural by x. 2, Prov. xvi. 23. The heart of a wise man, which is not hurried forward by dynastic oppression to a selfish forgetfulness of duty, but in quietness and hope (Lam. iii. 26) awaits the interposition of God, will come to the knowledge that there is an *eth*, a time, when oppression has an end, and a *mishpat*, when it suffers punishment. Well adapted to the sense in which *eth* is here used is the remark of Elia Levita in his *Tishbi*, that זְמָן corresponds to the German *Zeit* and the Romanic *tempo*, but עֵת to the German *Ziel* and the Romanic *termino*. The LXX. translates καιρὸν κρίσεως; and, in fact, עת ומ׳ is a hendidays, which, however, consists in the division of one conception into two. The heart of the wise man remaining true to duty will come to learn that there is a terminus and judicial decision, for everything has an end when it falls under the fate for which it is ripe, especially the sinner.

Ver. 6. "For there is a time and decision for everything, for the wickedness of man becomes too great." From 6*a* there follow four clauses with כִּי; by such monotonous repetition of one and the same word, the author also elsewhere renders the exposition difficult, affording too free a space for understanding the כי as confirming, or as hypothetical, and for co-ordinating or subordinating to each other the clauses with כי. Presupposing the correctness of our exposition of 5*a*, the clause 6*a* with כי may be rendered parenthetically, and that with כי in 6*b* hypothetically: "an end and decision the heart of the wise man will come to experience (because for everything there is an end and decision), supposing that the wickedness of man has become great upon him, *i.e.* his burden of guilt has reached its full measure." We suppose thereby (1) that רַבָּה, which appears from the accent on the ult. to be an adj., can also be the 3d pret., since before ע the tone has gone back to *áh* (cf. Gen. xxvi. 10; Isa. xi. 1), to protect it from being put aside; but generally the accenting of such forms of ע״ע hovers between the penult. and the ult., *e.g.* Ps. lxix. 5, lv. 22; Prov. xiv. 19. Then (2) that עָלָיו goes back to הָאָדָם, without distinction of persons, which has a support in vi. 1, and that thus a great רָעָה is meant lying upon man, which finally finds its punishment. But this view of the relation of the clauses fails, in that it affords no connection for ver. 7. It appears to be best to co-ordinate all the four כי as members of one chain of proof, which reaches its point in 8*b*, viz. in the following manner: the heart of a wise man will see the time and the judgment of the ruler, laying to his heart the temptation to rebellion; for (1) as the author has already said, iii. 17: "God will judge the righteous as well as the wicked, for there is with Him a time for every purpose and for every act;" (2) the wickedness of man (by which, as ver. 9 shows, despots are aimed at) which he has committed, becomes great upon him, so that suddenly at once the judgment of God will break in upon him; (3) he knows not what will be done; (4) no one can tell him how (*quomodo*) it, the future, will be, so that he might in any way anticipate it—the judgment will overwhelm him unexpectedly and irretrievably: wickedness does not save its possessor.

Vers. 7 and 8 thus continue the *For* and *For:* "For he knoweth not that which shall be; for who can tell him how it will be? There is no man who has power over the wind, to restrain the wind; and no one has authority over the day of death; and there is no discharge in the war; and wickedness does not save its possessor." The actor has the sin upon himself, and bears it; if it reaches the terminus of full measure, it suddenly overwhelms him in punishment, and the too great burden oppresses its bearer (Hitzig, under Isa. xxiv. 20). This עת ומשׁ comes unforeseen, for he (the man who heaps up sins) knoweth not *id quod fiet*; it arrives unforeseen, for *quomodo fiet*, who can show it to him? Thus, *e.g.*, the tyrant knows not that he will die by assassination, and no one can say to him how that will happen, so that he might make arrangements for his protection. Rightly the LXX. καθὼς ἔσται; on the contrary, the Targ., Hitzig, and Ginsburg: when it will be;[1] but בַּאֲשֶׁר signifies *quum*, iv. 17, v. 3, viii. 16, but not *quando*, which must be expressed by מָתַי (Mishnic אֵימָתַי, אֵימָה).

Now follows the concluding thought of the four כּי, whereby 5b is established. There are four impossibilities enumerated; the fourth is the point of the enumeration constructed in the form of a numerical proverb. (1) No man has power over the wind, to check the wind. Ewald, Hengst., Zöckl. and others understand רוּחַ, with the Targ., Jerome, and Luther, of the Spirit (רוח חיים); but man can limit this physically when he puts a violent termination to life, and must restrain it morally by ruling it, Prov. xvi. 32, xxv. 28. On the contrary, the wind הרוח is, after xi. 5, incalculable, and to rule over it is the exclusive prerogative of Divine Omnipotence, Prov. xxx. 4.

The transition to the second impossibility is mediated by this, that in רוח, according to the *usus loq.*, the ideas of the breath of animal life, and of wind as the breath as it were of the life of the whole of nature, are interwoven. (2) No one has power over the

---

[1] The Venet. ἐν ᾧ, as if the text had בַּאֲשֶׁר.

day of death: death, viz. natural death, comes to a man without his being able to see it before, to determine it, or to change it. With שַׁלִּיט there here interchanges שִׁלְטוֹן, which is rendered by the LXX. and Venet. as abstr., also by the Syr. But as at Dan. iii. 2, so also above at ver. 4, it is concr., and will be so also in the passage before us, as generally in the Talm. and Midrash, in contradistinction to the abstr., which is שִׁלְטָן, after the forms דָּרְבָן, אָבְדָן, etc., *e.g.* *Bereshith rabba*, c. 85 *extr.*: " Every king and ruler שלטון who had not a שולטן, a command (government, sway) in the land, said that that did not satisfy him, the king of Babylon had to place an under-Caesar in Jericho," etc.[1] Thus: no man possesses rule or is a ruler ...

A transition is made from the inevitable law of death to the inexorable severity of the law of war; (3) there is no discharge, no dispensation, whether for a time merely (*missio*), or a full discharge (*dimissio*), in war, which in its fearful rigour (*vid.* on the contrary, Deut. xx. 5-8) was the Persian law (cf. above, p. 214). Even so, every possibility of escape is cut off by the law of the divine requital; (4) wickedness will not save (מִלֵּט, causative, as always) its lord (cf. the proverb: "Unfaithfulness strikes its own master") or possessor; *i.e.* the wicked person, when the עת ומ' comes, is hopelessly lost. Grätz would adopt the reading עֹשֶׁר instead of רֶשַׁע; but the fate of the בַּעַל רֶשַׁע, or of the רָשָׁע, is certainly that to which the concatenation of thought from ver. 6 leads, as also the disjunctive accent at the end of the three first clauses of ver. 8 denotes. But that in the words *ba'al resha'* (not בַּעֲלֵי) a despotic king is thought of (בְּעָלָיו, as at v. 10, 12, vii. 12; Prov. iii. 27; cf. under Prov. i. 19), is placed beyond a doubt by the epilogistic verse:

Ver. 9. "All that I have seen, and that, too, directing my heart to all the labour that is done under the sun: to the time when a man rules over a man to his hurt." The relation of the clauses is mistaken by Jerome, Luther, Hengst., Vaih., Ginsburg, and others, who begin a new clause with עֵת: "there is a time," etc.; and Zöckl., who ventures to interpret עת וגו' as epexegetical of כָּל־מַעֲ' וגו' ("every work that is done under the sun"). The clause וְנָתוֹן is an adverbial subordinate clause (*vid.* under iv. 2): *et advertendo quidem animum*. עֵת is accus. of time, as at Jer. li. 33; cf. Ps. iv. 8, the relation of *'eth asher*, like מָקוֹם שׁ', i. 7, xi. 3. All that, viz. the wisdom of patient fidelity to duty, the perniciousness of revolutionary selfishness, and the suddenness with which the judgment comes, he has

---

[1] Regarding the distinction between שִׁלְטוֹן and שִׁלְטָן, *vid.* Baer's *Abodath Jisrael*, p. 385.

seen (for he observed the actions done under the sun), with his own eyes, at the time when man ruled over man לְרַע לוֹ, not: to his own [the ruler's] injury (Symm., Jerome), but: to the injury (LXX., Theod., τοῦ κακῶσαι αὐτόν, and thus also the Targ. and Syr.) of this second man; for after 'eth asher, a description and not a judgment was to be expected. The man who rules over man to the hurt of the latter rules as a tyrant; and this whole section, beginning with viii. 1, treats of the right wisdom of life at a time of tyrannical government.

It is with the Righteous as with the Wicked, and with the Wicked as with the Righteous,—it is best to enjoy Life as long as God grants it, viii. 10-15.

The theme of the following section shows itself by "and then" to be cognate. It is the opposition of the fate of the wicked and of the righteous to the inalienable consciousness of a moral government of the world; this opposition comes forth, under the unhappy tyrannical government of which the foregoing section treats, as a prominent phenomenon.

Ver. 10. "And then I have seen the wicked buried, and they came to rest; but away from the holy place they had to depart, and were forgotten in the city, such as acted justly: also this is vain." The double particle בְּכֵן signifies, in such a manner, or under such circumstances; with "I have seen" following, it may introduce an observation coming under that which precedes (בכן = Mishnic בְּכָךְ), or, with the force of the Lat. *inde*, introduce a further observation of that ruler; this temporal signification "then" (= אָז), according to which we have translated, it has in the Targ. (*vid.* Levy's *W. B.*).[1] Apparently the observation has two different classes of men in view, and refers to their fate, contradicting, according to appearance, the rectitude of God. Opposite to the רְשָׁ׳ ("the wicked") stand they who are described as אֲשֶׁר וגו׳: they who have practised what is rightly directed, what stands in a right relation (*vid.* regarding כֵּן, as noun, under Prov. xi. 19), have brought the morally right into practice, *i.e.* have acted with fidelity and honour (עָשָׂה כֵן, as at 2 Kings vii. 9). Koheleth has seen the wicked buried; ראה is followed by the particip. as predic. obj., as is שמע, vii. 21; but קְבוּרִים is not followed by וּבָאִים (which, besides not being distinct enough as *part. perfecti*, would be, as at Neh. xiii. 22, *part. praes.*), but, according to the

---

[1] Cf. וְכֵן, 2 Chron. xxxii. 31; Ewald, § 354*a*; Baer's *Abodath Jisrael*, pp. 384, 386.

favourite transition of the particip. into the finite, Gesen. § 134. 2, by וּבָאוּ, not וּבָאוּ ; for the disjunctive *Rebîa* has the fuller form with יְ; cf. Isa. xlv. 20 with Job xvii. 10, and above, at ii. 23. "To enter in" is here, after Isa. xlvii. 2, = to enter into peace, come to rest.[1] That what follows וּמִמְּ does not relate to the wicked, has been mistaken by the LXX., Aquila, Symm., Theod., and Jerome, who translate by ἐπῃνήθησαν, *laudabantur*, and thus read יִשְׁתַּבְּחוּ (the Hithpa., Ps. cvi. 47, in the pass. sense), a word which is used in the Talm. and Midrash along with יִשְׁתַּבְּחוּ.[2] The latter, testified to by the Targ. and Syr., is without doubt the correct reading : the structure of the antithetical parallel members is chiastic ; the naming of the persons in 1 *a a* precedes that which is declared, and in 1 *a β* it follows it ; cf. Ps. lxx. 5 *b*, lxxv. 9 *b*. The fut. forms here gain, by the retrospective perfects going before, a past signification. מְקוֹם קָדֹ', "the place of the holy," is equivalent to מָקוֹם קָדֹשׁ, as also at Lev. vii. 6. Ewald understands by it the place of burial : "the upright were driven away (cast out) from the holy place of graves." Thus *e.g.* also Zöckl., who renders : but wandered far from the place of the holy . . . those who did righteously, *i.e.* they had to be buried in graves neither holy nor honourable. But this form of expression is not found among the many designations of a burial-place used by the Jews (*vid.* below, xii. 5, and Hamburger's *Real-Encykl. für Bibel u. Talm.*, article "Grab"). God's-acre is called the "good place,"[3] but not the "holy place." The "holy place," if not Jerusalem itself, which is called by Isaiah II. (xlviii. 2), Neh., and Dan., *'ir haqqodesh* (as now *el-kuds*), is the holy ground of the temple of God, the τόπος ἅγιος (Matt. xxiv. 15), as Aquila and Symm. translate. If, now, we find *min* connected with the verb *halak*, it is to be presupposed that the *min* designates the point of departure, as also מן הָשְׁלַךְ, Isa. xiv. 19. Thus not : to wander far from the holy place ; nor as Hitz., who points יְהַלְּכוּ : they pass away (perish) far from the holy place. The subject is the being driven away from the holy place, but not as if יְהַלֵּ' were causative, in the sense of יוֹלִיכוּ, and meant *ejiciunt*, with an indef. subj. (Ewald, Heiligst., Elst.),—it is also, iv. 15, xi. 9, only the intens. of *Kal*,—but יְהַלֵּ' denotes, after Ps. xxxviii. 7, Job xxx. 28, cf. xxiv. 10, the meditative, dull, slow walk of those who are compelled

---

[1] Cf. Zunz, *Zur Gesch. u. Literatur*, pp. 356–359.

[2] The Midrash *Tanchuma*, Par. יתרו, *init.*, uses both expressions ; the Talm. *Gittin* 56 *b*, applies the passage to Titus, who took away the furniture of the temple to magnify himself therewith in his city.

[3] *Vid.* Tendlau's *Sprichw.*, No. 431.

against their will to depart from the place which they love (Ps. xxvi. 8, lxxxiv. 2 ff.). They must go forth (whither, is not said, but probably into a foreign country; cf. Amos vii. 17), and only too soon are they forgotten in the city, viz. the holy city; a younger generation knows nothing more of them, and not even a gravestone brings them back to the memory of their people. Also this is a vanity, like the many others already registered—this, viz., that the wicked while living, and also in their death, possess the sacred native soil; while, on the contrary, the upright are constrained to depart from it, and are soon forgotten. Divine rectitude is herein missed. Certainly it exists, and is also recognised, but it does not show itself always when we should expect it, nor so soon as appears to us to be salutary.

Ver. 11. "Because judgment against the work of the wicked man is not speedily executed, for this reason the heart of the children of men is full within them, to this, that they do evil." The clause with *asher* is connected first with the foregoing *gam-zeh havel*: thus vain, after the nature of a perverted world (*inversus ordo*), events go on, because ... (*asher*, as at iv. 3, vi. 12*b*; cf. Deut. iii. 24); but the following clause with '*al-ken* makes this clause with *asher* reflex. an antecedent of itself (*asher* = '*al-asher*)—originally it is not meant as an antecedent. פִּתְגָם[1] (here to be written after נַעֲשָׂה, with פ *raph.*, and, besides, also with ג *raph.*), in the postexilian books, is the Persian *paigam*, Armen. *patgam*, which is derived from the ancient Pers. *paiti-gama*: "Something that has happened, tidings, news." The Heb. has adopted the word in the general sense of "sentence;" in the passage before us it signifies the saying or sentence of the judge, as the Pers. word, like the Arab. *naban*, is used principally of the sayings of a prophet (who is called *peighámbar*). Zirkel regards it as the Greek φθέγμα; but thus, also, the words אָמָל, אַפִּרְיוֹן strangely agree in sound with σμίλη, φορεῖον, without being borrowed from the Greek. The long *a* of the word is, as Elst. shows, i. 20, invariable; also here פִּתְגָם is the constr. To point פִּתְגַם, with Heiligst. and Burg., is thus unwarrantable. It is more remarkable that the word is construed fem. instead of mas. For since אֵין is construed[2] neither in the bibl. nor in the Mishnic

---

[1] With ג *raph.* in H. P. and the older edd., as also Esth. i. 20; Dan. iii. 16. Thus also the punctuator Jekuthiél in his *En hakore* to Esth. i. 20.

[2] Ginsburg points in favour of נַעֲשָׂה as fin. to Ex. iii. 2, but there אָבַל is particip.; to Jer. xxxviii. 5, but there יוּבַל (if it is not to be read יְבַל) represents an attributive clause; and to Job xxxv. 15, but there the word is rightly pointed אַיִן, not אֵין; and this, like the vulg. Arab. *laysa*, is used as an emphatic לֹא.

style with the finite of the verb, נַעֲשָׂה is not the 3d *pret.*, but the particip. It is not, however, necessary, with Hitz., to read נֶעֶשְׂתָה. The foreign word, like the (Arab.) *firdans*, παράδεισος, admits of use in the double gend. (Ewald, § 174*g*); but it is also possible that the fem. נַעֲשָׂה is *per. attract.* occasioned by הָרָעָה, as Kimchi, *Michlol* 10*a*, supposes (cf. besides, under x. 15). מַעֲשֵׂה is const. governed by *phithgam*, and *hara'ah* is thus obj. gen. The LXX., Syr., and Jerome read מֵעֹשֵׂי, which would be possible only if *phithgam min*—after the analogy of the Heb.-Aram. phrase, *niphra'* (*'ithp^era'*) *min*, to take one's due of any one, *i.e.* to take vengeance on him, to punish him —could mean the full execution of punishment on any one; but it means here, as Jerome rightly translates, *sententia ;* impossible, however, with *me'ose hara'ah, sententia contra malos.* Hengst. supposes that not only the traditional text, but also the accentuation, is correct, for he construes: because a sentence (of the heavenly Judge) is not executed, the work of wickedness is haste, *i.e.* speedy. Thus also Dachselt in the *Biblia accentuata.* Mercerus, on the contrary, remarks that the accents are not in the first instance marks of interpunction, but of cantillation. In fact, genit. word-connections do not exclude the keeping them asunder by distinctives such as *Pashta* and *Tiphcha,* Isa. x. 2, and also *Zakeph,* as *e.g.* Esth. i. 4. The LXX. well renders: "Therefore the heart of the sons of men is fully persuaded in them to do evil;" for which Jerome, freely, after Symm.: *absque timore ullo filii hominum perpetrant mala.* The heart of one becomes full to do anything, is = it acquires full courage thereto (Luzzatto, § 590: *gli blastò l'animo*); cf. Esth. vii. 5: "Where is he who has his heart filled to do?" (thus rightly, Keil), *i.e.* whom it has encouraged to so bold an undertaking. בָּהֶם in itself unnecessarily heightens the expression of the inwardness of the destructive work (*vid. Psychol.* p. 151 f.). The sentence of punishment does not take effect *m^ehera,* hastily (adv. accus. for *bimherah,* iv. 12), therefore men are secure, and they give themselves with full, *i.e.* with fearless and shameless, boldness to the practice of evil. The author confirms this further, but not without expressing his own conviction that there is a righteous requital which contradicts this appearance.

Vers. 12, 13. "Because a sinner doeth evil an hundred times, and he becometh old therein, although I know that it will go well with them that fear God, that fear before Him: but it will not go well with the wicked, and he shall not live long, like a shadow; because he feareth not before God." Ewald (whom Heiligst., Elst., and Zöckl. follow), as among the ancients, *e.g.* Mendelssohn, translates ver. 12 : " Though a sinner do evil an hundred times, and live long, yet I know," etc. That an antecedent may begin with *asher* is admissible, Lev. iv. 22, Deut. xviii. 22 ; but in the case lying before us, still less acceptable than at ver. 11. For, in the first place, this *asher* of the antecedent cannot mean "although," but only "considering that;" and in places such as. vi. 3, where this "considering that" may be exchanged with "although," there follows not the part., but the fut. natural to the concessive clause; then, in the second place, by this antecedent rendering of *asher* a closer connection of 12a and 12b is indeed gained, but the mediation of ver. 12 and ver. 11 is lost; in the third place, כי גם, in the meaning "however" (*gam*, ὅμως, with affirmative *ki*), is not found; not *asher*, but just this *ki gam*,[1] signifies, in the passage before us, as at iv. 14, εἰ καί, although,—only a somewhat otherwise applied *gam ki*, Ewald, § 362b, as כי על־כן is a somewhat otherwise applied על־כן כי. Rightly, Hitzig : " In 12a, 11a is again resumed, and it is explained how tardy justice has such a consequence." The sinner is thereby encouraged in sinning, because he does evil, and always again evil, and yet enjoys himself in all the pleasures of long life. Regarding חֹטֶא for חֹטֵא, vid. above, p. 197, 1. מְאָת is = מֵאָה פְעָמִים, an hundred times, as אַחַת, Job xl. 5, is = פַּעַם אַחַת ; Hengst. and others, inexactly: an hundredfold, which would have required the word מָאתַיִם ; and falsely, Ginsburg, with the Targ.: an hundred years, which would have required מֵאָה, scil. שָׁנָה, Gen. xvii. 17. This *centies* (Jerome) is, like מֵאָה, scil. בָּנִים, vi. 3, a round number for a great many, as at Prov. xvii. 10, and frequently in the Talm. and Midrash, *e.g. Wajikra rabba*, c. 27: " an hundred deeply-breathed sighs (מאה פעיות) the mother gave forth."[2] The meaning of וּמַאֲרִיךְ לוֹ is in general clear: he becomes therein old. Jerome, improbable: *et per patientiam sustentatur*, as Mendelssohn: he experiences forbearance, for they supply אפו (Isa. xlviii. 9), and make God the subject. לוֹ is in any case the so-called *dat. ethic.*; and the only question is, whether the doing of evil has to be taken from עֹשֶׂה רָע,[3] as obj. to וּמא: he practises it to him long, or whether, which is more probable, יָמִים is

---

[1] That גַם is not pointed נָם, has its reason in the disjunctive *Jethîb* with כי, which is not interchanged with the conjunctive *Mahpach*. Thus, viii. 1, 'מִי כְּ, and viii. 7, 'כִּי כְּ.

[2] Vid. Jac. Reifmann in the *Zeitsch.*, המגיד, 1874, p. 342.

[3] We expect these two words (cf. Gen. xxxi. 12) with the retrogression of the tone ; but as this ceases, as a rule, with *Mercha* before *Tifcha* and *Pashta*, Gen. xlvii. 3, Ex. xviii. 5, Deut. iv. 42, xix. 4, Isa. x. 14 (cf. the penult. accent of יֹאכַל, Lev. xxii. 10, 19, and בָּנָה, Gen. iv. 17, with the ult. accent Lev. xxii. 14 ; Hab.

to be supplied after 13*a*, so that הַאֲרִיךְ signifies to live long, as at Prov. xxviii. 2, to last long; the *dat. ethic.* gives the idea of the feeling of contentment connected with long life: he thereupon sins wantonly, and becomes old in it in good health.

That is the actual state of the case, which the author cannot conceal from himself; although, on the other hand, as by way of limitation he adds *ki ... ani*, he well knows that there is a moral government of the world, and that this must finally prevail. We may not translate: that it should go well, but rather: that it must go well; but there is no reason not to interpret the fut. as a pure indic.: that it shall go well, viz. finally,—it is a postulate of his consciousness which the author here expresses; that which exists in appearance contradicts this consciousness, which, however, in spite of this, asserts itself. That to לְיִרְ' הָאֱלֹ' the clause אֲשֶׁר מִפְּ', explaining *idem per idem*, is added, has certainly its reason in this, that at the time of the author the name " fearers of God " [*Gottesfürchtige*] had come into use. "The fearers of God, who fear before (מִלְּפָנֵי, as at iii. 14) Him," are such as are in reality what they are called.

In ver. 13, Hitzig, followed by Elster, Burg., and Zöckl., places the division at יָמִים: like the shadow is he who fears not before God. Nothing can in point of syntax be said against this (cf. 1 Chron. xxix. 15), although בַּצֵּל אֲשֶׁר, " like the shadow is he who," is in point of style awkward. But that the author did not use so rude a style is manifest from vi. 12, according to which בצל is rightly referred to יָמִים ... וְלֹא־. Is then the shadow, asks Hitzig, because it does not "prolong its days," therefore קְצַר יָמִים? How subtle and literal is this use of יָמִים! Certainly the shadow survives not a day; but for that very reason it is short-lived, it may even indeed be called קצר ימים, because it has not existence for a single day. In general, *qetsel*, ὡς σκιά, is applicable to the life of all men, Ps. cxliv. 4, Wisd. ii. 5, etc. It is true of the wicked, if we keep in view the righteous divine requital, especially that he is short-lived like the shadow, "because he has no fear before God," and that in consequence of this want of fear his life is shortened by his sin inflicting its own punishment, and by the act of God. *Asher*, 13*b*, as at 11*a*, 12*a*, is the relative conj. Also in ver. 14, אשר (שׁ) as a pronoun, and אשר (שׁ) as a conj., are mixed together. After the author has declared the reality of a moral government of the world as an inalienable fact of human consciousness, and particularly of his own consciousness, he places over against this fact ii. 12), so with *Mercha* sometimes also before other disjunctives, as here before *Tebir*.

of consciousness the actual state of things partly at least contradicting it.

Ver. 14. "There is a vanity which is done on the earth; that there be just men, to whom it happeneth according to the conduct of the wicked; and that there be wicked men, to whom it happeneth according to the conduct of the righteous—I said, that also this is vain." The limiting clause with *ki gam*, 12*b*, 13, is subordinated to the observation specified in vers. 10–12*a*, and the confirmation of it is continued here in ver. 14. Regarding מַגִּיעַ, to happen, *vid.* above, p. 193, under נָגַע. Jerome translates כְּמַ׳ הָר׳ by *quasi opera egerint impiorum*, and כמ׳ הצ׳ by *quasi justorum facta habeant; instar operis* . . . would be better, such as is conformable to the mode of acting of the one and of the other; for כ is in the Semitic style of speech a *nomen*, which annexes to itself the word that follows it in the genitive, and runs through all the relations of case. This contradictory distribution of destiny deceives, misleads, and causes to err; it belongs to the illusory shadowy side of this present life, it is a *hevel*. The concluding clause of this verse: "I said, that also this is vain," begins to draw the *facit* from the observation, and is continued in the verse following.

Ver. 15. "And I commended joy, that there is nothing better for a man under the sun than to eat and drink and enjoy himself; and that this accompanies him in his labour throughout all the days of his life, which God hath given him under the sun." We already read the *ultimatum*, 15*a*, in a similar form at ii. 24, iii. 12, 22; cf. v. 17. With הוּא יִלְ׳ either begins a new clause, and the fut. is then jussive: "let this accompany him," or it is subordinate to the foregoing infinitives, and the fut. is then subjunctive: *et ut id eum comitetur.* The LXX. and other Greeks translate less appropriately indicat.: καὶ αὐτὸ συμπροσέσται αὐτῷ. Thus also Ewald, Hengst., Zöckl., and others: and this clings to him, which, however, would rather be expressed by והוא יתרון לו or וה׳ חלקו. The verb לוה (R. לו, to twist, to bend) does not mean to cling to = to remain, but to adhere to, to follow, to accompany; cf. under Gen. xviii. 16. The possibility of the meaning, "to accompany," for the *Kal*, is supported by the derivatives לְוָיָה and לוּי (particularly לְוָיַת הַמֵּתִים, convoy of the dead); the verb, however, in this signification extra-bibl. is found only in *Pih.* and *Hiph.*[1]

[1] *Vid.* Baer in *Abodath Jisrael*, p. 39.

The Fruitlessness of all Philosophizing, viii. 16, 17.

Like the distributions of destiny, so also labour and toil here below appear to the author to be on all sides an inextricable series of mysteries. Far from drawing atheistical conclusions therefrom, he sees in all that is done, viewed in its last causality, the work of God, *i.e.* the carrying out into execution of a divine law, the accomplishment of a divine plan. But this work of God, in spite of all his earnest endeavours, remains for man a subject of research for the future. Treating of this inexplicable difficulty, the words here used by the author himself are also hard to be understood.

Vers. 16, 17. "When I gave my heart to know wisdom, and to view the business which is done on the earth (for neither day nor night doth he see sleep with his eyes): then have I seen all the work of God, that a man is unable to find out the work which is done under the sun: therefore that a man wearieth himself to seek out, and yet findeth not; and although a wise man taketh in hand to know,—he is unable to find." A long period without a premeditated plan has here formed itself under the hand of the author. As it lies before us, it is halved by the *vav* in *v^eraithi* ("then I have seen"); the principal clause, introduced by "when I gave," can nowhere otherwise begin than here; but it is not indicated by the syntactical structure. Yet in Chron. and Neh. apodoses of כאשר begin with the second consec. modus, *e.g.* 1 Chron. xvii. 1, Neh. iv. 1, and frequently; but the author here uses this modus only rarely, and not (*vid.* iv. 1, 7) as a sign of an apodosis.

We consider, first, the protasis, with the parenthesis in which it terminates. The phrase נתן את־הלב ל, to direct the heart, to give attention and effort toward something, we have now frequently met with from i. 13 down. The aim is here twofold: (1) "to know wisdom" (cf. i. 17), *i.e.* to gain the knowledge of that which is wisdom, and which is to be regarded as wisdom, viz. solid knowledge regarding the essence, causes, and objects of things; (2) by such knowledge about that which wisdom is in itself "to see earthly labour," and—this arises from the combination of the two resolutions —to comprehend this labour in accordance with the claims of true wisdom from the point of view of its last ground and aim. Regarding *'inyan, vid.* under iii. 10. "On the earth" and "under the sun" are parallel designations of this world.

With כי גם begins a parenthetical clause. *Ki* may also, it is true, be rendered as at 17*a* : the labour on the earth, that he, etc. (Zöckl.); but this restlessness, almost renouncing sleep, is thereby

CHAP. VIII. 16, 17.   353

pressed too much into the foreground as the special obj. of the $r^e uth$ (therefore Ginsburg introduces "how that"); thus better to render this clause with *ki gam*, as establishing the fact that there is *'inyan*, self-tormenting, restless labour on the earth. Thus also אֵינֶנּוּ is easier explained, which scarcely goes back to *lāadam*, 15a (Hitz.), but shows that the author, by *'inyan*, has specially men in view. גַּם... וּבַלּ֑ is = גם בי' נם בל': as well by day as by night, with the negat. following (cf. Num. xxiii. 25; Isa. xlviii. 8): neither by day nor by night; not only by day, but also in the night, not. "To see sleep" is a phrase occurring only here; cf. Terence, *Heautontim.* iii. 1. 82, *Somnum hercle ego hac nocte oculis non vidi meis*, for which we use the expression: "In this whole night my eyes have seen no sleep." The not wishing to sleep, and not being able to sleep, is such an hyperbole, carrying its limitation in itself, as is found in Cicero (*ad Famil*. vii. 30): *Fuit mirifica vigilantia, qui toto suo consulatu somnum non vidit.*

With 'וֹרְ, "Then I have seen," begins the apodosis: *vidi totum Dei opus non posse hominem assequi.* As at ii. 24b, the author places the obj. in the foreground, and lets the pred. with *ki* follow (for other examples of this so-called antiposis, *vid.* under Gen. i. 4). He sees in the labour here below one side of God's work carrying itself forward amid this restless confusion, and sets forth this work of God, as at iii. 11 (but where the connection of the thoughts is different), as an object of knowledge remaining beyond the reach of man. He cannot come to it, or, as מצא properly means, he reaches not to it, therefore "that a man wearies himself to seek, and yet finds not," *i.e.* that the search on the part of a man with all his endeavours comes not to its aim. בכל אשר [Ewald's emendation, instead of the words of the text before us]: for all this, that *quantumcunque* (Ewald, § 362c), which seems to have been approved of by the LXX., Syr., and Jerome, is rightly rejected by Hitzig; *b*e*shel asher* is Heb., exactly equivalent to Aram. בְּדִיל דְּ, *e.g.* Gen. vi. 3; and is rightly glossed by Rashi, Kimchi, *Michlol* 47b, by בְּשֶׁבִיל שֶׁ and בַּעֲבוּר שֶׁ. The accent dividing the verse stands on *yim*e*tsa*, for to this word extends the first half of the apodosis, with *v*e*gam* begins the second. *Gam im* is = εἰ καί, as *gam ki* is = ἐὰν καί. יאמר is to be understood after 'אמ' אח, vii. 23: also if (although) the wise man resolves to know, he cannot reach that which is to be known. The characteristic mark of the wise man is thus not so much the possession as the striving after it. He strives after knowledge, but the highest problems remain unsolved by him, and his ideal of knowledge unrealized.

The Power of Fate, and the best possible Thing for Man in his Want of Freedom, ix. 1–12.

He cannot attain unto it, for to the thoughts as well as to the acts of man God has put a limit.

ix. 1. " For all this I brought to my consciousness, and all this I sought to make clear to me, that the righteous, and the wise, and their deeds, are in God's hands: neither love nor hatred stands in the knowledge of man, all lies before them." With *ki* follows the verification of what is said in viii. 17*b*, " is unable to find out," from the fact of men, even the best and the wisest of men, being on all sides conditioned. This conditioning is a fact which he layeth to his heart (vii. 2), or (since he here presents himself less as a feeling than as a thinking man, and the heart as reflecting) which he has brought to his consciousness, and which he has sought to bring out into clearness. וְלָבוּר has here not the force of an *inf. absol.*, so that it subordinates itself in an adverbial manner (*et ventilando quidem*)— for it nowhere stands in the same rank with the *inf. absol.*; but the inf. with לְ (לְ) has the force of an intentional (with a tendency) fut., since the governing הָיִיתִי, as at iii. 15*a*, הָיָה, and at Hab. i. 17*b*, יִהְיֶה, is to be supplied (*vid.* comm. on these passages, and under Isa. xliv. 14): *operam dedi ut ventilarem* (*excuterem*), or shorter: *ventilaturus fui*. Regarding the form לָבוּר, which is metapl. for לָבֹר, and the double idea of sifting (particularly winnowing, *ventilare*) of the R. בר, *vid.* under iii. 18. In the post-bibl. Heb. the words לְהַעֲמִיד עַל בּוּרְיוֹ would denote the very same as is here expressed by the brief significant word לָבוּר; a matter in the clearness of its actual condition is called דבר על בוריו (from בָּרִי, after the form חֲלִי, purity, *vid.* Buxtorf's *Lex. Talm.* col. 366). The LXX. and Syr. have read ולבי ראה instead of ולבור, apparently because they could not see their way with it: " And my heart has seen all this." The expression " all this " refers both times to what follows; *asher* is, as at viii. 12, relat. conj., in the sense of ὅτι, *quod*, and introduces, as at vii. 29, cf. viii. 14, the unfolding of the זֶה,—an unfolding, viz., of the conditioning of man, which viii. 17 declared on one side of it, and whose further verification is here placed in view with *ki*, 1*a*. The righteous, and the wise, and their doings, are in God's hand, *i.e.* power (Ps. xxxi. 16 ; Prov. xxi. 1 ; Job xii. 10, etc.); as well their persons as their actions, in respect of their last cause, are conditioned by God, the Governor of the world and the Former of history ; also the righteous and the wise learn to feel this dependence, not only in their being and in what befalls them, but also in their conduct; also this is not fully attained, לֹא

ידם, they are also therein not sufficient of themselves. Regarding 'avadēhĕm, corresponding to the Aram. 'ovadēhon, vid. 'avad, p. 194.

The expression now following cannot mean that man does not know whether he will experience the love or hatred of God, i.e. providences of a happy nature proceeding from the love of God, or of an unhappy nature proceeding from the hatred of God (J. D. Michaelis, Knobel, Vaih., Hengst., Zöckl.), for אַהֲבָה and שִׂנְאָ֫ה are too general for this,—man is thus, as the expression denotes, not the obj., but the subj. to both. Rightly, Hitz., as also Ewald: "Since man has not his actions in his own power, he knows not whether he will love or hate." Certainly this sounds deterministic; but is it not true that personal sympathies and antipathies, from which love and hatred unfold themselves, come within the sphere of man, not only as to their objects, in consequence of the divine arrangement, but also in themselves anticipate the knowledge and the will of man? and is it less true that the love which he now cherishes toward another man changes itself, without his previous knowledge, by means of unexpected causes, into hatred, and, on the other hand, the hatred into love? Neither love nor hatred is the product of a man's self-determination; but self-determination, and with it the function of freedom, begins for the first time over against those already present, in their beginnings. In הכל לפ׳, "by all that is before him," that is brought to a general expression, in which לִפְנֵי has not the ethical meaning proceeding from the local: before them, *prae = penes eos* (vid. Song, under viii. 12a), but the purely local meaning, and referred to time: love, hatred, and generally all things, stand before man; God causes them to meet him (cf. the use of הִקְרָה); they belong to the future, which is beyond his power. Thus the Targ., Symm., and most modern interpreters; on the contrary, Luther: "neither the love nor the hatred of any one which he has for himself," which is, linguistically, purely impossible; Kleinert: "Neither the love nor the hatred of things does man see through, nor anything else which is before his eyes," for which we ought at least to have had the words גם הכל אשר לפניו; and Tyler: "Men discern neither love nor hatred in all that is before them," as if the text were בכל אשר. The future can, it is true, be designated by אַחֲרִית, and the past by לְפָנִים, but according to the most natural way of representation (vid. Orelli's *Synon. der Zeit*, p. 14) the future is that which lies before a man, and the past that which is behind him. The question is of importance, which of the two words הכל לפ׳ has the accent. If the accent be on לפ׳, then the meaning is, that all lies before men deprived of their freedom; if the accent be on הכל, then the meaning is, that all things, events of all kinds, lie before them, and that God determines which shall happen to them. The latter is more accordant with the order of words lying before us, and shows itself to be that which is intended by the further progress of the thoughts. Every possible thing may befall a man—what actually meets him is the determination and providence of God. The determination is not according to the moral condition of a man, so that the one can guide to no certain conclusion as to the other.

Ver. 2. "All is the same which comes to all: one event happens to the righteous and the wicked, to the good and the pure and the impure; to him that sacrificeth, and to him that sacrificeth not: as with the good, so is it with the sinner; with him that sweareth, as with him that feareth an oath." Hitzig translates: "All are alike, one fate comes on all," adding the remark, that to make מקרה אחד at the same time pred. to הכל and subj. to כאשר לכל was, for the punctator, too much. This translation is indeed in matter, as well as in point of syntax, difficult to be comprehended. Rather, with Ewald, translate: All is as if all had one fate (death); but why then this useless *hevel haasher*, only darkening the thought? But certainly, since in הַכֹּל[1] the past is again resumed, it is to be supposed that it does not mean personally, *omnes*, but neut., *omnia*; and לַכֹּל, on the contrary, manifestly refers (as at x. 3) to persons. Herein agreeing with Ewald, and, besides, with Knobel, Zöckl., and others, we accept the interpunction as it lies before us. The apparently meaningless clause, *omnia sicut omnibus*, gives, if we separate *sicut* into *sic* and *ut*, the brief but pregnant thought: All is (thus) as it happens to all, *i.e.* there is no distinction of their experiences nor of their persons; all of every sort happens in the same way to all men of every sort. The thought, written in cyphers in this manner, is then illustrated; the *lameds* following leave no doubt as to the meaning of לכל. Men are classified according to their different kinds. The good and the pure stand opposite the impure; טָמֵא is thus the defiled, Hos. v. 3, cf. Ezek. xxxvi. 25, in body and soul. That the author has here in his mind the precepts of the law regarding the pure and the impure, is to be concluded from the following contrast: he who offers sacrifice, and he who does not offer sacrifice, *i.e.* he who not only does not bring free-will offerings, but not even the sacrifices that are obligatory. Finally, he who swears, and he who is afraid of an oath, are distinguished. Thus, Zech. v. 3, he who

---

[1] The LXX., Syr., and Aq. have read together the end of ver. 1 and the beginning of ver. 2. Here Jerome also is dependent on this mode of reading: *sed omnia in futurum servantur incerta* (הבל).

swears stands along with him who steals. In itself, certainly, swearing an oath is not a sin; in certain circumstances (*vid.* viii. 2) it is a necessary, solemn act (Isa. lxv. 16). But here, in the passage from Zechariah, swearing of an unrighteous kind is meant, *i.e.* wanton swearing, a calling upon God when it is not necessary, and, it may be, even to confirm an untruth, Ex. xx. 7. Compare Matt. v. 34. The order of the words יָרֵא שָׁב (cf. as to the expression, the Mishnic יְרֵא חֵטְא) is as at Nah. iii. 1; Isa. xxii. 2; cf. above, v. 8*b*. One event befalls all these men of different characters, by which here not death exclusively is meant (as at iii. 19, ii. 14), but this only chiefly as the same end of these experiences which are not determined according to the moral condition of men. In the expression of the equality, there is an example of stylistic refinement in a threefold change; כַּטּוֹב כַּח denotes that the experience of the good is the experience of the sinner, and may be translated, "*wie der Gute so der Sünder*" [as the good, so the sinner], as well as "*so der Gute wie der Sünder*" [so the good as the sinner] (cf. Köhler, under Hag. ii. 3). This sameness of fate, in which we perceive the want of the inter-connection of the physical and moral order of the world, is in itself and in its influence an evil matter.

Ver. 3. "This is an evil in all that is done under the sun, that one event happeneth to all: and also the heart of the children of men is full of evil; and madness possesseth their heart during their life, and after it they go to the dead." As זֶה, 1*a*, points to the *asher* following, in which it unfolds itself, so here to the *ki* following. We do not translate: This is the worst thing (Jerome: *hoc est pessimum*), which, after Josh. xiv. 15, Judg. vi. 15, Song i. 8, would have required the words הָרָע בְּכֹל—the author does not designate the equality of fate as the greatest evil, but as an evil mixed with all earthly events. It is an evil in itself, as being a contradiction to the moral order of the world; and it is such also on account of its demoralizing influences. The author here repeats what he had already, viii. 11, said in a more special reference, that because evil is not in this world visibly punished, men become confident and bold in sinning. *V*ᵉ*gam* (referable to the whole clause, at the beginning of which it is placed) stands beside *zeh ra'*, connecting with that which is evil in itself its evil influences. מָלֵא might be an adj., for this (only once, Jer. vi. 11), like the verb, is connected with the accus., *e.g.* Deut. xxxiii. 23. But, since not a statement but a *factum* had to be uttered, it is finite, as at viii. 11. Thus Jerome, after Symm.: *sed et cor filiorum hominum repletur malitia et procacitate juxta cor eorum in vita sua.* Keeping out of view the false *sed*, this translation corresponds to the accenting which gives the conjunctive *Kadma* to רָע. But without doubt an independent substantival clause begins with וְהֹל׳: and madness is in their heart (*vid.* i. 17) their life long; for, without taking heed to God's will and to what is pleasing to God, or seeking after instruction, they think only of the satisfaction of their inclinations and lusts.

"And after that they go to the dead"—they who had so given themselves up to evil, and revelled in fleshly lusts with security, go the way of all flesh, as do the righteous, and the wise, and just, because they know that they go beyond all restraining bounds. Most modern interpreters (Hitz., Ew., etc.) render *aharav*, after Jer. li. 46, adverbially, with the suffix understood neut.: afterwards (Jerome, *post haec*). But at iii. 22, vi. 12, vii. 14, the suffix refers to man: after him, him who liveth here = after he has laid down his life. Why should it not be thus understood also here? It is true בְּחַיָּיו precedes it; but in the reverse way, sing. and plur. also interchange in ver. 1; cf. iii. 12. Rightly the Targ., as with Kleinert and others, we also explain: after their (his) lifetime. A man's life finally falls into the past, it lies behind him, and he goes forth to the dead; and along with self-consciousness, all the pleasures and joy of life at the same time come to an end.

Ver. 4. "For (to him) who shall be always joined to all the living, there is hope: for even a living dog is better than a dead lion." The interrog. מִי אֲשֶׁר, *quis est qui*, acquires the force of a relative, *quisquis* (*quicunque*), and may be interpreted, Ex. xxxii. 33, 2 Sam. xx. 12, just as here (cf. the simple *mi*, v. 9), in both ways; particularly the latter passage (2 Sam. xx. 11) is also analogous to the one before us in the formation of the apodosis. The *Chethîb* יבחר does not admit of any tenable meaning. In conformity with the *usus loq.*, Elster reads מִי אֲשֶׁר יִבְחָר, "who has a choice?" But this rendering has no connection with what follows; the sequence of thoughts fails. Most interpreters, in opposition to the *usus loq.*, by pointing יְבֻחַר or יְבֻחָר, render: Who is (more correctly: will be) excepted? or also: Who is it that is to be preferred (the living or the dead)? The verb בָּחַר signifies to choose, to select; and the choice may be connected with an exception, a preference; but in itself the verb means neither *excipere* nor *praeferre*.[1] All the old translators, with right, follow the *Kerî*, and the Syr. renders it correctly, word for word: to every one who is joined (שׁוּתָּף, Aram. = Heb. חָבֵר) to all the living there is

---

[1] Luther translates, "for to all the living there is that which is desired, namely, hope," as if the text were מָה אֲשֶׁר יִבְחָר.

hope; and this translation is more probable than that on which Symm. ("who shall always continue to live?") and Jerome (*nemo est qui semper vivat et qui hujus rei habeat fiduciam*) proceed: Who is he that is joined to the whole? *i.e.* to the absolute life; or as Hitzig: Who is he who would join himself to all the living (like the saying, "The everlasting Jew")? The expression יֵשׁ בִּטָּ׳ does not connect itself so easily and directly with these two latter renderings as with that we have adopted, in which, as also in the other two, a different accentuation of the half-verse is to be adopted as follows:

כִּי מִי אֲשֶׁר יְחֻבַּר אֶל־כָּל־הַחַיִּים יֵשׁ בִּטָּחוֹן

The accentuation lying before us in the text, which gives a great disjunctive to יבחר as well as to הח׳, appears to warrant the *Chethîb* (cf. Hitzig under Ezek. xxii. 24), by which it is possible to interpret מי . . . יב׳ as in itself an interrog. clause. The *Kerî* יְ׳ does not admit of this, for Dachselt's *quis associabit se (sc. mortuis ? = nemo socius mortuorum fieri vult)* is a linguistic impossibility; the reflex may be used for the pass., but not the pass. for the reflex., which is also an argument against Ewald's translation: Who is joined to the living has hope. Also the Targ. and Rashi, although explaining according to the Midrash, cannot forbear connecting אל כל־הח׳ with יח׳, and thus dividing the verse at הח׳ instead of at יח׳. It is not, however, to be supposed that the accentuation refers to the *Chethîb;* it proceeds on some interpretation, contrary to the connection, such as this: he who is received into God's fellowship has to hope for the full life (in eternity). The true meaning, according to the connection, is this: that whoever (*quicunque*) is only always joined (whether by birth or the preservation of life) to all the living, *i.e.* to living beings, be they who they may, has full confidence, hope, and joy; for in respect to a living dog, this is even better than a dead lion. Symmachus translates: κυνὶ ζῶντι βέλτιόν ἐστιν ἢ λέοντι τεθνηκότι, which Rosenm., Herzf., and Grätz approve of. But apart from the obliquity of the comparison, that with a living dog it is better than with a dead lion, since with the latter is neither good nor evil (*vid.* however, vi. 5b), for such a meaning the words ought to have been: *chělěv hâi tov lo min ha'aryēh hammeth.*

As the verifying clause stands before us, it is connected not with יֵשׁ בִּטָּ׳, but with אֶל כָּל־הָ׳, of that which is to be verified; the לְ gives emphatic prominence (Ewald, § 310b) to the subject, to which the expression refers as at Ps. lxxxix. 19, 2 Chron. vii. 21 (cf. Jer. xviii. 16), Isa. xxxii. 1: A living dog is better than a dead lion, *i.e.* it is better to be a dog which lives, than that lion which is dead. The dog, which occurs in the Holy Scriptures only in relation to a shepherd's dog (Job xxx. 1), and as for the rest, appears as a voracious filthy beast, roaming about without a master, is the proverbial emblem of that which is common, or low, or contemptible, ·1 Sam. xvii. 43; cf. "dog's head," 2 Sam. iii. 8; "dead dog," 1 Sam. xxiv. 15; 2 Sam. ix. 8, xvi. 9. The lion, on the other hand, is the king, or, as Agur (Prov. xxx. 30) calls it, the hero among beasts. But if it be dead, then all is over with its dignity and its strength; the existence of a living dog is to be preferred to that of the dead lion. The art. in הָאֲרִי הַמֵּת is not that denoting species (Dale), which is excluded by *hamměth*, but it points to the carcase of a lion which is present. The author, who elsewhere prefers death and nonentity to life, iv. 2 f., vii. 1, appears to have fallen into contradiction with himself; but there he views life pessimistically in its, for the most part, unhappy experiences, while here he regards it in itself as a good affording the possibility of enjoyment. It lies, however, in the nature of his standpoint that he should not be able to find the right medium between the sorrow of the world and the pleasure of life. Although postulating a retribution in eternity, yet in his thoughts about the future he does not rise above the comfortless idea of Hades.

Vers. 5, 6. He sarcastically verifies his comparison in favour of a living dog. "For the living know that they shall die; but the dead know not anything, and have no more a reward; for their memory is forgotten. Their love, as well as their hatred and their envy, has long ago perished, and they have part no more for ever in all that is done under the sun." The description of the condition of death begins sarcastically and then becomes elegiac. "They have no reward further," viz. in this upper world, since there it is only too soon forgotten that they once existed, and that they did anything worthy of being remembered; Koheleth might here indeed, with his view shrouded in dark clouds, even suppose that God also forgot them, Job xiv. 13. The suff. of אַהֲבָ֫, etc., present themselves as subjective, and there is no reason, with Knobel and Ginsburg, to render them objectively: not merely the objects of their love, and hatred, and envy, are lost to them, but these their affections and strivings themselves have ceased (Rosenm., Hitzig, Zöckl., and others), they lie (*K^evar 'avadah*) far behind them as absolutely gone; for the dead have no part more in the history which is unfolding itself amid the light of the upper world, and they can have no more any part therein, for the dead as not living are not only without knowledge, but also without feeling and desire. The representation of the state after death is here more comfortless than anywhere else. For elsewhere we read that those who have been living here spend in *Sheol, i.e.* in the deep (R. שׁל, to be loose, to hang down, to go downwards) realm of the dead, as *rᵉphāim* (Isa. xiv. 9, etc.), lying beneath the upper world, far from the love and the praise of God (Ps. vi. 3, xxx. 10), a prospectless (Job vii. 7 f., xiv. 6-12 ; Ps. lxxxviii. 11-13), dark, shadowy existence; the soul in Hades, though neither annihilated nor sleeping, finds itself in a state of death no less than does the body in the grave. But here the state of death is not even set forth over against the idea of the dissolution of life, the complete annihilation of individuality, much less that a retribution in eternity, *i.e.* a retribution executed, if not here, yet at some time, postulated elsewhere by the author, throws a ray of light into the night of death. The apocryphal book of the Wisdom of Solomon, which distinguishes between a state of blessedness and a state of misery measured out to men in the future following death, has in this surpassed the canonical Book of Koheleth. In vain do the Targ., Midrash, and the older Christian interpreters refer that which is said to the wicked dead; others regard Koheleth as introducing here the discourse of atheists (*e.g.* Oetinger), and interpret, under the influence of monstrous self-deception, ver. 7 as the voice of the spirit (Hengst.) opposing the voice of the flesh. But that which Koheleth expresses here only in a particularly rugged way is the view of Hades predominating in the O. T. It is the consequence of viewing death from the side of its anger. Revelation intentionally permits this manner of viewing it to remain; but from premises which the revelation sets forth, the religious consciousness in the course of time draws always more decidedly the conclusion, that the man who is united to God will fully reach through death that which since the entrance of sin into the world cannot be reached without the loss of this present life, *i.e.* without death, viz. a more perfect life in fellowship with God. Yet the confusion of the O. T. representation of Hades remains; in the Book of Sirach it also still throws its deep shadows (xvii. 22 f.) into the contemplation of the future; for the first time the N. T. solution actually removes the confusion, and turns the scale in favour of the view of death on its side of light. In this history of the ideas of eternity moving forward amid many fluctuations to the N. T. goal, a significant place belongs to the Book of Koheleth; certainly the Christian interpreter ought not to have an interest in explaining away and concealing the imperfections of knowledge which made it impossible for the author spiritually to rise above his pessimism. He does not rise, in contrast to his pessimism, above an eudaemonism which is earthly, which, without knowing of a future life (not like the modern pessimism, without *wishing to know* of a future life), recommends a pleasant enjoyment of the present life, so far as that is morally allowable:

Vers. 7–10. " Go, eat thy bread with joy, and drink thy wine with a merry heart; for long ago hath God accepted thy work. Let thy garments be always white; and let not oil be wanting to thy head. Enjoy life with a wife whom thou lovest through all the days of thy vain life, which He hath given thee under the sun—through all thy vain days: for that is thy portion in life, and in thy labour wherewith thou weariest thyself under the sun. All that thy hand may find to do with thy might, that do ; for there is not work, and calculation, and knowledge, and wisdom, in the under world, whither thou shalt go." Hengstenberg perceives here the counterpart of the spirit; on the contrary, Oetinger, Mendelssohn, and others, discover also here, and here for the first time rightly, the utterance of an epicurean thought. But, in fact, this לֵךְ down to הוֹלֵךְ שָׁ֑ is the most distinct personal utterance of the author, his *ceterum censeo* which pervades the whole book, and here forms a particularly copious conclusion of a long series of thoughts. We recapitulate this series of thoughts: One fate, at last the same final event, happens to all men, without making any distinction according to their moral condition,—an evil matter, so much the more evil, as it encourages to wickedness and light-mindedness ; the way of man, without exception, leads to the dead, and all further prospect is cut off; for only he who belongs to the class of living beings has a joyful spirit, has a spirit of enterprise: even the lowest being, if it live, stands higher in worth, and is better, than the highest if it be dead ; for death is the end of all knowledge and feeling, the being cut off from the living under the sun. From this, that there is only one life, one life on this side of eternity, he deduces the exhortation to enjoy the one as much as possible; God Himself, to whom we owe it, will have it so that we enjoy it, within the moral limits prescribed by Himself indeed, for this limitation is certainly given with His approbation. Incorrectly, the Targ., Rashi, Hengst., Ginsb., and Zöckl. explain : For thy moral conduct and effort have pleased Him long ago—the person addressed is some one, not a definite person, who could be thus set forth as such a witness to be commended. Rather with Grotius and others : *Quia Deus favet laboribus tuis h. e. eos ita prosperavit, ut cuncta quae vitam delectant abunde tibi suppetant.* The thought is wholly in the spirit of the Book of Koheleth ; for the fruit of labour and the enjoyment of this fruit of labour, as at ii. 24, iii. 13, etc., is a gift from above; and besides, this may be said to the person addressed, since 7a presupposes that he has at his disposal heart-strengthening bread and heart-refreshing wine. But in these two explanations the meaning of כְּבָר is not comprehended. It was left untranslated by the old translators, from their not understanding it. Rightly, Aben Ezra: For God wills that thou shouldst thus do [indulge in these enjoyments]; more correctly, Hitzig: Long ago God has beforehand permitted this thy conduct, so that thou hast no room for scruples about it. How significant כבר is for the thought, is indicated by the accentuation which gives to it *Zakef*: from aforetime God has impressed the seal of His approbation on this thy eating with joy, this thy drinking with a merry heart.—The assigning of the reason gives courage to the enjoyment, but at the same time gives to it a consecration; for it is the will of God that we should enjoy life, thus it is self-evident that we have to enjoy it as He wills it to be enjoyed.

Ver. 8. The white garments, לְבָנִים, are in contrast to the black robes of mourning, and thus are an expression of festal joy, of a happy mood; black and white are, according to the ancients, colour-symbols, the colours respectively of sorrow and joy, to which light and darkness correspond.[1] Fragrant oil is also, according to Prov. xxvii. 9, one of the heart-refreshing things. Sorrow and anointing exclude one another, 2 Sam. xiv. 2; joy and oil stand in closest mutual relation, Ps. xlv. 8, Isa. lxi. 3; oil which smooths the hair and makes the face shine (*vid.* under Ps. civ. 15). This oil ought not to be wanting to the head, and thus the perpetuity of a happy life should suffer no interruption.

In 9*a* most translators render: Enjoy life with the wife whom thou lovest; but the author purposely does not use the word הָאִשָּׁה, but אִשָּׁה; and also that he uses חַיִּים, and not הַחַיִּים, is not without significance. He means: Bring into experience what life, what happiness, is (cf. the indetermin. ideas, Ps. xxxiv. 13) with a wife whom thou hast loved (Jerome: *quaecunque tibi placuerit feminarum*), in which there lies indirectly the call to choose such an one; whereby the

---

[1] Cf. *Shabbath* 114*a*: "Bury me neither in white nor in black garments: not in white, because perhaps I may not be one of the blessed, and am like a bridegroom among mourners; not in black, because perhaps I may be one of the blessed, and am like a mourner among bridegrooms." *Semachoth* ii. 10: Him who is outside the congregation, they do not bury with solemnity; the brothers and relatives of such must clothe and veil themselves in white; cf. *Joma* 39*b*. Elsewhere white is the colour of innocence, *Shabbath* 153*a*, *Midrash* under Prov. xvi. 11; and black the colour of guilt, *Kiddushin* 40*a*, etc.

pessimistic criticism of the female sex, vii. 26–28, so far as the author is concerned, falls into the background, since eudaemonism, the other side of his view of the world, predominates. The accus. designation of time, "through all the days of the life of thy vanity (*i.e.* of thy transient vain life)," is like vi. 12, cf. vii. 15. It is repeated in "all the days of thy vanity;" the repetition is heavy and unnecessary (therefore omitted by the LXX., Targ., and Syr.); probably like והדרך, Ps. xlv. 5, a *ditto;* Hitzig, however, finds also here great emphasis. The relative clause standing after the first designation of time refers to "the days which He (האלהים, 7*b*) has granted under the sun." *Hu* in 9*b* refers attractionally to חֶלְקְךָ (Jerome: *haec est enim pars*), as at iii. 22, v. 17, cf. vii. 2; הִיא of the Babyl. is therefore to be rejected; this enjoyment, particularly of marriage joys, is thy part in life, and in thy work which thou accomplishest under the sun, *i.e.* the real portion of gain allotted to thee which thou mayest and oughtest to enjoy here below.

Ver. 10. The author, however, recommends no continual *dolce far niente*, no idle, useless sluggard-life devoted to pleasure, but he gives to his exhortation to joy the converse side: "All that thy hand may reach (*i.e.* what thou canst accomplish and is possible to thee, 1 Sam. x. 7; Lev. xii. 8) to accomplish it with thy might, that do." The accentuation is ingenious. If the author meant: That do with all might (Jerome: *instanter operare*), then he would have said *b*ᵉ*chol-kohhacha* (Gen. xxxi. 6). As the words lie before us, they call on him who is addressed to come not short in his work of any possibility according to the measure of his strength, thus to a work straining his capacity to the uttermost. The reason for the call, 10*b*, turns back to the clause from which it was inferred: in Hades, whither thou must go (*iturus es*), there is no work, and reckoning (*vid.* vii. 25), and knowledge (וְדַעַת[1]), and no wisdom. Practice and theory have then an end. Thus: Enjoy, but not without working, ere the night cometh when no man can work. Thus spake Jesus (John ix. 4), but in a different sense indeed from Koheleth. The night which He meant is the termination of this present life, which for Him, as for every man, has its particular work, which is either accomplished within the limits of this life, or is not accomplished at all.

[1] Not וְדַעַת, because the word has the conjunctive, not the disjunctive accent, *vid.* under Ps. lv. 10. The punctuation, as we have already several times remarked, is not consistent in this; cf. וְדַעַת, ii. 26, and וְעֶרֶב, Ps. lxv. 9, both of which are contrary to the rule (*vid.* Baer in Abulwalîd's *Rikma* p. 119, note 2).

The Incalculableness of the Issues and of the Duration of Life, ix. 11, 12.

Another reflection, so far not without connection in the foregoing, as the fact of experience, that ability is yet no security for the issue aimed at and merited, is chiefly referred to wisdom:

Ver. 11. "Further, I came to see under the sun, that the race belongs not to the swift, and the war not to the heroes, and also not bread to the wise man, and not riches to the prudent, and not favour to men of knowledge; for time and chance happeneth to them all." The nearest preceding 'רָא, to which this 'שַׁבְ וְרָא suitably connects itself, is at viii. 17. Instead of *redii et videndo quidem = rursus vidi* (cf. viii. 9 and under ix. 1), we had at iv. 1 the simpler expression, *redii et vidi*. The five times repeated ל is that of property, of that, viz., by virtue of which one is master of that which is named, has power over it, disposes of it freely. The race belongs not to the swift (מֵרוֹץ, masc. to מְרוּצָה, only here), *i.e.* their fleetness is yet no guarantee that on account of it they will reach the goal. Luther freely: "To be fleet does not help in running," *i.e.* running to an object or goal. "The war belongs not to the heroes," means that much rather it belongs to the Lord, 1 Sam. xvii. 47.—God alone gives the victory (Ps. xxxiii. 16). Even so the gaining of bread, riches, favour (*i.e.* influence, reputation), does not lie in wisdom, prudence, knowledge of themselves, as an indispensable means thereto; but the obtaining of them, or the not obtaining of them, depends on times and circumstances which lie beyond the control of man, and is thus, in the final result, conditioned by God (cf. Rom. ix. 16 [1]); time and fate happen to all whose ability appears to warrant the issue, they both [time and fate] encounter them and bar to them the way; they are in an inexplicable manner dependent on both, and helplessly subject to them. As the idea of spiritual superiority is here expressed in a threefold manner by 'חָכְ (whence 'לְחָ' of the plur., also with the art. ix. 1; Ex. xxxvi. 4; Esth. i. 13), 'הַנְ, and 'הַיְ, so at Isa. xi. 2, the gifts of "wisdom," "counsel," and "knowledge" follow each other. '*Eth* is here "time" with its special circumstances (conjunctures), and *pega'*, "accident," particularly as an adversity, disappointment, for the word is used also without any addition (1 Kings v. 18) of misfortune (cf. שִׁיר פְּגָעִים, Ps. iii., xci.). The masc. 'יְקָ is regulated after 'וּם; '*eth* can, however, be used in the masc., Song ii. 12; Böttch. § 648, viz. "with the misapprehension of its origin" (v. Orelli).

---

[1] But not Jer. ix. 22; this passage, referred to by Bernstein, is of a different nature.

This limitation of man in his efforts, in spite of all his capacity, has its reason in this, that he is on the whole not master of his own life :

Ver. 12. "For man also knoweth not his time: like the fishes which are caught in an evil net, and like the birds which are caught in the snare—like them are the sons of men snared in an evil time, when it suddenly breaks in upon them." The particles כִּי גַּם are here not so clearly connected as at viii. 12, iv. 14, where, more correctly, the pointing should be כִּי גַּם (*ki* with the conjunct. accent); *ki* rules the sentence; and *gam*, as to its meaning, belongs to *eth-'itto*. The particular has its reason from the general: man is not master of his own time, his own person, and his own life, and thus not of the fruits of his capabilities and his actions, in spite of the previously favourable conditions which appear to place the result beyond a doubt; for ere the result is reached of which he appears to be able to entertain a certainty, suddenly his time may expire, and his term of life be exhausted. Jerome translates *'itto* (cf. vii. 17) rightly by *finem suum;* עֵת, with the gen. following, frequently (*vid.* under Job xxiv. 1) means the point of time when the fate of any one is decided,—the *terminus* where a reckoning is made; here, directly, the *terminus ad quem*. The suddenness with which men are frequently overtaken with the catastrophe which puts an end to their life, is seen by comparison with the fishes which are suddenly caught in the net, and the birds which are suddenly caught in the snare. With שֶׁנֶּאֱ (that are caught) there is interchanged, in two variations of expression, הָאֲחֻזוֹת, which is incorrectly written, by v. d. Hooght, Norzi, and others, הָאֲחֻז,[1] מְצוֹ, a net,—of which the plur. form vii. 26 is used,—goes back, as does the similar designation of a bulwark (14*b*), to the root-conception of searching (hunting), and receives here the epithet "evil." Birds, צִפֳּרִים (from a ground-form with a short terminal vowel; cf. Assyr. *iṣṣur*, from *iṣpur*), are, on account of their weakness, as at Isa. xxxi. 5, as a figure of tender love, represented in the fem.

The second half of the verse, in conformity with its structure, begins with בָּהֶם (which more frequently occurs as כְּמוֹהֶם). יוּקָשׁ is *part. Pu.* for מְיֻקָּשִׁים (Ewald, § 170*d*); the particip. מ is rejected, and פ is treated altogether as a guttural, the impracticable doubling of which is compensated for by the lengthening of the vowel. The use of the part. is here stranger than *e.g.* at Prov. xi. 13, xv. 32; the fact repeating itself is here treated as a property. Like the fish and the birds are they, such as are caught, etc. Otherwise Hitz. :

---

[1] *Vid.* Ed. König, *Gedanke, Laut u. Accent* (1874), p. 72.

Like these are they caught, during the continuance of their life in the evil time ... ; but the being snared does not, however, according to the double figure, precede the catastrophe, but is its consequence. Rightly, Ginsb.: "Like these are the sons of men ensnared in the time of misfortune." רָעָה might be adj., as at Amos v. 13, Mic. ii. 3 ; but since it lies nearer to refer 'כְּשֶׁתּ to *ra'ah* than to *'eth*, thus *ra'ah*, like the frequently occurring *yom ra'ah* (vii. 14 ; cf. Jer. xvii. 17 with xv. 11), may be thought of as genit. An example of that which is here said is found in the fatal wounding of Ahab by means of an arrow which was not aimed at him, so that he died "at the time of the going down of the sun," 2 Chron. xviii. 33, 34.

THE FURTHER SETTING FORTH OF EXPERIENCES, WITH PROVERBS INTERMIXED.—IX. 13–X. 15.

Experiences and Proverbs touching Wisdom and the Contrasts to it,
ix. 13–x. 3.

With the words, "further, I saw," 11*a*, the author introduced the fact he had observed, that there is not always a sure and honoured position in life connected with wisdom as its consequence; here he narrates an experience which, by way of example, shows how little wisdom profits, notwithstanding the extraordinary result it produces.

Ver. 13. "Also this have I come to see as wisdom under the sun, and it appeared great to me." The Venet. construes falsely : "This also have I seen: wisdom under the sun;" as also Hitzig, who reads זֶה (neut. as at vii. 27). There is no reason thus to break up the sentence which introduces the following experience. *Zoh* is connected with *hhochmah*, but not as Luther renders it : "I have also seen this wisdom," which would have required the words זאת 'הח, but, as Jerome does : *Hanc quoque sub sole vidi sapientiam;* this, however, since *gam-zoh*, as at v. 15, cf. 18, is attractionally related to *hhochmah* as its pred., is = "also in this I saw wisdom," as the LXX. translates, or as Zöckl.: "also this have I seen—come to find out as wisdom,"—also this, viz., the following incident narrated, in which wisdom of exceeding greatness presented itself to me. As Mordecai is called "great among the Jews," Esth. x. 3, so here Koheleth says that the wisdom which came to light therein appeared to him great (אֵלַי, as elsewhere בְּעֵינֵי or לִפְנֵי).

Now follows an experience, which, however, has not merely a

light side, but also a dark side; for wisdom, which accomplished so great a matter, reaped only ingratitude:

Vers. 14, 15. "A little city, and men therein only a few,—to which a great king came near, and he besieged it, and erected against it high bulwarks. And he met therein a poor wise man, and who saved the city by his wisdom; and no man thought of that poor man." What may be said as to the hist. reference of these words has already been noticed; *vid.* above, p. 215. The "great king" is probably an Asiatic monarch, and that the Persian; Jerome translates verbally: *Civitas parva et pauci in ea viri, venit contra eam*— the former is the subj., and the latter its pred.; the object stands first, plastically rigid, and there then follows what happened to it; the structure of the sentence is fundamentally the same as Ps. civ. 25. The expression בּוֹא אֶל, which may be used of any kind of coming to anything, is here, as at Gen. xxxii. 9, meant of a hostile approach. The object of a siege and a hostile attack is usually denoted by עַל, 2 Kings xvi. 5; Isa. vii. 1. Two Codd. of de Rossi's have the word מְצוּרִים, but that is an error of transcription; the plur. of מָצוֹר is fem., Isa. xxix. 4. מְצוֹדִים is, as at vii. 26, plur. of מָצוֹד (from צוּד, to lie in wait); here, as elsewhere, פַּח and דָּיֵק is the siege-tower erected on the ground or on the rampart, from which to spy out the weak points of the beleaguered place so as to assail it.

The words following וּמָצָא בָהּ are rendered by the Targ., Syr., Jerome, Arab., and Luther: "and there was found in it;" most interpreters explain accordingly, as they point to i. 10, יֹאמַר, *dicat aliquis*. But that מצא in this sequence of thought is = וְנִמְצָא (Job xlii. 15), is only to be supposed if it were impossible to regard the king as the subject, which Ewald with the LXX. and the Venet. does in spite of § 294*b*. It is true it would not be possible if, as Vaih. remarks, the finding presupposed a searching; but cf. on the contrary, *e.g.* Deut. xxiv. 1, Ps. cxvi. 3. We also say of one whom, contrary to expectation, a superior meets with, that he has found his match, that he has found his man. Thus it is here said of the great king, he found in the city a poor wise man—met therein with such an one, against whom his plan was shattered. חָכָם is the adjective of the person of the poor man designated by *ish miskēn* (cf. 2 Chron. ii. 13); the accents correctly indicate this relation. Instead of וּמִלַּט־הוּא, the older language would use וַיְמַלֵּט; it does not, like the author here, use pure perfects, but makes the chief factum prominent by the *fut. consec.* The *ē* of *millēt* is, as at xiii. 9, that of *limmēd* before *Makkeph*, referred back to the original *a*. The making prominent of the subject contained in *millat* by means of *hu* is favourable to the supposition that *umatsa'* has the king as its subject; while even where no opposition (as *e.g.* at Jer. xvii. 18) lies before us this pleonasm belongs to the stylistic peculiarities of the book (*vid.* above, p. 198, No. 3). Instead of *adam lo*, the older form is *ish lo;* perhaps the author here wishes to avoid the repetition of *ish*, but at vii. 20 he also uses *adam* instead of *ish*, where no such reason existed.

Threatened by a powerful assailant, with whom it could not enter into battle, the little city, deserted by its men to a small remainder capable of bearing arms (this idea one appears to be under the necessity of connecting with מעט ... 'ובא), found itself in the greatest straits; but when all had been given up as lost, it was saved by the wisdom of the poor man (perhaps in the same way as Abel-beth-maacha, 2 Sam. xx., by the wisdom of a woman). But after this was done, the wise poor man quickly again fell into the background; no man thought of him, as he deserved to have been thought of, as the saviour of the city; he was still poor, and remained so, and *pauper homo raro vivit cum nomine claro*. The poor man with his wisdom, Hengst. remarks, is Israel. And Wangemann (1856), generalizing the parable: "The beleaguered city is the life of the individual; the great king who lays siege to it is death and the judgment of the Lord." But sounder and more appropriate is the remark of Luther: *Est exemplum generale, cujus in multis historiis simile reperitur;* and: *Sic Themistocles multa bona fecit suis civibus, sed expertus summam ingratitudinem*. The author narrates an actual history, in which, on the one hand, he had seen what great things wisdom can do; and from which, on the other hand, he has drawn the following lesson:

Ver. 16. "And I said: Better is wisdom than strength; but the wisdom of the poor is despised, and his words are not heard." With the words, "I saw," the author introduces his observations, and with "I said" his reflections (*vid.* above, No. 3, p. 198). Wisdom is better than strength, since it does more for the wise man, and through him for others, than physical force,—more, as expressed in vii. 19, than ten mighty men. But the *respect* which wisdom otherwise secures for a man, if it is the wisdom of a poor man, sinks into *despect*, to which his poverty exposes him,—if necessity arises, his service, as the above history shows, is valued; but as a rule his words are unheeded, for the crowd estimate the worth of him whom they willingly hear according to the outward respect in which he is held.

To the lessons gathered from experience, are now added instructive proverbs of kindred contents.

Ver. 17. "The words of the wise, heard in quiet, have the superiority above the cry of a ruler among fools." Instead of *tovim min*, there stands here the simple *min, prae,* as at iv. 17, to express the superiority of the one to the other. Hitzig finds in this proverb the meaning that, as that history has shown, the words of the wise, heard with tranquillity, gain the victory over the cry of a ruler over fools. But (1) the contrast of נַחַת and זַעֲקַת require us to attribute the tranquillity to the wise man himself, and not to his hearers; (2) מוֹ' בַּ' is not a ruler over fools, by which it would remain questionable whether he himself was not a fool (cf. Job xli. 26), but a ruler among fools (cf. 2 Sam. xxiii. 3, מוֹ' בָּ', "a ruler among men;" and Prov. xxxvi. 30, גִּבּ' בַּ', "the hero among beasts"), *i.e.* one who among fools takes the place of chief. The words of the poor wise man pass by unheeded, they are not listened to, because he does not possess an imposing splendid outward appearance, in accordance with which the crowd estimate the value of a man's words; the wise man does not seek to gain esteem by means of a pompous violent deportment; his words נִשְׁ' בּ' are heard, let themselves be heard, are to be heard (cf. *e.g.* Song ii. 12) in quiet (Isa. xxx. 15); for, trusting to their own inward power of conviction, and committing the result to God, he despises vociferous pomp, and the external force of earthly expedients (cf. Isa. xlii. 2; Matt. xii. 19); but the words of the wise, which are to be heard in unassuming, passionless quietness, are of more value than the vociferation with which a king among fools, an arch-fool, a *non plus ultra* among fools, trumpets forth his pretended wisdom and constrains his hearers.

Ver. 18. The following proverb also leans on the history above narrated: "Better is wisdom than weapons of war; and one sinner destroyeth much good." The above history has shown by way of example that wisdom accomplishes more than implements of war, בְּלִי קְ =בְּלִי מְלְ (Assyr. *unut taḥazi*[1]), *i.e.* than all the apparatus belonging to preparation for war. But the much good which a wise man is accomplishing or has accomplished, one sinner (חוֹטֵא,[2] cf. above, p. 254, note) by treachery or calumny may render vain, or may even destroy, through mere malicious pleasure in evil. This is a synthetic distich whose two parts may be interpreted independently. As wisdom accomplishes something great, so a single villain may have a far-reaching influence, viz. such as destroys much good.

x. 1. The second half of the foregoing double proverb introduces what now follows: "Poisonous flies make to stink, make to ferment the oil of the preparer of ointment; heavier than wisdom,

[1] *Vid.* Fried. Delitzsch's *Assyr. Stud.* p. 129.

[2] The Syr. (not the Targ.) had חִטְאָא before it, and thus realized it, which appears to correspond better with the parall. חכמה.

than honour, weighs a little folly." We do not need to change זְבוּבֵי מָוֶת, on account of the foll. sing. of the pred., either into 'זבובי מ (as possible by Hitz.) or זב' יָמוּת (Luzz.); both are inadmissible, for the style of Koheleth is not adorned with archaisms such as *Chirek compaginis*; and also such an attrib. clause as זבוב ימות, "a fly which dies," is for him too refined; but both are also unnecessary, for a plur. of the subj., in which the plurality of the individuals comes less into view than the oneness of their character, is frequently enough followed by the sing. of the pred., *e.g.* Gen. xlix. 22; Joel i. 20; Isa. lix. 12, etc. It is a question, however, whether by זבובי מות, death-bringing, *i.e.* poisonous flies (LXX., Targ.,[1] Luther) or dead flies (Symm., Syr., Jerome) is meant. We decide in favour of the former; for (1) זבובי מות for זְבוּבִים מֵתִים (ix. 4; Isa. xxxvii. 36), "death-flies" for "dead flies," would be an affected poetic expression without analogy; while, on the contrary, "death-flies" for "deadly flies" is a genit. connection, such as כְּלֵי מוֶת [instruments of death, *i.e.* deadly instruments] and the like; Böttcher understands dung-flies; but the expression can scarcely extend to the designation of flies which are found on dead bodies. Meanwhile, it is very possible that by the expression 'זב' מ, such flies are thought of as carry death from dead bodies to those that are living; the Assyr. *syllabare* show how closely the Semites distinguished manifold kinds of זבובים (Assyr. *zumbi = zubbi*). (2) In favour of "dead flies," it has been remarked that that influence on the contents of a pot of ointment is effected not merely by poison-flies, but, generally, by flies that have fallen into it.

But since the oil mixed with perfumes may also be of the kind which, instead of being changed by a dead body, much rather embalms it; so it does not surprise us that the exciter of fermentation is thus drastically described by μυῖαι θανατοῦσαι (LXX.); it happens, besides, also on this account, because "a little folly" corresponds as a contrasted figure to the little destructive carcase,—wisdom תְּחַ' בְּעַ' ("giveth life," vii. 12), a little folly is thus like little deadly flies. The sequence of ideas 'יַבְ' יַבְ (maketh the ointment stink) is natural. The corrupting body communicates its foul savour to the ointment, makes it boil up, *i.e.* puts it into a state of fermentation, in consequence of which it foams and raises up small blisters, אבעבועות (Rashi). To the asyndeton 'יַבְ' יַבְ, there corresponds, in 1*b*, the asyndeton 'מֵחָ' מִפָּ; the Targ., Syr., and Jerome,[2] who translate by

---

[1] The Targ. interprets, as the Talm. and Mid. do, deadly flies as a figure of the *prava concupiscentia*. Similarly Wangemann: a mind buried in the world.

[2] The LXX. entirely remodels 1*b*: τίμιον κ.τ.λ. ("a little wisdom is more

"and," are therefore not witnesses for the phrase 'וּמִכּ, but the Venet. (καὶ τῆς δόξης) had this certainly before it; it is, in relation to the other, inferior in point of evidence.¹ In general, it is evident that the point of comparison is the hurtfulness, widely extending itself, of a matter which in appearance is insignificant. Therefore the meaning of 1*b* cannot be that a little folly is more weighty than wisdom, than honour, viz. in the eyes of the blinded crowd (Zöckl., Dächsel). This limitation the author ought to have expressed, for without it the sentence is an untruth. Jerome, following the Targ. and Midrash, explains: *Pretiosa est super sapientiam et gloriam stultitia parva*, understanding by wisdom and honour the self-elation therewith connected; besides, this thought, which Luther limits by the introduction of *zuweilen* ["folly is *sometimes* better than wisdom, etc."], is in harmony neither with that which goes before nor with that which follows. Luzz., as already Aben Ezra, Grotius, Geiger, Hengst., and the more recent English expositors, transfer the verbs of 1*a* zeugmatically to 1*b*: *similiter pretiosum nomine sapientiae et gloriae virum foetidum facit stoliditas parva*. But יביע forbids this transference, and, besides, מן יָקָר, "honoured on account of," is an improbable expression; also יקר מכ' presents a tautology, which Luzz. seeks to remove by glossing 'מכ, as the Targ. does, by מרוב עושר ונכסים. Already Rashi has rightly explained by taking יָקָר (Syr. *jakîr*, Arab. *wakur*, *wakûr*), in its primary meaning, as synon. of כָּבֵד: more weighty, *i.e.* heavier and weighing more than wisdom, than honour, is a little folly; and he reminds us that a single foolish act can at once change into their contrary the wisdom and the honour of a man, destroying both, making it as if they had never been, cf. 1 Cor. v. 6. The sentence is true both in an intellectual and in a moral reference. Wisdom and honour are

---

honour than the great glory of folly"), *i.e.* יקר מעט חכמה מכבוד סכלות רב (כבוד in the sense of "great multitude"). Van der Palm (1784) regards this as the original form of the text.

¹ מִפָּבוֹד; thus in the *Biblia rabb.* 1525, 1615, Genoa 1618, Plantin 1582, Jablonski 1699, and also v. d. Hooght and Norzi. In the Ven. 1515, 1521, 1615, וּמִפָּבוֹד is found with the copulat. *vav*, a form which is adopted by Michaelis. Thus also the Concord. cites, and thus, originally, it stood in J., but has been corrected to מִכָּבוֹד. F., however, has מִכָּבוֹד, with the marginal remark: מכבוד כן קבלתי מני שמשון (Simson ha-Nakdam, to whom the writer of the Frankf. Cod. 1294 here refers for the reading 'מכ, without the copul. *vav*, is often called by him his voucher). This is also the correct Masoretic reading; for if וּמִכּ' were to be read, then the word would be in the catalogue of words of which three begin with their initial letter, and a fourth has introduced a *vav* before it (*Mas. fin.* f. 26, *Ochla veochla*, Nr. 15).

swept away by a little *quantum* of folly; it places both in the shade, it outweighs them in the scale; it stamps the man, notwithstanding the wisdom and dignity which otherwise belong to him, as a fool. The expressive שֶׁמֶן רֹקֵחַ is purposely used here; the dealer in ointments (*pigmentarius*) can now do nothing with the corrupted perfume,—thus the wisdom which a man possesses, the honour which he has hitherto enjoyed, avail him no longer; the proportionally small portion of folly which has become an ingredient in his personality gives him the character of a fool, and operates to his dishonour. Knobel construes rightly; but his explanation (also of Heiligst., Elst., Ginsb.): "a little folly frequently shows itself more efficacious and fruitful than the wisdom of an honoured wise man," helps itself with a "frequently" inserted, and weakens מכ' to a subordinated idea, and is opposed to the figure, which requires a personality.

Vers. 2, 3. A double proverb regarding wisdom and folly in their difference: "The heart of a wise man is directed to his right hand, and the heart of the fool to his left. And also on the way where a fool goeth, there his heart faileth him, and he saith to all that he is a fool." Most interpreters translate: The heart of the wise man is at his right hand, *i.e.* it is in the right place. But this designation, meant figuratively and yet sounding anatomically, would be in bad taste[1] in this distinguishing double form (*vid.* on the contrary, ii. 14). The ל is that of direction;[2] and that which is situated to the right of a man is figuratively a designation of the right; and that to the left, a designation of the wrong. The designation proceeds from a different idea from that at Deut. v. 32, etc.; that which lies to the right, as that lying at a man's right hand, is that to which his calling and duty point him; הִשְׂ denotes, in the later Hebrew, "to turn oneself to the wrong side."

Ver. 3. This proverb forms, along with the preceding, a tetrastich, for it is divided into two parts by *vav*. The *Kerî* has removed the art. in כש' and שח', vi. 10, as incompatible with the שׁ. The order of the words *v^egam-baderek k^eshehsachal holek* is inverted for *v^egam k^eshehsachal baderek holek*, cf. iii. 13, and also *rav sh^eyihyn*, vi. 3; so

---

[1] Christ. Fried. Bauer (1732) explains as we do, and remarks, "If we translate: the heart of the wise is at his right hand, but the heart of the fool at his left, it appears as if the heart of the prudent and of the foolish must have a different position in the human body, thus affording to the profane ground for mockery."

[2] Accordingly, ver. 2 has become a Jewish saying with reference to the study of a book (this thought of as Heb.): The wise always turn over the leaves backwards, repeating that which has been read; the fool forwards, superficially anticipating that which has not yet been read, and scarcely able to wait for the end.

far as this signifies, "supposing that they are many." Plainly the
author intends to give prominence to "on the way;" and why, but
because the fool, the inclination of whose heart, according to 2b,
always goes to the left, is now placed in view as he presents himself in his public manner of life. Instead of חֲסַר לֵב־הוּא we have
here the verbal clause לִבּוֹ חָסֵר, which is not, after vi. 2, to be translated: *corde suo caret* (Herzf., Ginsb.), contrary to the suff. and also
the order of the words, but, after ix. 8: *cor ejus deficit, i.e.* his
understanding is at fault; for לב, here and at ver. 2, is thus used in
a double sense, as the Greek νοῦς and the Lat. *mens* can also be
used: there it means pure, formal, intellectual soul-life; here,
pregnantly (*Psychol.* p. 249), as at vii. 7, cf. Hos. iv. 11, the understanding or the knowledge and will of what is right. The fool takes
no step without showing that his understanding is not there,—that,
so to speak, he does not take it along with him, but has left it at
home. He even carries his folly about publicly, and prides himself
in it as if it were wisdom: he says to all that he is a fool, *se esse
stultum* (thus, correctly, most Jewish and Christian interpreters, *e.g.*
Rashi and Rambach). The expression follows the scheme of Ps.
ix. 21: May the heathen know *mortales se esse* (*vid. l.c.*). Otherwise
Luther, with Symm. and Jerome: "he takes every man as a fool;"
but this thought has no support in the connection, and would undoubtedly be expressed by סְכָלִים הֵמָּה. Still differently Knobel and
Ewald: he says to all, "it is foolish;" Hitzig, on the contrary, justly
remarks that סָכָל is not used of actions and things; this also is true
of כְּסִיל, against himself, v. 2, where he translates *qol k^esil* by "foolish
discourses."

The Caprice of Rulers and the Perverted World, x. 4–7.

Wisdom is a strong protection. To this thought, from which
the foregoing group proceeded, there is here subordinated the following admonition.

Ver. 4. This verse shows what is the wise conduct of a subject,
and particularly of a servant, when the anger of the ruler breaks
forth: "If the ill-humour of the ruler rise up against thee, do not
leave thy post; for patience leaves out great sins." Luther connects
ver. 4 and ver. 3 by "therefore;" for by the potentate he understands such an one as, himself a fool, holds all who contradict him
to be fools: then it is best to let his folly rage on. But the מוֹשֵׁל
is a different person from the סָכָל; and מְקוֹמְ׳ אַל־תַּנַּח does not mean,
"let not yourself get into a passion," or, as he more accurately ex-

plains in the *Annotationes:* "remain self-possessed" (similarly Hitzig: lose not thy mental state or composure), but, in conformity with אַל ... תלך, viii. 3, "forsake not the post (synon. מַצָּב and מַעֲמָד, Isa. xxii. 19, cf. 23) which thou hast received." The person addressed is thus represented not merely as a subject, but officially as a subordinate officer: if the ruler's displeasure (רוּחַ, as at Judg. viii. 3; Prov. xxix. 11) rises up against him (עָלָה, as elsewhere; cf. אַף, Ps. lxxiii. 21; or חֵמָה, 2 Sam. xi. 20), he ought not, in the consciousness that he does not merit his displeasure, hastily give up his situation which has been entrusted to him and renounce submission; for patience, gentleness (regarding מַרְפֵּא, *vid.* Prov. xii. 18) נַּד ... יַּ'.

This concluding clause of the verse is usually translated: "It appeaseth (pacifieth) great sins" (LXX. καταπαύσει, Symm. παύσει) The phrase (הֵנִיחַ אַף (חמה is not to be compared, for it signifies quieting by an exhausting outbreak; on the contrary, יניח in the passage before us must signify quieting, as the preventing of an outbreak (cf. Prov. xv. 1). It appears more correct to render הִנִּיחַ in both cases in the sense of ἐᾶν, *missum facere:* to leave great sins is = not to commit them, to give up the lust thereto; for *hinniahh* signifies to let go, to leave off, *e.g.* Jer. xiv. 9; and to indulge, Esth. iii. 8, here as at vii. 18, xi. 6, "to keep the hands from something." The great sins cannot certainly be thought of as those of the ruler; for on his part only one comes into view, if indeed, according to the old legal conception, it could be called such, viz. cruel proceeding with reference to him who wilfully withdraws from him, and thus proves his opposition; much rather we are to think of the great sins into which he who is the object of the ruler's displeasure might fall, viz. treason (viii. 2), insubordination, self-destruction, and at the same time, since he does not stand alone, or make common cause with others who are discontented, the drawing of others into inevitable ruin (viii. 3*b*). All these sins, into which he falls who answers wrath with wrath, patience avoids, and puts a check to them. The king's anger is perhaps justified; the admonition, however, would be otherwise expressed than by מק' אל־תנח, if it were not presupposed that it was not justified; and thus without μετάβασις εἰς ἄλλο γένος an *I*-section follows the reflection regarding wise deportment as over against the king's displeasure, a section which describes from experience and from personal observation the world turned upside down in the state.

Ver. 5. "There is an evil which I have seen under the sun, like an error which proceedeth from the ruler." The introduction by the virtual relative *räithi* is as at v. 12, cf. vi. 1. Knobel, Hengst., and others give to the ב of שֶׁ׳ the meaning of "according to," or "in consequence of which," which harmonizes neither with ra'ah nor with räithi. Also Kleinert's translation: "There is a misery—I have seen it under the sun—in respect of an error which proceedeth from the ruler," is untenable; for by this translation ra'ah is made the pred. while it is the subj. to שׁ, and kishgagah the unfolding of this subject. Hitzig also remarks: "as [wie ein] an error, instead of which we have: in respect to [um einen] an error;" for he confounds things incongruous. Hitz., however, rightly recognises, as also Kleinert, the ב as Caph veritatis, which measures the concrete with the ideal, Isa. xiii. 6, compares the individual with the general which therein comes to view, Ezek. xxvi. 10; Neh. vii. 2; cf. 2 Sam. ix. 8. Koheleth saw an evil under the sun; something which was like an error, appeared to him altogether like an error which proceedeth from the ruler. If we could translate שֶׁ׳ by quod exiit, then ב would be the usual Caph similitudinis; but since it must be translated by quod exit, בש׳ וגו׳ places the observed fact under a comprehensive generality: it had the nature of an error proceeding from the ruler. If this is correct, it is so much the less to be assumed that by הַשַּׁלִּיט God is to be understood (Dan. v. 21), as Jerome was taught by his Hebraeus: quod putent homines in hac inaequalitate rerum illum non juste et ut aequum est judicare. It is a governor in a state that is meant, by whom an error might easily be committed, and only too frequently is committed, in the promotion or degradation of persons. But since the world, with its wonderful division of high and low, appears like as it were an error proceeding from the Most High, there certainly falls a shadow on the providence of God Himself, the Governor of the world; but yet not so immediately that the subject of discourse is an "error" of God, which would be a saying more than irreverent. יָצָא = יָצָה is the metaplastic form for יְצָאָה or יָצְאָת (for which at Deut. xxviii. 57 incorrectly יֹצֵת), not an error of transcription, as Olsh. supposes; vid. to the contrary, above, No. 1, p. 197. מִלִּפְנֵי (Symm. ἐξ ἔμπροσθεν) with יצא is the old usus loq. There now follows a sketch of the perverted world.

Vers. 6, 7. "Folly is set on great heights, and the rich must sit in lowliness. I have seen servants upon horses, and princes like servants walking on foot." The word הַסֶּכֶל (with double seghol, Aram. סַכְלוּ) is used here instead of those in whom it is personified. Elsewhere a multiplicity of things great, such as עַמִּים, מַיִם, and the like, is heightened by רַבִּים (cf. e.g. Ps. xviii. 17); here "great heights" are such as are of a high, or the highest degree; rabbim, instead of harabbim, is more appos. than adject. (cf. Gen. xliii.

14; Ps. lxviii. 28, cxliii. 10; Jer. ii. 21), in the sense of "many" (*e.g.* Ginsburg: "in many high positions") it mixes with the poetry of the description dull prose.¹ *'Ashirim* also is peculiarly used: *divites = nobiles* (cf. יָשׁיעַ, Isa. xxxii. 5), those to whom their family inheritance gives a claim to a high station, who possess the means of training themselves for high offices, which they regard as places of honour, not as sources of gain. *Regibus multis*, Grotius here remarks, quoting from Sallust and Tacitus, *suspecti qui excellunt sive sapientia sive nobilitate aut opibus.* Hence it appears that the relation of slaves and princes to each other is suggested; *hoc discrimen*, says Justin, xli. 3, of the Parthians, *inter servos liberosque est quod servi pedibus, liberi nonnisi equis incedunt*; this distinction is set aside, princes must walk *'al-haarĕts*, i.e. *b⁰regel* (*b⁰raglēhĕm*), and in their stead (Jer. xvii. 25) slaves sit high on horseback, and rule over them (the princes),—an offensive spectacle, Prov. xix. 10. The eunuch Bagoas (*vid.* above, p. 214), long all-powerful at the Persian Court, is an example of the evil consequences of this reversal of the natural relations of men.

That which is Difficult exposes to Danger; that which is Improper brings Trouble; that which comes Too Late is not of use, x. 8-11.

How much time, thought, and paper have been expended in seeking to find out a close connection between this group of verses and that going before! Some read in them warnings against rising in rebellion against despots (Ginsb.); others (*e.g.* Zöckl.) place these proverbs in relation to the by no means enviable lot of those upstarts (Zöckl.); more simply and more appropriately, Luther here finds exemplified the thought that to govern (*regere homines et gerere res humanas*) is a difficult matter; on the other hand, Luzz. finds in 8–11 the thought that all depends on fate, and not on the wisdom of man. In reality, this section forms a member in the carrying forward of the theme which the author has been discussing from ix. 13: wisdom and folly in their mutual relations, particularly in difficult situations of life. The catchword of the foregoing section is מַרְפֵּא, patience, resignation, which guards against rendering evil for evil; and the catchword of the following section is הַכְשִׁיר, considerate and provisory straining of the means toward the accomplishment of that which one purposes to do. The author presents a prelude in

---

¹ Luzz. reads נָתַן: "Folly brings many into high places." The order of the words, however, does not favour this.

four sentences, which denote by way of example, that whoever undertakes any severe labour, at the same time faces the dangers connected therewith.

Vers. 8, 9. "He that diggeth a pit may fall into it; whoso breaketh down walls, a serpent may sting him. Whoso pulleth out stones may do himself hurt therewith; he who cleaveth wood may endanger himself thereby." The futures are not the expression of that which will necessarily take place, for, thus rendered, these four statements would be contrary to experience; they are the expression of a possibility. The fut. יִפּוֹל is not here meant as predicting an event, as where the clause 8a is a figure of self-punishment arising from the destruction prepared for others, Prov. xxvi. 27; Sir. xxvii. 26. גּוּמָּץ is, Prov. xxvi. 27, the Targum word for שַׁחַת, ditch, from שׁוּחַ = נָמַץ, *depressum esse*. גָּדֵר (R. גד, to cut), something cutting off, something dividing, is a wall as a boundary and means of protection drawn round a garden, vineyard, or farm-court; פָּרַץ גָּדֵר is the reverse of גָּדַר פֶּרֶץ, Isa. lviii. 12. Serpents are accustomed to nestle in the crevices and holes of walls, as well as in the earth (for a city-wall is called חומה and חֵל); thus he who breaks into such a wall may expect that the serpent which is there will bite him (cf. Amos v. 19). To tear down stones, *hissi'a*, is synon. of *hhatsav*, to break stones, Isa. li. 1; yet *hhotsēv* does not usually mean the stone-breaker, but the stone-cutter (stone-mason); *hissi'a*, from *nasa'*, to tear out, does not also signify, 1 Kings v. 31, "to transport," and here, along with wood-splitting, is certainly to be thought of as a breaking loose or separating in the quarry or shaft. *Ne'etsav* signifies elsewhere to be afflicted; here, where the reference is not to the internal but the external feeling: to suffer pain, or reflex.: to injure oneself painfully; the derivat. *'etsev* signifies also severe labour; but to find this signification in the *Niph.* ("he who has painful labour") is contrary to the *usus loq.*, and contrary to the meaning intended here, where generally actual injuries are in view. Accordingly יִסָּכֶן בָּם, for which the Mishn. יְסַכֵּן בְּעַצְמוֹ,[1] "he brings himself into danger," would denote, to be placed in danger of life and limb, cf. *Gittin* 65b, *Chullin* 37a; and it is therefore not necessary, with Hitzig and others, to translate after the *vulnerabitur* of Jerome: "He may wound himself thereby;" there is not a denom. סָכַן, to cut, to wound, derived from סַכִּין (שַׂכִּין), an instrument for cutting, a knife.[2]

---

[1] *Vid.* above, p. 194.

[2] The Midrash understands the whole ethically, and illustrates it by the example of *Rabsake* [we know now that the half-Assyr., half-Accad. word *rabsak*

The sum of these four clauses is certainly not merely that he who undertakes a dangerous matter exposes himself to danger; the author means to say, in this series of proverbs which treat of the distinction between wisdom and folly, that the wise man is everywhere conscious of his danger, and guards against it. These two verses (8, 9) come under this definite point of view by the following proverb; wisdom has just this value in providing against the manifold dangers and difficulties which every undertaking brings along with it.[1] This is illustrated by a fifth example, and then it is declared with reference to all together.

Ver. 10. "If the iron has become blunt, and he has not whetted the face, then he must give more strength to the effort; but wisdom has the superiority in setting right." This proverb of iron, *i.e.* iron instruments (בַּרְזֶל, from בָּרַז, to pierce, like the Arab. name for iron, *hadîd*, means essentially something pointed), is one of the most difficult in the Book of Koheleth,—linguistically the most difficult, because scarcely anywhere else are so many peculiar and unexampled forms of words to be found. The old translators afford no help for the understanding of it. The advocates of the hypothesis of a Dialogue have here a support in אִם, which may be rendered interrogatively; but where would we find, syntactically as well as actually, the answer? Also, the explanations which understand חֲיָלִים in the sense of war-troops, armies, which is certainly its nearest-lying meaning, bring out no appropriate thought; for the thought that even blunt iron, as far as it is not externally altogether spoiled (*lo-phanim qilqal*), or: although it has not a sharpened edge (Rashi, Rashbam), might be an equipment for an army, or gain the victory, would, although it were true, not fit the context; Ginsburg explains: If the axe be blunt, and he (who goes out against the tyrant) do not sharpen it beforehand (*phanim*, after Jerome, for *lephanim*, which is impossible, and besides leads to nothing, since *lephanim* means *ehedem* [formerly], but not *zuvor* [*prius*], Ewald, § 220*a*), he (the tyrant) only increases his army; on the contrary, wisdom hath the advantage by repairing the mischief (without the war being unequal);—but the "ruler" of the foregoing group has here long ago disappeared, and it is only a bold imagination which discovers in the *hu* of 10*a* the person addressed in ver. 4, and represents him as a rebel, and augments

---

means a military chief], whom report makes a brother of Manasseh, and a renegade in the Assyrian service.

[1] Thus rightly Carl Lang in his *Salom. Kunst im Psalter* (Marburg 1874). He sees in vers. 8-10 a beautiful heptastich. But as to its contents, ver. 11 also belongs to this group.

him into a warlike force, but recklessly going forth with unwhetted swords. The correct meaning for the whole, in general at least, is found if, after the example of Abulwalîd and Kimchi, we interpret גַּבֵּר חֲיָלִים of the increasing of strength, the augmenting of the effort of strength, not, as Aben-Ezra, of conquering, outstripping, surpassing; גַּבֵּר means to make strong, to strengthen, Zech. x. 6, 12; and חֲיָלִים, as plur. of חַיִל, strength, is supported by גִּבּוֹרֵי חֲיָלִים, 1 Chron. vii. 5, 7, 11, 40, the plur. of נבור חיל; the LXX. renders by δυνάμεις δυναμώσει [and he shall strengthen the forces], and the Peshito has חַיְלֵי for δυνάμεις, Acts viii. 13, xix. 11 (cf. Chald. Syr. אִתְחַיַּל, to strengthen oneself, to become strengthened). Thus understanding the words יְגַ׳ יְחַ׳ of *intentio virium*, and that not with reference to sharpening (Luth., Grotius), but to the splitting of wood, etc. (Geier, Desvoeux, Mendelss.), all modern interpreters, with the exception of a few who lose themselves on their own path, gain the thought, that in all undertakings wisdom hath the advantage in the devising of means subservient to an end. The diversities in the interpretation of details leave the essence of this thought untouched. Hitz., Böttch., Zöckl., Lange, and others make the wood-splitter, or, in general, the labourer, the subject to קֵהָה, referring וְהוּא to the iron, and, contrary to the accents, beginning the apodosis with *qilqal*: "If he (one) has made the iron blunt, and it is without an edge, he swings it, and applies his strength." לֹא־פָנִים, "without an edge" (*lo* for *b'lo*), would be linguistically as correct as לֹא בָנִים, "without children," 1 Chron. ii. 30, 32; Ewald, § 286*g;* and *qilqal* would have a meaning in some measure supported by Ezek. xxi. 26. But granting that *qilqal*, which there signifies "to shake," may be used of the swinging of an axe (for which we may refer to the Aethiop. *kualkuala, kalkala,* of the swinging of a sword), yet קִלְקֵל (קִלְקַל אֹתוֹ) could have been used, and, besides, פָנִים means, not like פִּי, the edge, but, as a somewhat wider idea, the front, face (Ezek. xxi. 21; cf. Assyr. *pan ilippi*, the forepart of a ship); "it has no edge" would have been expressed by וְהוּא לֹא פֶה (פִּיפִיוֹת), or by וְהוּא אֵינֶנּוּ מְלֻטָּשׁ (מוֹרָט, מוּחָד). We therefore translate: if the iron has become blunt, *hebes factum sit* (for the Pih. of intransitives has frequently the meaning of an inchoative or desiderative stem, like מָעֵט, to become little, *decrescere*, xii. 3; כֵּהָה, *hebescere, caligare,* Ezek. xxi. 12; Ewald, § 120*d*), and he (who uses it) has not polished (whetted) the face of it, he will (must) increase the force. וְהוּא does not refer to the iron, but, since there was no reason to emphasize the sameness of the subject (as *e.g.* 2 Chron. xxxii. 30), to the labourer, and thus makes, as with the other explanation, the change of subject noticeable (as *e.g.* 2 Chron. xxvi. 1). The order of the words קֵל ... וְהֹ, *et ille non faciem (ferri) exacuit,* is as at Isa. liii. 9; cf. also the position of *lo* in 2 Sam. iii. 34; Num. xvi. 29.

קִלְקֵל, or pointed with *Pattach* instead of *Tsere* (cf. *qarqar,* Num. xxiv. 17) in bibl. usage, from the root-meaning *levem esse,* signifies to move with ease, *i.e.* quickness (as also in the Arab. and Aethiop.), to shake (according to which the LXX. and Syr. render it by ταράσσειν, דָּלַח, to shake, and thereby to trouble, make muddy); in the Mishn. usage, to make light, little, to bring down, to destroy; here it means to make light = even and smooth (the contrast of rugged and notched), a meaning the possibility of which is warranted by נְח׳ קָלָל, Ezek. i. 7, Dan. x. 6 (which is compared by Jewish lexicographers and interpreters), which is translated by all the old translators "glittering brass," and which, more probably than Ewald's "to steel" (temper), is derived from the root *qal,* to burn, glow.[1] With *vahhaylim* the apodosis begins; the style of Koheleth recognises this *vav apod.* in conditional clauses, iv. 11, cf. Gen. xliii. 9, Ruth iii. 13, Job vii. 4, Mic. v. 7, and is fond of the inverted order of the words for the sake of emphasis, xi. 8, cf. Jer. xxxvii. 10, and above, under vii. 22.

In 10*b* there follows the common clause containing the application. Hitzig, Elster, and Zöckl. incorrectly translate: "and it is a profit wisely to handle wisdom;" for instead of the inf. absol. הַכ׳, they unnecessarily read the inf. constr. הַכְשִׁיר, and connect הַכְשִׁיר חָכְמָה, which is a phrase altogether unparalleled. *Hichsir* means to set in the right position (*vid.* above, p. 193, *kaser*), and the sentence will thus mean: the advantage which the placing rightly of the means serviceable to an end affords, is wisdom—*i.e.* wisdom bears this advantage in itself, brings it with it, concretely: a wise man is he who reflects upon this advantage. It is certainly also possible that הכש׳, after the manner of the *Hiph.* הצליח and השביל, directly means "to succeed," or causatively: "to make to succeed." We might explain, as *e.g.* Knobel: the advantage of success, or of the causing of prosperity, is wisdom, *i.e.* it is that which secures this gain. But the meaning prevalent in post-bibl. Heb. of making fit, equipping,—a predisposition corresponding to a definite aim or result, —is much more conformable to the example from which the *porisma* is deduced. Buxtorf translates the *Hiph.* as a Mishnic word by *aptare, rectificare.* Tyler suggests along with "right guidance" the meaning "pre-arrangement," which we prefer.[2]

[1] Regarding the two roots, *vid.* Fried. Delitzsch's *Indogerm.-Sem. Stud.* p. 91 f.
[2] Also the twofold Haggadic explanation, *Taanith* 8*a,* gives to *hachshir* the

Ver. 11. The last proverb of this series presents for consideration the uselessness of him who comes too late. "If a serpent bite without enchantment, the charmer is of no use." The Talm. interprets this אם, like that of ver. 10, also as interrog.: Does the serpent bite without its being whispered to, i.e. without a providential determination impelling it thereto? *Jer. Peah*, i. 1. But לחש, except at Isa. xxvi. 16, where whispering prayers are meant, signifies the whispering of formulas of charming; "serpents are not to be charmed (tamed)," לחש, Jer. viii. 17. Rather for בַּעַל הַלָּ׳ the meaning of slander is possible, which is given to it in the Haggada, *Taanith* 8a: All the beasts will one day all at once say to the serpent: the lion walks on the earth and eats, the wolf tears asunder and eats; but what enjoyment hast thou by thy bite? and it answers them: "Also the slanderer (לבעל הלשון) has certainly no profit." Accordingly the Targ., Jerome, and Luther translate; but if אִם is conditional, and the *vav* of *v*ᵉ*ēn* connects the protasis and the apodosis, then *ba'al hallashon* must denote a man of tongue, viz. of an enchanting tongue, and thus a charmer (LXX., Syr.). This name for the charmer, one of many, is not unintentional; the tongue is an instrument, as iron is, ver. 10: the latter must be sharp, if it would not make greater effort necessary; the former, if it is to gain its object, must be used at the right time. The serpent bites בְּלֹא לָ׳, when it bites before it has been charmed (cf. *b*ᵉ*lo yomo*, Job xv. 32); there are also serpents which bite without letting themselves be charmed; but here this is the point, that it anticipates the enchantment, and thus that the charmer comes too late, and can make no use of his tongue for the intended purpose, and therefore has no advantage from his act. There appropriately follow here proverbs of the use of the tongue on the part of a wise man, and its misuse on the part of a fool.

The Worthless Prating and the Aimless Labour of the Fool, x. 12–15.

It is wisdom, as the preceding series of proverbs has shown, to be on one's guard to provide oneself with the right means, and to observe the right time. These characteristics of the wise man ver. 11 has brought to view, by an example from the sphere of action in which the tongue serves as the instrument. There now follows, not unexpectedly, a proverb with reference to that which the words of a wise man and the words of a fool respectively bring about.

meaning of "to set, *à priori*, in the right place." Luther translated *qilqal* twice correctly, but further follows the impossible rendering of Jerome: *multo labore exacuetur, et post industriam sequetur sapientia.*

Ver. 12. "The words of a wise man's mouth are grace; but the lips of a fool swallow him up." The words from a wise man's mouth are חֵן, graciousness, *i.e.* gracious in their contents, their form and manner of utterance, and thus also they gain favour, affection, approbation, for culture (education) produces favour, Prov. xiii. 15, and its lips grace (pleasantness), which has so wide an influence that he can call a king his friend, Prov. xxii. 11, although, according to ix. 11, that does not always so happen as is to be expected. The lips of a fool, on the contrary, swallow him, *i.e.* lead him to destruction. The *Pih.* בַּלַּע, which at Prov. xix. 28 means to swallow down, and at Prov. xxi. 20 to swallow = to consume in luxury, to spend dissolutely, has here the metaphorical meaning of to destroy, to take out of the way (for that which is swallowed up disappears). שִׂפְתוֹת is parallel form to שִׂפְתֵי, like the Aram. סִפְוָת. The construction is, as at Prov. xiv. 3, " the lips of the wise תִּשְׁמֹר preserve them ;" the idea of unity, in the conception of the lips as an instrument of speech, prevails over the idea of plurality. The words of the wise are heart-winning, and those of the fool self-destructive. This is verified in the following verse.

Ver. 13. "The beginning of the words of his mouth is foolishness; and the end of his mouth is mischievous madness." From folly (absurdity) the words which are heard from a fool's mouth rise to madness, which is compounded of presumption, wantonness, and frenzy, and which, in itself a symptom of mental and moral depravity, brings as its consequence destruction on himself (Prov. xviii. 17). The adjective רָעָה is as in חֳלִי רָע, which interchanges with רָעָה חוֹלָ vi. 2, v. 12, etc. The end of his mouth, viz. of his speaking, is = the end of the words of his mouth, viz. the end which they at last reach. Instead of *holeloth*, there is here, with the adj. following, *holeluth*, with the usual ending of *abstracta*. The following proverb says how the words of the fool move between these two poles of folly and wicked madness: he speaks much, and as if he knew all things.

Ver. 14. "And the fool maketh many words: while a man yet doth not know that which shall be; and what shall be when he is no more, who can show him that?" The *vav* at the beginning of this verse corresponds to the Lat. *accedit quod.* That he who in 12*b* was named *k^esil* is now named *hassachal*, arises from this, that meanwhile *sichluth* has been predicated of him. The relation of 14*b* to 14*a*, Geier has rightly defined: *Probatur absurditas multiloquii a communi ignorantia ac imbecillitate humana, quae tamen praecipue dominatur apud ignaros stultos.* We miss before *lo-yeda'* an "although" (*gam,*

Neh. vi. 1, or *ki gam*, viii. 12); the clause is, after the manner of a clause denoting state or condition, subordinated to the principal clause, as at Ps. v. 10: "an open grave is their throat לְשׁ׳ יַחֲ׳, although they smooth their tongue, *i.e.* speak flatteringly." The LXX., Syr., Symm., and Jerome seek to rectify the tautology *id quod futurum est et quod futurum est* (cf. on the other hand, viii. 7), for they read יה׳ . . . מה שהיה. But the second *quod futurum* certainly preserves by מֵאַחֲ׳ its distinguishing nearer definition. Hitzig explains: "What is done, and what after this (that is done) is done." Scarcely correctly: *aharav* of the parallel passage, vi. 12, cf. vii. 14, ix. 3, requires for the suffix a personal reference, so that thus *meaharav*, as at Deut. xxix. 21, means "from his death and onwards." Thus, first, the knowledge of the future is denied to man; then the knowledge of what will be done after his death; and generally, of what will then be done. The fool, without any consciousness of human ignorance, acts as if he knew all, and utters about all and everything a multitude of words; for he uselessly fatigues himself with his ignorance, which remains far behind the knowledge that is possible for man.

Ver. 15. "The labour of the foolish wearieth him who knoweth not how to go to the city." If we do not seek to explain: labour such as fools have wearies him (the fool), then we have here such a *synallage numeri* as at Isa. ii. 8, Hos. iv. 8, for from the plur. a transition is made to the distributive or individualizing sing. A greater anomaly is the treatment of the noun עָמָל as fem. (greater even than the same of the noun *pithgam*, viii. 11, which admitted of attractional explanation, and, besides, in a foreign word was not strange). Kimchi, *Michlol* 10*a*, supposes that עמל is thought of in the sense of יְגִיעַת עָמָל; impossible, for one does not use such an expression. Hitzig, and with him Hengst., sees the occasion for the synallage in the discordance of the masc. יְיַגְּעֶנּוּ; but without hesitation we use the expressions יָיֵחַל, Mic. v. 6, 'יָם, Josh. vi. 26, and the like. '*Amal* also cannot be here *fem. unitatis* (Böttch. § 657. 4), for it denotes the wearisome striving of fools as a whole and individually. We have thus to suppose that the author has taken the liberty of using '*amal* once as fem. (*vid.* on the contrary, ii. 18, 20), as the poet, Prov. iv. 13, in the introduction of the Book of Proverbs uses *musar* once as fem., and as the similarly formed צָבָא is used in two genders. The fool kindles himself up and perplexes himself, as if he could enlighten the world and make it happy,—he who does not even know how to go to the city. Ewald remarks: "Apparently proverbial, viz. to bribe the great lords in the city." For us who, notwithstanding ver. 16, do not trouble ourselves any more with the tyrants of ver. 4, such thoughts, which do violence to the connection, are unnecessary. Hitzig also, and with him Elst. and Zöckl., thinks of the city as the residence of the rulers from whom oppression proceeds, but from whom also help against oppression is to be sought. All this is to be rejected. Not to know how to go to the city, is = not to be able to find the open public street, and, like the Syrians, 2 Kings vi. 18 f., to be smitten with blindness. The way to the city is *via notissima et tritissima*. Rightly Grotius, like Aben Ezra: *Multi quaestionibus arduis se fatigant, cum ne obvia quidem norint, quale est iter ad urbem.* אֶל־עִיר is vulgar for אֶל־הָעִיר. In the Greek language also the word πόλις has a definite signification, and Athens is called ἄστυ, mostly without the art. But Stamboul, the name of which may seem as an illustration of the proverbial phrase, " not to know how to go to the city," is = εἰς τὴν πόλιν. Grätz finds here an allusion to the Essenes, who avoided the city—*habeat sibi!*

THIRD CONCLUDING SECTION, WITH THE FINALE AND EPILOGUE

(*A.*) WARNINGS AGAINST IDLE REVELRY AND IMPROVIDENCE, AND A CALL TO A FRESH EFFORT AFTER A HAPPY IMPROVEMENT OF LIFE.— X. 16–XI. 7.

The Prosperity of a Country, its Misfortune, and Thoughtful Foresight, x. 16–20.

Interpreters have sought in every way to discover a close connection between the following proverbs of the bad and good princes, and those that precede. Hitzig, rightly dissatisfied with this forced attempt, cuts the knot by putting vers. 16–19 into the mouth of the fool, ver. 15 : Koheleth, ver. 20, refers to him this rash freedom of speech, and warns him against such language ; for, supposing that vers. 16–19 were the words of Koheleth, in ver. 20 he would contradict himself. This unworthy perversion of the contents of the section rectifies itself. The supposed words of the fool belong to the most peculiar, most impressive, and most beautiful utterances of the חכם which the Book of Koheleth contains, and the warning, ver. 20, against cursing the king, stands in no contradiction to the " woe," ver. 16 ; Isaiah under Ahaz, Jeremiah under Zedekiah, actually show how the two are in harmony; and the apostles even in the times of Nero acted on their " honour the king." Rather it may be said that the author in ver. 16, from fools in general (ver. 15) comes to speak of folly in the position occupied by a king and princes. But "folly" is not the characteristic name for that which is unseemly and indecorous which is blamed in these high lords. From x. 16, the Book of Koheleth turns toward the conclusion; since it represents itself as a discourse of Solomon's on the subject of the wisdom of life, and all through has a sharp eye on rulers and their surroundings, it is not strange that it treated of it in x. 4–7, and again now returns to the theme it had scarcely left.

Vers. 16, 17. "Woe to thee, O land, whose king is a child, and whose princes sit at table in the early morning! Happy art thou, O land, whose king is a noble, and whose princes sit at table at the right time, in manly strength, and not in drunkenness!" Regarding אִי, vid. above, p. 191. Instead of שֶׁנַּ׳, the older language would rather use the phrase אֲשֶׁר נַעַר מַלְכּוֹ; and instead of na'ar, we might correctly use, after Prov. xxx. 22, 'ĕvĕd; but not as Grätz thinks, who from this verse deduces the reference of the book to Herod (the "slave of the Hasmonean house," as the Talm. names him), in the same meaning. For na'ar, it is true, sometimes means—e.g. as Ziba's by-name (2 Sam. xix. 18 [17])—a servant, but never a slave as such, so that here, in the latter sense, it might be the contrast of בְּן־חוֹרִים; it is to be understood after Isa. iii. 12; and Solomon, Bishop of Constance, understood this woe rightly, for he found it fulfilled at the time of the last German Karolingian Ludwig III.[1] Na'ar is a very extensively applicable word in regard to the age of a person. King Solomon and the prophets Jeremiah and Zechariah show that na'ar may be used with reference to one in a high office; but here it is one of few years of age who is meant, who is incapable of ruling, and shows himself as childish in this, that he lets himself be led by bad guides in accordance with their pleasure. In 16b, the author perhaps thinks of the heads of the aristocracy who have the phantom-king in their power: intending to fatten themselves, they begin their feasting with the break of day. If we translate yochĕlu by "they eat," 16b sounds as if to breakfast were a sin,—with us such an abbreviation of the thought so open to misconception would be a fault in style, but not so with a Hebrew.[2] אָכֹל (for אֲכֹל לֶחֶם, Ps. xiv. 4) is here eating for eating's sake, eating as its own object, eating which, in the morning, comes in the place of fresh activity in one's calling, consecrated by prayer. Instead of אִשֵּׁ׳, 17a, there ought properly to have been אַשְׁרֶיךָ; but (1) אַשְׁרֵי has this peculiarity, to be explained from its interjectional usage, that with the suff.

---

[1] Cf. Büchmann's *Geflügelte Worte*, p. 178, 5th ed. (1868).
[2] Vid. *Gesch. d. jüd. Poesie*, p. 188 f.

added it remains in the form of the *st. constr.*, for we say *e.g.* אַשְׁרֵיךָ for אֲשָׁרֶיךָ; (2) the sing. form אֶשֶׁר, inflected אַשְׁרֵי, so substitutes itself that אַשְׁרֶיךָ, or, more correctly, אַשְׁרֵךְ, and אַשְׁרֵהוּ, Prov. xxix. 19, the latter for אַשְׁרָיו, are used (vid. under Song ii. 14). Regarding *bĕn-hhorim*, vid. above, p. 191; the root-word signifies to be white (vid. under Gen. xl. 16). A noble is called *hhor*, Isa. xxxiv. 12; and one noble by birth, more closely, or also merely descriptively (Gesen. Lehrgeb. p. 649), *bĕn-hhorim*, from his purer complexion, by which persons of rank were distinguished from the common people (Lam. iv. 7). In the passage before us, *bĕn-hhorim* is an ethical conception, as *e.g.* also *generosus* becomes such, for it connects with the idea of noble by birth that of noble in disposition, and the latter predominates (cf. Song vii. 2, *nadiv*): it is well with a land whose king is of noble mind, is a man of noble character, or, if we give to *bĕn-hhorim* the Mishnic meaning, is truly a free man (cf. John viii. 36). Of princes after the pattern of such a king, the contrary of what is said 16b is true: they do not eat early in the morning, but *ba'et*, "at the right time;" everywhere else this is expressed by *bᵉitto* (iii. 11); here the expression—corresponding to the Greek ἐν καιρῷ, the Lat. *in tempore*—is perhaps occasioned by the contrast *baboqĕr*, "in the morning." Eating at the right time is more closely characterized by *bighvurah vᵉlo vashshᵉthi*. Jerome, whom Luther follows, translates: *ad reficiendum et non ad luxuriam*. Hitz., Ginsb., and Zöckl. "for strengthening" (obtaining strength), not: "for feasting;" but that *beth* might introduce the object aimed at (after Hitz., proceeding from the *beth* of exchange), we have already considered under ii. 4. The author, wishing to say this, ought to have written לִגְבוּרָה וְלֹא לִשְׁתִי. Better, Hahn: "in strength, but not in drunkenness,"—as heroes, but not as drunkards (Isa. v. 22). Ewald's "in virtue, and not in debauchery," is also thus meant. But what is that: to eat in virtue, *i.e.* the dignity of a man? The author much rather represents them as eating in manly strength, *i.e.* as this requires it (cf. the plur. Ps. lxxi. 16 and Ps. xc. 10), only not *bashti* ("in drunkenness—excess"), so that eating and drinking become objects in themselves. Kleinert, well: as men, and not as gluttons. The Masora makes, under *bashti*, the note לֵית, *i.e.* שְׁתִי has here a meaning which it has not elsewhere, it signifies drunkenness; elsewhere it means the weft of a web. The Targ. gives the word the meaning of weakness (חַלָּשׁוּת), after the Midrash, which explains it by בְּחוּלְשֵׁי (in weakness); Menahem b. Saruk takes along with it in this sense נִשְׁתָּה, Jer. li. 30. The Talm. *Shabbath* 10a, however, explains it rightly by בִּשְׁתִיָּה שֶׁל־יַיִן.

Ver. 18. Since, now, ver. 19 has only to do with princes, the following proverb of the consequences of sloth receives a particular reference in the frame of this mirror for princes: " Through being idle the roof falleth; and through laziness of the hands the house leaketh." Ewald, Redslob, Olsh., Hitz., and Fürst, as already Aben Ezra, understand the dual עֲצַלְ׳ of the two idle hands, but a similar attribut. adject.-dual is not found in Heb.; on the contrary, *ephraim*, *m'rathaim* Jer. l. 21, *rish'athaim*, and, in a certain measure, also *riqmathaim*, speak in favour of the intensification of the dual; *'atsaltaim* is related to *'atslah*, as *Faulenzen* [being idle, living in idleness] to *Faulheit* [laziness], it means doubled, *i.e.* great, constant laziness (Gesen. *H. Wört.*, and Böttch. in the *N. Aehrenl.*, under this passage). If *'atsaltaim* were an attribut. designation of the hands, then *shiphluth yadaim* would be lowness, *i.e.* the hanging down of the hands languidly by the side; the former would agree better with the second than with the first passage. Regarding the difference between *hamm^eqareh* (the beams and joists of a house) and *hamqareh* (*contignans*), *vid.* note below.[1] Since exceeding laziness leaves alone everything that could support the house, the beams fall (יִמַּךְ, *Niph.* מָכַךְ), and the house drops, *i.e.* lets the rain through (יִדְלֹף, with *o*, in spite of the intrans. signification); cf. the Arab. proverb of the three things which make a house insufferable, under Prov. xix. 13. Also the community, whom the king and the nobles represent, is a בַּיִת, as *e.g.* Israel is called the house of Jacob. If the rulers neglect their duty, abusing their high position in obeying their own lusts, then the kingdom (state) becomes as a dilapidated house, affording no longer any protection, and at last a *machshelah*, a ruined building, Isa. iii. 6. It becomes so by slothfulness, and the prodigal love of pleasure associated therewith.

Ver. 19. "Meals they make into a pleasure, and wine cheereth the life, and money maketh everything serviceable." By עֹשִׂים, wicked princes are without doubt thought of,—but not immediately, since 16*b* is too remote to give the subject to ver. 19. The subject which *'osim* bears in itself (= *'osim hēm*) might be syntactically definite, as *e.g.* Ps. xxxiii. 5, אֹהֵב, He, Jahve, loves, thus: those princes, or, from ver. 18: such slothful men; but *'osim* is better rendered, like *e.g. omrim*, Ex. v. 16 (Ewald, § 200*a*), and as in the Mishna we read קוֹרִין and the like with gramm. indef. subj.: they make, but so that by it the slothful just designated, and those of a princely rank are meant (cf. a similar use of the *inf. abs.*, as here of the part. in the

---

[1] הַמְּקָרֶה, with *mem* Dagheshed (Masora: ליח דנש); in Ps. civ. 3, on the contrary, the *mem* has *Raphe*, for there it is particip. (*Michlol* 46*a;* Parchon's *Lex.* f. 3, col. 1).

historical style, Isa. xxii. 13). Ginsburg's rendering is altogether at fault: "They turn bread and wine which cheereth life into revelry." If עשה and לֶחֶם as its object stand together, the meaning is, "to prepare a feast," Ezek. iv. 15; cf. *'avad lᵉhĕm*, Dan. v. 1. Here, as there, *'osim lĕhĕm* signifies *coenam faciunt (parant)*. The ל of לְשׂ׳ is not the sign of the factitive obj. (as *lᵉēl*, Isa. xliv. 17), and thus not, as Hitz. supposes, the conditioning ל with which adv. conceptions are formed,—*e.g.* Lam. iv. 5, הָאֹכְ׳ לְמַעֲ׳, where Jerome rightly translates, *voluptuose* (*vid.* E. Gerlach, *l.c.*),—but, which is most natural and is very appropriate, it is the ל of the aim or purpose: *non ad debitam corporis refectionem, sed ad mera ludicra et stulta gaudia* (Geier). שְׂחוֹק is laughter, as that to which he utters the sentence (ii. 2): Thou art mad. It is incorrect, moreover, to take *lĕhĕm vᵉyaim* together, and to render *yᵉsammahh hayaim* as an attribut. clause to *yain*: this *epitheton ornans* of wine would here be a most unsuitable weakening of the figure intended. It is only an apparent reason for this, that what Ps. civ. 15 says in praise of wine the author cannot here turn into a denunciatory reproach. Wine is certainly fitted to make glad the heart of a man; but here the subject of discourse is duty-forgetting idlers, to whom chiefly wine must be brought (Isa. v. 12) to cheer their life (this sluggard-life spent in feasting and revelry). The fut. יְשַׂמַּח is meant in the same modal sense as יְנַבֵּר, 10*a*: wine must accomplish that for them. And they can feast and drink, for they have money, and money יַעֲ׳ ... הַכֹּל־. Luther hits the meaning: "Money must procure everything for them;" but the clause is too general; and better thus, after Jerome, the Zürich Bible: "unto money are all things obedient." The old Jewish interpreters compare Hos. ii. 23 f., where ענה, with *accus. petentis*, signifies, "to answer a request, to gratify a desire." But in the passage before us הַכֹּל is not the obj. accus. of *petentis*, but *petiti*; for *'anah* is connected with the accus. of that to which one answers as well as of that which one answers, *e.g.* Job xl. 2, cf. ix. 3. It is unnecessary, with Hitzig, to interpret יַעֲנֶה as *Hiph.*: Money makes all to hear (him who has the money),—makes it that nothing is refused to his wish. It is the *Kal*: Money answers to every demand, hears every wish, grants whatever one longs for, helps to all; as Menander says: "Silver and gold,—these are, according to my opinion, the most useful gods; if these have a place in the house, wish what thou wilt (εὖξαι τί βούλει), all will be thine;" and Horace, *Epod.* i. 6. 36 s.:

> "*Scilicet uxorem cum dote fidemque et amicos
> Et genus et formam regina pecunia donat.*"

The author has now described the king who is a misfortune and him who is a blessing to the land, and princes as they ought to be and as they ought not to be, but particularly luxurious idle courtiers; there is now a warning given which has for its motive not only prudence, but also, according to viii. 2, religiousness.

Ver. 20. "Curse not the king even in thy thought; and in thy bed-chamber curse not the rich; for the birds of the air carry away the sound, and the winged creature telleth the matter." In the Books of Daniel and Chronicles, מַדָּע, in the sense of γνῶσις, is a synon. of הַשְׂכֵּל and חָכְמָה; here it is rightly translated by the LXX. by συνείδησις; it does not correspond with the moral-religious idea of conscience, but yet it touches it, for it designates the quiet, inner consciousness (*Psychol.* p. 134) which judges according to moral criteria: even (*gam*, as *e.g.* Deut. xxiii. 3) in the inner region of his thoughts [1] one must not curse the king (cf. vii. 4 f.) nor the rich (which here, as at 6*b*, without distinction of the aristocracy of wealth and of birth, signifies those who are placed in a high princely position, and have wealth, the *nervus rerum*, at their disposal) in his bed-chamber, the innermost room of the house, where one thinks himself free from treachery, and thus may utter whatever he thinks without concealment (2 Kings vi. 12): for the birds of the air may carry forth or bring out (Lat. *deferrent*, whence *delator*) that which is rumoured, and the possessor of a pair of wings (cf. Prov. i. 17), after the *Chethîb* (whose ה of the art. is unnecessarily erased by the *Kerî*,[2] as at iii. 6, 10): the possessor of wings (double-winged), shall further tell the matter. As to its meaning, it is the same as the proverb quoted by the Midrash: "walls have ears."[3] Geier thinks of the swallows which helped to the discovery of Bessus, the murderer of his father, and the cranes which betrayed the murderer of Ibycus, as comparisons approaching that which is here said. There would certainly be no hyperbole if the author thought of carrier-pigeons (Paxton, Kitto) in the service of espionage. But the reason for the warning is hyperbolical, like an hundred others in all languages:

> "*Aures fert paries, oculos nemus: ergo cavere
> Debet qui loquitur, ne possint verba nocere.*"

---

[1] Hengst., not finding the transition from *scientia* to *conscientia* natural, gives, after Hartmann, the meaning of "study-chamber" to the word מַדָּע; but neither the Heb. nor the Aram. has this meaning, although Ps. lxviii. 13 Targ. touches it.

[2] הַבְּעַל with unpointed *He*, because it is not read in the *Kerî*; similarly הַחֲנִית (1 Sam. xxvi. 22). Cf. *Mas. fin.* f. 22, and *Ochla veochla*, No. 166.

[3] *Vid.* Tendlau's *Sprichwörter*, No. 861.

*Act Prudently, but not too Prudently—the Future is God's;
Enjoy Life—the World to come is Dark,* xi. 1–8.

There are interpreters (as *e.g.* Zöckl.) who regard the concluding part of the book as commencing with xi. 1, and do not acknowledge any connection with that which immediately precedes; but from x. 16 the book draws to its conclusion. לחם, x. 19, affords an external connection for the proverb here following; but, since the proverb x. 20 lies between, the sequence after the same catchword is uncertain. Whether there is here a more inward connection, and what it is, is determined by the interpretation of xi. 1, which proceeds in two fundamentally different directions, the one finding therein recommended unscrupulous beneficence, the other an unscrupulous spirit of enterprise. We decide in favour of the latter: it is a call, derived from commercial pursuits, to engage in fresh enterprise.

xi. 1. " Let thy bread go forth over the watery mirror: for in the course of many days shalt thou find it." Most interpreters, chiefly the Talm., Midrash, and Targ.,[1] regard this as an exhortation to charity, which although practised without expectation of reward, does not yet remain unrewarded at last. An Aram. proverb of Ben Sira's (*vid.* Buxtorf's *Florilegium,* p. 171) proceeds on this interpretation: " Scatter thy bread on the water and on the dry land; in the end of the days thou findest it again." Knobel quotes a similar Arab. proverb from Diez' *Denkwürdigkeiten von Asien* (Souvenirs of Asia), II. 106: " Do good; cast thy bread into the water: thou shalt be repaid some day." See also the proverb in Goethe's *Westöst. Divan,* compared by Herzfeld. Voltaire, in his *Précis de l'Ecclésiaste en vers,* also adopts this rendering:

> *Repandez vós bienfaits avec magnificence,*
> *Même aux moins vertueux ne les refusez pas.*
> *Ne vous informez pas de leur reconnaissance—*
> *Il est grand, il est beau de faire des ingrats.*

That instead of " into the water (the sea) " of these or similar proverbs, Koheleth uses here the expression, " on the face of (עַל־פְּנֵי) the waters," makes no difference; Eastern bread has for the most part

[1] The Midrash tells the following story: Rabbi Akiba sees a ship wrecked which carried in it one learned in the law. He finds him again actively engaged in Cappadocia. What whale, he asked him, has vomited thee out upon dry land? How hast thou merited this? The scribe learned in the law thereupon related that when he went on board the ship, he gave a loaf of bread to a poor man, who thanked him for it, saying: As thou hast saved my life, may thy life be saved. Thereupon Akiba thought of the proverb in Eccles. xi. 1. Similarly the Targ.: Extend to the poor the bread for thy support; they sail in ships over the water.

the form of cakes, and is thin (especially such as is prepared hastily for guests, *'ughoth* or *matstsoth*, Gen. xviii. 6, xix. 3); so that when thrown into the water, it remains on the surface (like a chip of wood, Hos. x. 7), and is carried away by the stream. But שַׁלַּח, with this reference of the proverb to beneficence, is strange; instead of it, the word הַשְׁלֵךְ was rather to be expected; the LXX. renders by ἀπόστειλον; the Syr., *shadar*; Jerome, *mitte*; Venet. πέμπε; thus by none is the pure idea of casting forth connected with שַׁלַּח. And the reason given does not harmonize with this reference: "for in the course of many days (*b^erov yamin*, cf. *mērov yamim*, Isa. xxiv. 22) wilt thou find it" (not "find it again," which would be expressed by תָּשׁוּב תִּמְ'). This indefinite designation of time, which yet definitely points to the remote future, does not thus indicate that the subject is the recompense of noble self-renunciation which is sooner or later rewarded, and often immediately, but exactly accords with the idea of commerce carried on with foreign countries, which expects to attain its object only after a long period of waiting. In the proper sense, they send their bread over the surface of the water who, as Ps. cvii. 33 expresses, "do business in great waters." It is a figure taken from the corn trade of a seaport (*vid.* p. 216), an illustration of the thought: seek thy support in the way of bold, confident adventure.[1] Bread in לֶחֶם is the designation of the means of making a living or gain, and bread in תִּמְצָאֶנּוּ the designation of the gain (cf. ix. 11). Hitzig's explanation: Throw thy bread into the water = venture thy hope, is forced; and of the same character are all the attempts to understand the word of agricultural pursuits; *e.g.* by van der Palm: *sementem fac juxta aquas* (or: *in loca irrigua*); Grätz even translates: "Throw thy corn on the surface of the water," and understands this, with the fancy of a Martial, of begetting children. Mendelssohn is right in remarking that the exhortation shows itself to be that of Koheleth-Solomon, whose ships traded to Tarshish and Ophir. Only the reference to self-sacrificing beneficence stands on a level with it as worthy of consideration. With Ginsburg, we may in this way say that a proverb as to our dealings with those who are above us, is followed by a proverb regarding those who are below us; with those others a proverb regarding judicious courageous venturing, ranks itself with a proverb regarding a rashness which is to be discountenanced; and the following proverb does not say: Give a portion, distribute of that which is thine, to seven and also to eight: for it is well done that thou gainest for thee friends with the unrighteous

---

[1] The Greek phrase σπείρειν πόντον, "to sow the sea" = to undertake a fruitless work, is of an altogether different character; cf. Amos vi. 12.

mammon for a time when thou thyself mayest unexpectedly be in want; but it is a prudent rule which is here placed by the side of counsel to bold adventure:

Ver. 2. "Divide the portion into seven, yea, eight (parts); for thou knowest not what evil shall happen on the earth." With that other interpretation, עָלָיו was to be expected instead of 'al-haarets; for an evil spreading abroad over the earth, a calamity to the land, does not yet fall on every one without exception; and why was not the רָעָה designated directly as personal? The impression of the words תֵּן ... לְשִׁמ׳, established in this general manner, is certainly this, that on the supposition of the possibility of a universal catastrophe breaking in, they advise a division of our property, so that if we are involved in it, our all may not at once be lost, but only this or that part of it, as Jacob, Gen. xxxii. 9, says. With reference to 1a, it is most natural to suppose that one is counselled not to venture his all in one expedition, so that if this is lost in a storm, all might not at once be lost (Mendelss., Preston, Hitz., Stuart); with the same right, since 1a is only an example, the counsel may be regarded as denoting that one must not commit all to one caravan; or, since in ver. 2 לחמך is to be represented not merely as a means of obtaining gain, that one ought not to lay up all he has gathered in one place, Judg. vi. 11, Jer. xli. 8 (Nachtigal); in short, that one ought not to put all into one business, or, as we say literally, venture all on one card. חֵלֶק is either the portion which one possesses, i.e. the measure of the possession that has fallen to him (Ps. xvi. 5), or נָתַן חֵלֶק means to make portions, to undertake a division. In the first case, the expression נתן ... לְ follows the scheme of Gen. xvii. 20: make the part into seven, yea, into eight (parts); in the second case, the scheme of Josh. xviii. 5: make division into seven, etc. We prefer the former, because otherwise that which is to be divided remains unknown; חֵלֶק is the part now in possession: make the much or the little that thou hast into seven or yet more parts. The rising from seven to eight is as at Job v. 19, and like the expression *ter quaterque*, etc. The same inverted order of words as in 2b is found in Esth. vi. 3; 2 Kings viii. 12.

Ver. 3. With this verse there is not now a transition, εἰς ἄλλο γένος (as when one understands ver. 1 f. of beneficence); the thoughts down to ver. 6 move in the same track. "When the clouds are full of rain, they empty themselves on the earth: and if a tree fall in the south, or in the north—the place where the tree falleth, there it lieth." Man knows not—this is the reference of the verse backwards—what misfortune, as *e.g.* hurricane, flood, scarcity, will come upon the earth; for all that is done follows fixed laws, and the binding together of cause and effect is removed beyond the influence of the will of man, and also in individual cases beyond his knowledge. The interpunction of 3 *a a* : אִם־יִמָּלְא֣וּ הֶעָבִ֣ים גֶּ֗שֶׁם (not as by v. d. Hooght, Mendelss., and elsewhere הֶעָבִים, but as the Venet. 1515, 21, Michael. הֶעָבִים, for immediately before the tone syllable *Mahpach* is changed into *Mercha*) appears on the first glance to be erroneous, and much rather it appears that the accentuation ought to be

אם־ימלאו העבים גשם על־הארץ יריקו

but on closer inspection גשם is rightly referred to the conditional antecedent, for "the clouds could be filled also with hail, and thus not pour down rain" (Hitz.). As in iv. 10, the fut. stands in the protasis as well as in the apodosis. If A is done, then as a consequence B will be done; the old language would prefer the words אם, (כי) נמלאו ... והריקו, Ewald, § 355*b* : as often as A happens, so always happens B. יָרִיקוּ carries (without needing an external object to be supplied), as internally transitive, its object in itself: if the clouds above fill themselves with rain, they make an emptying, *i.e.* they empty themselves downwards. Man cannot, if the previous condition is fixed, change the necessary consequences of it.

The second conditioning clause: *si ceciderit lignum ad austrum aut ad aquilonem, in quocunque loco ceciderit ibi erit.* Thus rightly Jerome (*vid.* above, p. 152). It might also be said: ואם־יפול עץ אם בדרום ואם בצפון, and if a tree falls, whether it be in the south or in the north; this *sive . . . sive* would thus be a parenthetic parallel definition. Thus regarded, the protasis as it lies before us consists in itself, as the two *v*e*im* in Amos ix 3, of two correlated halves: "And if a tree falls on the south side, and (or) if it fall on the north side," *i.e.* whether it fall on the one or on the other. The *Athnach*, which more correctly belongs to יריקו, sets off in an expressive way the protasis over against the apodosis; that a new clause begins with *v*e*im yippol* is unmistakeable; for the contrary, there was need for a chief disjunctive to בצ'. *M*e*qom* is *accus. loci* for *bimqom*, as at Esth. iv. 3, viii. 17. *Sham* is rightly not connected with the relat. clause (cf. Ezek. vi. 13); the relation is the same as at i. 7. The fut. יְהוּא is formed from הָוָה, whence ii. 22, as at Neh. vi. 6, and in the Mishna (*Aboth*, vi. 1;[1] *Aboda zara*, iii. 8) the part. הוֶה. As the jussive form יְהִי is formed from יִהְיֶה, so יְהוָה (יֶהֱוֶה) passes into יְהוּ, which is here written יְהוּא. Hitzig supposes that, according to the passage before us and Job xxxvii. 6, the word appears to have been written with א,

[1] *Vid.* Baer, *Abodath Jisrael*, p. 290.

in the sense of " to fall." Certainly הוה has the root-signification of *delabi, cadere*, and derives from thence the meaning of *accidere, exsistere, esse* (*vid.* under Job xxxvii. 6); in the Book of Job, however, הוה may have this meaning as an Arabism; in the *usus loq.* of the author of the Book of Koheleth it certainly was no longer so used. Rather it may be said that יְהוּ had to be written with an א added to distinguish it from the abbreviated tetragramm, if the א, as in אָבוּא, Isa. xxviii. 12, and הֵלִ֥ךְ, Josh. x. 24, does not merely represent the long terminal vowel (cf. the German-Jewish דוא = thou, דיא = the, etc.).[1] Moreover, יְהוּא, as written, approaches the Mishnic inflection of the fut. of the verb הוה; the sing. there is אֱהֵא, תֶּהֱא, יְהֵא, and the plur. יְהוּ, according to which Rashi, Aben Ezra, and Kimchi interpret יְהוּא here also as plur; Luzzatto, § 670, hesitates, but in his Commentary he takes it as sing., as the context requires: there will it (the tree) be, or in accordance with the more lively meaning of the verb הוה: there will it find itself, there it continues to lie. As it is an invariable law of nature according to which the clouds discharge the masses of water that have become too heavy for them, so it is an unchangeable law of nature that the tree that has fallen before the axe or the tempest follows the direction in which it is impelled. Thus the future forms itself according to laws beyond the control of the human will, and man also has no certain knowledge of the future; wherefore he does well to be composed as to the worst, and to adopt prudent preventive measures regarding it. This is the reference of ver. 3 looking backwards. But, on the other hand, from this incalculableness of the future—this is the reference of ver. 3 looking forwards—he ought not to give up fresh venturesome activity, much rather he ought to abstain from useless and impeding calculations and scruples.

Ver. 4. " He who observeth the wind shall not sow; and he that regardeth the clouds shall not reap." The proverb is not to be understood literally, but in the spirit of the whole *paraenesis*: it is not directed against the provident observation, guided by experience, of the monitions and warnings lying in the present condition of the weather, but against that useless, because impossible, calculation of the coming state of the weather, which waits on from day to day, from week to week, till the right time for sowing and reaping has passed away. The seed-time requires rain so as to open up and moisten the ground; he who has too much hesitation observes (שֹׁמֵר, as at Job xxxix. 1) the wind whether it will bring rain (Prov.

---

[1] Otherwise Ewald, § 192*b*: יְהוּא, Aram. of הוּא (as בּוֹא) = הָוֵא.

xxv. 23), and on that account puts off the sowing of the seed till it is too late. The time of harvest requires warmth without rain (Prov. xxvi. 1); but the scrupulous and timid man, who can never be sure enough, looks at the clouds (cf. Isa. xlvii. 13), scents rainy weather, and finds now and never any security for the right weather for the gathering in of the fruits of the field. He who would accomplish and gain anything, must have confidence and courage to venture something; the conditions of success cannot be wholly reckoned upon, the future is in the hand of God, the All-Conditioning.

Ver. 5. "As thou hast no knowledge what is the way of the wind, like as the bones in the womb of her who is with child; so thou knowest not the work of God who accomplisheth all." Luther, after Jerome, renders rightly: "As thou knowest not the way of the wind, and how the bones in the mother's womb do grow; so," etc. The clause, *instar ossium in ventre praegnantis*, is the so-called *comparatio decurtata* for *instar ignorantiae tuae ossium*, etc., like thy ignorance regarding the bones, *i.e.* the growth of the bones. בְּעֶ֫צֶם,[1] because more closely defined by בְּבֶ֫טֶן הַמְּ, has not the art. used elsewhere after כ of comparison; an example for the regular syntax (*vid.* Riehm, under Ps. xvii. 12) is found at Deut. xxxii. 2. That man has no power over the wind, we read at viii. 8; the way of the wind he knows not (John iii. 8), because he has not the wind under his control: man knows fundamentally only that which he rules. Regarding the origin and development of the embryo as a secret which remained a mystery to the Israel. Chokma, *vid. Psychol.* p. 209 ff. For עֶ֫צֶם, cf. Ps. cxxxix. 15 and Job x. 11. Regarding *m'leah*, pregnant (like the Lat. *plena*), *vid.* above, p. 193. With fine discrimination, the fut. לֹא תֵדַע in the apodosis interchanges with the particip. אֵינְךָ יוֹדֵעַ in the protasis, as when we say: If thou knowest not that, as a consequence thou shalt also not know this. As a man must confess his ignorance in respect to the way of the wind, and the formation of the child in the mother's womb; so in general the work of God the All-Working lies beyond his knowledge: he can neither penetrate it in the entireness of its connection, nor in the details of its accomplishment. The idea *'oseh kol*, Isa. xliv. 24, is intentionally unfolded in a fut. relat. clause, because here the fut. in the natural world, as well as in human history, comes principally into view. For that very reason the words אֶת־הַכֹּל are also used, not: (as in passages where there is a reference to the world of creation in its present condition) *eth-kol-elleh*, Isa. lxvi. 2. Also the growth of the

---

[1] The Targ. reads בְּעֶ֫צֶם, and construes: What the way of the spirit in the bones, *i.e.* how the embryo becomes animated.

child in the mother's womb is compared to the growth of the future in the womb of the present, out of which it is born (Prov. xxvii. 1 ; cf. Zeph. ii. 2). What is established by this proof that man is not lord of the future,—viz. that in the activity of his calling he should shake off anxious concern about the future,—is once again inferred with the combination of what is said in vers. 4 and 2 (according to our interpretation, here confirmed).

Ver. 6. "In the morning sow thy seed, and towards evening withdraw not thine hand; for thou knowest not which shall prosper, whether this or that, or whether both together shall well succeed." The cultivation of the land is the prototype of all labour (Gen. ii. 15*b*), and sowing is therefore an emblem of all activity in one's pursuit; this general meaning for יָדְךָ . . . אַל (like vii. 18 ; synon. with ידי . . . אל, Josh. x. 6, of the older language) is to be accepted. The parallel word to *babokĕr* is not *ba'ĕrĕv;* for the cessation from work (Judg. xix. 16 ; Ps. civ. 23) must not be excluded, but incessant labour (cf. Luke ix. 62) must be continued until the evening. And as ver. 2 counsels that one should not make his success depend exclusively on one enterprise, but should divide that which he has to dispose of, and at the same time make manifold trials; so here also we have the reason for restless activity of manifold labour from morning till evening: success or failure (v. 5*b*) is in the hand of God,—man knows not which (*quid*, here, according to the sense, *utrum*) will prosper (*vid.* regarding *kasher*, above, p. 193), whether (זֶה) this or (אוֹ) that, and whether (וְאִם), etc. ; *vid.* regarding the three-membered disjunctive question, Ewald, § 361 ; and regarding *kᵉĕhhad*, above, p. 192; it is in common use in the more modern language, as *e.g.* also in the last benediction of the *Shemone-Esra:* ברכנו . . . כאחד, "bless us, our Father, us all together." שְׁנֵיהֶם goes back to the two זה, understood neut. (as at vii. 18 ; cf. on the contrary, vi. 5). The LXX. rightly : καὶ ἐὰν (better : εἴτε) τὰ δύο ἐπὶ τὸ αὐτὸ ἀγαθά. Luther, who translates: "and if both together it shall be better," has been misled by Jerome.

The proverb now following shows its connection with the preceding by the copula *vav*. "The tendency of the advice in vers. 1, 2, 6, to secure guarantees for life, is justified in ver. 7: life is beautiful, and worthy of being cared for." Thus Hitzig; but the connection is simpler. It is in the spirit of the whole book that, along with the call to earnest activity, there should be the call to the pleasant enjoyment of life: he who faithfully labours has a right to enjoy his life ; and this joy of life, based on fidelity to one's calling, and consecrated by the fear of God, is the most real and the highest enjoyment here below. In this sense the *fruere vita* here connects itself with the *labora:*

Vers. 7, 8. "And sweet is the light, and pleasant it is for the eyes to see the sun: for if a man live through many years, he ought to rejoice in them all, and remember the days of darkness; that there will be many of them. All that cometh is vain." Dale translates the copula *vav* introducing ver. 7 by "yes," and Bullock by "truly," both thus giving to it a false colouring. "Light," Zöckler remarks, stands here for "life." But it means only what the word denotes, viz. the light of life in this world (Ps. lvi. 14; Job xxxiii. 30), to which the sun, as the source of it, is related, as מָאוֹר is to אוֹר. Cf. Eurip. *Hippol.*, ὦ λαμπρὸς αἰθὴρ κ.τ.λ., and *Iphigen. in Aulis*, 1218–19, μή μ' ἀπολέσῃς κ.τ.λ.: "Destroy not my youth; to see the light is sweet," etc. The ל in לְעֵ֫ין has the short vowel *Pattach*, here and at 1 Sam. xvi. 7, after the Masora.[1]

The *ki* beginning ver. 8 is translated by Knobel, Hitz., Ewald, and others by "*ja*" (yes); by Heiligstedt, as if a negative preceded by *immo;* but as the *vav* of 7a is copulative "and," so here the *ki* is causal "for." If it had been said: man must enjoy himself as long as he lives, for the light is sweet, etc., then the joy would have its reason in the opportunity given for it. Instead of this, the occasion given for joy has its reason in this, that a man ought to rejoice, viz. according to God's arrangement and ordinance: the light is sweet, and it is pleasant for the eyes to see the sun; for it ought thus to be, that a man, however long he may live, should continue to enjoy his fair life, especially in view of the night which awaits him. *Ki im* are not here, as at iii. 12, viii. 15, where a negative precedes, to be taken together; but *ki* assigns the reason, and *im* begins a hypothetical protasis, as at Ex. viii. 17, and frequently. *Im*, with the conclusion following, presents something impossible, as *e.g.* Ps. l. 12, *si esurirem*, or also the extreme of that which is possible as actual, *e.g.* Isa. vii. 18, *si peccata vestra sint instar coccini*. In the latter case, the clause with the concessive particle may be changed into a sentence with a concessive conjunctive, as at Isa. x. 22: "for though thy people, O Israel, be as numerous as the sand of the sea;" and here: "though a man may live ever so many years." The second *ki* after יִֽחְיֶ֫ה is the explicat. *quod*, as at ii. 24, iv. 4, viii. 17, etc.: he must remember the days of darkness, that there shall be many of them, and, at all events, not fewer than the many years available for the happy enjoyment of life. In this connection *kol-shebba'*

---

[1] Cf. on the contrary, at Gen. iii. 6 and Prov. x. 26, where it has the *Kametz*; cf. also *Michlol* 53b.

denotes all that will come after this life. If Hitz. remarks that the sentence: "All that is future is vanity," is a false thought, this may now also be said of his own sentence extracted from the words: "All that is, is transitory." For all that is done, in time may pass away; but it is not actually transitory (הֶבֶל). But the sentence also respects not all that is future, but all that comes after this life, which must appear as vain (hĕvĕl) to him for whom, as for Koheleth, the future is not less veiled in the dark night of Hades, as it was for Horace, i. 4. 16 s.:

> "*Jam te premet nox fabulaeque Manes*
> *Et domus exilis Plutonia.*"

Also, for Koheleth as for Horace, iv. 7. 16, man at last becomes *pulvis et umbra*, and that which thus awaits him is *hĕvĕl*. Tyler is right, that "the shadowy and unsubstantial condition of the dead and the darkness of Sheol" is thus referred to. הַבָּא signifies not that which is *nascens*, but *futurum*, e.g. Sanhedrin 27a, "from the present ולהבא and for the future" (for which, elsewhere, the expression לעתיד לבא is used). The Venet. construes falsely: All (the days) in which vanity will overtake (him); and Luther, referring בא as the 3d pers. to the past, follows the misleading of Jerome. Rightly the LXX. and Theod.: πᾶν τὸ ἐρχόμενον.

(*B.*) FINALE, WITH AN EPIPHONEMA.—XI. 9–XII. 7, 8.

In xi. 7, 8, having again reached the fundamental saying of his earthly eudaemonism, the author now discontinues this his *ceterum censeo*, and artistically rounds off his book; for having begun it with an *ouverture*, i. 2–11, he concludes it with a *finale*, xi. 9–xii. 7. Man, in view of the long night of death into which he goes forth, ought to enjoy the life granted to him. This fundamental thought of the book, to which the author has given a poetic colouring, xi. 7, 8, now amplifies itself into an animated highly poetical call to a young man to enjoy life, but not without the consciousness that he must render unto God an account for it. That the call is addressed not to a man as such, but to the young man,—including, however, after the rule *a potiori fit denominatio*, young women,— is explained from this, that the *terminus a quo* of an intelligent, responsible enjoyment of life stands over against the *terminus ad quem*, the night of death, with its pre-intimation in hoary old age. Without any connecting word, and thus as a new point of departure, the *finale* begins:

Ver. 9. "Rejoice, young man, in thy youth; and let thy heart cheer thee in the days of thy youth, and walk in the ways of thine heart, and in the sight of thine eyes: but know, that for all this God will bring thee to judgment." The parallel בִּימֵי shows that the *beth* in בְּיַלְד (with ד aspirated) does not introduce the reason of the joy, but the time suitable for it. Instead of *v*ᵉ*yithav libb*ᵉ*cha*, "let thy heart be of good cheer," as the expression might also be, the words are *vithiv*ᵉ*cha libb*ᵉ*cha*, "make thy heart of good cheer to thee,"—so, viz., that from this centre brightness may irradiate thy countenance (Prov. xv. 13) and thy whole personality, vid. *Psychologie*, p. 249. *V*ᵉ*hhuroth*, the period of youth, is here and at xii. 1 = Num. xi. 28, *v*ᵉ*hhurim*, as the only once occurring *n*ᵉ*uroth*, Jer. xxxii. 30, is = the elsewhere generally used *n*ᵉ*urim*; the form in *ôth* is the more modern (cf. *k*ᵉ*luloth*, Jer. ii. 2). "Ways of the heart" are thus ways into which the impulse of the heart leads, and which satisfy the heart. מַר׳ עֵינ׳, at vi. 9, designates the pleasure felt in the presence of the object before one; here, a sight which draws and fastens the eyes upon it. The *Chethîb* has the plur. מַרְאֵי, which is known to the language (Dan. i. 15; Song ii. 14), and which would here designate the multitude of the objects which delight the eyes, which is not unsuitable; the *Pih.* הִלֵּךְ denotes also elsewhere, frequently, e.g. Ps. cxxxi. 1, walking, in an ethical sense; Hitz., Zöckl., and others interpret the first ב as specifying the sphere, and the second as specifying the norm ("according to the sight of thine eyes"); but they both introduce that wherein he ought to act freely and joyfully: in the ways of thy heart, into which it draws thee; and in the sight of thine eyes, towards which they direct themselves with interest. The LXX. B. renders, "and not after the sight of thine eyes." This "not" (μή), which is wanting in A. C., is an interpolation, in view of the warning, Num. xv. 39, against following the impulse of the heart and of the eyes; the Targ. also therefore has: "be prudent with reference to the sight of thine eyes." But this moralizing of the text is superfluous, since the call to the youthful enjoyment of life is accompanied with the *nota bene:* but know that God will bring thee to an account for all this; and thus it excludes sinful sensual desire. In the midst of an address, where a yet closer definition follows, בְּמִשׁ׳ is thus punctuated, xii. 14, Job xiv. 3, Ps. cxliii. 3; here, in the conclusion of the sentence, it is בַּמִּשׁ׳. Hitzig supposes that there is denoted by it, that the sins of youth are punished by chronic disease and abandonment in old age; Knobel and others understand by the judgment, the self-punishment of sins by all manner of evil consequences, which the O. T. looks upon as divinely inflicted penalties. But in view of the facts of experience, that God's righteous requital is in this life too frequently escaped, viii. 14, the author, here and at iii. 17, xii. 14, postulates a final judgment, which removes the contradiction of this present time, and which must thus be in the future; he has no clear idea of the time and manner of this final judgment, but his faith in God places the certainty of it beyond all doubt. The call to rejoice is now completed by the call to avoid all that occasions inward and outward sorrow.

Ver. 10. "And remove sorrow from thy heart, and banish evil from thy flesh: for youth and age, not yet grown to grey hairs, are vain." Jerome translates: *aufer iram a corde tuo*, and remarks in his *Comm.*: *in ira omnes perturbationes animi comprehendit;* but כַּעַס (R. כס, *contundere, confringere*) does not signify anger, but includes both anger and sorrow, and thus corresponds to the specific ideas, "sadness, moroseness, fretfulness." The clause following, Jerome translates: *et amove malitiam a carne tua*, with the remark: *in carnis malitia universas significat corporis voluptates;* but רָעָה is not taken in an ethical, but in a physical sense: כעס is that which brings sorrow to the heart; and רעה, that which brings evil to the flesh (בשׂר, *opp.* לב, ii. 3, Prov. xiv. 30). More correctly than the Vulgate, Luther renders: "banish sorrow from thy heart, and put evil from thy body." He ought to free himself from that which is injurious to the inner and the outer man, and hurtfully affects it; for youth, destined for and disposed to joy, is *hevel, i.e.* transitory, and only too soon passes away. Almost all modern interpreters (excepting the Jewish), in view of Ps. cx. 3, give to שַׁחֲרוּת the meaning of "the dawn of the morning;" but the connection with יַלְדוּת would then be tautological; the Mishn.-Midrash *usus loq.*, in conformity with which the Targ. translates, "days of black hair," proves that the word does not go back to שַׁחַר, morning dawn, morning-red, but immediately to שָׁחוֹר, black (*vid.* above, p. 196), and as the contrast of שֵׂיבָה (non-bibl. שִׂיבוּת, סֵיב׳, סָב׳), *canities*, denotes the time of black hair, and thus, in the compass of its conception, goes beyond ילדות, since it comprehends both the period of youth and of manhood, and thus the whole period during which the strength of life remains unbroken.[1]

With xii. 1 (where, inappropriately, a new chapter begins,

---

[1] The Mishna, *Nedarim* iii. 8, jurist. determines that שְׁחוֹרֵי הָרֹאשׁ denotes men, with the exclusion of women (whose hair is covered) and children. It is disputed (*vid.* Baer's *Abodath Jisrael*, p. 279) whether תִּשְׁחֹרֶת, *Aboth* iii. 16, *Derech erez* c. II., *Midrash* under Lam. ii. 11, is = שַׁחֲרוּת, but without right; *ben-tishhoreth* is used for a grown-up son in full manly strength.

instead of beginning with xi. 9) the call takes a new course, resting its argument on the transitoriness of youth: " And remember thy Creator in the days of thy youth, ere the days of evil come, and the years draw nigh, of which thou shalt say: I have no pleasure in them." The *plur. majest.* בּוֹרְאֶיךָ is = עֹשִׂים as a designation of the Creator, Job xxxv. 10, Isa. liv. 5, Ps. cxlix. 2; in so recent a book it cannot surprise us (cf. above, p. 292), since it is also not altogether foreign to the post-bibl. language. The expression is warranted, and the Midrash ingeniously interprets the combination of its letters.[1] Regarding the words *'ad asher lo,* commonly used in the Mishna (*e.g. Horajoth* iii. 3; *Nedarim* x. 4), or *'ad shello* (Targ. *'ad d^elo*), *antequam, vid.* above, p. 195. The days of evil (viz. at least, first, of bodily evil, cf. κακία, Matt. vi. 34) are those of feeble, helpless old age, perceptibly marking the failure of bodily and mental strength; parallel to these are the years of which (*asher,* as at i. 10) one has to say: I have no pleasure in them (*bahĕm* for *bahĕn,* as at ii. 6, *mehĕm* for *mehĕn*). These evil days, adverse years, are now described symptomatically, and that in an allegorical manner, for the " ere " of 1*b* is brought to a grand unfolding.

Ver. 2. " Ere the sun becomes dark, and the light, and the moon, and the stars, and the clouds return after the rain." Umbreit, Elster, and Ginsburg find here the thought: ere death overtakes thee; the figure under which the approach of death is described being that of a gathering storm. But apart from other objections (*vid.* Gurlitt, " zur Erkl. d. B. Koheleth," in *Stud. u. Krit.* 1865), this idea is opposed by the consideration that the author seeks to describe how man, having become old, goes forth (הָלַךְ, 5*b*) to death, and that not till ver. 7 does he reach it. Also Taylor's view, that what precedes 5*b* is as a dirge expressing the feelings experienced on the day of a person's death, is untenable; it is discredited already by this, that it confuses together the days of evil, 1*b*, and the many days of darkness, *i.e.* the long night of Hades, xi. 8; and besides, it leaves unanswered the question, what is the meaning of the clouds returning after the rain. Hahn replies: The rain is death, and the return is the entrance again into the nothingness which went before the entrance into this life. Knobel, as already Luther and also Winzer (who had made the exposition of the Book of Koheleth one of the labours of his life), sees in the darkening of the sun, etc., a figure of the decay of hitherto joyful prosperity; and in the clouds after the

---

[1] It finds these things expressed in it, partly directly and partly indirectly: remember בְּאֵרְךָ, thy fountain (origin); בּוֹרְךָ, thy grave; and בּוֹרַאֲךָ, thy Creator. Thus *Jer. Sota* ii. 3, and Midrash under Eccles. xii. 1.

rain a figure of the cloudy days of sorrow which always anew visit those who are worn out by old age. Hitz., Ewald, Vaih., Zöckl., and Tyler, proceeding from thence, find the unity of the separate features of the figure in the comparison of advanced old -age, as the winter of life to the rainy winter of the (Palestinian) year. That is right. But since in the sequel obviously the *marasmus senilis* of the separate parts of the body is set forth in allegorical enigmatic figures, it is asked whether this allegorical figurative discourse does not probably commence in ver. 2. Certainly the sun, moon, and stars occur also in such pictures of the night of judgment, obscuring all the lights of the heavens, as at Isa. xiii. 10 ; but that here, where the author thus ranks together in immediate sequence וְהַ֫ ... חַשֶּׁ֫, and as he joins the stars with the moon, so the light with the sun, he has not connected the idea of certain corresponding things in the nature and life of man with these four emblems of light, is yet very improbable. Even though it might be impossible to find out that which is represented, yet this would be no decisive argument against the significance of the figures ; the *canzones* in Dante's *Convito*, which he there himself interprets, are an example that the allegorical meaning which a poet attaches to his poetry may be present even where it cannot be easily understood or can only be conjectured.

The attempts at interpreting these figures have certainly been wholly or for the most part unfortunate. We satisfy ourselves by registering only the oldest: their glosses are in matter tasteless, but they are at least of linguistic interest. A Barajtha, *Shabbath* 151–152a, seeking to interpret this closing picture of the Book of Koheleth, says of the sun and the light: "this is the brow and the nose ;" of the moon: "this is the soul ;" of the stars: "this the cheeks." Similarly, but varying a little, the Midrash to Lev. c. 18 and to Koheleth : the sun = the brightness of the countenance ; light = the brow ; the moon = the nose ; the stars = the upper part of the cheeks (which in an old man fall in). Otherwise, but following the Midrash more than the Talmud, the Targum: the sun = the stately brightness of thy countenance ; light = the light of thine eyes ; the moon = the ornament of thy cheeks ; the stars = the apple of thine eye. All the three understand the rain of wine (Talm.: בכי), and the clouds of the veil of the eyes (Targ.: " thy eye - lashes "), but without doing justice to שׁוּב אחר ; only one repulsive interpretation in the Midrash takes these words into account. In all these interpretations there is only one grain of truth, this, viz., that the moon in the Talm. is interpreted of the נִשָׁמָה, *anima*, for which the more correct word would have been נֶפֶשׁ ;

but it has been shown, *Psychol.* p. 154, that the Jewish, like the Arab. psychology, reverses terminologically the relation between רוּחַ (נְשָׁמָה), spirit, and נֶפֶשׁ, soul.

The older Christian interpretations are also on the right track. Glassius (as also v. Meyer and Smith in " The portraiture of old age ") sees in the sun, light, etc., emblems of the *interna microcosmi lumina mentis;* and yet better, Chr. Friedr. Bauer (1732) sees in 2*a* a representation of the thought: " ere understanding and sense fail thee." We have elsewhere shown that רוּחַ חַיִּים (נִשְׁמַת) and נֶפֶשׁ חַיָּה (for which nowhere נֶפֶשׁ חַיִּים) are related to each other as the *principium principians* and *principium principatum* of life (*Psychol.* p. 79), and as the root distinctions of the male and female, of the predominantly active and the receptive (*Psychol.* p. 103). Thus the figurative language of ver. 3 is interpreted in the following manner. The sun is the male spirit רוּחַ (which, like שֶׁמֶשׁ, is used in both genders) or נְשָׁמָה, after Prov. xx. 27, a light of Jahve which penetrates with its light of self-examination and self-knowledge the innermost being of man, called by the Lord, Matt. vi. 23 (cf. 1 Cor. ii. 11), " the light that is in thee." The light, viz. the clear light of day proceeding from the sun, is the activity of the spirit in its unweakened intensity: sharp apprehension, clear thought, faithful and serviceable memory. The moon is the soul; for, according to the Heb. idea, the moon, whether it is called יָרֵחַ or לְבָנָה, is also in relation to the sun a figure of the female (cf. Gen. xxxvii. 9 f., where the sun in Joseph's dream = Jacob-Israel, the moon = Rachel); and that the soul, viz. the animal soul, by means of which the spirit becomes the principle of the life of the body (Gen. ii. 7), is related to the spirit as female σκεῦος ἀσθενέστερον, is evident from passages such as Ps. xlii. 6, where the spirit supports the soul (*animus animam*) with its consolation. And the stars? We are permitted to suppose in the author of the Book of Koheleth a knowledge, as Schrader[1] has shown, of the old Babyl.-Assyr. seven astral gods, which consisted of the sun, moon, and the five planets; and thus it will not be too much to understand the stars, as representing the five planets, of the five senses (Mishn. הָרְגָּשׁוֹת,[2] later הֻשִּׁים, cf. the verb, ii. 25) which mediate the receptive relation of the soul to the outer world (*Psychol.* p. 233). But we cannot see our way further to explain 2*b* patholo.-anatom., as Geier is disposed to do: *Nonnulli haec accommodant ad crassos illos ac pituosos senum vapores ex debili ventriculo in cerebrum adscendentes continuo, ubi itidem imbres* (נשם) *h. e. destillationes creber-*

---

[1] Vid. " Sterne " in Schenkel's *Bib. Lex.* and *Stud. u. Krit.* 1874.
[2] Thus the five senses are called, *e.g. Bamidbar rabba,* c. 14.

rimae per oculos lippientes, per nares guttatim fluentes, per os subinde excreans cet., *quae sane defluxiones, tussis ac catharri in juvenibus non ita sunt frequentia, quippe ubi calor multo adhuc fortior, consumens dissipansque humores.* It is enough to understand עָבִים of cases of sickness and attacks of weakness which disturb the power of thought, obscure the consciousness, darken the mind, and which *ahhar haggĕshĕm*, after they have once overtaken him and then have ceased, quickly again return without permitting him long to experience health. A cloudy day is = a day of misfortune, Joel ii. 2, Zeph. i. 15; an overflowing rain is a scourge of God, Ezek. xiii. 13, xxxviii. 22; and one visited by misfortune after misfortune complains, Ps. xlii. 8 [7]: "Deep calleth unto deep at the noise of thy waterspouts: all thy waves and thy billows are gone over me."

Ver. 3. To the thought: Ere the mind and the senses begin to be darkened, and the winter of life with its clouds and storms approaches, the further details here following stand in a subordinate relation: "That day when the watchers of the house tremble, and the strong men bow themselves, and the grinders rest, because they have become few, and the women looking out of the windows are darkened." Regarding בַּיּוֹם with art.: *eo* (*illo*) *tempore, vid.* under Song viii. 8. What follows is regarded by Winzer, with Mich., Spohr, and partly Nachtigal, as a further description of the night to which old age, ver. 2, is compared: Watchers then guard the house; labourers are wearied with the labours and cares of the day; the maids who have to grind at the mill have gone to rest; and almost all have already fallen asleep; the women who look out from the windows are unrecognisable, because it has become dark. But what kind of cowardly watchers are those who "tremble," and what kind of (*per antiphrasin*) strong men who "bow themselves" at evening like children when they have belly-ache! Ginsburg regards vers. 2-5 as a continuation of the description of the consequences of the storm under which human life comes to an end: the last consequence is this, that they who experience it lose the taste for almonds and the appetite for locusts. But what is the meaning of this quaint figure? it would certainly be a meaningless and aimless digression. Taylor hears in this verse the mourning for the dead from ver. 2, where death is described: the watchers of the house tremble; the strong men bow themselves, viz. from sorrow, because of the blank death has made in the house, etc.; but even supposing that this picture had a connection in ver. 2, how strange would it be!—the lookers out at the windows must be the " ladies," who are fond of amusing themselves at windows, and who now—are darkened. Is there anything more comical than such little ladies having become darkened (whether externally or internally remains undetermined)? However one may judge of the figurative language of ver. 2, ver. 3 begins the allegorical description of hoary old age after its individual bodily symptoms; interpreters also, such as Knobel, Hitz., and Ewald, do not shrink from seeking out the significance of the individual figures after the old Haggadic manner. The Talm. says of *shomrē habbayith* : these are the loins and ribs; of the *anshē hehhayil* : these are the bones; of *harooth baarŭbboth*: these, the eyes. The Midrash understands the watchers of the house, of the knees of the aged man; the men of strength, of his ribs or arms; the women at the mill, of the digestive organs (הַמְסֵס,[1] the stomach, from *omasum*); those who have become few, of the teeth; the women looking out at the window, of the eyes; another interpretation, which by *harooth* thinks of the lungs, is not worth notice.

Here also the Targ. principally follows the Midrash: it translates the watchers of the house by " thy knees;" strong men by " thine arms;" the women at the mill by " the teeth of thy mouth;" the women who look out at the window by " thine eyes." These interpretations for the most part are correct, only those referable to the internal organs are in bad taste; references to these must be excluded from the interpretation, for weakness of the stomach, emphysema of the lungs, etc., are not appropriate as poetical figures. The most common biblical figures of the relation of the spirit or the soul to the body is, as we have shown, *Psychol.* p. 227, that of the body as of the house of the inner man. This house, as that of an old man, is on all sides in a ruinous condition. The *shomrē habbayith* are the arms terminating in the hands, which bring to the house whatever is suitable for it, and keep away from it whatever threatens to do it injury; these protectors of the house have lost their vigour and elasticity (Gen. xlix. 24), they tremble, are palsied (יְזֻעוּ, from זוּעַ, *Pilp.* זִעֲזֵעַ, bibl. and Mishn.: to move violently hither and thither, to tremble, to shake[2]), so that they are able neither to grasp securely, to hold fast and use, nor actively to keep back and forcibly avert evil. *Anshē hĕhhayil* designates the legs, for the *shoqē hāish* are the seat of his strength, Ps. cxlvii. 10; the legs of a man in the fulness of youthful strength are like marble pillars, Song x. 15; but those of the old man *hith'authu* (*Hithpa.* only here) have bowed themselves, they

---

[1] This *hamses* is properly the second stomach of the ruminants, the cellular caul.
[2] *Vid.* Friedr. Delitzsch's *Indogerm.-Se.n. Stud.* p. 65 f.

have lost their tight form, they are shrunken (בְּרָעוֹת, Job iv. 4, etc.) and loose ; 4 Macc. iv. 5 calls this τὴν ἐκ τοῦ γήρως νωθρότητα ποδῶν ἐπικύφων. To maidens who grind (cf. טֹחֲנֹ֖ת בָּ֑ר, Num. xi. 8 and Isa. xlvii. 2) the corn by means of a hand-mill are compared the teeth, the name of which in the old language is masc., but in the modern (cf. Prov. xxix. 19), as also in the Syr. and Arab., is fem.; the reference of the figure to these instruments for grinding is not to be missed ; the Arab. *ṭaḥinat* and the Syr. *ṭaḥonto* signify *dens molaris*, and we now call 6 of the 32 teeth *Mahlzähne* (molar teeth, or grinders); the Greeks used for them the word μύλαι (Ps. lvii. 7, LXX.). Regarding בְּטֵלוּ, LXX. ἤργησαν (= ἀεργοὶ ἐγενήθησαν), vid. above, p. 191.[1] The clause כִּי מִעֵטוּ (LXX. ὅτι ὠλιγώθησαν) assigns the reason that the grinders rest, *i.e.* are not at work, that they have become few : they stand no longer in a row ; they are isolated, and (as is to be supposed) are also in themselves defective. Taylor interprets *mi'etu* transitively : the women grinding rest when they have wrought a little, *i.e.* they interrupt their labour, because on account of the occurrence of death, guests are now no longer entertained ; but the beautiful appropriate allegory maintains its place against this supposed lamentation for the dead ; also מִעֵט does not signify to accomplish a little (Targ.), but to take away, to become few (LXX., Syr., Jerome, Venet., Luther), as such a *Pih.* as x. 10, קָהָה, to become blunt. And by הָרֹאוֹת בָּאֲ֯ we are not to think, with Taylor, of women such as Sisera's mother or Michal, who look out of the window, but of the eyes, more exactly the apples of the eyes, to which the *orbita* (LXX. ἐν ταῖς ὀπαῖς ; Symm. διὰ τῶν ὀπῶν) and the eyelids with the eye-lashes are related as a window is to those who look out ; אֲרֻבָּה (from אָרַב, R. רב, to entwine firmly and closely) is the window, consisting of a lattice of wood ; the eyes are, as Cicero (*Tusc.* i. 20) calls them, *quasi fenestrae animi*; the soul-eyes, so to speak, without which it could not experience what sight is, look by means of the external eyes ; and these soul-bodily eyes have become darkened in the old man, the power of seeing is weakened, and the experiences of sight are indistinct, the light of the eyes is extinguished (although not without exception, Deut. xxxiv. 7).

[1] We find a similar allegory in *Shabbath* 152a. The emperor asked the Rabbi Joshua b. Chananja why he did not visit בי אבידן (a place where learned conversation, particularly on religious subjects, was carried on). He answered : " The mount is snow (= the hair of the head is white), ice surrounds me (= whiskers and beard on the chin white), its (of my body) dogs bark not (the voice fails), and its grinders (the teeth) grind not." The proper meaning of בי אבידן, Levy has not been able clearly to bring to light in his *Neuhebr. u. Chald.* W. B.

Ver. 4. From the eyes the allegory proceeds to the mouth, and the repugnance of the old man to every noise disturbing his rest: "And the doors to the street are closed, when the mill sounds low; and he rises up at the voice of a bird; and all the daughters of song must lower themselves." By the door toward the street the Talm. and Midrash understand the pores or the emptying members of the body,—a meaning so far from being ignoble, that even in the Jewish morning prayer a *Beracha* is found in these words: "Blessed art Thou, O Lord our God, King of the world, who hast wisely formed man, and made for him manifold apertures and cavities. It is manifest and well known before the throne of Thy Majesty, that if one of these cavities is opened, or one of these apertures closed, it is impossible for him to exist and to stand before Thee; blessed art Thou, O Lord, the Physician of the body, and who doest wondrous works!" The words which follow 'הַפּ ... בְּשׁ are accordingly to be regarded as assigning a reason for this closing: the non-appearance of excretion has its reason in defective digestion in this, that the stomach does not grind (Talm.: בשביל ¹ קורקבן וג'). But the dual דְּלָתַיִם suggests a pair of similar and related members, and בַּשּׁוּק a pair of members open before the eyes, and not such as modesty requires to be veiled. The Targum therefore understands the shutting of the doors properly; but the mills, after the indication lying in 'הַפּ [grinding maids], it understands of the organs of eating and tasting, for it translates: "thy feet will be fettered, so that thou canst not go out into the street; and appetite will fail thee." But that is an awkward amalgamation of the literal with the allegorical, which condemns itself by this, that it separates the close connection of the two expressions required by בְּשִׁפַל, which also may be said of the reference of 'דלת to the ears, into which no sound, even from the noisy market, penetrates (Gurlitt, Grätz). We have for דלתים a key, already found by Aben Ezra, in Job xli. 6 [2], where the jaws of the leviathan are called דַּלְתֵי פָנָיו; and as Herzf. and Hitz. explain, so Samuel Aripol in his *Commentary*, which appeared in Constantinople, 1855, rightly: "He calls the jaws דלתים, to denote that not two דלתות in two places, but in one place, are meant, after the manner of a door opening out to the street, which is large, and consists of two folds or wings, דלתות, which, like the lips (הַשְּׂפָתַיִם, better: the jaws), form a whole in two parts; and the meaning is, that at the time of old age the lips are closed and drawn in, because the teeth have disappeared, or, as the

---

¹ Cf. *Berachoth* 61*b*: The stomach (קוּרְקְבָן) grinds. As *hamses* is properly the caul of the ruminant, so this word קֻוּרְקְבָן is the crop (bibl. מֻרְאָה) of the bird.

text says, because the noise of the mill is low, just because he has no teeth to grind with." The connection of סָפְרוּ and בְּשִׁפַל is, however, closer still: the jaws of an old man are closed externally, for the sound of the mill is low; *i.e.* since, when one masticates his food with the jaws of a toothless mouth, there is heard only a dull sound of this chewing (*Mumpfelns, vid.* Weigand's *Deut. W. B.*), *i.e.* laborious masticating. He cannot any more crack or crunch and break his food, one hears only a dull munching and sucking.—The voice of the mouth (Bauer, Hitz., Gurlitt, Zöckl.) cannot be the meaning of קול הֹם; the set of teeth (Gurlitt indeed substitutes, 3*b*, the cavity of the mouth) is not the organ of voice, although it contributes to the formation of certain sounds of words, and is of importance for the full sound of the voice.

בַּשּׁוּק, "to the street," is here = on the street side; שָׁפַל is, as at Prov. xvi. 19, infin. (Symmachus: ἀχρειωθείσης τῆς φωνῆς; the Venet.: ἐν τῷ ταπεινῶσθαι τὴν φωνήν), and is to be understood after Isa. xxix. 4; טַחֲנָה stands for רֵחַיִם, as the vulgar Arab. *taḥûn* and *maṭhana* instead of the antiquated *raḥâ*. Winzer now supposes that the picture of the night is continued in 4*b*: *et subsistit (vox molae) ad cantum galli, et submissius canunt cantatrices* (viz. *molitrices*). Elster, with Umbreit, supposes the description of a storm continued: the sparrow rises up to cry, and all the singing birds sink down (flutter restlessly on the ground). And Taylor supposes the lament for the dead continued, paraphrasing: But the bird of evil omen [owl, or raven] raises his dirge, and the merry voice of the singing girls is silent.

These three pictures, however, are mere fancies, and are also evidently here forced upon the text; for יקום קול cannot mean *subsistit vox*, but, on the contrary (cf. Hos. x. 14), *surgit (tollitur) vox;* and יקום לקול cannot mean: it (the bird) raises itself to cry, which would have required יקום לתת קולו, or at least לַקּוֹל, after קום לַמִּלְחָמָה, etc.; besides, it is to be presumed that צפור is genit., like קול עוגב and the like, not nom. of the subj. It is natural, with Hitz., Ewald, Heiligst., Zöck., to refer *qol tsippor* to the peeping, whispering voice ("childish treble" of Shakespeare) of the old man (cf. *tsiphtseph*, Isa. xxix. 4, xxxviii. 14, x. 14, viii. 19). But the translation: "And it (the voice) approaches a sparrow's voice," is inadmissible, since for קום לְ the meaning, "to pass from one state to another," cannot be proved from 1 Sam. xxii. 13, Mic. ii. 8; קום signifies there always "to rise up," and besides, *qol taḥhanah* is not the voice of the mouth supplied with teeth, but the sound of the chewing of a toothless mouth. If *l'qol* is connected with a verb of external movement, or of that of the soul, it always denotes the occasion of this movement, Num. xvi. 34; Ezek. xxvii. 28; Job xxi. 12; Hab. iii. 16. Influenced by this inalienable sense of the language, the Talm. explains ויקום ... צפ׳ by "even a bird awakes him." Thus also literally the Midrash, and accordingly the Targ. paraphrasing: "thou shalt awaken out of thy sleep for a bird, as for thieves breaking in at night." That is correct, only it is unnecessary to limit וְיָקוּם (or rather וְיָקֹום,[1] which accords with the still continued subordination of ver. 4 to the *eo die quo* of ver. 3*a*) to rising up from sleep, as if it were synonymous with וְיֵעֹור: the old man is weak (nervously weak) and easily frightened, and on account of the deadening of his senses (after the figure of ver. 2, the darkening of the five stars) is so liable to mistake, that if even a bird chirps, he is frightened by it out of his rest (cf. *hĕkim*, Isa. xiv. 9).

Also in the interpretation of the clause וַיִּשַּׁחוּ ... הַשִּׁיר, the ancients are in the right track. The Talm. explains: even all music and song appear to him like common chattering (שׂוּחָה or, according to other readings, שִׂיחָה); the proper meaning of ישחו is thus Haggad. twisted. Less correctly the Midrash: בנות השיר are his lips, or they are the reins which think, and the heart decides (on this curious psychol. conception, cf. *Chullin* 11*a*, and particularly *Berachoth* 61*a*, together with my *Psychol.* p. 269). The reference to the internal organs is *à priori* improbable throughout; the Targ. with the right tact decides in favour of the lips: "And thy lips are untuned, so that they can no more say (sing) songs." In this translation of the Talm. there are compounded, as frequently, two different interpretations, viz. that interpretation of בנ׳ הש׳, which is proved by the כל going before to be incorrect, because impossible; and the interpretation of these "daughters of song" of "songs," as if these were synonymous designations, as when in Arab. misfortunes are called *banatu binasan*, and the like (vid. Lane's *Lex.* I. p. 263); בַּת קֹול, which in Mish. denotes a separate voice (the voice of heaven), but in Syr. the separate word, may be compared. But יִשַּׁחוּ (fut. Niph. of שָׁחַח) will not accord with this interpretation. For that בנ׳ הש׳ denotes songs (Hitz., Heiligst.), or the sound of singing (Böttch.), or the words (Ewald) of the old man himself, which are now softened down so as to be scarcely audible, is yet

---

[1] Vav with *Cholem* in H. F. Thus rightly, according to the Masora, which places it in the catalogue of those words which occur once with a higher (יקוֹם) and once with a lower vowel (יקוּם), *Mas. fin.* 2*a b*, *Ochlaweochla*, No. 5; cf. also Aben Ezra's *Comm.* under Ps. lxxx. 19; *Zachoth* 23*a*, *Safa berura* 21*b* (where Lipmann is uncertain as to the meaning).

too improbable; it is an insipid idea that the old man gives forth these feeble "daughters of song" from his mouth. We explain יָשֹׁחוּ of a being bowed down, which is external to the old man, and accordingly understand b*e*noth hashshir not of pieces of music (Aq. πάντα τὰ τῆς ᾠδῆς) which must be lowered to *pianissimo*, but according to the parallel already rightly acknowledged by Desvoeux, 2 Sam. xix. 36, where the aged Barzillai says that he has now no longer an ear for the voice of singing men and singing women, of singing birds (cf. בַּר זְמִירָא of a singing bird in the Syrian fables of Sophos, and *banoth* of the branches of a fruit tree, Gen. xlix. 22), and, indeed, so that these are a figure of all creatures skilled in singing, and taking pleasure in it: all beings that are fond of singing, and to which it has become as a second nature, must lower themselves, viz. the voice of their song (Isa. xxix. 4) (cf. the *Kal*, Ps. xxxv. 14, and to the modal sense of the fut. x. 10, יַנֵּבַּר, and x. 19, יִשְׂמָח), *i.e.* must timidly retire, they dare not make themselves heard, because the old man, who is terrified by the twittering of a little bird, cannot bear it.

Ver. 5*a*. From this his repugnance to singing, and music, and all loud noises, progress in the description is made to the difficulty such aged men have in motion: "Also they are afraid of that which is high; and there are all kinds of fearful things in the way ..." The description moves forward in a series of independent sentences; that בְּיוֹם שׁ to which it was subordinate in ver. 3, and still also in ver. 4, is now lost sight of. In the main it is rightly explained by the Talm., and with it the Midrash: "Even a little hillock appears to him like a high mountain; and if he has to go on a journey, he meets something that terrifies him;" the Targ. has adopted the second part of this explanation. גָּבֹהַּ (falsely referred by the Targ. to the time lying far back in the past) is understood neut.; cf. 1 Sam. xvi. 7. Such decrepid old men are afraid of (יִרָאוּ, not *videbunt*, as the LXX., Symm., Ar., and the Venet. translate, who seem to have had before them the defective יראו) a height, —it alarms them as something insurmountable, because their breath and their limbs fail them when they attempt it; and *hathhhattim* (plur. of the intensifying form of חַת, *consternatio*, Job xli. 25), *i.e.* all kinds of *formidines* (not *formido*, Ewald, § 179*a*, Böttch. § 762, for the plur. is as in *salsilloth*, 'aph'appim, etc., thought of as such), meet them in the way. As the sluggard says: there is a lion in the way, and under this pretence remains slothfully at home, Prov. xxiv. 13, xxii. 13, so old men do not venture out; for to them a damp road appears like a very morass; a gravelly path, as full of neck-breaking hillocks; an undulating path, as fearfully steep and precipitous; that which is not shaded, as oppressively hot and exhausting—they want strength and courage to overcome difficulties, and their anxiety pictures out dangers before them where there are none.

5b. The allegory is now continued in individual independent figures: "And the almond tree is in blossom." The Talm. explains וינ׳ הש׳ of the haunch-bone projecting (from leanness); the Midrash, of the bones of the vertebral column, conceived of as incorruptible and as that round which will take place the future restoration of the human body,—probably the cross bone, *os sacrum*,[1] inserted between the two thigh bones of the pelvis as a pointed wedge; cf. Jerome in his *Comm.*: *quidam sacram spinam interpretantur quod decrescentibus natium cornibus spina accrescat et floreat;* לוּז is an Old Heb., Aram., and Arab. name of the almond tree and the almond nut (*vid.* under Gen. xxx. 37), and this, perhaps, is the reason of this identification of the emblematic שָׁקֵד with לוּז (the *os sacrum*, or *vertebra magna*) of the spine. The Targ. follows the Midrash in translating: the רִישׁ שֵׁזִי (the top of the spine) will protrude from leanness like an almond tree (viz. from which the leaves have been stripped). In these purely arbitrary interpretations nothing is correct but (1) that שָׁקֵד is understood not of the almond fruit, but of the almond tree, as also at Jer. i. 11 (the rod of an almond tree); (2) that יָנֵאץ (notwithstanding that these interpreters had it before them unpointed) is interpreted, as also by the LXX., Syr., Jerome, and the Venet., in the sense of blossoming, or the bursting out of blossoms by means of the opening up of the buds. Many interpreters understand שָׁקֵד of almond fruit (Winzer, Ewald, Ginsb., Rödiger, etc.), for they derive יָנֵאץ from נאץ, as Aben Ezra had already done, and explain by: *fastidit amygdalam (nucem),* or *fastidium creat amygdala.* But (1) יָנֵאץ for יְנָאֵץ (*Hiph.* of נאץ, to disdain, to treat scornfully) is a change of vowels unexampled; we must, with such an explanation, read either יִנָּאֵץ, *fastiditur* (Gaab), or יְנָאֵץ; (2) almond nuts, indeed, belong to the more noble productions of the land and the delicacies, Gen. xliii. 11, but dainties, κατ᾽ ἐξ., at the same time they are not, so that it would be appropriate to exemplify the blunted sensation of taste in the old man, by saying that he no more cracks and eats almonds. The explanation of Hitzig, who reads יְנָאֵץ, and interprets the almond tree as at Song vii. 9 the palm, to denote a woman, for he translates: the almond tree refuses (viz. the old man), we set aside as too ingenious; and we leave to those interpreters who derive ינאץ from

---

[1] The Jewish opinion of the incorruptible continuance of this bone may be connected with the designation *os sacrum;* the meaning of this is controverted, *vid.* Hyrtl's *Anatomie,* § 124.

נאץ, and understand הַשָׁקֵד¹ of the *glans penis* (Böttch., Fürst, and several older interpreters), to follow their own foul and repulsive criticism. יָנֵאץ is an incorrect reading for יָנֵץ, as at Hos. x. 14, קָאם for קָם, and, in Prov., רָאשׁ' for רָשׁ' (Gesen. § 73. 4); and besides, as at Song vi. 11, הֲנֵצוּ, regular *Hiph.* of נָצַץ (נִיץ, Lam. iv. 15), to move tremblingly (vibrate), to glisten, blossom (cf. נוס, to flee, and נִים, Assyr. *nisannu*, the flower-month). Thus deriving this verbal form, Ewald, and with him Heiligst., interprets the blossoming almond tree as a figure of the winter of life: "it is as if the almond tree blossomed, which in the midst of winter has already blossoms on its dry, leafless stem." But the blossoms of the almond tree are rather, after Num. xvii. 23, a figure of special life-strength, and we must thus, thrown back to יָנֵאץ from נאץ (to flourish), rather explain, with Furrer (in Schenkel's *B. L.*), as similarly Herzf.: the almond tree refuses, *i.e.* ceases, to blossom; the winter of old age is followed by no spring; or also, as Dale and Taylor: the almond tree repels, *i.e.* the old man has no longer a joyful welcome for this messenger of spring. But his general thought has already found expression in ver. 2; the blossoming almond tree must be here an emblem of a more special relation. Hengst. supposes that "the juniper tree (for this is the proper meaning of שָׁקֵד) is in bloom" is = sleeplessness in full blossom stands by the old man; but that would be a meaningless expression. Nothing is more natural than that the blossoming almond tree is intended to denote the same as is indicated by the phrase of the Latin poet: *Intempestivi funduntur vertice cani* (Luther, Geiger, Grot., Vaih., Luzz., Gurlitt, Tyler, Bullock, etc.). It has been objected that the almond blossoms are not pure white, but according to the variety, they are pale-red, or also white; so that Thomson, in his beautiful *Land and the Book*, can with right say: "The almond tree is the type of old age whose hair is white;" and why? "The white blossoms completely cover the whole tree." Besides, Bauer (1732) has already remarked that the almond blossoms, at first tinged with red, when they are ready to fall off become white as snow; with which may be compared a clause cited by Ewald from Bodenstedt's *A Thousand and One Days in the Orient:* "The white blossoms fall from the almond trees like snow-flakes." Accordingly, Dächsel is right when he explains, after the example of Zöckler: "the almond tree with its reddish flower in late winter, which strews the ground with its blossoms, which have gradually become white like snow-flakes, is an emblem of the winter of old age with its falling silvery hair."

---

¹ Abulwalid understands שקד and חגב sexually, and glosses the latter by *jundub* (the locust), which in Arab. is a figure of suffering and patience.

Ver. 5c. From the change in the colour of the hair, the allegory now proceeds to the impairing of the elasticity of the thighs and of their power of bearing a load, the *malum coxae senile* (in a wider than the usual pathological sense): "And the grasshopper (*i.e.* locust, חָגָב, Samar. חרגבה = חַרְגֹּל, Lev. xi. 22) becomes a burden." Many interpreters (Merc., Döderl., Gaab, Winz., Gesen., Winer, Dale) find in these words וְיִסְ׳ הֶחָ׳ the meaning that locust-food, or that the chirping of grasshoppers, is burdensome to him (the old man); but even supposing that it may at once be assumed that he was a keen aeridophagus (locusts, steeped in butter, are like crabs (shrimps) spread on slices of butter and bread), or that he had formerly a particular delight in the chirping of the τέττιξ, which the ancients number among singing birds (cf. Taylor, *l.c.*), and that he has now no longer any joy in the song of the *tettix*, although it is regarded as soothing and tending to lull to rest, and an Anacreon could in his old days even sing his μακαρίζομέν σε, τέττιξ,—yet these two interpretations are impossible, because יִסְ׳ may mean to burden and to move with difficulty, but not "to become burdensome." For the same reason, nothing is more absurd than the explanation of Kimchi and Gurlitt: Even a grasshopper, this small insect, burdens him; for which Zöckl., more naturally: the hopping and chirping of the grasshopper is burdensome to him; as we say, The fly on the wall annoys him. Also Ewald and Heiligstedt's interpretation: "it is as if the locust raised itself to fly, breaking and stripping off its old husk," is inadmissible; for הסתבל can mean *se portare laboriose*, but not *ad evolandum eniti*; the comparison (Arab.) *tahmmal* gains the meaning to hurry onwards, to proceed on an even way, like the Hebr. השכים, to take upon the shoulder; it properly means, to burden oneself, *i.e.* to take on one's back in order to get away; but the grasshopper coming out of its case carries away with it nothing but itself. For us, such interpretations—to which, particularly, the advocates of the several hypotheses of a storm, night, and mourning, are constrained— are already set aside by this, that according to the allegory וְיָנ׳ הֵשׁ׳, וְיִסְ׳ הֶחָ׳ must also signify something characteristic of the body of an old man. The LXX., Jerome, and Ar. translate: the locust becomes fat; the Syr.: it grows. It is true, indeed, that great corpulence, or also a morbid dropsical swelling of the belly (*ascites*), is one of the symptoms of advanced old age; but supposing that the (voracious) locust might be an emblem of a corpulent man, yet הסתבל means neither to become fat nor to grow. But because the locust in reality suggests the idea of a corpulent man, the figure cannot at the same time be intended to mean that the old man is like a skeleton, consisting as it were of nothing but skin and bone (Lyra, Luther, Bauer, Dathe); the resemblance of a locust to the back-bone and its joints (Glassius, Köhler, Vaih.) is not in view; only the position of the locust's feet for leaping admits the comparison of the prominent *scapulae* (shoulder-blades); but shoulder-blades (*scapulae alatae*), angular and standing out from the chest, are characteristics of a consumptive, not of a senile habit. Also we must cease, with Hitz., Böttch., Luzz., and Gratz, to understand the figure as denoting the φαλλός to be now impotent; for relaxation and shrinking do not agree with הסתבל, which suggests something burdensome by being weighty. The Midrash interprets החגב by "ankles," and the Targ. translates accordingly: the ankles (אִסְתְּוָרֵי, from the Pers. *ustuwâr*, firm) of thy feet will swell—unsuitably, for "ankles" affords no point of comparison with locusts, and they have no resemblance to their springing feet. The Talm., glossing החגב by "these are the buttocks" (*nates*) (cf. Arab. *'ajab*, the *os coccygis*, Syn. *'ajuz*, as the Talm. ענבות interchanges with עכוז), is on the right track. There is nothing, indeed, more probable than that חגב is a figure of the *coxa*, the hinder region of the pelvis, where the lower part of the body balances itself in the hip-joint, and the motion of standing up and going receives its impulse and direction by the muscular strength there concentrated. This part of the body may be called the locust, because it includes in itself the mechanism which the two-membered foot for springing, placed at an acute angle, presents in the locust. Referred to this *coxa*, the loins, יסתבל has its most appropriate meaning: the marrow disappears from the bones, elasticity from the muscles, the cartilage and oily substance from the joints, and, as a consequence, the middle of the body drags itself along with difficulty; or: it is with difficulty moved along (*Hithpa.* as pass., like viii. 10); it is stiff, particularly in the morning, and the old man is accustomed to swing his arms backwards, and to push himself on as it were from behind. In favour of this interpretation (but not deciding it) is the accord of חגב with ענב = κόκκυξ (by which the *os coccygis* is designated as the cuckoo's bone). Also the verbal stem (Arab.) *jaḥab* supplies an analogous name: not *jaḥab*, which denotes the air passage (but not, as Knobel supposes, the breath itself; for the verb signifies to separate, to form a partition, Mishn. מחיצה), but (Arab.) *jaḥabat*, already compared by Bochart, which denotes the point (dual), the two points or projections of the two hip-bones (*vid.* Lane's *Lex.*), which, together with the *os sacrum* lying between, form the ring of the pelvis.

Ver. 5d. From the weakening of the power of motion, the allegory passes on to the decay of sensual desires, and of the organs appertaining thereto: "And the caper-berry fails"... The meaning "caper" for הָאֲבִיּ is evidenced by the LXX. (ἡ κάππαρις, Arab. *alkabar*), the Syr., and Jerome (*capparis*), and this rendering is confirmed by the Mishnic אביונות, which in contradistinction to תמרות, i.e. the tender branches, and קפריסין, i.e. the rind of fruit, signifies the berry-like flower-buds of the caper bush,[1] according to Buxtorf (vid. above, p. 190). This Talm. word, it is true, is pointed אֲבִיּוֹנוֹת; but that makes no difference, for אֲבִיּוֹנָה is related to אֲבִיּוֹנָה merely as making the word emphatic, probably to distinguish the name of the caper from the fem. of the adj. אֶבְיוֹן, which signifies *avida, egena*. But in the main they are both one; for that אֲבִיּוֹנָה may designate "desire" (Abulwalîd:[2] *aliradat*; Parchon: התאוה; Venet.: ἡ ὄρεξις; Luther: *alle Lust*), or "neediness," "poverty" (the Syr. in its second translation of this clause), is impossible, because the form would be unexampled and incomprehensible; only the desiring soul, or the desiring, craving member (vid. Kimchi), could be so named. But now the caper is so named, which even to this day is used to give to food a more piquant taste (cf. Plutarch's *Sympos.* vi. qu. 2). It is also said that the caper is a means of exciting sexual desire (*aphrodisiacum*); and there are examples of its use for this purpose from the Middle Ages, indeed, but none from the records of antiquity; Pliny, *Hist. Nat.* xx. 14 (59), knew nothing of it, although he speaks at length of the uses and effects of the *capparis*. The Talm. explains האבי׳ by חמדה, the Midrash by תאוה, the Targ. by משכבא, interpreting the word directly without reference to the caper in this sense. If *haaviyonah* thus denotes the caper, we have not thence to conclude that it incites to sexual love, and still less are we, with the Jewish interpreters, whom Böttch. follows, to understand the word of the *membrum virile* itself; the Arab. name for the caper, *'itar*, which is compared by Grätz, which has an obscene meaning, designates also other aromatic plants. We shall proceed so much the more securely if we turn away from the idea of sexual impulse and hold by the idea of the impulse of self-preservation, namely, appetite for food, since אֶבְיוֹן (from אָבָה, the root-meaning of which, "to desire,"

---

[1] The caper-bush is called in the Mish. צָלָף, and is celebrated, *Beza* 25a, cf. *Shabbath* 30b (where, according to J. S. Bloch's supposition, the disciple who meets Gamaliel is the Apostle Paul), on account of its unconquerable life-power, its quick development of fruit, and manifold products. The caper-tree is planted, says *Berachoth* 36a, "with a view to its branches;" the eatable branches or twigs here meant are called שיתי (שׁוּתֵי). Another name for the caper-tree is נצפה, *Demai* i. 1, *Berachoth* 36a, 40b; and another name for the bud of the caper-blossom is פרחא דבוטיתא, *Berachoth* 36b (cf. Aruch, under the words *aviyonoth* and *tseˡlaph*).

[2] In his *Dictionary of Roots* (*kitâb el-uṣûl*), edited by Neubauer, Oxford 1873–4.

is undoubted[1]) denotes a poor man, as one who desires that which is indispensable to the support of life; the caper is accordingly called *aviyonah*, as being *appetitiva*, *i.e.* exciting to appetite for food, and the meaning will not be that the old man is like a caper-berry which, when fully ripe, bursts its husks and scatters its seed (Rosenm., Winer in his *R. W.*, Ewald, Taylor, etc.), as also the LXX., Symm. (καὶ διαλυθῇ ἡ ἐπίπονος, *i.e.* as Jerome translates it, *et dissolvetur spiritus fortitudo*, perhaps ἐπίπονος, the strength or elasticity of the spirit), and Jerome understand the figure; but since it is to be presupposed that the name of the caper, in itself significant, will also be significant for the figure: *capparis est irrita sive vim suam non exerit* (וְתָפֵר as inwardly trans. *Hiph.* of פרר, to break in pieces, frustrate), *i.e.* even such means of excitement as capers, these appetite-berries, are unable to stimulate the dormant and phlegmatic stomach of the old man (thus *e.g.* Bullock). Hitzig, indeed, maintains that the cessation of the enjoyment of love in old age is not to be overlooked; but (1) the use of artificial means for stimulating this natural impulse in an old man, who is here described simply as such, without reference to his previous life and its moral state, would make him a sensualist; and (2) moral statistics show that with the decay of the body lust does not always (although this would be in accordance with nature, Gen. xvii. 17; Rom. iv. 19) expire; moreover, the author of the Book of Koheleth is no Juvenal or Martial, to take pleasure, like many of his interpreters, in exhibiting the *res venereae*.

Ver. 5e. And in view of the clause following, the ceasing from nourishment as the last symptom of the certain approach of death is more appropriate than the cessation from sexual desire: "For," thus the author continues after this description of the enfeebled condition of the hoary old man, "man goeth to his everlasting habitation, and the mourners go about the streets." One has to observe that the *antequam* of the *memento Creatoris tui in diebus juventutis tuae* is continued in vers. 6 and 7. The words *'ad asher lo* are thrice repeated. The chief group in the description is subordinated to the second *'ad asher lo*; this relation is syntactically indicated also in ver. 4 by the subjective form וְיָקוּם, and continues logically in ver. 5, although without any grammatical sign, for וְיִנָּאֵץ and וְתָפֵר are indicative. Accordingly the clause with כִּי, 5b, will not be definitive; considerately the accentuation does not begin a new verse with כִּי: the symptoms of *marasmus* already spoken of are here explained by this, that man is on his way to the grave, and, as we say, has already one foot in it.

[1] *Vid.* Fried. Delitzsch's *Indogerman.-Sem. Stud.* I. p. 62 f. Also the Arab. *âby* in the language of the Negd means nothing else.

The part. הֹלֵךְ is also here not so much the expression of the *fut. instans* (*iturus est*), like ix. 10, as of the present (Venet.: ἄπεισι); cf. Gen. xv. 2, where also these two possible renderings stand in question. "Everlasting house" is the name for the grave of the dead, according to Diodorus Sic. i. 51, also among the Egyptians, and on old Lat. monuments also the expression *domus aeterna* is found (*vid.* Knobel); the comfortless designation, which corresponds[1] to the as yet darkened idea of Hades, remained with the Jews in spite of the hope of the resurrection they had meanwhile received; cf. Tob. iii. 6; *Sanhedrin* 19*a*, "the churchyard of *Husal*;" "to a churchyard" (*beth 'olam*);. "at the door of the churchyard" (*beth 'olam*), *Vajikra rabba*, c. 12. Cf. also above, p. 191, and Assyr. *bit 'idii* = בית עד of the under-world (Bab.-Assyr. Epic, "*Höllenfahrt der Istar*," i. 4).

The clause following means that mourners already go about the streets (cf. סָבַב, Song iii. 3, and *Pil.* Song iii. 2; Ps. lix. 7) expecting the death of the dying. We would say: the undertaker tarries in the neighbourhood of the house to be at hand, and to offer his services. For *hassophdim* are here, as Knobel, Winz., and others rightly explain, the mourners, *saphdanin* (*sophdanin*), hired for the purpose of playing the mourning music (with the horn שיפורא, *Moëd katan* 27*b*, or flute, חלילים, at the least with two, *Kethuboth* 46*b*; cf. Lat. *siticines*) and of singing the lament for the dead, *qui conducti plorant in funere* (Horace, *Poet.* 433), along with whom were mourning women, מקוננות (Lat. *praeficae*) (cf. Buxtorf's *Lex. Talm.* col. 1524 s.),—a custom which existed from remote antiquity, according to 2 Sam. iii. 31; Jer. xxxiv. 5. The Talm. contains several such lamentations for the dead, as *e.g.* that of a "mourner" (ההוא ספדנא) for R. Abina: "The palms wave their heads for the palm-like just man," etc.; and of the famed "mourner" Bar-Kippuk on the same occasion: "If the fire falls upon the cedar, what shall the hyssop of the walls do?" etc. (*Moëd katan* 25*b*[2])—many of the ספדנים were accordingly elegiac poets. This section of ver. 5 does not refer to the funeral itself, for the procession of the mourners about the bier ought in that case to have been more distinctly expressed; and that they walked about in the streets before the funeral (Isa. xv. 3) was not a custom, so far as we know. They formed a component part of the procession following the bier to the grave in Judea, as *Shabbath* 153*a* remarks with

---

[1] The Syr. renders *beth 'olam* by *domus laboris sui*, which is perhaps to be understood after Job iii. 17*b*.

[2] Given in full in *Wiss. Kunst Judenth.* p. 230 ff. Regarding the lament for the dead among the Haurans, *vid.* Wetzstein's treatise on the Syrian Threshing-Table in Bastian's *Zeitsch. für Ethnologie*, 1873.

reference to this passage, and in Galilee going before it; to mourn over the death, to reverse it, if possible, was not the business of these mourners, but of the relatives (Hitz.), who were thus not merely called הסופדים. The Targ. translates: "and the angels will go about, who demand an account of thee, like the mourning singers who go about the streets, to record what account of thee is to be given." It is unnecessary to change כְּסוֹפֵר into כְּסֹפֵר (*instar scribarum*). According to the idea of the Targumist, the *sophdim* go about to collect materials for the lament for the dead. The dirge was not always very scrupulously formed; wherefore it is said in *Berachoth* 62a, "as is the estimate of the dead that is given, so is the estimate of the mourners (singers and orators at the funeral), and of those who respond to their words." It is most natural to see the object of the mourners going about in their desire to be on the spot when death takes place.[1]

Vers. 6, 7. A third '*ad asher lo* now follows (cf. v. 1, 2); the first placed the old man in view, with his *désagrément* in general; the second described in detail his bodily weaknesses, presenting themselves as forerunners of death; the third brings to view the dissolution of the life of the body, by which the separation of the soul and the body, and the return of both to their original condition is completed. "Ere the silver cord is loosed, and the golden bowl is shattered, and the pitcher is broken at the fountain, and the wheel is shattered in the well, and the dust returns to the earth as that which it was, and the spirit returns to God who gave it." Before entering into the contents of these verses, we shall consider the form in which some of the words are presented. The *Chethîb* ירחק we readily let drop, for in any case it must be said that the silver cord is put out of action; and this word, whether we read it יִרְחַק or יֵרָחֵק (Venet. μακρυνθῇ), is too indefinite, and, supposing that by the silver cord a component part of the body is meant, even inappropriate, since the organs which cease to perform their functions are not removed away from the dead body, but remain in it when dead. But the *Keri* יֵרָתֵק ("is

---

[1] The Arab. funeral dirge furnishes at once an illustration of "and the mourners go about the streets." What Wetzstein wrote to me ought not, I believe, to be kept from the reader: "In Damascus the men certainly take part in the dirge; they go about the reservoir in the court of the house along with the mourning women, and behave themselves like women; but this does not take place in the villages. But whether the 'going about the streets' might seem as an evidence that in old times in the towns, as now in the villages, the *menaṣṣa* (bed of state) was placed with the mourning tent in the open street without, is a question. If this were the case, the *sôphdim* might appear publicly; only I would then understand by the word not hired mourners, but the relatives of the dead." But then מִפָּה, as at Ps. xxvi. 6 מִזְבֵּח, ought to have been joined to סבב as the object of the going about.

unbound") has also its difficulty. The verb רָתַק signifies to bind together, to chain; the bibl. Heb. uses it of the binding of prisoners, Nah. iii. 18, cf. Isa. xl. 19; the post-bibl. Heb. of binding = shutting up (contrast of פתח, *Pesikta*, ed. Buber, 176*a*, whence *Mezia* 107*b*, שורא וריתקא, a wall and enclosure); the Arab. of shutting up and closing a hole, rent, split (*e.g. murtatik*, a plant with its flower-buds as yet shut up; *rutûk*, inaccessibleness). The Targumist[1] accordingly understands יֵרָתֵק of binding = lameness (palsy); Rashi and Aben Ezra, of shrivelling; this may be possible, however, for נִרְתָּק, used of a "cord," the meaning that first presents itself, is "to be firmly bound;" but this affords no appropriate sense, and we have therefore to give to the *Niph.* the contrasted meaning of setting free, *discatenare* (Parchon, Kimchi); this, however, is not justified by examples, for a privat. *Niph.* is unexampled, Ewald, § 121*e*; נִלְבַּב, Job xi. 12, does not mean to be deprived of heart (understanding), but to gain heart (understanding). Since, however, we still need here the idea of setting loose or tearing asunder (LXX. ἀνατραπῇ; Symm. κοπῆναι; Syr. נתפסק, from פְּסַק, *abscindere*; Jerome, *rumpatur*), we have only the choice of interpreting *yērathēq* either, in spite of the appearance to the contrary, in the meaning of *constringitur*, of a violent drawing together of the cord stretched out lengthwise; or, with Pfannkuche, Gesen., Ewald, to read יִנָּתֵק ("is torn asunder"), which one expects, after Isa. xxxiii. 20; cf. Judg. xvi. 9, Jer. x. 20. Hitzig reaches the same, for he explains יֵרָתֵק = יֵחָרֵק, from (Arab.) *kharak*, to tear asunder (of the sound of the tearing[2]); and Böttcher, by adopting the reading יֵחָרֵק; but without any support in Heb. and Chald. *usus loq.* גֻּלָּה, which is applied to the second figure, is certainly[3] a vessel of a round form (from גָּלַל, to roll, revolve round), like the גֻּלָּה which received the oil and conducted it to the seven lamps of the candlestick in Zech. iv.; but to understand וְתָרֻץ of the running out of the oil not expressly named (Luther: "and the golden fountain runs out") would be contrary to the *usus loq.*; it is the metapl. form for וְתִרֹץ, *et confringitur*, as יָרוּץ, Isa. xlii. 4, for יָרֹץ, from רָצַץ, cogn. רעע, Ps. ii. 9, whence נָרֹץ, 6*b*, the regularly formed *Niph.* (the fut. of which, תֵּרוֹץ, Ezek. xxix. 7). We said that oil is

---

[1] Similarly the LXX. understands וְנָרֻץ, καὶ συντροχάσῃ (*i.e.* as Jerome in his *Comm.* explains: *si fuerit in suo funiculo convoluta*), which is impossible.

[2] *Vid.* my treatise, *Physiol. u. Musik, u.s.w.*, p. 31.

[3] The LXX., unsuitably, τὸ ἀνθέμιον, which, *per synecdochen partis pro toto*, signifies the capital (of a pillar). Thus, perhaps, also are meant Symm. τὸ περιφερίς, Jerome *vitta*, Venet. τὸ στέφος, and the Syr. "apple." Among the Arabs, this ornament on the capital is called *tabaryz* ("prominence").

not expressly named. But perhaps it is meant by הַזָּהָב. The *gullah* above the candlestick which Zechariah saw was, according to ver. 12, provided with two golden pipes, in which were two olive trees standing on either side, which sunk therein the tuft-like end of their branches, of which it is said that they emptied out of themselves *hazzahav* into the oil vessels. Here it is manifest that *hazzahav* means, in the one instance, the precious metal of which the pipes are formed; and in the other, the fluid gold of the oil contained in the olive branches. Accordingly, Hitzig understands *gullath hazzahav* here also; for he takes *gullah* as a figure of the body, the golden oil as a figure of the soul, and the silver cord as a figure of vital energy.

Thus, with Hitz., understanding *gullath hazzahav* after the passage in Zechariah, I have correctly represented the meaning of the figures in my *Psychol.* p. 228, as follows:—" The silver cord = the soul directing and bearing the body as living; the lamp hanging by this silver cord = the body animated by the soul, and dependent on it; the golden oil = the spirit, of which it is said, Prov. xx. 27, that it is a lamp of God." I think that this interpretation of the golden oil commends itself in preference to Zöckler's interpretation, which is adopted by Dächsel, of the precious *fluidum* of the blood; for if *hazzahav* is a metaphorical designation of oil, we have to think of it as the material for burning and light; but the principle of bright life in man is the spirit (*ruahh hhayim* or *nishmath hhayim*); and in the passage in Zechariah also, oil, which makes the candlestick give light, is a figure of the spirit (ver. 6, *ki im-b^eruhhi*). But, as one may also suppose, it is not probable that here, with the same genit. connection, הכסף is to be understood of the material and the quality; and *hazzahav*, on the contrary, of the contents. A golden vessel is, according to its most natural meaning, a vessel which is made of gold, thus a vessel of a precious kind. A golden vessel cannot certainly be broken in pieces, but we need not therefore understand an earthenware vessel only gilded, as by a silver cord is to be understood only that which has a silver line running through it (Gesen. in the *Thes.*); רָצִיץ may also denote that which is violently crushed or broken, Isa. xlii. 3; cf. Judg. ix. 53. If *gullath hazzahav*, however, designates a golden vessel, the reference of the figure to the body, and at the same time of the silver cord to the vital energy or the soul, is then excluded,—for that which animates stands yet above that which is animated,—the two metallic figures in this their distribution cannot be comprehended in this reference. We have thus to ask since *gullath hazzahav* is not the body itself: What in the human body is compared to a silver cord and to a golden vessel? What, moreover, to a pitcher at the fountain, and to a wheel or a windlass? Winzer settles this question by finding in the two double figures only in general the thoughts represented: *antequam vita ex tenui quasi filo suspensa pereat,* and (which is essentially the same) *antequam machina corporis destruatur.* Gurlitt also protests against the allegorical explanation of the details, but he cannot refrain from interpreting more specially than Winzer. Two *momenta,* he says, there are which, when a man dies, in the most impressive way present themselves to view: the extinction of consciousness, and the perfect cessation, complete ruin, of the bodily organism. The extinction of consciousness is figuratively represented by the golden lamp, which is hung up by a silver cord in the midst of a house or tent, and now, since the cord which holds it is broken, it falls down and is shattered to pieces, so that there is at once deep darkness; the destruction of the bodily organism, by a fountain, at which the essential parts of its machinery, the pitcher and windlass, are broken and rendered for ever useless. This interpretation of Gurlitt's affords sufficient support to the expectation of the allegorical meaning with which we approached ver. 6 ; and we would be satisfied therewith, if one of the figures did not oppose us, without seeking long for a more special allegorical meaning: the pitcher at the fountain or well (כַּד, not הַכַּד, because determined by *'al-hammabu'a*) is without doubt the heart which beats to the last breath of the dying man, which is likened to a pitcher which, without intermission, receives and again sends forth the blood. That the blood flows through the body like living water is a fact cognizable and perceptible without the knowledge of its course; fountain (מקור) and blood appear also elsewhere as associated ideas, Lev. xii. 7; and *nishbar,* as here *vᵉtishshabĕr,* used of a pitcher, is a usual scriptural word for the heart brought into a state of death, or near to death, Jer. xxiii. 9; Ps. lxix. 21. From this *gullath hazzahav* must also have a special allegorical sense; and if, as Gurlitt supposes, the golden vessel that is about to be destroyed is a figure of the perishing self-consciousness (whereby it is always doubtful that, with this interpretation, the characteristic feature of light in the figure is wanting), then it is natural to go further, and to understand the golden vessel directly of the head of a man, and to compare the breaking of the skull, Judg. ix. 53, expressed by *vataritz eth-gulgolto,* with the words here before us, *vatharutz gullath hazzahav;* perhaps by *gullath* the author thought of the cogn.—both as to root and meaning—גלגלת; but, besides, the comparison of the head, the bones of which form an oval bowl, with *gullath* is of itself also natural. It is true that, according to the ancient view, not the head, but the heart, is the seat of the life of the spirit; " in the heart, Ephrem said (*Opp. Syr.* ii. 316), the thinking spirit (*chuschobo*) acts as in its palace ; " and the understanding, the Arabians[1] also say, sits in the heart, and thus between the ribs. Everything by which בשׂר and נפשׁ is affected—thus, briefly formulated, the older bibl. idea—comes in the לב into the light of consciousness. But the Book of Koheleth belongs to a time in which spiritual-psychical actions began to be placed in mediate causal relation with the head; the Book of Daniel represents this newer mode of conception, ii. 28, iv. 2, vii. 10, vii. 15. The image of the monarchies seen in Nebuchadnezzar's dream, ii. 32, 38, had a golden head; the head is described as golden, as it is the *membrum praecipuum* of the human body; it is compared to gold as to that which is most precious, as, on the other hand, ראשׁ is used as a metaphorical designation of that which is most precious. The breaking to pieces of the head, the death-blow which it receives, shows itself in this, that he who is sick unto death is unable to hold his head erect, that it sinks down against his will according to the law of gravity; as also in this, that the countenance assumes the aspect which we designate the *facies hippocratica*, and that feeling is gradually destroyed; but, above all, that is thought of which Ovid says of one who was dying: *et resupinus humum moribundo vertice pulsat*.

If we now further inquire regarding the meaning of the silver cord, nothing can obviously be meant by it which is locally above the golden bowl which would be hanging under it; also גלת הכסף itself certainly admits no such literal antitype,—the concavity of the גלגלת is below, and that of a גלה, on the other hand, is above. The silver cord will be found if a component part of the structure of the body is pointed to, which stands in a mutually related connection with the head and the brain, the rending asunder of which brings death with it. Now, as is well known, dying finally always depends on the brain and the upper spinal marrow; and the ancients already interpreted the silver cord of the spinal marrow, which is called by a figure terminologically related to the silver cord, חוּט הַשִּׁדְרָה (the spinal cord), and as a cord-like lengthening of the brain into the spinal channel could not be more appropriately named; the centre is grey, but the external coating is white. We do not, however, maintain that *hakkĕsĕph* points to the white colour; but the spinal marrow is related, in the matter of its value for the life of man, to

[1] *Vid.* Noldeke's *Poesien d. alten Araber*, p. 190.

the brain as silver is to gold. Since not a violent but a natural death is the subject, the fatal stroke that falls on the spinal marrow is not some kind of mechanical injury, but, according as יֵרָתֵק [is unbound] is explained or is changed into יִנָּתֵק [is torn asunder], is to be thought of either as constriction = shrinking together, consuming away, exhaustion; or as unchaining = paralysis or disabling; or as tearing asunder = destruction of the connection of the individual parts. The emendation ינתק most commends itself; it remains, however, possible that ירתק is meant in the sense of morbid contraction (vid. Rashi); at any rate, the fate of the גלה is the consequence of the fate of the חבל, which carries and holds the *gullah*, and does not break without at the same time bringing destruction on it; as also the brain and the spinal marrow stand in a relation of solidarity to each other, and the head receives [1] from the spinal marrow (as distinguished from the so-called prolonged marrow) the death-stroke. As the silver cord and the bowl, so the pitcher and the well and the wheel stand in interchangeable relation to each other. We do not say: the wheel at the fountain, as is translated by Hitz., Ewald, and others; for (1) the fountain is called בְּאֵר, not בּוֹר (בְּאֵר), which, according to the usage (vid. Hitz. under Jer. vii. 9), signifies a pit, and particularly a hole, for holding water, a cistern, reservoir; but for this there was no need for a wheel, and it is also excluded by that which had to be represented; (2) the expression *galgal el-habor* is purposely not used, but *hagalgal el-habor*, that we may not take *el-habor* as virtual adj. to *galgal* (the wheel being at the בּוֹר), but as the designation of the place into which the wheel falls when it is shattered. Rightly, the LXX. renders 'al-hammabu'a by ἐπὶ τῇ πηγῇ, and *el-habor* by ἐπὶ τὸν λάκκον. The figure of a well (*mabbu'a*) formed by means of digging, and thus deep, is artistically conceived; out of this the water is drawn by means of a pitcher (כַּד, Gen. xxiv. 14, a word as curiously according with the Greek κάδος as those mentioned in pp. 12 and 74, whence (Arab.) *kadd*, to exhaust, to pitcher-out, as it were; syn. דְּלִי, a vessel for drawing out water; Assyr. *di-lu*, the zodiacal sign of the water-carrier), and to facilitate this there is a wheel or windlass placed above (Syr. *gilgla d^evira*), by which a rope is wound up and down (vid. Smith's Bibl. Dict. under "well").[2] The Midrash refers to the deep draw-

---

[1] Many interpreters (lately Ewald, Hengst., Zöckl., Taylor, and others) understand the silver cord of the thread of life; the spinal marrow is, without any figure, this thread of life itself.

[2] Wetzstein remarks, that it is translated by "cylinder" better than by "wheel," since the *galgal* is here not at a river, but over a draw-well.

well of the hill town of Sepporis, which was supplied with such rollers serving as a pulley (polyspast). Wheel and pitcher stand in as close mutual relation as air and blood, which come into contact in the lungs. The wheel is the figure of the breathing organ, which expands and contracts (winds and unwinds) itself like a draw-rope by its inhaling and exhaling breath. The throat, as the organ of respiration and speech, is called גָּרוֹן (Ps. cxv. 7) and גַּרְגְּרוֹת (*vid.* under Prov. i. 9), from גָּרָה or גָּרַר, to draw, σπᾶν (τὸν ἀέρα, Wisd. vii. 3). When this wheel makes its last laborious revolution, there is heard the death-rattle. There is a peculiar rattling sound, which they who once hear it never forget, when the wheel swings to an end—the so-called choking rheum, which consists in this, that the secretion which the dying cannot cough up moves up and down in the air-passage, and finally chokes him. When thus the breathings become always weaker, and sometimes are interrupted for a minute, and at last cease altogether, there takes place what is here designated as the breaking to pieces of the wheel in the pit within—the life is extinguished, he who has breathed his last will be laid as a corpse in the grave (בּוֹר, Ps. xxviii. 1, and frequently), the σῶμα has become a πτῶμα (Mark vi. 29; cf. Num. xiv. 32). The dust, *i.e.* the dust of which the body was formed, goes back to the earth again like as it was (originally dust), and the spirit returns to God who gave it. וְיָשֹׁב subordinates itself to the *'ad asher lo*, also in the form as subjunct.; the interchange of the full and the abbreviated forms occurs, however, elsewhere in the indic. sense, *e.g.* Job xiii. 27; Ewald, § 343*b*. *Shuv 'al* occurs also at 2 Chron. xxx. 9; and אֶל and עַל interchange without distinction in the more modern language; but here, as also at 6*b*, not without intention, the way downwards is to be distinguished from the way upwards (cf. iii. 21). כְּשֶׁהָיָה is = בַּאֲשֶׁר הָיָה, *instar ejus quod fuit*. The body returns to the dust from which it was taken, Gen. iii. 19, to the dust of its original material, Ps. civ. 29; and the spirit goes back to the God of its origin, to whom it belongs.

We have purposely not interrupted our interpretation of the enigmatical figures of ver. 6 by the citation and criticism of diverging views, and content ourselves here with a specification of the oldest expositions. The interpretation of *Shabbath* 152*a* does not extend to ver. 6. The Midrash says of the silver cord: זו חוט השדרה (as later, Rashi, Aben Ezra, and many others), of the golden vessel: זו גלגלת (as we), and it now adds only more in jest: "the throat which swallows up the gold and lets the silver run through." The pitcher becoming leaky must be כרס, the belly, which three days after death is wont to burst. And as for *hagalgal*, reference is made to the draw-wells of Sepporis; so for *el havor*, after Job xxi. 33, to the clods of Tiberias: he lies deep below, " like those clods of the deep-lying Tiberias." The Targ. takes its own way, without following the Midrash, and translates: " before thy tongue [this of חבל] is bound and thou art unable to speak any more, and the brain of thy head [this the גלה] is shattered, and thy gall [= כד] is broken with thy liver [= המבוע], and thy body [= הגלגל] hastens away [נרץ of רוץ] into the grave." These interpretations have at least historical and linguistic value; they also contain separate correct renderings. A *quodlibet* of other interpretations [1] is found in my *Psychol.* p. 229, and in Zöckler, *ad loc.* A principal error in these consists in this, that they read Koheleth as if he had been a disciple of Boerhaave, and Harvey, and other masters. Wunderbar in his *Bibl.-Talm. medicin* (1850) takes all in earnest, that the author knew already of the nervous system and the circulation of the blood; for, as he himself says, there is nothing new under the sun. As far as concerns my opinion, says Oetinger in his exposition (*Sämmt. Schrift. herausg. von Ehmann,* IV. p. 254), I dare not affirm that Solomon had a knowledge *systematis nervolymphatici,* as also *circuli sanguinis,* such as learned physicians now possess; yet I believe that the Holy Spirit spake thus through Solomon, that what in subsequent times was discovered as to these matters might be found under these words. This judgment also goes too far; the figure of death which Koheleth presents contains no anticipation of modern discoveries; yet it is not without its value for the historical development of anthropology, for science and poetry combine in it; it is as true to fact as it is poetically beautiful.

The author has now reached the close. His Koheleth-Solomon has made all earthly things small, and at last remains seated on this dust-heap of *vanitas vanitatum.* The motto-like saying, i. 2, is here repeated as a *quod erat demonstrandum,* like a summary conclusion. The book, artistically constructed in whole and in its parts, comes to a close, rounding itself off as in a circle in the epiphonema:

Ver. 8. " O vanity of vanities, saith Koheleth, all is vain." If we here look back to ver. 7, that which is there said of the spirit can be no consolation. With right, Hofmann in his *Schriftbeweis*, I. 490, says: "That it is the personal spirit of a man which returns to God; and that it returns to God without losing its consciousness, is an idea foreign to this proverb." Also, *Psychol.* p. 410, it is willingly conceded that the author wished here to

---

[1] Geiger in the *Deut. Morg. Zeitsch.* xxvii. 800, translates xii. 6 arbitrarily: and the stone-lid (נלגל) in the sense of the Mish.-Targ. גולל) presses on the grave.

express, first, only the fact, in itself comfortless, that the component parts of the human body return whence they came. But the comfortless averse of the proverb is yet not without a consoling reverse. For what the author, iii. 21, represents as an unsettled possibility, that the spirit of a dying man goes not downwards like that of a beast, but upwards, he here affirms as an actual truth.[1] From this, that he thus finally decides the question as an advantage to a man above a beast, it follows of necessity that the return of the spirit to God cannot be thought of as a resumption of the spirit into the essence of God (resorption or remanation), as the cessation of his independent existence, although, as also at Job xxxiv. 14, Ps. civ. 29, the nearest object of the expression is directed to the ruin of the soul-corporeal life of man which directly follows the return of the spirit to God. The same conclusion arises from this, that the idea of the return of the spirit to God, in which the author at last finds rest, cannot yet stand in a subordinate place with reference to the idea of Hades, above which it raises itself; with the latter the spirit remains indestructible, although it has sunk into a silent, inactive life. And in the third place, that conclusion flows from the fact that the author is forced by the present contradiction between human experience and the righteousness of God to the postulate of a judgment finally settling these contradictions, iii. 17, xi. 9, cf. xii. 14, whence it immediately follows that the continued existence of the spirit is thought of as a well-known truth (*Psychol.* p. 127). The Targ. translates, not against the spirit of the book: "the spirit will return to stand in judgment before God, who gave it to thee." In this connection of thoughts Koheleth says more than what Lucretius says (ii. 998 ss.):

> *Cedit item retro, de terra quod fuit ante,*
> *In terras, et quod missum est ex aetheris oris*
> *Id rursum caeli rellatum templa receptant.*

A comforting thought lies in the words אֲשֶׁר נְתָנָהּ. The gifts of God are on His side ἀμεταμέλητα (Rom. xi. 29). When He receives back that which was given, He receives it back to restore it again in another manner. Such thoughts connect themselves with the reference to God the Giver. Meanwhile the author next aims at showing the vanity of man, viz. of man as living here. Body and spirit are separated, and depart each in its own direction. Not only the world and the labours by which man is encompassed are "vain," and not only is that which man has and does and experiences "vain," but also

[1] In the Rig-Veda that which is immortal in man is called *manas*; the later language calls it *âtman*; vid. Muir in the *Asiatic Journal*, 1865, p. 305.

man himself as such is vain, and thus—this is the *facit*—all is הבל, "vain."

(*C*.) THE EPILOGUE.—XII. 9–14.

In an unexpected manner there now follows a postscript. Since the book closes with the epiphonema xii. 8 as having reached the intended goal, the supposition that what follows xii. 8 is from another hand is more natural than the contrary. Of the question of genuineness there cannot be here properly anything said, for only that which is not what it professes to be and ought to be, is spurious; the postscript is certainly according to tradition an integral part of the Book of Koheleth (Bullock), but not as an original organic formal part of it, and still less does it expressly bear self-evidence of this. At the least, those who regard Solomon as the author of the book ought to contend against the recognition in xii. 9 ff. of an appendix by a later hand. Hahn, however, regards the same Solomon who speaks in ver. 8 as continuing to speak in ver. 9, for he interprets אמר, which, however, only means *inquit*, as perf., looking back to the completed book, and regards this retrospect as continued in ver. 9 ff., without being hindered by the interchange of the *I* and of the following historical *he*, which is contained in " saith Koheleth." Dale even ventures the assertion, that the Book of Koheleth could have closed with the unsatisfying pure negative, ver. 8, as little as the Gospel of Mark with " and they were afraid " (xvi. 8). As if ver. 13 f. expressed postulates not already contained in the book itself! The epilogue has certainly manifestly the object of recommending the author of the book, Koheleth-Solomon, and of sealing the contents of the book. If Solomon himself were the author, the epilogue would stand in the same relation to the book as John xxi. 24 f. to the fourth Gospel, of the Johannean origin of which a voice from the apostolic church there bears witness.[1]

It is a serious anachronism when modern interpreters of Scripture occupy the standpoint of the old, who take the name of the man after whom the book is entitled, without more ado, as the name of its author from first to last.[2] To what childish puerilities a bigotry so uncritical descends is seen in the case of Christ.

---

[1] Hoelemann, in *Abth.* II. of his *Bibel-Studien* (1860), draws a parallel between these two epilogues; he regards them as original formal parts of the Solomonic Koheleth and of the Johannean Gospel, and seeks to prove that they stand in more than external and accidental relation to the two works respectively.

[2] Thus John Miller, in his *Commentary on the Proverbs* (New York, 1872), regards Solomon as the author of the entire Book of Proverbs and also of Ecclesi-

Fried. Bauer (1732). In this section, vers. 9–12, he says Solomon turns especially to his son Rehoboam, and delivers to him this *Solennel*-discourse or sermon as an instruction for his future life. He recommends it [the sermon] at once on account of the author, ver. 9, and of its contents, ver. 10, which accord, ver. 11, with his other writings, and from which altogether Rehoboam could find sufficient information, so that to write to him several books would be unnecessary. After this apostrophe to his son the preacher turns round to the entire *auditorio*, and addresses them in הַכֹּל נִשְׁמָע. But we are all permitted to hear what is the final aim and intention of this sermon: Fear thou God, and keep His commandments; for such ought every man to be, etc.

A rationalism not less fruitful in wonderful conceits appeared over against this dreamy irrationalism. Döderlein (1784) says of Koheleth: "As it appears, so the author feigned, that this was a lecture or treatise which Solomon delivered before his literary academy; for this academy I am inclined to understand under the name 'Koheleth.'" The epilogue appears to him as an appendage by another hand. Such is the opinion also of J. E. Ch. Schmidt (1794), Bertholdt (in his *Einleit.* 1812 ff.), Umbreit (1818, 20), and Knobel (1836), who maintain that this appendage is aimless, in form as in doctrine, out of harmony with the book, revealing by the "endless book-making" a more recent time, and thus is an addition by a later author. This negative critical result Grätz (1871) has sought, following Krochmal (in his *More nebuche hazeman*, 1851, 54), to raise to a positive result. Vers. 9–11 are to him as an apology of the Book of Koheleth, and vers. 12–14 as a clause defining the collection of the Hagiographa, which is completed by the reception into it of the Book of Koheleth; and this bipartite epilogue as an addition belonging to the period of the Synod of Jabneh, about A.D. 90 (*vid*. above, p. 189).

If, nevertheless, we regard this epilogue as a postscript by the author of the book himself, we have not only Herzfeld on our side, who has given his verdict against all Knobel's arguments, but also Hitzig, who (Hilgenfeld's *Zeitsch.* 1872, p. 566) has rejected Grätz' Herod-hypothesis, as well as also his introduction of the epilogue into the history of the canon, or, as Geiger (*Jüd. Zeitsch.* 1872, p. 123) has expressed himself, has dealt with it according to its

---

astes. His interpretation of Scripture proceeds on the fundamental principle, in itself commendable, that the Scripture never expresses trivialities ("each text must be a brilliant"); but it is not to be forgotten that the O. T., in relation to the high school of the New, is in reality a *trivium*, and that the depth of the words of Scripture is not everywhere the same, but varies according to the author and the times.

merit. Also in Bloch's monograph on the Book of Koheleth (1872) there are many striking arguments against placing the authorship of the book in the Herod-Mishn. period, although the view of this critic, that the book contains notes of Solomon's with interpolations, and an epilogue by the collector, who sought to soften the impression of the gloomy pessimism of these notes, is neither cold nor hot.

We have already (p. 206) shown that the epilogue is written quite in the same style as the book itself; its language is like that of the chronicler; it approaches the idiom of the Mishna, but, with reference to it, is yet somewhat older. That the first part of the epilogue, vers. 9–11, serves an important end, is also proved (p. 206), —it establishes the book as a production of the Chokma, which had Solomon as its pattern; and the second part, vers. 12–14, bears on it the stamp of this Chokma, for it places all the teaching of the book under the double watchword: "Fear God," and "There is a judgment" (Job xxviii. 28, xix. 29; cf. Eccles. v. 6, xi. 9). In the book, Koheleth-Solomon speaks, whose mask the author puts on; here, he speaks, letting the mask fall off, of Koheleth. That in his time (the Persian) too much was done in the way of making books, we may well believe. In addition to authors by profession, there have always been amateurs; the habit of much writing is old, although in the course of time it has always assumed greater dimensions. A complaint in reference to this sounds strange, at least from the mouth of an author who has contented himself with leaving to posterity a work so small, though important. We nowhere encounter any necessity for regarding the author of the book and of the epilogue as different persons. The spirit and tone of the book and of the epilogue are one. The epilogue seals only the distinction between the pessimism of the book and the modern pessimism, which is without God and without a future.

Ver. 9. In connection with ver. 8, where Koheleth has spoken his last word, the author, who has introduced him as speaking hitherto, continues: "And, moreover, because Koheleth was wise, he taught the people knowledge; he applied and searched out and formed many proverbs." The postscript begins with "and" because it is connected with the concluding words of the book—only externally, however; nothing is more unwarrantable than to make ver. 8 the beginning of the postscript on account of the *vav*. The LXX. translate καὶ περισσὸν (Venet. περιττὸν) ὅτι; as Hitz.: "it remains (to be said) that Koheleth was a wise man," etc.; and Dale may be right, that ויתר is in this sense as subj., pointed with *Zakeph gadhol* (cf. Gen. xvi. 16, xx. 4, and the obj. thus pointed, Ex. xxiii. 3). But that Koheleth was "a wise man" is nothing remaining to be said, for as such he certainly speaks in the whole book from beginning to end; the עוֹד, unconnected, following, shows that this his property is presupposed as needing no further testimony. But untenable also is the translation: So much the greater Koheleth was as a wise man, so much the more, etc. (Heinem., Südfeld); עוֹד does not signify *eo magis;* the Heb. language has a different way of expressing such an intensification: כל הנדול מחברו יצרו גדול ממנו, *i.e.* the higher the position is which one assumes, so much the greater are the temptations to which he is exposed. Rightly, Luther: "This same preacher was not only wise, but," etc. וְיֹתֵר signifies, vii. 11, "and an advance (benefit, gain);" here ויתר שֶׁ, "and something going beyond this, that," etc.—thought of as accus.-adv.: "going beyond this, that = moreover, because" (Gesen., Knobel, Vaih., Ginsb., Grätz); *vid.* above, p. 192. Thus *'od* is in order, which introduces that which goes beyond the property and position of a "wise man" as such. That which goes beyond does not consist in this, that he taught the people knowledge, for that is just the meaning of the name *Koheleth;* the statement which *'od* introduces is contained in the concluding member of the compound sentence; the after-word begins with this, that it designates the Koheleth who appears in the more esoteric book before us as חכם, as the very same person who also composed the comprehensive people's book, the *Mishle*. He has taught the people knowledge; for he has placed, *i.e.* formed ("*stellen,*" to place, as "*Schriftsteller*" = author; modern Heb. מְחַבֵּר; Arab. *muṣannif*),[1] many proverbs, as the fruit of mature reflection and diligent research. The obj. *mᵉshalim harbēh* belongs only to *tiqqēn*, which ἀσυνδέτως (according to the style of the epilogue and of the book, as is shown above, p. 207) follows the two preparative mental efforts, whose *resultat* it was. Rightly, as to the syntax, Zöckler, and, as to the matter, Hitzig: "Apparently the author has here not 1 Kings v. 12, but the canonical Book of Proverbs in his eye." The language is peculiar. Not only is תָּקֵן exclusively peculiar (*vid.* above, p. 196) to the Book of Koheleth, but also אזן, *perpendere* (cf. Assyr. *uzunu*, reflection), to consider, and the *Pih.* חִקֵּר. Regarding the position of *harbeh, vid.* above, p. 230.[2]

---

[1] Cogn. in the meaning "*verfassen*" = to compose, is יסד; *vid.* Zunz' *Aufs.:* "To compose and to translate," expressed in Heb. in *Deut. Morg. Zeitsch.* xxv. p. 435 ff.

[2] *Harbeh bĕchĕh*, Ezra x. 1, which signifies "making much weeping," makes no exception in favour of the scribe. Cf. *hatsne'a lecheth*, Mic. vi. 8; *haphlē vaphĕlĕ*, Isa. xxix. 14.

Ver. 10. It is further said of Koheleth, that he put forth efforts not only to find words of a pleasant form, but, above all, of exact truth: "Koheleth strove to find words of pleasantness, and, written in sincerity, words of truth." The unconnected beginning *biqqesh Koheleth* is like *dibbarti ani*, i. 16, etc., in the book itself. Three objects follow *limtso*. But Hitz. reads the *inf. absol.* וְכָתוֹב instead of וְכָתוּב, and translates: to find pleasing words, and correctly to write words of truth. Such a continuance of the *inf. const.* by the *inf. absol.* is possible; 1 Sam. xxv. 26, cf. 31. But why should וְכָתוּב not be the continuance of the finite (Aq., Syr.), as *e.g.* at viii. 9, and that in the nearest adverbial sense: *et scribendo quidem sincere verba veritatis*, *i.e.* he strove, according to his best knowledge and conscience, to write true words, at the same time also to find out pleasing words; thus sought to connect truth as to the matter with beauty as to the manner? *V^echathuv* needs no modification in its form. But it is not to be translated: and that which was right was written by him; for the ellipsis is inadmissible, and כָּתוּב מִן is not correct Heb. Rightly the LXX., καὶ γεγραμμένον εὐθύτητος. כָּתוּב signifies "written," and may also, as the name of the Hagiographa כְּתוּבִים shows, signify "a writing;" *kakathuvah*, 2 Chron. xxx. 5, is = "in accordance with the writing;" and *b^elo kăkathuv*, 2 Chron. xxx. 18, "contrary to the writing;" in the post-bibl. the phrase הַכָּתוּב אֹמֵר = ἡ γραφὴ λέγει, is used. The objection made by Ginsburg, that *kathuv* never means, as *k^ethav* does, "a writing," is thus nugatory. However, we do not at all here need this subst. meaning, וכתוב is neut. particip., and יֹשֶׁר certainly not the genit., as the LXX. renders (reading וּכְתוּב), but also not the nom. of the subj. (Hoelem.), but, since יֹשֶׁר is the designation of a mode of thought and of a relation, the accus. of manner, like *v^eyashar*, Ps. cxix. 18; *emeth*, Ps. cxxxii. 11; *emunah*, Ps. cxix. 75. Regarding the common use of such an accus. of the nearer definition in the passive part., *vid.* Ewald, § 284c. The asyndeton *v^echathuv yosher divre emeth* is like that at x. 1, *mehhochmah michvod*. That which follows *limtso* we interpret as its threefold object. Thus it is said that Koheleth directed his effort towards an attractive form (cf. *avne-hephets*, Isa. liv. 12); but, before all, towards the truth, both subjectively (יֹשֶׁר) and objectively (אֱמֶת), of that which was formulated and expressed in writing.

Ver. 11. From the words of Koheleth the author comes to the words of the wise man in general; so that what he says of the latter finds its application to himself and his book: "Words of the wise are as like goads, and like fastened nails which are put together in collections—they are given by one shepherd." The LXX., Aq., and Theod. translate *darvonoth* by βούκεντρα, the Venet. by βουπλῆγες; and that is also correct. The word is one of three found in the Jerus. Gemara, *Sanhedrin* x. 1, to designate a rod for driving (oxen) —דרבן (from דרב, to sharpen, to point), מַלְמֵד (from למד, to adjust, teach, exercise), and מַרְדֵּעַ (from רדע, to hold back, *repellere*); we read *ka-dārᵉvonoth;* Gesen., Ewald, Hitz., and others are in error in reading *dorvonoth;* for the so-called light *Metheg*, which under certain circumstances can be changed into an accent, and the *Kametz chatuph* exclude one another.¹ If דרבן is the goad, the point of comparison is that which is to be excited intellectually and morally. Incorrectly, Gesen., Hitz., and others: like goads, because easily and deeply impressing themselves on the heart as well as on the memory. For goads, *aculei*, the Hebrews use the word קוֹצִים; *darᵉvonoth* also are goads, but designed for driving on, thus *stimuli* (Jerome); and is there a more natural commendation for the proverbs of the wise men than that they incite to self-reflection, and urge to all kinds of noble effort? *Divre* and *darᵉvonoth* have the same three commencing consonants, and, both for the ear and the eye, form a paronomasia. In the following comparison, it is a question whether *ba'ale asuppoth* (plur. of *ba'al asuppoth*, or of the double plur. *ba'al asuppah*, like *e.g. sare missim*, Ex. i. 11, of *sar mas*) is meant of persons, like *ba'al hallashon*, x. 11, cf. *ba'al kᵉnaphayim*, x. 20, or of things, as *ba'al piphiyoth*, Isa. xli. 15; and thus, whether it is a designation parallel to חכמים or to דברי. The Talm. *Jer. Sanhedrin* x. 1, wavers, for there it is referred first to the members of assemblies (viz. of the *Sanedrium*), and then is explained by "words which are spoken in the assembly." If we understand it of persons, as it was actually used in the Talm. (*vid.* above, p. 191), then by *asuppoth* we must understand the societies of wise men, and by *ba'ale asuppoth*, of the academicians (Venet.: δεσπόται ξυναγμάτων; Luther: "masters of assemblies") belonging to such academies. But an appropriate meaning of this second comparison is not to be reached in this way. For if we translate: and as nails driven in are the members of the society, it is not easy to see what this wonderful comparison means; and what is then further said: they are given from one shepherd, reminds us indeed of Eph. iv. 11, but, as said of this perfectly unknown great one, is for us incomprehensible. Or if we translate, after Isa. xxviii. 1: and (the words of

---

¹ The *Kametz* is the *Kametz gadhol* (opp. *Kametz chatuph*), and may for this reason have the accent *Munach* instead of *Metheg*. *Vid. Michlol* 153*b*, 182*b*. The case is the same as at Gen. xxxix. 34, where *mimmachŏrāth* is to be read. Cf. Baer's *Metheg-Setz.* § 27 and § 18.

the wise are) like the fastened nails of the members of the society, it is as tautological as if I should say: words of wise men are like fastened nails of wise men bound together in a society (as a confederacy, union). Quite impossible are the translations: like nails driven in by the masters of assemblies (thus *e.g.* Lightfoot, and recently Bullock), for the accus. with the pass. particip. may express some nearer definition, but not (as of the genit.) the effective cause; and: like a nail driven in are the (words) of the masters of assemblies (Tyler: "those of editors of collections "), for ellipt. genit., dependent on a governing word carrying forward its influence, are indeed possible, *e.g.* Isa. lxi. 7, but that a governing word itself, as *ba'ale*, may be the governed genit. of one omitted, as here *divre*, is without example.[1] It is also inconsistent to understand *ba'ale asuppoth* after the analogy of *ba'ale masoreth* (the Masoretes) and the like. It will not be meant of the persons of the wise, but of the proverbs of the wise. So far we agree with Lang and Hoelem. Lang (1874) thinks to come to a right understanding of the "much abused" expression by translating, "lords of troops,"—a designation of proverbs which, being by many acknowledged and kept in remembrance, possess a kind of lordship over men's minds; but that is already inadmissible, because *asuppoth* designates not any multitude of men, but associations with a definite end and aim. Hoelem. is content with this idea; for he connects together " planted as leaders of assemblies," and finds therein the thought, that the words of the wise serve as seeds and as guiding lights for the expositions in the congregation; but *ba'ale* denotes masters, not in the sense of leaders, but of possessors; and as *ba'ale b^erith*, Gen. xiv. 13, signifies " the confederated," *ba'ale sh^evu'ah*, Neh. vi. 18, " the sworn," and the frequently occurring *ba'ale ha'ir*, "the citizens;" so *ba'ale asuppoth* means, the possessors of assemblies and of the assembled themselves, or the possessors of collections and of the things collected. Thus *ba'ale asuppoth* will be a designation of the "words of the wise" (as in *shalishim,* choice men = choice proverbs, Prov. xxii. 20, in a certain measure personified), as of those which form or constitute collections, and which stand together in order and rank (Hitz., Ewald, Elst., Zöckl., and others). Of such it may properly be said, that they are like nails driven in, for they are secured against separation,—they are, so to speak, made nail-fast, they stand on one common ground; and their being fixed in such connection not only is a help to the memory,

---

[1] Regarding this omission of the *mudâf* [the governing noun], where this is naturally supplied before a genitive from the preceding, cf. Samachschari's *Mufaṣṣal,* p. 43, l. 8–13.

but also to the understanding of them. The Book of Koheleth itself is such an *asuppah;* for it contains a multitude of separate proverbs, which are thoughtfully ranged together, and are introduced into the severe, critical sermon on the nothingness of all earthly things as oases affording rest and refreshment; as similarly, in the later Talmudic literature, Haggadic parts follow long stretches of hair-splitting dialectics, and afford to the reader an agreeable repose.

And when he says of the "proverbs of the wise," individually and as formed into collections: נִתְּנוּ מֵרֹעֶה אֶחָד, *i.e.* they are the gift of one shepherd, he gives it to be understood that his "words of Koheleth," if not immediately written by Solomon himself, have yet one fountain with the Solomonic Book of Proverbs,—God, the one God, who guides and cares as a shepherd for all who fear Him, and suffers them to want nothing which is necessary to their spiritual support and advancement (Ps. xxiii. 1, xxviii. 9). "*Mēro'eh ehad,*" says Grätz, "is yet obscure, since it seldom, and that only poetically, designates the Shepherd of Israel. It cannot certainly refer to Moses." Not to Moses, it is true (Targ.), nor to Solomon, as the father, the pattern, and, as it were, the patron of "the wise," but to God, who is here named the ἀρχιποίμην as spiritual preserver (provider), not without reference to the figure of a shepherd from the goad, and the figure of household economy from the nails; for רעה, in the language of the Chokma (Prov. v. 21), is in meaning cogn. to the N. T. conception of edification.[1] Regarding *masmᵉroth* (iron nails), *vid.* above, p. 193; the word is not used of tent spikes (Spohn, Ginsb.), —it is masc., the sing. is מַשְׂמֵר (מַסְמֵר), Arab. *mismâr.* נְטוּעִים is = תְּקוּעִים (cf. Dan. xi. 45 with Gen. xxxi. 25), post-bibl. (*vid. Jer. Sanhedrin*) קְבוּעִים (Jerome, *in altum defixi*). *Min* with the pass., as at Job xxi. 1, xxviii. 4, Ps. xxxvii. 23 (Ewald, § 295*b*), is not synonymous with the Greek ὑπό (*vid.* above, p. 67). The LXX. well: "given by those of the counsel from one shepherd." Hitzig reads מִרְעֶה, and accordingly translates: "which are given united as a pasture," but in *mēro'eh ehad* there lies a significant apologetic hint in favour of the collection of proverbs by the younger Solomon (Koheleth) in relation to that of the old. This is the point of the verse, and it is broken off by Hitzig's conjecture.[2]

---

[1] *Vid.* my Heb. *Römerbrief,* p. 97.

[2] J. F. Reimmann, in the preface to his Introduction to the *Historia Litterarum antediluviana,* translates, ver. 11: "The words of the wise are like hewn-out marble, and the beautiful *collectanea* like set diamonds, which are presented by a good friend." A *Disputatio philologica* by Abr. Wolf, Königsberg 1723, contends against this παρερμηνεία.

Ver. 12. With *v*ᵉ*yother mehemmah* the postscript takes a new departure, warning against too much reading, and finally pointing once more to the one thing needful: "And besides, my son, be warned: for there is no end of much book-making; and much study is a weariness of the body." With "my son," the teacher of wisdom here, as in the Book of Proverbs, addresses the disciple who places himself under his instruction. Hitzig translates, construing *mehcmmah* with *hizzaher*: "And for the rest: by these (the 'words of Koheleth,' ver. 10) be informed." But (1) נִזְהַר, according to usage, does not signify in general to be taught, but to be made wiser, warned; particularly the imper. הִזָּהֵר is cogn. with הִשָּׁמֵר (cf. *Targ. Jer. Ex.* x. 28, הִשָּׁמֶר לְךָ = אִזְדְּהַר לָךְ), and in fact an object of the warning follows; (2) *min* after *yothēr* is naturally to be regarded as connected with it, and not with *hizzaher* (cf. Esth. vi. 6, *Sota* vii. 7; cf. Ps. xix. 12). The punctuation of *v*ᵉ*yother* and *mehemmah* is thus not to be interfered with. Either *hēmmah* points back to *divre* (ver. 11): And as to what goes beyond these (in relation thereto) be warned (Schelling: *quidquid ultra haec est, ab iis cave tibi*, and thus *e.g.* Oehler in Herzog's *R. E.* vii. 248); or, which is more probable, since the *divre* are without a fixed beginning, and the difference between true and false "wise men" is not here expressed, *hemmah* refers back to all that has hitherto been said, and *v*ᵉ*yother mehemmah* signifies not the result thereof (Ewald, § 285*e*), but that which remains thereafter: and what is more than that (which has hitherto been said), *i.e.* what remains to be said after that hitherto said; Lat. *et quod superest, quod reliquum est*.

In 12*b*, Hitzig also proposes a different interpunction from that which lies before us; but at the same time, in the place of the significant double-sentence, he proposes a simple sentence: "to make many books, without end, and much exertion of mind (in making these), is a weariness of the body." The author thus gives the reason for his writing no more. But with xii. 8 he has certainly brought his theme to a close, and he writes no further; because he does not write for hire and without an aim, but for a high end, according to a fixed plan; and whether he will leave off with this his book or not is a matter of perfect indifference to the readers of this one book; and that the writing of many books without end will exhaust a man's mind and bring down his body, is not that a flat truism? We rather prefer Herzfeld's translation, which harmonizes with Rashbam's: "But more than these (the wise men) can teach thee, my son, teach thyself: to make many books there would be no end; and much preaching is fatiguing to the body." But נִזְהַר cannot mean to

CHAP. XII. 13.   437

"teach oneself," and *ēn qētz* does not mean *non esset finis*, but *non est finis*; and for *lahach* the meaning "to preach" (which Luther also gives to it) is not at all shown from the Arab. *lahjat*, which signifies the tongue as that which is eager (to learn, etc.), and then also occurs as a choice name for tongues in general. Thus the idea of a double sentence, which is the most natural, is maintained, as the LXX. has already rendered it. The *n. actionis* עֲשׂוֹת with its object is the subject of the sentence, of which it is said *ēn qēts*, it is without end; Hitzig's opinion, that *ēn lach qētz* must mean *non est ei finis*, is not justified; for *ēn qēts* is a virtual adj., as *ēn 'avel*, Deut. xxxiii. 4, and the like, and as such the pred. of the substantival sentence. Regarding לַהַג, *avidum discendi legendique studium*, *vid.* above, p. 193. C. A. Bode (1777) renders well: *polygraphiae nullus est finis et polymathia corpus delessat*. Against this endless making of books and much study the postscript warns, for it says that this exhausts the bodily strength without (for this is the reverse side of the judgment) truly furthering the mind, which rather becomes decentralized by this πολυπραγμοσύνη. The meaning of the warning accords with the phrase coined by Pliny (*Ep.* vii. 9), *multum non multa*. One ought to hold by the "words of the wise," to which also the "words of Koheleth," comprehended in the *asuppah* of the book before us, belong; for all that one can learn by hearing or by reading amounts at last, if we deduct all that is unessential and unenduring, to a *unum necessarium*:

Ver. 13. "The final result, after all is learned, (is this): Fear God and keep His commandments; for this is the end of every man." Many expositors, as Jerome, the Venet., and Luther, render נִשְׁמָע as fut.: The conclusion of the discourse we would all hear (Salomon); or: The conclusion of the whole discourse or matter let us hear (Panzer, 1773, de Wette-Augusti); Hitzig also takes together *soph davar hakol* = *soph davar kol-haddavar*: The end of the whole discourse let us hear. But הכל for כֻּלָּנוּ is contrary to the style of the book; and as a general rule, the author uses הכל for the most part of things, seldom of persons. And also *soph davar hakol*, which it would be better to explain ("the final word of the whole"), with Ewald, § 291*a*, after *y^emē-olam mosheh*, Isa. lxiii. 11 (cf. *Proverbs*, vol. II. p. 267, note), than it is explained by Hitzig, although, in spite of Philippi's (*Stat. const.* p. 17) doubt, possible in point of style, and also exemplified in the later period of the language (1 Chron. ix. 13), is yet a stylistic crudeness which the author could have avoided either by writing *soph d^evar hakol*, or better, *soph kol-haddavar*. נִשְׁמָע, Ewald, § 168*b*, renders as a particip. by *audiendum*; but that also does not commend itself, for נִשְׁמָע signifies nothing else than *auditum*, and acquires the meaning of *audiendum* when from the empirical matter of fact that which is inwardly necessary is concluded; the translation: The final word of the whole is to be heard, *audiendum est*, would only be admissible if also the translation *auditum est* were possible, which is not the case. Is נִשְׁמָע thus possibly the pausal form of the finite נִשְׁמַע ? We might explain: The end of the matter (*summa summarum*), all is heard, when, viz., that which follows is heard, which comprehends all that is to be known. Or as Hoelem.: Enough, all is heard, since, viz., that which is given in the book to be learned contains the essence of all true knowledge, viz., the following two fundamental doctrines. This retrospective reference of *hakol nishm'a* is more natural than the prospective reference; but, on the other hand, it is also more probable that *soph davar* denotes the final *resultat* than that it denotes the conclusion of the discourse. The right explanation will be that which combines the retrospective reference of *hakol nishm'a* and the resultative reference of *soph davar*. Accordingly, Mendelss. appears to us to be correct when he explains: After thou hast heard all the words of the wise ... this is the final result, etc. *Finis (summa) rei, omnia audita* is = *omnibus auditis*, for the sentence denoting the conditions remains externally undesignated, in the same way as at x. 14; Deut. xxi. 1; Ezra x. 6 (Ewald, § 341*b*). After the clause, *soph ... nishm'a, Athnach* stands where we put a colon: the mediating *hocce est* is omitted just as at vii. 12*b* (where translate: yet the preference of knowledge is this, that, etc.).

The sentence, *eth-haelohim y^era* (" fear God "), repeating itself from v. 6, is the kernel and the star of the whole book, the highest moral demand which mitigates its pessimism and hallows its eudaemonism. The admonition proceeding therefrom, "and keep His commandments," is included in *lishmo'a*, iv. 17 [v. 1], which places the hearing of the divine word, viz. a hearing for the purpose of observing, as the very soul of the worship of God above all the *opus operatum* of ceremonial services.

The connection of the clause, *ki-zeh kol-haadam*, Hitzig mediates in an unnecessary, roundabout way: "but not thou alone, but this ought every man." But why this negative here introduced to stamp כִּי as an *immo* establishing it? It is also certainly suitable as the immediate confirmation of the rectitude of the double admonition finally expressing all. The clause has the form of a simple judgment, it is a substantival clause, the briefest expression for the thought which is intended. What is that thought? The LXX.

renders: ὅτι τοῦτο πᾶς ὁ ἄνθρωπος; also Symm. and the Venet. render *kol haadam* by πᾶς ὁ ἄνθρ., and an unnamed translator has ὅλος ὁ ἄνθρ., according to which also the translation of Jerome is to be understood, *hoc est enim omnis homo*. Thus among the moderns, Herzf., Ewald, Elst., and Heiligst.: for that is the whole man, viz. as to his destiny, the end of his existence (cf. as to the subject-matter, Job xxviii. 28); and v. Hofmann (*Schriftbew.* II. 2, p. 456): this is the whole of man, viz. as Grotius explains: *totum hominis bonum;* or as Dale and Bullock: "the whole duty of man;" or as Tyler: "the universal law (כֹּל, like the Mishnic כְּלָל) of man;" or as Hoelem.: that which gives to man for the first time his true and full worth. Knobel also suggests for consideration this rendering: this is the all of man, *i.e.* on this all with man rests. But against this there is the one fact, that *kol-haadam* never signifies the whole man, and as little anywhere the whole (the all) of a man. It signifies either "all men" (πάντες οἱ ἄνθρωποι, οἱ πά. ἄνθρ. οἱ ἄνθρ. πά.), as at vii. 2, *hu soph kol-haadam*, or, of the same meaning as *kol-haadam*, "every man" (πᾶς ἄνθρωπος), as at iii. 13, v. 18 (LXX., also vii. 2: τοῦτο τέλος παντὸς ἀνθρώπου); and it is yet more than improbable that the common expression, instead of which *haadam kullo* was available, should here have been used in a sense elsewhere unexampled. Continuing in the track of the *usus loq.*, and particularly of the style of the author, we shall thus have to translate: "for this is every man." If we use for it: "for this is every man's," the clause becomes at once distinct; Zirkel renders *kol-haadam* as genit., and reckons the expression among the Graecisms of the book: παντὸς ἀνθρώπου, viz. πρᾶγμα. Or if, with Knobel, Hitz., Böttch., and Ginsburg, we might borrow a verb to supplement the preceding imperat.: "for this ought every man to do," we should also in this way gain the meaning to be expected; but the clause lying before us is certainly a substantival clause, like *meh haadam*, ii. 12, not an elliptical verbal clause, like Isa. xxiii. 5, xxvi. 9, where the verb to be supplied easily unfolds itself from the ל of the end of the movement.

We have here a case which is frequent in the Semitic languages, in which subj. and pred. are connected in the form of a simple judgment, and it is left for the hearer to find out the relation sustained by the pred. to the subj.—*e.g.* Ps. cx. 3, cix. 4, "I am prayer;" and in the Book of Koheleth, iii. 19, "the children of men are a chance."[1] In the same way we have here to explain: for that is every man,

---

[1] *Vid.* Fleischer's *Abh. u. einige Arten der Nominalapposition*, 1862, and Philippi's *St. const.* p. 90 ff.

viz. according to his destiny and duty; excellently, Luther: for that belongs to all men. With right, Hahn, like Bauer (1732), regards the pronoun as pred. (not subj. as at vii. 2): "this, *i.e.* thus constituted, that they must do this, are all men," or rather: this = under obligation thereto, is every man.[1] It is a great thought that is thereby expressed, viz. the reduction of the Israelitish law to its common human essence. This has not escaped the old Jewish teachers. What can this mean: *zeh kol-haadam?* it is asked, *Berachoth* 6*b*; and R. Elazar answers: "The whole world is comprehended therein;" and R. Abba bar-Cahana: "This fundamental law is of the same importance to the universe;" and R. Simeon b. Azzai: "The universe has been created only for the purpose of being commanded this."[2]

Ver. 14. As we render *zeh kol-haadam* as expressive of the same obligation lying on all men without exception, this verse appropriately follows: "For God shall bring every work into the judgment upon all that is concealed, whether it be good or bad." To bring into judgment is, as at xi. 9 = to bring to an account. There the punctuation is בַּמִּשְׁ׳, here בְּמִשְׁ׳, as, according to rule, the art. is omitted where the idea is determined by a relative clause or an added description; for *b'mishpat 'al kol-ne'llam* are taken together: in the judgment upon all that is concealed (cf. Rom. ii. 16; 1 Cor. iv. 5, τὰ κρυπτά). Hitzig, however, punctuates here בַּמִּשְׁ׳, and explains עַל as of the same meaning as the distributive לְ, *e.g.* Gen. ix. 5, 10; but in this sense עַל never interchanges with לְ. And wherefore this subtlety? The judgment upon all that is concealed is a judgment from the cognition of which nothing, not even the most secret, can escape; and that משפט על is not a Germanism, is shown from xi. 9; to execute judgment on (Germ. *an*) any one is expressed by בְּ, Ps. cxix. 84, Wisd. vi. 6; judgment upon (*über*) any one may be expressed by the genit. of him whom it concerns, Jer. li. 9; but judgment upon anything (Symm. περὶ παντὸς παροραθέντος) cannot otherwise be expressed than by עַל. Rather עַל may be rendered as a connecting particle: "together with all that is concealed" (Vaih., Hahn); but כל־מעשה certainly comprehends all, and with כל־נעלם

---

[1] Hitz. thus renders הִיא, Jer. xlv. 4*b*, predicat.: "And it is such, all the world."

[2] Cf. *Jer. Nedarim* ix. 3: "Thou oughtest to love thy neighbour as thyself," says R. Akiba, is a principal sentence in the Law. Ben-Azzai says: "The words *zĕh . . . adam* (Gen. v. 1) are it in a yet higher degree," because therein the oneness of the origin and the destiny of all men is contained. Aben Ezra alludes to the same thing, when at the close of his *Comm.* he remarks: "The secret of the non-use of the divine name יהוה in Gen. i.–ii. 3 is the secret of the Book of Koheleth."

this comprehensive idea is only deepened. The accent dividing the verse stands rightly under נֶעְלָם;[1] for *sive bonum sive malum* (as at v. 11) is not related to *ne'llam* as disjoining, but to *kol-ma'aseh*.

This certainty of a final judgment of personal character is the Ariadne-thread by which Koheleth at last brings himself safely out of the labyrinth of his scepticism. The prospect of a general judgment upon the nations prevailing in the O. T., cannot sufficiently set at rest the faith (*vid. e.g.* Ps. lxxiii., Jer. xii. 1–3) which is tried by the unequal distributions of present destiny. Certainly the natural, and particularly the national connection in which men stand to one another, is not without an influence on their moral condition; but this influence does not remove accountability,—the *individuum* is at the same time a person; the object of the final judgment will not be societies as such, but only persons, although not without regard to their circle of life. This personal view of the final judgment does not yet in the O. T. receive a preponderance over the national view; such figures of an universal and individualizing personal judgment as Matt. vii. 21–23, Rev. xx. 12, are nowhere found in it; the object of the final judgment are nations, kingdoms, cities, and conditions of men. But here, with Koheleth, a beginning is made in the direction of regarding the final judgment as the final judgment of men, and as lying in the future, beyond the present time. What Job xix. 25–27 postulates in the absence of a present judgment of his cause, and the Apocalyptic Dan. xii. 2 saw as a dualistic issue of the history of his people, comes out here for the first time in the form of doctrine into that universally-human expression which is continued in the announcements of Jesus and the apostles. Kleinert sees here the morning-dawn of a new revelation breaking forth; and Himpel says, in view of this conclusion, that Koheleth is a precious link in the chain of the preparation for the gospel; and rightly. In the Book of Koheleth the O. T. religion sings its funeral song, but not without finally breaking the ban of nationality and of bondage to this present life, which made it unable to solve the mysteries of life, and thus not without prophesying its resurrection in an expanded glorified form as the religion of humanity.

---

[1] Thus rightly pointed in F. with *Dagesh* in *lamed*, to make distinct the ע as quiescent (cf. 1 Kings x. 3; and, on the other hand, Neh. iii. 11, Ps. xxvi. 4). Cf. 'שֶׁתִּח with *Dagesh* in *shin*, on account of the preceding quiescent guttural, like 'יָח, ix. 8; 'הֵתְּ, Lev. xi. 16; 'נְחָ, Num. i. 7, etc.; cf. *Luth. Zeitsch.* 1863, p. 413.

The synagogal lesson repeats the 13th verse after the 14th, to gain thereby a conclusion of a pleasing sound. The Masoretic *Siman* (*vox memorialis*) of those four books, in which, after the last verse, on account of its severe contents, the verse going before is repeated in reading, is יח״קק. The י refers to ישעיה (Isaiah), ת to תריסר (the Book of the Twelve Prophets), the first ק to קהלת, the second ק to קינות (Lamentations). The Lamentations and Koheleth always stand together. But there are two different arrangements of the five *Mcgilloth*, viz. that of the calendar of festivals which has passed into our printed editions: the Song, Ruth, Lamentations, Koheleth, and Esther (*vid.* above, p. 3); and the Masoretic arrangement, according to the history of their origin: Ruth, the Song, Koheleth, Lamentations, and Esther.

THE END.

www.ingramcontent.com/pod-product-compliance
Lightning Source LLC
Chambersburg PA
CBHW052137300426
44115CB00011B/1416